Fifth Edition

JUVENILE DELINQUENCY

Peter C. Kratcoski
Department of Justice Studies
Kent State University

Lucille Dunn Kratcoski
Research Associate

PEARSON
Prentice
Hall

Upper Saddle River, New Jersey 07458

Library of Congress Cataloging-in-Publication Data

Kratcoski, Peter C.
  Juvenile delinquency / Peter C. Kratcoski, Lucille Dunn Kratcoski.—
5th ed.
    p. cm.
Includes index.
  ISBN 0-13-033673-4
  1. Juvenile delinquency—United States. 2. Juvenile justice,
Administration of—United States. I. Kratcoski, Lucille Dunn II.
Title.
  HV9104 .K7 2004
  364.36'0973—dc22

                                        2003018112

Publisher: Nancy Roberts
Managing Editor (Editorial): Sharon Chambliss
Production Liaison: Joanne Hakim
Senior Marketing Manager: Marissa Feliberty
Marketing Assistant: Adam Laitman
Manufacturing Buyer: Mary Ann Gloriande
Cover Art Director: Jayne Conte
Cover Design: Suzanne Behnke
Cover Illustration/Photo: Noma / SIS, Inc.
Cover Image Specialist: Karen Sanatar
Composition/Full-Service Project Management: Jessica Balch/Pine Tree Composition
Printer/Binder: Hamilton Printing Company

> *This book is dedicated to our daughter and our son, Deborah Kratcoski Ricker and Peter Christopher Kratcoski, who have shown love, compassion, and concern for children in their personal and professional lives.*

Pearson Education LTD., London
Pearson Education Singapore, Pte. Ltd
Pearson Education, Canada, Ltd
Pearson Education—Japan
Pearson Education Australia PTY, Limited

Pearson Education North Asia Ltd
Pearson Educación de Mexico, S.A. de C.V.
Pearson Education Malaysia, Pte. Ltd
Pearson Education, Upper Saddle River, New Jersey

10 9 8 7 6 5 4 3 2 1
ISBN 0-13-033673-4

CONTENTS

PREFACE   xi
INTRODUCTION   xv

PART ONE   DEFINING AND EXPLAINING DELINQUENCY

1   DEFINITIONS, SCOPE, AND TRENDS IN JUVENILE DELINQUENCY   1

    DEFINING DELINQUENCY 2
    SOCIETAL REACTION TO YOUTHFUL MISBEHAVIOR   5
    DELINQUENT AND STATUS OFFENSES   6
    SCOPE OF JUVENILE DELINQUENCY   7
        Officially Recorded Delinquency   7   •   Self-Reported Delinquency Studies   9   •
        Victimization Surveys   10
    TRENDS IN DELINQUENT BEHAVIOR   11
        Total Arrest Trends   11   •   Crimes of Violence by Juveniles   11   •   Substance
        Abuse   13   •   Minority-Group Crime   15   •   Female Delinquency   15   •
        Delinquency in Suburban and Rural Areas   15
    SUMMARY   17
    DISCUSSION QUESTIONS   18
    NOTES   19

2   HISTORICAL PERSPECTIVES ON DELINQUENCY CAUSATION   21

    THE THEORY-DEVELOPMENT PROCESS   23
    THEORIES OF DELINQUENCY AND CRIMINALITY 25
        The Classical School   25   •   Neoclassical Thought   26   •   The Biological
        School   27   •   Heredity-Based Theories   29   •   Current Biological Explanations
        of Delinquency   30
    SUMMARY   34
    DISCUSSION QUESTIONS   35
    NOTES   35

3   PSYCHOLOGICAL THEORIES OF DELINQUENCY CAUSATION   37

    PSYCHOANALYTIC THEORIES   39
    MORAL DEVELOPMENT AND DELINQUENCY   40
        Moral-Development Theories   40   •   Cognitive-Development Theories   41   •
        Adolescent Coping Mechanisms   42

PERSONALITY-TRAIT EXPLANATIONS OF DELINQUENCY   43
Early Personality-Trait Theories   44   •   The Quay Classification System   45   •
Personality Measurement as a Method of Ascertaining Behavior Disorders   45   •
The Criminal Personality   46   •   The Psychopathic Personality   48
MENTAL ILLNESS AND DELINQUENCY   48
SUMMARY   50
DISCUSSION QUESTIONS   51
NOTES   51

4 SOCIOLOGICAL PERSPECTIVES ON DELINQUENCY CAUSATION   53

SOCIAL STRAIN THEORY   54
Poverty, Family Disruption, and Delinquency   54   •   Environmental Influences
on Delinquency   56   •   Anomie and Delinquency   59   •   Reaction Formation
Defense Mechanisms   60   •   Delinquency and Opportunity   60   •   Stress
and Delinquency   60
LEARNING THEORY, CULTURAL TRANSMISSION, AND DELINQUENCY   61
Social Learning Theory   61   •   Differential Association Theory   62   •   Differential
Reinforcement Theory   63
THE INFLUENCE OF TELEVISION VIOLENCE ON AGGRESSIVE
   DELINQUENT BEHAVIOR   64
THE CULTURE OF VIOLENCE   65
SOCIAL-PSYCHOLOGICAL EXPLANATIONS OF DELINQUENCY   66
The Gluecks' Multiple-Factor Approach   66   •   Containment Theory   66   •   Social
Control/Bonding Theory   67   •   Self-Concept   68   •   Labeling Theory   70
SUMMARY   70
DISCUSSION QUESTIONS   71
NOTES   71

PART TWO   DELINQUENCY AND THE SOCIAL ENVIRONMENT

**5 CONTROLLING CHILDREN: THE CHANGING ROLE OF CHILDREN
   IN AMERICAN SOCIETY   74**

CHILDREN IN THE MIDDLE AGES   76
THE RENAISSANCE AND THE EMERGENCE OF INTEREST
   IN CHILDREN   77
CHILDHOOD IN COLONIAL AMERICA   78
CHILDHOOD DURING THE PERIOD OF INDUSTRIALIZATION
   AND IMMIGRATION   79
Houses of Refuge   80   •   Compulsory Education   80
ORIGINS OF THE JUVENILE COURT   81
The Child Savers   82   •   Creation of the First Juvenile Court   83
JUVENILE COURT PHILOSOPHY   84
Focus on Treatment   84   •   The *Kent, Gault, Winship,* and *McKeiver* Decisions   85
   •   The Juvenile Court Today   88
SUMMARY   90
DISCUSSION QUESTIONS   91
NOTES   91

6 GANG DELINQUENCY AND VIOLENCE 93

THE SCOPE OF THE PROBLEM 96
What Is a Gang? 96 • How Widespread Is Gang Membership? 97
THE HISTORY OF GANG DEVELOPMENT 97
GANG BEHAVIOR IN THE 1970s 100
GANG BEHAVIOR IN THE 1980s, 1990s, AND 2000s 101
THEORIES OF GANG FORMATION 103
Thrasher's Theory of Gang Development 103 • Research of the Chicago School 104
• Lower-Class Culture 105 • Delinquency and Opportunity 106 • The
Underclass as a Generating Milieu for Gang Formation 115 • Needs Theory 117
STRUCTURE OF THE GANG 118
VARIATIONS IN GANG BEHAVIOR 120
Female Gangs 120 • Suburban and Small-Town Gangs 123
GANG ACTIVITY CONTROL 125
Community Organization for Gang Control 125 • Social Intervention 126 •
Opportunities Provision 126 • Suppression 127 • Legislation for Youth
Gang Prevention and Control 129
SUMMARY 130
DISCUSSION QUESTIONS 131
NOTES 131

7 FAMILY FUNCTIONING AND DELINQUENCY 136

THE CONTEMPORARY FAMILY AS A SOCIALIZATION AGENCY 137
THE CHANGING AMERICAN FAMILY 139
THE INFLUENCE OF THE FAMILY ON DELINQUENT BEHAVIOR 140
Conditions that Contribute to Family Disruption 140 • Financial Aid
for Economically Deprived Children 141 • Delinquency and Disrupted Family
Structure 142 • Socialization and Delinquency 143 • Family Violence and
Delinquency 144 • Delinquency and Parental Rejection 146 • Relation
of Consistent and Adequate Discipline to Delinquency 147
VALUES AND DELINQUENCY 150
SUMMARY 151
DISCUSSION QUESTIONS 152
NOTES 152

8 FEMALE DELINQUENCY 155

THE CASE OF SUSAN FRYBERG 156
THE EXTENT OF FEMALE DELINQUENCY 158
Official Statistics 158 • Self-Reported Delinquency 159
THE NATURE OF FEMALE DELINQUENCY 160
CAUSES OF FEMALE DELINQUENCY 160
The Unique Characteristics of the Adolescent Girl 161 • The Double Standard
in American Sexual Definitions 161 • Influence of the Family 163 • Sex-
Related Offenses by Females 164
JUVENILE JUSTICE SYSTEM HANDLING OF DELINQUENT GIRLS 170
Differential Treatment of Males and Females 170 • Programs Designed
for the Unique Problems of Delinquent Girls 171

SUMMARY   171
DISCUSSION QUESTIONS   172
NOTES   172

9   THE SCHOOL AND DELINQUENCY   **175**

THE SCHOOL AS A DELINQUENCY-PRODUCING INSTITUTION   179
Schools' Failure in Socialization   179   •   Victimization at School   183   •
Students' Failure in Academic Endeavors   186
THE RELATION OF DROPPING OUT TO DELINQUENCY   189
SCHOOL VANDALISM   190
THE RELATION OF SCHOOL INVOLVEMENT TO DRUG
   AND ALCOHOL USE   191
DEFINING THE APPROPRIATE ROLE OF THE SCHOOLS
   IN DELINQUENCY PREVENTION   192
Social Networking   193   •   Safe School Initiatives   194   •   Drug
Education   195   •   Alternative Programs   196   •   Levels of Delinquency
Prevention and Control by the Schools   197
SUMMARY   199
DISCUSSION QUESTIONS   200
NOTES   200

10   MALTREATED/ENDANGERED CHILDREN   **204**

WHAT ARE CHILD ABUSE AND NEGLECT?   207
MANDATORY VERSUS PERMISSIVE REPORTING OF CHILD ABUSE   208
EXTENT AND NATURE OF CHILD MALTREATMENT   209
The Distinction between Child Punishment and Child Maltreatment   209   •
Documentation of Child Maltreatment   210
SEXUAL EXPLOITATION AND ABUSE OF CHILDREN   211
The Incidence of Sexual Abuse of Children   212   •   Characteristics of Sexual Abuse
of Children   213
WHO ARE THE ABUSED AND NEGLECTED CHILDREN?   216
WHO ARE THE ABUSERS?   218
THE RELATIONSHIP BETWEEN BEING ABUSED AND DELINQUENT
   AND CRIMINAL BEHAVIOR   220
DISCOVERY OF CHILD ABUSE AND NEGLECT AND SEXUAL ABUSE   221
LEGISLATION DIRECTED TOWARD PROTECTING
   MALTREATED CHILDREN   222
THE ROLE OF CHILD PROTECTIVE SERVICES   223
JUVENILE COURT PROCESS IN ABUSE AND NEGLECT CASES   224
Steps in the Process   224   •   Special Considerations in Abuse and Neglect Cases   226
WHAT CAN BE DONE?   228
SUMMARY   229
DISCUSSION QUESTIONS   231
NOTES   231

PART THREE DELINQUENCY AND THE JUVENILE JUSTICE PROCESS

11 KEY ISSUES IN THE JUVENILE JUSTICE PROCESS 234

THE STATUS-OFFENDER DILEMMA 235
Categorization of Status Offenders 235 • History of the Treatment of Status Offenders by the Juvenile Court 236 • Runaway Behavior—Should the Juvenile Court Intervene? 237 • Other Status Offenses—The Role of the Juvenile Court 239 • Proposed Changes in the Handling of Status Offenders 241
HANDLING SERIOUS DELINQUENT OFFENDERS 247
Scope of the Problem 247 • Legislation Directed to Control Habitual and Violent Juvenile Offenders 248 • Court Action against Habitual and Violent Juvenile Offenders 249 • Methods of Working with Habitual Violent Offenders 252
SUMMARY 253
DISCUSSION QUESTIONS 254
NOTES 254

12 THE POLICE ROLE IN DELINQUENCY PREVENTION AND CONTROL 257

THE NATURE OF POLICE WORK WITH JUVENILES 259
POLICE DISCRETION IN DEALING WITH JUVENILES 261
Police Juvenile Diversion Programs 263 • The Decision to Take a Juvenile into Custody 264 • Interrogation Procedures 265 • Identification Procedures 265 • Fingerprinting and Photographing Juveniles 266
INVESTIGATING OFFENSES AGAINST CHILDREN 267
THE POLICE JUVENILE UNIT 268
YOUTH GANG UNITS 269
POLICE ROLE IN DELINQUENCY PREVENTION 272
Community Policing 273 • Debate over the Appropriate Role of the Police in Delinquency Prevention 274
SUMMARY 275
DISCUSSION QUESTIONS 276
NOTES 276

13 JUVENILE COURT PROCESS AND ISSUES 279

SOURCES OF JUVENILE COURT REFERRALS 281
NATURE AND NUMBER OF CASES PROCESSED BY JUVENILE COURTS 281
THE JUVENILE COURT PROCESS 283
Total Diversion from Court Involvement 283 • Entering the Juvenile Court Process 283 • The Petition 287 • Temporary Detention 291 • The Intake Process 293 • Partial Diversion/Unofficial Probation 295 • Juvenile Court Hearings 298 • Adjudication Hearings 309 • Dispositional Hearings 310 • Sentencing of Juveniles Adjudicated in Criminal Court 316
SUMMARY 318
DISCUSSION QUESTIONS 319
NOTES 319

14 PROBATION AND COMMUNITY-BASED PROGRAMS   **322**

HISTORICAL DEVELOPMENT OF PROBATION   325
DEFINITION OF PROBATION   325
EXTENT OF PROBATION USE   326
ROLE OF THE PROBATION OFFICER   327
THE PROBATION PROCESS   328
     The Probation Officer as Investigator   329   •   The Probation Officer
     as Supervisor   334   •   Intensive Probation   340
PROBATION REVOCATION   341
ALTERNATIVE COMMUNITY-BASED SUPERVISION   341
     Early Experiments with Community-Based Services for Delinquents   341   •   Current
     Community Supervision Programs   343   •   Specialized Treatment Programs   345
     •   Services for Multiproblem Youths   349   •   Community Residential
     Treatment   350
THE EFFECTIVENESS OF PROBATION AND OTHER
     COMMUNITY-BASED ALTERNATIVES   352
SUMMARY   353
DISCUSSION QUESTIONS   355
NOTES   355

15 SECURE FACILITIES FOR JUVENILES   **358**

HISTORY OF JUVENILE INSTITUTIONS IN AMERICA   361
THE ORGANIZATION OF JUVENILE DETENTION AND CORRECTIONAL
     FACILITIES   363
     Short-Term Incarceration Facilities   363   •   Long-Term Incarceration Facilities   371
THE JUVENILE'S RESPONSE TO INSTITUTIONAL LIFE   378
     Violence in Institutions   379   •   Adaptation to Institutional Life   380   •
     Institutional Effectiveness   382   •   Normalization   384
SUMMARY   385
DISCUSSION QUESTIONS   386
NOTES   386

16 AFTERCARE AND NONSECURE RESIDENTIAL PLACEMENT   **389**

THE JUVENILE AFTERCARE DECISION   391
THE AFTERCARE PROCESS   392
     Preparation for Release   393   •   The Aftercare Treatment Plan   395   •   General
     and Special Rules of Aftercare   395   •   Discharge from Aftercare   396
AFTERCARE REVOCATION   396
     The Revocation Process   396   •   Youths' Rights at a Revocation Hearing   397
AFTERCARE EFFECTIVENESS   397
INTENSIVE AFTERCARE FOR HIGH-RISK JUVENILES   399
     Developing Intensive Case Management Plans   399   •   Implementing Intensive Case
     Management   400   •   Effectiveness of Intensive Aftercare   400
AFTERCARE AND RESIDENTIAL TREATMENT   401
     History of the Halfway House Movement   402   •   Highfields   403   •
     Community Hostels   403

SUMMARY   404
DISCUSSION QUESTIONS   405
NOTES   406

PART FOUR   PREVENTING, TREATING, AND CONTROLLING DELINQUENCY

17   TREATING THE JUVENILE OFFENDER   407

DEFINITION OF TREATMENT   410
THE APPLICATION OF MANAGEMENT PRINCIPLES TO THE TREATMENT
  OF JUVENILES   411
  Management of Treatment Programs   412   •   The Decision to Use Individual
  or Group Treatment   413
THE ROLE OF TREATMENT PERSONNEL   414
SPECIFIC TREATMENT TECHNIQUES   416
  Psychotherapy   416   •   Reality Therapy   416   •   Crisis Intervention   418   •
  Assertiveness Training   418   •   Behavior Modification   419   •   Milieu
  Therapy   422   •   Group Work   422   •   Guided Group Interaction and Positive
  Peer Culture   423   •   Family Counseling   423   •   Anger Management   424   •
  Treatment Techniques for Specific Types of Offenders   425
TREATMENT EFFECTIVENESS   430
SUMMARY   432
DISCUSSION QUESTIONS   433
NOTES   433

18   DELINQUENCY PREVENTION AND CONTROL   436

DELINQUENCY PREVENTION PROGRAM   437
  The Evolution of Delinquency Prevention Programming   437   •   Contemporary
  Delinquency Prevention Programming   440
THE ROLE OF VOLUNTEERS IN DELINQUENCY PREVENTION   443
DELINQUENCY PREVENTION THROUGH DETERRENT METHODS   443
DELINQUENCY CONTROL   444
  Juvenile Code Revision and Juvenile Court Administration   445   •   Possible Changes
  in the Jurisdiction of the Juvenile Court   445   •   The Balanced Approach/Restorative
  Justice Approach   447   •   Privatization in Juvenile Corrections   448
PLANNING FOR DELINQUENCY PREVENTION AND CONTROL   448
SUMMARY   450
DISCUSSION QUESTIONS   451
NOTES   452

NAME INDEX   454

SUBJECT INDEX   457

PREFACE

Publication of this fifth edition of *Juvenile Delinquency* provided an opportunity to reflect on the changes in the amount and types of juvenile misbehavior and the juvenile justice responses to it that have taken place since the first edition was published 25 years ago. The cyclical nature of delinquency and the increased formalization of juvenile court procedures and juvenile justice system approaches became apparent in this examination.

The first edition explored the problems of youth deviance and unlawful behavior in the United States at the close of the 1970s and the methods used at that time to inhibit, detect, punish, deter, or reduce this activity. It reported trends and developments in the amount and nature of delinquency that are still occurring, including increased similarities in the amount and types of offenses committed by males and females; involvement of younger age groups in delinquent activity; and increases in middle class suburban and rural youths' misbehavior, gang activity, and substance abuse. It was noted that treatment strategies had moved beyond the "medical model" and had begun to focus on minimization of penetration into the system, community treatment, deinstitutionalization, and the "right to punishment."

The second edition focused on delinquency in the mid-1980s. The continuing narrowing of the gap between the rates of male and female offending and overrepresentation of minority group members in arrests for property crime and violent crime were important trends. Key issues were the pressures for removal of both status offenders (those who commit offenses that are unlawful only for juveniles) and serious violent delinquents from juvenile court jurisdiction, and revision of juvenile codes to formalize processing of serious offenders and mandate their referral to adult criminal courts or specialized youth courts. For other offenders, the emphasis was on diversion, community treatment, and deinstitutionalization.

At the beginning of the 1990s, the third edition noted increases in arrests of juveniles for offenses related to substance abuse and substantial increases in gang activity, which was regarded as a serious threat to safety in the schools and inner-city neighborhoods. As a result of policies for separate handling of delinquent and status offenders at all levels of the juvenile justice system, the debate over status offenders had largely subsided. Increased attention was given to physical and sexual abuse as threats to the welfare of children and the juvenile court procedures for dealing with these problems became important. Firmer handling of serious offenders and more severe dispositions for habitual, serious offenders had been initiated, leading to increases in the number of juveniles held in long-term institutions. Treatment in institutions now focused on education, job skills, and preparation for return to the community rather than on the personal problems of the offenders. For other offenders, restitution, community service, and intensive probation were used. Privatization of juvenile corrections was a new trend.

When the fourth edition appeared in the mid-1990s, increases in arrests of juveniles for serious and violent crimes and overrepresentation of minority group youths in these types of offenses, new surges in gang activity and expansion in the age ranges of gang members, and rapid increases in female delinquency were noted. These trends were seen as creating an identity crisis for the juvenile courts. Many states lowered the upper age of juvenile court jurisdiction so that older adolescent offenders could be referred directly to adult courts. Juvenile court procedures were formalized and there were new pressures for complete removal of status offenders from juvenile court jurisdiction. Increases in the number of abuse, neglect, and dependency cases required the juvenile courts to devote more attention to these cases. The demands for harsher penalties for serious juvenile offenders resulted in waiver of more cases to adult criminal courts. The trend toward more severe dispositions for habitual, serious offenders continued, with increases in the number of institutionalized juveniles and close supervision of them when they were released. Institutional treatment continued to focus on the skills needed for reintegration into the community. Privatization of juvenile corrections increased. The schools began to take greater responsibility for delinquency prevention programming.

As this fifth edition of *Juvenile Delinquency* appears at the beginning of the 21st century, it is apparent that the problems of youth have not changed appreciably over the past 25 years, but certain trends can be identified. Juvenile arrests for both violent and property crimes declined considerably in the late 1990s, but offenses related to the personal, family and community behavior of youths, including substance abuse, offenses against family, and disorderly conduct, increased. School-related violence and gang activity continued to capture the headlines, minority group youths were still overrepresented in every facet of the juvenile justice system, and involvement of females in gang activity and serious and violent delinquencies showed strong increases. The reductions in arrests for violent and property crimes have been attributed to the strong economy in the late 1990s, harsher dispositions for and closer supervision of serious offenders, and the institutionalization of many habitual serious offenders. However, as the economy declined in the early 2000s, serious and violent delinquency began to increase again, underlining the connection between poverty and lack of opportunities and delinquency.

The formalization of juvenile court procedures has continued and some legal scholars have questioned the wisdom of having a separate juvenile justice system. Many states have lowered the upper age of juvenile court jurisdiction so that older adolescent offenders are referred directly to adult courts. Judicial waiver (transfer of juveniles' cases to adult criminal courts), statutory exclusion (giving criminal courts original jurisdiction over certain offenses by juveniles, so that they are automatically excluded from the juvenile court), and concurrent jurisdiction (both the juvenile and criminal courts have jurisdiction, but the prosecutor has the discretion to file the case in either type of court) have resulted in the removal of many serious delinquency cases from the juvenile courts. The renewed call for removal of status offenders from juvenile court jurisdiction is a challenge to the purposes of the court, which was originally designed to intervene in and touch the lives of any youths believed to be disposed toward unacceptable or inappropriate conduct. The challenges facing today's juvenile courts, court decisions that have influenced changes in their procedures, and discussion of their future are presented in Chapters 13 and 18.

More severe dispositions for habitual, serious offenders frequently take the form of institutionalization. Treatment strategies in institutions that focus of preparing the incarcerated youths for return to the community are described in Chapter 17. Such programs as restitution, community service, and intensive probation promote greater involvement of the community in delinquency prevention and control. New programs designed for these purposes are described in Chapters 14 and 18.

Police and the courts are developing diversion programs and intensive supervision possibilities based on the "balanced approach," which gives equal consideration to protecting the community and rehabilitating offenders. The schools, which have become a focal point for meeting the needs of many children who have no other agency contacts, have developed programs to feed needy children during the school day, reach out to their families, and provide for their safety as they travel to and from school, through patrol of areas near the schools and by use of in-school police officers who present classes on drug- and alcohol-abuse prevention and avoiding sexual exploitation. Schools are also offering opportunities for teenage mothers to continue their education and peer influence groups are formed to encourage youths to stay in school and avoid gang influences.

The conditions early theorists associated with delinquency, such as poverty, crowded living conditions, and lack of educational opportunities, can still be accepted as explanations for a portion of delinquent behavior, but they have little validity in explaining middle-class delinquency. The influence of portrayals of violent and morally permissive subject matter in the mass media, violent video games, lack of supervision of young people brought on by the need for both parents to contribute to the family income or parents' desires for self-fulfillment, rootlessness and lack of extended family ties, the impersonality of large school systems, and the lack of opportunities for meaningful work for teenagers, or various combinations of these factors, have been demonstrated to be conditions that contribute to the misbehavior of certain young people. It is apparent that delinquency is still a complex phenomenon that defies easy explanations.

In this fifth edition of *Juvenile Delinquency*, these matters and many others related to juvenile delinquency in contemporary society were examined with the help of professionals in the juvenile justice field, including juvenile court judges, probation and aftercare officers, police officers, youth leaders, social workers, researchers, and those involved in special diversion or community treatment programs. Their candor, assistance, and encouragement helped us to develop *Juvenile Delinquency's* fifth edition into a book that we believe presents a picture of delinquency and the juvenile justice system as they were, as they are, and as they may exist in the future. We thank the following persons for their contributions, cooperation, and suggestions: Former Judge Saundra Robinson, Summit County (Ohio) Juvenile Court; former Judge Leodis Harris of the Court of Common Pleas of Cuyahoga County (Ohio);

Rod Schneider, Administrator, Multi-County Juvenile Attention System; Commander Sollie Vincent, Gang Unit, Chicago Police Department; Captain James Albrecht, New York City Police Department; Sergeant Lawrence J. Bobrowski, Chicago Police Department; Dr. Jacqueline Y. Warren, Counseling Psychologist and Family Therapist, Cuyahoga County (Ohio) Juvenile Court; Anthony Leone, former Director, Tobin Attention Center; Thomas Cerne, Probation Supervisor, Summit County Juvenile Court; Micholas DelGrosso, Director, Restitution Program, Summit Count Juvenile Court; Kristal Y. Brown; James Dunn; Annette Kratcoski; Peter Christopher Kratcoski; Leonard Kratcoski; Carrie Lavery; Heidi Kay Ott; Deborah Ricker; Lynaia Romeo; and Jacqueline Ullmer.

Our editor from Prentice Hall, Sharon Chambliss, and our project coordinator from Pine Tree Composition, Jessica Balch, provided invaluable suggestions and assistance.

Peter C. Kratcoski

Lucille Kratcoski

INTRODUCTION

A go-go dancer who had been left in charge of her young cousins was charged with child endangerment Monday after one boy's corpse was found in a plastic storage bin and his two starving brothers were rescued from a locked room. Sherry Murphy, 41, is accused of beating and burning the three boys. . . . Faheem's body was found in a basement storage bin. . . . A day earlier, Faheem's twin brother Raheem [age 7] and another brother, Tyrone [age 4], were found locked in a basement room in the same house. . . . Tyrone had burns from his neck down his body. Melinda Williams [the boys' mother] told police she put the children in Murphy's [her cousin's] care in March when she went to the Essex Country jail to serve time.[1]

*   *   *

Twaun Asphy was hanging out on the playground before school when he saw them—a crowd of students from a rival elementary school, approaching fast and swinging baseball bats and planks of wood at any child in their path. . . .

"They grabbed my friend and hit him with a two-by-four in the back and in the eye," Twaun said. That boy was one of 18 Songhai students treated for cuts and bruises at hospitals after Thursday's fight. . . . Even some Chicago police veterans were startled at the age of the children involved.[2]

*   *   *

Pictures of Robert Williams' 17-year-old son sit on the kitchen table of his tidy home in South Los Angeles. . . . The teenager was gunned down by gang members on his way to a neighborhood store last week. . . .

Friends and neighbors said Williams, a high school senior and computer whiz, had no connection to gangs, regularly attended church with his father, and did chores in the neighborhood. His slaying occurred during a recent surge of primarily gang-related violence that saw 16 people killed in six days. Some of the victims, like Williams, were not gang members but simply people who appeared to be in the wrong place at the wrong time.[3]

*   *   *

Dale A. Reed, 15, was indicted Thursday in the murder of Jaden Lacher, who police say was shaken so severely that he later died. . . . Reed was arrested September 30 for allegedly shaking the 4-month-old boy two days earlier. . . . Prosecutors are trying to classify Reed as a "serious youthful offender," which opens the door to a so-called "blended sentence.". . . That means Reed would receive a juvenile sentence and an adult sentence if he's convicted. If he violated his juvenile sentence by breaking a law or prison rule, he could be thrown into an adult prison to serve the adult penalty. Since he could receive an adult sentence, Reed is entitled to a trial by jury.[4]

As shown by these news accounts, many juveniles in contemporary America live in family situations that are far different from those of the ideal or "typical" American family. One-parent families, those blended through divorce and remarriage, families made up of young people and grandparents who have assumed responsibility for their upbringing, and even situations where young people live independently because they have been "thrown away" or forced out of their former home situations exist. Poverty is a reality of life for many children and, as we also saw in these news stories, the environments in which some children grow up are plagued by violence, fear of physical harm from family members or in the neighborhood, and too early familiarity with the problems of adult life. Others have parents who are so absorbed in work or their own personal needs that they have little time for or interest in their children. Even for young people who are maturing in stable, safe, and caring environments, the preteen and teen years can be times of inner conflict, self-doubt, and even fear of the future. Of course, they are also years of excitement, emerging physical and mental capabilities, testing of values, strong peer influence, desire for status, and a search for one's place in the larger society.

As part of the maturation process, youths are sure to feel pulled toward activities that may be defined as inappropriate, extreme, shocking, or completely unacceptable by parents or other adults responsible for regulating youths' behavior. While certain young people may be known in their own neighborhoods or schools as "bad influences," "wild kids," or even members of loosely organized gangs responsible for periodic outbreaks of malicious mischief, they manage to move through the adolescent years into adulthood without any official involvement with juvenile authorities. They have no recorded offenses, are certainly not regarded as *juvenile delinquents* in the strictest sense, and their escapades become the basis of stories about the "good old days" as the years pass.

Other young people, who have been involved in similar or even less serious offenses, may discover that their lives are deeply affected when they are caught up in official involvement with the juvenile justice system and are subjected to treatment, rehabilitation, punishment, or whatever handling is judged appropriate for them. The effect may vary from determination never to commit another offense and a positive change in environmental or school situations to little or no change in the young person's life, and association with more hardened or experienced offenders, who may draw a young person toward continued or extended delinquent involvement.

Certain youths are exposed to and adopt patterns of deviant behavior that become increasingly serious as they mature. Others, who appear to have received strong family support and exposure to appropriate values, may also become involved in serious delinquency. These young people pose special problems for the juvenile justice system and for society.

When the juvenile court was created at the beginning of the 20th century, it embraced the concept of *parens patriae,* which implies that the function of the court is to serve as a parent substitute. As illustrated in the cases presented earlier, juvenile justice is not concerned only with juveniles who violate the law, but also with those who are in need of protection. The juvenile court was established to address the problems in the social existence of immature youths that may lead to deviant behavior and also to provide them with protection and assistance. To accomplish this, the juvenile justice system, with the juvenile court or family court as its heart, has parameters that extend to include all of the legal, educational, and social service agencies that in some way have responsibility for youths who are deviant or those in need of assistance or protection. The system has responsibility for delinquents; status offenders; and abused, dependent, and neglected children.

In *Juvenile Delinquency,* we explore the problem of delinquency by examining the backgrounds and problems of those officially regarded as delinquents, as well as the more general needs of juveniles who are acting within the larger population of unreported or unrecorded delinquents. Part One of this book, "Defining and Explaining Delinquency," reports the current trends in officially reported and self-reported delinquency and the biological, psychological, and sociological theories that have been formulated to explain delinquency. In Part Two, "Delinquency and the Social Environment," we examine the changing role of children in our society and consider the arenas of juvenile interaction where problems of unacceptable behavior may arise—the family, the neighborhood peer group, the school, and the larger community. Physical and sexual abuse and neglect are given considerable attention and the types of family situations in which abuse is most likely to occur are described. Justice system handling of abuse cases and methods for protecting abused and neglected children are presented.

Part Three, "Delinquency and the Juvenile Justice Process," presents key issues in the juvenile justice process, including the propriety of applying to children legal penalties that would not be given to adults engaged in the same activity and the options for dealing with violent juvenile offenders and those whose repeated serious offenses seem to make them too hardened or "hardcore" for handling by the juvenile court. The juvenile justice process is described and discussed in detail, with attention to diversion, arrest, referral to the juvenile court, disposition, probation, institutionalization, aftercare, and community treatment. The case history of a juvenile offender is followed from apprehension through disposition. Interviews with juvenile court judges, intake officers, probation officers, and directors of diversion programs give a picture of the wide diversity of possibilities available within the juvenile justice system. In Part Four, "Preventing, Treating, and Controlling Delinquency," we describe traditional and innovative treatment techniques and present the evaluative research conducted to measure their effectiveness. We also describe delinquency-prevention programs and we discuss trends in delinquency control, including juvenile code revision and possible changes in the jurisdiction of the juvenile court.

Throughout this book, the juvenile is the center of attention. As he or she comes into conflict with community norms, an action-reaction chain of events begins to occur. If impulses toward delinquency can be blunted or the energy spent on them can be channeled into other directions, the child remains within the bounds of socially tolerated behavior. Continued advance beyond these bounds increases the likelihood of some interaction with justice system personnel, penetration into the system, envelopment in the system, and perhaps, loss of freedom or initiation into a lifelong pattern of deviance.

The juvenile justice system must balance the needs of the community and society in general with the needs of individual youths. In this book, we demonstrate how changes in philosophy, thought, and political climate resulted in changes of emphasis in the juvenile justice system. Currently, the system is moving toward a balanced approach and "restorative justice," a philosophy that gives equal consideration to the needs and rights of offenders and victims and the safety of the community.

NOTES

1. Steve Strunsky, "Woman Charged after Boy Found Dead," *Akron Beacon Journal*, January 7, 2003, A5.
2. Martha Irvine, "Elementary Schools Brawl; 18 Hurt," *Akron Beacon Journal*, April 6, 2002, A6.
3. Paul Chavez, "Los Angeles Gang Violence Fueling Wave of Murders," *Akron Beacon Journal*, November 27, 2002, A6.
4. Stephen Dyer, "Stark Teen Denies Killing Infant," *Akron Beacon Journal*, December 7, 2002, B1.

CHAPTER 1

DEFINITIONS, SCOPE, AND TRENDS IN JUVENILE DELINQUENCY

(Photo credit: Nick J. Cool, The Image Works)

DEFINING DELINQUENCY
SOCIETAL REACTION TO YOUTHFUL MISBEHAVIOR
DELINQUENT AND STATUS OFFENSES
SCOPE OF JUVENILE DELINQUENCY
    Officially Recorded Delinquency
    Self-Reported Delinquency Studies
    Victimization Surveys
TRENDS IN DELINQUENT BEHAVIOR
    Total Arrest Trends
    Crimes of Violence by Juveniles
    Substance Abuse
    Minority-Group Crime
    Female Delinquency
    Delinquency in Suburban and Rural Areas

Juvenile misbehavior occurs in every city, town, and rural area throughout the United States. Although violent, aggressive acts by juveniles capture the spotlight, juvenile delinquency extends beyond these acts and encompasses a wide range of inappropriate activities by young people. In spite of the growing public concern about juvenile crime, even those who seek to explain and prevent it may be at a loss when called upon to define exactly what juvenile delinquency is. In this chapter, we will discuss the social and legal definitions of juvenile delinquency, with emphasis on our society's response to various types of juvenile misbehavior. We will compare the amount of officially recorded delinquency with data from self-reported delinquency surveys (anonymous reports by young people) and victimization studies (surveys of crime victims). We will also look at the troubling recent trends in the amount, types, location, and severity of juvenile delinquency.

DEFINING DELINQUENCY

Broadly considered, juvenile delinquency could mean any type of behavior by those socially defined as juveniles that violates the norms (standards of proper behavior) set by the controlling group. From this viewpoint, juveniles could be considered delinquent if they adopted modes of hairstyle, dress, or action that were opposed to the standards set by those in authority.

In a narrower sense, juvenile delinquency is defined as any action by someone designated a juvenile (nonadult) that would make such a young person subject to action by the juvenile court. Even here there are problems of definition, since many youths who commit such acts are not reported or subjected to official juvenile court action. Are we to consider every young person guilty of such misbehavior a juvenile delinquent, or does this apply only if the guilty party is apprehended and processed? If we take the broader view, virtually every child in America would have to be considered a juvenile delinquent, since the following types of behavior could make him or her subject to juvenile court action:

2

Skipping school

Making anonymous telephone calls

Gambling for money

Staying out past curfew

Running away from home

Purchasing or drinking wine, beer, or liquor

Buying, using, or selling illicit drugs

Setting fire to buildings or other property to damage it

Driving a car without a license or permit

Driving too fast or recklessly

Using threat of force to get something from someone else

Drag racing

Taking or riding in a person's car without permission

Taking any item from a store without paying for it

Carrying a dangerous weapon

Taking part in a gang fight

Having a fist fight

Using or accepting something that another has taken without permission

Deliberately damaging or destroying another's property

Trespassing

Sending in a false fire alarm

Deliberately disobeying parents

Having sexual relations with a person of the opposite sex

Having homosexual relations

Breaking into or forcibly entering a residence or place of business

Although all these actions cause young people to be brought to the attention of the juvenile court, a youth is not normally considered a juvenile delinquent unless he or she has been officially processed by the juvenile court and judged (adjudicated) as such.

Even the word "juvenile" can have a variety of connotations when it is combined with "delinquent." Sixteen states have established minimum ages for juvenile court referral. These range from 6 through 10 years, with 11 of the states setting the minimum age at 10 years.[1] Although common law presumes that a child younger than 7 cannot be held criminally responsible, the matter has not been defined in state statutes. The upper age of the juvenile status is not uniform in federal and state codes. All states set upper age limits for original juvenile court jurisdiction. This refers to the youth's age at the time an offense was committed. For example, a youth who committed an offense while within the upper age limit of the juvenile court, but was not apprehended until after he or she exceeded the upper age limit, could still be subject to juvenile court jurisdiction. Thirty-seven states and the District of Columbia, as well as federal codes, use age 17; 10 states use age 16, and three states use age 15.[2] Thus, in the majority of states a person is legally defined as a juvenile until his or her 18th birthday, and legally becomes an adult at that point.

All states allow juveniles to be tried as adults in criminal courts under certain circumstances. In several states, if the offense is a very serious felony, such as homicide, the juvenile court does not have *original* jurisdiction. In New York, juveniles charged with murder may be tried as adults. In a Bath, New York, case involving a 14-year-old charged with bludgeoning and strangling a 4-year-old boy, the defense argued that the youth suffered from a disorder that made him prone to uncontrollable rages. The jury rejected this explanation, and convicted him of second-degree murder, with a possible sentence of nine years to life in prison. A newspaper account of the 14-year-old's confession reported that the older boy coaxed the victim into a wooded area on the pretext that it was a shortcut to a day camp he attended, then squeezed his neck, stuffed a paper towel and a lunch bag in his mouth, and crushed his skull with a 26-pound rock.[3]

A juvenile may also be tried in an adult court in a case of *concurrent jurisdiction*. In such instances, which usually involve serious, violent, or repeated offenses, the prosecutor has the choice of filing charges against a youth in either the juvenile court or the adult criminal court. But the predominant means by which cases involving juveniles come to adult criminal courts is through *judicial waiver*, or transfer from the juvenile court, which has original jurisdiction. Eighteen states and federal statutes do not specify a lower age limit at which juvenile cases can be waived to adult courts, but for those states with a lower age limit, this age ranges from 10 to 14.[4]

In some instances, the criminal court may elect to transfer a case to the juvenile court. For example, a very young child charged with a serious offense would be a candidate for transfer. This process is sometimes termed *reverse waiver*.

In an appendix to the *Kent* v. *U.S.* decision, the U.S. Supreme Court set the following criteria to be used by states in deciding on transfers of juveniles to criminal courts for trial:

1. The seriousness of the alleged offense and the need to protect the community.

2. Whether the alleged offense was committed in an aggressive, violent, premeditated, or willful manner.

3. Whether the alleged offense was against persons or against property, greater weight being given to offenses against persons, especially if personal injury resulted.

4. The prosecutive merit of the complaint (i.e., the likelihood of conviction).

5. Whether the juvenile's associates in the alleged offense are adults who will be charged with crimes in the adult court.

6. The sophistication and maturity of the juvenile as determined by consideration of his or her home, environmental situation, emotional attitude, and pattern of living.

7. The record and previous history of the juvenile.[5]

SOCIETAL REACTION TO YOUTHFUL MISBEHAVIOR

Concern about the behavior of the youth of a country is a universal phenomenon, regardless of the society in question or the point in history. In some societies, cultural values, beliefs, customs, and material possessions do not change much from one generation to another, whereas in other cases, change is very rapid. But no matter how stable or traditional a society appears to be, people do not remain exactly the same from one generation to the next. New attitudes, behavior patterns, clothing styles, and values are constantly appearing, and most often the younger generation introduces these changes. They are not always readily accepted by those in the society who have already established a comfortable way of life and wish to maintain the current standards.

Behavior by a society's young people that deviates from accepted standards will often be tolerated or even encouraged if it does not appear to threaten the well-being of the society as a whole. When those in authority decide that certain actions by some youths are threatening to the common good, however, the behavior is no longer tolerated and attempts are made to suppress it and punish the violators. If "normal" behavior is behavior that is considered acceptable at a particular time in a certain society, then a juvenile delinquent is, in a sociological sense, "any child who deviates from normal behavior so as to endanger himself, his social career, or the community."[6]

The types of behavior by youth that are defined as unacceptable may range from extremely antisocial actions to only minor nonconformity; and the society's response to this youthful behavior may range from strong condemnation to mild disapproval. In a highly urbanized, mobile, industrialized society, the degree of conformity to standards and values held by the society is not absolute. Children are not expected to be perfect, and deviation is tolerated if the behavior is not viewed by adults as particularly threatening. In fact, children who conform exactly to the expectations set up for them tend to be viewed by both adults and their peers as somewhat abnormal. Occasional disobedience, mischief, violating parents' or the city's curfews, or fighting when provoked generally do not lead to official action. As the degree of nonconforming behavior moves farther away from accepted standards, however, the tolerance of such behavior declines. Even though a youth may not be subject to official action at this stage, he or she may be characterized by adults as "a bad influence," or "looking for trouble." The more serious misbehavior that may occur at this stage may be handled by the parents, the school, or as an unofficial action by the police.

When youthful misbehavior reaches the point of frequent dishonesty, deceitful or destructive activity, theft, or serious assault, the violator begins to feel the full weight of public disapproval. Parents and school officials may feel inadequate to handle the problems. When the police decide to treat these more serious matters officially, the juvenile court enters the picture. Attempts may first be made to counsel and assist the child through programs outside official court action. If an unconforming youth is brought into juvenile court and adjudicated delinquent, this label is an additional sign of the public's rejection and disfavor. Eventually, a youth who continues to violate the society's values and norms in serious matters may be socially isolated from society through placement in an institution for juveniles.

An additional consideration is the fact that the acceptable standard of behavior varies from society to society—and even within the same society for children of various social classes or according to the sex of the child. For example, parents who know that their teenage son is having sexual encounters with various girls may express disapproval but inwardly feel a certain sense of pride that the son is so virile and is such a "ladies' man." However, if the same parents discover that their teenage daughter is involved in sexual activity with a number of young men, they are apt to take immediate action to stop her behavior and may take official action to have the boys punished.

DELINQUENT AND STATUS OFFENSES

Those who fit the "juvenile" status as defined by their state of residence are subject to arrest for two broad types of offenses. The first type is that for which adults also may be arrested—murder, arson, rape, robbery, shoplifting, auto theft, and so on. But young people may also be arrested, referred to juvenile court, and even institutionalized for activities that would not be considered criminal for adults—such as truancy, incorrigibility, running away from home, violations of curfew laws, purchase or drinking of alcoholic beverages, or various sexual acts. In juvenile codes, a distinction is made between the two types of offenses. Those that would be criminal for adults are termed "delinquent" offenses, whereas those that are law violations only if committed by juveniles are called "status," "unruly," or "beyond control" offenses. Some states have developed such categories as Minors in Need of Supervision (MINS), Persons in Need of Supervision (PINS), Children in Need of Supervision (CHINS), or Juveniles in Need of Supervision (JINS) to differentiate status offenders from delinquent offenders. Even though most states make distinctions between delinquent and status offenses in their juvenile codes, status offenders are still subject to juvenile court action. In some states, the status offender problem is approached by *decriminalization* of some of these behaviors, so that they are no longer grounds for juvenile court referrals. If it is felt that some court intervention or supervision is required, the youths involved are classified as dependent or neglected children and the primary responsibility for working with them is given to child protective services by the juvenile court.[7]

Status offending can have more serious repercussions if juveniles who have been referred to juvenile courts for status offenses and placed on probation commit new offenses and are brought back to the court as probations violators. Since violation of probation is a delinquent offense, the youths have now been recategorized as delinquent offenders.

The matter of the legal definition of delinquency is of great concern and a debate over the referral of status offenders to juvenile courts rages in legal, judicial, and social-service circles. This controversy is explored in detail in Chapter 11.

Even within the group of offenses categorized as "delinquent" (offenses that would also be unlawful for adults), most states have not developed juvenile codes that make distinctions between felony and misdemeanor offenses, or between offenses that are punishable by institutionalization and those that are not. We shall see that this situation is a result of the philosophy adopted by the juvenile court at its beginning, which is discussed in detail in Chapter 5.

SCOPE OF JUVENILE DELINQUENCY

The total number of offenses by juveniles in any given period of time is impossible to ascertain. Although the Federal Bureau of Investigation (FBI) records and statistically analyzes the number of juvenile arrests for various offenses each year, the illegal behavior by juveniles that is not detected or reported to the police is not accounted for in any statistical report. Information about the amount and nature of juvenile misbehavior comes from three major sources. First, official statistical information is provided by police departments to the FBI and reports by other agencies that deal with juvenile offenders are summarized by the Department of Justice. A second way of obtaining information about delinquency is through surveys that ask juveniles whether they have committed acts that resulted in or could have resulted in arrest or referral to the juvenile court. The findings of such surveys are called "self-reported delinquency" data. Research of this type has certain shortcomings, including the difficulty of knowing whether youths are overreporting or underreporting the amount and types of behavior in which they have engaged. Some self-reported delinquency studies have sought to verify the data collected by comparing them with juvenile court records for the same sample of youths. This technique is also limiting, however, because it does not allow the anonymity that respondents need if they are to reply truthfully, without fear of punishment. Crime victimization surveys provide a third source of information about offenses committed by juveniles. These surveys, usually conducted by telephone, solicit information from a random sample of people about their experiences as victims of crime. Those surveyed are asked to provide information on the types and number of offenses committed against them and to estimate the ages of the offenders. Again, the possibility of ascertaining the actual amount and nature of juvenile illegal activity is limited, since the victim must be willing to discuss the crime and must have seen the perpetrator in order to make an age estimate.

Officially Recorded Delinquency

In its Uniform Crime Report, *Crime in the United States*, each year the FBI provides information on the arrests made by law enforcement agencies in the United States. These annual arrest figures do not actually measure the number of persons taken into custody, since a person may be arrested several times during a given year for a number of offenses. Of those arrested in 2001, approximately 17 percent were under age 18. More than 15 percent of the arrests for violent crime in the same year (murder and manslaughter, forcible rape, robbery, and aggravated assault) were of those under 18, as were approximately 30 percent of all arrests for property crime (burglary, larceny, theft, and motor vehicle theft).[8] The 2001 Uniform Crime Report also noted that 12 percent of the violent crime *clearances* and 21 percent of the property crime *clearances* in that year involved only persons under age 18.[9] Clearance by arrest for an offender under 18 is recorded when a youth is cited to appear in juvenile court or before other juvenile authorities, even though no physical arrest may have been made.

Table 1–1 shows the number of persons under 18 years of age arrested by each type of offense reported in the Uniform Crime Report for 2001, ranked from highest to lowest number of arrests, and the percentage of all arrests of those under 18 for each offense.

As shown in Table 1–1, individual offense categories showing high percentages of arrests of those under 18 included arson (49%), vandalism (39%), motor vehicle theft (33%), suspicion (32%), burglary (31%), and larceny-theft (30%). Those under age 18 were arrested for all of the status offenses included in the report (curfew and loitering law violations, runaways).[10] These arrest figures are not identical to

Table 1–1. Arrests of Persons under 18 Years of Age in 2001

Offense Charged	Number under Age 18 Arrested	Percent of All Arrests for This Offense
All other offenses (except traffic)	269,317	11%
Larceny-theft	238,605	30%
Other assaults	163,142	18%
Drug abuse	139,238	13%
Disorderly conduct	117,635	28%
Curfew and loitering law violations	100,701	100%
Liquor law violations	92,326	23%
Runaway	91,168	100%
Vandalism	71,962	39%
Burglary	61,623	31%
Aggravated assault	44,815	14%
Motor vehicle theft	33,563	33%
Carrying or possessing weapons	25,861	23%
Buying, receiving, possessing stolen property	18,467	22%
Robbery	18,111	24%
Drunkenness	13,971	3%
Driving under the influence	13,397	1%
Sex offenses other than rape and prostitution	12,381	20%
Arson	6,313	49%
Offenses against the family and children	6,286	7%
Fraud	5,830	3%
Forgery	3,975	5%
Forcible rape	3,119	17%
Vagrancy	1,607	8%
Prostitution and commercialized vice	1,034	2%
Gambling	1,000	13%
Murder and non-negligent manslaughter	957	10%
Suspicion	834	32%

Source: Developed by Lucille Kratcoski from Federal Bureau of Investigation, *Crime in the United States, 2001* (Washington, DC: U.S. Department of Justice, 2002), 244.

those for juvenile arrests, since in a number of states the juvenile status extends only to age 16 or 17.

Another tabulation of officially recorded delinquency appears in *Juvenile Court Statistics*, compiled by the National Center for Juvenile Justice for the Office of Juvenile Justice and Delinquency Prevention within the U.S. Department of Justice. The 1996 statistics revealed that nearly 2 million cases of persons under age 18 were referred to juvenile courts in that year, 92 percent for delinquent offenses, and 8 percent for status offenses. The ratio of male to female referrals was approximately 4.3 to 1 for delinquent offenses and 2.4 to 1 for status offenses.[11]

Even if youths come to the attention of the police, there is a good chance that they will escape processing by the juvenile court and thus avoid the "delinquency" label. The majority of police contacts with youths are handled informally, with the youths being given warnings, told to leave the area, or released to their parents without being taken into custody. Of the juveniles formally taken into custody by police in 2001, 19 percent were handled within police departments and released, 2 percent were referred to welfare or other agencies, 72 percent were referred to juvenile courts, and 7 percent were referred to criminal or adult courts.[12]

Although in any given year the likelihood of a youth's being referred to a juvenile court is relatively slight (1 in 25), if the youth is followed through the entire 10-through-17 age period, the chances of referral increase. Two longitudinal studies of boys in the city of Philadelphia, involving a sample of youths born in 1945 and another sample born in 1958, found that 33 percent of the first group and 35 percent of the second group had at least one police contact before reaching their 18th birthday.[13]

Self-Reported Delinquency Studies

Self-report studies of delinquency are usually conducted by asking groups of youths to respond anonymously to a checklist of acts they may have performed that could, if discovered, have resulted in referral to juvenile authorities. The respondents are asked to indicate whether they have engaged in these types of behavior and, if so, how often. The participants are assured that the information will not be revealed in such a way that they could be identified. Interviews are sometimes used in self-report delinquency studies, but this is more frequently done when the youths involved have already come to the attention of the courts or counseling services.

Self-report studies consistently reveal that the amount of juvenile illegal activity is much greater than officially recorded. The most extensive attempt to collect and compare self-reports nationally is a project developed by the Institute for Social Research of the University of Michigan. Since 1975, annual self-report surveys of high schools seniors' behavior have been conducted using a random sample of high school seniors in public and private schools throughout the United States. The sample members are asked to report their involvement in specific activities during the past 12 months. A comparison of the seniors' responses from 1989 through 2001 reveals only small variations from year to year. In each of the years surveyed, close to 32 percent of the youths had taken something worth under $50 from another, approximately 25 percent had gone into a house or building when they were not supposed to be there, approximately 30 percent had taken something from a store without paying for it, 20 percent had been involved in a fight at school or at work, and 20 percent had been involved in a fight with friends against another group. Approximately 32 percent had received a ticket for speeding, running a red light, or improper passing. The greatest variations in self-reported behavior over these years occurred on items related to alcohol and drug use. Alcohol use showed a consistent pattern of decline (83% in 1989, 73% in 2001). Drug use declined from 1989 through 1992, but increased from 1993 through 2001.[14]

Some self-report studies have found that, although many youths are involved in illegal activities that are never discovered or reported, the majority of such activity is related to personal conduct, rather than actions against others. For example, the National Youth Survey Project gathered self-reported delinquency information from a representative national sample of American youths. The project began in 1976, when the youths were ages 11 to 17. They were contacted for a reassessment of their activities in succeeding years, when their ages were 18 to 24. Over the years, their highest levels of illegal involvement were in alcohol use, public drunkenness, marijuana use, disorderly conduct, truancy, and vandalism. Few of the sample members reported involvement in violent crime or serious property crimes.[15]

The notion that unreported illegal behavior by juveniles generally involves only minor misbehavior was challenged by a self-report study conducted by Peter C. and John E. Kratcoski, who analyzed the self-reported delinquency of 11th and 12th grade students in three public schools and an institution for delinquents. It was discovered that the high school students had committed an average of 8.8 offenses each and an average of 5.6 delinquent offenses each, whereas the institutionalized youths had committed 15 offenses and 10.3 delinquent offenses each.[16]

The value of self-report studies, particularly those conducted over long periods of time, would seem to be the identification of trends in juvenile misbehavior and development of strategies to deal with sudden increases in certain types of misbehavior. They can also be used to gauge the effectiveness of programs for delinquency prevention and control.

Victimization Surveys

In contrast to self-reported delinquency studies, victimization surveys contact random samples of citizens to discover whether they have been victims of crime. As part of the information gathered in these surveys, crime victims are asked to estimate the age of the offender.

The National Crime Survey is conducted each year for the Bureau of Justice Statistics by the U.S. Bureau of the Census. The information is gathered from a survey of a representative sample of housing units in the United States. In the 1999 survey, victims of crimes of violence (rape, robbery, and assaults) perceived offenders who acted alone to be ages 12 to 18 in about 22 percent of the reported incidents and, in multiple offender cases of the same types, more than 40 percent of the victims perceived the offenders as being ages 12 to 20.[17]

Although official statistics, self-report surveys, and victimization studies are all helpful in providing information about the nature of delinquency, it is impossible to discover accurately and control all delinquent behavior. Juvenile justice and law enforcement agencies can only act on the cases referred to them. Other offenses of equal or greater gravity or frequency go unreported.

TRENDS IN DELINQUENT BEHAVIOR

Total Arrest Trends

In 2001, 17 percent of all persons arrested were under age 18. These youths accounted for 15 percent of the arrests for violent crimes and 30 percent of the arrests for property crimes.[18]

In the 10-year period 1992–2001, there was a 2.5 percent reduction in the total number of arrests of persons under 18 years of age. Youth arrests for violent crimes fell 21 percent and property crime arrests fell 32 percent. These reductions have been attributed to the strong economy during those years, which provided more opportunities for youths, stronger law enforcement, and harsher penalties for repeat serious offenders. Drug abuse arrests of juveniles showed a strong upward trend in the same time period, increasing more than 121 percent. Increases were also noted in offenses against family and children (up 108%), curfew and loitering law violations (up 34%), disorderly conduct up (34%), violations of liquor laws (up 21%), and driving under the influence (35%).[19]

Crimes of Violence by Juveniles

Crimes of violence by juveniles reached an all-time high in 1994 and have declined since that time, but violence by juveniles is still an important problem. In the 2000s, violence in and near schools and gang-related violence are major concerns.

Seven widely publicized school shootings occurred within a 19-month period in 1998 and 1999, including the incidents at Columbine High School in Littleton, Colorado (13 killed, 23 wounded) and Jonesboro, Arkansas (5 dead, 10 wounded).[20] These events focused attention on the problems of violence in or near schools that have created a climate of fear in many communities. School responses to this problem have included the use of uniformed security officers within the schools, installation of metal detectors, heightened school security measures, including locking all doors during school hours and allowing access at only one entrance, zero-tolerance policies, under which a student who has brought anything that could be construed as a weapon to school or has made any type of written or verbal threat can be excluded from school, and development of prevention programs through which youths who are identified as possibly violence-prone can be counseled. The problem of school violence is examined in detail in Chapter 9.

Gangs are also involved in violence in and near schools, as well as in drive-by shootings and turf wars that are frequently related to drug dealing. Such incidents may claim innocent victims who happen to be in the areas where violence occurs. There is evidence of a trend toward violent behavior by groups of youths acting together. These may or may not be "gangs," but they pose a serious threat to public safety. The problem of gang violence is discussed in detail in Chapter 6.

Research on the causes and progression of violent juvenile careers has noted that the offenders begin unlawful behavior at young ages. The following characteristics of chronic violent offenders were identified:

Family—The offenders are less attached to and less monitored by their parents.

School—The offenders have less commitment to school and attachment to teachers.

Peers—They have more delinquent peers and are more apt to be gang members.

Neighborhood—They are more likely to reside in poor, high-crime-rate areas.[21]

Although many violent crimes are committed by youths who have long histories of inappropriate behavior and court involvement, violent incidents also occur in which a youth, who to all outward appearances has been a model student and child, well liked by teachers and peers, commits a bizarre crime of violence with no apparent provocation or motive. The following news account describes such an incident.

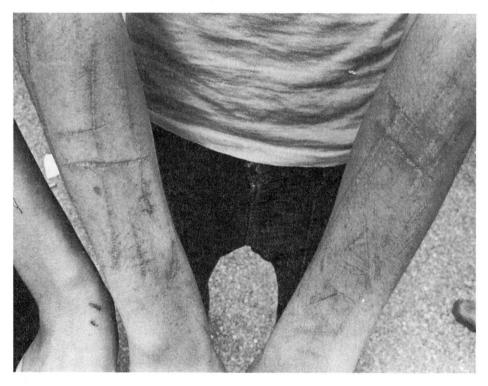

Some youths bear physical scars related to their violent deviant behavior. *(Photo credit: Jay Paris)*

> A 12-year-old . . . boy came to school Tuesday with a loaded shotgun, tied up and robbed 31 other pupils and then fled in a teacher's car, police said.
>
> The boy, who also had a hunting knife, threatened the teacher and students at . . . Middle School by pointing the 16-gauge shotgun at them, according to police.
>
> The boy drove the teacher's [car] to . . . where he was arrested when he hit a police cruiser being used as a roadblock. . . .
>
> [A classmate] described . . . as quiet and said he was liked by most everyone . . . [The police chief] knew of no previous offenses by the boy. [The school superintendent] said the boy had had no apparent problems in school.[22]

It is difficult to analyze the reasons behind youth violence. Explanations include the influence of the mass media, the easy availability of dangerous weapons, the frustrations and anxieties youths experience as part of growing up, lack of parental supervision of or interest in the youth, failure of parents to instill any sort of value system or sense of accountability in their children, and a need for recognition and status that cannot be gained through acceptable behavior.

Teasing and bullying by peers have also been identified as having an impact on youth violence. It was discovered that the youths involved in the seven highly publicized 1998–1999 school shootings had been bullied or teased and/or were regarded as outcasts.[23] The violent incident described below appeared to have similar roots.

> A 13-year-old boy who complained that he was being bullied is charged with shooting one teen to death and injuring two others. . . . Obryant Carr was charged as a juvenile with one count of murder and two counts of felonious assault, police said. . . .
>
> A heated argument took place before the shooting occurred about 6:35 in front of a store. . . . An uncle and grandmother of Carr said the juveniles he is accused of shooting had bullied him since last summer.[24]

Theories of violent behavior causation are discussed in detail in Chapters 2, 3, 4, and 6.

Substance Abuse

Substance abuse by juveniles has long been recognized as a pervasive problem. Self-report studies have revealed that high school students routinely use alcohol and that many are involved in heavy drinking. About one third of high school seniors reported using alcohol before age 13, but the most frequent school level at which they began to use alcohol was the ninth grade.[25] Reported alcohol use by students decreased from 1989 through 2001, but involvement in drug use steadily increased.[26] This is reflected in the finding that, although alcohol-related offenses increased somewhat from 1992 through 2001, drug abuse arrests increased more than 120 percent.[27]

Marijuana is the drug most frequently used by juveniles, followed in frequency of use by amphetamines, hallucinogens, tranquilizers, sedatives, cocaine, inhalants, and other narcotics. The drug ecstasy has become popular with youths from all types of socio-economic backgrounds. Its described effects explain its appeal to adolescents.

> Ecstasy is marketed as a "feel good" drug. Devotees say it produces profoundly positive feelings, empathy for others, elimination of anxiety, and extreme relaxation—hence the name "Hug Drug" or "Love Drug."[28]

The relation of substance abuse to delinquency is a complex one. Although self-report data has shown that youths who used drugs were more frequently involved in many types of delinquencies than those who did not, alcohol and drug abuse can also be seen as one facet of the lifestyles of delinquency-endangered youths, rather than the direct causes of their misbehavior. In Chapters 6 and 9 we examine the relation of substance abuse to school violence and gang activities.

Street drug price list. (Drawings by youth at the Stark Attention Center from "A Call to Action.")

Minority-Group Crime

Another trend in delinquency is the overrepresentation of juveniles who are minority-group members in arrests for both property and violent crime. For example, although blacks made up 13 percent of the juvenile population in 2001, they accounted for 28 percent of the property crime and 43 percent of the violent crime arrests of persons under age 18 in that year. Within the violent crime category, they were involved in 58 percent of the arrests for robbery, 48 percent of those for murder and nonnegligent manslaughter, 36 percent of those for forcible rape, and 36 percent of those for aggravated assault.[29]

When a proportion of a racial or ethnic group larger than its proportion in the juvenile population is present at various stages of juvenile justice system activity (including intake, detention, and residential placement), that group is said to be *overrepresented*.[30] *Overrepresentation* of black juveniles occurs at every stage of the juvenile justice system, as shown in Figure 1–1. This *overrepresentation* may be the result of discrimination on the part of juvenile court personnel in making arrest or detention decisions, or it may be related to the seriousness of their offenses and their offense histories. This question is considered in Chapters 6 and 11.

Female Delinquency

Both official statistics and self-report studies reveal that, with the exception of running away and prostitution/commercialized vice, females commit fewer offenses than males in every juvenile offense category.[31] However, the differences in the sexes in the number and types of offenses committed have been narrowing. For example, the ratio of male to female arrests was 6-to-1 in 1960 and stood at approximately 3.5-to-1 in the 1970s, 1980, and 1990s. In 2001, it was 2.5 to 1.[32] There has been an increased tendency for females to commit violent offenses and more and more females are now involved in offenses that were formerly committed chiefly by males, including property crimes, assaults, disorderly conduct, and curfew and loitering law violations.[33]

The growing involvement of females in violent behavior and other serious offenses is of great concern. Such factors as the greater freedom now experienced by girls as a result of relaxation of social and sexual mores, the declining importance of the family as a controlling influence in the lives of female adolescents, more involvement of girls in gang activity, and the growth of an "underclass" of young single mothers and their children who live in poverty and may resort to deviant behavior as a survival technique may be related to these changes in the nature of female delinquency.

Delinquency in Suburban and Rural Areas

Until recently, delinquency in the United States was considered to be predominantly a product of inner-city poverty, family disorganization, high population density, overcrowded living conditions, and high rates of unemployment. Although these circumstances have continued to contribute to high delinquency rates in the cities,

Figure 1–1. Black juveniles are overrepresented at all stages of the juvenile justice system, compared with their proportion in the population. Sources: Howard N. Snyder and Melissa Sickmund, *Juvenile Offenders and Victims*, 1999 National Report (Washington, DC: Office of Juvenile Justice and Delinquency Prevention, 1999), 192. Authors' analysis of Bureau of the Census' *Estimates of the population of States by age, sex, race, and Hispanic origin: 1990–1997* [machine-readable data files] for 1991 and 1997, Bureau of Justice Statistics' *National Crime Victimization Survey* [machine-readable data files] for 1991 and 1996, FBI's *Crime in the United States* reports for 1991 and 1997, OJJDP's *Juvenile court statistics* reports for 1991 and 1996, OJJDP's *Children in Custody Census of public and private juvenile detention, correctional, and shelter facilities 1990/91* [machine-readable data file], and OJJDP's *Census of Juveniles in Residential Placement 1997* [machine-readable data file].

delinquency is also increasing in suburban and rural areas. In 2001, 18 percent of all arrests in cities were of persons under 18 years of age, while those under 18 accounted for 13 percent of suburban arrests and 11 percent of rural arrests.[34] Delinquency in suburban and rural areas may be greater than reported in arrests statistics, since much of it may be handled informally.[35] Gang activity has also been noted outside urban settings. In the National Youth Gang Survey, active gangs were reported by police agencies in 57 percent of suburbs, 34 percent of small cities, and 25 percent of rural areas.[36] Some research has attributed the increases in delinquent behavior and gang activity in suburban and rural areas to diffusion of delinquent activities from urban areas. Highways may channel delinquent activity from cities to some rural areas, particularly to vacation spots. In addition, industry relocation and population growth have brought many "outsiders" to suburban and rural areas and changed the makeup of the population in those areas.[37]

Control of suburban and rural delinquency presents special problems. Because of the distances from their homes to the nearest city or large consolidated school, many youths own and drive cars and this decreases the possibility of close supervision of their activities by parents. Increases in the numbers of mothers who work outside the home and the long hours both parents may have to spend commuting to jobs leave young people unsupervised for extended periods of time before and after school. Large suburban shopping malls have emerged as centers of adolescent social life, with the attendant problems of opportunities for shoplifting, malicious mischief, or contacts with drug dealers, and their large parking lots are often the sites of motor vehicle thefts and carjackings.

Delinquencies by youths who seem to have had every advantage in upbringing and education are difficult to understand. What motivates the kind of juvenile misbehavior described next, committed by youths from a wealthy suburban school district?

> . . . School Superintendent . . . said Saturday that many parents are disappointed and their children are remorseful about a shoplifting spree that occurred last weekend on the three-day field trip to Williamsburg, VA.
>
> Fourteen of 150 . . . Middle School pupils stole hundreds of dollars' worth of jewelry and souvenirs from Williamsburg shops. The misdemeanors came to light when a chaperone overheard some of the pupils talking about their escapade.
>
> The school chaperones returned to the shops with the pupils—all eighth graders—who confessed and returned the stolen merchandise.
>
> . . . The merchants were surprised by what had happened and surprised the pupils returned the items.[38]

Chapters 2, 3, and 4 are devoted to discussions of theories of delinquency causation.

SUMMARY

Juvenile delinquency may be defined as any action by a person considered a juvenile that would make him or her subject to action by the juvenile court. Most young people are involved in some unlawful behavior during the adolescent years but escape detection, apprehension, or court involvement. Only those who have been officially adjudicated as such by a juvenile court are normally designated "juvenile delinquents."

The definition of the juvenile age status differs in various states. A lower age limit has been set in 16 states; in the others, the age of 7, the common-law minimum for criminal responsibility, is normally applied. The upper age limit of juvenile court jurisdiction is 17 in 37 states and the District of Columbia, 16 in 10 states, and 15 in 3 states. Juveniles guilty of certain serious crimes may be tried in adult criminal courts in every state. This may occur when state statutes give juvenile courts no jurisdiction over certain offenses; when concurrent jurisdiction of the adult and juvenile courts exists and the prosecutor decides to try the case in the adult court; or by judicial waiver, in which the case is transferred from the juvenile court to an adult criminal court.

Juvenile deviation from societal norms has existed throughout history, and it is usually tolerated unless the behavior becomes so extreme that the common good is threatened. As behavior becomes more seriously antisocial, sanctions may be applied by parents or the school, or by police in an unofficial manner. But if such methods fail, arrest and referral to court may follow.

Juveniles may be referred to courts for two broad types of offenses. Acts that would also be illegal for adults are termed "delinquent" offenses; violations of regulations that apply only to juveniles are variously known as "status," "unruly," or "beyond control" offenses. Both types of offenses can lead to court involvement, adjudication as a delinquent, and even institutionalization. The question of whether status offenses should be removed from juvenile court jurisdiction is a hotly debated issue in juvenile justice today, and will be discussed in detail in Chapter 11.

The actual amount of delinquent activity by juveniles each year is impossible to estimate, since so much of it is not reported to police or made known to the courts. Self-reported delinquency surveys have shown that delinquent behavior exists in all social environments, and is committed by both males and females. Victimization surveys have revealed that victims of crimes of violence perceived many of the offenders who acted against them either alone or in multiple offender incidents to be juveniles.

Official measurements of delinquency have identified crimes of violence in and near schools, gang-related violence, substance abuse, and delinquency in suburban and rural areas as presenting significant problems. Violent behavior by female juveniles has increased substantially and minority group members are overrepresented in arrests for both violent and property crime in relation to their proportion in the general population.

DISCUSSION QUESTIONS

1. Virtually every person in the United States could have been or could be labeled a juvenile offender if his or her behavior history as a juvenile were known to authorities. Discuss.

2. Why are officially recorded statistics, such as those found in the FBI's Uniform Crime Report, *Crime in the United States,* misleading when one is trying to determine the scope of juvenile delinquency in the United States?

3. In your opinion, which method of gathering information about delinquent behavior, arrest and juvenile court statistics, victimization surveys, or self-reported delinquency studies most accurately reflects the true amount of juvenile misbehavior that is occurring?

4. Identify three conditions or trends in contemporary society that are possible explanations for the increased rates of violent delinquency among females. Which of these do you believe has the strongest influence on this behavior?

5. What conditions in suburban and rural life are conducive to the development of delinquency?

NOTES

1. Howard N. Snyder and Melissa Sickmund, *Juvenile Offenders and Victims: 1999 National Report* (Washington, DC: Office of Juvenile Justice and Delinquency Prevention, 1999), 93.
2. *Ibid.*
3. *Akron Beacon Journal*, August 17, 1994, A6.
4. P. Griffin, P. Torbet, and L. Szymanski, *Trying Juveniles as Adults in Criminal Court: An Analysis of State Transfer Provisions* (Washington, DC: Office of Juvenile Justice and Delinquency Prevention, 1998), reported in Snyder and Sickmund, *Juvenile Offenders and Victims, 1999*, 104.
5. *Kent v. United States*, 383 U.S. 541 (1966).
6. Ruth Shonle Cavan and Theodore N. Ferdinand, *Juvenile Delinquency*, 3rd ed. (Philadelphia: J.B. Lippincott, 1975), 26.
7. Snyder and Sickmund, *Juvenile Offenders and Victims: 1999*, 166.
8. Federal Bureau of Investigation, *Crime in the United States, 2001* (Washington, DC: U.S. Department of Justice, 2002), 244.
9. *Ibid.*, 228.
10. *Ibid.*, 244.
11. Snyder and Sickmund, *Juvenile Offenders and Victims, 1999*, 167.
12. FBI, *Crime in the United States, 2001*, 291.
13. Paul E. Tracy, Marvin E. Wolfgang, and Robert M. Figlio, *Delinquency in Two Birth Cohorts* (Washington, DC: U.S. Department of Justice, 1985), 5.
14. Lloyd D. Johnston, Jerald G. Bachman, and Patrick M. O'Malley, *Monitoring the Future* (Ann Arbor, MI: Institute for Social Research, University of Michigan), reported in U.S. Department of Justice, *Sourcebook of Criminal Justice Statistics, 2001* (Washington, DC: U.S. Government Printing Office, 2002), pp. 226, 227 251.
15. Delbert S. Elliott, *The Prevalence and Incidence of Delinquent Behavior: 1976–1980*, National Youth Survey Report 26 (Boulder, CO: Behavioral Research Institute, 1983), 413–422.
16. Peter C. and John E. Kratcoski, "The Balance of Social Status Groupings within Schools as an Influencing Variable on the Frequency and Character of Delinquent Behavior," in Paul C. Friday and V. Lorne Stewart, *Youth Crime and Juvenile Justice* (New York: Praeger, 1977), 160–171.
17. U.S. Bureau of Justice Statistics, *Criminal Victimization in the United States, 1999 Statistical Tables*, reported in U.S. Department of Justice, *Sourcebook of Criminal Justice Statistics, 2001*, 205, 206.
18. FBI, *Crime in the United States, 2001*, 244.
19. *Ibid.*, 238
20. Gordon A. Crews and Reid H. Montgomery, Jr., *Chasing Shadows: Confronting Juvenile Violence in America* (Upper Saddle River, NJ: Prentice Hall, 2001), 4.
21. *Comprehensive Strategy for Serious, Violent, and Chronic Juvenile Offenders* (Washington, DC: U.S. Department of Justice, 1994), 14.
22. *Akron Beacon Journal*, April 11, 1984, A1, A6.
23. Crews and Montgomery, *Chasing Shadows*, 5.
24. "Boy, 13, Charged in Fatal Shooting," *Akron Beacon Journal*, February 22, 2003, B4.
25. L. Kann, S. Kinchen, B. Williams, J. Ross, R. Lowry, C. Hill, J. Grunbaum, P. Blumston, J. Collins, and L. Kolbe, "Youth Risk Behavior Surveillance—United States, 1997. Reported in Snyder and Sickmund, *Juvenile Offenders and Victims, 1999*, 72.
26. Lloyd D. Johnston, Patrick M. O'Malley, and Jerald G. Bachman *National Survey Results on Drug Use from the Monitoring the Future Study, 1975–2001*, reported in U.S. Department of Justice, *Sourcebook of Criminal Justice Statistics 2001*, 251.
27. FBI, *Crime in the United States, 2001*, 238.

28. Publishers Group, *Street Drugs* (Plymouth, MN: Publishers Group, 2002), 2.
29. FBI, *Crime in the United States, 2001*, 253.
30. Snyder and Sickmund, *Juvenile Offenders and Victims, 1999*, 192.
31. See FBI, *Crime in the United States, 2001*, 243, and "Youth Risk Behavior Surveillance—United States, 2001," reported in U.S. Department of Justice, *Sourcebook of Criminal Justice Statistics, 2001*, 244.
32. FBI, *Crime in the United States, 2001*, 243.
33. *Ibid.*
34. FBI, *Crime in the United States, 2001*, 256, 264, 273.
35. L. Edward Wells and Ralph A. Weisheit, "Gang Problems in Nonmetropolitan Areas: A Longitudinal Assessment," *Justice Quarterly* 28, 4 (December 2001), 759–790.
36. Snyder and Sickmund, *Juvenile Offenders and Victims, 1999*, 78.
37. J. F. Donnermeyer, "Crime and Violence in Rural Areas," paper presented at the annual meeting of the Academy of Criminal Justice Sciences, Chicago, 1994.
38. *Akron Beacon Journal*, June 5, 1994, B1.

CHAPTER 2

HISTORICAL PERSPECTIVES ON DELINQUENCY CAUSATION

(Photo credit: Ernie Mastroianni)

THE THEORY-DEVELOPMENT PROCESS
THEORIES OF DELINQUENCY AND CRIMINALITY

The Classical School
Neoclassical Thought
The Biological School
Heredity-Based Theories
Current Biological Explanations of Delinquency

We noted in Chapter 1 that adults in every society have been concerned about behavior by youth that deviates from that society's norms to such an extent that it causes problems of social control. Such behavior is labeled undesirable, and sanctions are imposed in the hope of reducing its incidence and severity.

Explanations for youthful deviance have varied according to the characteristics of the society in question, the period of history, the philosophical and social backgrounds of the theorists, and the degree of sophistication reached in sampling and data-analysis methods at the time the research was conducted. For example, low intelligence was hypothesized to be a cause of delinquency in the early 20th century,[1] but the intelligence of delinquents and nondelinquents could not be meaningfully compared until the development of intelligence tests. The theory of Lombroso that a "criminal type" existed,[2] with such physical characteristics as protruding ears, abundant body hair, and broad cheekbones, was later put to a scientific test by Goring, who found no significant anatomical differences in the physical measurements of 3,000 English prisoners and a comparison group of Cambridge and Oxford graduates.[3] Other early theories, which seemed in their time to be important breakthroughs in discovering the causes of delinquency, were disproved or displaced by later researchers with more sophisticated techniques. For example, the research of Sheldon and Eleanor Glueck, which employed a number of scientific controls in the selection of samples, has been criticized in recent years as not being broad enough in scope to substantiate the conclusions drawn.[4] Similarly, more recent theories, such as the XYY chromosome theory, which sought to link the existence of an extra Y chromosome in some males to their involvement in aggressive and violent behavior,[5] and theories that the diet of an offender, particularly a high amount of sugar ingestion, could be related to inappropriate behavior,[6] were not substantiated when extensive controlled research examined them.

The development of any theory is an elaborate process, involving the gathering and analysis of data to discover the interrelationships of certain variables and their degree of importance in producing the observed condition. The end product of this activity—the theory—is a scientifically acceptable general principle or group of principles. Theories, then, provide explanations for the relation between two or more variables. For example, if we assume that delinquency is caused by a lack of recreational opportunities, this assumption might be tested by locating a group of adolescents who have ample recreational facilities and opportunities and comparing the amount and nature of their delinquent behavior with those of a group of adolescents who have little or no opportunity for recreational activities. We would have to standardize or match every possible factor other than the recreational variable that could conceivably contribute to delinquent behavior. If, after an observation period and careful recording of the behavior of both groups, the nonrecreational group was shown to have a level of delinquency significantly higher than that of the other group, then lack of recreational opportunities could be advanced as the explanation for the delinquency of this particular sample.

A search for cause is essentially a search for those things that make something happen. In the social sciences, it is difficult to isolate those factors that produce a specific result—in this case, delinquency. In fact, it is customary to think of a delinquent as the end product of a whole variety of causes or factors that independently might not have a drastic influence but that in a specific combination produce the observed undesirable result.

THE THEORY-DEVELOPMENT PROCESS

A very rigid definition of theory would accept only those explanations that have been empirically tested, with the causative variables being isolated and all other possible explanations being eliminated. This view would exclude most of the explanations of delinquency causation. In this text, theory will be considered in a more general sense as encompassing any attempt to understand and/or explain why something happens. We will apply Shoemaker's wide definition, in which an explanation of delinquency is regarded as a theory "if it attempts to explain or understand delinquency, regardless of the level of its causal assumptions and irrespective of the sophistication of its concepts and propositions."[7]

Much of the research on delinquency causation does not venture beyond finding correlations—that is, showing that two or more variables are associated with each other and that a change in the independent variable (the cause) is likely to result in a change in the dependent variable (the effect). Even when a factor has been defined as statistically significant as a cause of some type of juvenile misbehavior, its importance in proportion to other causes must be taken into account. As Nettler observed, rather than viewing certain behavior correlations as "the cause," we should consider them "candidates nominated to be causes."

> Correlation is a necessary sign of causation, but it is not a sufficient sign. It is not even a clear sign, for we do not know from the correlations that social scientists compute "how much *power* is demonstrated by the finding of a significant association."[8]

Cohen noted that many explanations of delinquency that were accepted at one time were eventually discarded because they failed to respect the truth that

> if one wants to explain something which has a number of distinct parts, his explanation must fit all the parts and not just some facet of the thing which happens, for some reason, to intrigue him. . . . If one fails to keep in mind the whole, he is not likely to find a satisfactory explanation of the part.[9]

Cavan and Ferdinand made a similar observation in their discussion of delinquency theories:

> All theories rest upon distinct perspectives, and to evaluate any particular theory adequately it is necessary to examine its basic assumptions as well as its conclusions regarding the natural world.[10]

A theorist, whether a psychologist, social psychologist, social worker, or sociologist, will draw upon those concepts and methods of investigation that are the basic foundation stones of his or her particular discipline. These will tend to provide the perspectives that guide the scientist in developing theories of causation. For example, a psychologist may tend to focus on traits and characteristics that are internal to the individual (feelings of inferiority, negative self-concept, emotional stress, peculiar personality traits) and attempt to associate them with the presence or absence of delinquency. By contrast, a sociologist may look at factors external to the individual (poverty, slums, peer-group influences, broken family, effects of the mass media) and their relation to delinquency.

Researchers investigating the problems of delinquency generally agree that it is a complex subject and that no single theory is going to offer plausible explanations for all varieties of deviant behavior. Each pattern of delinquency may be the result of a host of interrelated factors.

In Chapter 1, we saw that in self-reported delinquency studies, virtually every youth involved admitted having performed one or more acts violating the law as it applies to juveniles. We also saw that the vast majority of these youthful offenses were ignored or considered too trivial to warrant official action. Some were never detected, and others that did come to the attention of law enforcement officials were not officially processed. The reasons why some offenders are brought into the juvenile justice system, labeled delinquent, and officially handled, while others who commit comparable offenses are not, will be considered in later chapters. Chance, luck, or extenuating circumstances may well enter into the matter; therefore, it would be unwarranted to attribute the behavior of an apprehended youth to an intricately related set of causative factors while ignoring the fact that youths not labeled delinquent have engaged in exactly the same behavior.

Youths may engage in a deviant act on impulse, because of the influence of peers, or in a fit of anger, and later may be unable to give a logical explanation for their action. In some cases, a reasonable causative explanation simply does not exist, and such behavior must be regarded as an impulsive response.

Cavan and Ferdinand identified six problem areas that delinquency theorists might seek to address:

1. What are the personality patterns that give organization and direction to delinquent behavior?
2. What are the socializing pressures that create the personality patterns underlying delinquent behavior?

3. What are the immediate social situations that shape and influence delinquent behavior?

4. What are the broad social processes that engender the social situations that shape delinquency?

5. How are these four basic processes (social organization, social disorganization, cultural disorganization, and cultural deviance) affected by the organization of the surrounding society?

6. Can we affect the level or characteristics of delinquency in any significant way?[11]

THEORIES OF DELINQUENCY AND CRIMINALITY

Researchers who have sought explanations of delinquent and criminal behavior have formulated their hypotheses and conducted their studies according to their areas of interest (philosophical, biological, psychological, or sociological). Their methods and conclusions have been influenced by the eras in which they lived, the earlier research or theories with which they were familiar, and their access to various delinquent or criminal populations for testing and comparison. The theories touched on in this chapter will be treated under the general headings of the classical school, the biological school, heredity-based theories, and current biological explanations. Many of the studies were not confined to examining the influence of one set of factors. Rather, they took into account ideas from other schools of thought and their relation to the hypotheses under investigation. Theorists from the biological and psychological schools tended to seek the causes of delinquency within the individual, while the classical school, rather than focusing on the causes of delinquent behavior, examined the nature of the act and explored measures that might be taken to persuade the individual not to repeat it.

The Classical School

During the 16th and 17th centuries, European criminal justice was geared toward punishment and deterrence. Severe penalties were provided even for trivial offenses. Capital punishment was dictated for over 200 offenses in 17th-century England, with lesser offenses punished by such horrors as burning a hole in the tongue or ears, cutting out the tongue, or severing a limb.[12] Prisons were used to detain political prisoners and those awaiting trial, rather than as places of incarceration for those convicted of crimes.

Against this background, the thinking of Cesare Beccaria (1738–1794), an Italian university professor, seemed revolutionary indeed. Beccaria developed the "pleasure-pain" principle—the idea that each human behavior choice involves a decision between the amount of pleasure that would accompany an act and the pain (physical or psychological) that could result. He maintained that the punishments for various crimes should be just severe enough to deter people from the criminal act and that punishments should be applied equally to all citizens, regardless of their social status. Those who knew in advance exactly what the consequences of their illegal behavior would be could then exercise their free will (a popular concept in that era) to decide on the proper course of action. Children under 7 and the insane were to be excluded from these punishments as incapable of making rational choices of pleasure or pain.[13] The "right to punishment" concept in juvenile justice follows many of Beccaria's ideas regarding the need for a set punishment for each offense to be impartially administered to all offenders.[14]

Beccaria is regarded by some as the founder of modern penology. He saw imprisonment as a deterrent to criminal activity, and he believed it would be most effective if it were applied impartially, without exception, and in a degree appropriate for the severity of the offense.[15]

While Beccaria was writing in Italy, in England Jeremy Bentham (1748–1832) was developing a theory of "utilitarianism" that was in virtual agreement with Beccaria's idea. He also emphasized the setting of specific punishments applicable to all, which would serve as deterrents. He assumed that a rational man, through exercise of free will, would be disposed to choose pleasure over pain. Bentham expanded his concept to include "the greatest good for the greatest number," noting that behavior must be controlled by a set system of punishments for the good of the larger society. In an era when most convicts were assigned to galley ships, transported to penal colonies, or punished by some form of physical mutilation or flogging, Bentham developed the concept of the prison as a "correctional" institution. He urged that the prison be located near the center of the city, so that citizens would observe it in their daily activities and ponder their own behavior according to the "pleasure-pain" ratio. He also advocated that prisoners be kept busy during their incarceration, taught trades, and classified according to their offenses.[16]

Neoclassical Thought

The neoclassical thinkers believe that the justice system should focus on the act and not on the offender. They maintain that it is not the concern of the justice system to change the offender, only to assure that the offender receives his or her "just deserts." The utilitarian theorists also assert that punishment deters potential criminal behavior. They believe that most people would commit crimes if they dared. For them, society is held together by an implied social contract. Humans are social beings who must follow the rules and regulations set by law if order is to be maintained. Conduct prohibited by law must be punished, because each violation threatens the welfare of the whole society.

Fogel put these ideas into a theoretical concept known as the "justice model," in which justice and compliance with the law are the standard by which both offenders and law enforcement and correctional personnel should be judged. The justice model suggests that offenders, in addition to being punished, should make restitution or compensation to the victim. *Just punishment*, quickly applied and harsh enough to deter future illegal activity, is the central focus of the justice model.[17] Wilson reiterated the idea of just punishment, noting that serious offenders should receive a punishment that would remove them from the community and put a stop to their criminal careers for a substantial period of time.[18] Bailey, Martin, and Gray found that *certainty of punishment* and the potential offender's perceptions of the *probability of detection and punishment* were the keys to deterrence. For example, signs in department stores beside television surveillance cameras or mirrors stating that all shoplifters will be prosecuted should deter shoplifting by youths, even if the cameras are not in operation.[19]

The ideas of the neoclassical theorists are reflected in certain revisions of the juvenile code. For example, requiring mandatory institutionalization of youths charged with serious offenses and "career criminals" (those with an extensive history of delinquent offenses) or setting exact penalties (determinate dispositions) for certain offenses, which cannot be shortened or lifted, are consistent with neoclassic theory. The movement to remove from juvenile court jurisdiction status offenses that pose no threat to public safety or order and handle them instead through social agencies is another reflection of the application of neoclassic theory.

The Biological School

Classical and neoclassical thought on criminal behavior emphasizes that since people "choose" to commit criminal acts, their "free-will" decisions must be directed toward choices of noncriminal behavior through the setting of specific standards of punishment for certain offenses. The biological school, by contrast, holds that in most cases, criminals are predetermined, or at least predisposed, toward criminal behavior by factors within their biological makeup.

Although biological theories of criminality have been advanced for hundreds of years, no one has definitively identified the causative links or internal biological factors that bring about unacceptable behavior. Many theorists do not distinguish between biological and psychological traits or discuss the degree to which the characteristics may intertwine to produce criminality. The early biological theorists believed that certain physical characteristics, such as the shape of the head or hands, body type, or chemical imbalances in the system, were indications of a predisposition toward criminal behavior. The modern biological theorists also see a cause-and-effect relationship between certain biological factors and the occurrence of criminality, although they recognize that the destructive potential of these factors can be affected by environmental conditions. For example, hyperactivity in children, which can result in impulsive delinquent acts such as vandalism or assault, can be controlled by behavior modification or by medication.

Cesare Lombroso (1835–1909) was the founder of the school of delinquency and criminality that held that criminals are born as such and that the criminal is a result of "atavism," a throwback to an earlier level of civilization. Lombroso was obviously influenced by the theories of Charles Darwin regarding evolution. He maintained that criminals, or "undermen," as he termed them, could be differentiated from noncriminals by the shape of their skulls, a long lower jaw, a flattened nose, and various other physical features. These indicators of criminal predisposition (called "stigmata" by Lombroso) existed in various combinations. The presence of five or more of them "branded" an individual as predisposed to criminal behavior, while lesser combinations of them were suggestive rather than indicative.[20]

Lombroso, a physician, formulated his theory by observing the physical characteristics of criminals with whom he came in contact. After the death of a particularly notorious prisoner, he performed an autopsy and observed that the interior of the skull was abnormal, with a depression where there should have been a protrusion. This finding led Lombroso to believe that in criminals, the evolutionary process had somehow been arrested, and that the brains of criminals were biological throwbacks to the savage man, or atavist.

> At the sight of that skull, I seemed to see all of a sudden, lighted up as a vast plain under a flaming sky, the problem of the nature of the criminal—an atavistic being who reproduces in his person the ferocious instincts of primitive humanity and the inferior animals. Thus were explained anatomically the enormous jaws, high cheekbones, prominent superciliary arches, solitary lines in the palms, extreme size of the orbits, handle-shaped or sessile ears found in criminals, savages and apes, insensibility to pain, extremely acute sight, tattooing, excessive idleness, love of orgies, and the irresistible craving for evil for its own sake, the desire not only to extinguish life in the victim, but to mutilate the corpse, tear its flesh and drink its blood.[21]

The abnormalities or "stigmata" that Lombroso thought were characteristics of criminals were not the causes of the criminal behavior but rather identification marks of those born with the atavistic condition. He declared that female atavists could also be differentiated by such characteristics as excessive body hair, moles, and masculine traits.

The first attempt to relate body traits systematically to juvenile delinquency came from the work of William Sheldon in the 1940s. He differentiated three body types, or "somatotypes," and associated each with certain personality traits. The first type, endomorphic, is characterized by a fat, soft, round body; this type of person is extroverted and a lover of comfort. The second body type, mesomorphic, is muscular and hard; persons of the type Sheldon considered assertive and aggressive. Finally, ectomorphic types are frail, thin, and weak and described as shy, sensitive, and introverted.

Sheldon rated juvenile offenders on a scale of 1 to 7 on each body type. Then, after comparing 200 delinquent boys in a rehabilitation home with 4,000 college students, he concluded that the large majority of the delinquents were "decidedly mesomorphic."[22] In contrast, his nondelinquent comparison group was more evenly distributed among the somatotypes. Sheldon viewed body types as inborn and stated that there is a very strong correlation between physique and temperament. The assertive-aggressive temperament he associated with the mesomorphic body type explained the violent offenses of the delinquents. He also noted that their assertive-aggressive temperaments helped these youths survive in the unfavorable sociocultural environment in which many of them lived.

Sheldon and Eleanor Glueck also employed body-type designations in their research on delinquents. Like Sheldon, they found that the majority of the 500 institutionalized delinquent boys they studied were mesomorphic. When they compared these boys with a sample of 500 boys believed to be nondelinquent, 60 percent of the delinquents were categorized as mesomorphic, compared to 31 percent of the nondelinquents.[23]

A later analysis of the same samples of delinquents and nondelinquents led the Gluecks to conclude that personality and family characteristics must be considered along with body type when attempting to explain the causes of delinquency. For example, they found that mesomorphic delinquents tended to come from homes that were disorganized. These delinquents were also characterized as emotionally unstable. Thus, the mesomorphic delinquents exhibited severe psychological and social problems, while the nondelinquent mesomorphs did not. For a boy growing up in a harsh sociocultural environment such as the inner city, the aggressiveness and muscular build of the mesomorph could be a key to survival.[24]

The specific physiological connection between body type and delinquent behavior has never been empirically established. When social and psychological factors are taken into consideration, the importance of body type appears insignificant.

Heredity-Based Theories

Theorists who claim a basis in heredity for delinquent behavior believe that the tendency to delinquency and other aberrations, such as mental illness and alcoholism, is genetically transmitted from parents to children.

When various researchers began to challenge the conclusions reached by Lombroso, the emphasis of those who continued to support the biological explanations shifted to inherited lack of mental capacity as a possible cause of criminality. The most colorful of these studies, Richard Dugdale's (1841–1883) tracing of the descendants of the Jukes family[25] and Henry Goddard's examination of the foibles of the Kallikak family,[26] sought to document long histories of illegitimacy, idiocy, prostitution, alcoholism, and other social aberrations in certain families. Goddard maintained that feeblemindedness is inherited and causes crime because those who are mentally inferior are unable to assess the consequences of their behavior.[27] He developed the following summary of the Kallikak family traits:

> Martin Kallikak, Sr., a Revolutionary soldier, and a man of good stock, became the father of an illegitimate boy, Martin Kallikak, Jr. The mother was a feeble-minded girl. To 1912 the known descendants from this source were 480. Thirty-six of these were illegitimate; 33 sexually immoral; 24 alcoholics; 3 epileptics; 3 were criminal. There is conclusive proof that 143 (29.7%) of these were feeble-minded while only 46 were certainly known to be normal. The rest are doubtful.[28]

Goddard also tested the intelligence of delinquents and concluded that at least 25 percent of them, and perhaps as many as 70 percent, were of inferior intelligence, using the mental age of 12 or under as a standard for feeblemindedness. When Zeleny applied the same standard to thousands of draftees for military service, however, he found that more than 30 percent of them were also feebleminded according to Goddard's standards. Goddard retreated from his original position and decided that only about 5 percent of all delinquents could be considered feebleminded.[29]

In the 1930s, a Harvard anthropologist named Earnest Hooton renewed the notion first promoted by Lombroso that criminals could be identified by certain physical characteristics and stated that they were also mentally inferior to noncriminals.

On the basis of a comparison of 13,000 inmates of reformatories and jails with a sample of more than 3,000 noncriminals, he defined a list of physical characteristics, quite similar to those of Lombroso, which were indicative of criminals. He even related the criminal's particular physical characteristics to the type of crime committed. For example, tall, heavy men are most inclined to be killers, while men with small, undersized builds are likely to be thieves.[30]

The theories that related delinquent and criminal behavior to heredity were attacked by sociologists and psychologists as being defective in their research methods, the reasoning employed to develop their conclusions, and the lack of consideration given to personality and environment. Nevertheless, they had profound effects on juvenile court and correctional practices. Because intelligence tests were used as the basis for determining mental deficiency or defectiveness, the courts and correctional administrators tended to go along with the results obtained. The IQ test had an aura of scientific reliability in their eyes, and conclusions that youths were mentally deficient or defective that were based on this test were given considerable weight. Consequently, those tested and found to be "defective" were isolated from their families and placed in institutions, where it was felt that the inferior intelligence they possessed could be used to develop some skills. Early testing of children who showed delinquent tendencies was encouraged so that these children could be isolated before they had an opportunity to become deeply involved in unacceptable behavior. Sterilization was used to prevent the procreation of new generations of these "feebleminded" and "inferior" children.

More than 30 states passed laws allowing sterilization of the feebleminded, the mentally ill, epileptics, and certain categories of criminal and delinquent offenders. Although these laws were eventually declared unconstitutional, as late as 1970 more than 20 states still retained them in their statutory law.[31]

Current Biological Explanations of Delinquency

Interest in biological and heredity-linked explanations of deviant behavior has increased in recent years, as methods of genetic research and machinery for observing brain waves and other types of biological functioning have become increasingly sophisticated. Researchers have abandoned the earlier assumptions of direct causal links between biological traits and deviance, and instead are exploring the interaction of genetic and environmental factors on the functioning of the nervous system.

Gender and Age. We noted in Chapter 1 that males are much more likely than females to engage in delinquent behavior, and they do so at an earlier age. However, for both males and females misbehavior peaks at age 16 or 17, and from this point on their behavior generally begins to conform more and more to accepted norms. Both biological and sociological explanations have been developed to explain these variations. Male hormonal changes during puberty have been used to explain the fact that males become more aggressive and less subject to control at that time. Physical and mental development (maturation) may also help to explain why behavior changes for the better during the late teens. However, many social factors, including family structure, physical and cultural environment, peer group influences, and unique personality factors may be interrelated with gender and age to produce these results.

Biochemical Explanations.   The "biochemical" or "orthomolecular" explanation of delinquency, which has gained popularity in recent years, suggests that chemical deficiencies or abnormalities in the body can affect the entire nervous system and directly or indirectly lessen a youth's ability to perform in a socially acceptable manner. Brain damage caused by injury or disease can alter brain patterns. Vitamin deficiencies or the effects of certain foods or food additives may also be related to aggressive or out-of-control behavior. Hypoglycemia (a low blood-sugar count) has also been associated with violent delinquency.[32]

Causative links have been sought between delinquency and exposure to high levels of lead, complicated births, water fluoridation, smoking and/or use of alcohol during pregnancy, and other forms of drug use. A study conducted in Mexico revealed that children born to mothers with a history of exposure to lead were at risk for low birth weight, a powerful predictor of child behavior problems and learning disabilities.[33]

Kosofsky reviewed the research studies on the effects of children being exposed to cocaine in the uterus. These "crack babies" were found to have language and behavioral deficits, short attention spans, and impulsivity. The extent of these problems was found to be related to the amount and length of cocaine use by the mothers. Kosofsky characterized the effects of these problems on future behavior in the following way:

> . . . the subtle behaviors that may be compromised [by prenatal cocaine exposure] are important for socialization, educability, and the adaptive skills required for individuals to become enfranchised in schools, communities, and society.[34]

Alcohol use by mothers during pregnancy has also been linked to children's physical and behavior problems. A research study on drinking by adolescents reached the conclusion that:

> . . . many risk factors commonly linked to serious drinking in adolescence—including impulsivity, conduct disorder, and brain dysfunction—could result, at least in part, from exposure to alcohol during prenatal development.[35]

Hyperactivity and Learning Disabilities.   Hyperactivity, or hyperkinesis, has also been advanced in recent years as a biological explanation for some delinquent activity. This type of minimal brain dysfunction has been observed in many youngsters who are discipline problems in school because of their highly impulsive behavior.

A possible link between learning disabilities and delinquency has also been explored. Recent attempts to link academic failure with delinquency have centered on the topic of learning disabilities. The National Advisory Committee on Handicapped Children has defined learning disabilities in the following way:

> Children with special learning disabilities exhibit a disorder in one or more of the basic psychological processes involved in understanding or using spoken or written languages. These

may be manifested in disorders of listening, thinking, talking, reading, writing, spelling, or arithmetic. They include conditions which have been referred to as perceptual handicaps, brain injury, minimal brain dysfunction, dyslexia, developmental aphasia, etc. They do not include learning problems which are due primarily to visual, hearing, or motor handicaps, to mental retardation, emotional disturbance, or to environmental disadvantage.[36]

Three types of learning disabilities have been broadly recognized and defined: dyslexia, aphasia, and hyperkinesis. *Dyslexia*, sometimes termed "word blindness," refers in a broad sense to defective language achievement in reading, writing, and spelling.[37] It may include such problems as poor ability to discriminate between words in which only one letter differs (*some, same*), writing or perceiving words or letters backwards or upside down (*b* for *d*, *saw* for *was*, *w* for *m*), and spelling words with letters out of sequence.[38] *Aphasia* involves hearing and speaking difficulties in ascertaining and pronouncing words. *Hyperkinesis* refers to excessive muscular movement in the performance of activities.[39] Males have been estimated to outnumber females four to one in the incidence of learning disabilities. Experts have estimated that from 5 to 10 percent of all children under 10 years of age have such disabilities.[40]

The effect of learning disabilities on school behavior may begin when teachers perceive these physically awkward youths as discipline problems, or when a child who has normal or above-average intelligence is placed in the slow-learning group because of a disability and experiences the frustration of falling behind classmates, in spite of his or her best efforts. A child's reaction may be despair, frustration acted out in disruptive behavior, avoidance of school by feigning sickness or deliberate truancy, or eventual involvement in delinquent activity as a method of gaining acceptance or recognition. Certain other personality characteristics of learning-disabled children may also make them prone to delinquent behavior, such as their poor ability to learn from experience and their tendency to act on impulse.[41]

A number of researchers have identified a high proportion of learning disabled youngsters among populations already defined as delinquent, and have attempted to establish a causal relationship between delinquency and learning disabilities. Testing of 100 juveniles referred to the Norfolk (Virginia) Juvenile Court for incorrigibility, truancy, and runaway behavior revealed that 57 percent had a general learning disability.[42] William Mulligan, who surveyed the reading abilities of 60 juveniles placed with the Sonoma County (California) Special Supervision Unit, designed to supervise the more severely delinquent children on probation, discovered that 80 percent of them were reading below grade level, even though they were typically of average or superior intelligence.[43] This jurisdiction now refers children with truancy or school-related problems for a screening test for learning disabilities, and it also interviews the child's mother to attempt to uncover any conditions in the child's early life that may have been responsible for minimal brain damage or neurological handicaps that may contribute to such disabilities.[44] Referrals are then made to appropriate remedial programs.

Twin Research.   Other attempts to isolate the relative effects of heredity and environment on deviant behavior have been made through studies of twins. Research has compared twins developed from the same egg (monozygotic) with twins developed from two eggs (dizygotic) and discovered that the monozygotic twins, who have the identical genetic makeup, are more similar in their criminal or delinquent behavior than the dizygotic twins. Studies of this type conducted by Dalgard and Kringler in Norway found that rates of involvement in such criminal acts as violence, theft, and sexual assault were more similar for pairs of monozygotic twins than for dizygotic twins. Further research into the environmental factors of their childhoods revealed that the monozygotic twins generally felt that they were reared and treated alike and experienced closeness and common identity much more than the dizygotic twins, indicating that both their genetic and environmental backgrounds were more similar than those of the dizygotic twins.[45] Studies of alcoholism among twins have revealed similar patterns. Monozygotic twins are more likely to both be alcoholic than dizygotic twins, according to researchers.[46]

Studies of Adopted Children.   The question of the relative influence of heredity and environment on deviant behavior has also been explored through studies of youths adopted shortly after birth. Their degree of criminality in later years was compared to that of their genetic parents and their adoptive parents to determine which they more closely resembled. It must be noted that at the time of adoption, most agencies make efforts to match children as closely as possible with their adoptive parents in terms of race, socioeconomic background, and physical appearance. For this reason, the results of adoptee studies may not be as valid as if the children had been randomly placed in homes other than their own. Nevertheless, such controlled experiments have yielded interesting results. Bohman, for example, found that adoptees whose natural mother or father (or both) had a criminal record were more likely to be involved in criminal behavior than adoptees whose genetic parents had no criminal record. He related much of the criminality of the adoptees to alcohol abuse, a trait he found more often among the adoptees' genetic parents than among their adoptive parents. Since genetic factors are considered to contribute to alcohol abuse, they may thus have influenced the adoptees' criminality.[47]

Hutchings, who compared the genetic and adoptive fathers of adopted males with criminal records, found that 31 percent of the genetic fathers also had criminal records, compared to only 11 percent of the adoptive fathers. The fathers of a comparison group of unadopted offspring in the general population were found to have the same percentage of criminal convictions (11%) as the adoptive fathers of adoptees with criminal convictions. This study's findings support the idea that genetics have some significant relationship to criminal behavior.[48]

With regard to the onset of alcoholism, studies have shown a biological link between adopted children and their birth parents. Studies in several countries followed adopted children separated from their birth parents before the children were six months old. Alcoholism occurred much more frequently in the children whose biological parents were alcoholics, while alcoholism in the adoptive parents was not strongly related to alcoholism in the adopted children.[49]

A four-year study of nearly 900 adopted adolescents and their families, funded by the National Institute of Mental Health, found that birthparents' problems with alcohol and drugs, or psychological difficulties, were not significantly linked to the psychological health of the adopted children in the study. However, in the component of the study that dealt with self-reported behaviors it was discovered that adopted adolescents were slightly more prone to delinquent and aggressive behavior and such internal problems as withdrawn, anxious/depressed behavior and somatic complaints than were the youths in a comparable national sample of nonadopted adolescents.[50]

SUMMARY

In this chapter, we have examined the process by which a theory of delinquency develops, taking note of the difficulties inherent in assigning causal properties to various factors in the production of delinquency. Even when correlations between or among various factors have been established to indicate that a certain factor has causal properties, the strength or power of its impact on the life of a juvenile has yet to be assessed.

The theories of delinquency causation discussed in this chapter include those of the classical and neoclassical schools, the biological school, heredity-based theories, and the current biological theories.

Beccaria and Bentham, the classical theorists, believed that the decision to become involved in delinquent or criminal behavior is a rational one, and that criminality can be deterred by establishing a system of sure and quickly administered punishments severe enough to outweigh any pleasure or gain received from committing an illegal act.

This "pleasure-pain" principle is also embraced by the neoclassical thinkers, who support the notion of "just desserts." Those who are found guilty of delinquent or criminal acts, according to this idea, must receive exact punishments set by law, which may include mandatory institutionalization for certain offenses. The certainty and severity of punishment are regarded as deterrents to future crime.

In contrast to the freedom of choice stressed by the classical and neoclassical theorists, the biological theorists believe that offenders are predetermined, or at least predisposed, toward criminality by features of their biological makeup, and that certain physical characteristics can be noted in individuals who have this predisposition. The early biological theorists focused on particular physical features, while later ones developed "body types" characteristics of criminals or delinquents.

Those who promote heredity-based theories follow a similar line of reasoning, claiming that the tendency toward delinquency and other aberrations such as mental illness and alcoholism is genetically transmitted from parents to children.

Through the use of comparison studies, researchers have disproved the conclusions reached by the early biological theorists. But current genetic research has focused on new theories of delinquency causation. These include the influence of brain damage, vitamin deficiencies, chemical imbalances in the body, hyperactivity, and learning disabilities. Controlled experiments with twins and adopted children have been used to attempt to establish the relative influences of heredity and environment.

Searches for biological explanations of delinquency continue at more sophisticated levels today, bolstered by new genetic research techniques and more detailed methods. To date, however, no specific biological or physiological trait has been found to be a definite predisposing or influencing factor for delinquency and criminal behavior.

DISCUSSION QUESTIONS

1. Describe how a theory of delinquency is developed. How did early theories of delinquency, which seemed logical and sound at the time they were developed, come to be disproved or rejected?

2. What types of current biological research are exploring the relative influences of heredity and environment on delinquency? Do you believe that a tendency to delinquency and criminality is inherited?

3. Some researchers have suggested that many children are mistakenly diagnosed as hyperactive when their behavior problems have other explanations. Discuss.

4. Several studies have found that identical twins separated early in life who have grown up in widely different economic and cultural circumstances still exhibit similar behavior patterns. Do these findings strongly support the idea that a tendency to delinquency or criminality is inherited, or are there other possible explanations?

5. Discuss how the theories of the classical and the biological schools were related to the concepts of free will and determinism, which were widely debated at the time these theories were advanced.

NOTES

1. For a description of the theories of Willem Bonger on this topic, see J. M. van Bemmelen, "Willem Adriaan Bonger," *Journal of Criminal Law, Criminology, and Police Science* 46, 5 (September–October 1955).

2. For a description of Cesare Lombroso's theories, see Marvin E. Wolfgang, "Pioneers in Criminology: Cesare Lombroso (1835–1909)," *Journal of Criminal Law, Criminology, and Police Science* 52, 6 (November–December 1961), 361–391.

3. For a detailed description of Charles Goring's research, see Stephen Schafer and Richard D. Knudten, *Juvenile Delinquency: An Introduction* (New York: Random House, 1970), 60–61.

4. The research efforts of Sheldon and Eleanor Glueck are presented in their books *Unraveling Juvenile Delinquency* (New York: Commonwealth Fund, 1950), and *Physique and Delinquency* (New York: Harper & Row, 1956).

5. Saleem A. Shah and Loren H. Roth, "Biological and Psychophysiological Factors in Criminality," in Daniel Glaser, ed., *Handbook of Criminology* (Chicago: Rand McNally, 1974), 137.

6. Richard Milich and William Pelham, "Effects of Sugar Ingestion on the Classroom and Playgroup Behavior of Attention Deficit Disordered Boys," *Journal of Counseling and Clinical Psychology* 54 (1986), 714–718, cited in Larry J. Siegel and Joseph J. Senna, *Juvenile Delinquency* (St. Paul, MN: West, 1991), 93.

7. Donald J. Shoemaker, *Theories of Delinquency* (New York: Oxford University Press, 1984), 8.

8. Gwynn Nettler, *Explaining Crime* (New York: McGraw-Hill, 1978), 119–120.

9. Albert K. Cohen, *Delinquent Boys: The Culture of the Gang* (New York: Free Press, 1955), 21.

10. Ruth Shonle Cavan and Theodore N. Ferdinand, *Juvenile Delinquency*, 3rd ed. (Philadelphia: J. B. Lippincott, 1975), 67.

11. *Ibid.*, 68–72.

12. Sue Titus Reid, *Crime and Criminology* (Hinsdale, IL: Dryden Press, 1976), 106.

13. Edwin H. Sutherland and Donald R. Cressey, *Criminology* (Philadelphia: J. B. Lippincott, 1974), 50.

14. Sanford J. Fox, "The Reform of Juvenile Justice: The Child's Right to Punishment," *Juvenile Justice*, 25, 3 (Fall 1974), 4.

15. Schafer and Knudten, *Juvenile Delinquency*, 43.

16. Reid, *Crime and Criminology*, 111–112.

17. David Fogel, *We Are the Living Proof* (Cincinnati, OH: Anderson Publishing Company, 1975), 247.

18. James Q. Wilson, *Thinking about Crime* (New York: Basic Books, 1975), 210–243.
19. W. C. Bailey, J. D. Martin, and L. N. Gray, "Crime and Deterrence: A Correlation Analysis," *Journal of Research in Crime and Delinquency*, 11, 2 (July 1974), 140.
20. Sutherland and Cressey, *Criminology*, 53.
21. G. Ferrero, *Lombroso's Criminal Man* (New York: Putnam, 1911), 10.
22. William H. Sheldon, et al., *The Varieties of Delinquent Youth* (New York: Harper & Row, 1949), 726–729.
23. Glueck and Glueck, *Unraveling Juvenile Delinquency*, 193.
24. *Ibid.*, 224–225.
25. Richard Louis Dugdale, *The Jukes: A Study in Crime, Pauperism, and Heredity* (New York: Putnam, 1877).
26. Henry H. Goddard, *Feeblemindedness: Its Causes and Consequences* (New York: Macmillan, 1914).
27. *Ibid.*, 8–9.
28. Robert H. Gault, *Criminology* (Boston: D. C. Heath, 1932), 281.
29. Lamar T. Empey, *American Delinquency* (Homewood, IL: Dorsey Press, 1982), 166.
30. Earnest A. Hooton, *Crime and the Man* (Cambridge, MA: Harvard University Press, 1931), 376–378.
31. Charles H. McCaghy, *Deviant Behavior* (New York: Macmillan, 1976), 20.
32. William H. Philpott, "Ecological Aspects of Anti-social Behavior," in Leonard J. Hippchen, ed., *Ecologic-Biochemical Approaches to Treatment of Delinquents and Criminals* (New York: Van Nostrand Reinhold, 1978), 116–137.
33. T. Gonzalez-Cossio, K.E. Peterson, L.H. Sanin, E. Fishbein, E. Palazuelos, A. Aro, M. Hernandez-Avila, and H. Ho, "Decrease in Birth Weight in Relation to Maternal Bone-lead Burden," *Pediatrics*, 100, 5 (November 1997), 856–862.
34. Barry E. Kosofsky, "Cocaine-induced Alterations in Neuro-development," *Seminars in Speech and Language*, 19, 2 (1998), 121.
35. John S. Baer, Helen M. Barr, Fred L. Bookstein, Paul D. Sampson, and Ann P. Streissguth, "Prenatal Alcohol Exposure and Family History of Alcoholism in the Etiology of Adolescent Alcohol Problems," *Journal of Studies on Alcohol*, 59 (September 1998), 542.
36. Charles A. Murray, *The Link between Learning Disabilities and Juvenile Delinquency* (Washington, DC: U.S. Government Printing Office, 1976), 12.
37. William Mulligan, "Dyslexia, Specific Learning Disability and Delinquency," *Juvenile Justice* 23, 3 (November 1972), 21.
38. *Ibid.*, 23–25.
39. Murray, *The Link between Learning Disabilities and Juvenile Delinquency*, 13–14.
40. *Ibid.*, 11, 14.
41. *Ibid.*, 26.
42. W. Chris Love and Gary H. Bachara, "A Diagnostic Team Approach for Juvenile Delinquents with Learning Disabilities," *Juvenile Justice* 26, 1 (February 1975), 28.
43. Mulligan, "Dyslexia," 22–23.
44. *Ibid.*, 23.
45. Odd Steffen Dalgard and Einar Kringler, "Criminal Behavior in Twins," in Leonard D. Savitz and Norman Johnston, eds., *Crime in Society* (New York: Wiley, 1978), 292–307.
46. Norman Miller and Doug Toft, *The Disease Concept of Alcoholism and Other Drug Addiction* (Center City, MN: Hazelden, 1990), 10.
47. Martin Bohman, "A Study of Adopted Children, Their Background, Environment, and Adjustment," *Acta Paediatrica Scandinavia* 61 (1972), 90–97.
48. Bernard Hutchings and S. A. Mednick, "Criminality in Adoptees and Their Adoptive and Biological Parents: A Pilot Study," in S. Mednick and K. O. Christiansen, eds., *Biosocial Basis of Criminal Behavior* (New York: Gardner, 1977), 127–141.
49. Miller and Toft, *The Disease Concept of Alcoholism and Other Drug Addictions*, 10.
50. Peter L. Benson, Anu R. Sharma, and Eugene C. Roehlkepartain, *Growing Up Adopted* (Minneapolis, MN: Search Institute, 1994), 79, 90.

CHAPTER 3

PSYCHOLOGICAL THEORIES OF DELINQUENCY CAUSATION

(Photo credit: Nick J. Cool, The Image Works)

PSYCHOANALYTIC THEORIES
MORAL DEVELOPMENT AND DELINQUENCY
Moral-Development Theories
Cognitive-Development Theories
Adolescent Coping Mechanisms
PERSONALITY-TRAIT EXPLANATIONS OF DELINQUENCY
Early Personality-Trait Theorists
The Quay Classification System
Personality Measurement as a Method of Ascertaining Behavior Disorders
The Criminal Personality
The Psychopathic Personality
MENTAL ILLNESS AND DELINQUENCY

A 13-year-old pleaded no contest Wednesday to a homicide charge in the . . . death of a 7-year-old playmate who was shot while riding a snowmobile. . . . The boy pleaded no contest to a charge of criminal homicide, a felony charge similar to murder, in the shooting death of Jessica Ann Carr. Jessica was killed as she rode a snowmobile in a field next to the boy's home. . . . At the time, Cameron [the offender] was a couple of months shy of his 10th birthday. . . . The boy had an argument with Jessica, went home, unlocked his father's gun cabinet, and removed a high-powered rifle that his father had taught him to shoot. He loaded it, rested his weapon on a window sill, and fired at the girl 100 yards away. She was struck in the back and the bullet pierced her spine and right lung.

After the shooting, according to testimony . . ., Cameron cleaned the weapon and put it back into the gun cabinet.[1]

* * *

Two boys accused of bludgeoning their father to death with a baseball bat pleaded guilty to reduced charges and got up to eight years in prison Thursday after a judge threw out their convictions and spared them a much harsher sentence. In strong, clear voices, Derek King, 14, and his brother, Alex, 13, admitted to third-degree murder, as well as arson, for burning down the house around their father's body last year.

Derek was sentenced to eight years in prison, Alex to seven years—well below the 12½-year minimum specified under state guidelines. . . . The boys, who were 12 and 13 at the time, gave detailed confessions to police: Derek said he swung the bat and Alex said he had urged his brother to kill their father because they were afraid of being punished for running away from home.[2]

* * *

A grand jury indicted 17-year-old Lee Boyd Malvo on murder charges that could bring the death penalty for his alleged role in the sniper attacks that terrorized the Washington area. . . . Malvo and John Allen Muhammad, 42, are accused of killing 13 people and wounding five in Alabama, Georgia, Louisiana, Maryland, Virginia, and Washington, D.C. . . . Police said that fingerprints from a rifle, notes to police, and phone calls from Malvo link him to at least four of the sniper shootings.[3]

These descriptions of murders carried out by juveniles with precision, planning, and apparent lack of remorse suggest the possibility of extreme psychological disturbance in the offenders. But other less serious types of juvenile misbehavior, including running away, sexual promiscuity, and other offenses may also be related to psychological disturbances.

In Chapter 2 we examined the theories of delinquency causation that involve biological explanations of misbehavior and noted that, while the conclusions reached by early biological theorists have been disproved, current research on genetics continues to seek some causative links between the physical makeup of delinquent youths and their behavior. Psychological theories of delinquency causation have followed a similar pattern. The human personality has been exhaustively examined by psychologists and psychiatrists, who claim to have traced the various stages of its development, defined its component parts, outlined its functioning, sought the causes of the development of various personality traits, and related certain patterns of deviant behavior to the malfunctioning of the personality.

While explanations of behavior that can be broadly categorized as psychological theories are numerous and diverse, they generally share some common assumptions. First, they view delinquent behavior as caused by some disturbance or trauma in the youth's development. Second, they regard this psychological disturbance as beginning not later than early childhood and continuing during the maturation process. And third, they see delinquency as a problem *within* the individual that must be approached through direct treatment of this person rather than modification of external environmental factors.[4]

PSYCHOANALYTIC THEORIES

A great deal of the personality-development theory that is applied to the existence of juvenile delinquency is based on the psychoanalytic theories of Sigmund Freud (1856–1939). Freud defined the personality as having three structural components—the id, the ego, and the superego. Brenner described them in the following way:

> The id comprises the psychic representatives of the drives, the ego consists of those functions which have to do with the individual's relation to his environment, and the superego comprises the moral precepts of our minds as well as our ideal aspirations.[5]

Psychoanalytic theory places great emphasis on early childhood as the critical period in personality formation and defines various stages of psychological development that correspond to the child's mastery of certain bodily functions and drives (e.g., oral, anal, and genital phases of development). The parents are viewed as crucial factors in the child's personality formation and conduct disorders and neuroses are regarded as reflections of the effects of inadequate parenting. Critical parent-child relationship deficiencies that may result in personality and conduct disorders, according to the psychoanalysts, are the absence of the mother or her rejection of the child during infancy and very early childhood, lack of affection and discipline by both parents during the first five years of life, and, for boys, absence or lack of influence of a father figure during the pre-adolescent years.[6]

The parents are also regarded as important influences in the formation of the superego (somewhat similar to the conscience). Schoenfeld described the relation of superego formation to delinquency in the following way:

> The vast majority of delinquent acts reflect the presence not of an unduly strict superego or of a superego with criminal tendencies but rather of a superego that is somehow so weak, defective, or incomplete that it proves unable to control properly the primitive and powerful urges of early childhood that are resurrected just before puberty, with the result that some of these antisocial urges . . . are expressed in delinquent behavior.[7]

Freud tested and modified his theories during his lifetime, and his coresearchers and followers, including Anna Freud, Heinz Hartman, and Eric Erikson, continued to examine and apply them after his death. Erikson defined eight ages in the life of a human being that require adjustment and adaptation and maintained that failure to progress successfully from one stage to the next can set off unacceptable behavioral activity. These eight stages include the development of trust by an infant in his or her caretakers; gaining control over the basic bodily functions; experimentation by a child with various behavioral roles in his or her environment; attempts to master physical, social, and cognitive skills; development by an adolescent of an identity and sense of purpose; development by an adult of intimacy with others; acceptance of adult caretaking activities in which the family and external relations are the absorbing preoccupations; and last, development of the personal integrity needed to face life's final crisis, that of illness and death.[8] The Freudians and neo-Freudians have based their theories on the assumption that interruption of this sequential order of development, or inability to proceed past a given stage, can trigger unacceptable behavior. Erikson postulated the development of a "negative identity" by some youths, who deliberately embrace the roles or lifestyles that parents and significant others in their lives have characterized as unacceptable.[9] According to White, this negative identity is a defense mechanism, a method of coping with self-doubt and fear of not being able to live up to expectations. Such youths tend to seek each other out, develop relationships based on their "mutual rejection of society's norms," and become involved in a delinquent subculture.[10]

MORAL DEVELOPMENT AND DELINQUENCY

Moral-Development Theories

Researchers since the neo-Freudians have concentrated on the concept of the superego, or moral-judgment-development stage of personality. For example, Piaget viewed the internalization of moral values as involving two stages, which he termed "moral realism" and "moral relativism." At the stage of moral realism, a child realizes that he or she is required to obey rules set by some authority (most often the parents); with the development of moral relativism, the child becomes cognizant of the reasons behind certain requirements and begins to develop an internalized set of moral precepts. Piaget believed that moral relativism begins to develop at about the age of 8.[11] Concurrent with this moral development, according to Piaget, is the intellectual growth of the child, which moves from sensory-motor responses to the world to what Piaget terms *concrete operations*, or reality-based, logical efforts to understand the world, beginning at about the age of 7.[12] The child's experiences in the family and in society obviously have strong influences on both moral and intellectual development.

Kohlberg believed that the internalization of moral judgment occurs later, during adolescence. He saw the moral-development process as involving three periods of personal growth: a *premoral* period, normally completed by age 7, in which avoiding punishment is the motivation for conformity and a child is completely caught up in a search for self-gratificaton; the period of *conventional conformity*, beginning in the preadolescent and continuing into the adolescent period, when deviant behavior is avoided because there are rules against it and a child comes to respect the authorities who enforce the rules; and a period of *autonomy*, when a young person conforms to a specific set of norms or moral principles that has been internalized.[13] If this theory of moral development is considered, juvenile misbehavior may be attributed to the failure of the young person to progress beyond, or in some instances even reach, the premoral level of conformity, where conformity is motivated by fear of punishment. The reasons for this failure may be related to negative life experiences, a lack of interaction with persons who hold the values of conventional conformity, or even conscious decisions to pursue self-gratification and thrills rather than conform.

Perhaps the major contribution of the psychoanalytic and moral-development theorists is the notion that personality and moral-judgment development are gradual conditions, influenced by many factors in a child's life, and that *internalization* of moral values rather than mere exposure to moral influences (religion, social programs, parents' concepts of morality) is the key to the development of a nondelinquent personality.

Cognitive-Development Theories

Cognitive development applies to decision making and judgment. Psychological researchers have defined these as developmental processes and discovered that children, pre-adolescents, and younger teenage youths differ substantially in their capacities to make appropriate decisions and judgments. They have found that many children may be quite deviant in their preteen and early teen years, but are not deviant or delinquent in their later teens. The theory explaining these variations targets potential cost and rewards associated with engaging in deviant behavior. In early adolescence, children may be rebellious and destructive because they perceive this behavior as a way of gaining some independence from adults. They do not perceive their unacceptable behavior as having long-range negative effects on their goals or life styles. As they develop cognitively and are capable of making better judgments and decisions, and as they come closer to the goals they have established for themselves (graduating from high school, going to college, getting a good job), they begin to realize the potential costs associated with delinquency and misbehavior in general. Scott and Grisso content that it is necessary to understand the youth's cognitive developmental process to gain insight into the choices that children make.[14] Citing Moffit's theory, they note:

. . . youthful antisocial risk-taking acts are personal statements of independence by individuals who are precluded from yet assuming legitimate adult roles. Desistance in young adulthood is explained under the theory as the adaptive response to changed contingencies, as more legitimate adult roles become available. Delinquent behavior becomes costly rather than rewarding, as many young adults perceive that it threatens now-available conventional opportunities and may foreclose future goals. In short, they come to realize that they have something to lose.[15]

Adolescent Coping Mechanisms

The developmental process involves repeated testing of self and of the limits set by parents and the larger society. In adolescence, young people are constantly questioning the values and standards presented to them and making their own judgments as to whether they wish to adhere to them or deviate from them. Internal conflict and conflicts with others, including parents, peers, teachers, employers, and others who have power over them, are inevitable parts of growing up. However, if adolescents deal with the pressures and conflicts in their lives in inappropriate ways, the results may be psychological disturbances and/or delinquent behavior.

Just as a person under physical attack will ordinarily defend himself, a youth experiencing conflicts may use psychological defense mechanisms to deal with the stress and conflict being experienced. Some of the defense mechanisms commonly used by adolescents are shown in Table 3–1.[16]

As a young person seeks to understand, accept, or deal with a stressful situation, employment of these defense mechanisms may be a positive response. Repression or

Table 3–1.   Commonly Used Defense Mechanisms

Repression—The automatic or unconscious screening out of unacceptable wishes, drives, images, and impulses. Repression begins in childhood and is one of the basic defense mechanisms.
Suppression—Consciously tuning out unpleasant feelings, ideas, or emotions by trying not to work it out. Suppression is conscious, whereas repression is unconscious.
Denial—Denial usually refers to the screening out of unpleasant external values or feelings generated by unpleasant external realities. Repression usually refers to intrapsychic feelings. All defenses involve some degree of repression or denial.
Displacement—A shift of feelings from one object to another. The second object becomes a more acceptable target of such feelings as anger or hostility.
Rationalization—The assessment of a socially acceptable explanation for our behavior so we appear to be acting rationally or logically.
Intellectualization—Dealing with anxiety and stress-provoking problems as if they were intellectually interesting, emotionally neutral events.
Projection—Attributing one's own anxiety, arousal, or unacceptable or acceptable motives to someone else.
Sublimation—Channeling unacceptable aggressive and sexual energies into socially approved behaviors such as athletics, school, or the performing arts.
Acting out—Poorly controlled release of sexual, aggressive, or angry impulses to reduce tension.
Regression—Retreating to earlier ways of behaving when one is under stress.

Source: Joseph L. White, *The Troubled Adolescent* (New York: Pergamon Press, 1989), p. 21.

Table 3–2. Maladaptive Coping Behavior and Possible Triggering Conflicts

Depression—Conflicts which are preventing the emergence of self-worth, hope, confidence, and feelings of being capable, powerful, and lovable.

Suicide—Suicide in adolescents represents the ultimate loss of hope. Core conflicts involve deficits in connectedness to others, unconditional love, and a sense of belonging.

Anorexia and eating disorders—Conflicts around body image and nurturance.

Schizophrenia—Core conflict involves difficulties in perceptual, cognitive, and emotional organization which may be caused by a combination of biochemical and psychological vulnerabilities and predispositions. Schizophrenia can also be a defense against further hurt by withdrawing from reality.

Excessive use of drugs and alcohol—Core conflict involves the inability or unwillingness to cope with the demands of adolescent life and feel good about one's self without using substances.

Delinquency and conduct disturbances—Conflicts between the adolescent and the rules of society. If delinquent behavior persists, society has the power to create adverse consequences by restricting personal freedom and punishment.

Source: Joseph L. White, *The Troubled Adolescent* (New York: Pergamon Press, 1989), p. 31.

suppression of painful feelings may help a youth to get through the immediate situation and, as time goes by, other ways of coping may be used. For example, trying out for a sports team and not being chosen can be a stressful occurrence, but if the young person tries not to think about it (suppression), or decides that it wouldn't have been that exciting anyway (rationalization), the lack of acceptance may be less traumatic. In contrast, acting out through aggressive or angry behavior toward those who selected the team members would be an unacceptable use of a defense mechanism.

Facing and dealing with conflicts and stress are parts of the maturation process, and most adolescents are resilient and able to handle many problem situations without lasting psychological difficulties. However, others respond to the pressures of growing up by *maladaptive behavior*.[17] Table 3–2 describes some maladaptive behavior responses to adolescent problems and the types of difficulties that may bring on these responses.

As shown in Table 3–2, the maladaptive coping behaviors are serious enough to warrant active concern by those who observe their occurrence. For example, anorexia and other eating disorders, if left untreated, can be life threatening, and excessive use of drugs and/or alcohol requires appropriate intervention. Delinquency or suicidal behavior, if discovered, may result in efforts at intervention and treatment. All of these maladaptive responses are indications of conflicts within the youths that go beyond the ordinary problems associated with adolescence.

PERSONALITY-TRAIT EXPLANATIONS OF DELINQUENCY

Psychologists have devoted considerable attention to discovering the configuration of personality traits that are characteristic of persons involved in deviant behavior. The personality-trait approach assumes that delinquents are different from "normal" youths and that the differences can be found in their personality makeup. Although personality theorists do not consider delinquents mentally ill, they regard them as

Expressions of individuality are part of the adolescent coping mechanism. *(Photo credit: RubberBall Productions)*

having personality disturbances that interfere with their normal functioning in the family, school, and community.

Early Personality-Trait Theorists

Among the first personality-trait theorists were Richard L. Jenkins and Lester E. Hewitt. On the basis of their experience with young people in a child-guidance clinic, they defined three distinct maladjusted personality types among their clients. These included the *unsocialized aggressives,* who displayed assaultive, malicious tendencies and openly defied authority; the *socialized delinquents,* whose misbehavior was peer related; and the *overinhibited delinquents,* who were shy, apathetic children that came from repressive family situations.[18]

We noted in Chapter 2 that Sheldon and Eleanor Glueck analyzed the body types of 500 delinquents they compared with 500 nondelinquents and related the mesomorphic body type (muscular, hard) to delinquency. They found that the delinquents exhibited such personality traits as extroversion, suspicion or hostility toward authority, defiance, resentfulness, and fear of failure more often than nondelinquents.[19]

The Quay Classification System

Persons involved in the classification and handling of delinquents incorporated the ideas of these early theorists into testing and classification systems that came to be widely used in diagnosis and treatment. After extensive research on the personality patterns manifested by delinquents, Herbert Quay identified four dimensions of delinquent behavior that occurred frequently. Those delinquents who were *unsocialized aggressives* displayed constant conflict with parents, peers, and social institutions. The *neurotic-conflicted* youths, in contrast, expressed strong feelings of unhappiness, anxiety, and distress, and had many physical complaints. Those who were *inadequate-immatures* were the objects of aggression and ridicule from other children and withdrew from stressful situations through daydreaming and apathy. The *socialized delinquents* committed their offenses in the company of peers and were drawn to delinquency by social rather than psychological pressures. Quay's personality theories were incorporated into a system used for classifying and treating offenders that came to be used in youth training schools and adult institutions.[20]

Personality Measurement as a Method of Ascertaining Behavior Disorders

Clinical psychologists or psychiatrists attached to juvenile justice agencies or institutions and social workers and counselors who work with adolescents in school or general counseling have viewed delinquency in terms of reaction to personal emotional problems of various kinds. They have observed that delinquents frequently have difficulty establishing close relationships with peers and adults, and that they tend to be insecure and experience feelings of inferiority, inadequacy, or rejection, coupled with strong resentment of authority figures. Also characteristic of many delinquents is a sole concern for the present, with unrealistic ideas of what the future will bring for them, or a lack of interest in making future plans.

Much time and energy have been devoted to the development of various types of tests to measure facets of the personality (self-image, aspirations, values, ego strength, interest) and uncover precisely how young people with difficulties differ from "normal" youths. Inherent in the development of such tests are the problems of whether specific test items really measure what they are designed to measure (validity) and whether the items are interpreted and applied in the same way by all young people taking the tests (reliability).

An example of a personality test that has been widely used as a diagnostic tool for older adolescents in juvenile court services and institutions is the Minnesota Multiphasic Personality Inventory (MMPI). The self-rating schedule contains 550 statements designed to uncover the possible existence of depression, paranoia, a psychopathic personality, and various other behavioral ills. Once the major difficulty of the young person has been disclosed by this diagnostic tool, programs are applied that are designed to overcome or reduce the emotional difficulty.

Another instrument used to identify personality traits is the Jesness Inventory. It consists of a series of written statements that are checked as "true" if the respondent agrees or "false" if he or she disagrees. One section of the inventory, referred to as the *asocial index*, attempts to measure potential or susceptibility for delinquent behavior. The 155 items pertain to control of anger, response to authority figures, and the mechanisms used for problem solving. The asocial index is structured in such a way that affirmative answers to the items indicate the possession of deviant personality traits. Thus, the higher the score of "true" responses on the asocial index, the more likely it is that the youth being tested would use delinquent ways to solve problems.[21] When sex and age differences of the respondents were taken into account, Jesness asserted that the inventory was more than 80 percent accurate in predicting delinquency.[22]

Van Ness used a modified version of the Jesness Inventory in her study of more than 1,500 institutionalized delinquents who had been involved in predatory violence. She operationally defined predatory delinquents as those with clear descriptions in their case files of five or more nondefensive, nonaccidental physical attacks on others or attempted uses of force that could lead to physical injury to a human victim. She found that these youths scored significantly higher on the Jesness Inventory's asocial index than did nonviolent delinquents who were included in the study.[23] Her findings suggest that the Jesness Inventory is not only useful in identifying personality traits that may be predictive of delinquent behavior, but also helpful in differentiating potentially violent, predatory delinquents from those who, while engaging in some deviant activity, are not likely to persist with their unlawful behavior through their later adolescence and adulthood.[24]

The Criminal Personality

Publication of the books *The Criminal Personality: A Profile for Change* and *The Criminal Personality: The Change Process* in the 1970s brought about a renewed interest in personality theories of crime and delinquency. The authors, Yochelson and Samenow, were a neuropsychiatrist and a psychologist at St. Elizabeth's Hospital in Washington, DC. Their research spanned 16 years of work with patients who had committed serious criminal offenses. The authors contended that certain deviant thinking patterns were present to an extreme degree in all the criminals they studied and identified 52 "errors of thinking" present in all these offenders. The criminals they studied regarded everyday interaction with family, friends, or coworkers as dull and sought excitement by doing something forbidden. For them, crime was the ultimate excitement. They appeared to enjoy thinking about crime, talking about crime, planning crime, carrying it out, and even getting caught.[25]

The researchers focused on the notion that the erroneous thinking patterns of criminals, which are different from those of "normal" persons, show up in early childhood. Although the exact cause for the development of the criminal mind has not been established, the authors concluded that it is futile to search for causes of delinquency and crime outside the individual (in poverty, the environment, family, or school).

In a subsequent book, *Inside the Criminal Mind*, Samenow described the criminal personality in the following way:

> Beginning during the preschool years, patterns evolve that become part of a criminal life style. As a child, the criminal is a dynamo of energy, a being with an iron will, insistent upon taking charge, expecting others to indulge his every whim. . . . He takes risks, becomes embroiled in difficulties, and then demands to be bailed out and forgiven. . . .
>
> As a child, the criminal has contempt not only for his parents' advice and authority but also for the way they live, no matter what their social and economic circumstances. . . . To him, having a good time is what life is all about. . . .
>
> As the personality of the criminally inclined child unfolds, his parents are gripped by a gnawing fear that something terrible is going to happen. . . . Every time the phone rings, their hearts sink. . . . As their concerns mount, parents try new ways to cope with the youngster's misbehavior. They restrict his movement and privileges, but end up suffering more than the child, who blatantly and sneakily circumvents the restrictions or flouts them.[26]

Samenow also noted that lawbreakers frequently claim to have been rejected by their parents, schools, or other authorities in their lives, but see no link between their behavior and this purported rejection.[27]

The premise that a specific "criminal personality" type can be identified has come under attack from other researchers. Most of this research maintains that aggression and violence are learned responses rather than innate personality traits. Aggression, violence, and deviance are learned from a variety of sources, including the family, peers, and through the mass media, particularly television.

Paul Mones, a Santa Monica, CA attorney who specializes in patricide cases, said his experience has shown that most adolescent murderers learn about—and become desensitized—to violence in the home. Mones, who recently wrote a book on parricide, *When A Child Kills*, has been involved in about 200 parricide trials. The violence does not necessarily have to be directed against the child, Mones said. Many children who kill have learned about violence by watching their parents, aunts, uncles, and siblings.[28]

A person who is currently serving a life sentence in a California prison, reflecting on his feelings about his first gang fight involving an ambush of a rival gang in which several youths were killed, noted that he looked forward to the fight and the possibility of killing members of the other gang, but later experienced feelings of guilt. He described his feelings in the following way:

> The seriousness of what I had done that evening did not dawn on me until I was alone at home that night. My heart had slowed to its normal pace and the alcohol and pot had worn off. I was left then with just myself and the awesome flashes of light that lip up my mind to reveal bodies in abnormal positions and grotesque shapes, twisting and bending in arcs that defied bone structure. The actual impact was on my return back past the bodies of the first fallen, my first real look at bodies torn to shreds. It did little to me then, because it was all about survival. But as I lay wide awake in my bed, safe, alive, I felt guilty and ashamed of myself. Upon further contemplation, I felt that they were too easy to kill. Why had they been

out there? I tried every conceivable alibi within the realm of reason to justify my actions. There was none. I slept very little that night.[29]

The Psychopathic Personality

Psychologists have identified a type of disturbed individual quite similar to Yochelson and Samenow's "criminal personality," terming this person a "psychopath." The psychopath is an aggressive, impulsive person who has developed no bond of affection with others and experiences no feelings of guilt for delinquent acts. The search for pleasure or personal gratification, frequently conducted at the expense of others, is the hallmark of this personality type. McCord and McCord, who did extensive research on the psychopathic personality, noted that the two traits of guiltlessness and lovelessness make the psychopath different from other people.[30]

The term "sociopath" is now being used in lieu of "psychopath" in a good deal of research literature. Cleckley defined sociopaths as

> chronically antisocial individuals who are always in trouble, profiting neither from experience nor punishment and maintaining no real loyalties to any person, group, or code. They are frequently callous and hedonistic, showing marked emotional immaturity, with lack of responsibility, lack of judgment, and an ability to rationalize their behavior so that it appears warranted, reasonable, and justified.[31]

While Yochelson and Samenow advanced no explanation for the existence of a criminal personality in a given individual, McCord and McCord suggested that the psychopathic personality has its origins in brain damage or other physical trauma, or, most commonly, extreme emotional deprivation in childhood.[32] Whereas the research on psychopathic behavior has identified its presence in a relatively small percentage of the total population of delinquent and criminal offenders, Yochelson and Samenow declared that the criminal personality existed in all the offenders they studied.

MENTAL ILLNESS AND DELINQUENCY

The notion that misbehaving young people are "ill" and in need of "diagnosis" and "treatment" has been very popular in juvenile justice work. Sometimes termed the "medical model," such an approach presupposes that some problem within the individual rather than in the external environment is the cause of misbehavior and that once this condition is uncovered, it can be treated in some manner to make the young person "healthy" again. The medical model has been challenged in recent years by those who believe that environmental influences or situational factors play a more important role in delinquency than mental or emotional ills.

To examine this question, research was conducted on all the juvenile patients referred to a psychiatric ward of a hospital over a four-year period for diagnosis and treatment of behavior problems. Referrals had been made by parents, social workers, or the juvenile courts. Although the vast majority of these youngsters had been diagnosed as having personality disorders and had been given treatment programs, the researchers, in conversations with them, discovered that most of them did not feel that they had emotional problems or were in need of treatment, and most of them regarded the treatment they had received as of little benefit. The researchers also observed that the majority of the youths referred for psychiatric treatment were given this disposition as an alternative to a more severe handling of their cases and that by accepting the option of psychiatric treatment, they received either dismissal of the charges against them or informal handling of their cases. It follows that such referrals may simply be used as a device to avoid giving certain children a juvenile record.[33]

Studies of homicide suggest that most juvenile murderers are not extremely psychotic. A study of 72 Michigan youths charged with murder concluded that only five were psychotic when they committed their crimes.[34] Extensive participation in delinquent activities or involvement in violent peer groups, rather than mental illness, were advanced as alternative explanations for juvenile homicide offenses.

The deviant behavior of delinquents who suffer from some form of mental illness is generally so bizarre, extreme, or unpredictable that it can readily be differentiated from general delinquency. Acts of torture, brutality, murder, sadistic rape, and arson may signal the presence of mental illness. A study by Sorrells of juvenile murderers led him to classify youths who kill into three personality types: the *nonempathic*, who have no feelings of sympathy toward or identification with others; the *prepsychotic*, who are trapped in painful and conflict-ridden interpersonal situations, usually in their families, and see no possibility of escaping; and the *neurotically fearful*, who are so insecure that they overreact to threatening circumstances as though they were potentially lethal.[35]

The causes of mental illness in children are varied. They include inadequate diet, neurological injury, excessive drug or alcohol use, physical or emotional deprivation, emotional traumas (sexual abuse, death of a parent), or physical or emotional abuse. Other factors related to juvenile mental illness include a violent, chaotic family,[36] and emotionally disturbed, alcoholic, or incompetent parents.[37]

If some youths who commit delinquent acts are mentally ill, then the question arises concerning their responsibility for their actions. In many juvenile court jurisdictions, the defense of insanity is being considered in juvenile cases. The logic behind this plea is that if mental illness negates an adult's culpability because intent cannot be established, the same privilege should be available for juveniles. Some juvenile court judges are receptive to this defense, while others feel that it is still improper for youths. Those in favor of allowing an insanity defense in juvenile cases believe that this defense would prevent mentally ill juveniles from receiving negative sanctions. Those who feel that the insanity plea is inappropriate note that the juvenile justice system is still oriented toward protection and rehabilitation and can provide appropriate treatment for mentally disturbed young people.

Although the U.S. Supreme Court has not ruled on this issue, the use of the insanity plea in a Wisconsin juvenile court was upheld by the state court of appeals. *In re Winburn* was a case involving a juvenile accused of killing his mother. At the adjudicatory hearing, the defendant's sanity was questioned. After a psychiatric examination of the youth was conducted, the court found him to be mentally ill and committed him to a state mental hospital. The original petition alleging delinquency was dismissed. The state appealed the dismissal, arguing that the insanity defense did not apply in the juvenile court. The appeals court ruled that the defense did apply and that the dismissal was proper.[38] However, in a New Jersey case, *In re H.C.*, a juvenile's request to enter a plea of insanity was denied.[39] The kinds of evidence used to determine whether a juvenile is competent or incompetent owing to mental illness are discussed in Chapter 13.

SUMMARY

In this chapter, we examined the psychological theories of delinquency causation, which have sought the explanation for delinquency within the human personality and have related it to problems in the youth's mental and/or emotional development.

The psychoanalytic theories of delinquency place great emphasis on early childhood and relate delinquency to deficiencies in parent-child relationships or interruptions in a young person's progress through specific emotional-development stages.

Those who advance moral-development theories emphasize the importance of the internalization of moral values in a gradual, developmental sequence. Cognitive development theorists maintain that the ability to make appropriate choices and judgments is a gradual, maturation process, related to perceived costs and rewards. Adolescents use psychological defense coping mechanisms to deal with the stresses in their lives. These can be positive or maladaptive.

Personality-trait theorists, including Jenkins and Hewitt and Sheldon and Eleanor Glueck, have identified certain personality traits as characteristic of delinquents. The Quay Classification System is based specifically on separation and treatment of offenders according to the specific personality characteristics they display. Personality tests are widely used to identify the existence of undesirable personality traits. In their book, *The Criminal Personality*, Yochelson and Samenow, maintained that criminals display erroneous thinking patterns and that criminal personality characteristics are present in delinquents from a very early age. Although the criminal-personality theory has strong appeal as an explanation of criminal behavior in youths who have suffered no apparent psychological deprivation, it cannot be accepted uncritically. There is evidence that even those who display many of the traits of a "criminal personality" have had negative influences in their lives that could have triggered their deviant behavior, or these offenders have indicated that they did experience feelings of guilt about their actions.

Psychopathic individuals, who apparently experience no guilt feelings for delinquent acts and display no bonds of affection with others, are regarded as having experienced extreme emotional deprivation or physical trauma in childhood. This personality disorder has been identified in a small percentage of the total delinquent population.

The question of whether a plea of insanity should be allowed in juvenile courts has not yet been acted on by the U.S. Supreme Court. Some juvenile court jurisdictions allow a defense of insanity, while others consider it improper.

DISCUSSION QUESTIONS

1. Define personality and discuss the various meanings the term can have. Why is it so difficult to measure or categorize personality?
2. Many psychologists believe that anyone who commits a deviant act has a character disorder, and thus should be considered abnormal. Do you agree?
3. Discuss the theories of criminality set forth in Yochelson and Samenow's books on the criminal personality. Why does this theory have such strong appeal today?
4. Define "psychopath" and discuss some of the traits that make psychopaths different from normal persons.
5. Is a plea of insanity currently allowed in juvenile courts? Discuss the arguments for and against allowing juveniles to enter insanity pleas.

NOTES

1. *Daily Kent Stater*, September 3, 1992, 3.
2. Bill Kaczor, "Boys Sentenced for Dad's Death," *Akron Beacon Journal*, November 15, 2002, A14.
3. "Jury Indicts Teen Suspect in Sniper Case," *Akron Beacon Journal*, January 23, 2003, A7.
4. Donald J. Shoemaker, *Theories of Delinquency* (New York: Oxford University Press, 1955), 45.
5. Charles Brenner, *An Elementary Textbook of Psychoanalysis* (New York: International Universities Press, 1955), 45.
6. C. G. Schoenfeld, "A Psychoanalytic Theory of Juvenile Delinquency," in Edward E. Peoples, ed., *Readings in Correctional Casework and Counseling* (Pacific Palisades, CA: Goodyear, 1975), 24–26.
7. *Ibid.*, 23.
8. Eric H. Erikson, *Identity and the Life Cycle* (New York: International Universities Press, 1959), 35–46; summarized in James K. Whittaker, *Social Treatment* (Chicago: Aldine, 1974), 69–70.
9. Eric H. Erikson, *Identity: Youth and Crisis* (New York: Norton, 1968).
10. Joseph L. White, *The Troubled Adolescent* (New York: Pergamon Press, 1989), 307.
11. Jean Piaget, *The Moral Judgment of the Child* (New York: Free Press, 1948).
12. B. Inhelder and J. Piaget, *The Growth of Logical Thinking from Childhood to Adolescence* (New York: Basic Books, 1958).
13. Lawrence Kohlberg, "Moral Development and Identification," in *Child Psychology: A Yearbook of the National Society for the Study of Education* (Chicago: University of Chicago Press, 1963), 277–333.
14. Elizabeth S. Scott and Thomas Grisso, "The Evolution of Adolescence: A Developmental Perspective on Juvenile Justice Reform," *Journal of Criminal Law and Criminology* 88, 1 (1997), 137–145.
15. *Ibid.*, 138.
16. See Joseph L. White, *The Troubled Adolescent*, 19–23 for a detailed discussion of these defense mechanisms.
17. *Ibid.*, 30–31.
18. Lester E. Hewitt and Richard L. Jenkins, *Fundamental Patterns of Maladjustment: The Dynamics of Their Origin* (Springfield, IL.: State of Illinois, 1946).
19. Sheldon and Eleanor Glueck, *Unraveling Juvenile Delinquency* (New York: Commonwealth Fund, 1950), 281–282.
20. Roy Gerard, "Institutional Innovations in Juvenile Corrections," *Federal Probation*, 34, 4 (December 1970), 37–44.

21. Carl F. Jesness, *Manual, The Jesness Inventory* (Palo Alto, CA.: Consulting Psychologists Press, 1966), 16–17.
22. Carl F. Jesness, "An Empirical Approach to Offender Classification," *Contemporary Psychology* 29 (1984), 709–720.
23. Shela R. Van Ness, "Theoretical Origins of Predatory Violence Phenomenon: A Study of Juvenile Offenders in Ohio," unpublished doctoral dissertation, Kent State University, May, 1987, 15, 136.
24. *Ibid.*, 135–141.
25. Samuel Yochelson and Stanton E. Samenow, *The Criminal Personality*, Vol. 1 (New York: Jason Aronson, 1976).
26. Stanton E. Samenow, *Inside the Criminal Mind* (New York: Times Books, 1984), 26, 39, 42.
27. *Ibid.*, 35.
28. Michael D. Biskup and Charles P. Cozic, eds., *Youth Violence* (San Diego, CA: Greenhaven Press, 1992), 63.
29. Sanyika Shakur, *Monster: The Autobiography of an L.A. Gang Member* (New York: Penguin Books, 1993), 13.
30. William McCord and Joan McCord, *The Psychopath* (Princeton, NJ: D. Van Nostrand, 1964), 3.
31. Hervey M. Cleckley, "Psychopathic States," in Silvano Arieti, ed., *American Handbook of Psychiatry* (New York: Basic Books, 1954), 567–588.
32. McCord and McCord, *The Psychopath*, 8–10.
33. Robert Miller and Emmet Kenney, "Adolescent Delinquency and the Myth of Hospital Treatment," *Crime and Delinquency* 12, 1 (January 1966), 38–48.
34. Biskup and Cozic, *Youth Violence*, 62.
35. James Sorrells, Jr., "What Can Be Done about Juvenile Homicide," *Crime and Delinquency*, 26, 2 (April 1980), 154–157.
36. Ismail B. Sendi and Paul G. Blomgren, "A Comparative Study of Predictive Criteria in the Predisposition of Homicidal Adolescents," *American Journal of Psychiatry* 132, 4 (April 1975), 423–427.
37. Sorrells, "What Can be Done about Juvenile Homicide," 158–160.
38. *In re Winburn*, 32 Wis. 2d 152, 245 N.W. 2d 178 (1966).
39. *In re H.C.*, 106 N.J. Super. 583, 256A. 2d 322 (Juvenile and Domestic Relations Court, Morris County, 1969).

CHAPTER 4

SOCIOLOGICAL PERSPECTIVES ON DELINQUENCY CAUSATION

(Photo credit: Ernie Mastroianni)

SOCIAL STRAIN THEORY
      Poverty, Family Disruption, and Delinquency
      Environmental Influences on Delinquency
      Anomie and Delinquency
      Reaction Formation Defense Mechanisms
      Delinquency and Opportunity
      Stress and Delinquency
LEARNING THEORY, CULTURAL TRANSMISSION, AND DELINQUENCY
      Social Learning Theory
      Differential Association Theory
      Differential Reinforcement Theory
THE INFLUENCE OF TELEVISION VIOLENCE ON AGGRESSIVE DELINQUENT BEHAVIOR
THE CULTURE OF VIOLENCE
SOCIAL-PSYCHOLOGICAL EXPLANATIONS OF DELINQUENCY
      The Gluecks' Multiple-Factor Approach
      Containment Theory
      Social Control/Bonding Theory
      Self-Concept
      Labeling Theory

We noted in Chapter 3 that psychological theories of delinquency locate the problem within the individual or in the developmental phase of human life. In contrast, the sociological theories of delinquency presented in this chapter suggest that external factors or combinations of factors act to heighten the possibility of delinquency. These factors include inadequate family functioning, poverty, school problems, environmental factors, and the influence of delinquent peers.

SOCIAL STRAIN THEORY

Poverty, Family Disruption, and Delinquency

Contemporary American families vary in structure, economic status, racial and ethnic group membership, family customs, traditions, and styles of life. Children are less likely to live in a two-parent family than in the past. From 1970 to 1997, the proportion of children in the United States living in two-parent homes declined from 85 to 68 percent. In 1997, 85 percent of the children in single-parent households lived with their mother, but the percentage living with only their father increased from 9 percent in 1970 to 15 percent in 1997. In 1997, 38 percent of the children in one-parent families were living with a never-married parent.[1] The problems that face the young, never-married female heads of one-parent families often include dropping out of school, inability to work outside the home, and an environment of poverty and social deprivation for the children.

Children who live in poverty present a compelling social problem in American society. In 1997, 14.1 million children (approximately one fifth of the juvenile population) lived in poverty. Poverty rates were highest for children of black families (34% in poverty) and Hispanic families (24% in poverty).[2] During a two-year period beginning in 2000, the United States experienced an economic decline, resulting in significant increases in unemployment, homelessness, and poverty. At the end of 2002, the unemployment rate in the United States was 6 percent, the highest in eight years, and the number of people living in poverty increased, compared to 2000. Federal guidelines define poverty as a family of four or more with an annual income of less than $18,104, a family of three with income less than $14,128, a family of two with income less than $11,569, or a single person with income less than $9,039. In 2002, children younger than 18 make up 36 percent of the nation's poor, although they constitute only 26 percent of the population.[3]

A report on homelessness completed by the U.S. Department of Housing and Urban Development revealed that homelessness is increasing and that minorities and children are the most affected segments of the population. Blacks constituted 40 percent of the homeless, but only 11 percent of the population; Hispanics made up 11 percent of the homeless, but only 9 percent of the population; and 8 percent of the homeless were American Indians, although they represent less than 1 percent of the population. The report also revealed that 15 percent of all of the homeless were part of a family, with the family head being a woman in 84 percent of the families. The average number of children attached to the homeless families was 2.2.[4]

Changes in the structure of the American family and the economic deprivation that many families are experiencing have resulted in the creation of a permanent segment of the American population that can be characterized as an *underclass*. Living on welfare or Aid for Dependent Children (AFDC), residing in substandard housing or homeless, being poorly educated, lacking job skills or the desire to obtain them, or seeking employment without success, a large segment of this population is clustered in the large cities of the United States. The following account of conditions in which 19 children were found to be living in Chicago is indicative of the problems of social disorganization that occur.

> The four-room apartment was littered with filth and crawling with cockroaches, its windows broken and covered with blankets that flapped in the wind. It was home to 19 children—the oldest 14 years old, the youngest just 1.

> When police barged in on a drug raid, they found five of the children sleeping in their underwear on a bare floor. Others fought with a German shepherd dog for scraps of meat on bones scattered on the floor.

> Six adult relatives of the children—four mothers, a father, and an uncle—were charged with contributing to child neglect, a misdemeanor. A fifth mother of some of the children was in custody but had not been charged, and a sixth mother was in the hospital giving birth, police said.

> Inside the apartment was a world that the public pays for and that the welfare system, as it is structured in Illinois, monitors only from a distance, asking almost nothing of the people who receive their monthly checks. . . . Almost $2,500 in cash payments are mailed out each month to six of the seven women. . . . In addition, the women receive nearly $2,000 monthly in food stamps. And Medicaid paid for more than $20,000 in medical care and prescription drugs for the women and children in the last 13 months, the records showed. . . .

Doubling up in living quarters is common in low-income neighborhoods. In this case, the families lived cheaply in an apartment where the landlord asked only $380 in rent.

Three of the 19 children found in the apartment were expelled from school earlier this week because their immunizations were not up to date. . . .

When mothers are receiving cash payments and food stamps, yet the children are hungry and neglected, workers increasingly say they sense the same problem: Drugs. At . . . a social service agency on the city's West Side, some workers say they often unwrap new clothes they give out to the mothers, fearing that packaged clothes will be sold to get money for drugs. And women come in asking for bottles of free infant formula—too much and too often for just feeding babies. Other clients tell them the formula is sold to get money for drugs.[5]

Children living in poverty are vulnerable to a wide variety of problems, including poor nutrition, inadequate housing, substandard medical attention, lack of proper supervision, and physical or emotional abuse. Adolescents from these backgrounds become part of a cycle of low income or unemployment. Black and Hispanic teenagers have particularly acute problems obtaining employment.

Criminal and delinquent activity may also be an accepted part of the total picture for deprived children. It is difficult to emerge from such surroundings unscarred. Just how strong is the influence of these experiences on the production of delinquency? Many researchers have sought to locate the causes of delinquency in the environment and the effects poverty and social disorganization can have on young people.

Environmental Influences on Delinquency

Much of the early sociological research on delinquency focused on the environment within which individuals act and on the factors in social organization and social processes that they develop to adapt to the environment. Researchers concentrated on adaptation to slums, deteriorated housing, high population density, areas with heterogeneous populations and cultural conflicts because of uprooting, effects of urbanization, unemployment, poverty, broken families, and other factors.

The theoretical assumptions of many sociological studies were borrowed from ecology, which is concerned with the distribution of certain organisms and their relationship to their environment. Human ecology is the sociological evaluation of relations between the social and institutional distribution of human beings and their geographical environment.[6]

A number of researchers studied social disorganization, industrialization, population movements, and changes in neighborhoods to determine their influence on delinquency and crime in cities. In their study, *The Polish Peasant*, Thomas and Znaniecki examined social disorganization in a Polish neighborhood of Chicago. They noted the failure of existing social rules and norms to control behavior, and they documented the fact that the home, neighborhood, church, and friendship patterns lost their influence when rapid social change occurred.[7]

The term "social disorganization" is used to denote a breakdown in conventional institutional controls within a community and the inability of organizations, groups, or individuals within that community to solve common problems.[8] Several approaches to studying social disorganization and its effects were developed by the Chicago School—a group of sociologists who used the city of Chicago as a natural laboratory for their research on all facets of social interaction.

Delinquency Areas. Burgess showed the uses and activities of various parts of a large city in a pattern moving from the center of the city outward. His "concentric zone" concept divided the city into different zones. Zone I, the inner city, contained the downtown area, where business and government buildings were located. Zone II, the zone in transition, was characterized by factories, tenement buildings, transportation lines, and ghettos. Zone III, the area of working-class homes, was a residential area of multiple-family dwellings. Zone IV, also a residential area, was made up of single-family dwellings for the middle class. Zone V was a suburban commuter area. Delinquency was most likely to occur in Zone II, the least stable area in terms of permanent residents, strong community feeling or control, and church or neighborhood involvement.[9]

The term "delinquency area" is used to designate a geographical part of a city that has delinquency rates higher than average for that city. It frequently is separated from other sections by a physical boundary such as a railroad track or highway. The values and traditions of the persons who live in a delinquency area have been found to support or even encourage delinquent and criminal behavior in many instances.

Clifford Shaw attempted a geographic analysis of the distribution of juvenile court petitions filed in the city of Chicago, according to the areas of residence of the alleged delinquents, as part of the Chicago Area Project, a joint effort during the 1930s by the University of Chicago and residents of high-delinquency neighborhoods to control delinquent behavior and discover its causes. On the basis of his analysis, he developed a theory that juvenile delinquency occurs most frequently in the center of the city, decreasing as one moves out toward the peripheral suburban areas. He also asserted that the high-delinquency areas were those in which the population was declining and that were deteriorating physically, with a consequent movement from residential to business zoning. Shaw termed such an area "interstitial."[10]

Shaw was later joined in his research by Henry D. McKay; the two sought to apply the same approach to analysis of the distribution of delinquency in other major American cities. The findings of these studies appeared to be consistent with Shaw's analysis of Chicago, although later researchers questioned their validity on the basis of the omission of certain important variables from the research design, including whether the delinquency petitions were found to be true, and whether agencies for diversion of juveniles were more likely to exist in the fringe areas than in the central city. Shaw and McKay's analysis of the Chicago delinquency areas continued periodically for 35 years (1927–1962). Data from various time periods within this 35-year span showed remarkable consistency in the characteristics and delinquency rates of those "interstitial" areas of the city initially identified by Shaw and McKay. These areas tended to maintain the characteristics of mobility, high population density, and slum conditions, regardless of the ethnic or racial makeup of the population.[11]

A number of more recent researchers have also sought to locate the delinquency areas of large cities. A comparison of data from Indianapolis, Baltimore, and Detroit revealed that despite other dissimilarities, the cities all tended to have zones with high levels of delinquency and that these were characterized by a transient population residing in overcrowded, substandard housing. The residents of these zones were chiefly those with low incomes and minimal occupational skills.[12]

Bloom, in a survey of delinquent behavior in an American city, found that the areas in which family, marital, economic, environmental, and educational disruption were most prevalent were those that had the highest delinquency rates.[13]

Wolfgang and his associates analyzed the police contacts of nearly 10,000 boys born in Philadelphia in 1945 and 14,000 males born in Philadelphia in 1958. They discovered that for both cohorts, delinquency was more prevalent among nonwhites and that residential instability, poor school achievement, and failure to graduate from high school were related to involvement in delinquency.[14]

Delinquency and Drift.   Environmental conditions that contribute to delinquency are not confined to urban settings. Suburban and rural youths also may become caught up in delinquent behavior as a result of their surroundings. Matza, who developed the theory of delinquency and drift, theorized that many juveniles are not committed to a delinquent lifestyle, but become involved in situations and circumstances that lead to delinquent behavior.[15] Rural youths may break into summer homes when the owners are away, vandalize school buildings, drag race on deserted highways late at night, or steal from unsecured garages or warehouses; suburban youths may shoplift from mall stores; and urban youngsters may vandalize or hang out in vacant apartments. All become caught up in activities that seem to be profitable or fun at a particular moment.

According to Sykes and Matza, the youths *neutralize* or *rationalize* their behavior by contending that they didn't really mean any harm that the person from whom they stole deserved it, that school officials "had it coming" because they treated the youths badly, or that they simply got caught up in the excitement of the moment under peer pressure.[16]

Routine Activities.   The theory of routine activities, closely allied to delinquency and drift, would help explain why youths living in various environments engage in different types of delinquent activities. According to this theory, delinquent behavior occurs when opportunities for the activities are available, there is a lack of supervision of the youths or of the targets of the activities, and youths who would consider becoming involved in unlawful behavior are present.[17] Thus, inner-city youths are drawn to form gangs or engage in unlawful activities that they observe adults performing in their neighborhoods, while rural youths resort to underage drinking, theft, or vandalism. Studies of delinquencies committed by rural youths have shown that their offenses are less serious than those committed by urban youths.[18]

In summary, environmental conditions have been identified as contributing to the delinquency of some youths, regardless of the specific settings in which they live. Urban, suburban, and rural youths are at risk. However, the strength of the influence of environmental conditions and the opportunities to commit delinquent acts vary. Many youths who live in deplorable environments avoid delinquent involvement. Thus, environmental conditions cannot be regarded as a sole cause of delinquency, but they may be an important contributing factor.

Anomie and Delinquency

The term *anomie* was used by the French sociologist Emile Durkheim to describe a way of life in which many of the old customs, values, and beliefs have been discarded, and a new value or belief system has not yet been ingrained.[19] Individuals exist in a state of "normlessness," lacking moral convictions and not responding to social controls such as the influence of neighbors, community leaders, church representatives, or teachers.

Merton identified such conditions as existing among disadvantaged persons in the late 1930s. He maintained that members of all social classes seek success, defined in terms of economic affluence and manifested by possession of material status symbols. Those living in areas characterized by rapid changes in the population, lack of interpersonal interaction, poverty, and family disruption have limited opportunities to achieve through legitimate means, so they react by seeking success through illegitimate means. The social disorganization that exists around them reduces their response to social controls and in many instances causes them to seek success or pleasure without regard for the rules of society.[20]

Social strain theory implies that there are circumstances arising within both the physical and the social environment of an individual or group that create confusion, disruption, breakdown of norms and values, or lack of direction. Changes in family structure, economic situation, or opportunities can produce these problems. In his studies of the relation of economic factors to rates of crime and delinquency for black males, Sampson concluded that their commitments to family life and marital commitment are affected by their lack of opportunities for steady, good paying jobs.[21] Chilton also suggested that urban life and the isolation of poor families in disadvantaged areas of the cities limit the types of socialization that serve as positive influences for children living in suburban areas and small towns.[22]

Robert Agnew broadened the scope of social strain theory by introducing the concepts of vicarious and anticipated strain. He contended that vicarious experiences (interacting with persons who describe being treated in a negative manner, especially if they are close family members, friends, or neighbors) may have a significant impact on an individual, even though that person has not actually witnessed the incidents or been treated in this manner. Anticipated strain refers to a person's expectation that the strain he or she is currently experiencing will continue or intensify in the future. Agnew's study of adolescent boys concluded that both actual physical victimization and experiencing certain types of vicarious and anticipated physical victimization (assaults on family members or friends, presence of drug addicts or dealers or other undesirables in the neighborhood, violence in their schools, or fear of physical attacks) were associated with delinquent behavior.[23]

Reaction Formation Defense Mechanisms

In his book, *Delinquent Boys*, Cohen noted that youths who realize they cannot achieve their goals develop various behavior characteristics in reaction to their failure. They not only defy conventional norms but deliberately seek to oppose them. This "reaction formation" behavior may involve engaging in delinquent behavior that seems to have no purpose other than to express rebellion and display disregard for conventional norms. It may include involvement in activities that are deliberately undertaken to shock or outrage those in authority or take the form of self-destructive behavior.[24]

Delinquency and Opportunity

Cloward and Ohlin also noted that youths may seek gratification through illegitimate methods without regard for the social acceptability of their activities. Their "opportunity theory" stressed the importance of the social environment in determining which of the opportunities open to them youths will follow. When opportunities for success by following conventional norms appear to be blocked, they may engage in an apparently normless lifestyle that includes violence, con games, drug or alcohol abuse, or prostitution, without regard for the conventional values of society, which define such activities as improper.[25]

Today, anomic behavior is not restricted to youths living in poverty areas or those lacking educational or social advantages. Changes in American life, notably in the stability of family life, have caused young people of all social classes to experience a lack of structure, continuity, and goal orientation in their day-to-day existence. Parents chiefly concerned with their own professional or personal development frequently lack the motivation or time to provide strong control and guidance. The youth culture offers the appeal of drug and alcohol use as a means of coping with personal problems. The emphasis on personal gratification and immediate pleasure, which can be sought without concern for the needs, wishes, and rights of others, promotes normlessness as a way of life.

Stress and Delinquency

Stress theorists view violent behavior as a means of coping with intolerable stress, which may occur when youths are faced with pressure from a single trauma or when pressure has gradually accumulated from several sources. The ensuing violence may be directed against intimates or toward strangers. Such violent incidents tend to be unplanned and unintended. Mawson theorized that aggressive violent behavior may be directed toward family members or peer-group members when an aggressor experiencing stress wishes to maintain intense physical and emotional contact with the victim. This may be true even when the person toward whom the violence is directed is the source of the stress.[26]

In his study of the impact of community violence on African-American children and families, Isaacs found that African-American children were more likely than non-African-American children to experience or witness violence, and that the family and the school are no longer safe havens for a large number of African-American children. As a result, they expressed feelings of fatalism and acceptance of death, felt powerless to prevent being victimized, and experienced psychological problems. The possible factors identified as helping children who had experienced these stresses were their own personal resources, positive role models, support from family and peers, and internalization of good community values and beliefs.[27]

LEARNING THEORY, CULTURAL TRANSMISSION, AND DELINQUENCY

One of the first theorists to associate the origins of crime with a learning process was Gabriel Tarde. In his book, *The Law of Imitation*, Tarde argued that crime results from one person's imitating the actions of another. Although he also took into account biological and psychological factors, he believed that crime is essentially a social product.

Social Learning Theory

Social learning explanations of violent behavior hold that early childhood experiences are related to behavior patterns later in life. Physical abuse of children by parents or violence of spouses toward each other is internalized by the children as the appropriate reaction to problems. A study that followed the offense careers of nearly 1,600 persons from childhood until they became adults found that being abused or neglected as a child increased the likelihood of being arrested as a juvenile by 53 percent and being arrested as an adult by 38 percent. It also discovered that such mistreatment increased the likelihood of being arrested for a violent crime by 38 percent.[28] Kratcoski's study of institutionalized delinquents revealed that 26 percent of the youths in his sample had experienced physical abuse and that the abused delinquents tended to direct their violence toward members of their immediate families or significant others in their lives (teachers, youth counselors, friends).[29] Another study by Kratcoski of self-reported violent behavior by high school students and youths referred to a juvenile court revealed that those who had experienced violence from their parents and who lived in families characterized by low levels of family functioning were more likely to have committed violent acts than those who had not had such experiences.[30]

Researchers who have examined the family situations of youths who threatened to kill or actually killed their parents found that the youths' family environment was characterized by physical abuse of children, heavy drinking by parents, and constant verbal and physical fighting between parents.[31]

A history of drug abuse has also been identified as being related to violent delinquency. When drug-use histories of incarcerated youths were explored according to the types of offenses they had committed, it was found that those who had abused drugs were more likely to have been involved in violent offenses against persons than in property offenses.[32] A veteran police officer described the influence of drugs on youth violence.

"Drugs have changed everything," Van Horn said. "You used to get an 18- or 20-year-old for murder. You'd bring him up to an interrogation room in handcuffs. You'd tell him he was being charged with murder, that he might go to the electric chair, and he would cry."

"Now we get 15-year-olds and killing doesn't faze them. They don't cry no more. They simply don't have feelings. They've never had a childhood. They've gone from being a baby to being a street person, someone selling or using drugs."[33]

All of these explanations of youth violence involve causative influences throughout a youth's lifetime. They emphasize the difficulties encountered by the courts in making decisions on the appropriate dispositions and treatment for these offenders, using the limited options and resources at their disposal. The following incident illustrates this dilemma.

In the juvenile court of a large metropolitan county, the judge was holding a detention hearing for a 17-year-old male charged with robbery and attempted rape. After listening to some of the particulars of the alleged offense, presented by an assistant prosecutor, the judge asked if a judicial waiver would be requested by the Prosecutor's Office. The assistant prosecutor noted that the boy had a previous conviction for rape and several other delinquency convictions and that he was currently on probation.

The judge then asked the public defender, who represented the boy, if he had any recommendations concerning the need for detention while the boy was awaiting a hearing on the current charge. The defense counsel tried to convince the judge that the youth respected his mother and would listen to her if he was released to her custody. The judge then consulted the boy's probation officer. He stated that the youth had not adhered to probation rules and wanted to do as he pleased. He recommended that the youth be held in detention until the hearing.

The judge informed the boy that he would be detained until the hearing and transferred to the county jail because of the aggressive nature of his behavior, an option allowed by state law if the youth in question is age 16 or older. As the youth was being led away by Sheriff's deputies, he broke free and began pounding a wall with his fists. He then rushed toward the probation officer, his fists swinging wildly. The deputies needed the assistance of several others to subdue him.

When the youth had left the room, the judge commented that he recognized in this boy a potential for out-of-control behavior and that by keeping him in secure detention he was both protecting the community and preventing the boy from lashing out at others and further complicating his own problems.[34]

Differential Association Theory

Edwin Sutherland developed a broad, general theory of crime and delinquency grounded in the learning process. According to this theory, criminal behavior is learned through association with persons who are law violators, or through observing the mechanisms of criminal activity. This learning involves both internalization of attitudes that are favorable toward criminal behavior and specific techniques for performing criminal actions.[35]

According to Sutherland, a person may have many associations, some of them having a pro-criminal-behavior influence and others having essentially an anti-criminal-behavior influence. A person may thus experience internal conflict in trying to decide which set of values, attitudes, and codes of behavior to accept and internalize. For example, to a youth living in a neighborhood that has many criminal types, these people may be symbols of economic and social success because they have money, expensive clothes, flashy cars, and other material possessions that inspire respect and envy. The young may be drawn to the criminal lifestyle of these people because they want the same symbols of success for themselves. At the same time, a number of youths in the neighborhood may have good relationships with parents or other adults who are noncriminal in their lifestyles and who try to instill nondelinquent values in them. A young person exposed to both types of influences must balance out their merits and decide whether to accept the values of one set of associates or those of the other.

Although Sutherland originally developed this *differential-association* theory to apply within the context of a single disorganized community in which normative values and attitudes and societal controls were weak, the theory was later applied to explain the learning process for white-collar crime.[36]

The theory of differential association has received a good deal of criticism. It has been faulted as being too broad and vague, not taking into consideration personality factors as causes of crime, failing to explain the exact process by which criminal behavior is learned, and ignoring crimes that result from mental illness or compulsive behavior. Why do some youths exposed to criminal influences succumb to them while others do not? And why do some who have no criminal associations in their social background turn to crime? The answer to the first question may lie in defining the strength of influences that operate on some youngsters to counteract criminal associations; the answer to the second may be that the results or "rewards" of some types of criminal activity serve as powerful reinforcement, comparable to the praise or approval of criminal associates. For example, being able to use loot from a burglary to improve one's lifestyle may serve as a stimulant to further criminal behavior.

Leader believed that personality factors and need satisfaction were the basic causal elements in the production of acceptable or unacceptable behavior. If a person's needs are not met by acceptable behavior, that person turns to alternative forms of behavior that do meet those needs and conform to the person's value system.[37]

Differential Reinforcement Theory

Others have said that Sutherland overemphasized the role of intimate association in the learning of criminal techniques and internalization of values that justify criminal behavior. Jeffery maintained that criminal behavior can be learned without ever associating with those who commit crimes (e.g., through the influence of television portrayals of crime).[38] Jeffery advanced his own theory of *differential reinforcement*:

> Criminal behavior is maintained by its consequences, both material and social. Such social variables as age, sex, social class, ethnic membership, and residential area influence the manner in which criminal behavior is conditioned.

> Punishment decreases a response rate only if it is used in a consistent manner and is applied near the time of the occurrence of the forbidden act. As it is used to control criminal behavior, punishment is likely to create avoidance and escape behaviors rather than law-abiding behaviors.[39]

In summary, differential association serves as the cornerstone for learning and crime- and delinquency-causation theories. Sutherland's work has produced a good deal of interest and research. The application of differential-association principles to gang formation and peer-group influences in general is considered in Chapter 6.

THE INFLUENCE OF TELEVISION VIOLENCE ON AGGRESSIVE DELINQUENT BEHAVIOR

Although a cause-and-effect relationship between exposure to violence and aggression on television and aggressive delinquencies by juveniles has not been confirmed by research studies, many people are convinced that such a relationship exists.

Various explanations have been advanced for the appeal television violence holds for children. One is the so-called "catharsis theory"—the belief that by observing characters working out their aggressions on television, children are able to discharge their own aggressive impulses in ways that are socially acceptable. According to Lopiparo:

> It helps [them] cope with [their] feelings of powerlessness. . . . If they want to do something, they must ask an adult; if they want something changed, they have to hope adults feel the same way. . . . It is for this reason that children are drawn to TV violence. Many of the frustrations they feel can be very effectively worked out via the TV screen. It is safe, the person you're attacking cannot retaliate, you can be a hero or a villain with just a flip of the dial, and, most important, you can experience that elusive feeling of power.[40]

While noting that for a small minority of children, viewing television violence may trigger an unacceptable level of aggression, Lopiparo further observed that

> with all of us—child and adult alike—there reposes a potential for violence, TV or no TV. Once this is accepted, we may then be more receptive to the notion that the expression of this aggression, whether via fantasy or outright overt behavior, is not only normal, but, in many respects, quite beneficial.[41]

Another explanation of the appeal of television violence for young people is that it makes the brutality and violence that may be present in their own lives seem less terrible. By observing television violence, which in most cases is far worse than the aggression they experience in their own lives, they begin to feel that what they are going through is not so unusual. Life in an urban ghetto may seem less terrible after television heroes are viewed in more difficult situations and have shown that they can overcome their problems through aggression.

A third explanation of the attraction of young people to violent portrayals is that watching these "adventure stories" provides the excitement and danger that is missing in their own day-to-day existence. In much the same way that youths of an earlier era pored over Western adventure stories or mysteries, the contemporary youth "escapes" into the world of television violence, lives vicariously, and apparently emerges and returns to his own world without being seriously affected.

A number of research studies have explored the effects of the portrayal of aggressive behavior on television on the behavior of children and adults. Perhaps the best known is that conducted by Bandura in the early 1960s. One experiment involved four groups of nursery-school-age children who observed an adult performing acts of aggression toward a large doll. One group observed the adult kick and punch the doll, a second group saw a movie of the adult doing exactly the same thing, and the third group watched a movie on television in which the adult, costumed as a cartoon cat, performed the same aggressive acts toward the doll. A fourth (control) group did not observe any presentation. Bandura discovered that during a 20-minute period after observing various forms of the aggressive behavior, the children who had seen the in-person performance and those who had seen the movie used toys that were available in the observation room to imitate the adult's actions more frequently than did those who had observed the cartoon character. The children in the control group, who had not witnessed any form of aggressive behavior in the experiment, displayed the least aggression.[42] In another experiment, the adult who performed aggressive acts was shown to one group of children receiving candy and soda immediately after the aggressive behavior and to another group receiving a spanking and scolding after the aggression; a third group was shown only the aggressive behavior. The play activity of the children immediately afterward was observed. Aggressive behavior by the children was most frequent in the group that had seen the aggressive adult rewarded, and least frequent among the group that had seen him punished.[43]

Viewing aggressive behavior on television influences some children more strongly than it does others. Bandura found that boys were more likely than girls to imitate aggressive behavior seen on television.[44] Chaffee and McLeod found that the family backgrounds of children who viewed aggression on television influenced its effects. They discovered only a slight relationship between viewing violence on television and aggressive behavior in children from families that stressed nonaggressive behavior, but a strong relationship between them among children from families that did not.[45]

Additional research is needed to clarify the true role of television violence in producing delinquent behavior. There is agreement that viewing aggression on television can result in delinquent behavior by certain youths who are stimulated by such portrayals to commit aggressive acts. Television programs that show actual violent events and police responses to them; emergency service responses to gory shootings, stabbings, automobile accidents, or other calamities; and reenactments of murders, robberies, or abductions, under the guise of informing the public about at-large criminals or catching "most wanted" fugitives are a popular trend on television and may also affect juveniles in negative ways. Will they come to view such events and behaviors as commonplace occurrences in most people's lives? Will they become desensitized to suffering and tragedy? Is it possible that some youths will imitate offenses they see performed? These are important questions the agencies that regulate the television industry must address.

THE CULTURE OF VIOLENCE

Ferracuti and Wolfgang hypothesized that expressions of violence are part of the norms of the lower socioeconomic classes and are a learned response to pressures of survival. According to this theory, young males, particularly those in female-headed households in socially deprived areas, frustrated in their search for self-esteem and material goods, turn to violence as a means of achieving status. These researchers made a distinction between "idiopathic" violent crimes (committed by youths who suffer from a major psychological disorder) and "normatively prescribed" violent crimes (committed by members of a subculture of violence who are goal-oriented). They estimated that less than 10 percent of violent youth crime is idiopathic.[46]

In their study of child abuse and aggressive behavior within the family, Glasser and Galvin hypothesized that children who have weak affectional family bonds are prime candidates for gang delinquency and peer-oriented violent delinquent behavior.[47]

SOCIAL-PSYCHOLOGICAL EXPLANATIONS OF DELINQUENCY

A number of delinquency theorists have regarded sociological and psychological factors as contributing in combination to the occurrence of delinquency.

The Gluecks' Multiple-Factor Approach

One of the first major efforts to develop a multiple-factor approach to explanations of delinquency causation was that of Sheldon and Eleanor Glueck. In their comparison of 500 chronic delinquents with 500 nondelinquents of matched age, intelligence, ethnic and racial origin, and residence neighborhoods, they emphasized physique—specifically the mesomorphic body type (muscular, athletic, bony)—as an indication of delinquency proneness. They also stressed the bearing and interaction of other factors in delinquency production. Their extensive research led them to conclude that delinquents can be distinguished from nondelinquents in the following ways:

1. Physically, in being essentially mesomorphic;
2. Temperamentally, in being restless, impulsive, aggressive, destructive;
3. Emotionally, in being hostile, defiant, resentful, assertive, nonsubmissive;
4. Psychologically, in being direct, concrete learners;
5. Socioculturally, in being reared by unfit parents.[48]

Reckless termed the Gluecks' schema the "4 to 1 Causal Law," since they saw four individual factors and one situational factor (number 5) combining to produce delinquency.[49] It is difficult to apply this law to the general population, since the sample was limited to lower class youths so delinquent that they had been institutionalized. The Gluecks' characterization nevertheless offers an example of an early effort to develop a multiple-factor approach to juvenile delinquency causation.[50]

Containment Theory

Reckless proposed another multiple-factor theory, which he termed a "containment theory." To "contain," or prevent, delinquent activity, he said, certain factors must be present in a child's life. They may take the form of "inner containment" (a positive self-concept, well-developed superego, strong sense of responsibility, positive goal orientations) within the child or "outer containment" (factors in the child's social environment that resist delinquency). Outer-containment factors could include strong parental supervision and support of nondelinquent activities, reinforcement of the youngster's positive self-concept by the school and other social institutions, opportunities to interact with other nondelinquents who share the youth's goals and ambitions, and a sense of personal identity and belonging within the social circle. Reckless believed that both inner and outer containment could serve as buffers against what he termed the "pulls" toward delinquency—the delinquent subculture, acquaintance with patterns of deviance, temptations, and other prodelinquency environment influences. He maintained that the existence of both inner- and outer-containment elements in a youth's life would be the most effective antidelinquency factors, but that the presence of strong inner containment could compensate for poor or defective outer containment, and vice versa. He believed that this theory of containment could be used effectively to explain the nondelinquency of some youths who were exposed to strong delinquent influences in their environments and that those who were noted at an early age to be delinquent-endangered because of a lack of either inner- or outer-containment factors in their lives could be identified and helped.[51]

Social Control/Bonding Theory

Hirschi used social control/bonding theory as an explanation of why some youths become delinquent and others do not. He contended that those young people who have established strong social bonds with their families and in the community will be more likely to accept the norms and values of the community and abide by the rules and laws of society, while youths with weak social bonds become prime candidates for delinquency.[52]

Hirschi described four elements of social bonding: attachment (based on an emotional feeling of respect and caring for others, particularly parents and family members, including the development of a conscience and the ability to differentiate between right and wrong); commitment (acceptance of conventional goals, including wanting to succeed in school and developing career aspirations and a personal reputation for being honest and virtuous); involvement (the investment of time and effort in pursuit of conventional goals); and belief in the moral worth of the values, norms, and laws of society.[53] In his research, Hirschi explored the social bonding and delinquency involvement of more than 4,000 students. His comparison of delinquent and nondelinquent youths revealed that the delinquent youths were less attached to parents, peers, and teachers; less involved in conventional behavior; and less conforming to community norms.[54] Other researchers replicated Hirschi's research and their findings generally supported his conclusions.[55] Junger and Marshall tested social control theory in a study of youths in four countries, and they found that the propositions of social bonding advanced by Hirschi were applicable and virtually interrelated in the same matter for the youths in their research.[56]

Self-Concept

In a research effort to test the hypothesis that a positive self-concept serves as an insulator against delinquency whereas a poor self-concept may enhance the chances for delinquency to occur, Reckless conducted an experiment involving sixth grade boys, their teachers, and their parents. Thirty teachers who taught sixth grade in schools in the highest delinquency areas of a medium-sized western city were asked to name male, white students in their classes who, in their opinion, would not ever have contact with the police and the juvenile courts, and to give the reasons why they considered their choices "good boys." A sample of those named by the teachers was selected for study. All youths who actually had police or juvenile court records were eliminated. The sample of "good boys" was given a battery of tests measuring delinquency proneness; social responsibility; occupational preference; and the boys' conceptions of self, family, and other interpersonal relationships.[57] Also, the boys' mothers were interviewed to check the information received from teachers and from the standardized tests.

In response to self-evaluation items, the boys reported themselves to be law-abiding and obedient. They felt they had moral standards about principles of right and wrong, did not feel they would ever become delinquents, had not participated in delinquent activities to any appreciable extent, and chose friends who had similar orientations. Their homes were characterized as economically stable and their parents were found to offer careful supervision. The researchers concluded that the youths' positive self-concepts and the stability and control offered by their family situations enabled them to remain law-abiding in spite of the strong prodelinquency influences in their neighborhood.

A follow-up study of the "good boys" four years later found that teachers and parents still considered the vast majority of them to be "good boys," and that they continued to have positive self-images and stable families.[58]

At the time the "good boys" were originally selected, the researchers also selected a sample of "bad boys" who were regarded by their teachers and parents as likely to have police contacts or become involved with the juvenile courts. One fourth of this sample was found to have had police or juvenile court contacts by the age of 12. Testing revealed that the "bad boys" had less positive self-concepts and less stable family backgrounds than the "good boys."[59] Four years later, a follow-up study of the "bad boys" found that 39 percent of those who were located had had serious and frequent police and court contacts by the age of 16, and interviews with the boys, their teachers, and their parents revealed that they were considered likely to experience further problems.[60]

It can also be argued that a negative self-concept is the product of social interaction. In his description of a "developmental" theory of delinquency, Hackler argues that children in a recognizable status, such as "lower class," are expected by significant persons in their lives, particularly their teachers, to behave in a certain way. The youths perceive these expectations, and they influence their developing self-concepts. He cites an example from his own experience of a girl with a Spanish accent, the daughter of a migrant worker, who transferred to a new school without records from her previous school. The school counselor placed the girl in a slow-learner section, automatically assuming that she must be academically deficient because of her parent's occupation. Subsequently, it was discovered that she was very bright and had no academic problems.[61] When teachers and other important members of society anticipate that certain children will be failures or problems and communicate these expectations to the youths directly or indirectly, the young people may embrace the self-concepts presented to them.

Jackie's Story

This passage from an essay written by a woman reflecting on her childhood illustrates the importance of self-concept and how one views his or her "place" in society. This woman revealed that she had a positive view of herself and how she fit into both primary and secondary groups. In a subsequent interview, some additional information was obtained. Jackie stated that she always liked to take on responsibility. Even though she was the youngest family member, she liked to help her mother and organize things around the house. She recalled that, at church events, she would help the adults set the tables and do other things instead of playing with the other children. She felt that she might have done this to gain adult approval.

My mother and I always talked about adult things—like her personal problems. She seemed to be more confident in my answers than she was in her own. It certainly didn't matter what the subject was, we talked about it. She would even dress me like a little adult. When I was sent to school the kids thought I was the teacher. I was tall for my age and I dressed more conservatively than the teachers. Those were just some of the things that contributed to my feeling weird. Even earlier than that, my Dad set up an account at the local candy store (named John's) where I didn't have to use money; I just went and got what I wanted and he paid for it every Friday morning. I bought for everyone, even my Mom. I felt rich. I could buy just what I wanted. At that point, I could say I was special because no other kid in the neighborhood had it that good, so quite naturally everyone wanted to be my friend.

. . . Different people, on many separate occasions, have let me know just how unusual I really am. I mean, here I was, a young, black, 23-year-old woman, unmarried, working two full-time jobs, a high school graduate, who was teased about my age, and having my first child. I was unique or classified as a misfit, especially within my family and the black community. You see, back in 1986, 23 was old to be having a first child; most young women were on their third and fourth child, mainly within the black community. In addition to being viewed as a misfit, I had two jobs and a high school education. Really, I've always felt different, not better than, but different from everybody else. You know, the more I think about it, the more apparent it is that it could've been because of the way my mother always used to dress me, or maybe because of the way she used to talk to me about adult things, or maybe because I had my own candy credit account at the corner store . . . or maybe because I was sickly at various points of my life, or just maybe cause of something within.

This essay was written by a university student for a class assignment. The student is now in her mid-30s and is self-assured, determined, and very successful in her academic career.

Labeling Theory

Those who adhere to the "labeling theory" concentrate on the consequences of a delinquent act in an offender's life rather than on the act itself or the social and psychological characteristics of the offender. Thus, the processing of the youth through the juvenile justice system and the labeling as delinquent are the primary focuses of their attention.

Schur refers to this as the "patterned-reaction" approach to the study of delinquency.[62] There is considerable evidence that most adolescents commit acts that could lead to involvement with the police and other juvenile justice officials. Most youths escape the delinquent label, however, since they are not formally processed. The labeling theorists argue that there is no great difference between the characteristics of those youths who are labeled delinquent and those who commit delinquent acts but are not caught, or who escape official handling for various other reasons. The labeling theorists are interested in studying why some offenders are selected for official processing by juvenile justice agencies and others are not. They seek to measure the effects of official processing on self-image; on relationships with peers, family, the school, and other individuals in the community; and on the character and amount of subsequent delinquent behavior. They try to discover how much involvement with the justice system must occur before a young person accepts the "deviant" label and regards himself or herself as a "delinquent" rather than a "nondelinquent" person.

Sociological research has tended to emphasize the negative consequence of being labeled. However, some research has noted that the labeling process can have positive effects in leading youths to recognize the seriousness of their deviant behavior and turn away from it.[63]

SUMMARY

Those who advance sociological explanations for delinquency locate them in the youth's environment and social relationships. Social disorganization, which is a breakdown in conventional institutional controls within a community and the inability of organizations, groups, or individuals there to solve common problems, is an important influence on delinquency. Radical changes in the American family, including a huge increase in the number of children living in one-parent families; the emergence of an underclass of poorly educated, inadequately housed, and unemployed persons living in poverty and depending on the government for support; and a lack of personal commitment on the part of many parents to care for and supervise their children, are evidence of such disorganization. Environmental theorists, including Burgess, Shaw and McKay, Bloom, and Wolfgang, all regarded the conditions of poverty, deteriorated and crowded housing, family disorganization, educational disruption and deprivation, and lack of opportunity as important factors contributing to the occurrence of delinquency.

Other theorists, including Merton, Cohen, and Cloward and Ohlin, noted that youths who live in highly disruptive environments, with few stabilizing influences, are likely to develop a "normless" attitude toward their social interactions and engage in activities that are illegal, provided they produce some short-run feelings of status or well-being.

Other researchers maintain that delinquent activity is a learned process and results from association with persons involved in delinquent or criminal activity and who display symbols of economic and social success that appear to have been gained by illegal means. Sutherland described the delinquent and nondelinquent values present in youths' lives as "differential associations." Ferracuti and Wolfgang described expressions of violence as part of the norms of the lower socioeconomic classes and termed this behavior a "culture of violence."

Social psychologists have viewed juvenile delinquency as a result of multiple influences in the child's life and have advanced containment theory and social control/bonding theory to support the idea that both the inner strength of the child and the positive or negative supportive influences of the environment make the difference between opting for or against delinquency. If a child becomes involved with the juvenile justice system, the effects of this contact on the self-image and future behavior of the youth are examined by labeling theorists.

DISCUSSION QUESTIONS

1. Anomie denotes a state of normlessness with a lack of direction and no definitive values or goals. Can you think of examples in present-day society that would illustrate such a state?
2. Although poverty cannot be considered the only cause of delinquency, many believe it is a major cause. Discuss the ways in which poverty affects the lives of youths to turn them toward delinquent behavior.
3. Why is it important to have a positive self-concept? Do you think delinquents generally have a positive or a negative self-concept?
4. Discuss the major assumptions underlying labeling theory. What are some criticisms of this theory?
5. Discuss the arguments for and against the theory that viewing television violence produces aggressive behavior by children. What are some practical ways in which the amount of aggressive violence viewed by children can be controlled?

NOTES

1. U.S. Bureau of the Census, "Population Characteristics: Marital Status and Living Arrangements," *Current Population Reports* (Washington, DC: U.S. Government Printing Office, 1998. Cited in Howard N. Snyder and Melissa Sickmund, *Juvenile Offenders and Victims: 1999 National Report* (Washington, DC: Office of Juvenile Justice and Delinquency Prevention, 1999), 8.
2. U.S. Bureau of the Census, "Poverty in the United States: 1997," *Current Population Reports: Consumer Income,*" (Washington, DC: U.S. Government Printing Office, 1998). Cited in Snyder and Sickmund, *Juvenile Offenders and Victims,* 5.
3. Tony Pugh, "Poverty Numbers Increase in 2001," *Akron Beacon Journal,* September 25, 2002, A8.
4. Timothy Williams, "Homelessness Breaking NYC," *Akron Beacon Journal,* August 21, 2002, A9.

5. *Akron Beacon Journal*, February 5, 1994, A2.
6. Donald R. Taft, *Criminology*, 3rd ed. (New York: Macmillan, 1956), 204.
7. W. I. Thomas and Florian Znaniecki, *The Polish Peasant in Europe and America* (New York: Alfred A. Knopf, 1918.
8. Donald J. Shoemaker, *Theories of Delinquency* (New York: Oxford University Press, 1984), 73–74.
9. R. E. Park, E.W. Burgess, and R.D. McKenzie, *The City* (Chicago: University of Chicago Press, 1925).
10. Clifford Shaw, *Delinquency Areas* (Chicago: University of Chicago Press, 1929).
11. Henry D. McKay, "A Note on Trends in Rates of Delinquency in Certain Areas in Chicago," Appendix F in *Task Force Report: Juvenile Delinquency and Youth Crime* (Washington, DC: U.S. Government Printing Office, 1967), 114–118.
12. R. J. Chilton, "Delinquency Area Research in Baltimore, Detroit, and Indianapolis," *American Sociological Review* 37 (1972), 93–99.
13. B. L. Bloom, "A Census Tract Analysis of Socially Deviant Behaviors," *Multivariate Behavioral Research* 1 (1966), 307–320.
14. Paul E. Tracy, Marvin E. Wolfgang, and Robert M. Figlio, *Delinquency in Two Birth Cohorts* (Washington, DC: U.S. Department of Justice, 1985), 23.
15. David Matza, *Delinquency and Drift* (New York: Wiley, 1964).
16. Gresham M. Sykes and David Matza, "Techniques of Neutralization: A Theory of Delinquency," *American Journal of Sociology* 22 (1957), 664–670.
17. Lawrence Cohen and Marcus Felson, "Social Change and Crime Rate Trends: A Routine Activities Approach," *American Sociological Review* 44 (1979), 588–608.
18. Michael P. Roche, *Rural Police and Rural Youth* (Charlottesville, VA: University Press of Virginia, 1985), 40.
19. Emile Durkheim, *The Division of Labor in Society*, trans. George Simpson (London: Free Press of Glencoe, 1933).
20. Robert K. Merton, "Social Structure and Anomie," *American Sociological Review* 3 (October 1938), 672–682.
21. Robert J. Sampson, "Urban Black Violence: The Effect of Male Nobleness and Family Disruption," *American Journal of Sociology*, 93 (1987), 348–382.
22. Ronald Chilton, "Urban Crime Trends and Criminological Theory," *Criminal Justice Research Bulletin* 6, 3 (1991).
23. Robert Agnew, "Experienced, Vicarious, and Anticipated Strain: An Exploratory Study on Physical Victimization and Delinquency," *Justice Quarterly*, 19, 4 (Dec. 2002), 603–632.
24. Albert K. Cohen, *Delinquent Boys* (New York: The Free Press, 1955), 24–31.
25. Richard A. Cloward and Lloyd E. Ohlin, "Illegitimate Means, Differential Opportunity and Delinquent Subculture," in *Delinquency and Opportunity: A Theory of Delinquent Gangs* (New York: Free Press, 1961); reprinted in Rose Giallombardo, *Juvenile Delinquency*, 3rd ed. (New York: Wiley, 1976), 126.
26. Robert Mawson, "Aggression, Attachment Behavior, and Crimes of Violence," in Travis Hirschi and Michael Gottfredson, eds., *Understanding Crime* (Beverly Hills, CA: Sage, 1981), 12.
27. Mareasa R. Isaacs, *Violence: The Impact of Community Violence on African-American Children and Families* (Arlington, VA: National Center for Education in Maternal and Child Health, 1992).
28. Cathy Spatz Widon, *The Cycle of Violence* (Washington, DC: U.S. Department of Justice, 1992), 1.
29. Peter C. Kratcoski, "The Relationship of Victimization through Child Abuse to Aggressive Delinquent Behavior," *Victimology* 7 (March 1983), 199–203.
30. Peter C. Kratcoski, "Perspectives on Intrafamily Violence," *Human Relations* 37, 8 (1984), 443–454.
31. See J. Duncan and G. Duncan, "Murder in the Family: A Study of Some Homicidal Adolescents," *American Journal of Psychiatry* 127 (1971), 1498–1502; James M. Sorrells, "Kids Who Kill," *Crime and Delinquency* 23, 2 (1977), 312–320; E. Tanay, "Adolescents Who Kill Parents: Reactive Parricide," *Australian and New Zealand Journal of Psychiatry* 7 (1973), 263–277.

32. Allen J. Beck, Susan A. Kline, and Lawrence A. Greenfeld, *Survey of Youth in Custody, 1987* (Washington, DC: U.S. Department of Justice Statistics, 1988), 8.

33. Robert Hoiles, "Retired Cop Remembers the Faces," *Akron Beacon Journal*, February 22, 1994, B4.

34. Peter C. Kratcoski, personal observation of juvenile court activity, Cuyahoga County Juvenile Court, Cleveland, OH, May 1986.

35. Edwin H. Sutherland and Donald R. Cressey, *Criminology* (Philadelphia: J. B. Lippincott, 1975), 75–77.

36. Edwin H. Sutherland, *White Collar Crime* (New York: Dryden Press, 1949).

37. A. Leader, "The Role of Intervention in Family Group Treatment," *Social Casework* 45, 4 (1964), 327–333.

38. C. R. Jeffery, "Criminal Behavior and Learning Theory," in Edward E. Peoples, ed., *Readings in Correctional Casework and Counseling* (Pacific Palisades, CA: Goodyear, 1975), 38–39.

39. *Ibid.*, 44.

40. Jerome J. Lopiparo, "Aggression on TV Could be Helping Our Children," *Intellect* 105, 2383 (April 1977), 346.

41. *Ibid.*

42. Albert Bandura, "What TV Violence Can Do to Your Child," *Look*, October 22, 1963, 48.

43. Albert Bandura, "Influence of Model's Reinforcement Contingencies on the Acquisition of Imitative Responses," *Journal of Personality and Social Psychology* 1 (1965), 589–595.

44. *Ibid.*

45. S. Chaffee and J. McLeod, "Adolescents, Parents, and Television Violence," paper presented at the annual meeting of the American Psychological Association, Washington, DC, 1971.

46. Franco Ferracuti and Marvin Wolfgang, *Violence in Sardinia* (Rome: Bulzoni, 1970), 71.

47. Paul Glasser and Charles Galvin, "A Framework for Family Analysis Relevant to Child Abuse, Neglect and Juvenile Delinquency," in Robert J. Munner and Yvonne Elder Walker, *Exploring the Relationship Between Child Abuse and Delinquency* (Montclair, NJ: Allanheld, Osmun, 1981), 101–109.

48. Walter C. Reckless, "A New Theory of Delinquency and Crime," in Ruth Shonle Cavan, ed., *Readings in Juvenile Delinquency*, 3rd ed. (Philadelphia: J.B. Lippincott, 1969), 169.

49. *Ibid.*

50. Sheldon and Eleanor Glueck, *Unraveling Juvenile Delinquency* (New York: Commonwealth Fund, 1950), 281–282.

51. Reckless, "A New Theory of Delinquency and Crime," 164–174.

52. Travis Hirschi, *Causes of Delinquency* (Berkeley: University of California Press, 1969).

53. *Ibid.*, 20, 22, 83, 198.

54. *Ibid.*, 108, 180, 205.

55. M. Wiatrowski, D.B. Griswald, and M.K. Roberts, "Social Control Theory and Delinquency, *American Sociological Review* 46 (1981), 525–541.

56. M. Junger and I. H. Marshall, "The Inter-ethnic Generalizability of Social Control Theory: An Empirical Test," *Journal of Research in Crime and Delinquency*, 34 (February 1997), 79–112.

57. Walter C. Reckless, Simon Dinitz, and Ellen Murray, "Self-Concept as an Insulator against Delinquency," in James E. Teele, ed., *Juvenile Delinquency: A Reader* (Itasca, IL: F.E. Peacock, 1970), 317.

58. *Ibid.*, 318–319.

59. Simon Dinitz, Walter C. Reckless, and Barbara Kay, "A Self-Gradient among Potential Delinquents," *Journal of Criminal Law, Criminology, and Police Science* 49 (1958), 231.

60. *Ibid.*

61. James C. Hackler, "A Developmental Theory of Delinquency," *Canadian Review of Sociology and Anthropology* 8, 2 (1971), 61–75.

62. Edwin M. Schur, *Radical Non-intervention: Rethinking the Delinquency Problem* (Englewood Cliffs, NJ: Prentice Hall, 1973), 19.

63. Bernard A. Thorsell and Lloyd W. Klemke, "The Labeling Process: Reinforcement and Deterrent?" *Law and Society Review* 6, 2 (1972), 403.

CHAPTER 5

CONTROLLING CHILDREN: THE CHANGING ROLE OF CHILDREN IN AMERICAN SOCIETY

(Photo credit: Robert Brenner/PhotoEdit)

CHILDREN IN THE MIDDLE AGES
THE RENAISSANCE AND THE EMERGENCE OF INTEREST IN CHILDREN
CHILDHOOD IN COLONIAL AMERICA
CHILDHOOD DURING THE PERIOD OF INDUSTRIALIZATION AND IMMIGRATION
    Houses of Refuge
    Compulsory Education
ORIGINS OF THE JUVENILE COURT
    The Child Savers
    Creation of the First Juvenile Court
JUVENILE COURT PHILOSOPHY
    Focus on Treatment
    The *Kent, Gault, Winship,* and *McKeiver* Decisions
    The Juvenile Court Today

In American society today, the roles of "child," "adolescent," and "adult" are clearly defined. Children are those in the preteen years who must be cared for and supervised by adults. Adolescents (often considered synonymous with "teenagers") are those in a state of transition from childhood to adulthood. They are experiencing the biological and psychological changes associated with this developmental stage and, although they are allowed a certain degree of independence, are still considered subject to control by parents. Adults are those who have completed schooling, left the family unit to secure employment, and established themselves as mature, independent individuals.

A closer look at these definitions reveals some inconsistencies. Boys and girls are developing physically at younger ages than in previous generations, with the onset of puberty occurring before the teen years, hastening the beginning of adolescence. At the same time, our system of compulsory education requires many older teenagers who have little interest in or aptitude for high school studies to remain in school until they reach a state-specified age. Unmarried teenage mothers who are either living with their own parents or living on their own are still juveniles in terms of age and subject to compulsory education requirements and other laws that apply to juveniles only, even though their life experiences and responsibilities more closely resemble those of adults. Child-labor laws carefully regulate the number of hours and the conditions under which those under 16 can work, making them financially dependent on and responsible to parents. For many youths who pursue higher education, this period of dependence extends into the early 20s, postponing the time when they can assume the full adult role. High unemployment among school dropouts and minority group members in the late teens who have completed school also makes many of them dependent upon their families and delays their movement from adolescence to full adulthood.

The term "juvenile delinquent" commonly refers to a young person, usually a teenager, who has committed acts at variance with the laws or norms of a particular group or area. Yet the idea of considering "juvenile" delinquents somehow different from adult lawbreakers has been in vogue only since the middle of the 19th century and is closely related to the contemporary conception of childhood and adolescence as periods in life distinct from adulthood. Before the mid-19th century, children who came into contact with the police or the courts were housed with, tried with, and given dispositions similar to those for adult offenders. The juvenile court, a unique American creation designed to serve as a "benevolent parent" safeguarding the well-being of children and adolescents, has been in operation slightly more than a century.

In this chapter, we will explore the origins of the roles of children and adolescents in American society by examining the manner in which children were regarded and treated in earlier times. We will explore how children came to be seen as being in need of special types of supervision, care, and handling. And we will examine the events that led to the creation of the first juvenile court, an institution charged with acting in the best interests of the child, unfettered by rules of law or recognition of the civil rights of children.

CHILDREN IN THE MIDDLE AGES

The division of the human life cycle into periods of childhood, adolescence, adulthood, middle age, and old age is a social phenomenon of relatively recent vintage. Life-span and life-expectancy levels remained rather constant at only 25 or 30 years until the 15th century, with the majority of babies and young children succumbing to the ravages of such diseases as smallpox or diphtheria or falling victim to malnutrition.[1] The number of children was further controlled and reduced by infanticide and child abandonment, with illegitimate or defective children and females most frequently the victims of these fates.

Certain child-care practices also contributed to infant mortality. These included swaddling and wet-nursing. The swaddling procedure is documented in the biblical account of the birth of Christ, when his mother wrapped him in swaddling clothes and laid him in a manger. Swaddling involved the tight wrapping of the child's body in cloths, making it virtually impossible for the baby to move its limbs. Explanations of this practice include the notions that the baby had to be kept warm or that direct sunlight was bad for a baby's skin,[2] but the practice may also have been used as a matter of convenience, since it prevented a child from moving away from the spot where it was placed. The dangers to children in this practice, in addition to the possible retardation of development because of restricted body movement, were the health hazards caused by infrequent washing and changing of the infants.

Wet-nursing was another common practice. Instead of caring for children in their own homes, women who could afford it hired "wet nurses" who nursed and cared for babies almost from the moment of birth. These women from the lower social strata also had children of their own to care for, and in many instances did not provide the babies in their charge with the needed attention and were not particularly concerned about hygiene.

The seeming lack of interest in close contact and involvement with children, evidenced by such practices as wet-nursing, may have been a psychological defense mechanism employed by parents to divorce themselves from strong emotional attachment to children in an era when the odds were very much against the survival of an infant to adulthood. The birth of many children and the probability that quite a number of them would not survive were accepted as facts of life. Children grew up with and were socialized by persons other than members of the immediate family. Similar practices were used in the American South up until the Civil War, when children born on large plantations were nursed and cared for by slaves and spent a great deal of time growing up in their company.

The value of children in the Middle Ages was often viewed in material terms. Land-holding families were controlled and governed by the fathers as strong authority figures. Sons were needed to work the land and eventually inherit it. Daughters, in contrast, could be a drain on a family's wealth, since a sizable dowry of land or money was needed to assure the arrangement of a desirable marriage. Apprenticeship was an important activity for youths. Beginning at ages as young as 7, children were "bound out" and sent into the homes of others to work and learn skills. This practice, extending to all social classes, separated a child from the family of kinship for very long periods of time, further weakening the bond between parent and child.[3] Children who did not serve as apprentices worked the land or performed household duties.

In the Middle Ages, children were not shielded or protected from the realities or difficulties of life. The innocence of children in matters of sex was not safeguarded, and there is documented evidence that children were frequently the objects of sexual abuse. The socialization of young children, including those of the well-to-do, in crowded, lower class settings virtually assured that they would be exposed to and even involved in sexual activity at an early age. Children who failed to work, or who were found to be disobedient or rebellious, were subjected to beatings, and the penalties for crimes were meted out without age distinctions.

THE RENAISSANCE AND THE EMERGENCE OF INTEREST IN CHILDREN

Historians note that an increased interest in children can be detected beginning in approximately the 13th century and becoming apparent in the 15th century, at the time of the Renaissance. The historical indicators include the introduction into various languages of words describing children as separate or different from adults and the depiction of children in paintings in a realistic manner, rather than as small bodies with adult faces. The many realistic representations of the Madonna and Child in Renaissance art are examples of this change. As the Renaissance and the Enlightenment progressed, a renewed interest in learning and the extension of the privilege of education to persons other than nobles and the clergy created a desire to begin formal education as early as possible and to set aside a period of a youth's life for schooling.

The variety of ideas discussed and debated at the time of the Protestant Reformation also had an influence on the handling and treatment of children. The concept of original sin was stressed, highlighting the need to shape an individual's moral development virtually from the moment of birth. This created an interest in training children at much earlier ages than was formerly the case. Their instruction involved not only moral training but also education and discipline. Children began to be viewed as different from adults and in need of intensive supervision and attention.

The movement from an agrarian to an industrialized society also contributed to the emergence of a concept of childhood. The differentiation of skills and occupations created a need for better educated and skilled workers, so public education began to be introduced. Young people placed in schools were removed from the constant association and identification with adults, which had been the norm under the apprenticeship system. Industrialization created an urbanizing trend, with families forsaking life on the land to move to cities. Parents brought their children with them to the cities and kept them in their own households for longer periods of time, creating more intense and prolonged contact between parents and children. Although children were used as workers in factories and mines beginning at very early ages, continued urbanization provided large numbers of adults who competed for these jobs. As the mechanization of tasks became more complex, a number of the activities performed by children were no longer needed. Many children were subsequently removed from the labor force and placed in schools, where they were differentiated by age and status from adults. The notion that the activities of children should be different from those of adults was further reinforced.

The ideals of democracy, as expressed by the leading figures of the French and American revolutions, also contributed to patterns of behavior that resulted in the conception of childhood and adolescence as distinct and privileged periods. Education was seen as the vehicle by which children rich and poor could be given equal opportunities for virtually unlimited social, esthetic, political, and moral achievement.

CHILDHOOD IN COLONIAL AMERICA

In Puritan society, the handling of children was dominated by the belief that a child is a creature whose tendency to mischief and sin must be repressed by careful training and discipline. Children and servants were viewed in the same manner in this regard. The family had the responsibility for seeing that they conformed to norms. If the family failed, the church or the community intervened through the use of publicly applied punishments and sanctions. The Massachusetts Stubborn Child Law, enacted in 1646, detailed severe punishments for youths who were disobedient toward their parents, for rude or disorderly children, and for children who profaned the Sabbath.[4] Whipping was the most commonly applied punishment, and parents could be fined if their children were found guilty of stealing.[5] Incorrigibility was viewed as a capital offense for certain children. The Connecticut Blue Laws of 1650 contained the following legal remedy for such behavior:

> If any man have a stubborne and rebellious sonne of sufficient years and understanding which will not obey the voice of his father or the voice of his mother, and that when they have chastened him will not harken unto them, then may his father and mother lay hold of him and bring him to the Magistrates assembled in Courte, and testifie unto them that their sonne is stubborne and rebellious and will not obey theire voice and Chastisement, but lives in sundry notorious Crimes, such a sonne shall bee put to death.[6]

Work was the chief activity of Puritan children, and they were introduced to it early in life. The Puritans brought the apprenticeship system with them from England, but gradually the more affluent families abandoned its use for their own children in favor of schooling. There were few dependent or homeless children. Social control of all children was handled within the family or the local community.

Methods of controlling children throughout the American colonies were similar to those used in New England, although the other colonies had no special punishments or laws that applied only to children. Youths involved in serious offenses received the same penalties as adults and children could be put to death for certain offenses. Disobedience to parents was regarded as evidence that a child was on the path to a life of waywardness and sin. Benjamin Wadsworth, author of a popular treatise on child rearing, "The Well Ordered Family," published in 1712, noted:

> When children are disobedient to parents, God is often provoked to leave them to those sins which bring them to the greatest shame and misery. . . . When persons have been brought to die at the gallows, how often have they confessed that disobedience to parents led them to those crimes.[7]

Execution sermons were used as a powerful warning to all citizens of the consequences of sin, and executions of children had particular significance for the young. On one such occasion in Connecticut, the minister stated the message clearly:

> Let all children . . . beware of disobedience. . . . Appetites and passions unrestricted in childhood become furious in youth; and ensure dishonor, disease, and an untimely death.[8]

During the Colonial period, the emphasis on a strong family life, religion, and the work ethic fostered a climate of rigid social control of children. Beginning in the mid-19th century, however, changes in American life created new conditions, needs, and problems.

CHILDHOOD DURING THE PERIOD OF INDUSTRIALIZATION AND IMMIGRATION

During the 19th century, the United States experienced an expansion in population that made the closely knit family life of small towns and communities during the Colonial period difficult to maintain. After the American Revolution, waves of immigrants from Europe came to the new country and settled predominantly in the urban centers of the Northeast and Midwest. Between 1850 and 1900, the urban population increased 700 percent. Those in positions of control viewed the resulting overcrowding, poverty, and crime with alarm, feeling that the ideals of stable family and community life were threatened. Children who lived in crowded city tenements could not be assigned the types of daily work so readily available in rural settings. Their idleness, lack of ambition, and neglected moral training alarmed those in power. Juvenile lawbreakers were arrested, housed, tried, and imprisoned with adult criminals, creating conditions of sexual exploitation of these youths and fostering their schooling in crime. As the number of homeless children increased, the need to provide for their care and supervision promoted one of the key movements in the history of the control of juveniles—the creation of "Houses of Refuge."

Houses of Refuge

New York was the first state to respond to the pressures for removing children from prisons and jails and for establishing places of residence for homeless youths. In 1824, the New York legislature granted a charter to the Society for the Reformation of Juvenile Delinquents, authorizing it to build and maintain a House of Refuge. The goals of the Society were twofold: to rescue children of the poor, whether deviant or homeless, from the influence of adult criminals encountered in the courts and jails, and to provide them with "homelike" care and discipline to arrest and reverse their movement toward criminality.[9] Houses of Refuge were soon built in Philadelphia, Boston, and other major cities. They were viewed as the panacea for correcting the evils afflicting youths in a changing society. Private orphan asylums were also established. By 1850, New York State alone had 27 public and private childcare institutions.[10]

Admission to an orphan asylum or a House of Refuge was not contingent upon proved deviant behavior or lack of parental control.

> The trustees quickly spread their nets to catch a wide variety of dependent children. They admitted the abandoned as well as the orphaned child and those whose widowed or deserted mothers, hard pressed to make ends meet, had little time for supervision. They accepted minors whose parents were quite alive but very poor and those from families that seemed to be morally, if not financially, inadequate to their tasks. . . . [The Houses of Refuge], like the orphan asylum, maintained a flexible admissions policy, prepared to accept the commitment decisions of a judicial body, the less formal recommendations of overseers of the poor, or the personal inclinations of the head of a household. Its administrators expressed no fear about a possible miscarriage of justice. . . . A good dose of institutionalization could only work to the child's benefit.[11]

Once a child was committed to an orphanage or House of Refuge, his or her release was dependent upon the judgment of the institution's administrators that the child had been reformed or properly trained according to the prevailing moral and ethical precepts. Obedience and conformity were required in these institutions, and strictly applied discipline was considered the best method for preparing children for productive lives. We shall see that the use of indeterminate stays in institutions until youths were judged ready for release by administrators became an established practice in juvenile corrections, which has continued to the present time.

Compulsory Education

The movement toward compulsory education for all children was also important in differentiating childhood and adolescence as distinct life stages. Massachusetts and New York passed compulsory education laws early in the 19th century, and by the century's close, compulsory public education for those between the ages of 6 and 16 was the law in many states.[12] Public school officials enforced attendance laws and had the right to suspend, expel, or punish students for improper behavior. Compulsory schooling removed young people from their homes and the influence of their parents for long daily periods and brought them under the authority of the state. Laws prohibiting child labor, promoted by the newly organized labor unions, were ineffective at first, but gradually resulted in a substantial reduction in the number of children used in factories and mines, reaffirming the notion that childhood should be devoted to activities different from those of adult life.

ORIGINS OF THE JUVENILE COURT

Although the creation of orphan asylums and Houses of Refuge resulted in the removal of many homeless and uncontrolled children from the public eye, these institutions were incapable of handling the growing number of youths in the crowded cities who, in the eyes of the middle class, presented a serious threat to the public welfare by their idleness, poverty, and criminal activity.

> The low level of "morality" of the new occupants of the burgeoning cities was a matter of frequent comment. Drinking, sexual immorality, vagrancy, and crime were not only intrinsically threatening to orderliness, but were also particularly distressing influences on the young. The rapid breeding, the continuing threat of "street Arabs," evoked a cry that the state intercede in restraining and training the young.[13]

At the same time, social forces were set in motion to separate and differentiate juvenile offenders from adults. The concept of a "juvenile delinquent" as a distinct entity began to emerge.

We noted earlier that in Europe and Colonial America, children who broke laws could be treated in the same manner as adult offenders. Under English law, which formed the basis for treatment of juveniles by the courts in America, children under the age of 7 were regarded as incapable of forming criminal intent (legally *mens rea*, "a guilty mind"). A child between the ages of 7 and 14 could be charged with crimes and tried in criminal courts like an adult if it was demonstrated that the child could distinguish between right and wrong. Youths over 14 were considered adults and subject to the criminal law as such. If a child tried as an adult was found guilty, the judge was required to impose the penalty set by law without taking into account the age of the offender.[14]

Certain devices were frequently used, however, to save children from the severest penalties of the criminal law. One of these was the chancery court, which was developed in the 13th and 14th centuries. This court operated under the doctrine of *parens patriae* (literally, "father of his country"), which was applied to mean that the king, acting through his representative, the chancellor of the court, could depart from the due process of law and, as a benevolent parent, not only exempt children from the penalties set for various criminal offenses, but also take control over children who had not committed crimes but were involved in vagrancy, idleness, incorrigibility, or association with undesirable persons. Under the concept of *parens patriae*, all children are regarded as subject to the benevolent protection of the courts. The viability of the principle of *parens patriae* was confirmed in 1838 by a Pennsylvania

Supreme Court decision in the case *Ex parte Crouse*. When Mary Ann Crouse was committed to a House of Refuge as unmanageable by her mother, her father appealed the decision on the ground that she had been sent there by decision of a justice of the peace, without a jury trial. The Pennsylvania Supreme Court upheld the commitment, stating that no trial was necessary because the court, applying the *parens patrae* principle, was acting in the best interests of the child.

> The object of the charity is reformation, by training its inmates to industry; by imbuing their minds with principles of morality and religion; by furnishing them with means to earn a living; and, above all, by separating them from the corrupting influence of improper associates. To this end may not the natural parents, when unequal to the task of education, or unworthy of it, be superseded by the *parens patriae* or common guardian of the community? It is to be remembered that the public has a paramount interest in the virtue and knowledge of its members, and that of strict right, the business of education belongs to it.[15]

In England, the chancery court, with its *parens patriae* orientation, was used chiefly as a vehicle for disposing of or safeguarding the estates of children whose wealthy parents had died before the children reached the age of majority. In the late 19th century, certain social philosophers in the United States seized upon the idea as the basis for the development of a new kind of court that would consider only the cases and behavior of juveniles.

The Child Savers

A group of reformers, characterized as the "child savers," was instrumental in pressuring various state legislatures to provide separate detention facilities and hearings for juveniles, and eventually to establish juvenile courts. The child savers, among whom Jane Addams and Louise DeKoven Bowen are the best known, were upper- and middle-class women who were dedicated to improving the lot of the less fortunate and to bringing the poverty-stricken children they encountered closer to middle-class standards of morality and conduct. They viewed juvenile delinquency as the outgrowth of slum living and the horrible conditions under which youths labored in the factories and mines.[16] Although many of these women were persons of high principles who were genuinely concerned about the needs and problems of the poor, the Child Saving Movement was also motivated by the desire to control the lower classes and preserve the privileged position of its middle-class advocates. Some viewed these troublesome juveniles as a genuine present and future threat to society and sought to gain influence over their lives as a means of self-protection and preservation. The prevailing notion among the child savers was that these children must be brought under proper influences as soon as possible so that they could be exposed to middle-class morality and work habits and brought into conformity with accepted lifestyles. They reasoned that such intervention in the lives of children could be made without regard for legal procedures or the rights of the children, since they were acting in the children's best interest.

> The unique character of the Child-Saving Movement was its concern for predelinquent offenders . . . and its claim that it could transform potential criminals into respectable citizens

by training them in "habits of industry, self-control, and obedience to law." This policy justi-fied the diminishing of traditional procedures and allowed police, judges, probation officers, and truant officers to work together without legal hindrance. If children were to be rescued, it was important that the rescuers be free to pursue their mission without the interference of defense lawyers and due process. Delinquents had to be saved, transformed, and reconsti-tuted.[17]

The efforts of the reformers soon bore fruit. In 1870, separate hearings were re-quired for juveniles brought to trial in Boston. Seven years later, the New York Soci-ety for the Prevention of Cruelty to Children was successful in gaining a prohibition on housing youths under the age of 16 in any prison, jail, or courtroom where adult offenders were kept or tried, unless officers were present at all times.[18]

Creation of the First Juvenile Court

Legislation that is generally credited with creating the first juvenile court in the United States was enacted on July 1, 1899, by the Illinois legislature. An Act to Reg-ulate the Treatment and Control of Dependent, Neglected, and Delinquent Chil-dren provided that in any jurisdiction with a population of 500,000 or over, one cir-cuit judge should be designated to hear all juvenile cases in a separate courtroom, with its own records. Since Cook County (Chicago) was the only jurisdiction with a population of this size, it became the site of the first juvenile court. The jurisdiction of this court extended to delinquent, neglected, and dependent children. The Act stated that

the words "dependent child" and "neglected child" shall mean any child who for any reason is destitute or homeless or abandoned; or dependent upon the public for support; or has not proper parental care or guardianship; or who habitually begs or receives alms; or who is found living in any house of ill fame or with any vicious or disreputable person; or whose home, by reason of neglect, cruelty, or depravity on the part of its parents, guardian, or other person in whose care it may be, is an unfit place for such a child; and any child under the age of 8 years who is found peddling or selling any article or singing or playing any musical in-strument upon the streets or giving any public entertainment.

The Act specified appropriate dispositions for youths found to be dependent, neglected, or delinquent.[19]

In the same year, the Colorado School Laws provided that youthful offenders would be charged with improper conduct, rather than with crimes, and that truant officers or teachers would supervise their activities.[20] The idea of juvenile courts caught on rapidly, and by 1917, all but three states had enacted legislation establish-ing them. In 1932, there were more than 600 juvenile courts and over 2,000 juvenile sessions of other courts. Wyoming was the last state to establish a juvenile court sys-tem, in 1945.[21]

JUVENILE COURT PHILOSOPHY

Focus on Treatment

The first juvenile courts were established on the premise that it was the court's right and duty to intercede on a child's behalf to eliminate undesirable social influences leading to antisocial behavior. From 1899 until the mid-1960s, the juvenile courts exercised the authority and enforcement power granted to them but placed little emphasis on the legal rights of the accused. The assurances of due process characteristic of adult criminal proceedings were frequently absent from juvenile courts, as "treatment" rather than punishment became the center of court philosophy.

Julian Mack, one of the original judges of the Cook County Juvenile Court, summarized the idealism vested in the juvenile court's philosophy:

> Why is it not just and proper to treat these juvenile offenders, as we deal with the neglected children, as a wise and merciful father handles his own child whose errors are not discovered by the authorities? Why is it not the duty of the state, instead of asking merely whether a boy or a girl has committed a specific offense, to find out what he is, physically, mentally, morally, and then if it learns that he is treading the path that leads to criminality, to take him in charge, not so much to punish as to reform, not to degrade but to uplift, not to crush but to develop, not to make him a criminal but a worthy citizen.[22]

In efforts to view the child in this treatment framework, in which the youth's behavioral ills were diagnosed and "cures" were attempted through various types of therapy and treatment strategies, the terms used in adult court proceedings were modified to make juvenile court proceedings seem less like those of adult courts. The term "petition" was substituted for "criminal complaint," but a juvenile against whom a petition was filed was still required to appear in court. Trials became "hearings," pleas available became "true" or "not true" rather than "guilty" or "not guilty," and sentences became "dispositions." Hearings were held in private as a way of protecting the child's reputation, but the private nature of the hearings also made it possible for judges to exercise the broadest possible range of discretion in dispositions and to hear all sorts of testimony without having its admissibility or the legality of the proceedings questioned.

The mandate given to juvenile courts was so broad, and juvenile codes were written in such general terms, that some of the behavior of nearly all American youths *could* have brought them to the attention of the juvenile court. Discretionary practices of police and court workers, however, often made it possible for youths of good reputation or the "right" social-class background to escape court involvement, while others who had committed similar offenses were drawn into formal processing. Since those referred to the court were not advised of their right to remain silent or to have counsel present at every stage of court procedure, judges, probation officers, and other court officials could act arbitrarily, coercively, in a discriminatory manner, or even maliciously without observation or review of their methods. Once a youth came under the court's jurisdiction, officials could do as they wished, under the philosophy that their decisions would serve the best interests of the child. For example, a judge might order a youth charged with school truancy or incorrigibility to spend an indeterminate period in a boy's industrial school, so that he could develop good work habits and principles of conduct. Unfortunately, the abuses in these institutions and their potential as schools for crime frequently proved far more damaging to the child than getting away with the initial misconduct would have been. And such commitments to institutions could be made on the basis of testimony by parents or school officials, without giving the youth a chance for rebuttal.

During the 1960s and early 1970s, when many groups were demanding their civil rights, the juvenile court process was questioned in several important matters brought to the U.S. Supreme Court. The decisions of the Court in these cases had far-reaching effects in altering juvenile court procedure and philosophy. The *parens patriae* orientation of the past gave way to a new philosophy, which gave equal weight to guaranteeing youths their rights under the Constitution; answering their need for treatment, guidance, punishment, or rehabilitation; and protecting the community.

The *Kent, Gault, Winship,* and *McKeiver* Decisions

In 1966, the case of *Kent* v. *U.S.* brought before the Supreme Court for the first time the question of whether youths involved in juvenile court proceedings should be granted the essentials of due process of law given to adults. The case involved a 16-year-old boy, Morris Kent, who was charged with a 1961 forced entry into a Washington, DC, apartment, where he allegedly raped the occupant and stole her wallet. When Kent was arrested and charged, the juvenile court judge decided to waive (voluntarily relinquish) jurisdiction and transfer the case to an adult criminal court, where Kent would be tried as an adult. The judge made this determination without holding a hearing on the issue of waiving jurisdiction or discussing the matter with the youth's lawyer. Kent was subsequently tried as an adult and sentenced to a term of 30 to 90 years in prison.

On the appeal of Kent's case to the Supreme Court in 1966, the Court's decision set forth specific conditions for a valid waiver of jurisdiction by a juvenile court:

> An opportunity for a hearing which may be informal, must be given to the child prior to entry of a waiver order. . . . The child is entitled to counsel in connection with a waiver proceeding. . . . The hearing must measure up to the essentials of due process and fair treatment. . . . It is incumbent upon the Juvenile Court to accompany its waiver order with a statement of the reasons or considerations therefore. . . . The statement should be sufficient to demonstrate that the statutory requirement of "full investigation" has been met; and that the question has received the careful consideration of the Juvenile Court; and it must set forth the basis for the order with sufficient specificity to permit meaningful review.[23]

In reaching its decision, the Court made the point that the question of whether Kent's case should have been transferred to an adult court was not the issue, but rather the fact that the decision was made without the types of safeguards listed earlier. It also made the following observation about the type of "justice" received in juvenile courts:

There is evidence, in fact, that there may be grounds for concern that the child receives the worst of both worlds: that he gets neither the protection accorded to adults nor the solicitous care and regenerative treatment postulated for children.[24]

All states allow juveniles to be tried as adults in criminal court under certain circumstances.[25] The report .of the Task Force on Juvenile Justice and Delinquency Prevention of the National Advisory Committee on Criminal Justice Standards and Goals set the following conditions as a standard for transfer of a juvenile for trial in an adult criminal court:

1. The juvenile is charged with a delinquent act (an act which would also be a law violation if committed by an adult).
2. The juvenile was 16 years or older at the time of the alleged commission of the delinquent act.
3. The alleged delinquent act is (a) aggravated or heinous in nature or (b) part of a pattern of repeated delinquent acts.
4. There is probable cause to believe that the juvenile committed acts that are to be the subject of the adult criminal proceedings if waiver and transfer are approved.
5. The juvenile is not amenable, by virtue of maturity, criminal sophistication, or past experience in the juvenile justice system, to services provided through the family court.
6. The juvenile has been given a waiver and transfer hearing that comports with due process. The *Kent* v. *United States* criteria should be the minimum specific criteria on which these decisions are based.[26]

Sixteen months after the *Kent* decision, the landmark case in juvenile court law, *In re Gault*, was decided by the Supreme Court. Gerald Gault was a 15-year-old boy, on probation from an Arizona juvenile court for having been in the company of a youth who had stolen a wallet, when a new charge was made against him. A neighbor alleged that she recognized his voice in an indecent telephone call made to her home. In an informal juvenile court hearing, at which Gault was not represented by counsel and at which the woman who made the accusation was not required to appear, Gault was committed to a state industrial school for the period of his minority (until age 21 in Arizona), "unless sooner discharged." This amounted to a six-year commitment for an offense that for an adult carried a maximum sentence of a $50 fine or two months' imprisonment.

In its 1967 opinion of Gault's appeal, the Supreme Court ruled that Gault had not been granted due process. It set forth specific rights to which juveniles are entitled. These include:

1. The right to written notice of the charges in sufficient time for preparation of a defense;

2. In cases where commitment to an institution is a possible disposition, the right of the child and parents to be advised to their right to counsel, either their own or court-appointed;

3. The privilege against self-incrimination:

4. In the absence of a valid confession, the right to confront witnesses and cross-examine them on their sworn testimony.[27]

The next constitutional question of juvenile court procedures to come before the Court occurred in *In re Winship* in 1970. Up until that time, the standard of proof required in the juvenile court was the same as that in civil law—"a preponderance [majority] of the evidence"—rather than the "proof beyond a reasonable doubt" required in adult criminal proceedings. The *Winship* matter involved a 1967 New York case in which a 12-year-old boy had entered a locker and stolen $112 from a woman's pocketbook. The judge, who acknowledged that his decision was based upon a preponderance of the evidence, ordered the youth placed in a training school for a period of 18 months, subject to annual extensions of the commitment until his 18th birthday. When Winship's appeal reached the Supreme Court in 1970, the Court ruled that when a child is charged with an act that would make him or her liable to confinement, the charge must be proven beyond a reasonable doubt.[28]

In the *Kent, Gault*, and *Winship* decisions, the Supreme Court clearly moved away from the doctrine of *parens patriae* (benevolent paternalism), upon which the juvenile court was founded, toward giving juveniles all the constitutional rights of an adult at juvenile court hearings. The next logical challenge in this direction came when the appeal of Joseph McKeiver reached the Court. McKeiver, aged 16, had been charged in 1968 with robbery, larceny, and receiving stolen goods. His counsel at a juvenile court hearing on the matter requested a jury trial, which was denied. McKeiver was subsequently adjudicated delinquent.

In its 1971 decision on McKeiver's appeal, the Court halted its movement toward remaking the juvenile court on the model of the adult criminal court and declared that juveniles do not have a constitutional right to a jury trial. The chief rationale behind the Court's decision was its fear that the assurance of jury trials to juveniles would

> remake the juvenile proceeding into a full adversary process and put an effective end to what has been the idealistic prospect of an intimate, informal protective proceeding.[29]

The Court noted, however, "there is nothing to prevent a juvenile court judge in a particular case where he feels the need, or when the need is demonstrated, from using an advisory jury."[30] A 1976 decision by the Illinois Supreme Court confirmed the position of the juvenile court judge as having fact-finding responsibility in juvenile cases and declared that this responsibility cannot be bypassed by the judge by ordering a jury trial.[31] Although a number of states have statutory provisions for jury trials of juveniles, this right is not guaranteed by the Constitution.

The seeming reversal in *McKeiver v. Pennsylvania* of the trend toward granting juveniles all the constitutional right of adults has made the current situation an ambiguous one. Justice Stewart, in his dissent to the *Gault* decision, predicted the dilemma:

> I possess neither the specialized experience nor the expert knowledge to predict with any certainty where may lie the brightest hope for the progress in dealing with the serious problems of juvenile delinquency. But I am certain that the answer does not lie in the Court's opinion in this case, which serves to convert a juvenile proceeding into a criminal prosecution.[32]

In *McKeiver v. Pennsylvania*, the Court described the situation that still exists:

> There have been, at one and the same time, both an appreciation for the juvenile court judge who is devoted, sympathetic, and conscientious, and a disturbed concern about the judge who is untrained and less than fully imbued with an understanding approach to the complex problems of childhood and adolescence. There has been praise for the system and its purposes, and there has been alarm over its defects.[33]

The Juvenile Court Today

As a result of the *Kent, Gault,* and *Winship* decisions, juveniles are now assured the right to have counsel, to receive notice of the charges against them, to confront and cross-examine witnesses, and to have their guilt established beyond a reasonable doubt. Jury trials, however, are not available to juveniles as a constitutional right (although they are permitted by statute in some states),[34] and youths may be charged with offenses that would not be illegal if performed by adults (status offenses).

Contemporary views of the direction the juvenile court should take vary widely. Those who actively promote removing status offenders and minor delinquent offenders from juvenile court jurisdiction believe that any positive effects the juvenile court may have on the lives of the young people referred there are counterbalanced by the detrimental effects of being labeled delinquent. Even in instances of serious delinquency, such persons feel that the principle of "minimization of penetration" must be applied. According to this principle, any youth's case should be pursued into the justice system only as far as necessary to assure that some action is taken. They contend that delinquency is part of the growing-up process, and that most delinquents, even the majority of those involved in rather serious misbehavior, will move away from this unacceptable activity as they mature.

In sharp contrast to this view, those who promote "just deserts" for juvenile offenders feel that uniform and quickly administered punishments should be applied for all offenders. They also see the juvenile court process as ineffective, because in their view it has not demonstrated its deterrent effect on delinquency. These people promote lowering of the age at which a youth may be referred to and tried by adult courts, determinate (exact-length) sentences for juveniles, and mandatory referral of juveniles to adult criminal courts for certain violent offenses as ways of bringing juvenile offenders to justice.

Finally, some persons involved in juvenile justice believe that the juvenile court system should be retained without major changes in its structure, the types of juveniles over whom it has jurisdiction, or its procedures. They are convinced that the court must continue to follow the "benevolent parent" philosophy upon which it was founded and see rehabilitation and treatment of both minor and serious offenders as the court's continuing mission.

Throughout this chapter, we noted that changes in the status and treatment of children reflected changes in the larger society. For example, when children were no longer needed as part of the workforce, a compulsory public education system emerged. The creation of orphanages and Houses of Refuge was a response to public pressures to control the "immoral" behavior of poor children in crowded urban areas. In many instances, alterations in the way children were handled were not necessarily beneficial to them, and this continues to be true. As Hackler observed:

> We probably make greater efforts to understand and help juveniles than we did in the past. Can we assume, however, that there will be steady progress, that we will continue to be wiser, more humane, and more effective in our handling of troubled and troublesome youth? In North America, for example, can we assume that the last 20 years has brought improvement? Or should we be cautious and somewhat skeptical about those institutions and practices that we take for granted?
>
> Can we have faith in courts, in laws, in governments, in social workers, in universities? As we talk with people in powerful positions about changing legislation and creating programs to help young people, and in so doing influence the quality of life of the entire society, should we be cautious about placing too much faith in our major institutions? One must consider the possibility that democratically elected governments will find it more convenient to give the *impression* that they are doing something, and that has often taken the form of "getting tough on crime." Long-term programs that might help problem juveniles are often seen as "soft" and rarely win votes.[35]

Even though research studies and other sources have pointed out appropriate measures that could help to reduce juvenile misbehavior, and those who work in the juvenile court system and its related agencies have ideals that are consistent with the basic philosophy and underlying assumptions on which the court was established, they may find that they do not have the power to insist on the types of programs and processes that they believe would be effective. As Hackler noted, short-term solutions may be promoted for political expediency. The "just deserts" model was adopted by various states, even though there was no evidence that it would have any deterrent effect on juvenile delinquency. In fact, at the time that many state legislatures were changing laws and policies to hop on the "get tough" bandwagon, delinquency rates were in a pattern of decline.[36]

The growth in popularity of philosophies of juvenile justice that seem to place the needs of the community above those of the individual child and that stress punishment rather than treatment indicate that the pendulum has swung away from the strong interest in children's rights and welfare that reached a high point in the 1970s. This is apparent in demands for "get tough" policies in the courts in dealing with juveniles, revision of many state juvenile codes to provide for determinate sentences for certain types of juvenile offenders, and a lack of public response to the call by federal agencies and reformers for removal of status offenders from juvenile court jurisdiction and of juvenile offenders from jails.

Nowhere is this trend toward making youth totally responsible for their actions more apparent than in the call for "restorative justice." Under restorative justice, juvenile offenders are held accountable to the victims as well as to the state and crime victims and other community members are involved in decision making pertaining to the control, prevention, and sanctioning of delinquent offenses.[37] Linked to restorative justice is the "balanced approach," which gained strong support in the late 1990s and in the 2000s. The balanced approach is a back-to-basics attitude toward a community's need to concurrently sanction and rehabilitate youthful offenders and ensure public safety. This takes in three goals: accountability, public safety, and competency development. Resources are equitably allocated toward the achievement of each goal.[38] Community and victim involvement may take the form of mediation meetings between offenders and victims where victims express their feelings and needs, offenders apologize to their victims, and agreements for restitution are formulated; or development of community service projects in which offenders are required to participate. The youth's accountability may also take the forms of obeying curfews and submitting to drug screenings.[39]

SUMMARY

In this chapter, we explored the origins of the roles of children and adolescents in American society by examining the manner in which children were regarded and treated in earlier times. Before the 15th century, childhood and adolescence did not exist as distinct life stages, since short life spans made age-status divisions of life impractical. At the time of the Renaissance and the Protestant Reformation, there was an increased interest in children and concern for setting aside a period in youth for education and moral development. Children in Colonial America were subject to rigid family and community controls of their behavior. The immigration and urbanization trends of the 19th century, however, resulted in large numbers of homeless or poorly supervised children, who were viewed as a threat to the public welfare. In response, Houses of Refuge and orphanages were built to house and train children placed there and reformers termed "child savers" pressured local and state governments to separate youthful offenders from adults in the courts and jails. The juvenile court was an outgrowth of this movement.

The origins of the juvenile court can be found in the English chancery courts of the 13th and 14th centuries. The American juvenile court was founded on the principle of *parens patriae* and was designed to act as a benevolent parent, concerned not with legal sanctions or procedures but with promoting the welfare of the child.

Since challenges to the authority and procedures of the juvenile court began to be mounted in the 1960s, the court has moved away from its *parens patriae* beginnings toward procedures that more closely resemble those of adult criminal courts. Juveniles, however, may still be referred to the court for offenses that would not be illegal if committed by adults (status offenses), and they are not assured jury trials as a constitutional right.

Contemporary thinkers are divided as to the course the juvenile court should now take. Some believe that it should relinquish jurisdiction over all but the most serious offenders, while others promote its continued operation in its present form. Critics of the juvenile court maintain that many serious offenders are given dispositions of treatment or long periods of supervision when immediate and just punishment is a better solution. Others feel that the juvenile court has been ineffective in making any real changes in the youths referred there and should be completely abolished. The debate over the future of the court and its proper role has not yet been resolved.

DISCUSSION QUESTIONS

1. Discuss the status and value of children in the Middle Ages. Why was there a seeming lack of interest in close contact and involvement with children? Why was the value of children viewed in material terms?
2. What was the Puritan view of the basic nature and tendencies of children? What types of punishments were used in New England for children who were disobedient or disorderly?
3. Why were Houses of Refuge established? What practice related to release from these houses was adopted in juvenile corrections and is still used today?
4. Describe the social conditions in late-19th century America that led reformers to pressure legislatures for differential handling of juveniles? What standards of morality and conduct did the "child savers" wish to enforce?
5. Do you believe that the *parens patriae* principle of the juvenile court should be totally abandoned in favor of a formalized, legalistic principle of operation? Discuss.

NOTES

1. Dean G. Rojek and Gary F. Jensen, "The Social History of Delinquency," in Dean G. Rojek and Gary F. Jensen, eds., *Readings in Juvenile Delinquency* (Lexington, MA: D.C. Heath, 1982), 25.
2. Pricilla Robertson, "Home as a Nest: Middle-Class Childhood in Nineteenth-Century Europe," in Lloyd de Mause, ed., *The History of Childhood* (New York: Psychohistory Press, 1974), 411.
3. Lamar T. Empey, *American Delinquency* (Homewood, IL: Dorsey Press, 1982), 30.
4. Edwin Powers, "Crime and Punishment in Early Massachusetts," in Paul Lerman, ed., *Delinquency and Social Policy* (New York: Praeger, 1970), 9.
5. William E. Thornton, Jr., Jennifer A. James, and William G. Doerner, *Delinquency and Justice* (Glenview, IL: Scott, Foresman, 1982), 8.
6. Larry Cole, *Our Children's Keepers* (Greenwich, CT: Fawcett, 1974), 13.
7. David J. Rothman, *The Discovery of the Asylum* (Boston: Little, Brown, 1971), 16.
8. *Ibid.*, 17.
9. Society for the Reformation of Juvenile Delinquents, "The Founding of the New York House of Refuge," in Lerman, *Delinquency and Social Policy*, 12–14.
10. Rothman, *Discovery of the Asylum*, 207.
11. *Ibid.*, 207–209.
12. David Bakan, "Adolescence in America: From Idea to Social Fact," in Rojek and Jensen, *Readings in Juvenile Delinquency*, 30–31.

13. *Ibid.*, 29.
14. Thomas A. Johnson, *Introduction to the Juvenile Justice System* (St. Paul, MN: West Publishing Co., 1975), 1–2.
15. *Ex parte Crouse*, 4, Wharton (Pa.), 9, 1838.
16. Anthony Platt, *The Child Savers: The Invention of Delinquency* (Chicago: University of Chicago Press, 1969), 4.
17. Anthony Platt, "The Triumph of Benevolence: The Origins of the Juvenile Justice System in the United States," in Rojek and Jensen, *Readings in Juvenile Delinquency*, 41.
18. H. H. Lou, *Juvenile Courts in the United States* (Chaptel Hill, NC: University of North Carolina Press, 1927), 14.
19. Ill. Laws 1899, 131–37, Sections 1, 7, 9.
20. Sophia M. Robinson, *Juvenile Delinquency* (New York: Holt, Rinehart and Winston, 1964), 250–251.
21. U.S. Children's Bureau, "Report to the U.S. Congress on Juvenile Delinquency," 1960, cited in "The Conflict of *Parens Patriae* and Constitutional Concepts of Juvenile Justice," *Lincoln Law Review* 6, 1 (December 1970), 67.
22. Julian W. Mack, "The Juvenile Court," *Harvard Law Review* 23 (1909), 104.
23. *Kent v. U.S.*, 383 U.S. 541 (1966).
24. *Ibid.*
25. Howard N. Snyder and Melissa Sickmund, *Juvenile Offenders and Victims: 1999 National Report* (Washington, DC): Office of Juvenile Justice and Delinquency Prevention, 1999, 102.
26. Task Force on Juvenile Justice and Delinquency Prevention, National Advisory Committee on Criminal Justice Standards and Goals, *Juvenile Justice and Delinquency Prevention* (Washington, DC: U.S. Government Printing Office, 1977), 303.
27. *In re Gault*, 376 U.S. 1 (1967).
28. *In re Winship*, 397 U.S. 358 (1970).
29. *McKeiver v. Pennsylvania*, 403 U.S. 528 (1971).
30. *Ibid.*
31. *People ex re Carey v. White*, 357 N.E. 2d 512 (Ill. 1976).
32. *In re Gault*.
33. *McKeiver v. Pennsylvania*.
34. Douglas J. Besharov, *Juvenile Justice Advocacy* (New York: Practicing Law Institute, 1974), 287.
35. Jim Hackler, "Responding to Juveniles in Trouble," in *Official Responses to Problem Juveniles: Some International Reflections* (Onati, Spain: Onati International Institute for the Sociology of Law, 1991), 16.
36. Peter C. Kratcoski and Lucille Kratcoski, "The Impact of Social Change on Juvenile Justice Policy in the United States," in *Official Responses to Problem Juveniles: Some International Reflections* (Onati, Spain: Onati International Institute for the Sociology of Law, 1991), 194.
37. Peter C. Kratcoski, *Correctional Counseling and Treatment*, 4th ed. (Prospect Heights, IL: Waveland Press, 2000), 110.
38. Peter C. Kratcoski, *Evaluation of the Ashtabula County Juvenile Court and Programs*; Unpublished research report, Kent, OH: 1997, 1.
39. Gordon Bazemore and Susan E. Day. "Restoring the Balance: Juvenile and Community Justice," *Juvenile Justice*, 3, 1 (1996), 3–4.

CHAPTER 6

GANG DELINQUENCY
AND VIOLENCE

(Photo credit: Nick J. Cool, The Image Works)

THE SCOPE OF THE PROBLEM
     What is a Gang?
     How Widespread is Gang Membership?
THE HISTORY OF GANG DEVELOPMENT
GANG BEHAVIOR IN THE 1970s
GANG BEHAVIOR IN THE 1980s, 1990s, AND 2000s
THEORIES OF GANG FORMATION
     Thrasher's Theory of Gang Development
     Research of the Chicago School
     Lower-Class Culture
     Delinquency and Opportunity
     The Underclass as a Generating Milieu for Gang Formation
     Needs Theory
STRUCTURE OF THE GANG
VARIATIONS IN GANG BEHAVIOR
     Female Gangs
     Suburban and Small-Town Gangs
GANG ACTIVITY CONTROL
     Community Organization for Gang Control
     Social Intervention
     Opportunities Provision
     Suppression
     Legislation for Youth Gang Prevention and Control

When I was 8 years old I did my first job in the racket. . . . That day I was hanging around with the oldest brother and his gang. . . . The big guys got to talking about stealing, and my brother said he had a good place spotted where we would get some easy "dough" (money). . . . My brother had been in the place a few days before to see how to get in and where the cash register was. . . . We all went up to the back door, and then my brother got a box and stood on it and tried the transom—and it opened. It was too little for my brother or the other guys to get through. Then I was thrilled when they said I'd have to crawl through the transom. . . .

My brother lifted me up on his shoulders and I crawled through. . . . The door was locked with a padlock and chain, but I was able to unlock the window and let the big guys in that way. . . . I felt like a "big-shot" after that night and the big guys said I could go with them every time they went robbin' . . . and many times I had to crawl through transoms and one time through an ice-box hole. That's why the big guys called me the "baby bandit."[1]

*   *   *

Officers found Robert Sandifer in a pool of blood beneath a railroad overpass yesterday. He was 11.

Robert's body—not yet 5 feet, not quite 70 pounds—lay about seven blocks from where police believe he opened fire Sunday at two groups of boys, fatally hitting a 14-year-old girl. . . .

Robert was suspected of having gang ties and two gun-shot wounds—one to the back of the head, one to the top—led police to suggest that fellow gang members had killed him.[2]

In the end, police said, the loyalty of the street gang for which . . . Robert Sandifer had been willing to kill melted in the heat of police and media attention about the death of an innocent girl during two shootings he had carried out at the gang's urging.

Investigators said two fellow gang members who had been harboring him after those shootings have been charged in his murder. Police said the suspects apparently acted on the instruction of gang leaders, who feared Sandifer eventually would be arrested and cause them legal problems. . . . The two suspects harbored Sandifer at safehouses and an abandoned building when he was on the run for three days. . . . After it was determined that Sandifer was to be slain, the suspects, who said they had been gang members since they were 10 or 11 years old, drove to the place Robert was hiding. . . . It was his understanding that he was being taken out of town. . . . Instead, he was driven to the viaduct and shot.[3]

These two descriptions of very young boys involved in gang activity, one in the 1930s and the other in the 1990s, reveal that gang formation and loyalties, and the appeal of gang membership, have long existed. Gang formation has been a consistent element in juvenile reaction to urban life and gangs have also been found to exist in suburban and rural areas in the past. Currently, gangs pose a serious threat in urban areas and suburban and rural gang membership is on the increase. Although gang members still come predominantly from the "underclass" and lower and working classes, certain types of gangs have strong appeal for middle-class youths.

The signs are everywhere: kids bringing guns onto junior high and high school campuses and shooting each other; teenagers forming sex posses and racking up "body counts" of the number of girls they have "scored with" or "sacked"; mall rats rampaging through suburban shopping arcades, "streaming," as it is called, through the aisles of department stores and grabbing stacks of clothing before making a quick getaway; tagger crews "mapping the heavens," spray painting their three-letter monikers on overhead freeway signs. The "cry for help" of punk rockers and their offshoots, ignored, as they were by families and society that do not take time to listen. And these are just the good kids!

And what about the others? Racist teenage skinheads plot revenge on unsuspecting fellow students at suburban high schools for no other reason than that they dislike them because of their skin color, nationality, or presumed sexual orientation. White, youthful, stoner gang members adrift, wander aimlessly with the suburban "homies," or homeboys, looking for the next high, surviving on dope and booze. Juvenile satinists, participating in a fad, find themselves caught up in a cult.[4]

In Houston, two girls, aged 14 and 16, taking a shortcut home from a pool party, were raped and strangled by six teenage gang members, the youngest of them 14 years old. One 17-year-old defendant in the case, when told that he might be charged with murder, allegedly told another boy: "Hey, great! We've hit the big time."[5]

There are certain factors that make contemporary gangs more threatening to the common good than gangs of the past. The use of firearms by gang members has greatly increased, and there has been a sharp rise in the levels of gang violence. While gang fights and violent interactions have been documented throughout the history of gangs in the United States, gang activity now frequently involves random attacks against persons or places that have little or no connection to the gang itself, and gang-related drive-by shootings carried out without concern for innocent bystanders have become everyday occurrences in major cities.

In this chapter, we will discuss in detail the magnitude and seriousness of gang behavior; the reasons for gang formation; various theories explaining gang development and behavior; and methods for preventing, controlling, or refocusing gang activities.

THE SCOPE OF THE PROBLEM

What is a Gang?

The definitions of "gang" vary, depending upon who is doing the defining. The term "gang" has been used to denote a neighborhood street corner group or highly organized criminals who are oriented toward profit-making through their criminal activity. According to Moore, a gang is:

> A friendship group of adolescents who share common interests, with a more or less clearly defined territory, in which most of the members live. They are committed to defending one another, the territory, and the gang name in the status-setting fights that occur in school and on the streets.[6]

The Chicago Police Department, concerned with controlling illegal behavior by gang members, defines a "street gang" as

> An association of individuals who exhibit the following characteristics in varying degrees:
> - A gang name and recognizable symbols
> - A geographic territory
> - A regular meeting pattern
> - An organized, continuous course of criminality.[7]

Beyond the basic fact that a gang is a group of persons who have joined together for mutual benefit, other characteristics of gangs are readily apparent. There is some type of organizational structure and leadership, a name and some type of insignia or "colors" to identify gang members, a specific "turf" or area where the gang meets and seeks to be in control, and involvement in some type of illegal or undesirable behavior that is frowned upon by the larger society.

From the perspective of gang members, the name and "colors" of the group may be the most significant characteristic.

> Each street gang in Chicago has its own distinct symbols and emblems. These are used to distinguish rival gangs and to decorate territorial objects. Signs, signals, sweaters, colors, jewelry, and forms of dress are used to promote gang recognition and solidarity.[8]

One contemporary research study found that the development of many of today's gangs was almost identical to the process described in research on gangs in Chicago in the 1920s. That is, a group of adolescent friends gathered on the street corner, having nothing to do, perhaps skipping or excluded from school, drinking or getting high, and occasionally fighting with other groups.[9] At first spontaneous, the groups later become identified as gangs once they adopt names and some identifiable insignias. When asked how his gang got started, a member gave this description:

You know we were just standing on the corner, then we got to just getting together every day, and then we came up with something called the 34th Street Players. And as we kept going north, the gangs got to coming around and they got to have gang fights and they got to robbing and just carrying on.[10]

How Widespread Is Gang Membership?

The National Youth Gang Center conducts an annual survey of youth gang activity in all United States cities with populations of 25,000 or more, all suburban counties, and a randomly selected sample of smaller cities and rural counties, collecting information from police and sheriff's departments. The 2000 survey estimated that there were more than 24,500 gangs with 772,500 active members in more than 3,330 jurisdictions.[11] In the years from 1995 through 2000, gang membership in large cities increased slightly, while the numbers declined slightly in suburban and rural areas.[12] An analysis of the distribution of gangs revealed that 60 percent of the police agencies located in metropolitan areas reported the presence of gangs, compared to approximately 30 percent of the police agencies in nonmetropolitan areas. Chronic gang activity (constant and persistent presence of gangs) was reported by more than half of the metropolitan police agencies but less that 25 percent of the nonmetropolitan police agencies.[13]

In 2,000, 94 percent of the members were male; six percent were female. Thirty-nine percent of all gangs had female members, but only two percent were identified as predominantly female.[14]

In 1999, the race/ethnicity of gang members was identified as 47 percent Hispanic, 31 percent African-American, 13 percent white, 7 percent Asian, and 3 percent "other."[15] Gang members may range in age from 10 or younger to 25 or older. The peak age is believed to be about 17, but in cities with long-established gangs many members are adults.[16] In 1999, 50 percent of the gang members were older than 18.[17] It is estimated that up to 74 percent of Chicago gang members are adults.[18]

How and why have gang membership and activities become such a pressing social problem? What is the appeal of gang membership? Are the characteristics of gang members and the activities of today's gangs similar to those in other eras? To explore these questions, let us first view gang activity from a historical perspective.

THE HISTORY OF GANG DEVELOPMENT

The existence of gangs in New York City and Boston in the early 19th century, and the bitter feuds that took place between gangs from various sections of the cities, have been documented.[19] In *The Gangs of New York*, Asbury described how, during the draft riots in New York City in 1863, the gangs joined forces against the police in efforts to pillage the city. In the Bowery section of New York, where gang membership was principally Irish, battles between rival gangs sometimes raged for two or three days, streets were barricaded, and both hand-to-hand combat and gun battles took place.[20]

Of particular interest in the accounts of early gang battles is the presence of girls. In this early era, the girls carried the weapons and reserve ammunition, a service that, as we shall see, became an ascribed activity of girl members and persists today. However, some of the girls also took part in the fighting, as documented by this graphic account:

> Often these Amazons fought in the ranks, and many of them achieved great renown as ferocious battlers. They were particularly gifted in the art of mayhem, and during the Draft Riots it was the women who inflicted the most fiendish tortures upon Negroes, soldiers, and policemen captured by the mob, slicing their flesh with butcher knives, ripping out eyes and tongues, and applying the torch after the victims had been sprayed with oil and hanged to trees.[21]

Thrasher was one of the first sociologists to conduct extensive systematic research on gang formation and behavior. His book, *The Gang,* published in 1926, focused on 1,313 cases of gang activity in the Chicago area during the early decades of the 20th century. Thrasher maintained that gangs tended to develop in the slums of the city, where a large number of youths were forced to live in crowded conditions, and that the majority of gangs developed from conflicts between spontaneous play groups over territory, play space, and privileges to exploit or claim new territory.[22]

Whyte identified other factors in his book *Street Corner Society,* which examined gang behavior in an Italian neighborhood in Boston during the Depression years of the 1930s. He found that the gang members (the "corner boys") provided each other with protection, status, and material assistance within the neighborhood community.[23]

In the 1950s, gang organization and activity seemed to center around defense of territory and proof of strength through fighting. In the book *Manny,* the author describes the test of personal valor that won him the position of "warlord" (arranger of fights with other gangs) at the tender age of 13:

> I walk into this movie; I'm with this girl and we buy some popcorn and stuff and walk up into the balcony to watch the flick. And there's a bunch of Italian dudes sittin' up there. They say, "Hey guys, look at the goddam Spic."
>
> I thought there would be some of my gang at the movie. I take off my jacket so the Italians can see my sweater, and I holler, "Young Star here!"
>
> They say, "Yeah, Young Star!"
>
> Only one problem. I jump up, but I'm the only Young Star in the place. I was the only one standing, the only Spic in the balcony, and they just pick me up and heave me over. Wow! I woke up in the hospital. Had several broken bones and a bad concussion. They almost killed me.
>
> . . . When I woke up in that hospital I thought I was a big deal. Guys and debs would come up to see Manny, the kid that defended the honor of the Young Stars against all odds. I was a big hero. It got me elected warlord.[24]

The social concerns among the general population during the 1960s found echoes in gang activity. Members of gangs developed an intensified spirit of brotherhood and camaraderie and were more conscious of the ethnic or racial qualities enhanced by gang membership. In his study of a black Chicago gang called the Vice

Lords, Keiser identified the elements of the gang's culture as heart ideology, soul ideology, brotherhood ideology, and game ideology. "Heart" has reference to the total devotion of individuals to the gang, in which they are willing to follow the leadership and suggestions of the chieftains, regardless of the personal risk involved. "Soul" refers to both the black experience and the stripping away of pretense to bare one's most intense feelings and emotions. "Brotherhood" involves the concept of mutual help and is frequently reinforced through ritualistic behavior. "Game" has reference to the ability to manipulate others through craftiness.[25]

In the late 1960s, the energies of the Vice Lords were channeled toward improving the lot of the black community. Dawley documented these efforts in the book, *A Nation of Lords:*

> In 1964 the Lords vowed to see that our community and children get a chance, and three years later, as spokesman for the Nation, Bobby said:
>
> "We could not turn our backs on them. We were and are the last resort for many, and if we didn't listen, who would? . . .
>
> ". . . As black people, we gotta start worryin' about what's happening, where our real humbug is and the way to humbug with it. . . .
>
> ". . . In the three years from 1964 to 1967 we stopped gang wars and started to build a new kind of Vice Lord Nation. . . . Between 1967 and 1969 we opened several businesses and community programs. The police never thought they would see the day when we'd put our minds to do something like that. . . . Not even the younger fellas thought we could change."[26]

The involvement of gangs in social programs was viewed with suspicion by the Chicago police, who insisted that the gangs were using such activities as a front for illegal behavior. For example, in 1967, the U.S. Office of Economic Opportunity allocated more than $900,000 for a job-training and employment-opportunity program for members of the gangs known as the Blackstone Rangers and the Devil's Disciples. In the summer of 1968, a Senate investigating committee heard testimony from a former gang leader that the gang used the job-training center as a storage site for arms and marijuana. Testimony was also given that part of the money was used to pay off gang members not to riot, and that gang members enrolled in the program were required to kick back part of their pay to the gang for the purchase of guns.[27]

Gang activity in the 1960s gained little public attention, since other forms of youth protest and rebellion had captured the headlines and the interest of social researchers. Some crime analysts took the position that the wide use of drugs by gang members had weakened gang cohesion and diminished members' fighting spirit.[28] Others felt that involvement in policy protests and social programs did in fact lead to a decline in gang activity. Miller contended that gang activity did not decrease significantly during the 1960s but simply received less public attention because of the other overwhelming social problems facing the nation.[29] The "resurgence" of gang activity that seemed to occur in the 1970s, he said, was merely a return to the spotlight of a form of youthful deviance that had never really declined.

GANG BEHAVIOR IN THE 1970s

Whether gang activity increased in the 1970s or merely captured renewed public interest is a matter open to debate. The gangs of the 1970s, however, had distinctive characteristics that set them apart from their predecessors of earlier decades. A study of street gangs operating in New York City in the period 1971–1976 revealed that this "new" gang had "bigger and better organizations, more sophisticated weapons, and a greater propensity for crime and violence than its ancestor, the 'fighting gang' of the 1950s."[30]

Miller researched the youth-gang activities of the 1970s to ascertain what proportion of crime in the cities could be attributed to gangs and how effective the police and service agencies were in controlling their activities. His study extended to 12 major cities in the United States. Information was obtained from a variety of sources, including representatives of police departments, Youth Gang Divisions of Youth Service Bureaus, criminal justice planning agencies, outreach workers, judicial representatives, probation officers, youth-aftercare departments, juvenile courts, and public schools. The following definition of "gang" was used in the research:

> A gang is a group of recurrently associating individuals with identifiable leadership and internal organization, identifying with or claiming control over territory in the community, and engaging either individually or collectively in violent or other forms of illegal behavior.[31]

Miller's research defined the age range of gang members as from 12 to about 21. Reports that many gang members were in their late 20s or early 30s did not seem to be substantiated by the research. In fact, the gang age distribution appeared to be quite similar to the age range traditionally associated with gang members, with the largest concentration in the 16- to 17-year-old age group.[32]

Miller found that urban youth gangs were predominantly male (90% or more of the membership). Autonomous female gangs were not identified, although female "auxiliaries" or "branches" of male gangs were quite evident.[33] When the racial and ethnic compositions of the gang membership were compared, more than 80 percent of gang members were found to be of black or Hispanic background.[34]

The primary locus of serious gang activity was found to be in the slum areas of cities. These areas were not necessarily concentrated in the central city, however; they were found to exist also in formerly middle-class and working-class neighborhoods that had deteriorated.

Gang violence was identified as assuming four forms:

1. "Normal" gang violence (attacks in which both assailants and victims are gang members);
2. Victimization of nongang members with social characteristics similar to those of gang members;
3. Crimes against the general public;
4. Victimization of young children, the elderly, females, or those who are not community members.[35]

An increased tendency of gang members to victimize innocent children and adults appeared to be one important aspect of gang behavior in the 1970s that was different from the behavior of gangs of earlier eras. Nongang members (teenagers, children, adults) were the victims of nearly 40 percent of gang activity.[36]

In the late 1970s, Miller expanded his research into a nationwide study of youth gangs. He concluded that by 1980 there were more gang members in the United States than at any time in the past and that gangs were active in more cities than at any earlier time. He also found that in the 1970s more people were the victims of gang-related killings than in any previous 10-year period and that property destruction by gangs in the 1970s was more extensive than in any earlier decade.[37]

GANG BEHAVIOR IN THE 1980s, 1990s, AND 2000s

The trend toward increased violence and use of more sophisticated weapons by certain types of gangs continued in the 1980s, 1990s, and 2000s. A study of gang activity in seven large Ohio cities identified three typologies: informal, *hedonistic gangs,* concerned with having a good time and getting high on drugs and alcohol; *instrumentally oriented gangs,* focused on property crimes for economic gain; and *predatory gangs,* which commit robberies and other crimes of opportunity, and whose members' use of highly addictive drugs contributes to their violent, assaultive behavior.[38]

Although members of these gangs and those identified in other large cities have been found to be predominantly blacks or Hispanics,[39] other distinct types have also emerged. These included gangs of Asians (Vietnamese, Chinese) involved in crimes against property, extortion for protection, and kidnapping, with members of their own ethnic group usually the targets of their activity.[40] Other new gang variations are the heavy metal, punk rockers, and Satanic groups. Their members are predominantly white youths devoted to heavy metal rock music and behavior chosen for its shock value. Their gang activities have included drug trafficking, parent abuse, grave robbing, and desecration of animal and human remains. Their potential for violence is recognized by those who must deal with them.

> Punk rock and heavy metal youngsters come from all socio-economic classes. They're of average intelligence and they're capable youngsters. They have very little parental authority. They're angry youngsters. Their dance is violent. Their behavior is violent. They enjoy shock value. They're into anarchy.[41]

The escalating violence of gang activity has been of great concern in many large cities. The situation in Chicago parallels that in many other cities.

> The type of crime committed by today's gangs includes the sale of narcotics, running guns, rapes, murder,. . . robbery, burglary, theft, harassment, intimidation and extortion.
>
> Some of the gangs' activities have become so sophisticated that they are thought by law enforcement officials to be linked to organized crime. . .[42]

Homicides committed by gang members have distinctive characteristics. They are more likely than nongang homicides to take place in public areas, with consequent danger to innocent bystanders, and to involve automobiles and firearms. An example of such activity is the drive-by shooting, when one gang seeks out the home, automobile, or hangout of a rival gang member, and sprays it with bullets from assorted weapons in the gangland style of the 1920s. Victims and assailants in these criminal events, although they are not likely to be personally known to each other, are of the same racial or ethnic background, with the relationship between offenders and victim likely to be based on gang affiliations.[43]

Since 2000, gang-related homicides, involving gang members killing each other or killing persons caught in the crossfire of gang violence, have increased sharply in several large cities. Declines in the number of homicides in large cities in the late 1990s were attributed in part to police pressure on gangs, the strong economy, and a decline in trafficking in crack cocaine. Many large cities reduced the size of their gang units or abolished them because the gang problem seemed to be under control. The resurgence in gang activity and violence since 2000 is attributed to law enforcement's focus on terrorism, a declining economy, and the gang members being released from prison and returning to the community.[44] A gang detail police officer commented on gang violence control:

> We had a stranglehold on it and we allowed them to breathe. We relaxed our grip, and now they're back.[45]

Drug involvement and trafficking have been identified as factors in the violence of gangs, but researchers differ in their assessments of the strength of the connection. In a survey conducted by the National Youth Gang Center, law enforcement officials estimated that 43 percent of drug sales in their jurisdictions involved gang members,[46] but several researchers have concluded that gang violence is more closely related to intergang and interpersonal conflict than to "drug wars."[47]

The ability of juveniles to easily acquire firearms has also been recognized as a factor in the deadliness of gang violence. In a recent study, which included serious offenders who were incarcerated in juvenile correctional facilities in four states and male students from 10 inner-city high schools located near the correctional facilities, it was found that most of those surveyed from either group stated it would be "easy to acquire a gun." Fifty-five percent of the incarcerated juveniles had carried guns "all or most of the time" in the year or two before being incarcerated, 12 percent of the high school students routinely carried guns, and another 13 percent carried them "now and then."[48] While this study did not specifically focus on gangs and gang behavior, it was determined that 68 percent of the institutionalized juveniles and 22 percent of the students were affiliated with a gang or quasi-gang. More than 80 percent of the incarcerated gang members reported that they owned a revolver, automatic weapon, or semi-automatic handgun.[49] The researchers concluded that:

> For the inmates, and to a lesser extent the students as well, movement from nongang member to member of a gang was associated with increases in possessing and carrying guns.[50]

Changes in the focus of gang activity have been observed. Large-scale gang fights for turf are rarely reported, partly because blighted inner-city areas formerly used as gang hangouts have been razed in many cities to make way for redevelopment projects or parking lots. The sites of gang warfare appear to have shifted in some instances to the schools. With the consolidation of middle schools and high schools, members of gangs from diverse sections of large cities are thrown together in a common school location, where they victimize other students and teachers and challenge each other for control.

The types of gang activity reported within the schools include attacks upon members of other gangs, nongang members, and teachers; intimidation of teachers; charging protection money from nongang members or extorting money from them for use of school facilities; school vandalism; and general classroom disruption. Gang fighting in schoolyards and adjoining areas and attacks upon youths going to and from school also occur. The increase in gang activity in or close to schools has been attributed in part to the greater holding power of schools, which now (as a result of various legal decisions related to students' rights) cannot legally exclude many youths who formerly would have been expelled.

Outside the schools, street hustling appears to be a major activity of youth-gang members. It is undertaken for economic survival, support of drug habits, or status. Hustling involves a broad range of illegal income-generating activities such as burglary, disposal of stolen property, shoplifting, prostitution, con games, and drug sales. Interviews with gang leaders reveal that they take pride in their hustling skills:

> Like, I haven't worked in a hell of a long time, you know, on a job. I have no means of getting no money without that knowledge that I know in the streets. My game is hustling, period. See, I'm a good flim-flam man, you know. I know various things about various different arts that you all just heard about and read about.[51]

Gang members regard their activities as necessary for survival, and may view the victimization of others as just "part of a day's work":

> Catch a man or woman coming down the street and they've been counting a little money, and I'd run and take it from them, knock them down and go in their pocket and get their money. You know, this kind of thing. And burglarize people's houses, you know, and it was a thing, whereas, like, I mean, I had to survive and had to get to that money, and this is what I did to get it.[52]

Is the appeal of gang membership today based on the same factors that led youths to become involved in gangs in the past? To explore this question, we now turn to the theories formulated over the years to explain gang development.

THEORIES OF GANG FORMATION

Thrasher's Theory of Gang Development

The pioneer of gang-formation research, Frederic M. Thrasher, contended that gangs develop from spontaneous play groups, when threats from youthful enemies lead them to protect their territory through mutual support. Groups that evolve into gangs develop a formalized structure, complete with defined leadership status, division of labor, distinctive styles of dress, and well-defined goals. Threats from others were found to be a unifying force. Thrasher identified marriage as the most potent cause of attrition from gangs.[53]

Thrasher maintained that those play groups that eventually become gangs go through an evolutionary process, in which a loosely organized group develops into a closely knit gang with strong group loyalty, ready to present a united front against enemies. He characterized gangs as being either *diffuse* or *solidified*. Diffuse gangs are loosely organized; those that are solidified have developed a strong internal structure and *esprit de corps*. Solidified gangs were identified as being "conventional," "criminal," or "secret societies."[54]

Thrasher described the movement of one group from a diffuse to a solidified status:

> A crowd of about fifteen Polish lads from fourteen to sixteen years old were accustomed to meet on a street corner in front of a store. From loafing, smoking, and "rag-chewing," they turned to shooting craps, which excited hostility toward them.
>
> "Jigs, de bulls!" someone would shout, and they would scatter. As the group grew, business men and residents regarded as a nuisance the crowd which blocked the way on the sidewalk, interfered with traffic on the street, and hung about at night, keeping people awake with their noise. The crowd had now become a rudimentary gang.
>
> The next step in their development was to organize a ball team to which they gave the name "Pershing Tigers." With a name, group-consciousness increased, for they could say proudly, "We belong to the Pershings!"
>
> One night the Altons, a gang from another neighborhood, swooped down for a raid and attempted to "clean out" their corner. Bitter enmity developed, and the Pershings cleaned out the Altons' alley with rocks, guns, and daggers. With about six months of fighting the gang became fully solidified.[55]

Research of the Chicago School

A number of early research projects on gang behavior were undertaken by the members of the Chicago School of sociological theorists described in Chapter 4. As we have seen, Shaw developed a geographical analysis of the distribution of juvenile court petitions filed in Chicago, which showed that delinquency occurred most often in the areas of the city that were deteriorating physically and decreased in proportion to one's distance from the center of the city.[56] Shaw, later joined in his research by McKay, sought to apply the same approach to analysis of the distribution of delinquency in other American cities. The findings of these studies appeared to be consistent with Shaw's analysis of Chicago, although later researchers questioned their validity on the basis of the omission of certain important variables from the research design, including whether the delinquency petitions were found to be true and whether agencies for diversion were more likely to exist or be used in suburban areas than in the cities.[57]

Tannenbaum, another member of the Chicago School, regarded the gang as fulfilling a need for primary-group involvement that was missing in the lives of youths from physically or psychologically broken homes who resided in high-delinquency areas.[58] For such youths, group solidarity is attained by identifying enemies of the group and acting against them. These enemies may be individuals from other gangs, the police, the adult establishment, or merely the broad rules and regulations of society that seem too restrictive and confining to the youthful gang members.

In *Street Corner Society*, another classic study of gang formation, Whyte documented the activities of a group he called the Norton gang, unemployed young Italian men who used gang activity as a method of survival. Whyte's contribution to the development of gang-formation theory was his identification of the brotherhood or mutual-assistance aspects of gang development. The "corner boys" from the Norton gang were poor and underprivileged in comparison to young men in the community who could afford to go to college; they received their status, recognition, and economic assistance within the gang and the local community, whereas the college-bound youths developed broader reference groups and values. A number of the college-bound youths eventually became doctors, lawyers, and politicians, while some gang members exercised the type of upward mobility open to them by moving into the rackets.[59]

Lower-Class Culture

In his book *Delinquent Boys*, Cohen contended that working-class youths who have failed to win status through achieving goals set by the middle class turn to delinquent behavior to gain some measure of status and recognition from their peers, engender respect by being feared, or receive public attention. Cohen believed that the middle-class lifestyle is held in high esteem and desired by members of all social classes, and that when youths realize that they cannot achieve the approved middle-class goals, they develop various behavior characteristics as a reaction to their failures.

In Cohen's "reaction-formation" behavior, a youth tries to turn the middle-class value system upside down by engaging in activity that displays its antithesis. For example, the middle-class value of academic success is flouted by engaging in truancy, and respect for property is defied by vandalism.[60]

Miller, on the other hand, did not view juvenile delinquency as predominantly a reaction to the inability to achieve middle-class standards, but saw it instead as the natural outgrowth of being socialized with a lower-class culture. He theorized:

> A large body of systematically interrelated attitudes, practices, behaviors, and values characteristic of lower-class culture are designed to support and maintain the basic features of the lower-class way of life. . . . Action oriented to the achievement and maintenance of the lower-class system may violate norms of middle-class culture and be perceived as deliberately nonconforming.[61]

In other words, delinquency occurs not because youths are trying to topple middle-class values, but because they are following a *different* value system, one that conflicts with that of the middle class on many points. Miller believed that the predominant concerns of lower-class youths include trouble, toughness, smartness, excitement, fate, and autonomy. These concerns permeate the working-class and lower-class way of life, and people in these social strata, both adults and juveniles, develop means of adapting to situations related to these concerns as part of their socialization process. Some of the concerns (such as trouble) are met through avoidance, while others (toughness, smartness, and autonomy) require the development of skills and style in dealing with the problems of life.

The cultural practices followed in dealing with these basic concerns may violate the law, but since they appear to be appropriate to the situations encountered, they are frequently practiced anyway. Miller maintained that not all youths adapt to their cultural situations in the same way. He delineated three forms of adaptation: (1) acceptance of the lower-class culture as a reference and internalization of lower-class norms; (2) aspiration to middle-class lifestyle and values, and embracing opportunities to achieve the goals set by the middle class; or (3) aspiration to the middle-class system of material rewards and values, then failure to achieve them owing to lack of opportunities or lack of needed skills and personal characteristics, followed by reversion to the lower-class lifestyle.[62]

Lewis disagreed with some of Miller's assumptions; he formulated a modified gang theory, based on acceptance or rejection of a number of Miller's premises. Lewis maintained that lower-class culture is not so completely distinct from middle-class culture that following the norms of the lower class automatically violates the laws set up in support of the middle-class culture. Rather, he took the position that lower-class gang members were in fact following the norms set by the middle class but were using deviant ways to achieve these norms:

> The gang . . . is not delinquent in response to deviant norms; but it is delinquent to the extent that its members are socialized to mainstream norms while at the same time they find themselves impeded from expressing their commitments in the manner of the middle class.[63]

Delinquency and Opportunity

Cloward and Ohlin's theory of delinquency, sometimes termed "opportunity theory," combines and expands elements of Shaw and McKay's theory of delinquency areas and Cohen's conception of the universal acceptance of middle-class values. According to Cloward and Ohlin, youths who experience frustration of their efforts to achieve the middle-class goals delineated by society may resort to various illegitimate methods of achieving them. The form their reaction to blockages of their aspirations will take is dependent upon the opportunities open to them in their environment.

Cloward and Ohlin held that delinquent behavior is a search for solutions to the problem of adjustment that arises when lower-class youths must face and recognize a discrepancy between their aspirations and the opportunities open to them for achieving their goals. In exploring the reasons why different types of delinquent subcultures or gangs develop in lower-class urban areas, these researchers identified three types that may emerge, depending on the opportunity, or lack of opportunity, to engage in illegitimate means of obtaining material rewards. The three types of gangs delineated by Cloward and Ohlin are the criminal gang, the conflict gang, and the retreatist gang.

The *criminal* gang is apt to develop in neighborhoods where there is a tradition of organized crime; where organized crime operates fairly openly, is accepted by the residents, and is protected by the political structure; and where there is close communication among the various age groups in the population. According to Cloward and Ohlin:

> The "big shots"—conspicuous successes in the criminal world—become role-models for youth, much more important as such than successful figures in the conventional world, who are usually socially and geographically remote from the slum area . . . structural connections between delinquents, semimature criminals, and the adult criminal world, where they exist, provide opportunities for upward mobility. . .[64]

The *conflict* subculture may emerge when it is difficult for youths to succeed through either legitimate or criminal channels. The ensuing frustration and discontent are manifested in violent behavior as a means of achieving status by being feared or by showing independence of social control by the larger community. The conflict gang's behavior includes violent confrontations with other groups, unpredictable and destructive assaults on persons and property, freedom from conventional societal norms, and in-group solidarity, with the immediate motive a reputation of toughness—as a group to be feared.

Those who do not have the criminal contacts or the strength to become part of either a criminal or a conflict subgroup may abandon efforts to achieve status through either legitimate or illegitimate means and become involved in a *retreatist* subculture or gang, which relies on alcohol or drugs to escape from the awareness of aspirational failures. Others may join retreatist gangs after growing weary of the violence and danger associated with other types of gang activity. Such youths try to develop a sophisticated lifestyle in the world of alcohol and drug use or through other unusual ("cool") experiences. They may engage in criminal behavior such as con games, drug sales, or pimping to support their lifestyle, but their distinctive characteristic is an apparent desire to withdraw from conventional activities and norms valued by the larger society.[65]

Research Findings on Criminal Gangs. The attempts to empirically document the existence of criminal, conflict, and retreatist gangs, as delineated by Cloward and Ohlin, have met with limited success. However, in some cases the close links between gangs and organized crime described by Cloward and Ohlin as part of their criminal gang structure have been demonstrated.

There has been research that suggests some gangs focus their activities predominantly on crimes for profit. In a study of street gang crime in Chicago, Block and Block found that 40 major street gangs were active in the city. Many of the members of the four "super gangs" (Black Gangster Disciples Nation, Latin Disciples, Latin Kings, and Vice Lords) began their gang careers as adolescents, continued on into their late teens and 20s, and are now adult criminals.[66] Since many of the gangs operate out of the large public housing projects, they have opportunities to organize and control drug sales there.

The degree to which the illegal activities of the gangs were drug related varied. Block and Block found that:

. . . More incidents of cocaine possession (the most common offense) were attributed to the Vice Lords or to the Black Gangster Disciples Nation than to all other street gangs combined. The Vice Lords were also active in heroin possession offenses, with twice as many incidents attributed to them than to all other street gangs combined.[67]

In his study of Detroit gangs, Carl S. Taylor used the term "corporate gang" to describe a gang structure that closely resembles the "criminal gang" of Cloward and Ohlin. Taylor categorized the Detroit gangs as "scavenger," "territorial," and "corporate." While scavenger gangs were loosely organized thrill seekers who chose petty and spontaneous crimes, and territorial gangs were committed to turf defense, the corporate gangs went far beyond these activities and boundaries.[68]

Describing the corporate gangs, Taylor stated:

> These well-organized groups have very strong leaders and managers. The main focus of their organization is participation in illegal money-making ventures. Membership is based on the worth of the individual to the organization. . . . Different divisions handle sales, marketing, distribution, enforcement, and so on. . . . Criminal actions are motivated by profit. . . . Crimes are committed for a purpose, not for fun.[69]

Organized criminal activity among gangs has been documented in other large cities in the United States. Apparently, crack cocaine is the most readily available and profitable drug for sale. The large supply of this drug and the search for markets have led to expansion of the corporate gangs into other cities and smaller communities.

> When young Detroiters invade the state of Ohio, they are in pursuit of the American dream. That dream may appear distorted to middle-class or working-class America, yet it is truly business, the spirit of American entrepreneurship. Cocaine rocks in Detroit sell for $5.00, while in Cleveland, Toledo, or Cincinnati the same rocks will bring $20.00—supply and demand.[70]

The gangs that are profit-oriented and migratory expand their operations into new areas where they believe they can gain control, because the law enforcement presence there is perceived as ineffective or inadequate to control them. For example, it was reported that the Gangster Disciples, based in Chicago, have branches as far away as Colorado Springs, Colorado, and Mobile, Alabama. Federal investigators uncovered evidence of members of this gang operating in at least 50 cities throughout the United States. They tend to locate in cities connected by interstate highways to facilitate their drug trade operations.[71]

Another characteristic of the well-organized, profit-oriented gangs is their total lack of fear for law enforcement and the juvenile justice system. Discussions with the Cleveland, Ohio, Caribbean Gang Task Force revealed that they felt that the juvenile gang members involved in drug dealing have no regard for the legal system, and, in fact, can be very threatening to police officers. Even if they are arrested, they know that, if they remain under the jurisdiction of the juvenile court, the likelihood of remaining incarcerated for any significant period of time is slim. These gang members have ties with the "headpins" of the drug traffickers, and they are provided with attorneys and are assured that, even if convicted, they will soon be out on the streets again. If sent to a juvenile institution, they have friends there who will look after them. They do not "rat" on each other.[72]

Although gangs in certain cities fit Cloward and Ohlin's description of criminal gangs, in other instances the gangs' criminal activities do not seem to be highly organized. In Milwaukee, it was found that the Vice Lords, for a short period of time, focused on shoplifting, purse snatching, and other activities for profit, but this stopped after the police began to seriously monitor the Vice Lords' activities. The researchers concluded that the Vice Lords had gone through a phase of criminal activity that was only one facet of the gang's behavior.[73] Many of the gang members viewed drug sales and other criminal acts as a means of day-to-day survival. When asked how important the gang was to him, one ex-member confirmed this.

> I feel it was real important, 'cause you know when I was in the gang, it was about hustling. . . . We really didn't do a lot of fighting, but when we had fights it was about the hustling. I used to have new clothes every day, money in my pocket every day.[74]

A youth's artwork illustrating feelings of power and invincibility of gang members. *(Source: Art work provided by Ron Schneider from the publication "Feel My Pain.")*

Research Findings on Conflict Gangs.   Conflict or violence is the single defining characteristic of youth gangs, and there is considerable evidence that conflict is a theme of gang activity. However, contrary to the message communicated by the mass media and by police officials in large cities concerned about controlling youth gangs, the major activity of most gangs is not violent confrontation. In addition, even for those gangs that have been identified as involved in violence, the actual violent activity may only be carried on by core leaders.

Jackson and McBride note that gathering accurate information on the violent activities of gangs is a difficult task.

> Identification of the various gangs and their members is an on-going process. The very nature of gang membership is transitory. As members gravitate away from gang involvement or are sent to jail, new, younger members join who must be identified.[75]

In regard to determining the amount of gang violence, they state:

> Drive-by attacks, five to ten suspects robbing one or two victims, ambushes and snipings do not lend themselves easily to inclusion within gang crime statistics inasmuch as such crimes can be, and are, committed by individuals other than gang members.[76]

Gang violence tends to involve homicide and aggravated assault, and is not equally distributed throughout the cities, but concentrated in certain neighborhoods. While this violence may be directly connected to disputes related to other types of criminal activities, such as drug distribution, studies seem to confirm that in most instances turf battles are its focus.[77]

> Erodito Musse Jr., 19, is a big fellow, with a neat mustache and short brown hair. He lives in Brooklyn, in a neighborhood in which drugs and guns are more plentiful than fresh air. . . .
>
> "My primary concern," said Erodito, "is just staying alive. I didn't think, when I was growing up, that it could get this bad. I've lost 19 friends.
>
> "I was 12 when I first witnessed a murder. It was right in front of me, right out on the sidewalk. We lived in East Flatbush then. I knew the guy who killed the person. He came right up to him and shot him in the back of the head. I just ran up the stairs. I was shocked. I told the cops I didn't know nothing."
>
> "I was 14 the first time a friend of mine got killed. We called him Tazz. He moved to New Jersey, but he came back to Brooklyn and he got shot up. He died, and then suddenly people just started dying, to tell you the truth. . . ."
>
> Mariano Esquilin is tall and thin and a bearer of hair-raising stories delivered in a matter-of-fact tone. "Crime happens every other minute," he said.
>
> "You could be coming out of the grocery store and just catch a stray bullet. Last year I got shot myself. May 4. A young kid on a bicycle, no older than 15 or 16, pulled a .380 automatic from his waist and began shooting. I don't know why. Nobody said nothing to him. Maybe somebody stared at him."[78]

Researchers have sought to differentiate violent gangs from other types and determine why they focus on violence.

In his book *The Violent Gang,* Yablonsky developed a three-pronged classification of gangs, characterizing them as social, delinquent, or violent. *Social* gangs are composed of youths who seek to realize their individual social goals in a gang atmosphere, *delinquent* gangs have as their primary objective material profit as a result of delinquent activity, and *violent* gangs are those that seek emotional gratification through violent behavior.[79] Even in such a classification scheme, it becomes difficult to characterize a particular gang as purely social, delinquent, or violent, since elements of all three types of activity may be present during various stages of the gang's activity or development. Retreatist characteristics are also found at various stages of the development and activity of delinquent and violent gangs.

Lewis highlighted the importance of making distinctions between "amorphously structured" peer groups (youths who hang around together for fun, excitement, and companionship) and "organized" gangs, which have structures, rules, defined goals, and distinctive concerns. Lewis maintained that the organized gangs behave as they do not in an irrational effort to get back at society, but to pursue very definite purposes and goals. Their delinquency occurs when, in this pursuit, they violate laws formulated on the basis of middle-class standards. As Lewis noted:

> The organized gang is a far cry from the rebellious congeries of individuals implied in Cohen's treatment and also in Miller's lower-class street corner group, depicted as pursuing distinctive normative concerns into certain conflict with middle-class morality and legality. The gangs of which I write are organizationally sophisticated in a manner not unlike middle-class collectives. They emphasize universalistic task rationality in their allocation of roles, the necessity for rational planning, and obedience to rules of collective action and individual demeanor.[80]

The major goal of the organized juvenile gang is to maintain sovereignty or control over its turf. To this end, rules and norms must be developed, and a division of labor takes place. The concept of sovereignty, according to Lewis, implies control over a physical territory established as the gang's turf. Those who live within the boundaries of the territory and fall within an age category established by the gang are candidates for gang membership (in-group) or subjection to the power of the gang (out-group). Organized gangs, according to Lewis, normally do not try to subject all residents of the turf, but concentrate on gaining the respect and fear of members of their peer group. Although rules for the activities of the gang members are well defined, dealings with the out-group are relatively normless, and may involve violence, property destruction, extortion, intimidation—virtually any means that the gang can conceive of as useful. Thus, the organized gang is in essence a miniature society establishing its own rules, regulations, and value system, which apply only to its members and serve the gang's needs.[81]

Well aware of the differences in handling and penalties for juvenile and adult offenders, gangs frequently use very young members for tasks that pose a strong possibility for arrest, if the offender is detected, as evidenced by the follow case:

> At 4-foot-11, with dark eyes and an eager smile, Yuen Tung Chui exuded a disarming sweetness. It was a quality, authorities said, that helped make the 13-year-old dropout deft at his

profession: gangland enforcer. Chui is accused of terrorizing Chinatown [New York] street vendors with a box cutter to extort cash for the Flying Dragons gang. . . .

Chui was charged with offenses including attempted robbery, grand larceny, and attempted kidnapping. As a juvenile, he could be kept behind bars until his 18th birthday. . . .

The Dragons select baby-faced boys, some as young as 10, to carry guns, deliver messages, and watch for police, said Peter Kwong, a Hunter College professor who has studied China-town gangs. "They get the kids to do their dirty work so they themselves don't get impli-cated," Kwong said.[82]

Although the potential for conflict and violence is always present in the youth-gang setting, much of the gang members' activity is not violent and in many ways re-sembles the behavior of other adolescents. Moore, in her study of gangs in Los Ange-les, discovered that the frequency and severity of violent behavior varied tremendously from gang to gang. Even for the gangs considered the most violent by the police and the mass media, less time was spent in violent pursuits than in such activities as hanging around and getting high.[83] Haagedorn and Macon noted that Puerto Rican gangs in Milwaukee went to great lengths to avoid large-scale gang warfare and that several Hispanic gang-related homicides reported in Milwaukee were the result of intra-gang conflicts rather than inter-gang warfare.[84]

Jackson and McBride analyzed how conflict becomes enmeshed with the rou-tine activities of gang members.

> "Partying" and "getting down with the home boys" is an integral part of gang life and offers members social contacts not previously available. Loyalty outweighs personal interests. An individual cannot merely assimilate into the gang without proving his toughness and worth to the group. He must see himself as a soldier protecting his turf in an ongoing war with rival gangs. He is expected to prove himself in battle. It is not uncommon for a gang member to seek out situations where he can build his reputation. Often these incidents follow a party or other gang function. When the member is accepted by the gang, he is expected to share with fellow members. This includes narcotics, alcohol, and money. The gang is the first and most important part of his life.[85]

Research on Retreatist Gangs.   Most accounts of youth gang activities reveal that the use of various kinds of drugs by members is quite common. However, the con-tention that this drug use is a way of retreating or withdrawing from society does not seem to be true. Rather, the drug use is part of the day-to-day activity, along with the other socially unacceptable practices, in which members indulge.

Commenting on youth street gangs in Detroit, Taylor states:

> Drug usage by scavengers [youths in loosely organized gangs] is normal. If youngsters are not using drugs, then they are trying to sell them.[86]

Huff found alcohol, marijuana, and crack cocaine use to be frequent among the members of all three different types of gangs he identified [hedonistic, instrumental, and predatory] as operating in Cleveland and Columbus, Ohio.[87]

A Miami gang study found that:

Drug and alcohol use are closely associated with gang activity. *(Photo credit: Jay Paris)*

Of the first 308 youths interviewed, 95.5 percent reported having used crack at least once, and 87.3 percent reported current regular use—i.e., in the 90 days prior to being interviewed, used three or more times a week.[88]

In a study of youth gangs in Milwaukee, it was found that:

Sixty percent of the gang members interviewed admitted they used drugs (mainly marijuana) most or all of the time, meaning at least every other day. Nearly one third said they used drugs every day. Less than 5 percent of those interviewed said that at this time they "never used drugs."[89]

Research has also discovered that the gang drug users are involved in the sale of drugs, particularly crack cocaine. In the Milwaukee study, nearly half of the gang members interviewed said that they sold drugs "now and then," and drug sales were seen as ventures for profit. As one gang member observed:

You know, I use drugs because right now that's really one of the biggest ways for me to get money. The black society today is drugs. You know, and it's strange, cause there ain't that many jobs, but you notice it's always drugs. There's always money, but there ain't that many jobs, so how is that?[90]

A Miami study revealed that a youth's involvement in crack cocaine sales was highly correlated with drug use. Of youths who said they did not deal in crack cocaine, only 2 percent were daily users, while 87 percent of those who were crack dealers were also daily users.[91] The majority of the youths who were involved in robberies were also frequent drug users. When asked, "Of the money you make illegally, how much goes to buying drugs?", nearly two-thirds of the youths in the study said that 90 percent or more of their profits went for drugs.[92] A 17-year-old robber described how he acquired money for drugs:

To get enough money for whatever we wanted to do [whatever drugs], sometimes me and a friend would go downtown, maybe down the street from some nice restaurants, and wait for them [potential victims] to go to their cars. We'd know what cars they'd be goin' to. It was the rental cars—Hertz, Alamo, you know, those cars—for the tourists. When the guy would bend down to unlock the door, we'd run from across the street real fast, knock him with a club an' kick him a few times, take his wallet, jewelry. And the guy would always have a lady with him, and she would stand there in shock, so I'd run around the car an' take her bag, a chain from the neck if she had it.[93]

It seems, on the basis of recent research, that retreatist gangs, who use drugs to withdraw from society and establish a drug-centered way of life, are uncommon today, particularly in the inner cities. Some suburban youth gangs may still fit this pattern, but even there the drug involvement is only part of their lifestyle and not their chief reason for existence.

In summary, the work of Thrasher, in which he stated that many gangs develop out of neighborhood play groups, with some evolving into more formalized structures with defined leadership and concerned with turf protection, and others becoming more oriented toward criminal behavior as the members mature and become more sophisticated, may be an adequate description of the larger majority of contemporary gang formation activities in the inner cities. Much of the research considered here points out that the activities of gang members usually involve an intermeshing of social interactions, such as hanging around, partying, and drug use, with delinquent behavior that initially is recreational in nature.

Mercer L. Sullivan researched street gangs in Brooklyn. He pointed out that the gangs did not start out as groups oriented toward economic crime. When youths first became involved in gang activities, their primary motivation was the excitement of committing the acts, and only later did the profit motive emerge.

Many stole initially in order to enjoy direct use of the stolen objects. Stealing that took place in adolescent street fights, for example, usually involved the appropriation of youth culture consumer items—radios, bicycles, sneakers, coats—which were then as likely to be used directly as to be sold. . . . Some youths who snatched gold jewelry on the streets and subways did so initially in order to wear it themselves. . . . After the first few experiences with economic crime, however, their motivations began to change. . . . Crime proved a viable way to make money at the same time that they were beginning to perceive a need for more regular income. . . . Stealing for direct use gave way to conversion of stolen goods into cash. . . . The risks and rewards associated with specific criminal opportunities were weighed against those associated with opportunities for other types of crime or for legitimate work.[94]

The Underclass as a Generating Milieu for Gang Formation

The identification of an "underclass" in contemporary American society has important implications. William Wilson, who has written extensively on the inner-city black population, considers the underclass to be those who lack education and training and are children of families who are likely to have been in the poverty category for generations. They depend on welfare and apparently have little opportunity to break the cycle of poverty and welfare dependency.[95] Hagedorn and Macon define the underclass as "a category of men and women who are permanently excluded from participation in mainstream occupations."[96]

The emergence of this underclass, particularly in the eastern and midwestern cities of the United States referred to as the "rust belt," is related to a drastic decline in employment opportunities in the large cities, primarily through the loss of the types of factory jobs that provided employment for the unskilled, poorly educated children of the immigrants who came to these cities at the height of the industrial revolution. Hagedorn and Macon contend that the black and Hispanic gangs of Milwaukee resemble the immigrant gangs of the past who lived in the inner-city, deteriorated neighborhoods, but the one major difference from the gangs of the past is that those youths had job opportunities and gradually matured out of gang behavior. With the industrial jobs greatly reduced or eliminated, the present gang members do not have the education or skills to find employment in the highly skilled professional or service occupations, and are destined to remain in the underclass. As a result of the welfare reforms of the late 1990s, millions of single mothers who formerly qualified for welfare benefits are now working in low paying jobs that do not provide health benefits. Shelden et al. termed this the "feminization of poverty" and noted that these women find it very difficult to find affordable child care and provide supervision for their children while they are at work.[97]

In the past, adolescents who dropped out of school might take up street life for a while, but it was possible for them to find factory jobs and eventually become self-supporting. Today, such jobs are scarce, and, if work is available, it is low paying or part-time. Fox and Pierce note that:

> Adolescents, particularly those in the major cities, are beset with idleness and, for some, hopelessness. A growing number of teens and pre-teens see few attractive alternatives to violence, drug use, and gang membership. For them, the American Dream is a nightmare. There may be little to hope for and live for, but plenty to die for and even kill for.[98]

A study of 125 homeless male street youths who were runaways or throwaways found that most of these youths were unemployed or underemployed. They spent considerable time without shelter, hung out in public places (streets, parks, or shopping malls), and experienced poverty and hunger as daily conditions. The researchers discovered that these youths developed subcultural rules that favored violence as a way to meet their daily needs or settle conflicts that occurred in their lives. Interviews with these youths revealed that they generally came from family backgrounds where violence was frequently used as a disciplining strategy and had developed the outlook that intimidation and violence were appropriate methods of self-protection. Their continuous interaction with other homeless, angry youths and their perceptions of threats to their security increased the likelihood that they would use violence. When their violence produced a successful outcome, it reinforced the likelihood that they would use it again in similar situations.[99]

It is recognized that adolescents in all social classes may be susceptible to the lure of gang membership, in terms of the expected excitement, status, and camaraderie. However, as they mature, youths who have family support and other opportunities open to them may disengage from the gang and turn away from the types of deviant activity they pursued as gang members. Those from the underclass, having few options or opportunities, are more likely to remain within the gang structure. In these families, younger brothers follow older ones into the gang and remain with the gang after they have reached adulthood. As Moore observed:

> The opportunities available in the community at the time probably determine what fraction "matures out" and what fraction remains. Thus the gang becomes an institutionalized feature of some poverty communities, and plays a role in the perpetuation of the underclass.[100]

For underclass youths, the gang becomes a "family," as well as an avenue for economic survival. The money made from selling drugs or robberies, activities that gang members participate in, helps provide for some basic needs, and the companionship, recognition, and status enhancement from gang membership fulfill other needs of the youth that are not met at home, at school, or in a job situation.

The Compound, a book describing the lifestyles of a number of gangs in New York City, highlights the attempts of gang members to explore the middle-class activities they perceive as important and to gain information about the more structured aspects of family life. For example, two police officers assigned to the gang intelligence unit noted that the gang members, and the girls in particular, repeatedly questioned them about their personal lives, asking if they were married, if they had children, and what sort of homes they had. They liked to look at snapshots of the officers' families and seemed pathetically eager to know what a stable family life was like.[101] In some cases, the gang developed elaborate ceremonies that simulated middle-class "rites of passage," but with a touch of individuality added to suit the gang's needs. The following description of a gang wedding from *The Compound* highlights this imitative activity:

> Slick presented his bride with a plastic orchid, and Bricktop . . . wrapped around Amelia's head the white towel which was to the outlaw-style wedding what the white veil is to a traditional wedding. "You're the first bride we have who wears a white towel," said Bricktop. "White's for virgins, and we never had one before." . . .

> "You take Slick to be your husband?" . . . "You take Candy to be your wife?". . . Then Slick took Amelia's hand in his, and together they moved a few steps closer to the prez . . . King Cobra, who was short and husky and not much taller than Amelia, climbed up on a chair,

held a can of beer aloft, and proceeded to pour it over their heads. . . . "Kiss!" the prez commanded, and Slick kissed her hard on the lips, after which King Cobra threw the first piece of vanilla cake straight into Slick's face—the sign that he was now a husband. It was official.[102]

Even though these gang members were capable of murder, rape, and many other forms of criminal activity, and repeatedly committed violent offenses without any show of remorse, elements of the values and norms of the larger society touched and affected them. The author of *The Compound* noted that at a conference on gang violence sponsored by the National Urban League, present and former gang members agreed that underemployment, oppression, idleness, and despair all contribute to the existence of gangs.

Needs Theory

Maslow believed that a person's behavior can be explained in terms of that individual's response to five basic human needs. These include physiological needs (basic items required for physical survival such as food and water), things needed for safety and security (environmental factors, such as a place to live and protection from harm), belonging needs (membership in family, friendship, or other groups), self-esteem needs (recognition or approval from others), and self-actualization needs (desires to achieve and excel).[103]

Maslow placed these needs in a pyramidal hierarchy, with the needs of physiological survival and safety and security being the most basic, and needs of belonging, self-esteem, and self-actualization met or gratified in successive order after the basic needs are satisfied. Thus, a person's motives for engaging in a specific behavior at any given time can be interpreted as an attempt by that person to use the behavior to satisfy his strongest need at that moment.

It should not be concluded that lower level needs must be completely satisfied before one becomes motivated to attempt to fill a higher level need. In general, most people are partially satisfied at all levels, but not completely satisfied at any need level. At times individuals may defer gratification of a lower level need in order to focus on fulfilling the higher level needs of self-esteem and self-actualization.

Jackson and McBride developed a theory of gang formation that employed Maslow's hierarchy of needs levels. They stated that what they termed Level I needs (physiological needs for survival, such as food and clothing) are often obtained by future gang members' parents through illegal acts, and the young people, at an early age, begin to develop mindsets that approve antisocial behavior. For Level II (safety and security), these youths initially look to family members, but, finding what is provided inadequate, may see the gang as the way to obtain security in a hostile environment. Thus, when they reach Level III (belonging needs), they gravitate toward gang membership as a way of "socializing with others who have also learned to use unacceptable means to satisfy their needs for survival and security."[104] As the group becomes more cohesive, the levels of criminal activity rise. Jackson and McBride theorized that a lack of parental guidance and a lack of love from family members drives youths to seek friendship and respect in a gang setting. Once involved with a gang, a youth seeks Level IV needs (the desire for self-esteem, the need to attain recognition by displaying skills and talents) through turf fights, displays of "colors," graffiti writing, and criminal activities. These lead to Level V (self-actualization), in the form of efforts to be the toughest, most violent, most feared gang member, with the goal of winning the admiration of fellow members.[105]

Short and Strodtbeck, in their study of Chicago gangs, also discovered that the gang members had needs and aspirations that they hoped to fulfill. For example, many gang boys revealed their desires for good jobs, material rewards, stable family life, and opportunities for their children. There was ambivalence in their value system, however, since they also enjoyed the activities of the lower-class way of life (excitement, freedom, concentration on fun) and their acceptance of middle-class standards was rather superficial. They did not perceive that their delinquent behavior would have an effect on their future opportunities. Their aspirations tended to be rather unrealistic in light of the amount of preparation they were making to achieve them; few were studying to achieve in school or working at a part-time job to have enough money to buy some of the things they desired.[106]

STRUCTURE OF THE GANG

We have already noted the development of gangs from small groups that interact and come to recognize their common interests. While the gang theorists have emphasized the importance of neighborhood groups in the evolution of gang activity, Huff observed that the word "neighborhood" now has an expanded definition.

> Forerunners of the current gangs in Cleveland and Columbus [Ohio] were neighborhood streetcorner groups and "turf"-oriented gangs who fought against one another over turf issues, ethnic and racial conflict, and other issues . . . "Neighborhood" no longer conveys the same kind of meaning. . . . If still in school, they [gang members] attend schools whose pupils come from various neighborhoods. Gang membership is no longer confined to the neighborhood, but involves confederates recruited at school, at skating rinks, and elsewhere throughout the city.[107]

Thrasher made the observation that a gang does not become one until it "begins to excite disapproval and opposition, and thus acquires a more definite group consciousness."[108]

Various levels of involvement in gang activity have been identified. Yablonsky presented evidence that the average gang is composed of a number of "hard-core" members (estimated to be 10 to 15% of the gang) who lead, plan, and manage the day-to-day activities of the gang and a much larger group of "marginal" members who are their followers:[109] A study by Esbensen and Huizinga supported Yablonsky's theory of impermanence of commitment on the part of many gang members. In their survey of urban gang members, more than half of the youths indicated that they did not want to be or did not expect to be gang members in the near future.[110] Hardman expanded the involvement levels to three: (1) a core leadership elite; (2) regulars or full-time members; and (3) hangers-on, fringe, or peripheral members. He also noted the presence of a few adult hangers-on, who tried to become involved in gang activities and exploit the gang members for their own advantage.[111]

The hard-core leaders are those responsible for recruiting new members and holding the marginals in line through use of various manipulative and fear tactics. Since fear of enemies (members of other gangs or the police) is an integrating factor, the hard-core leaders may fabricate threats or exaggerate dangers to solidify the marginal members' loyalty to the group.

A hierarchy of levels within the gang leadership has also been identified in gang studies. Collins outlined the following power structure in gangs:

> The President is surrounded by several distinct positions that are delegated and have individual responsibilities. Next in line to the President is the Vice-President, administrative assistant to the leader; War Counselor, second in command in peace time, but assumes command in time of conflict; Advisor, who acts as a "confidant" and bodyguard to the President; Gang Armorer, who is charged with the responsibility of having weapons that function properly; Spokesman, who represents the Prez at meetings, alliances and treaties and also acts as the gang's intelligence officer, and a few other hard core members who comprise the nucleus of the gang.
>
> . . . A new type of leader has come upon the youth gang scene . . . He is the "Top Prez," "Godfather," or "Supreme Prez." This title applies to the supreme leader of large cliques of gangs that have divisions in several boroughs or throughout the entire city. He is chief of operations and coordinates all gang activity and policy.[112]

Retention of the top leadership position in the gang may depend upon meeting the physical challenges presented by other candidates, demonstrating "heart" by fearlessly leading the gang into battle, or showing the ability to "look out for" the other gang members through cunning and manipulation. The other leadership positions are frequently conferred as a result of extraordinary performance in the gang's behalf.

Entrance into the gang frequently involves an elaborate initiation rite, which may include demonstrations of personal valor. For example, a Los Angeles gang called the Cripplers requires candidates for admission to furnish evidence that they have physically injured someone.[113] Sex-oriented gangs may require new members to demonstrate their virility by having sexual relations with a number of girls. The Savage Skulls, a South Bronx gang, developed an initiation rite that involved hanging a new member upside down from a pipe or tree and beating him to see how much physical pain he could endure.[114]

In San Antonio, Texas, teenaged girls described a gang initiation in which they demonstrated their toughness by having sex with male members of the gang who had tested positive for HIV, the virus that causes AIDS.[115] In one gang initiation rite, the girls had a choice of being "rolled in" or "jumped in."

> Those who choose to get "rolled in" roll a pair of dice and the number rolled is the number of gang members that they will have sex with, beginning with the gang leader.
>
> "It's not so bad, considering it's a one time deal," said a girl who had rolled a nine.
>
> Getting "jumped in" means getting beaten and kicked by a half-dozen or so gang members for about a minute. Cracked ribs and other injuries, one girl said, is a small price to pay for having a gang "be there for you after that."[116]

A member of another gang described the practice "sexing in" the female members.

Describing this initiation, Jermaine explained that the girl has to have sex with "anybody that wants to. . . ."

RB: Suppose everybody wants to?

Jermaine: She ain't gonna let everybody do it. Half probably get in it, though. . . .

If they get sexed in, they don't really get no respect."[117]

Symbolic efforts to heighten group solidarity center around names of gangs and distinctive patterns of dress. A gang's name may refer to the turf the gang claims as its own (West Side Devils) or to claims of superior strength (Invincibles). A gang emblem may be developed and used to indicate the group's presence or domination, by being spray-painted or written on walls. Distinctive styles of dress are also characteristic of well-developed gang structures.

The primary appeal of social or violent gangs is status enhancement. Social gangs offer opportunities for developing a sense of belonging to youths who may never have experienced such a feeling in their family or school situations. The existence of rules and taboos also has an appeal to those who have known little control at home or in the community. Brotherhood, protection from neighborhood toughs, opportunities to "get even" with members of other gangs or adults who are perceived as threatening are all part of the gang appeal. Self-preservation is a strong motive in violent-gang membership. One Puerto Rican gang member in Chicago revealed the "why" of his gang membership in the following words: "Protection, man, protection. I was a skinny little kid, and I was tired of having hassles. You don't last long if you don't belong to a club. You can always count on having someone stand up for you."[118]

Gang solidarity and a sense of security are enhanced for delinquent or violent gangs by the amassing of a large collection of weapons, which are handled, concealed, and made ready for use. The stockpile of weaponry for the gang is obtained in various ways. Guns taken in burglaries form an important part of the collection, and others are purchased with the proceeds from drug sales and robberies. We noted earlier in this chapter that many of the gang members carry guns with them as part of their daily routines.

The meeting place of the gang is another important feature in its development of group cohesion. It serves as the location for planning and setting gang activities in motion; concealing loot; and taking part in sexual activities, drinking, drug use, and general socialization. Abandoned buildings or apartments of older members of the gang may serve this function.

VARIATIONS IN GANG BEHAVIOR

Female Gangs

Although involvement of females in gang activity has long been documented, their attachments to gangs has usually been in the roles of weapons carriers or girlfriends of gang members. Often they were part of female auxiliaries of male gangs.

Over the years, gang behavior researchers have given female gangs only cursory analysis. Thrasher's 1927 study did locate several gangs whose membership was entirely female, but only one of these was oriented toward delinquent behavior.[119] Bernard's study of New York juvenile gangs in the 1940s found that girls were associated with many of the juvenile male gangs. They served as sex objects for male members and some occasionally carried weapons or lured victims into isolated spots so that male members could rob or beat them. He also identified a few girl gangs that had names and wore distinctive colors.[120]

In the 1950s and 1960s, Walter B. Miller studied two female gangs—an all-white gang of Catholic girls called the Molls and a black female gang known as the Queens. Each was affiliated with a male gang, but also performed delinquent acts on its own.[121]

In the 1970s, Miller's survey of youth-gang activities in major cities reported the same pattern. The activities of the female gangs were described as complementing the male gang members by serving as weapon carriers or decoys. Only occasionally were they found to be involved in gang fights or organized criminal activities.[122]

At the end of the 1970s, Campbell summarized the research on female gangs that had taken place. She noted that girls always were found to have a "marginal status" and that "sexual objectification" is a second major theme.

> Girls join gangs to meet boys. Innocent girls are corrupted by sex and as "fallen women" slip into the underworld of gang life. Girls in gangs perform sexual roles (lures, spies), are "passive, property, and promiscuous," are sexually and physically abused by men, want to excel as females by having sex with as many members as possible, get pregnant, and work as prostitutes.[123]

In the 1980s, however, there was evidence that independent female gangs were springing up. In Chicago, at least six such gangs were identified by the agency that had the responsibility for monitoring gang activity. They were known to carry and use weapons, especially carpet knives. The Chicago Police Department noted substantial increases in violent crimes by females up to 20 years of age in the late 1980s and attributed the increase in female gangs to organizing activity by females who had worked with male gangs, increases in female imprisonment, high teen pregnancy rates, and the young females' drive to establish their independence.[124]

In the 1980s and 1990s, there were indications that female gangs were attracting younger members. In a Milwaukee study of two female gangs, the 2-7 Syndicates and the V-L Queens, which were auxiliaries of male gangs, the girls performed most of the traditional functions of such groups, including serving as sexual partners for the males. Girls in these gangs were 12, 13, and 14 years old.[125] In San Antonio, Texas, female gang members, imitating a practice of the California male Spur Posse gang, who kept scorecards of their sexual encounters, tried to have sex with as many males as possible. Authorities confiscated lists containing as many as 60 names from 14- and 15-year-old girls.[126]

In 2000, the National Youth Gang Survey reported that only two percent of gangs were identified as predominantly female and 82 percent of the police

A youth's artwork depicting female gang members
(Source: Art work provided by Rod Schneider from the publication "Feel My Pain.")

agencies that provided the data reported no predominantly female gangs in their jurisdictions.[127]

Walter Miller classified female gangs into three types—mixed gender gangs, female gangs affiliated with male gangs (auxiliary gangs), and independent female gangs.[128] Jody Miller found that females' attachment to the gang lifestyle and other gang members and involvement in drug use and violence varied by gang type. Females affiliated with male gangs had a low status. In the mixed gender gangs their status varied with the number of girls in the gang. Females still had a lower status than the males, but they were treated with more respect than those affiliated with all male gangs. The females in the mixed gender gangs were rarely directly involved in violence or even in serious criminal acts. The independent female gangs appeared to be less criminal and violent than the other types, but members of these gangs associated with members of other types of gangs.[129]

The ability of female gangs to organize and act on their own or to attain positions of leadership or recognition in largely male gangs is still hampered by traditions and ethnic customs. For example, in their studies of Hispanic gangs, Jackson and McBride discovered:

> Equal rights and thoughts of equal rights for women play no part in Hispanic gangs. Females have their place within the gang structure and adhere strictly to that place. The female members are, by and large, separate cliques of the larger male gang. There are also very few female gangs that are totally separate entities.[130]

Earlier in this chapter, we noted that the appeal of the gang for many members is related to its creation of a "family" situation for youths who have never had such experiences. This is particularly true for female gang members. Girls involved in gangs have been found to have higher levels of social isolation and lower levels of self esteem than nongang members.[131] The bonding with male members, sometimes recognized by mock "wedding" ceremonies, and the feeling that they belong somewhere and can depend on someone to protect or support them, draws girls to become involved. However, as Campbell observed in *The Girls in the Gang*, this proves to be an illusion.

> For these girls, there was no escape in the gang from the problems they faced: their female role could not be circumvented, their instability remained and was magnified, their isolation was covered by a rough veneer. The gang was no alternative life for them. It was a microcosm of the society beyond. Granted, it was one that had a public image of rebellion and excitement and offered a period of distraction (discussion of gang feuds and honor and death). But in the end, gang or no gang, the girls remained alone with their children, still trapped in poverty and in a cultural dictate of womanhood from which there was no escape.[132]

Suburban and Small-Town Gangs

Traditionally, gangs have been regarded as an urban phenomenon. Although ganging did occur in suburban areas and in small towns, the behavior of these youths was more anti-social than criminal, and the delinquent behavior in which they were involved was mostly nonviolent. In recent years, however, the presence of violent and criminal gangs has been reported in smaller communities, particularly those that are adjacent to large urban centers.

We noted earlier in this chapter that street gangs from large cities have migrated to smaller ones, motivated chiefly by the possibilities of high profits from drug sales.[133] In addition, members of big-city gangs may be commuting from the cities to suburban malls and small towns to commit crimes, then returning to their home bases. Thad Alexander, a member of the Columbus, Ohio gang control unit, remarked that when he recognized a gang member he had worked with in Columbus at a shopping center in a middle-class, suburban town, he approached the boy and said, "You shouldn't be here, this isn't your turf." The gang member responded, "Our house is where we want it to be."[134]

The National Youth Gang Survey revealed that suburbs, small cities, and rural areas have noted gang activity, and this has occurred in areas with no previous gang experience. In 1995, 57 percent of the suburbs, 34 percent of the small cities, and 25 percent of the rural areas in the survey reported the presence of active gangs.

Although some migration of gangs from large cities to small towns and rural areas occurs, chiefly in the form of gangs engaged in drug trafficking that are expanding their operations, the suburban and small town gangs are mostly "homegrown."[135] Youths who are residents of suburbs and small towns are forming their own gangs, hanging out in malls and parks, acting boisterously, displaying distinctive garb and "colors" vandalizing property, writing graffiti, and engaging in other delinquent activity.

Juvenile gangs that develop in suburban areas and small towns may take various forms, as documented by researchers.

Hardman's Study of Small-Town Gangs.   Hardman examined the characteristics of four youthful gangs that were formed in a small midwestern community. The small-town gangs were found to differ from defined urban types in a number of respects. They were all delinquent, aggressive, *and* retreatist, rather than definable as one distinct type. Girls were incorporated into the gangs as full members rather than given auxiliary status. Instead of defying or putting down middle-class norms, the gang members respected and supported them and applauded gang members who strove for middle-class achievements.[136]

Middle-Class Gangs.   Loosely structured middle-class gangs that develop in suburbs, small towns, or rural areas may take various forms. Wooden divided the suburban gang members he studied into "renegade kids" or "suburban outlaws." The "renegade kids," whom he regarded as "identity seekers," engaged in relatively harmless behaviors, while the "suburban outlaws" were nonconformists, rebellious, and had developed deviant and delinquent identities and behavior.[137] The types of suburban outlaws he differentiated included tagger crews (graffiti painters competing to identify their turf); stoners (drug abusers also involved with heavy metal music); Satanists (devil worshippers and cult members); and skinheads (white supremacists, racists).[138] Of the youths who purport to be members of such gangs, some are deeply committed to them and others are only marginal members.

Mark Hamm, who studied American neo-Nazi skinheads, traveled to large cities where skinheads were known to be active, developed contacts with them in street settings, interviewed some, and sent questionnaires to leaders of the groups. He was able to gather information from 36 leaders and groups from major cities and smaller towns.

Hamm characterized the groups as terrorist or nonterrorist on the basis of their degree of involvement in violent or dangerous acts for the purpose of intimidating or coercing officials or the civilian population. Of the 36 groups he identified, he classified 22 as terrorist and 14 as nonterrorist. The terrorist and nonterrorist group members did not differ significantly by age, but the terrorists were predominantly male, from blue-collar families, had a high school or less than a high school education, and, if they were employed, did blue-collar work. The nonterrorist groups were about equally divided in male and female membership, made up of youths predominantly from white-collar families, with high school educations, and, if employed, were in white-collar occupations. Most of the terrorists were older adolescents who had been academically successful, were gainfully employed, and did not report friction with their parents. The basis of their involvement in the groups seemed to be ideological commitment.[139]

GANG ACTIVITY CONTROL

Typically, the control of gang activity has been defined as a police matter. However, those who have observed and researched gang behavior conclude that its prevention and control is a complex task and must involve the entire community.

Measures used to reduce and control gang activities may be proactive or reactive. Proactive control focuses on preventing gangs from forming. The appeal of gang membership is strong, particularly for inner-city youngsters who have few other options to channel their energy and meet their needs. If young people are to resist the gangs' appeal, positive alternatives must be provided. These may include sports, youth clubs, afterschool programs at churches or civic centers, or extension of the hours that schools are open. Since the school is the point of contact with the community for all children, provision of late afternoon and evening athletic, fine arts, tutoring, computer training, and life-skill programs, well organized and supervised, can help meet the needs of children who have empty hours to fill. In addition, neighborhood residents may be organized to observe and report suspected drug sale or use or identify places where gangs gather.

Reactive gang control, which occurs when gangs are recognized as present in a community, may include formation of special police gang control units, gang streetworker programs, and implementation of firm justice system responses to unlawful gang activity.

Spergel and Curry, in a major research project titled, "National Youth Gang Suppression and Intervention Research and Development," identified the strategy areas for gang suppression and control as community organization, social intervention, opportunities provision, and suppression.[140] Activity in all of these areas is needed.

Community Organization for Gang Control

Until the mid-1980s, most communities, and even some large cities, did not have serious gang problems, at least in terms of random violence, set off with little or no warning or provocation. Although gangs existed, and they were regarded as troublesome and at times destructive, through their vandalism and graffiti writing, they did not pose a major threat to the physical well-being of most community residents. With the sudden upsurge in violent behavior by gangs in the late 1980s and 1990s and the spread of gangs from large cities to medium-sized and even smaller cities, a whole new situation was recognized.

Youths who had few opportunities—who were not succeeding in school or were out of school and unemployed—found role models in the charismatic gang leaders and were eager to be identified with notorious gangs. Television programs and rap music brought gang activities to the attention of these youths and endowed them with a certain glamour. The communities and neighborhoods in which these young people resided provided no activities or opportunities to match the appeal of the gangs.

Police gang units are an important part of gang control. *(Photo credit: Nick J. Cool, The Image Works)*

Now that the peril posed by gangs has aroused community awareness, quick action must be taken to combat the gangs' appeal. There are no "quick fix" solutions, and the problems faced are formidable. As Block and Block observed:

> Street gang patterns and trends reflect not only chronic problems, such as racial and class discrimination and adjustment of immigrants, but also acute, often rapidly changing problems stemming from the existing economic situation, weapon availability, drug markets, and the spatial arrangement of street gang territories across a city.[141]

Social Intervention

Mentoring programs, in which children from disadvantaged neighborhoods are introduced to lifestyles and role models that would otherwise be unavailable to them, can be used. Successful professionals, businessmen and women, or college students are paired one-on-one with youths. The mentors may take the youths to their places of employment or may interact with them at social or athletic events. Such activities give the youths visions of life beyond their everyday experiences and may motivate them to work hard to achieve new goals.

Opportunities Provision

Most social scientists agree that opportunities are the key to resisting gang influence. Government, community organizations, schools, and businesses must work together to make meaningful opportunities available to at-risk youths, and the potential for misuse or ineffective use of funds that are provided for such programs is very great. Apprenticeship programs, in which employers and the schools cooperate in training youths for jobs that hold real opportunities, would be one solution. Unfortunately, very few placements of this type exist, and many high school students are too poorly prepared academically to succeed in those that are available. Providing youths with quality education is the best possible solution, but there are many obstacles to their academic success, including lack of student or parent interest, lack of knowledge about what employment in jobs other than service occupations actually involves, poor preparation for school entry, no quiet places or resources in the home for study, peer influences that pull youths toward "easy money" and downplay deferred gratification, lack of positive adult role models, poorly financed and administered schools, and tracking of disadvantaged youths into school programs that do not prepare them for college or additional schooling.

Suppression

One approach to reducing and controlling gang activity is the development of "gang-intelligence" units, which work out of the police departments of large cities and seek to discover who the core leaders of various gangs are, what their plans and habits may be, and how their influence on other youths and propensity toward violence can best be counteracted. The 2000 National Youth Gang Survey reported that 37 percent of police agencies in jurisdictions that were experiencing gang activity operated a specialized gang unit with two to four officers. The units' activities included patrol/enforcement, intelligence gathering, and investigation.[142]

An important facet of intelligence gathering is identifying the type of gang activity that is taking place in specific areas, so that programs to reduce or eliminate the activity can be implemented[143] As Block and Block pointed out in their research on gangs in Chicago, instituting a program to reduce gang involvement in drug sales would not be warranted in an area where it is discovered that the violence is predominantly related to turf defense.[144] Because gang activities may change quickly or may shift to new neighborhoods without warning, gang intelligence units are vital.

Archbold and Meyer cautioned against overestimating gang problems. When groups of adolescents are observed gathering in certain areas and episodes of violence or property destruction occur, a gang problem may be defined when one does not actually exist. They researched the development of a gang-suppression unit in a small midwestern community and found that the police department's failure to accurately distinguish between crimes committed by individual youths and those that were gang related led to erroneous conclusions about the extent of gang problems in their community. After a gang suppression unit was established, the police realized that there was little evidence that organized gangs existed or presented a serious threat to the community.[145]

Making weapons less easily available is another method of suppressing gang violence. Although such legislation as the Brady Law, which mandated a five-day waiting period between application for and purchase of firearms and a criminal background check for the applicant, and other legislation, which banned the sale of certain semiautomatic weapons, is a tangible move toward reducing the availability of weapons to youths, it cannot prevent such purchases from occurring. As Hechinger notes:

> In the world of embattled streets, housing projects, and schools, firearms are not bought through legal commercial channels: they are traded like drugs in alleys, from vans and through a host of illegal suppliers.[146]

Others believe that punishing the hard-core leaders of gangs and isolating them from the other youths through institutionalization is needed for effective control of violent gangs. This view is likely to be received enthusiastically by the public, particularly residents of communities that have been harassed, terrorized, or vandalized by gangs.

On the basis of his findings from a study of youth gangs in seven Ohio cities, Huff developed a number of policy recommendations for gang membership reduction and control of gang activities. These included identification of at-risk areas of cities and development of prevention programs to reach youths before they become involved in gangs; development of school curriculum that presents situational ethics to students in relation to the problems they face in everyday life, stressing teacher and principal assertiveness and the need to hold students accountable for their behavior; establishment of a statewide intergovernmental task force on gangs, organized crime, and narcotics as a preventive measure; aggressive but professional police behavior in dealing with gangs; intensive probation, supplemented by telephone or electronic monitoring for gang members who have been found delinquent but who do not pose a threat to public safety; development of school board policies that clearly forbid all types of weapons in school; close cooperation of schools with local police to assure that the school is a safe environment; and implementation of programs that will offer young people who live in inner-city poverty areas opportunities to become involved in positive experiences that will help counter the appeal of gang membership.[147]

California's State Task Force on Youth Gang Violence had similar recommendations for schools and communities plagued by gang activity. It also suggested that local law enforcement agencies form special units of officers whose sole responsibility is gang crime prevention and investigation, and that the agencies recruit officers who have bilingual skills and represent a variety of ethnic groups. Coordination of efforts and cooperation with other local agencies and state and local officials were encouraged. The Task Force suggested that county and city district attorneys form special gang prosecution units, with attorneys trained and experienced in prosecution of these cases. Edwin Miller, District Attorney for the Country of San Diego, noted the special features of gang cases which differentiate them from other criminal cases.

> First, gang cases are characterized by an extraordinarily high level of witness intimidation. Second, gang cases exist in a world which appears unfathomable to most citizens. Third, most gang cases are multi-defendant cases involving between two to ten defendants. Fourth, most such cases involve virtually simultaneous proceedings in both the adult and juvenile courts.[148]

Legislation for Youth Gang Prevention and Control

State legislation enacted to deal with the gang problem varies by state in purpose, scope, and definition, but generally includes one or more of the following provisions:

- Makes it a crime to belong to a gang organization that is known to be involved in random crimes of violence, terrorism, or intimidation or takes part in criminal activity for economic gain.
- Calls for enhanced penalties if a crime is committed as part of a gang action.
- Allows for an increased bail figure or preventive detention if an accused offender is charged with a gang-related crime.
- Supports civil courses of action against gang leaders and members, so that individuals or the state can pursue civil actions to seize proceeds and instrumentalities accumulated by or used by street gangs and allows the government to recover compensatory damages and all court costs of filing these suits.
- Allows juveniles accused of gang-related crimes to be fingerprinted and photographed, and requires gang members and leaders convicted of gang-related offenses to register with local law enforcement officials when they are released back into the community.
- Provides for curfew laws as a gang control mechanism.
- Provides funds to local law enforcement agencies that can be used to protect victims and witnesses who are aiding in the prosecution of those involved in gang crimes.
- Provides for creation of multilaw enforcement violent crime task forces that focus on gang-related drug trafficking, terrorism, and violence.
- Prohibits youths under 18 from exhibiting tattoos that have gang symbols or markings without parental consent.
- Provides funds for anti-gang counseling programs and prevention activities in schools and the community.[149]

The descriptions of gang behavior and the characteristics of gang members presented in this chapter testify to the difficulty of generalizing about the nature, motivations, and extent of gang activity. Various types of gangs have defined their goals as status, companionship, protection, recognition, or material gain.

Any attempt to discover the most effective method of preventing or controlling gang behavior must take into account not only the wide range of gang types and levels of commitment and solidarity within gangs, but also the orientations of those who are seeking to reduce or eliminate gang behavior. Opinions of the most proper or effective methods will vary with the professional status of those involved, such as police officers, social workers, ministers, poverty workers, or politicians. Extreme gang control measures could range from attempts at destruction of the gangs and institutionalization of all core members to rechanneling gang activities through socially acceptable behavior. Another view is that gang behavior will become less appealing and destructive in nature when its social and economic causes, including poverty, slum living, and lack of educational and employment opportunities, are attacked. There are no easy solutions.

SUMMARY

A review of the history of gang development reveals that gangs have existed in the urban areas of this country virtually from the time cities became large enough to develop slum areas. Conflict over control of territory was the chief concern of the earliest gangs and is still important. Contemporary gangs, however, may be competing for control of a particular area for the purpose of profiting from the drug sales there. The levels of gang violence escalated markedly in the late 1980s and 1990s, and gangs' increased use of firearms created threats to innocent bystanders.

Although gang members are predominantly blacks or Hispanics, involvement of Asians and white youths is also apparent. The age range of gang members is expanding, with preteen youngsters now becoming gang members and youths in their 20s remaining active in gangs. Violent crimes and drug trafficking by gangs are of great concern. Gang activity has been reported in the schools in many large cities, and in-school robberies and assaults on teachers and students frequently involve youths acting in groups. Street crime is also a major activity of youth-gang members. Gang theorists include the members of the Chicago School (Thrasher, Shaw, McKay, and Tannenbaum), Whyte, Cohen, Miller, Lewis, Cloward and Ohlin, Yablonsky, Jackson and McBride (applying Maslow's "needs theory" to gang formation), and Short and Strodtbeck. They developed contrasting or complementary theories of gang-behavior causation. The emergence of an underclass of impoverished, poorly educated, unemployed persons who seem to have few options for breaking out of a cycle of welfare dependency and hopelessness has also been recognized as contributing to gang formation.

Gang structure most frequently involves an inner circle of leaders who plan strategy and control the gang's decision making, a group of regular members, and other youths who remain on the fringes of gang activity and participate only occasionally. Leaders must frequently justify their positions by demonstrations of strength or courage. Gang solidarity is developed by use of initiation rites; distinctive patterns of dress, emblems, and names; and collection of a large cache of weapons.

Although gang activity is most frequently associated with inner-city males, females are involved in male-dominated gangs in various roles and sometimes form independent female gangs. Gang activity occurs in suburbs, small cities, and rural areas as well as in urban settings, and middle-class youths who do not fit the gang member profile of "disadvantaged youths" also create gangs.

Approaches to gang control may be proactive or reactive. Proactive efforts focus on preventing gang formation by developing community and school activities and programs to meet the needs of youths who might fall prey to the gangs' appeal. Reactive control occurs when gangs are recognized as present in the community. Reactive approaches may take the form of collection of intelligence and attempts to destroy the gang, isolation of the leaders through arrest and institutionalization, and debunking of romanticized versions of gang behavior in the mass media. Because of the violent nature of a good deal of current gang activity, legislation for transfer of gang members' cases to adult criminal courts, development of special units of prosecutors to work on gang cases, and determinate sentences for certain violent crimes have been implemented. The schools are regarded as the best avenue for reaching youths who may be in danger of gang involvement and seek to influence them in a positive way by providing educational and employment opportunities. Although control programs may have limited successes, real solutions to the problem of gang delinquency depend on a broad, sweeping attack on the social problems that breed it.

DISCUSSION QUESTIONS

1. Describe the levels of membership and leadership in a typical gang. What are the methods used by leaders to inspire loyalty and produce feelings of group solidarity?
2. Discuss the possible explanations for the strong pull toward gang involvement for certain youths in disadvantaged neighborhoods, while other youths who live in the same area do not seek such attachments.
3. Describe the three types of gangs identified by Cloward and Ohlin in their studies of delinquency and opportunity. Why do different types of gangs develop?
4. How have the activities and interests of gangs in the inner cities of large metropolitan areas changed in the last several decades?
5. What mechanisms are used by police and the courts to control gangs? How effective do you think these are?

NOTES

1. Clifford Shaw, "Juvenile Delinquency: A Group Tradition," in James F. Short, Jr., ed., *Gang Delinquency and Delinquent Subcultures* (New York: Harper & Row, 1968), 86–87.
2. *Baltimore Sun*, September 2, 1994, 3A.
3. *The Times Leader*, September 2, 1994, B1.
4. Wayne S. Wooden, *Renegade Kids, Suburban Outlaws* (New York: Wadsworth, 1995), 2–3.
5. Fred M. Hechinger, "Saving Youth from Violence," *Carnegie Quarterly* 39, 1 (Winter 1994), 4.
6. Joan Moore, "Gangs and the Underclass: A Comparative Perspective," in John Hagedorn and Perry Macon, *People and Folks* (Chicago: Lakeview Press, 1988), 5.
7. Carolyn Rebecca Block and Richard Block, *Street Gang Crime in Chicago* (Washington, DC: U.S. Department of Justice, 1993), 3.
8. Gad J. Bensinger, "Chicago Youth Gangs: A New Old Problem," *Journal of Crime and Justice* 7 (1984), 3.
9. John Hagedorn and Perry Macon, *People and Folks*, 60.
10. *Ibid.*, 61.
11. Arlen Egley, Jr., and Mehala Arjunan, "Highlights of the 2000 National Youth Gang Survey," *OJJDP Fact Sheet #4* (Washington, DC: Office of Juvenile Justice and Delinquency Prevention, February 2002), 1.
12. *Ibid.*, 2.
13. L. Edward Wells and Ralph A. Weisheit, "Gang Problems in Nonmetropolitan Areas: A Longitudinal Assessment," *Justice Quarterly* 18, 4 (2001), 805, 811.
14. Arlen Egley, Jr. "National Youth Survey Trends from 1996 to 2000," *OJJDP Fact Sheet* (Washington, DC: Office of Juvenile Justice and Delinquency Prevention, February 2002), 2.
15. *Ibid.*

16. James C. Howell, "Gangs," *OJJDP Fact Sheet #12* (Washington, DC: Office of Juvenile Justice and Delinquency Prevention, April, 1994), 1.
17. Egley, "National Youth Survey Trends from 1996 to 2000," 2.
18. James C. Howell, "Gangs," 2.
19. Herbert Asbury, *The Gangs of New York* (New York: Capricorn Books, 1928); Walter B. Miller, "White Gangs," in James F. Short, Jr. *Modern Criminals* (New York, Chicago: Aldine, 1970), 46.
20. Asbury, *The Gangs of New York*, 29.
21. *Ibid.*
22. Frederick M. Thrasher, *The Gang* (Chicago: University of Chicago Press, 1927), 23–24.
23. William F. Whyte, *Street Corner Society*, 2nd ed. (Chicago: University of Chicago Press, 1955).
24. Richard R. Rettig, Manuel J. Torres, and Gerald R. Garrett, *Manny: A Criminal Addict's Story* (Boston: Houghton Mifflin, 1977), 19.
25. R. Lincoln Keiser, *The Vice Lords* (New York: Holt, Rinehart and Winston, 1969).
26. David Dawley, *A Nation of Lords* (Garden City, NY: Anchor Books, 1973), 109, 110, 113.
27. Gad J. Bensinger, "Chicago Youth Gangs: A New Old Problem," 4–5.
28. Walter B. Miller, *Violence by Youth Gangs and Youth Groups as a Crime Problem in Major American Cities* (Washington, DC: U.S. Government Printing Office, 1975), 1.
29. *Ibid.*, 2.
30. H. Craig Collins, "Street Gangs of New York: A Prototype of Organized Youth Crime," *Law & Order* 25 (1977), 5, 10–11.
31. Walter B. Miller, *Violence by Youth Gangs*, 9.
32. *Ibid.*, 21–23.
33. *Ibid.*
34. *Ibid.*, 26.
35. *Ibid.*, 35–36
36. *Ibid.*, 39
37. Walter B. Miller, *Crime by Youth Gangs and Groups in the United States* (Washington, DC: Office of Juvenile Justice and Delinquency Prevention, 1982).
38. C. Ronald Huff, "Youth Gangs and Public Policy in Ohio: Findings and Recommendations," paper presented at the Ohio Conference on Youth Gangs and the Urban Underclass, Columbus, Ohio, May 25, 1988, 8.
39. *Ibid.*, 3.
40. *Final Report, State Task Force on Youth Gang Violence* (Sacramento, CA: California Council on Criminal Justice, 1986), 11.
41. *Ibid* 12.
42. Gad J. Bensinger, "Chicago Youth Gangs: A New Old Problem," 7.
43. Malcolm W. Klein, Margaret A. Gordon, and Cheryl L. Maxson, "The Impact of Police Investigations on Police-Reported Rates of Gang and Nongang Homicides," *Criminology* 24, 3 (August 1986), 495–96.
44. Brian Skoloff, "Killings Jump in Some Cities; Gang Violence Blamed," *Akron Beacon Journal*, December 11, 2002, A13
45. *Ibid.*
46. James C. Howell and Debra K. Gleason, "Youth Gang Drug Trafficking," *OJJDP Juvenile Justice Bulletin* (Washington, DC: U.S. Department of Justice, December 1999), 3.
47. See S. H. Decker and B. Van Winkle, "Slinging Dope: The Role of Gangs and Gang Members in Drug Sales," *Justice Quarterly* 11, 4 (1994), 583–604 and J.C. Howell and S. H. Decker, *The Youth Gangs, Drugs, and Violence Connection* (Washington, DC: U.S. Department of Justice, 1999).
48. Joseph F. Sheley and James D. Wright, *Gun Acquisitions and Possession in Selected Juvenile Samples* (Washington, DC: U.S. Department of Justice, 1993), 1.
49. *Ibid.*, 9.
50. *Ibid.*

51. Barry Krisberg, "Gang Youth and Hustling: The Psychology of Survival," in Barry Krisberg and James Austin, *The Children of Ishmael* (Palo Alto, CA: Mayfield, 1978), 244.
52. *Ibid.*, 245.
53. Thrasher, *The Gang*, 31, 33.
54. *Ibid.*, 52.
55. *Ibid.*, 47–48.
56. Clifford Shaw, *Delinquency Areas* (Chicago: University of Chicago Press, 1929).
57. Henry D. McKay, "A Note on Trends in Rates of Delinquency in Certain Areas in Chicago," Appendix F, in *Task Force Report: Juvenile Delinquency and Youth Crime* (Washington, DC: U.S. Government Printing Office, 1967), 114–18.
58. Frank Tannenbaum, *Crime and the Community* (New York: Columbia University Press, 1939), 9–13.
59. Whyte, *Street Corner Society*.
60. Albert K. Cohen, *Delinquent Boys* (New York: Free Press, 1955), 24–31.
61. Walter Miller, "Lower Class Culture as a Generating Milieu of Gang Delinquency,' *The Journal of Social Issues* 14, 3 (1958), 10.
62. *Ibid.*, 17.
63. Michael Lewis, "Structural Deviance and Normative Conformity: The 'Hustle' and the Gang," in Daniel Glaser, ed., *Crime in the City* (New York: Harper & Row, 1970), 189.
64. Richard A. Cloward and Lloyd E. Ohlin, "Illegitimate Means, Differential Opportunity and Delinquency Subcultures," in *Delinquency and Opportunity: A Theory Of Delinquent Gangs* (New York: Free Press, 1961).
65. *Ibid.*
66. Block and Block, *Street Gang Crime in Chicago*, 2–3.
67. *Ibid.*, 3.
68. Carl S. Taylor, "Gang Imperialism," in C. Ronald Huff, ed., *Gangs in America* (Newbury Park, CA: Sage Publications, 1990), 105.
69. *Ibid.*, 108.
70. *Ibid.*, 115.
71. *ABC Nightly News*, February 8, 1995.
72. Peter C. Kratcoski, interview with members of the Cleveland, OH, Caribbean Gang Task Force, February 8, 1995.
73. Hagedorn and Macon, *People and Folks*, 100.
74. *Ibid.*, 101.
75. Robert K. Jackson and Wesley D. McBride, *Understanding Street Gangs* (Placerville, CA: Custom, 1990), 90.
76. *Ibid.*, 91.
77. Howell, *Gangs*, 2.
78. Bob Herbert, "A River of Blood Links the Street to the Capitol," *Akron Beacon Journal*, August 26, 1994, A9.
79. Lewis Yablonsky, *The Violent Gang* (Baltimore: Penguin Books, 1966), 141–147.
80. Lewis, "Structural Deviance," 194–95.
81. *Ibid.*, 194–98.
82. "Juvenile Charged as Asian Gang Enforcer," *IAACI News* 8, 6 (January/February 1995), 15.
83. Moore, "Gangs and the Underclass," 12–13.
84. Hagedorn and Macon, *People and Folks*, 142.
85. Jackson and McBride, *Understanding Street Gangs*, 25–26.
86. Taylor, "Gang Imperialism," 113
87. C. Ronald Huff, "Youth Gangs and Public Policy," *Crime and Delinquency* 35 (October 1989), 528–529.
88. James A. Inciardi, Ruth Horowitz, and Anne E. Pottieger, *Street Kids, Street Drugs, Street Crime: An Examination of Drug Use and Serious Delinquency in Miami* (Belmont, CA: Wadsworth, 1993), 98.

89. Hagedorn and Macon, *People and Folks*, 142.
90. *Ibid.*
91. Inciardi, Horowitz, and Pottieger, *Street Kids, Street Drugs, Street Crime*, 102.
92. *Ibid.*, 105
93. *Ibid.*
94. Mercer L. Sullivan, "Greed Causes Youth Violence," in Michael D. Biskus, ed. *Youth Violence* (San Diego, CA: Greenhaven Press, 1992), 93.
95. William J. Wilson, "Cycles of Deprivation and the Underclass Debate," *Social Service Review* 59, 4 (1996), 541–559.
96. Hagedorn and Macon, *People and Folks*, 142.
97. Randall G. Shelden, Sharon K. Tracy, and William B. Brown, *Youth Gangs in American Society* (Belmont, CA: Wadsworth, 2001), 191.
98. James Alan Fox and Glenn Pierce, "American Killers Are Getting Younger," *USA Today* 122, 2484 (January 1994), 25.
99. Stephen W. Baron, Leslie W. Kennedy, and David R. Forde, "Male Street Youths' Conflict: The Role of Background, Subcultural, and Situational Factors," *Justice Quarterly* 18, 4 (December 2001), 759–790.
100. Moore, *Gangs and the Underclass*, 8.
101. William Gale, *The Compound* (New York: Rawson Associates Publishers, 1977), 14–16.
102. The quotation from "The Compound" by William Gale is used by permission of Rawson Associates Publishers, Inc., 52–53.
103. Abraham H. Maslow, *Motivation and Personality* (New York: Harper and Row, 1954) in John Klofas, Stan Stojkovic, and David Kalinich, *Criminal Justice Organizations: Administration and Management* (Pacific Grove, CA: Brooks/Cole, 1989), 81–82.
104. Jackson and McBride, *Understanding Street Gangs*, 6.
105. *Ibid.*, 5–8.
106. James F. Short, Jr. and Fred L. Strodtbeck, *Group Process and Gang Delinquency* (Chicago: University of Chicago Press, 1965), 25–46.
107. Huff, "Youth Gangs and Public Policy in Ohio," 11.
108. Thrasher, *The Gang*, 26.
109. Yablonsky, *The Violent Gang*, 227.
110. Finn-Aage Esbensen and David Huizinga, "Gangs, Drugs, and Delinquency in a Survey of Urban Youth," *Criminology* 31, 4 (1993), 565–590.
111. Dale G. Hardman, "Small Town Gangs," *Journal of Criminal Law, Criminology, and Police Science* 60, 2 (June 1969), 176.
112. H. Craig Collins, "Street Gangs of New York: A Prototype of Organized Youth Crime," *Law & Order* 25 (1977), 10–11.
113. *Time*, July 11, 1977, 20.
114. Collins, "Street Gangs of New York," 11.
115. *Akron Beacon Journal*, April 27, 1993, A1–4.
116. *Akron Beacon Journal*, July 8, 1993, A6.
117. Jody Miller and Rod K. Brunson, "Gender Dynamics in Youth Gangs: A Comparison of Males' and Females' Accounts," *Justice Quarterly* 17, 3 (September 2000), 438–439.
118. *Time*, July 11, 1977, 20.
119. Thrasher, *The Gang*, 161.
120. William Bernard, *Jail Bait* (New York: Breenberg, 1949).
121. Walter B. Miller, "The Molls," *Society* 11 (1973) 32–35; E. Ackely and B. Fliegel, "A Social Work Approach to Street Corner Girls," *Social Work* 5 (1960), 29–31.
122. Walter B. Miller, *Violence by Youth Gangs and Youth Groups*, 23.
123. Anne Campbell, *The Girls in the Gang* (New York: Basil Blackwell, 1984), 28.
124. "Girl Gangs on Rise and Dangerous," *CJ the Americas* 1, 4 (August–September 1988), 11.
125. Hagedorn and Macon, *People and Folks*, 86.
126. *Akron Beacon Journal*, April 27, 1993, A4.
127. Egley and Arjunana, "Highlights of the 2000 National Youth Gang Survey," 2.

128. Miller, *Violence by Youth Gangs and Youth Groups as a Crime Problem in Major American Cities*, 2.
129. Jody Miller, *One of the Guys* (New York: Oxford University Press, 2001).
130. Jackson and McBride, *Understanding Street Gangs*, 37.
131. Finn-Aage Esbensen and Elizabeth Piper Deschenes," A Multisite Examination of Youth Gang Membership: Does Gender Matter?" *Criminology* 36, 4 (1998), 799–828.
132. Campbell, *The Girls in the Gang*, 266.
133. Howell, *Gangs*, 1.
134. Thad Alexander, Panelist, "Violence in the Schools Seminar," Columbus, OH, October 21, 1994.
135. Howard N. Snyder and Melissa Sickmund, *Juvenile Offenders and Victims: 1999 National Report* (Washington, DC: Office of Juvenile Justice and Delinquency Prevention, 1999), 78.
136. Hardman, "Small Town Gangs," 176–177.
137. Wooden, *Renegade Kids, Suburban Outlaws*, 3.
138. *Ibid.*, 115–185.
139. Mark S. Hamm, "A Modified Social Control Theory of Terrorism: An Empirical and Ethnographic Assessment of the American Neo-Nazi Skinheads," in *Hate Crime: International Perspectives on Causes and Control*, Mark S. Hamm, ed., (Cincinnati, OH: Anderson Publishing Company, 1994), 105–149.
140. Irving A. Spergel and G. David Curry, "Reducing Gang Violence: An Overview," in Michael D. Biskup, ed., *Youth Violence* (San Diego, CA: Greenhaven Press, 1992), 175.
141. Block and Block, *Street Gang Crime in Chicago*, 9.
142. Egley and Arjunan, "Highlights of the 2000 National Youth Gang Survey," 3.
143. Block and Block, *Street Gang Crime in Chicago*, 9.
144. *Ibid.*
145. Carol A. Archbold and Michael Meyer, "Anatomy of a Gang Suppression Unit: The Social Construction of an Organizational Response to Gang Problems," *Police Quarterly* 2, 2 (June 1999), 201–224.
146. Hechinger, "Saving Youth from Violence," 14.
147. Huff, "Youth Gangs and Public Policy in Ohio," 11–14.
148. Final Report, *State Task Force on Youth Gang Violence*, 40–45.
149. Summarized by Peter C. Kratcoski from *Gang Related Legislation*, www.iir.com/nygc/ganglegis/Miscellaneous%20Gang%20Legislation.htm, February 16, 2003.

CHAPTER 7

FAMILY FUNCTIONING AND DELINQUENCY

(Photo credit: Mike Mazzaschi/Stock Boston)

THE CONTEMPORARY FAMILY AS A SOCIALIZATION AGENCY
THE CHANGING AMERICAN FAMILY
THE INFLUENCE OF THE FAMILY ON DELINQUENT BEHAVIOR
     Conditions that Contribute to Family Disruption
     Financial Aid for Economically Deprived Children
     Delinquency and Disrupted Family Structure
     Socialization and Delinquency
     Family Violence and Delinquency
     Delinquency and Parental Rejection
     Relationship of Consistent and Adequate Discipline to Delinquency
VALUES AND DELINQUENCY

Studies of delinquency causation conducted by psychological and sociological researchers have invariably touched in some way on the influence of the family, and particularly parents, on the development or prevention of delinquency. We noted in Chapter 5 that the juvenile court was developed around the principle of *parens patriae*, meaning that the court adopts the posture of a "benevolent parent" toward youths whose training and supervision by their natural parents have apparently been inadequate to prevent the occurrence of unacceptable behavior.

Psychologists, in their studies of the relationship of family life to delinquency development, have concentrated on testing the effects of early childhood influences on delinquent behavior in adolescence, the effect of family size and ordinal position of a child within the family on juvenile misbehavior patterns, and the role of various child-rearing and disciplining factors in character formation. Sociologists have tended to concentrate their research on such matters as the relation delinquency may have to broken homes, mothers' employment outside the home, social class, poverty, urban or rural residence, educational levels of parents, and parental expectations.

Much of the early research on family conditions contributing to delinquency stressed such factors as the difficulties encountered by families that were attempting to adapt to hostile environments (rural families that had emigrated to cities, immigrant families from foreign countries) or the detrimental effects of criminal or alcoholic tendencies of the parents.[1] Such research based its definitions of family disruption on the assumption that the "typical" American family was one in which both parents lived in one residence, with definite status positions existing within the family—including the father as chief breadwinner and authority figure, the mother as the source of emotional support for other family members, and the children as the objects of the parents' efforts to prepare them for an adulthood not radically different from their own. Economic and geographic stability were also regarded as indicative of family integration.

THE CONTEMPORARY FAMILY AS A SOCIALIZATION AGENCY

Today, it is apparent that the "typical American family" no longer exists (if, in fact, it ever did). The most obvious change is that the number of mothers employed full-time has increased dramatically, so that, in 2000, it was estimated that four out of five American infants and schoolage children had working mothers.[2] The U.S. Census Bureau estimated that more than 500,000 children between the ages of 6 and 11 must care for themselves at home alone between the time they return from school and their parents get home from work.[3] Three out of 10 children lived in single parent homes in 1997 and in 85 percent of these homes, the single parent was the mother. Never-married parents are also becoming more common. Of children living in single parent homes in 1997, about the same percentage were living with never married parents (38%) as with divorced parents (36%).[4]

Obviously, modifications in family life and activities are necessary to deal with and adjust to divorce or separation of the spouses, frequent mobility, situations in which parents alternate or even exchange various role functions, blending of children from previous marriages into the new family unit, and varied social and cultural settings. A contemporary family can offer stability, emotional support, and satisfaction to its members when the members cooperate in striving toward a common set of goals. This remains true even though the family must constantly adjust to the demands and pressures of modern life. The family can best adapt and adjust when it functions as a system.

The notion that a family constitutes a system is developed from a comparison of the family with a living body having interrelated parts that support and complement each other's functions. Just as a malfunction of one body part affects the entire physical system and may require compensation by other parts to keep the system functioning, or may eventually lead to morbidity or death, difficulties within a family regarded as a system may have analogous results. The common values and goals of a family make it possible for it to function as a system and meet the challenges that confront the individual members of the entire unit. The specific structure and mechanisms a family adopts to meet these challenges and problems, however, may vary widely from one family unit to the next.

When a family has a set pattern of operation that involves establishing limits on the behavior of each member and achieving mutually satisfying modes of interaction by all members, the family is said to be in a state of *homeostasis,* and the processes by which families develop predictable patterns of interaction are known as *homeostatic mechanisms.*[5] For example, the fact that the mother prepares breakfast for the children each morning and is always there to greet them when they return from school could be a crucial homeostatic mechanism in one family but simply not apply to another. Regardless of the particular homeostatic mechanisms a family has developed, dramatic changes in these mechanisms may result in undesirable reactions by the children. For example, suppose a father who has established a pattern of closely supervising his children and devoting a great amount of attention to their activities takes a new job that requires him to be away from home for extended periods. The absence of the close supervision and attention the children are accustomed to receiving from the father may lead to misbehavior or other bizarre behavior patterns as a means of gaining from some other adult the attention they have lost.

Family counselors often use the concept of "healthy family" to designate a functioning family. Jacqueline Cook, a family therapist, described some of the characteristics of a healthy family.

- A healthy family provides for nurturing and emotional well-being of the parents or authority figures. . . . New research is showing that if the parents are supportive and caring of each other, then it has a very beneficial impact on the children. . . . The parents' needs should be met as well as the children's.
- The healthy family has good communication, which . . . sets the stage for success in all of the other areas. . . . The parents do provide some leadership and set some ground rules. . . . Parents should strive to provide authoritative, rather than authoritarian, leadership. . . . The healthy family works together to resolve difficulties.
- The healthy family encourages family time in which an atmosphere is created for fellowship, communication, as well as problem solving.
- The healthy family also makes time for play and humor.
- The American family is being reconfigured, . . . Previously, families were expected to focus solely on the physical survival of their members. Now, they are expected to provide a great deal of emotional and social support as well.[6]

The early involvement of a child within a family provides the framework in which the child learns about the culture, develops personality traits, and forms a character and a sense of morality. Not only does the child depend upon its parents for food, clothing, and shelter, but the child's self-image, and feelings of worth and of being loved or rejected are developed within the family. Parents are responsible for the behavior of their children, with the widest possible application of the word "responsible." This implies not only their acceptance of responsibility for the children's supervision, but also their realization that they contribute to their children's moral and educational development in a manner that external agencies cannot duplicate.

The teaching process between parent and child is most often not a formal instructional exercise but a day-to-day exchange of cues as to what is appropriate and what is not for a member of their particular family. From observation of their parents, children internalize notions about how a husband should treat a wife and a wife should treat a husband; what the place of a child is in a family setting; how to respond to crisis situations; how to regard and relate to neighbors, acquaintances, and strangers; and many other complex lessons in human interaction.

THE CHANGING AMERICAN FAMILY

Of course, the family does not exist or perform its socialization functions in a vacuum. On the contrary, it reflects and relates to economic, governmental, educational, and religious institutions. As the society in which the family unit functions has changed, family structures and processes have also been altered and adapted to new social and cultural situations. The following factors have had dramatic effects on the contemporary American family:

1. *Urbanization.* For the socially disadvantaged, the problems of urban living include overcrowded and substandard housing, crime and victimization, and so-

cial isolation from neighbors. For the more affluent, the difficulties involve long commuting distances to work for parents, with a resulting lack of before- and afterschool supervision of children, and the lure of large shopping malls, which may be locations for drug dealing.

2. *Industrialization.* Effects of industrialization on the family include children's lack of familiarity with adult work, the impersonality and repetitiousness of work skills, and the increasing number of women in the work force.

3. *Changes in transportation and communication.* Americans, regardless of their place of residence, are increasingly aware of lifestyles and behavior patterns of people in all social strata. Young people are made aware of changing moral values and behavior in our society and can observe trends in dress, popular music, violent behavior, and drug or alcohol use that would have been communicated to them much more slowly and guardedly in earlier eras. Easy access to transportation has compounded the problem of runaway activity.

4. *Changing values:*
   (a) A more liberal attitude toward premarital sex and children born to unmarried mothers. This in turn has led a larger proportion of unmarried mothers to keep their babies rather than give them up for adoption.
   (b) Acceptance of divorce as an alternative to an unworkable family situation, and reduction of the stigma and ill feeling that formerly characterized a divorce action.
   (c) Recognition of women as important breadwinners for the family and acceptance of the working mother not only as one who is contributing to the family income, but also as an individual who has a right to seek self-fulfillment in the world of work rather than in the home.
   (d) Development of new marriage styles, including trial periods of cohabitation before marriage, postponement of childbearing, and marriages that are childless by design.
   (e) Alteration of the family from a child-centered institution to one in which parents also seek to develop and fulfill their aspirations.
   (f) Realization that a broken home or an arrangement in which separated or divorced parents alternate responsibility for care of the children need not be a negative or harmful aspect of a child's development.
   (g) A new view of the place of women in the family unit and in the larger society.

THE INFLUENCE OF THE FAMILY ON DELINQUENT BEHAVIOR

Conditions that Contribute to Family Disruption

In Chapters 5 and 6, we considered how such factors as unemployment, poverty, overcrowded, dilapidated housing or homelessness, poor health, and inadequate health care may be related to juvenile delinquency. The same conditions have obvious detrimental effects on parents and caregivers. Suicide, alcoholism, drug addiction, family violence, and desertion are prevalent in families who have had to face such conditions. Even if the parents are conscious of their roles and try very hard to do the right things for their children, opportunities for bonding, positive interaction, and activity as a family may be lacking because of the pressures of these other problems.

Families may be physically disrupted by the loss of either parent through death, desertion, separation, or divorce. The increases in unemployment, homelessness, and poverty that are occurring (a 6% unemployment rate in the United States in 2002, a poverty rate of 11.7%, and an ever-increasing number of homeless people)[7] are sure to have strong influences on family functioning and stability. Fifteen percent of all homeless are part of a family, often headed by a woman (84%). The average number of children attached to homeless families was 2.2.[8]

Financial Aid for Economically Deprived Children

Throughout most of the history of the United States, the task of providing economic assistance and social services to families in need was carried out by private agencies, chiefly by church-related organizations. However, state governments have always had some concern with the plight of the poor, especially of poor families with children. In the early 1900s, the states began giving financial support to widows, their children, and orphans.[9] In 1909, President Theodore Roosevelt convened the first White House Conference on Children for the purpose of deterring child labor and providing public assistance to widows with young children through "mothers' pensions" so it would not be necessary for the mothers to work outside the home.[10] The Social Security Act of 1935 established Aid to Dependent Children. This program, commonly referred to as welfare, consisted of federal/state involvement in jointly funded aid. This funding was administered by the state and local governments.[11] In 1962, Aid to Dependent Children was officially renamed Aid for Dependent Children (AFDC) and the program was designed to help keep the children in their own homes whenever possible. It also more clearly defined who were the "deserving poor," compared to the "undeserving poor." Previously, eligibility varied according the conditions set down by the various states. Families headed by widowed mothers were considered to be the "deserving poor," compared to families headed by never-married or divorced women, who were frequently defined as the "undeserving poor" by those administering the programs.[12] This change in focus broadened the eligibility population for this assistance and continued the trend to provide for care of the dependent children in their own homes.

The political debate over who is "deserving" or "undeserving" of assistance continues today. Legislation enacted in the 1960s and 1970s created incentives for families on AFDC to gain work skills and experiences, but later legislation required that the benefits of mothers who were employed would be reduced in proportion to their incomes.[13] Such stipulations negatively affected the welfare recipients' incentives to seek employment and often resulted in "welfare fraud." Gradually, dependence on welfare became a way of life and several generations of mothers and children came to view this support as an entitlement and ceased making efforts to provide for themselves. This led to the emergence of what has been termed a "culture of poverty" that profoundly affects the socialization, opportunities, and aspirations of children conditioned to this way of life.

Delinquency and Disrupted Family Structure

Families may be physically disrupted by the loss of either parent through death, desertion, separation, or divorce. Rosen and Neilson reviewed 15 studies published over a 43-year period that investigated the relationship of a broken home (a home characterized by the absence of at least one natural parent or stepparent) to male delinquency. They found that broken homes were only weakly related to delinquency when comparisons were made by race, social class, and age of the sample members[14] Hardy and Cull noted that loss of either parent through death does not seem to be as harmful an experience for children as loss of a parent through divorce or separation.[15]

Although youths from broken homes tend to be referred to juvenile courts more often than youths from intact ones, this fact cannot be taken at face value as an indicator that broken homes foster delinquent activity. Instead, it may be a reflection of differential treatment of young people by the police and the courts. When interacting with young people from broken homes, police officers and court officials may decide to handle a case officially rather than informally because they believe that a single parent needs more support in controlling a child's behavior. Hirschi found that, of boys who experienced police contacts, fatherless boys were more likely to be picked up by the police than were boys with fathers or stepfathers.[16] In light of these findings, it seems reasonable to suggest that studies of the relation between delinquency and broken homes would have greater validity if the researchers relied on self-reported delinquency measures rather than analyses of juvenile court or police-contact records. A self-reported delinquency study of high school students by Van Voorhis et al. found that a broken home was less important in determining delinquency than was the quality of family life.[17]

Studies that have examined the relation between broken homes and delinquency have consistently noted that female delinquents are more likely than male delinquents to come from dysfunctional families. It may be that family disintegration has a more profound effect on girls, who are normally more carefully supervised and have fewer opportunities than boys to develop extensive peer-group contacts outside the home that can serve as family substitutes. Another possibility is that parents in a disintegrating family structure feel helpless in minor instances of rebellion or undesirable behavior by their daughters and seek help from the juvenile court in handling them, whereas behavior of comparable severity by their sons is not regarded so seriously. Such referrals of females frequently take the form of "incorrigibility" or runaway cases. Findings regarding the sexual abuse of girls in the family setting by natural fathers or by stepfathers[18] highlight the fact that a large number of female runaways from physically or psychologically broken homes who are charged and labeled as delinquents may be taking flight as a self-preservation tactic.

Research by Canter has challenged the notion that a broken home has a greater impact on the behavior of females than of males. Her National Youth Survey, a longitudinal study of delinquent behavior in a national probability sample of adolescents, revealed that a broken home has a comparable impact on boys and girls and that it has a greater impact on males than on females in the area of offenses that reflect a lack of parental supervision or control.[19] The difficulties faced by delinquent girls whose families are characterized as "dysfunctional" are discussed in detail in Chapter 8.

A family unit that is physically intact but characterized by internal conflict and constant tension may also contribute to delinquency. In her study of delinquent behavior by affluent youths, Freeman observed that all the boys she studied came from intact, middle-class families where parents had never had contacts with law enforcement or social agencies, but that their family lives were nevertheless beset with serious psychological problems. Fathers of these boys tended to be aggressive and hostile in their relations with other family members, yet in the majority of the families, the mother made the major decisions. The parents were found to be inconsistent in their child-rearing practices and the boys viewed neither parent as "dependable."[20]

Socialization and Delinquency

Analysis of the socialization of children within families can offer considerable insight into the causes and motivations for delinquent behavior. Parents' attitudes, behavior, communication or lack of communication with their children, and manner and consistency of disciplining are all factors associated with developing self-control, respect for authority, responses to stressful events, acceptance of responsibility, and realization of consequences for behavior.[21] Hirschi noted that attachment to parents is a

Family dysfunction frequently results in family violence. *(Photo credit: Ernie Mastroianni)*

central variable of control theory, since children's attachment to parents helps explain the process through which norms are internalized by the child.[22] He drew on the work of Nye, who theorized that:

> . . . if the child is alienated from the parent, he will not learn or will have no feelings for moral rules, he will not develop an adequate conscience or superego.[23]

Hirschi found that strong attachment to parents is closely related to a lack of deviance. He also found that this holds true regardless of the social class of the parents. Children of lower class parents are as likely to be attached to their parents as children from the middle class and:

> . . . the child attached to a low-status parent is no more likely to be delinquent than the child attached to a high-status parent.[24]

In another study testing the relation of attachment to parents and delinquency, Hope gathered self-report data from more than 1,000 middle school and high school students from a semi-rural university town that was predominantly white. She explored the relationship of family characteristics of the students and their membership or lack of membership in gangs. Hope found that parental deviance had a direct effect on gang members. She concluded that "those who live in violent homes are at a greater risk for gang membership."[25] Gang members, however, did not differ significantly from nongang members on measures of attachment to their parents or being poorly supervised. Gang members did measure significantly lower on self-control.[26]

Family Violence and Delinquency

Physical violence directed by children toward parents has also been found to be closely related to high levels of emotional tension within the family and physical abuse of children by parents. A number of researchers have documented the fact that deviant or unacceptable behavior by youths is closely related to emotional stress and high levels of tension in the family environment.[27]

A study completed by Straus compared the amount of corporal punishment used by two nationwide samples of parents 10 years apart and found that the proportion of parents using corporal punishment of any kind was virtually the same for the two samples. However, he found a decrease in the more severe forms of corporal punishment such as hitting a child with an object.[28] He also discovered rather drastic decreases in the frequency with which corporal punishment was used in the later sample.

Despite the fact that almost all American children have been hit, there are large differences between families in three aspects of corporal punishment:

- The frequency of hitting. For some it is a rare event; for others it occurs daily.
- The severity of the hitting. For some it is a mild slap on the hand or buttocks, for others it is being hit with a belt or paddle.

- The duration of the attacks; that is, the number of years parents continue to hit. Some stop when the child is about school age; others continue to hit for many years.[29]

Straus found that mothers hit both younger and older children more often than fathers did, possibly because they spend so much more time with the children. Parents who were hit by their own parents tended to hit their own children at a higher rate.[30] Parents who were violent toward each other were more likely than other parents to hit their children, and marital violence also increased the probability that older children (ages 16 and older) would be hit by their parents. Almost all parents hit toddlers, although the spankings tended to be very mild. He also found that there was no relationship between socio-economic status and the use of corporal punishment. He concluded that the differences in the social classes in several aspects of life styles have been decreasing, and the use of corporal punishment may be one of these.[31] Straus concluded that, while the majority of children who are spanked do not become delinquent, and perhaps for most children mild spanking may be harmless, nevertheless receiving corporal punishment as a child is significantly related to marital violence as an adult.[32]

Straus used a self-report questionnaire to ask 385 college students if they had received corporal punishment and whether they had committed any delinquent offenses. He found that:

> Students who were hit were more likely to be involved in both violent crime and property crime. Similar results were found for the other delinquent acts.[33]

Mann, who researched the murder of pre-school-age children by their mothers, discovered that children under age six accounted for 61 percent of the children murdered by their mothers.[34] According to Straus, the extensive time the mothers must spend with young children, the stress involved, early age of marriage and the birth of unwanted children, lack of parenting skills, and social isolation are factors that contribute to this extreme violence against young children.[35]

Children who have been the subjects of abusive treatment frequently become child abusers when they become parents because they have internalized the notion that severe physical punishment is an acceptable part of child rearing. In the same way, delinquent behavior by children, while not necessarily imitative of the conduct of parents, may be a direct result of adaptations to life learned or experienced at home. For example, drug or alcohol abuse by children may be an imitation of the methods they have seen their parents use to deal with or escape from pressures, even though the parental conduct is far less extreme in degree or style than that of the children.

The relation of family functioning to violent behavior of family members toward each other was highlighted in a study of levels of family functioning and intrafamily violence. Families in the study were rated as having low, moderate, or high functioning levels, based on such factors as frequency of communication, interaction in and sharing of social activities, and amount of mutual support and concern. It was found that intrafamily violence (defined as an act toward another family member or family members which threatened or inflicted physical harm) was most likely to occur in homes characterized by low levels of family functioning. Problems in the low-functioning families included disagreements over money matters, inappropriate discipline measures, substance-abuse problems, and lack of meaningful communication between family members.[36]

A national study of family violence conducted by the URSA Institute, based on victims' accounts, concluded that exposure to domestic violence during childhood, as either victim or witness, is the strongest predictor of future violence toward other family members.[37] A study of homicides in which the assailant and the victim were members of the same family revealed that 19 percent of the killings were performed by persons under 24 years of age, usually young males. The incidents tended to occur in the home, during or after a quarrel, in a spontaneous manner. The assailants tended to have previous delinquency records that included violent behavior, and in many instances they had experienced disruptive family lives.[38]

Delinquency and Parental Rejection

A number of researchers have found a relationship between parental rejection and aggressive delinquent behavior. Davids emphasized the important role a father can play in preventing delinquency by establishing strong and meaningful contacts with

Family violence can have profound effects on children.
(Photo credit: Michael Newman/PhotoEdit)

his children. He maintained that if the father accepts his role of parent with all of the responsibilities attached, the socialization process should produce a firmer identification with the desired roles and values on the part of the children.[39]

Davids advocated a training program to teach fathers to become more effective parents and pointed out two areas in which many fathers display ignorance. First, according to Davids, it is important for fathers to better understand the nature of the social environment of the contemporary urban adolescent, which includes high school, television, and peer groups. How does each of these influences affect the identity and attitudes of adolescents? And second, many fathers need to become more aware of the dynamics of the parent–child relationship, particularly during late childhood and adolescence. Davids suggested certain techniques for improving communication between father and child, helping promote a stronger sense of identity through parental role modeling, and encouraging growth in healthy and fulfilling directions through consistent positive reinforcement. To aid in the development of parental effectiveness, he advocated training fathers through role playing, group discussions with peers, and instruction in basic child and adolescent psychology.[40]

Other innovative programs are designed to offer guidance to young unwed fathers. The Responsive Fathers Program, a national demonstration project partially funded by the Ford Foundation, explores ways to help such men take legal, financial, and emotional responsibility for their children. Since many of those involved are inner-city men with limited education and little work experience, they are encouraged to complete Graduate Equivalency Diplomas (GEDs) from high school and become involved in job training programs. They are also provided opportunities to interact with and care for their children. Many of these men had received little or no attention from their own fathers and need assistance in learning how to relate to their children.[41]

Relationship of Consistent and Adequate Discipline to Delinquency

The mechanisms used within families for controlling youthful behavior can have a significant bearing on the activities of children. Hirschi found that the incidence of delinquency increased with the number of hours mothers were employed outside the home. Those youths whose mothers were employed full time were most prone to delinquency, followed by those with mothers who were employed part time. Those whose mothers were housewives had the lowest rates of delinquency. Hirschi attributed this finding to the fact that mothers who were not employed spent more time directly supervising their children's activities and behavior.[42]

The commonly held belief that boys commit more delinquent acts than girls because they are not as closely supervised and controlled was tested by Jensen and Eve by means of a self-reported delinquency study. First, they categorized all subjects in the sample as being subjected to either low, moderate, or high levels of parental supervision; then, they compared the boys and girls in each category. The delinquent

The relation of parental rejection to future deviant behavior is dramatically illustrated by these descriptions of the childhood experiences of an abused wife who killed her husband. They reveal a great deal about the ways in which parental rejection and other mistreatment affected her.

June had been dumped at the front door of her grandparents' home the day she was born, as had her sister six years earlier. Their mother, Ann Jackson, was neither capable nor interested in raising children—she only enjoyed making them. Diane was sired by one man, June by another, and Dan, who came along three years later, by yet another unnamed and unknown father whom Ann had met and bedded after one of her nightly drinking bouts in an equally undistinguished local bar. . . .

"A complete absence of love" was how June characterized her childhood. "And quiet. It was too quiet in our house. My grandparents never spoke. They just didn't care about us, couldn't be bothered. There was no interaction between us: no input, no punishment when we misbehaved, nothing. We never went anywhere or did anything: no beach, amusement park, picnics—none of the normal things families did. We even made our own breakfast when we were little."

"I remember climbing up on the stool in the morning to get the cereal down from the cupboard. And when I took a bath, I took it alone. I didn't have rubber duckies or anything like that to play with. My grandmother would leave me and come back thirty minutes later to see me shivering in the cold water." . . .

[When her mother visited], June's routine was always the same: kneel by her mother's chair and tug at her sleeve to get her attention, saying over and over, "Mama, mama, I'm so glad you're here. I have so much to tell you." But Mama was never interested in her

younger daughter and always turned her attention to Diane.

"I think I spent most of my childhood trying to get my mother's attention. And I never quit. Any normal kid would have given up at some point, but, considering the source, I wasn't what you would call normal. I kept hoping against hope that my mother—or my grandmother or grandfather or somebody—would love me. They never did."

No one knew where Ann Jackson lived or what she did, but one thing they knew was that she was an alcoholic. And she was not an attractive woman. Perhaps the two issues were related. "She didn't have a very pretty face. And she was uneducated. I don't know if she went to school or for how long. I remember hearing something about reform school or a juvenile detention center."

As an adolescent, June and a friend ran away. After a week of living on the streets, a man who had befriended them gave them bus fare to return home. Her comments on what happened when they returned reveal how much she yearned for someone to care about her.

Deborah [her runaway companion] expected her mother to be livid when she picked her up at the bus station, and she was not disappointed. The first thing the woman did was slap her daughter hard across the face the moment she was within reach. June watched almost with envy as Deborah's mother berated and continued to hit her daughter for running away. It was something June had never experienced from her grandparents, and though humiliating, it was the type of concern she had always longed for but never received.

Source: From FIGHTING BACK by Robert Davidson, copyright © 2000 by Robert Davidson. Used by permission of Ballantine Books, a division of Random House, Inc.

activity of the boys was greater than that of the girls regardless of the degree of parental supervision. For this sample, degree of supervision was not a significant factor in the amount of delinquent activity.[43]

The trend for unmarried adolescent mothers to keep their babies rather than give them up for adoption has created a new type of family situation in many areas, particularly in the cities. Unwed girls with one or more small children are leaving home and setting up independent households with male companions or other unmarried young women. The children of these young women, who are frequently supported by AFDC payments, are reared in environments of poverty and unstructured family life. Sometimes termed the "new underclass," this population of child-mothers—school dropouts with minimal education and skills—and their children presents problems for educational and social institutions which are unique to our time. The mothers lack the personal resources or commitment to discipline their children adequately. The children become streetwise at an early age and are endangered for involvement in delinquent activity. Juvenile courts and family courts that become involved in such cases are severely limited in their options for handling these children, as illustrated by the following case.

> Two brothers—ages 11 and 12—appeared yesterday in _____ _____ Juvenile Court to face charges in connection with a stolen car.
>
> They appeared alone. . . . They had no attorney. None of their relatives had come to court to be with them.
>
> "We've had no inquiries from their family about their whereabouts," _____ said after the hearing. "We've been unable to contact a parent or guardian."
>
> The boys and their 8-year-old brother were all picked up by _____ police in a [car] that had been reported stolen about an hour earlier. . . .
>
> All three boys—and two other siblings—have been in the custody of their grandmother.
>
> The boys' mother has eight children and does not have custody of any of them, said their aunt.[44]

Researchers who have examined inadequate parental discipline as a factor in delinquent behavior have found that when parents physically punish their children, or threaten to, the result may be aggressive behavior on the part of the children. This physical punishment is the termination of a chain of events in the parent–child relationship that begins when parents have unrealistic expectations about what can and should be expected of children at early stages of development. Acts which are normal for a child are viewed by such parents as disobedient or disrespectful, or as evidence of the child's tendency toward nonconformity, and are punished accordingly. Over time, the continued criticism and rejection of the child's behavior begins to be reflected in the child's interaction with peers, siblings, and even with adults, with physical aggression internalized as the proper reaction to frustration.[45]

Other studies have concluded that the level of parental control is related to delinquent behavior. Wells and Rankin found that direct controls of adolescents' behavior, in the form of setting rules, monitoring the youths' activities, and punishing them for violating rules, were related to involvement in delinquency. However, very strong or very weak parental involvement led to greater frequency of delinquency.[46] Similar findings were reported by Loeber and Stouthamer-Loeber[47] and Rollins and Thomas.[48] These researchers also concluded that very strict discipline or very low levels of parental control were less effective in obtaining desired behaviors from children than were moderately strict parental rules.[49]

VALUES AND DELINQUENCY

The challenging of parents' opinions and beliefs and the outright rejection of some of their values by young people have come to be recognized as a normal part of the maturation process in American society. However, *excessive* hostility toward parents and the *total* rejection of their values have been noted as characteristic of some delinquents.

Megargee and Golden compared the attitudes toward parents of three groups of juveniles—nondelinquents, subcultural delinquents (youths with essentially normal personality development who had internalized values at variance with conventional middleclass norms), and psychopathic delinquents (youths who had failed to develop the usual inhibitions against acting out their desires and were impulsive and guilt-free in their behavior). The nondelinquents expressed the most favorable attitudes toward both their mothers and their fathers, and the psychopathic delinquents the most negative. The subcultural delinquents displayed attitudes toward their mothers that were as favorable as those of nondelinquents, but were as negative in their attitudes toward their fathers as were the psychopathic delinquents. This finding pointed to the possibility that subcultural delinquents may identify with a delinquent peer group (frequently a gang) as a source of reinforcement because of problems in relating to their fathers. The positive attitudes of subcultural delinquents toward their mothers suggested that their mothers might be enlisted effectively in treating them.[50]

A study of the influence of family normlessness on the occurrence of delinquency discovered that such a condition correlates strongly with all types of delinquent behavior and that normlessness is more strongly related to delinquency by males than by females. Large differences were discovered in the incidence of felony property offenses and violent offenses among normless boys and girls, with the males displaying a much higher inclination toward these offenses.[51]

Piliavin, Vadum, and Hardyck developed a "costs-and-rewards" theory of delinquency by exploring the hypothesis that the greater a person's potential costs from committing a juvenile offense, the less likely he or she is to commit the offense. They compared both black youths' and white youths' needs for approval from their fathers, mothers, teachers, and school acquaintances. Using self-reported delinquency files, they also discovered the incidence of delinquent behavior among the student population. The researchers found that the greater the white youths' concern with approval by their fathers and mothers and at school, the less likely they were to have had police contacts, to have engaged in delinquent activity, or to have been officially referred to juvenile authorities. Among the black youths in this sample, however, the relationship between the need for approval and low delinquent activity held only in the case of concern with approval at school. Concern with approval by either parent did not significantly relate to involvement in delinquent activity. The authors interpreted this finding as indicating that virtually all white parents of the youths studied severely condemned and punished delinquency among their children, while a large number of the black parents tolerated it. The presence of such tolerance lowered the potential cost of delinquent behavior for the black children and increased the probability that it would occur.[52]

SUMMARY

In this chapter, we noted the changing nature of the American family and the stresses that contemporary living places on parental efforts to achieve stability in the family unit. The dynamic balance in the interaction of family members, known as homeostasis, may be achieved by widely varied homeostatic mechanisms, depending upon the lifestyle and role ascriptions or acceptances in that particular household. Loss of this balance caused by rapid or unforeseen changes may contribute to the development of juvenile misbehavior.

Parents have been identified as the first and most influential educators of their children in cultural, personality, and moral development. Such teaching may include the inculcation of undesirable as well as desirable attitudes and values. Delinquent behavior may result from youths' internalization of attitudes or behavior patterns that are at variance with accepted community norms.

A number of changes in contemporary society have been identified as affecting American family structures and practices. These include urbanization, industrialization, mobility, complex communication networks, and changing value systems. Most notable among observed changing values are the greater relaxation of sexual standards, the acceptance of divorce and varied marriage styles, a turning away from child-centered family life, and new views on the appropriate roles for women in the family unit and in the larger society.

Research studies of the influence of the family on delinquent behavior have documented the relation between the development of delinquency and the physical or psychological disruption of the family structure. Some studies have found female delinquents to be more deeply influenced by broken homes than males. Psychological disruption of the family through alcoholism, mental illness, emotional disturbance of parents, or home atmospheres characterized by internal conflict and constant tension have been identified as factors in delinquency production. Conversely, a number of studies have shown that a happy and well-structured family life is related to lack of delinquency and successful adjustment to society. Socialization was also identified as an important factor. Attachment to parents was found to be closely related to a lack of deviance, and children who observed and/or experienced family violence and excessive corporal punishment were found to be more prone to violent acts.

A number of researchers have established a relation between parental rejection and aggressive delinquent behavior. The important role of the father in delinquency prevention has also been stressed. Lack of consistent and adequate discipline has been documented in many cases of delinquent behavior. Finally, the extensive use of physical punishment is a recognized factor in the production of aggressive delinquent activity.

Although some testing and rejection of parental values is recognized as a normal part of the maturation process, excessive hostility toward parents and rejection of their values has been noted as a characteristic of certain types of delinquents, while the desire for approval by parents and school authorities has been documented as a delinquency-inhibiting factor. The "costs-and-rewards" theory of delinquency holds youths to be inhibited from delinquent behavior by their recognition of the potential costs of such activity. Researchers have discovered, however, that the costs-and-rewards factor was a more potent delinquency-reducing variable for white youths than for blacks, and suggested that socialization factors might be responsible for this variation. Successful family adjustment was also found to be related to lack of involvement in the drug subculture.

On the basis of these observations, it can be seen that the contemporary family, regardless of its style and structure, continues to be a potent force in delinquency prevention or generation. In combination with the influence of the school, the community, and the economic and social structure, it contributes greatly to the milieu in which each child is socialized and prepared for adult life.

DISCUSSION QUESTIONS

1. Compare the family as a system to the operation of a living body. What are some of the homeostatic mechanisms that might be part of the activities of a family with very small children?
2. Discuss how changing values and economic necessities in American life have altered the conception of the "typical American family."
3. How has the growth of an "underclass" of very young unwed mothers and their children created special problems for juvenile courts and social agencies? How can these problems be addressed?
4. Discuss how a strong family unit can serve as a buffer against delinquency.
5. Is it appropriate for parents to use physical punishment (spanking) as a means of controlling their misbehaving children?

NOTES

1. See W. Healy and A. L. Bronner, *Delinquents and Criminals: Their Making and Unmaking* (New York: Macmillan, 1926); Clifford R. Shaw and Henry D. McKay, "Social Factors in Juvenile Delinquency," in *Report on the Causes of Crime* (Washington, DC: U.S. Government Printing Office, 1931), 266–276; C. R. Shaw and H. D. McKay, *Juvenile Delinquency and Urban Areas* (Chicago: University of Chicago Press, 1942); Sheldon Glueck and Eleanor Glueck, *Unraveling Juvenile Delinquency* (New York: Commonwealth Fund, 1950); and Jackson Toby, "The Differential Impact of Family Disorganization," *American Sociological Review* 22 (October 1957), 505–512.
2. Theodora Lurie, "Improving the Quantity and Quality of Child Care," *USA Today* 120, 2554 (July 1991), 68.
3. *Akron Beacon Journal*, September 5, 1995, D5.
4. Howard N. Snyder and Melissa Sickmund, *Juvenile Offenders and Victims: 1999 National Report* (Washington, DC: Office of Juvenile Justice and Delinquency Prevention, 1999), 8.
5. Alfred P. French, *Disturbed Children and Their Families* (New York: Human Sciences Press, 1977), 21–22.
6. Jacqueline Cook, "What Makes Families Happy and Stable?" *USA Today* 212, 2575 (April 1993), 1–2.
7. U.S. Bureau of the Census Report, cited in the *Akron Beacon Journal*, September 25, 2002, A8.
8. U.S. Department of Housing and Urban Development, cited in Timothy Williams, "Homelessness Breaking NYC," *Akron Beacon Journal*, August 21, 2002, A9.
9. Susan Gluck Mezey, *Children in Court* (Albany, NY: State University of New York Press, 1996), 32.

10. *Ibid.*
11. *Ibid.*, 33.
12. *Ibid.*
13. *Ibid.*, 34.
14. Lawrence Rosen and Kathleen Neilson, "The Broken Home and Delinquency," in Leonard D. Savitz and Norman Johnston, *Crime in Society* (New York: Wiley, 1978), 406–413.
15. Richard E. Hardy and John G. Cull, *Climbing Ghetto Walls* (Springfield, IL: Charles C. Thomas, 1973), 22.
16. Travis Hirschi, *Causes of Delinquency* (Berkeley, CA: University of California Press, 1969), 242–243.
17. Patricia Van Voorhis, Francis T. Cullen, Richard A. Mathers, and Connie Chenoweth Garner, "The Impact of Family Structure and Quality on Delinquency: A Comparative Assessment of Structural and Functional Factors," *Criminology* 26, 2 (May 1988), 235–262.
18. David Finkelhor, *Sexually Victimized Children* (New York: Free Press, 1979), 88–89.
19. Rachelle J. Canter, "Family Correlates of Male and Female Delinquency," *Criminology* 20, 2 (August 1982), 163–164.
20. Beatrice Freeman, George Savastano, and J.J. Tobias, "The Affluent Suburban Male Delinquent," *Crime and Delinquency* 16 (1970), 262–272.
21. Kevin Lamb, "The Causal Factors of Crime: Understanding the Subculture of Violence," *The Mankind Quarterly*, 36 (1995), 105–116.
22. Hirschi, *Causes of Delinquency*, 86.
23. William Nye, "Family Relationships," in William and Joan McCord, *Origins of Crime* (New York: Columbia University Press, 1959), 71.
24. Hirschi, *Causes of Delinquency*, 108.
25. Trina L. Hope, "Do Families Matter?" in Thomas C. Calhoun and Constance L. Chapple, *Readings in Juvenile Delinquency and Juvenile Justice* (Upper Saddle River, NJ: Prentice Hall, 2003), 180
26. *Ibid.*
27. See Peter C. Kratcoski and Lucille Dunn Kratcoski, "The Relationship of Victimization through Child Abuse to Aggressive Delinquent Behavior," paper presented at the annual meeting of the American Society of Criminology, San Francisco, 1980; Richard J. Gelles and Murray A. Straus, "Determinants of Violence in the Family: Toward a Theoretical Integration," in Wesley R. Burr, ed., *Contemporary Theories about the Family* (New York: Free Press, 1979), 549–581.
28. Murray A. Straus, *Beating the Devil Out of Them* (New York: Lexington Books, 1994) 26, 28
29. *Ibid.*, 32.
30. *Ibid.*, 54, 58.
31. *Ibid.*, 60, 62.
32. *Ibid,* 119
33. *Ibid.*, 108.
34. Coramae Richey Mann, *When Women Kill* (Albany: State University of New York Press, 1996), 71.
35. Murray A. Straus, "Domestic Violence and Homicide Antecedents," *Bulletin of the New York Academy of Medicine* 62, 5 (1986), 459.
36. Peter C. Kratcoski, "Perspectives on Intrafamily Violence," *Human Relations* 37, 6 (1984), 443–454.
37. J. A. Fagan, D. K. Stewart, and K. V. Hansen, *Violent Men or Violent Husbands: Background Factors and Situational Correlates of Domestic and Extra-domestic Violence* (San Francisco: URSA Institute, 1982).
38. Peter C. Kratcoski, "Families Who Kill," *Marriage and Family Review* 12, 1/2 (1987), 47–70.
39. Leo Davids, "Delinquency Prevention through Father Training: Some Observations and Proposals," in Paul C. Friday and V. Lorne Steward, eds., *Youth Crime and Juvenile Justice: International Perspectives* (Chicago: University of Chicago Press, 1977).
40. *Ibid.*

41. Theorora Lurie, "Father and Families: Forging Ties That Bind," *USA Today* 121, 2576 (May 1993), 30–33.
42. Hirschi, *Causes of Delinquency,* 237–39.
43. Gary J. Jensen and Raymond Eve, "Sex Differences in Delinquency," *Criminology* 13, 3 (February 1976), 427–448.
44. *Akron Beacon Journal,* September 22, 1994, B1.
45. Susan Saunders, *Violent Individuals and Families* (Springfield, IL: Charles C. Thomas, 1984), 88.
46. L. Edward Wells and Joseph H. Rankin, "Direct Parental Controls and Delinquency," *Criminology* 26, 2 (May 1988), 263–286.
47. Rolf Loeber and Magda Strouthamer-Loeber, "Family Factors as Correlates and Predictors of Juvenile Conduct Problems and Delinquency," in Michael Tonry and Norval Morris, eds., *Crime and Justice: An Annual Review of Research,* Vol. 7 (Chicago: University of Chicago Press, 1986), 187–193.
48. Boyd Rollins and Darwin Thomas, "Parental Support, Power, and Control Techniques in the Socialization of Children," in Wesley Burr, Reuben Hill, F. Ivan Nye, and Ira Reiss, eds., *Contemporary Theories about the Family* (New York: Free Press, 1979), 35–43.
49. Wells and Rankin, "Direct Parental Controls and Delinquency," 263–286.
50. Edwin I. Megargee and Roy E. Golden, "Parental Attitudes of Psychopathic and Subcultural Delinquents," *Criminology* 10, 3 (February 1973), 427–439.
51. Canter, "Family Correlates of Male and Female Delinquency," 155–157.
52. Irving M. Piliavin, Arlene C. Vadum, and Jane Allyn Hardyck, "Delinquency, Personal Costs, and Parental Treatment: A Test of a Reward-Cost Model of Juvenile Criminality," *Journal of Criminal Law, Criminology, and Police Science* 60, 2 (June 1969), 172.

CHAPTER **8**

FEMALE DELINQUENCY

(Photo credit: Ryan McVay/Getty Images, Inc.–Photodisc)

THE CASE OF SUSAN FRYBERG
THE EXTENT OF FEMALE DELINQUENCY
     Official Statistics
     Self-Reported Delinquency
THE NATURE OF FEMALE DELINQUENCY
CAUSES OF FEMALE DELINQUENCY
     The Unique Characteristics of the Adolescent Girl
     The Double Standard in American Sexual Definitions
     Influence of the Family
     Sex-Related Offenses by Females
JUVENILE JUSTICE SYSTEM HANDLING OF DELINQUENT GIRLS
     Differential Treatment of Males and Females
     Programs Designed for the Unique Problems of Delinquent Girls

THE CASE OF SUSAN FRYBERG

The name and certain details of the following case have been altered to protect the identity of the person involved, but all the basic facts of this story are true and were revealed by the girl to one of the authors.

Susan's first contact with the juvenile authorities occurred when she was 9. At that time, she was removed from her mother's care and placed in a foster home, after it was determined that her home situation was deficient.

Susan had spent her early childhood in a rural area of Tennessee. She recalls that her father left home when she was very young and that she, with her six older brothers and two older sisters, had to run the household. Her recollections of her mother from this early age were that she was pretty and that she had many men visitors. This did not present a real difficulty for the little girl, because she and her siblings liked having company and receiving occasional treats from these men. The one disturbing thing she remembers is that some of the men who visited her mother were black, although her mother was white. Other neighborhood children ridiculed and taunted her because of this.

By the time Susan was 9, most of her older brothers and sisters had left home. About this age, she began to realize that her mother was receiving money from the men who visited her. Susan began to get into trouble at school, was caught shoplifting a small item from a local store, and began to act in a rebellious manner toward her mother, who by this time had developed a severe drinking problem. It was at this point that the juvenile authorities first intervened in her life and placed her in a foster home.

Susan ran away from this foster home, and from two subsequent placements. Eventually she was placed in an institution for delinquent girls. There she was rebellious and unable to adjust to the routine. Finally, at the age of 13, she was returned to her mother, and she remained with her for three years. During this period, there were intermittent difficulties with the juvenile authorities. At the age of 16, she left home for good and ran away to a large city in Ohio. Her reason for running, as she explained it, was that her mother was grooming her to share her boyfriends in return for money.

Apparently no one was too concerned about her leaving home, because no action was taken to find her. She remained in the city, did not attend school, and earned money working at a fast-food restaurant. She also began receiving money from various men. Before long, she gave up her job and used shoplifting and prostitution as her means of support. At the age of 17, she was prostituting for a man who arranged contacts for her. On one occasion, she and two girlfriends overpowered a woman in the restroom of a bus terminal and stole her purse. When she was apprehended by a store detective for shoplifting, a check of her identity and records revealed that she was a juvenile. After a hearing, she was placed in an institution for delinquent girls.

This case study is typical in many respects of the patterns and progression of delinquency among girls. Many of the danger signals that appeared in this girl's life indicating that she badly needed help in managing her problems were ignored by those who had authority to intervene. For example, even though her mother was known to be a prostitute, the juvenile authorities returned the girl to her at the age of 13, certainly a highly impressionable and dangerous time for a girl to be thrust into such a home situation.

Delinquent activity by girls has received much less attention by researchers than misbehavior by boys. Although W.I. Thomas's book, *The Unadjusted Girl*, appeared in the 1920s, female delinquency received little attention until the 1960s. When it was discussed, it was in relation to improper sexual behavior and regarded, as Thomas suggested, as a search for love and security or using sexual favors as a way to obtain money or things, rather than rebellion against parents or social norms.[1] Such important early delinquency research as Cohen's *Delinquent Boys*, Cloward and Ohlin's *Delinquency and Opportunity*, and Sheldon and Eleanor Glueck's *Physique and Delinquency* made no mention of whether the theories developed applied to females. As late as 1966, Voss's study of self-reported delinquent behavior by junior high school students concentrated its analysis on the portion of the results received from the 284 male respondents and virtually ignored the data from the 336 females who also participated in the study.[2]

When girls did receive attention from the justice system, it was most often for behavior in the areas of incorrigibility, running away, or sexual activity; boys were seldom arrested or held for such offenses.

The offenses with which girls were most often charged might be termed "victimless offenses," in the sense that they harmed no one but the girls themselves. Since their misbehavior was not as overtly threatening to society as the property crime or violent misbehavior of boys, it was not as closely examined. In addition, girls who did come to the attention of the juvenile justice system did not receive the same levels of treatment or rehabilitation given to boys. They were frequently "warehoused" away until the age of majority in institutions where they spent a good deal of time doing nothing or engaged in activities related to domestic work (sewing, cooking) rather than in training for jobs or professions. Cosmetology was frequently the only type of employment preparation offered. Such inequalities of opportunity continue to exist in juvenile institutions. For example, a survey of various state institutions revealed that nationwide training programs offered in institutions for boys were much more varied than those for girls. Thirty-six different types of programs for boys were identified, compared to 17 for girls.[3]

Finally, it must be noted that those who have studied delinquency and its implications have overwhelmingly been males. Until Konopka produced *The Adolescent*

Girl in Conflict in 1966, no in-depth study of delinquent girls had been attempted by a woman.[4]

THE EXTENT OF FEMALE DELINQUENCY

Official Statistics

A number of the assumptions about female delinquency that have caused theorists to minimize its importance need to be reexamined to test their validity. The first of these is the belief that girls are much less likely than boys to engage in delinquent activity. The most definitive sources of information regarding official involvement of girls and boys in delinquent behavior over the years are the *Uniform Crime Reports* compiled by the FBI. They reveal that, beginning in the 1960s, the number of arrests of female juveniles rose dramatically. In 1960, there was a 6-to-1 ratio of male to female juvenile arrests. The ratio declined steadily from that point until the mid-1970s, when it leveled off at approximately 3.5 to 1, and remained in a similar range in the 1980s and 1990s. In 2001, it stood at 2.5 to 1.[5] As shown in Table 8.1, an analysis of the 2001 arrests of youths under 18 years of age reveals that the majority of arrests for offenses traditionally associated with females (prostitution/commercialized vice [70%] and running away [60%]) were arrests of females. However, for types of crimes that have usually been associated with males, the percentage of these offenses committed by females is increasing. Females under age 18 were arrested for 32 percent of the property crimes, 32 percent of other assaults, 30 percent of the disorderly conduct offenses, 32 percent of the curfew and loitering law violations, and 32 percent of the liquor law violations. Relatively high percentages of offenses

Table 8–1.   A Gender Comparison of Arrests of Youths Under Age 18, 2001 (Percentage Comparison)

Offense	Male	Female
Violent offenses (murder, forcible rape, robbery, aggravated assault)	82%	18%
Property crime	68%	32%
Other assaults	68%	32%
Motor vehicle theft	82%	18%
Disorderly conduct	70%	30%
Curfew and loitering laws violations	68%	32%
Liquor laws violations	68%	32%
Drug abuse violations	83%	17%
Offenses against family	63%	37%
Forgery and counterfeiting	63%	37%
Prostitution/commercialized vice	30%	70%
Running away	40%	60%

Source: Compiled by Lucille Kratcoski from "Current Year over Previous Year Arrest Trends," *Crime in the United States, 2001* (Washington, DC: U.S. Government Printing Office, 2002), 243.

against family (37%) and forgery and counterfeiting (37%) were also committed by females.

Referrals to the juvenile courts have been increasing for both males and females, but the growth in cases involving females has been greater. In the 10-year period from 1987 to 1996, female referrals increased 76 percent, compared to a 42 percent increase for males.[6]

Self-Reported Delinquency

Official reports may not be accurate measures of the amount of female delinquency, since law enforcement officials may be less inclined to arrest or officially process girls because of the nondestructive nature of much of their misbehavior and because of paternalistic attitudes toward the damage that arrest or official handling might do to the girls' reputations. In addition, a good deal of the misbehavior traditionally regarded as female delinquency is easily concealed. Because of these factors, self-report studies of delinquent activity may be truer measures of the amount of female delinquency than arrest statistics or numbers of juvenile court referrals. Self-report studies usually involve anonymous responses to survey questions that ask if a youth has committed a certain act and if the act has been committed within a specific time period (e.g., the last 30 days or the last 12 months). Those conducting the survey select a representative sample of youths in the age group being questioned.

The National Longitudinal Survey of Youth involved 9,000 youths ages 12 through 16. This self-report data revealed that the percentages of males and females who ever drank alcohol, used marijuana, or ran away from home were nearly the same, but males were much more likely to have carried a handgun, purposely destroyed property, stolen something worth over $50, sold drugs, and committed assaults.[7] In 2001, the Youth Risk Behavior self-report survey of high school students revealed that female high school students are engaging in violent behavior. Twenty-four percent of the females had been in a physical fight in the past 12 months, compared to 43 percent of the males, and six percent of the females had carried a weapon in the past 30 days, compared to 29 percent of the males. Females also appeared to be at risk for self-destructive behavior. Twenty-four percent of the females reported that they had seriously considered suicide, compared to 14 percent of the males.[8] The Monitoring the Future survey of high school seniors in 2001 revealed similar patterns of violent activity by females. During the preceding 12 months, 13 percent of the females had gotten into a serious fight in school or at work, compared to 19 percent of the males, and 17 percent of females had taken part in a fight with a group of friends against another group, compared to 24 percent of the males.[9]

As we noted in Chapter 6, the number of females involved with male gangs or in independent female gangs has been increasing, and the female gang members now are more likely to be directly involved in gang fights and other criminal behaviors, including robberies, assaults, drug abuse, and drug trafficking.

On the basis of both official statistics and self-reported delinquency studies, it appears that, except for the offenses of running away and prostitution/commercialized vice, females under age 18 do commit fewer offenses than males, but the differences between the sexes are narrowing, both in the number of offenses committed and in the types of delinquent behavior in which youths engage.

THE NATURE OF FEMALE DELINQUENCY

We noted earlier that there has been an increased tendency for female juveniles to commit violent offenses and offenses against property, and that the delinquencies of females are becoming more and more like those associated with males. Sharp increases have occurred in the number of female juveniles involved in disorderly conduct, curfew and loitering law violations, and liquor law violations.

These changes in the nature of female delinquency are related to the fact that many of these young offenders, while technically juveniles and under the jurisdiction of the juvenile courts, have in fact assumed adult roles. We noted in earlier chapters that the emerging "underclass," made up of children and young single mothers who have limited education, few financial or family resources, and little incentive to make efforts to escape from what has become a multigenerational cycle of poverty, is increasingly involved in deviant behavior. A good deal of this activity, including shoplifting, passing bad checks, purse snatching, welfare fraud, receiving or selling stolen property, using and selling drugs, and prostitution, is viewed as "survival" activity, without any regard for its unlawfulness. Runaway females—who may have left home for various reasons, including physical or sexual abuse by members of the parent(s)' household, or may have gone off on their own because their family disintegrated or they were no longer wanted in the parent(s)' home—frequently become involved in the same patterns of activity.

CAUSES OF FEMALE DELINQUENCY

Defining the causes of female delinquency today cannot really begin without a glance backward. The lower rates of female delinquency in the past have been attributed to the much closer supervision given to girls. Thus, the increases in female delinquency observed in recent years seem to parallel the declining influence of the family as a social-control mechanism. In the past, it was considered normal for boys to become involved in delinquent activity as part of their growing-up process, but girls were not allowed to seek, or were discouraged from seeking, such outlets for youthful energies. Here again, the movement toward a unisex view for adolescents, or at least one of sexual equality, may have filtered down to the level of delinquent activity and caused some girls to seek status through violent crime, property crime, or drug or alcohol abuse. We have also noted the utilitarian nature of some of the offenses committed by female adolescents today and the life situations that have contributed to their involvement in property crimes, drug offenses, and prostitution.

Even when such explanations of increased delinquency by females are given a good deal of weight, we are left with the reality that female delinquency still has many unique facets and background factors that differentiate it from the delinquency of males. These matters deserve close examination and analysis.

The Unique Characteristics of the Adolescent Girl

Gisela Konopka, in her detailed and sensitive study *The Adolescent Girl in Conflict*, sought to identify the factors that bring young girls into conflict with society and cause them to become involved in behaviors defined as unacceptable. Konopka studied adolescent girls between 14 and 19 years of age who were institutionalized or on probation or parole. She conducted in-depth interviews with the girls, which were supplemented by examinations of their case histories, diaries, and original poetry.

Konopka defined four key factors that contributed to delinquency among girls:

1. *The unique dramatic biological onset of puberty.* In girls, this onset is marked and often frightening. From that time on, fear of the consequences of the sex act is always present.
2. *The complex identification process.* The delinquent girls were found to have special difficulty identifying with their mothers, particularly in early adolescence. This difficulty was often brought on by competitiveness with the mother or disdain for her weakness. The absence of a father or brutal treatment by a father contributed to these identification difficulties.
3. *The changing cultural position of women.* Konopka regarded the following as having great impact on the behavior of girls who came from the lower socio-economic classes:
   (a) Lack of traditional or vocational training of women
   (b) Stereotyped and low-paying employment for women
   (c) Thwarted ambition
   (d) Lack of legitimate outlets for aggressive drives
   (e) Increased awareness and resentment of the double standard
4. *"Faceless" adult authority and the resulting loneliness.* The delinquent girl feels that no one listens to her, but that authorities at home, in school, and in the community keep telling her what to do. The delinquent girl has no source of high self-esteem.[10]

The Double Standard in American Sexual Definitions

In spite of the strides made in promotion of the rights of women, the adolescent girl's treatment by parents, the police, and officials of the juvenile court is still strongly influenced by the fact of her gender. Although there has been a relaxation of standards, premarital sex by girls is still frowned upon by most parents, and most juveniles are pressured to go along with their parents' views. Consequently, police are more likely to arrest girls than boys for sexual offenses, parents are more likely to refer a daughter whom they suspect of sexual activity to the juvenile courts than a son, and a juvenile court judge is likely to deal more harshly with a girl charged with sexual misbehavior than a boy charged with the identical conduct.

Parents frequently bring females to the juvenile court and charge them with incorrigibility or domestic violence when they are really concerned about their sexual activities. Strouse observed:

Adolescent girls face unique problems in their developmental years. *(Photo credit: Jay Paris)*

Attempts to "protect" young females from sexuality—often their own—reflect society's profound confusion and ambivalence about both females and their sexuality. Side-by-side with the judge who regards girls as the "cause" of sexual deviation in boys . . . is all the rhetoric about protection of females and children and crimes such as "seduction" and "statutory rape." . . . That the "victims" of seduction and statutory rape are always females reflects society's judgment that girls under a certain age are not capable of making responsible decisions to engage in sexual intercourse; it makes no similar judgment about boys.[11]

Institutionalization of females for status offenses has been the most obvious application of the double standard by the juvenile court. Until 1972, the New York State Persons in Need of Supervision law provided different upper age limits for the institutionalization of males and females. Females could be institutionalized until the age of 18, while the upper age limit for males was 16. This law was declared unconstitutional by the New York Court of Appeals, which held that there are no factual differences between males and females that could justify such differential treatment.[12] In Oklahoma, females were formerly under juvenile court jurisdiction until age 18, while males left juvenile court jurisdiction after the age of 16. The juvenile code in that state was changed when the 10th Circuit Court of the U.S. Court of Appeals, in

Lamb v. *Brown* (1972), declared that there was no constitutional justification for having different age limits for the juvenile status on the basis of sex.[13]

Influence of the Family

Most studies of delinquency among females have concluded that the family situation of the girl is a crucial factor in her delinquent behavior. Sociologists have long recognized that the family is the major socializing institution for youth. The process of internalizing the norms and rules of society is generally developed within the family context. Nye pointed out that the parents' role as a socializing agent is exercised through the *direct control* they impose upon their children by means of restrictions, rewards, and punishments; through the *internalized control* they have brought about by developing the child's superego or conscience; as well as through the *indirect control* they exert when their child refrains from a certain type of behavior because he or she does not want to hurt, upset, or disillusion them.[14]

To test the strength of various degrees of parental control, Jensen and Eve compared the delinquency of males and females according to the amount of control exercised over them by their families. They found that males had higher proportions of delinquency than females in every level of supervision (low, moderate, or high), but they also discovered that for both white and black females, the proportion of those who had committed delinquent acts steadily decreased as the degree of maternal supervision increased.[15]

Hill and Atkinson discovered that support from either parent reduced involvement in delinquency for both males and females, but that girls were more influenced by maternal support and boys more affected by support from their fathers. They also found gender-related patterns in parents' control of adolescents. Girls were more carefully monitored and supervised than boys, with parental activity concentrated on preventing unacceptable activity, while parental concern regarding boys' misbehavior tended to occur after the fact, when their misbehavior was discovered and punished.[16]

There is strong evidence that suggests the differences in behavior between girls and boys can be attributed more to the gender socialization process than to biological sex differences. Hagen, Simpson, and Gillis found that girls who had developed a masculine role identification were more likely to engage in delinquent behavior than girls who identified with the feminine role. In addition, they found that masculine or feminine role identification for children differed by class strata, with girls in the upper class more likely to develop a masculine role identification than those in the middle class. This was attributed to the parents of upper-class children allowing them to take risks and in general subjecting them to less strict parental control.[17]

Researchers have also explored the relationship between disrupted family structure and delinquent behavior. A study involving a national sample of nearly 2,000 adolescents found that divorce or separation and parents' remarriage, particularly during a youth's adolescent years, was strongly associated with status offending (e.g., incorrigibility or running away) and the author suggested that failure of the adolescents to accept or adjust to the new family situation may have triggered feelings of depression, rebelliousness, or desire to escape that manifest themselves in these offenses.[18]

Kovar demonstrated that the delinquent girls she worked with tended to come from homes in which there was little love for the girl, to have been abandoned or misused by their families, and to have in their family history patterns of neglect and deprivation.[19] It has been observed that a boy can more easily escape a bad home situation and find companionship and status within his peer group; a girl tends to tolerate the home situation as long as she can, until a crisis occurs and she attempts to escape by running away.[20]

The case history of Jamie, a juvenile incarcerated in a women's prison for a serious offense, illustrates the type of family situation that can motivate runaway behavior.

> My dad came and kidnapped me and my sister from my mom when I was 4 and my sister was 2. And we was down there living with my dad for 5 years. My dad had my mom's phone number, but my mom didn't know where we were. My mom called this children thing and found us 5 years later. I was 9 and my sister was 7. We came back and my mom had had two more kids since then and was living with my stepdad. And everything was all right, until when I was 11, my stepdad started molesting me. I told my mom and she didn't believe me. I just kept telling her and she didn't want to believe me. So I started running away. I don't remember how many times I ran away because I ran away so much. Because my mom wouldn't listening to me, I kept running away to let him know. When she finally believed me, she said it was my fault. . . . They'd take me to juvenile jail, and they'd let me go the next day. They'd keep me overnight. I've been in and out of so many foster homes because I didn't like living with people I don't know.[21]

Gaarder and Belknap, who completed extensive interviews with 22 juvenile girls confined in a women's prison after being tried and convicted in adult criminal courts for such offenses as aggravated murder, involuntary manslaughter, robbery, kidnapping, aggravated felonious assault, and some less serious offenses (possession of drugs, theft, receiving stolen property) noted the presence of abuse, neglect, and family disruption in the girls' backgrounds:

> Some of the most significant experiences in the lives of the young women interviewed were the interlocking oppressions of gender, race, class, and sexuality that brought them to this blurred domain of victimization and offending. Incidents of sexual and physical abuse, neglect and disorder in the family, school problems, and chemical dependency were persistent themes in their lives.[22]

Sex-Related Offenses by Females

Victimization of girls through prostitution, sexual abuse, and their use in child pornography is a serious problem and must be considered in any discussion of sex-related offenses by females.

The Extent of Child Prostitution.   The amount of exploitation of children through sexual misuse is impossible to determine, with estimates of the number of adolescent prostitutes ranging as high as 1 million.[23] Both boys and girls are involved in this activity, with male prostitutes tending to be street hustlers who work as "independents," while female prostitutes may be independent or may work for a pimp who recruits, organizes, and controls the girls' activities. Recruitment of female prostitutes by pimps is more often made through other girls than by a direct approach, but pimps or girls who represent them frequently seek out girls in spots such as big-city bus stations, where runaways may arrive with little money and no friends.[24] Chesney-Lind and Belknap, after an extensive review of the research studies, concluded that:

> Prostitution among girls, then, is not so much a choice as a survival mechanism for those who have few other options once forced unto the street.[25]

The youthful experiences of a woman who eventually murdered her husband illustrate the problems and fears faced by young girls on the streets. After she was raped, this girl's grandparents, with whom she lived, gave her no emotional support. She felt shamed, depressed, and angry. Shortly after her 13th birthday she and another girl stole money from family members and ran away. She described their experiences on the street.

> I don't know how we managed on so little money, but we did. We tried to get jobs at McDonald's by saying we were 18 but the manager just laughed at us. . . . We slept in doorways most of the time. Deborah was scared to death all night long. She'd say, "Someone's going to rape us. They're going to kill us." And I'd tell her that I'd stay awake all night so no one could get us.[26]

When a young man who met and befriended them took them to a bar, they experienced firsthand the perils of life on the street:

> "Hey, Snake man," said the bartender as the trio walked into the dimly lit bar. "Whatcha got there? Jailbait?" Everyone laughed and turned to look at the girls.
>
> "No, just a couple of thirsty little birds that flew away from home. How about a few beers?"
>
> "Why not? How about a few lines, too?" said the bartender, pulling out a tiny silver spoon that was hanging on a gold chain around his neck. . . . June watched the bartender, who removed from his pocket a small plastic bag containing white powder. "How about a snort for the little ladies" he said, ignoring Deborah and fixing his gaze on June. She didn't say anything, and had no idea what he was talking about anyway.[27]

Sexual abuse of girls at an early age has been found by various researchers to be related to entrance into teenage prostitution. In a study of girls age 13 to 15 detained in New York secure detention facilities, it was found that 80 percent of the girls who were prostitutes had their first intercourse experience at the age of 13 or under.[28] Early intercourse, in combination with other life events, was found by James and Davis to be strongly related to entrance into prostitution. These researchers interviewed two groups of women, a group involved in street prostitution and another group involved in criminal activities not related to sex activities. They explored the relation of such events as broken homes, withdrawal from school, early intercourse (age 15 or less), having a juvenile record, and early drug use (age 15 or less) to becoming a prostitute. They found that prostitutes had higher frequencies of all of these events than did the nonprostitutes. There was a strong association between coming from a broken home, early intercourse, departure from school, and prostitution, and between having a juvenile record, coming from a broken home, and prostitution. Early drug use, combined with a juvenile record, was also strongly related to becoming a prostitute. The authors concluded that these combinations of negative events contributed to the females' development of a devalued sense of self-worth.[29]

The destructive effects of child sexual abuse include development of a negative self-image, feelings of powerlessness or worthlessness, and the creation of a psychological defense mechanism of distancing oneself from involvement in the sexual experience, so that it is viewed unemotionally. In a study of runaways and homeless women, it was found that child sexual abuse increased the probability of involvement in prostitution and also elevated the risk of running away, substance abuse, and other deviant behavior.[30]

The following story, revealed to one of the authors in an interview, describes the kind of sexual exploitation to which young victims may be exposed.

> When I was 10 years old my father (not my real father, but my mother's second husband) took me into his bedroom and told me he was going to show me how children were made. He took off my jeans and panties and pushed his finger into me. When I started crying he told me to stop it or he would slap me. After that time he would try to get me to go in his bedroom with him whenever my mother and sisters weren't home. He told me that I would have to do as he said or I would not be allowed to go anywhere and would have to do all of the housework. Sometimes when I refused to go in the room and take off my clothes he would hit me in the stomach with his fist.

> After a few months of sticking his finger in me, he forced me to have intercourse with him. We engaged in sex for five years. If I refused he wouldn't let me go on dates. I ran away when I was 15 because he wouldn't let me go out with my boyfriend.

> I decided not to tell on him because the social workers were going to make me go back home, and I was afraid of being beaten again. I also wanted to protect my younger sisters from being forced into sex with my father.[31]

The lack of a supportive family or strong family relationships also appears closely related to entrance into prostitution. In her study of "baby-pros," Bracey discovered that most girls choose to become prostitutes because they know other girls who are involved or because of the charm or flattery of a pimp who offers money, protection, companionship, and emotional closeness, all elements missing in the girls' lives.[32] A study of girls housed in a temporary shelter care facility in Chicago for sexually abused and exploited children found that the majority of the girls who have been involved in prostitution came from broken or recombined homes, were likely to have grown up in families where emotional conflict and parental neglect occurred, and had experienced other types of physical abuse in addition to sexual abuse.[33]

Chesney-Lind and Shelden concluded that, for a large number of girls, running away from home is preceded by a long history of family conflict, physical or sexual abuse, extremely strict discipline, or a combination of these factors. They stated:

> It is clear that many young women are on the streets in flight from sexual victimization at home. Once there, they often resort to crime in order to survive, but they do not have much

attachment to their delinquent activities. Angry about being labeled delinquent, most still engage in illegal acts.[34]

Janus et al. found that girls were six times more likely than boys to cite sexual abuse as the reason for running away.[35]

Physical or sexual victimization of girls tends to occur in the home, with the perpetrator being a parent, other relative, or close acquaintance. While a direct causal relationship between physical or sexual abuse and delinquency cannot be easily established, there are numerous research studies that show statistical correlations between the two, particularly with regard to females engaging in sex-related delinquency or other delinquent behavior. Sexually abused children become higher risks for offending than nonabused youths as a consequence of their attempts to deal with the abuse, which may take the form of anger and aggression toward all adults, particularly caretakers or others in authority positions, running away, engaging in substance abuse, becoming alienated from peers, or even attempting suicide.

In a study of the relationship between maltreatment during childhood and delinquency, Ireland et al. found that maltreatment during adolescence or persistent maltreatment throughout childhood and adolescence were both highly predictive of delinquent behavior. This finding would appear to support the significance of the sexual maltreatment of girls during adolescence as a predictor of future delinquency.[36] An extensive nationwide study of the relationship between childhood abuse and delinquency found that childhood abuse increased the odds of future delinquency and adult criminality by 40 percent.[37] It also found that the impact of abuse on females was profound:

> Being abused or neglected in childhood increased the likelihood of arrest for females by 77 percent over comparison group females. As adults, abused and neglected females were more likely to be arrested for property, drug, and misdemeanor offenses such as disorderly conduct, curfew violations, or loitering, but not for violent offenses.[38]

Research on girls who associate with gang members or belong to gangs reveals that there is a likelihood that these girls were sexually abused at home or within their neighborhoods and they followed this pattern of being used as sex objects within the gangs. Moore found that most of the girls who were involved with male gangs did not believe that they were being sexually exploited, but the majority of the male gang members stated that the girls were mere sex objects or that the girls were worthless and deserved whatever abusive treatment they received.[39] Miller and Brunson reported that the members of all-male gangs were "those most likely to describe girls primarily as sex objects or individuals to be exploited,"[40] as illustrated by the comments of a member of an all-male gang.

> Most girls are just for pleasure, fun and pleasure for real. We don't see girls like we see dudes . . . .[41]

The gang member reported that the male gang members associated with girls "to have sex with them and stuff like that."[42]

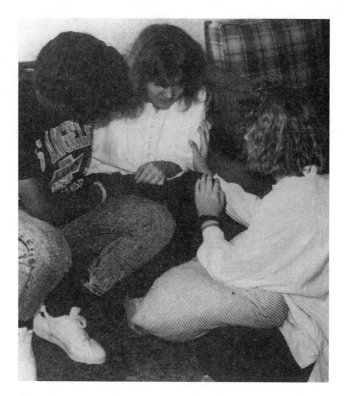

Group counseling is frequently used to help physically or sexually abused girls. *(Photo credit: Bill Sherlock, courtesy of the American Correctional Association)*

Sadly, previously abused girls who become prostitutes continue to be caught up in a cycle of victimization. The victimization suffered by these girls extends beyond their sexual use and may include physical abuse by customers, who beat them or force them to perform sadistic acts. The fact that they frequent inner-city areas at late hours and are assumed to carry money makes them targets for muggers or addicts. Pimps may also exploit them by physical abuse. They are rarely dressed for inclement weather, and their diet usually consists of junk food purchased in the areas where they work.[43]

Prostitution and its related lifestyle makes these girls highly vulnerable to venereal disease and AIDS. A study of female prostitutes found that 87 percent of the girls reported a median of 200 acts of prostitution. There was also a high correlation between prostitution and drug use. It was found that their initial exposure to alcohol and marijuana began at the ages of 8 to 10, with experimentation with cocaine and heroin occurring by age 12. Forty-two percent of the females in the study reported exchanging sex for crack six or more times, and 29 percent reported one to five such exchanges. The authors noted that these findings indicate very high levels of involvement in HIV risk behavior by these females, because of their frequent acts of prostitution and their intravenous drug use.[44]

Child Pornography. It is estimated that 7 percent of the pornography market in the United States involves activity between children and other children and adults, and that between 40,000 and 120,000 children are involved each year in pornography and/or prostitution.[45] It has also been estimated that more than 100,000 runaway youths in this country have had some involvement with child pornography.[46]

Child pornography includes magazines sold in adult bookstores or through mailorder houses, films, and still photos. The children involved may be posed or filmed in the nude, or presented engaged in sexual acts with adults, other children, or animals. The performers may range in age from as young as age 2 or 3 through the teens. Some films also show children being mistreated or tortured.[47]

The availability or exploitability of young children for pornography is directly related to a lack of supervision by adults, lack of knowledge that the children are being used for these purposes, or the willingness of parents or other adult caretakers to allow children to be used in this manner.

Involvement in pornography by older youths may be related to a life of prostitution, or they may see it as a way to make some quick money. Contact with the industry usually occurs in such instances through peers who have already worked for the filmmakers or photographers, or may be arranged by a pimp. The Internet is also used as mechanism to recruit gullible, immature girls, frequently under the guise of preparing them for modeling careers.

What Can Be Done? Efforts to deal with child pornography and prostitution have increased, as revelations of the magnitude of the problems have aroused public concern. The federal Protection of Children Against Sexual Exploitation Act prohibits the transportation of children across state lines for the purpose of prostitution or pornography. A number of states have also enacted statutes that provide strong penalties for exploiting children for sexual purposes.[48] Large cities, including Los Angeles, have established sexual exploitation units within their police departments to coordinate investigative activities, increase public awareness of the problem, and develop a network of community agencies that can offer intervention and treatment possibilities for exploited children.

In October 2002, a White House Conference on Missing, Exploited, and Runaway Children was held in Washington, DC. The conference participants included officials from various government departments, law enforcement personnel, families of child victims, researchers, and corporate leaders. The topics discussed included "child abductions, domestic and international parental kidnapping, sex trafficking of children, child pornography, runaway and homeless youth, Internet safety, and corporate and community involvement."[49] Technologies now available to track missing children, law enforcement efforts, and community strategies that have been demonstrated to be effective in reducing harm to children from abduction or exploitation, were highlighted.

Child prostitution and pornography have been identified as closely related to the runaway problem. Diversion programs for runaways (see Chapter 13) may help to remove them from the streets and lessen the risk of sexual exploitation.

JUVENILE JUSTICE SYSTEM HANDLING OF DELINQUENT GIRLS

Differential Treatment of Males and Females

There has always been differential treatment of males and females by the juvenile justice system, with females receiving more restrictive handling and harsher dispositions. The greatest injustices to females have occurred when they have been held in detention and institutionalized for status offenses. In the past, the typical response to misbehavior by girls was involvement by the juvenile court or a social service agency. For example, it was very common for the police to take official action in cases involving runaway females and virtually ignore those cases involving males. Such action was justified on the ground that the juvenile court was predominantly a protective and service agency rather than a punishment agency, and that it was often necessary to hold a girl in detention for her own safety and well-being. Girls picked up as runaways were held if the parents could not be reached immediately. A girl who was fleeing from a punishing or sexually aggressive parent might need the protection offered by the detention center. When it seemed imperative not to return a girl to her home and a temporary foster home was not readily available, the detention center was utilized. The court personnel and police said that some girls found the detention center environment more comfortable and less threatening than their own homes. Differential treatment of female offenders, in their view, was the juvenile court's response to girls' special needs and the limited alternatives available.

Many juvenile justice officials felt that, since a large proportion of delinquency among girls has its roots in problems in the home environment, the immediate solution to the problem was to remove the girl from the home and place her in a secure setting until a more permanent solution, such as foster-home placement, could be worked out.

Federal legislation, notably the U.S. Juvenile Justice and Delinquency Prevention Act of 1974, and changes in juvenile justice codes in various states designed to reduce or eliminate the practice of youths being held in detention centers or institutions with delinquent offenders, have reduced the differential treatment of boys and girls that formerly occurred. However, these legislative safeguards do not guarantee that differential treatment has been eliminated. Beginning from the point of contact with the police or referral to the juvenile court by parents or the school, females may continue to be affected by the paternalistic attitude that, for their own protection, they must be arrested, held in detention, declared "incorrigible," or removed from their homes. For example, even though self-report surveys consistently show that an equal number of boys and girls run away from home, the number of females arrested for this offense continues to exceed the number of males. In 1992, 104,300 youths under age 18 were arrested as runaways and in 2001 the number was 78,407. Girls accounted for 57 percent of the runaway arrests in 1992, and 60 percent of those in

2001.[50] In this 10-year period, the number of male runaway arrests declined by nearly 30 percent and the number of female runaway arrests was reduced by more than 21 percent. These figures could be interpreted as revealing a decline in the number of youth who are running away from home, but it is more likely that the reduced numbers are related to changes in methods of handling status offenders. However, females still account for much higher percentages of runaway arrests (60% for females in 2001, compared to 40% for males). A more detailed discussion of the juvenile justice system's response to female misbehavior will be given in Chapters 11, 14, and 15.

Programs Designed for the Unique Problems of Delinquent Girls

Many communities have developed community-based programs that offer opportunities for supervision of female juvenile offenders while they remain in their own homes. When their family situation or conduct calls for removal from home, group-home placement offers an alternative to institutionalization. These programs are developed as diversion alternatives to juvenile court processing, or may be used as a dispositional alternative for cases that have been officially handled by the juvenile court. The varieties and types of group homes developed as alternatives to institutionalization and the types of programs developed as community-based responses and alternatives to institutionalization are discussed in detail in Chapter 14.

For older adolescents, some programs have focused on possibilities for them to live independently. Housing and employment needs and training in the skills needed for such placements are emphasized. Although those who have been physically, sexually, or emotionally victimized may require specialized counseling, the emphasis of the programs is on developing the skills needed for personal independence.[51]

SUMMARY

In this chapter, we discovered that it was only in the late 1960s and the 1970s that female delinquency began to receive its proper attention from researchers and juvenile justice planners. In the past, delinquencies of girls were largely self-destructive activities rather than ones that threatened the well-being of the community, and as a result, inadequate attention was given to investigation of their causes or exploration of effective means of treatment. The steadily declining differentials in the ratio of boy-to-girl delinquencies and the increasing amounts of violent crime and property crime by female juveniles evident from official statistics and self-reported delinquency studies, however, have highlighted the need for more careful attention to female delinquency.

In addition to the conditions in American life that are conducive to delinquent behavior for both males and females, a number of factors are uniquely related to the occurrence of unacceptable behavior by adolescent girls. These include the special stresses adolescent girls undergo at the time of puberty, the double standard in

American sexual definitions, the changing cultural position of women and convergence of the male and female roles, and the influence of family disorganization.

The exploitation of female juveniles through child prostitution and pornography is a serious problem. Researchers have discovered that female adolescent prostitutes tend to be runaways or girls whose families have failed to provide the needed physical or emotional support. Sexual abuse of girls has been identified as a factor which contributes to entrance into teenage prostitution in some cases.

There has always been differential treatment of males and females by the juvenile justice system, with females receiving more restrictive handling and harsher dispositions. The greatest injustices to females have occurred when they have been held in detention and institutionalized for status offenses. New juvenile justice standards have identified the inequalities in treatment of males and females and have proposed remedies. One hopeful trend is the use of community-based treatment, which allows girls to be supervised and counseled while remaining in their own homes or living in residential group homes that provide an atmosphere of control, involvement, and preparation for adult living.

DISCUSSION QUESTIONS

1. What are some of the ways in which females and males have been handled and treated differently by the juvenile justice system? How do juvenile justice system officials justify this differential treatment?

2. In *The Adolescent Girl in Conflict*, Gisela Konopka defined four key factors that contribute to delinquency among girls. List these factors and discuss their possible relationship to delinquent activity.

3. Disruptions of the family structure and family tensions and conflict have been established as being related to female delinquency. Why might such conditions within the family have a more devastating effect on a female than on a male juvenile?

4. What factors in a female's family life or home environment have been found to be related to entrance into teenage prostitution?

5. Official statistics show a wide divergence between males and females in the numbers who engage in delinquent behavior. Are these statistics accurate reflections of the amount of female delinquent activity?

NOTES

1. W.I. Thomas, *The Unadjusted Girl* (New York: Harper & Row, 1923).
2. Harwin L. Voss, "Socio-economic Status and Reported Delinquent Behavior," *Social Problems* 13, 3 (Winter 1966).
3. Richard Flaste, "Girls Get Short End of Juvenile Justice," *Quarterly Journal of Corrections* 1, 4 (Fall 1977), 41.
4. Gisela Konopka, *The Adolescent Girl in Conflict* (Englewood Cliffs, NJ: Prentice Hall, 1966), 119.
5. Federal Bureau of Investigation, *Crime in the United States, 2001* (Washington, DC: U.S. Government Printing Office, 2001), 243.

6. Howard N. Snyder and Melissa Sickmund, *Juvenile Offenders and Victims: 1999 National Report* (Washington, DC: Office of Juvenile Justice and Delinquency Prevention, 1999), 148.

7. U.S. Bureau of Labor Statistics, "The National Longitudinal Survey of Youth 1997," reported in Snyder and Sickmund, *Juvenile Offenders and Victims: 1999*, 59.

8. "Youth Risk Behavior Surveillance—United States, 2001," reported in Bureau of Justice Statistics, *Sourcebook of Criminal Justice Statistics, 2001* (Washington, DC: U.S. Government Printing Office, 2002), 244.

9. Lloyd D. Johnston, Jerald G. Bachman, and Patrick M. O'Malley, *Monitoring the Future, 2001*, reported in *Sourcebook of Criminal Justice Statistics, 2001*, 229.

10. Konopka, *The Adolescent Girl in Conflict*, 119.

11. Jean Strouse, "To be Minor and Female: The Legal Rights for Women under 21," in Barry Krisberg and James Austin, eds., *The Children of Ishmael* (Palo Alto, CA: Mayfield, 1978), 374.

12. *In re Patricia A.*, New York Court of Appeals, 1972.

13. *Lamb v. Brown*, 456 F 2d 18 (1972).

14. F. Ivan Nye, *Family Relations and Delinquent Behavior* (New York: Wiley, 1958).

15. Gary J. Jensen and Raymond Eve, "Sex Differences in Delinquency," *Criminology* 13, 1 (February 1976), 426.

16. Gary D. Hill and Maxine P. Atkinson, "Gender, Familial Control, and Delinquency," *Criminology* 26, 1 (February 1988), 127–147.

17. John Hagen, John Simpson, and A. R. Gillis, "Class in the Household: A Power-control Theory of Gender and Delinquency," *American Journal of Sociology* 92, 4 (1987), 788–816.

18. Cesar J. Rebellon, "Reconsidering the Broken Homes/Delinquency Relationship and Exploring its Mediating Mechanism(s)," *Criminology* 40, 1 (2002), 103–136.

19. Lillian Kovar, *Faces of the Adolescent Girl* (Englewood Cliffs, NJ: Prentice Hall, 1966).

20. Ruth Shonle Cavan, *Juvenile Delinquency* (New York: J. B. Lippincott, 1969).

21. Emily Gaarder and Joanne Belknap, "Tenuous Borders: Girls Referred to Adult Court," *Criminology* 40, 3 (August 2002), 493.

22. Ibid., 508–509.

23. Shirley O'Brien, *Child Pornography* (Dubuque, IA: Kendall-Hunt Publishing Company, 1983), 2.

24. Dorothy Heid Bracey, *Baby Pros* (New York: John Jay Press, 1979), 23.

25. Meda Chesney-Lind and Randal G. Shelden, *Girls, Delinquency, and Juvenile Justice* (Belmont, CA: Wadsworth Publishing Company, 1998), 40.

26. From FIGHTING BACK by Robert Davidson, copyright © 2000 by Robert Davidson. Used by permission of Ballantine Books, a division of Random House, Inc., 37.

27. Ibid., 36.

28. Daria S. Bour, Jeanne P. Young, and Rodney Henningsen, "A Comparison of Delinquent Prostitutes and Delinquent Non-Prostitutes on Self-Concept," Paper presented at the Annual Meeting of the Academy of Criminal Justice Sciences, San Antonio, Texas, March, 1983.

29. Jennifer James and Nannette J. Davis, "Contingencies in Female Sexual Role Deviance; The Case of Prostitution," *Human Organization* 41, 4 (Winter, 1902), 345–349.

30. Ronald L. Simons and Les B. Whitbeck, "Sexual Abuse as a Precursor to Prostitution and Victimization Among Adolescent and Adult Homeless Women," *Journal of Family Issues* 12, 3 (September 1991), 361–379.

31. Interview with anonymous juvenile conducted by Peter C. Kratcoski, June 11, 1984.

32. Bracey, *Baby Pros*, 23.

33. Mangus J. Seng, "Child Sexual Abuse and Adolescent Prostitution: A Comparative Analysis," *Adolescence* 24, 95 (Fall 1989), 665–673.

34. Chesney-Lind and Shelden, *Girls, Delinquency, and Juvenile Justice*, 36.

35. M. Janus, F. X. Archambault, S. Brown, and L. Welsh, "Physical Abuse in Canadian Runaway Adolescents," *Child Abuse and Neglect* 19 (1995), 433–447.

36. Timothy O. Ireland, Carolyn A. Smith, and Terence P. Thornberry, "Developmental Issues in the Impact of Child Maltreatment on Later Delinquency and Drug Use," *Criminology* 40, 2 (2002), 359–400.

37. Cathy Spatz Widon, *The Cycle of Violence* (Washington, DC: U.S. Department of Justice, 1992), 1.
38. *Ibid.*, 2.
39. J. W. Moore, *Going Down to the Barrio: Homeboys and Homeboys in Change* (Philadelphia, PA: Temple University Press, 1991).
40. Jody Miller and Rod K. Brunson, "Gender Dynamics in Youth Gangs: A Comparison of Males' and Females' Accounts," *Justice Quarterly* 17, 3 (September 2000), 435.
41. *Ibid.*
42. *Ibid.*
43. Bracey, *Baby Pros*, 61–63.
44. James A. Inciardi, Anne E. Pottieger, Mary Ann Forney, Dale D. Chitwood, and Duane C. McBride, "Prostitution, IV Drug Use, and Sex-For-Crack Exchanges among Serious Delinquents: Risks for HIV Infection," *Criminology* 29, 1 (1991), 221–235.
45. O'Brien, *Child Pornography*, 19.
46. J. O'Conner, "Child Pornography, Social Disease," *New York Times*, February 24, 1981, C19.
47. O'Brien, *Child Porngraphy*, 20.
48. See Ariz. Rev. Stat. Ann. Sec. 13–3552 (Supp. 1980), and Maryland Code Ann. Art 27, Sec. 35A (supp. 1980).
49. U.S. Department of Justice, "White House Holds Conference on Missing, Exploited, and Runaway Children," *OJJDP News at a Glance* 1, 5 (September/October 2002), 2.
50. Federal Bureau of Investigation, *Crime in the United States, 2001*, 238–239.
51. Chesney-Lind and Shelden, *Girls, Delinquency, and Juvenile Justice*, 227.

CHAPTER 9

THE SCHOOL
AND DELINQUENCY

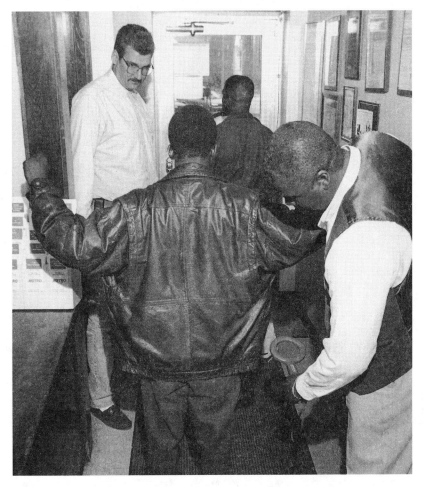

(Photo credit: Nick J. Cool, The Image Works)

THE SCHOOL AS A DELINQUENCY-PRODUCING INSTITUTION
    Schools' Failure in Socialization
    Victimization at School
    Students' Failure in Academic Endeavors
THE RELATION OF DROPPING OUT TO DELINQUENCY
SCHOOL VANDALISM
THE RELATION OF SCHOOL INVOLVEMENT TO DRUG AND ALCOHOL USE
DEFINING THE APPROPRIATE ROLE OF THE SCHOOLS IN DELINQUENCY PREVENTION
    Social Networking
    Safe School Initiatives
    Drug Education
    Alternative Programs
    Levels of Delinquency Prevention and Control by the Schools

---

The April 1999 shootings at Columbine High School in Littleton, Colorado and the March 1998 shootings at a Jonesboro, Arkansas Middle School were among seven cases of multiple shootings by students in U.S. schools that received widespread media coverage over a 19-month period.

In addition to reporting the details of the shootings, newspaper journalists attempted to answer the questions that occupied many minds; "Why? Why this shooting? Why this rash of shootings in schools? Experts, politicians, and parents indicted the general culture of violence in the United States, a southern culture of violence, media violence in the news and entertainment industries, a generation of kids out of control, gangs, individual psychopathology, family problems, and guns.

. . . these seven shootings, by nine male students, resulted in the deaths of 13 female and nine male students as well as one female and one male teacher and injuries to 32 female and 24 male students and two female teachers.[1]

Although school violence has captured strong media attention, a recent Gallup Report on citizens' views regarding the biggest problems in public schools in their community revealed that respondents with children in public schools ranked lack of financial support/funding/money as their greatest concern and overcrowded schools/large schools as their second greatest concern.[2]

The Head Start early education program will be able to enroll 4,000 fewer children under the next two-year state budget, Governor Bob Taft said Friday. Taft also said 15,000 fewer families would be eligible for child care help under proposed changes meant to slow the growth of the state's child care subsidy program.[3]

*   *   *

When school lets out, Renae Walker walks downstairs to the basement to pick up her 7-month-old daughter. Walker is one of 11 girls in the district who participate in the Learning Center, a day-care center and transportation program. It's designed to keep teen mothers in school, but the district said it can't afford the $104,000 annual cost. . . . The district will keep the center open through the end of this school year and will make a decision on its future then.

176

... Donna Holt, who helped start the center in 1987, wants it to stay open. "People need to ask, 'How much does it cost society later if we won't do something to get these girls an education?'"[4]

The examples just given illustrate the contrasting problems facing public schools today. The threat of extreme school violence still exists and national attention regarding school problems tends to focus on such "infamous school violence," which refers to "violent acts in schools that generate widespread media attention."[5] However, the day-to-day problems of victimization faced by the more than one million students who attend public schools (bullying by peers, fist fights, physical abuse by peers, character assassination, sexual harassment, fear of victimization going to and returning from school) are also of great concern for school administrators. Inadequate funding, large classes, dilapidated buildings, lack of equipment and books, and discipline problems are far more pressing matters than being prepared for the types of dramatic incidents highlighted by the media.

In this chapter, we examine the role of education in American society, particularly its function as a means to advance economically, socially, and culturally, and discuss the problems that inhibit the achievement of these goals for some children.

The American dream, as forged and promulgated from the beginning of our national existence, has always included reference to education as the "great equalizer," the ladder by which the poorest immigrant, ghetto dweller, or deprived rural child could climb to the pinnacle of success, as measured by occupational status, cultural attainment, or conspicuous consumption. Public schools, designed to assist in the realization of this dream, existed even in Colonial times, and the child-saving reforms at the turn of the 20th century included pressures for enactment of compulsory-attendance laws, regulations against child labor that would encourage young people to remain in school, and community pride in the education system.[6]

Now, Americans are bombarded daily with bulletins that something has gone wrong and that the dreams and visions of earlier eras are taking on the trappings of a national nightmare. Studies of the reading levels of high school graduates—and even of college students—have revealed that many young people do not possess the most rudimentary skills. Financial crises force many school districts to operate in an atmosphere of uncertainty, constantly appealing to taxpayers for levies that will provide funds to avert teachers' strikes or pay for badly needed physical-plant repairs. The results have been larger classes; the elimination of "nonessential" programs such as classical and foreign languages, music, and art; pressures on teachers with many years of experience to take early retirement and reduce the financial burden their salaries place on the district; and the hiring of inexperienced new teachers whose entry-level salaries will fit more comfortably into the school budget.

Even more devastating than the financial crises and achievement problems has been the discovery that our schools have become the sites of crime and violence, drug dealing, and general lawlessness, which are so difficult to control that in too many cases teaching must take second place to maintaining order and preserving the physical well-being of students and staff. In 1996, students ages 12–18 were the victims of 2.1 million in-school thefts and 255,000 serious violent crime incidents (such as sexual assault, robbery, and aggravated assault).[7] In a 2001 survey of students in grades 6 through 12, approximately 3 percent reported that they had carried a gun to school; 13 percent said they had carried a knife, club, or other weapon; 5 percent revealed that they had threatened another student with a gun, knife, or club; 37 percent said they had threatened another student by hitting, slapping, or kicking; 3 percent said they had hurt another student using a gun, knife, or club; and 29 percent said they had hurt another student by hitting, slapping, or kicking.[8] The danger of victimization by serious violent crime is greatest for students in urban schools and greater in large schools (more than 1,000 students) than in smaller ones, but student vulnerability to theft is similar in urban, suburban, and rural schools.[9] Teachers are also victims of school crime. In the years 1992 through 1996, teachers were victims of 123,800 violent crimes (30 for every 1,000 teachers) and 18,000 (4 of every 1,000 teachers), were victims of serious violent crime (robbery, aggravated assault, rape, or sexual assault). Teachers were also victims of an average of 192,400 thefts per year (46 for every 1,000 teachers).[10]

The costs of school vandalism and crime must be measured not only in terms of damage estimates, but in the school funds that must be diverted from educational purposes to pay for security guards and protective devices at a time when many school districts are facing financial crises. Schools have responded to the threats to the welfare of students and teachers by installing metal detectors and other security measures and by having armed security guards or police officers present in the schools.

In addition to financial considerations, there are costs in terms of time and concentration lost from educational activities, and of the personal traumas that make learning more difficult. These cannot even be estimated. An associate superintendent of Los Angeles schools observed:

> The fear of violence, both physical and psychological, is reflected in students' inability to concentrate on classroom activities due to apprehension and anxieties regarding incidents which have and may take place in the halls, on the campus, and to and from school.[11]

The atmosphere of many city schools also presents something less than a stimulating, creative environment for teachers. The following excerpt from a handbook published by the New York United Federation of Teachers offers a helpful suggestion for female teachers:

> If a rapist is armed, the police urge that his victim offer no resistance, lest she be maimed or fatally injured. If he is not armed, a woman should remember that her knee or almost any instrument can become a weapon: A Bic pen will open a beer can—or a kidney or an eye.[12]

Teachers have reasons to be concerned about their personal safety. The following story illustrates just how dangerous the school environment can be.

> An elementary school janitor is accused of killing an occupational therapist who police say struggled with her killer in her bloodstained classroom. Martin Saiz, 20, was arrested Saturday. . . .

Carolyn Thurman Rustvold, 28, of Albuquerque was last seen Friday at Montezuma Elementary School. Her body had not been found as of Monday morning, and police were trying to determine what type of weapon, if any, was used.[13]

Although the information presented up to this point has painted a dreary picture of the American educational system, the system's many successes must not be overlooked. In a report by the National Center for Education Statistics, the introduction of metal detectors and surveillance cameras is credited with reducing weapons and crime in the schools. In the years from 1995 through 2001, there was a steady decline in the number of students carrying weapons at school, and the percentages of students reporting streets gangs in their schools was also reduced. The only major increase was in the number of students who reported being threatened or bullied. School officials were praised for balancing prevention programs and crime intervention.[14]

We will now examine the monumental tasks of socialization and education that have been assigned to the schools and explore the conditions in contemporary life that have contributed to the present recognized difficulties; we will also describe programs designed to attack and reduce the problems of delinquency that are identified and intensified in the schools.

THE SCHOOL AS A DELINQUENCY-PRODUCING INSTITUTION

The indictment of many schools as delinquency-producing institutions seems to center on two types of accusations: (1) that the schools have failed as socialization institutions; that is, delinquency is produced because young people have not been taught the social skills that enable them to interact appropriately with peers and adults; or (2) that failure in academic subjects leads to situations in which youths are shamed or downgraded by peers and teachers or in which they develop such negative self-images that they undertake delinquent behavior as a defense mechanism or a method of gaining attention or status. Each of these charges will be examined in detail in the following sections.

Schools' Failure in Socialization

Outside the family, the school is the scene of most youthful activity from childhood through adolescence. The school provides a much more complex socialization setting than the family unit does, since more varied forces interact and pull against each other there for a youth's loyalty and attention. Although schools are established and administered by adults and their organizational goals are set by adults, they are also the focal point of interaction for the peer culture, which in many instances has goals different from, or at least not in total accord with, the goals set by school administrators and pursued by the faculty.

The school provides the first location of socialization away from the family unit, where a child can be exposed to ideas at variance with those learned at home, and where choices of behavior and companions must be made without dependence on parents.

The criticism of the American school system as an agent of socialization has centered on its apparent inability in many instances to meld the divergent elements presented to it by the family and the community, to serve as the location of peer-culture formation, and to produce a socially acceptable citizen. It appears that somewhere in the process, the tendency toward deviance promoted by forces brought into the school from the family, the neighborhood, or peers overcomes the efforts exerted by the school toward positive socialization, and delinquent behavior results.

Within the school environment, enforcement of discipline is recognized as a pressing social-interaction problem. Explanations for the perceived breakdown in discipline include a lessening of respect by youths for adults in general; development of sophistication and disillusionment at increasingly earlier ages; parents' failure to support school personnel in their attempts to maintain discipline; students' increasing demands for their "rights" without concomitant realization of their responsibilities; home environments that are lacking in supervision and discipline; and the need to be entertained, brought on by constant exposure to the mass media, and related to decreased attention spans and the inability to sit still or concentrate for extended periods of time.

Another cause of discipline problems in school is student apathy. School is viewed by many young people as a necessary evil that must be endured but in which they are not bound to take an active interest. They are there to pass the time, and they lack the motivation to achieve or even actively participate. Somewhere in the process of socialization within the school experience, they have ceased to view themselves as a vital part of the activity within the school setting. They come to function as spectators rather than participants in the social interactions of the school.

The problems of socialization faced by school systems in some areas go far beyond basic educational activities. In disadvantaged urban settings in particular, the schools may be regarded by parents as free babysitters and expected to assume responsibility for many types of training that should have been accomplished long before the child enters school. Children may enter school without having experienced or mastered the basic skills needed to succeed there, including the ability to listen, to answer a direct question, or to go through elementary problem-solving processes. In extreme cases, children may not even know their own names.

Amos noted the impossible burdens too often placed upon the schools:

> The school, through a combination of public apathy, home neglect, and public pressure, has attempted to become all things to all children without the resources, knowledge, or public support to succeed. The school may feed, clothe, teach, treat, transport, and counsel our young. These services have been influenced and molded by the middle-class philosophy of our school as the principal agency to shape our youth.[15]

Parents with serious financial problems may turn to the school as the obvious source of some kinds of help for their children, particularly in cases where the lack of shoes or clothing is keeping the children from attending school. Although some schools have well-organized programs to assist such children, others do not. Rebuffs received when requests of this type are made known to insensitive or uncaring school personnel may serve to alienate parents and children from close involvement with the schools.

In spite of what may seem at times to be insurmountable odds, schools must continue to provide a social milieu that supplies many experiences and benefits not available in the home if they are to function as delinquency-preventing rather than delinquency-producing institutions. An example of a program that seeks to provide positive socialization of this type is the Youth Gentleman's Club, designed by the Cleveland Task Force on Violent Crime, and developed in two Cleveland elementary schools. The club is designed to improve the members' attitudes, behavior, and academic performance through counseling, group discussion, role playing, and after-school activities. The boys discuss real problems they might face, such as what to do if someone offers them a ride in a stolen car or how to respond when another person tries to provoke violence. Since many of the boys have experienced problems in their family situations, the club focuses on developing their self-esteem, pride, and sense of community. In its five years of operation, the club has influenced hundreds of boys in a positive way.[16]

School Environment and Delinquency.   The increasing amount of delinquent behavior within the schools has been attributed to the impersonal, repressive atmosphere created there. Particularly on the junior and senior high school levels, styles of building construction, consolidation of districts into huge central schools, budget crunches that have forced the creation of large classes and formalized student-teacher contacts, and even computerization of scheduling and grading have reduced opportunities for positive social interaction between school personnel and students.

Two major factors determine the climate or environment of a school. These are the characteristics of the students, parents, and community from which the students are drawn and the manner in which the school is administered. Not all schools are alike, either in physical structure or administration. As noted earlier, funding and resources are major concerns for parents with school-age children. Funding for school systems in the United States is a joint venture between the states and the local communities. Therefore, the physical plant of a school, the equipment, and the quality of instruction are dependent on the wealth of the community in which the school is located. Other than the core curriculum and programs required by the state boards of education, the variety of courses, special programs offered, and the quality of the teachers will be a reflection of the priorities of the citizens within the community, particularly the value they place on education.

Generally, the more wealthy a community is, the more likely it is that an enriched educational program will exist. Schools in upper middle-class communities have swimming pools, gyms with state-of-the-art equipment, and science labs comparable to those found in universities, as well as programs for gifted children that may even include semesters in foreign countries. In contrast, other schools have the atmosphere of prisons. Students may have to pass through metal detectors as they enter buildings, drug-sniffing dogs are periodically called in to check students' lockers, and security guards or uniformed police officers are present. If these conditions of repressive control are not utilized, the alternative may be a climate of fear that makes the school experience one of daily dread of physical harm. These schools are likely to be located in communities with high rates of crime, poverty, and unemployment; many single-parent households; and poorly educated parents. The communities where they are located may have limited resources to invest in the schools and, more important, these communities are generally not structurally stable and have few strong leaders interested in promoting quality education. Typically, the parents living in such communities have not been involved in school matters or policies or have felt powerless to influence them. The students attending such schools bring with them the values, norms, expectations, and attitudes about the value of education they have learned through interaction with parents, peers, and others within the community.

The communities in which the large majority of school systems in the United States operate fall between the extremes of wealth or socio-economic deprivation. Problems related to physical plants, educational resources, quality of teachers, and violence and disruption within the schools exist in varying degrees.

School Climate and School Disorder.   The school experience produces life-long memories. For some it was pleasant, exciting, and rewarding, and the goal of becoming educated was accomplished. For others it was miserable, boring, uneventful, and unrewarding. Very little learning occurred. Most youths pass through their school years without experiencing trauma on a daily basis. Researchers believe that the combined efforts of school administrators, teachers, parents, students, and community groups can make attending school a rewarding experience. The end result of their efforts can be improvement in the school climate and reductions in school disruption.

School climate includes communication patterns, norms about what is appropriate behavior, patterns of influence, role relationships between staff and students, friendship patterns between student peers, protection from victimization, and discipline measures used within the school.[17] Welsh conducted a study of the relationship between school climate and school disruption in Philadelphia middle schools. More than 5,000 students, the majority of whom were minority group members, were involved in the research. The school climate measurement scale consisted of items related to student characteristics, including involvement in school activities, positive peer associations, belief in school rules, effort at school, and school rewards given. The psychosocial climate measurement items included perception of school safety, clarity of the rules, fairness of rules, respect for students, student influence in school affairs, and administrative planning and action. It was found that those students who expressed greater belief in school rules, were motivated to achieve, and had positive peer associations had much lower levels of misconduct than students who did not have these characteristics. It was found that students' perceptions of respect for students, fairness of rules, clarity of rules, and planning and action were associated with low levels of student victimization. Even though the youths in the sample came from very similar backgrounds (Philadelphia schools), the researcher found considerable variation within the schools in the amount of disorder and misconduct that occurred. He concluded that a positive social climate can reduce social disorder within schools and this climate can be created by cooperative and coordinated efforts of administrators, teachers, parents, and other community members.[18]

Use of Medication As a Control Technique.   The use of medication to alter the behavior of students is another control technique that has great potential for abuse. One of the most frequently diagnosed disorders handled with drug therapy is attention deficit disorder (ADD), estimated to affect as many as 5 percent of all children, but about four times more common in boys than in girls. This problem, characterized by a combination of inattentive, impulsive, and hyperactive behavior,[19] is frequently handled with drug therapy, particularly use of Ritalin.

Instances of parents requesting and receiving prescriptions for drugs to help them control highly active children seem to be increasing. As Bratter noted:

> The penalty for active and curious elementary students who "disrupt" the serenity of the classroom . . . is to be labelled "hyperkinetic," which is the term used to describe overactive, easily distractable, excitable children. Once this syndrome—which cannot be diagnosed by any standard neurological or psychological test—has been identified, referral is made to either a pediatrician or a child psychiatrist who has a more potent armentarium—medication.[20]

Indiscriminate referrals for drug therapy have the potential for introducing the child to a lifetime of drug dependency or addiction. There is also the possibility that drugs may be used to subdue children who have no drug-treatable disorder simply to make classroom control easier. Both possibilities are cause for concern.

Victimization at School

> A second grader at L_____ school took his uncle's gun to school and shot another second grader. He is seven years old. The victim was only shot in the hand, so luckily he will be okay. It is just so sad these days. I mean, how do you prosecute and detain a seven-year-old?[21]

Schools are faced with the challenge of providing an atmosphere where children can concentrate, learn, and interact with caring teachers and their peers. In many instances they are succeeding, but schools today must deal with problems that were less severe in the past. Among these are violent and threatening behavior by some youths and the increasing presence of gangs in the schools and near school buildings.

The sensational school shootings that were widely reported drew attention to the problem of violence in the schools. However, the violence encountered by most children occurs in much less dramatic forms. In many schools, violence happens on a daily basis, and even when it is detected by authority figures it is difficult to control. Much of this violence takes the form the bullying, which is defined as "behaviors that treat other persons abusively or affect others by means of force or coercion."[22] This definition includes such common occurrences as fist fighting, sexual harassment, and character assassination.

Research indicates that boys engage in direct physical bullying more often that girls do. Girls are more involved in indirect methods of harassment, such as verbal abuse. Boys tend to be bullied by other boys, while girls are bullied by both girls and boys.[23] These forms of violence may establish a climate of fear and cause absenteeism. Some children do not attend because they fear for their personal safety on the way to and from school, and also in the school building. The National Crime Victimization Survey found that 12 percent of students in urban schools feared being harmed or attacked at school or going to or from school, and the same percentage reported avoiding certain places at school (e.g., the entrance, certain hallways or stairs, rest rooms) because they feared they might be victimized there.[24]

Danner and Carmody completed a content analysis of 230 newspaper articles related to the seven most infamous school violence cases with the purpose of abstracting what the writers concluded was the motivation for the shootings. They found that approximately 20 percent of the writers identified the motivations for the killings as a response to being bullied or picked on, or the fact that the bullying made being in that particular school environment a painful experience. Other major motivational factors delineated were easy availability of guns; widespread approval of guns and modeling of gun use by family and relatives (16%); school officials, police, and parents ignoring the youth murderers' warnings that they would do something desperate (13%); retaliations against girlfriends (9%); and the whole act defies explanations (15%).[25] This may illustrate how violence in the school leads to escalation of the level of violence and retaliation.

Fears Related to Guns, Drugs, and Gangs. The presence of youths within the schools who belong to gangs, carry weapons, or are involved in drug-related activities increases the likelihood of students being victimized and contributes to a climate of fear. In a nationwide survey of students in grades 6 through 12, 17 percent claimed that street gangs were present in their schools. The gangs were reported to be most prevalent in urban schools (25%) and in public schools (19%). Gangs were slightly more prevalent in the middle schools than in the high schools.[26]

We noted earlier that the preventive measures taken by the school have resulted in a substantial decrease in the number of students who carry handguns and in the number of weapons that get into buildings.[27] Still, the National Youth Risk Behavior Survey found that half of the youths who carried a weapon at any time carried it onto school grounds.[28] Another national study reported that, in the 2000–2001 school year, 3 percent of the students claimed to have carried a gun to school one or more times; 5 percent reported that they had threatened a student with a deadly weapon; and 4 percent said they used this weapon to injure another student one or more times.[29]

Youth self-report behavior surveys have also found connections between drug use, carrying guns, and gang membership. In a nationwide longitudinal survey of school children between the ages of 12 and 16, more than one fifth of the students reported using marijuana within the past year and 21 percent of the marijuana users claimed to have sold it. Those who used or sold drugs were more likely to be involved in carrying handguns and gang membership. For example, 21 percent of the marijuana users reported carrying a handgun and 14 percent of the marijuana users belonged to gangs. The proportion of nonmarijuana users who reported carrying a handgun or belonged to a gang was significantly lower.[30] The National Survey of

Youth Risk Behavior found that one third of high school students had been offered, sold, or given an illegal drug on school property in the past year.[31] In all of the studies, there was considerable variation in the youths' involvement with guns, drugs, or gangs by the size and locations of their schools and the ethnic and racial composition of the student body.

Fear of Social Failure.   In addition to the fear of physical violence, the fear of social failure may act as a strong force for many young people to withdraw from school through truancy, or to dissociate themselves from the mainstream of "socially successful" students through either drug or alcohol use or apathy toward school activities. Such young people may already have passed the boundaries of defined delinquent behavior or can readily be influenced to show their disregard for the school social situation by rebelling against it.

Those who have a low social standing in the school setting have little to lose by misbehavior, in contrast to the socially successful adolescents who have a high stake in behaving properly so that they do not jeopardize their positions as class officers, athletic-team members, cheerleaders, or members of the most prestigious academic or social cliques.

Aspirations and Delinquency.   The continued emphasis on "going on to college" as a definition of high school success may also serve as a stimulus to deviant behavior for those who have little hope of achieving this status. A study of violence against teachers by high school youths found that 65 percent of those who had attacked teachers still regarded graduation from high school as "very important." In the light of this finding, the students' violence toward teachers might be interpreted as a manifestation of frustration by students who aspire to academic success but are frustrated in their efforts to achieve it.[32]

The fact that attending college extends the period of dependence on parents beyond the high school years creates a role-conflict situation for high school students who expect to go on to college. Although many youths, particularly those from affluent families, have already achieved a number of the symbols of adulthood—their own cars, part-time jobs that give them money to spend exclusively on themselves, and a good deal of freedom from adult control—they must still assume a posture of submission and respect while in school as the price of their "ticket of admission" to college. Placed in such a situation, young people who are outwardly conforming may explode in paradoxical behavior—vandalism, sexual promiscuity, or drug or alcohol abuse—as a means of expressing their adulthood and desire for independence, which seem to be denied them.

Young people who are not planning to go on to college, on the other hand, may not feel the same constraints to maintain an outward demeanor of conforming behavior. They may anticipate the full status of adulthood that will be theirs upon high school graduation and may regard many of the activities and regulations of high school as meaningless and having little relationship to their future plans.

Students' Failure in Academic Endeavors

The inability to succeed academically has also been correlated with delinquency development. Many children enter school from home and neighborhood environments that have predisposed them toward academic failure. They may come from homes where the degree of environmental disorganization is such that any sort of serious intellectual pursuit is a near impossibility. Overcrowded, noisy, substandard housing; lack of attention from parents; and inexperience with books, writing materials, exchange of ideas, or conversation with adults all may handicap a child and make it difficult for him or her to succeed at school.

Social control theory[33] suggests that a student whose ties to conventional society are weak could become a prime candidate for delinquency, substance abuse, and gang involvement. Those without strong attachments to school, family, or community organizations are at risk.

A national study of children identified by school teachers and counselors as "at risk" for academic failure found that, if a child came from a family where a parent was alcoholic or lost a job during the year, the parents were employed in low-level jobs, or the parents were not high school graduates, the odds were overwhelming that this student would be at risk in many areas, such as being suspended from school, using drugs, or having low self-esteem.[34]

The report summarized the dilemmas schools face every day:

> The school does not cause children to come to school hungry every day. The school did not create conditions that require some children to go home to an empty house every day after school. The school did not cause an increase in the divorce rate or alcohol consumption or parental conflict or adolescent suicide. The school did not promote the inanity of much of television programming today. The school did not push the National Rifle Association's agenda of no restrictions on gun sales and no registration of handguns. . . .

> Educators have to deal with problems that youngsters bring to school every day. . . . The problems will be solved only if society changes in ways that enhance children's lives rather than endanger them.[35]

Tracking and Delinquency.   Environmental disadvantages may also result in poor showings on achievement and intelligence tests, which in turn result in placement in schools, or in ability groups within the schools, where disadvantaged youths interact almost exclusively with those from the same social backgrounds. One school practice of this type that has been roundly criticized and challenged as contributing to delinquent and disruptive behavior in school is known as "tracking." This involves separating students into groups called "tracks," at the time of entrance into junior or senior high school, of those who plan to attend college, those who plan to enter vocational schools, those who anticipate careers in business or industry, those who are undecided about career plans (general students), and those who are in need of remedial work. Young people assigned to the various tracks receive course schedules that are judged appropriate for their needs and generally attend classes almost exclusively with others who are assigned to the same track. Although junior and senior high school students participate in deciding what tracks they are assigned to, they and their parents are guided by suggestions from teachers and guidance counselors and these suggestions may be based not only on such objective factors as past academic records and intelligence and achievement test scores, but also on the counselors' and teachers' perceptions of the family's social-class status and the real potential of the child.

Critics of the tracking system maintain that such placement is in fact an ascribed-status assignment that has far-reaching implications for the student's entire school career and great bearing on future career aspirations. Through various cues given in the school social environment, the youths in the lower tracks perceive themselves as less prestigious, intelligent, and successful than those in the college-prep sections; the students categorize their fellow students and develop friendship patterns on the basis of track; and teachers generally use different teaching techniques in college-prep and lower-track classes.

Kelly regards tracking as a major delinquency-producing variable within the schools and uses the term "status degradation ceremonies" to describe the manner in which certain students are informed that they are "not college material" or assigned to tracks within the school that label them "slow," "educationally disadvantaged," or "not academically inclined." Once placed in tracks where they are not expected to achieve, students begin meeting these expectations. A self-fulfilling prophecy begins to mold these young people into the image others have of them. Kelly states:

> Once a pupil is assigned to a low school status or deviant career line, that student must become subject to and be influenced by the prevailing value system, the general content of which is frequently nonacademic in nature. It is in this way that a deviant, delinquent, and perhaps ultimately a criminal career, is launched.[36]

Kelly also observed:

> These pupils must, if they expect to become a member in good standing, act in accordance with the anti-academic values that characterize a school's deviant statuses. It is this very demand for conformity that will guarantee the continued production of nonconformity.[37]

A study of tracking in high schools characterized the practice as "harming millions of students in American society."[38] Tracking was found to be particularly destructive for students with middle-range abilities. It was discovered that many Latino and African American students and about 20 percent of white students who performed well on the eighth grade tests used to determine high school track placements are misplaced in courses below their abilities and that the proportion of high-ability black and Hispanic students not taking college prep courses in math and science was more than twice that of white and Asian-American students who had the same level of ability. The study also discovered that students who planned to go to college and their parents were often unaware that the youths had been tracked out of college-prep science and math classes. Deceptive course titles often hid the fact that the courses were not geared toward preparation for college.[39]

The study concluded that being placed in the lower tracks contributes to lack of achievement.

Being at the bottom of the high track appears to bring better educational results than being at the top of the low track. High-ability students in the lower tracks learn little and get lower grades than those of equal ability in the higher track. Most kids can learn a lot, but aren't learning much, and too often schools use lack of ability as an excuse for poor performance.[40]

Various types of educational groupings have been tested in court actions and ruled to be inappropriate. In *Anthony v. Marshall County Board of Education* (1970), a court of appeals ruled against the use of achievement-test scores for assignment of students to certain schools because it resulted in the segregation of black children who had received their earlier education in an inferior school system.[41] In *Moses v. Washington Parish School Board et al.*, the court ruled that the testing used at a particular elementary school to assign students to ability groups violated the 14th Amendment rights of the black children there and made the judgment that "homogeneous grouping is educationally detrimental to students assigned to lower sections and blacks comprise a disproportionate number of the students in the lower sections."[42]

Exploration of a Possible Link Between Learning Disabilities and Delinquency. In Chapter 2 we discussed the research efforts that have been undertaken to attempt to establish some link between hyperactivity, learning disabilities, and delinquency, and noted that, to date, the evidence for a link between them is suggestive rather than documented. A study involving nearly 1,700 youths examined the delinquency records and self-reported delinquencies of comparison groups of learning-disabled youngsters and those without such disabilities. It was found that those with learning disabilities and those without them reported being involved in, and had been referred to the police for, about the same amount of delinquent behavior.[43]

In spite of the apparent lack of definitive data to make a connection between learning disabilities and delinquency, some juvenile court administrators and personnel have been sufficiently convinced that a causal relationship exists between the two to set up special programs for learning-disabled youths referred to them. A manual for juvenile court judges prepared by the National Council of Juvenile and Family Court Judges notes that learning disabilities contribute to academic underachievement and frustration and can also have a variety of social consequences, including poor impulse control, little frustration tolerance, inability to understand social cues, and aggressive behavior.[44]

If the existence of a learning disability is uncovered, referrals may be made to developmental optometrists, audiologists, ophthalmologists, psychiatrists, clinical psychologists, or occupational therapists.

The difficulties that may inhibit children's ability to succeed academically may also include various types of health problems. Inadequate prenatal care or postnatal diet can result in retardation or bad health.

Although a good deal of longitudinal comparative research would be needed to establish definite causal relationships between learning disabilities and delinquency, or between health or emotional problems and delinquency, enough evidence of such problems among children who have been defined as delinquent already exists to prompt action by the schools. Early definition of these problems and placement in remedial programs, or referral for help to other community agencies before the child is defined by the peer group as "different" or develops a negative self-image, is a logical first step. Testing children involved in school-related delinquencies to determine whether learning disabilities or health problems exist is another course of action that can be followed by remedial referrals where the need is indicated.

THE RELATION OF DROPPING OUT TO DELINQUENCY

Although compulsory-attendance laws in the various states set school-attendance requirements at ages ranging from 6 through 18, not only do many students drop out before the upper age of compulsory attendance or before graduation, but a surprisingly high number never "drop in." These include severely handicapped children never identified or not receiving services and children of illegal immigrants who have not enrolled them in school. Other youths never return to school after they have been expelled or suspended or are not re-enrolled by their parents when they move from one school district to another. The potential for unacceptable behavior in this large group of young people who are idle, receiving no formal education of any kind, and isolated from positive socialization is a cause for great concern.

Our discussion here will focus on youths who "dropped in" before dropping out; that is, young people who have been enrolled in school but leave at some point before graduation. In 1996, 86 percent of students had completed high school by age 24. Of these, 10 percent had finished their studies by passing a high school equivalency exam such as the GED test. The rate of high school completion was lower among Hispanics (63%) than for non-Hispanic whites (92%) or blacks (83%).[45] Language problems appeared to be one factor related to noncompletion of high school. In a 1995 study, 80 percent of foreign born Hispanic youths reported that they spoke English "not well" or "not at all." Forty-four percent of the foreign born Hispanic students ages 16 to 24 had dropped out of school, compared to 29 percent of all Hispanic youths in this age group. The dropout rates for black (13%) and white youths (7%) were much lower.[46] Socio-economic factors also were found to be related to high school completion. Ninety-seven percent of youths from high-income families had completed high school, compared to 87 percent of those from middle-income families and 75 percent of those from low-income families.[47]

In many instances, dropping out is the final step in a progressive alienation from the school that may begin with failure or difficulty with subjects in the elementary grades, progress to apathy or disruptive behavior in junior high school, then to periods of absenteeism that become progressively longer, and culminating in dropping out. Studies of youths who have dropped out of school have attempted to identify their characteristics. Frymer summarized the findings of several studies.

> The general findings were that dropouts had been retained in grade or were overage, were involved in pregnancy, worked more than 20 hours outside the school, had low reading test scores, had parents who had not finished high school, and had lower self-concepts than students who had not dropped out of school.[48]

Another study of dropouts found that 4 out of 10 youths left school because they were failing or did not like school. Although an equal number of males and females said they dropped out because they could not get along with their teachers, more males than females in the study left school because of suspension or expulsion, while many of the females (27%) left because they became pregnant. Males were more likely than females to drop out because they found a job (36%, compared to 22%).[49]

Youths who drop out may not have lost their desire to succeed educationally or complete their education in the hope of improving their economic status. In a later section of this chapter we will discuss options or programs that are designed to prevent dropping out or provide opportunities for youths who seem unable to succeed in conventional school settings.

SCHOOL VANDALISM

School vandalism is a pervasive problem. Although the problem is more intense in large urban districts, it also occurs in suburban and rural schools. Students are also the victims of vandalism. They may experience damage to their personal property (cars, clothing, or other items) while they are on school campuses.

The replacement costs of items destroyed by vandalism are only a portion of the total costs to the schools of this misbehavior. Insurance rates for school property have skyrocketed, and the cost of hiring security guards and installing electronic sensors and alarm equipment is also highly burdensome to school budgets.

Since school vandalism has increased alarmingly in recent years, it has come to be viewed as another result of family disintegration, the influence of the mass media, and the changing climate within the schools. Much of this destructive behavior is undertaken as a way of "getting even" with school personnel who are perceived as repressive or unjust. In addition to the obvious motive of revenge against school personnel, the problem of vandalism has been variously attributed to drug and alcohol use by juveniles, which reduces their inhibitions; lack of supervision by parents or their failure to punish a youth found to have engaged in this activity; and the permissiveness of the courts in dealing with school vandals.

Schools have introduced increased forces of security guards, guard dogs within school buildings, alarm systems, sensing devices, and expanded security lighting at great cost in the hope of reducing vandalism. Shattered windows are frequently replaced with break-resistant plastic ones.

Some districts have reported successes with student involvement in vandalism prevention. Since the use of expanded security systems and surveillance forces has not resulted in impressive reductions in vandalism, expanded programs of student involvement, parent participation, and community awareness of the problems of vandalism in the schools may produce the desired results. Initiation of positive programs aimed at beautifying the school grounds and buildings in which students are meaningfully involved may also help exert peer pressure against vandalism.

THE RELATION OF SCHOOL INVOLVEMENT TO DRUG AND ALCOHOL USE

The use of drugs and alcohol by high school students has been documented by a number of self-reported-use research studies. On the basis of their findings, it appears that the vast majority of adolescents experiment with various kinds of illegal substances (alcohol, marijuana, other drugs) during their school years. Self-reports by high school seniors showed that 73 percent had used alcohol and 37 percent had used marijuana during the past 12 months.[50] A higher percentage of males (57%) than of females (47%) had used alcohol in the past 30 days, and heavy drinking (five or more drinks in a row in the previous two weeks) was reported by two of every five males and one of every four females.[51] More males than females had used marijuana in the past 12 months (42%, compared to 33%), but use of other drugs in the past year was similar for males and females (22% for males and 18% for females).[52]

A nationwide study of youth risk behavior explored the question of how early youths had used alcohol or marijuana. About a third of the students (31%) reported that they had used alcohol before age 13. Ten percent had used marijuana and 1 percent had used cocaine before age 13. Initiation into alcohol and marijuana use occurred most frequently in the ninth grade. Thirty-two percent of the students reported that they have been offered, sold, or given drugs on school property during the past 12 months.[53]

Self-report data from high school seniors have also provided convincing evidence of a link between drug use and delinquency. When those who used drugs were compared with those who reported no drug use on items that described unlawful behavior, drug users were more frequent offenders in every instance. These items included taking something from a store without paying, damaging school property, taking a car without the owner's permission, setting fires, and striking an instructor or supervisor. Drug users also reported being more involved in violent offenses, including taking part in fights with a group of friends against another group, hurting someone badly enough that they needed bandages or a doctor, and using a knife or gun to some other weapon to get something from another person.[54]

Rather than being an isolated cause of delinquency, substance abuse must be viewed as another facet of the process of alienation and removal from the mainstream of successful students that results in delinquent behavior. As a result of her study of marijuana use in a suburban community, Tec concluded that the more involved and committed adolescents are to education and their school, the more satisfied they are with school, and the more optimistic they are about their future plans, the less likely they are to use marijuana regularly. She noted that:

> When involved, interested, and satisfied, an adolescent may have neither the inclination nor the time to bother with illegal drugs. Being detached and dissatisfied with school may not necessarily be so unbearable as to lead to extensive drug involvement, but nevertheless leaves one open to experimentation.[55]

Polk and Burkett, who reached similar conclusions about the relation between school success and alcohol use, also made the following suggestions about educational programs designed to make youths aware that they have problems and need help:

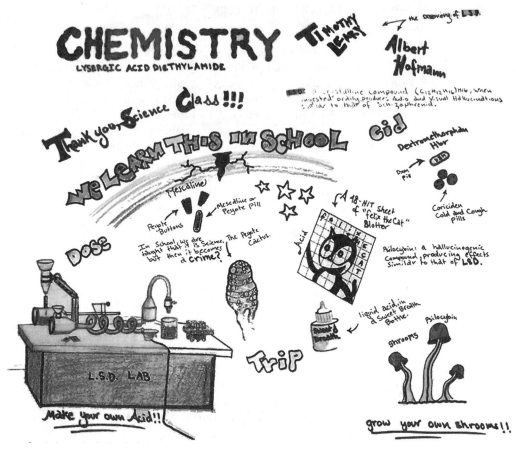

This youth's drawing demonstrates familiarity with the drug culture. *(Source: Rod Schneider, Administrator, Stark Attention Center)*

The adolescents most likely to drink are those who have withdrawn psychologically from the school and have developed elaborate peer defenses against adult attempts to guide and control their behavior. From this we can conclude that the typical lecture, film, and pamphlet approach to alcohol education runs the risk of missing the group for whom its message is most appropriate. Approaches through the classroom are likely to find an attentive audience of eager and cooperative youth who will do little drinking anyway, along with a bored, apathetic—if not antagonistic—tuned-out group who probably will be little affected by the experience.[56]

DEFINING THE APPROPRIATE ROLE OF THE SCHOOLS IN DELINQUENCY PREVENTION

Earlier in this chapter, we noted that the school has been called upon to meet and deal with many problems in children's lives that are not directly related to teaching the prescribed subject matter. Many schools have recognized and responded to these needs by introducing such programs as preschool education, efforts to develop codes of conduct and define students' rights, drug-abuse and venereal-disease education, social and psychological services, truancy- and dropout-prevention efforts, and alternative schools.

Unfortunately, many of these programs, while well-intentioned, are doomed to failure because those who design them are not aware of the extent and the complexity of the problems at-risk children face. In some school districts, particularly in the inner cities, where a large number of students come from dysfunctional and disadvantaged home situations, the school, family members, community agencies, law enforcement agencies, and civic leaders must become involved in cooperative efforts to address these problems.

Social Networking

Krohn used the concepts of social network and personal network to describe and analyze the social and personal relationships of individuals. The social network is a set of persons or organizations linked by social relationships of a specific type, while a personal network represents an individual's link to other people. The term "multiplexity" is used to refer to the number of different role relations any two people have with one another or the number of shared activities they have. Networking theory proposes that the more a person interacts with another person in a variety of situations and contexts, the more the behavior in one context is likely to influence the behavior in another context. For example, if a youth goes to church with his or her parents, asks the parents for help with homework, invites friends to the parents' home, attends school-related functions with parents, and engages in community-sponsored recreationship activities with parents, the youth has a multiplexity network system operating because of the overlapping and interdependence of the role relationships. Both the parents and the child are likely to have personal relationships with a number of the individuals belonging to the various groups mentioned. Krohn hypothesized that "the greater the number of foci over which there is network multiplexity, the lower the probability of delinquent behavior.[57]

Another important factor to consider in networking is network density. This is defined as the extent to which everyone in a social network is in direct relation with each other. A network reaches maximum density when everyone knows everyone else. For example, in a typical family every member usually has direct, personal contact with every other member on a daily basis. On the other hand, it is conceivable that network density may be low for a teacher in a large urban high school, so that the teacher may not know members of his or her classes by name.

While high density can generally be considered a buffer to delinquency, high density can actually have the opposite effect if it is not coupled with network multiplexity. For example, if youths who are members of a delinquent group are highly organized, interact frequently, and have broken their ties with conventional institutions such as the family, church, and school, they have low network multiplexity. The high network density (constantly interacting with delinquent peers) can lead to a weakening of the personal and social controls that tend to inhibit antisocial and illegal behavior.

For many children, strong ties with parents, churches, community agencies, or family friends are nonexistent. They need assistance if they are to develop networks of persons with whom they can interact in a positive manner. The schools can take the lead in helping these youngsters by introducing them to programs in which they can succeed and come to know positive role models. The school buildings could be appropriate locations for this activity.

> The school remains the institution to which parents look for help in their daily struggle to do the best for their children. . . . Some experts believe schools should expand from the traditional 8:00 A.M. to 3:00 P.M. teaching institutions to become all-day community centers concerned with their clients' mental, physical, and emotional needs as well.[58]

Safe School Initiatives

Many students experience violence or other victimization in school or on the way to and from school. In some instances, the victimizers are not other students. They are persons who are in the vicinity of the schools to sell drugs or engage in gang fights. Most offenses by juveniles are committed after 3 P.M. on school days and on non-school days (during summer vacations, holidays, or weekends). The number of school days is almost equal to the number of days when school is not in session. More than half of the violent crimes occur on school days and about 20 percent of them occur in the hours between 3 P.M. and 7 P.M. on school days.[59] These findings suggest that after-school programs or programs for youths during weekends and vacation periods have the potential to reduce violent youth crimes in these at-risk hours.

Even within schools, some classroom situations are out of control, with students and teachers experiencing verbal and physical assaults. According to Dr. Ronald Stephens of the National School Safety Center, clear expectations about what sort of behavior is allowed in the schools must be established. He noted;

> We tend not only to get what we deserve, what we expect, but also what we put up with in terms of the kind of intimidation that occurs on a school campus.[60]

Huff also observed that clear, firm discipline practices and policies play an important part in keeping the schools safe. He found that teachers who were fair but firm were less likely to be assaulted than those who backed down in the face of threats or intimidation.[61]

The Safe Schools/Healthy Students Initiative, a federal program, provides funding for projects designed to prevent violence and substance abuse in the schools and to promote healthy youth development through a joint effort of educators; law enforcement; and juvenile justice, mental health, and social service agencies.[62] A study by the Justice Policy Institute found that the political responses to high-profile incidents of school violence had included eliminating after-school programs, assigning police officers to the schools, increasing security by locking doors and allowing no outsiders to enter the schools without clearance, not allowing students to leave the school during lunch periods, imposing suspensions and expulsions in cases of threats of violence, and zero tolerance for such behavior as carrying firearms or other types of weapons to school. The Institute's report suggested that this was a "moral panic" response to the problem and noted that the risk of violence and death in the schools is much lower than the risk of violence and death through family violence at home. The Institute suggested that instead of stopping after-hour programs in schools, these activities should be expanded. It also recommended prohibition of mass gun sales and encouraged the media to stop sensationalizing school violence cases and report the facts of these incidents in the proper context.[63]

Many schools now have police officers assigned to patrol inside the building and on the school grounds. Students tend to react in a positive way to the officers' presence. In Cleveland, Ohio, officers assigned to the Cleveland Police Mini-Station Program work with selected schools in the city as Police School-Community Resource Officers. The program was developed as a cooperative venture of the Cleveland Police Department, the Cuyahoga County Juvenile Court, the Cleveland Task Force on Violent Crime, and Case Western Reserve University. It was instituted in response to incident reports that indicated problems of truancy, suspension, drugs, peer pressure, gang activity, and a less-than-safe environment within the schools. The program's goals include keeping at-risk youths from dropping out of school, increasing involvement of parents who are effective role models, improvement of students' basic academic skills, development of career orientations on the part of students, and breaking through student alienation to attempt to impede present and future criminal activity. The officers meet regularly with groups of youths who appear to be endangered for involvement in gang- and drug-related activities and are physically present in the school buildings at established times during the day, Although their function as counselors is important, their chief contribution appears to be the security they provided for students coming to and leaving the school grounds.[64]

Drug Education

Created in 1983 by the Los Angeles Police Department, Drug Abuse Resistance Education (D.A.R.E.) has been used in classrooms throughout the United States. D.A.R.E. uses uniformed police officers to present 17 hour-long weekly lessons to fifth and sixth graders. More than half of the nation's school districts have adopted the program. D.A.R.E.'s chief success, according to an evaluation of the program sponsored by the National Institute of Justice, lies in increasing students' knowledge about drugs. The study described its effects on attitudes toward drugs, attitudes toward the police, and self-esteem as "more modest," and only in the case of tobacco use were its effects on substance abuse statistically significant.[65] Another study confirmed that the D.A.R.E. curriculum is effective in reducing smoking by elementary age children. Students who completed the program were five times less likely to start smoking than a comparison group who did not participate in D.A.R.E. Suggestions for improvement of the program's effectiveness have included more interaction with students rather than lecture techniques and expansion of the topics covered to include violence prevention or anger control in addition to drug-related topics.[66]

Alternative Programs

Alternative programming uses creative instructional techniques and activities to promote learning. Such programming usually involves small class sizes, testing to determine the student's entering level of competency and potential, individual attention, behavioral contracting, and assistance with the special problems students may face, such as providing day care for small children, so that their teenage mothers can attend classes.

During the 1970s, more than 2,500 alternative schools were developed in the United States as options to the existing "conventional" school experience in the hope that the "high risk student drop-out population" would have its needs better served.[67]

Although many of the programs lost funding and were eliminated, the alternative schools that are currently operating effectively seek to meet various types of student needs, including security (a safe and orderly learning environment), social needs (through development of new peer and adult networks), self-esteem (by encouraging both academic and social achievement), and self-actualization needs (increasing the student's motivation toward becoming a socially integrated individual).[68] These needs, important at all students, are given intensive attention in alternative programs, with the goal of helping at-risk adolescents succeed and remain in school. The alternative programs described in the following sections are designed to address these needs.

Longfellow Alternative Learning Center Programs.   The Longfellow Center provides three distinct programs. The first, in which students may not be enrolled for more than one year, is designed for students with multiple suspensions and expulsions; the second program, for students with histories of school failure, excessive absences, or academic achievement two or more years below grade level, can be attended for up to two years. A third program, for pregnant students, limits enrollment to six weeks prior to and six weeks after delivery, unless the students wish to remain in the program until the end of the current semester or year. Students are referred to the program from the local juvenile court, group homes for juveniles, juvenile detention centers, or local public or private schools. The academic, vocational, medical, and psychological needs of each student are assessed and considered by the center's Review Panel, which decides on the specialized treatment program for each student. Students are required to attend classes; to meet with personnel specified in their individualized program, who might be counselors, attendance officers, or medical doctors; pursue the course or study designed for them; and modify their behavior to a level appropriate for entry into a regular school setting.[69]

An assessment of the Center's success over a five-year period revealed that 45 percent of the students placed there had been able to complete requirements for high school graduation, either by returning to their home school or completing their studies at Longfellow.[70]

The Phoenix Program.   The Phoenix Program, an alternative project for delinquent youths in Summit County, Ohio, has demonstrated success in attacking the drop-out problem. The program involves an academic program that stresses basic reading, writing, and math skills; a behavior-change component, which includes a point-accumulation system for acceptable behavior and rule compliance in school and at home; and individual and group counseling. Support-group counseling is also used to teach parents management skills for dealing with their children. More than 80 percent of the students in the Phoenix Program are referred by the Ohio Department of Youth Services or the Summit County Juvenile Court, with various school districts making the remaining referrals. More than 90 percent of them have been involved in serious delinquency and 60 percent of the students had committed at least one violent offense before coming to the program. Although many of the students are able to return to their home school, Phoenix has been chartered as a high school and can offer a regular high school diploma.[71]

Levels of Delinquency Prevention and Control by the Schools

Ernst A. Wenk defined four levels of possible school intervention to prevent delinquency: (1) primary prevention, (2) prevention, (3) treatment, and (4) rehabilitation.[72] Wenk's concept of *primary prevention* involves the use of programs that are applied to all children as an insulator against delinquency, without singling out any groups or individuals. Such programs might include preschool head start programs, recreational activities outside school hours, reading clubs, or other programs designed to involve children in the total school experience. Primary prevention could also include in-school presentations of programs on drug and alcohol abuse, and even courses on the workings of the criminal justice system.

At the level of *prevention*, specific children may already have been identified as "at risk" for delinquent behavior, but at this stage they should be regarded as children in need of help rather than potential delinquents. The teacher's role seems all-important in recognizing conditions that may produce the frustration and negative experiences that lead to unacceptable behavior. Diagnosis of reading difficulties at their earliest stages and implementation of effective remedial measures is an important preventive tactic. Response to signals from potential dropouts that they are badly in need of help, and their referral to programs in which they can succeed, is another. Research studies of dropouts have consistently reported their inability to establish supportive relationships with teachers and other adults as a factor in eventual school withdrawal.

At the next level, *treatment*, the children have already been involved in some sort of unacceptable behavior or even criminal acts. In addition to juvenile court diversion programs, which may involve interaction with the school counselors, efforts by teachers and administrators to include the entire family in treatment efforts may have a positive effect. The types of difficulty experienced by a youth should be care-

Alternative schools provide opportunities for individualized instruction. *(Photo credit: The Image Works)*

fully analyzed to determine if placement in a work-study program or tutoring could provide the change needed to break the cycle of failure.

At the fourth level of intervention, *rehabilitation*, a youth who has already been adjudicated delinquent and placed on probation or been institutionalized is returning to school. In such cases, every effort should be made by administrators and teachers not to duplicate the climate of rejection that the young person may have already experienced in his or her own family or peer group. Assignment of a specific teacher as this child's in-school counselor, transfer to a new school in the district where the child's past misbehavior is not known to other students, or placement in a work-study program may have some desirable effects.[73]

Since the school has been identified as the primary site of peer-culture development, efforts to involve all students in extracurricular activities may reduce feelings of isolation from the social environment. Expansion of the range of school-sanctioned activities to include those that might be of greater interest to youths from blue-collar backgrounds could help in this regard—for instance, wider development of intramural sports activities, to allow involvement and success in athletics for far more students, and school honors convocations, which make a point of recognizing the outstanding students in all programs rather than concentrating on college-prep students. Since removal from the mainstream of successful students was identified over and over again by researchers as a factor in school-related delinquency, providing more opportunities for success may prove to be a compensating factor in some instances.

SUMMARY

In this chapter the problems of school-related delinquency have been examined. The dramatic amounts of violent behavior, vandalism, and drug and alcohol use by high school students were highlighted, as well as the financial difficulties, falling achievement levels, truancy, absenteeism, and dropout problems encountered by the schools.

When delinquency is school-related, it may be the result of socialization difficulties experienced there by some children. Those from disadvantaged backgrounds may come to school without mastery of the basic skills needed to succeed, and perhaps without needed clothing and food. The inability of the schools to provide resources that are not their responsibility may handicap efforts to teach these children. Insensitivity of some teachers to the backgrounds and problems of such children is also destructive of school progress. In many instances, parents identify the school as the nearest and most accessible source of assistance with their problems and rely on the social and counseling services provided there, which may be minimal.

The impersonal, bureaucratic atmosphere in some schools is also blamed for student socialization problems. Large classes, strict regulations regarding movement within the school, and lack of opportunity for interaction with teachers on a one-to-one basis all contribute to the problems of student noninvolvement that may breed unacceptable behavior.

Fear of physical violence going to or from school or within the school itself may contribute to truancy, absenteeism, or a climate that makes both teaching and learning difficult.

Lack of social standing in the school is another variable in the production of delinquent behavior. Whereas socially successful students must be careful to preserve their reputations and maintain their images, those who are not so defined have little to lose by not conforming. Young people who do not see a relationship between school programs and their future status, or who are not involved in school activities, have been found to have higher rates of delinquency. Those who are defined as "college-bound" are less likely to engage in delinquency than those whose future activities are not clearly defined.

Academic failure has also been correlated with delinquency. Tracking, which separates students into groups according to their abilities and future plans, has been found to reduce academic achievement and raise levels of misbehavior among those placed in the lower tracks, regardless of the youths' academic ability and social class.

Learning disabilities, including dyslexia, aphasia, and hyperkinesis, have been noted in a large number of delinquent children. Children with these reading and perception difficulties, but with normal or above-average intelligence, experience frustration and defeat in their efforts to read and write, which may result in school failures. Although a causal link has not been established between learning disabilities and delinquency, their presence in a substantial number of delinquent children has led to the establishment of identification and remedial programs by a number of juvenile courts.

The relation between dropping out of school and delinquency is a complex one. Dropping out emerges as another progressive step in a delinquency-endangered youth's alienation and isolation from society.

School vandalism, another school-related facet of delinquency, has caused great expense to school districts. The causes of vandalism have been defined as a desire to strike back against school personnel viewed as unjust or repressive (vindictive vandalism); reduction of inhibitions brought on by alcohol or drug use; and failure of authorities to punish known vandals, which has made others feel they can get away with it. In addition, youths often do it "for fun." Schools have responded to this problem with increased security measures and personnel, but the most effective programs have been found to be those that involve the students themselves in prevention efforts.

Drug and alcohol use has also been identified as contributing to school misbehavior. Increased school involvement and commitment have been cited as the best methods for reducing drug and alcohol use among school-age youngsters.

Various studies have attempted to define the appropriate role schools should play in delinquency prevention. Social networking, which involves interaction of the schools, parents, and community organizations in efforts to provide a strong support and reinforcement for acceptable behavior, is effective. In-school drug education and involvement of law enforcement officers as resource officers in the schools have also yielded good results.

Alternative education for youths with intense personal, behavioral, or academic problems has also demonstrated success. Individualized instruction and counseling have helped at-risk youths remain in or return to school.

DISCUSSION QUESTIONS

1. What are the changes in American society that have forced the schools to assume a number of the socialization functions that were formerly performed by the family?

2. How does fear of physical violence affect student attendance and involvement in school activities? Describe some programs that have been initiated to make schools safer for teachers and students.

3. Discuss the effects that school tracking assignments may have on academic achievement and the likelihood that young people will become involved in delinquent behavior.

4. What are the most important factors that influence youths to drop out of school? What should schools do to reduce the influence of these factors?

5. Several experts on education have recommended that compulsory school attendance laws be changed so that a youth could drop out of school around the age of 14 or 15. Do you agree? What are the possible negative consequences of such a policy?

NOTES

1. Mona J. E. Danner and Dianne Cyr Carmody, "Missing Gender in Cases of Infamous School Violence: Investigating Research and Media Explanations," *Justice Quarterly* 18, 1 (March 2001), 88.

2. George Gallup, Jr., "The 33rd Annual Phi Delta Kappa/Gallup Poll of the Public's Attitudes Toward the Public Schools," reported in *Sourcebook of Criminal Justice Statistics 2001* (Washington, DC: Bureau of Justice Statistics, 2002), 104.

3. "Head Start to Take Hit with Taft Plan," *Akron Beacon Journal*, February 1, 2003, B4.

4. "Teen Moms May Lose Day Care," *Akron Beacon Journal*, January 21, 2003, B4.

5. Danner and Carmody, "Missing Gender in Cases of Infamous School Violence," 88.

6. For a detailed discussion of the Child-Saving Movement, see Anthony Platt, *The Child Savers: The Invention of Delinquency* (Chicago: University of Chicago Press, 1969).

7. Howard N. Snyder and Melissa Sickmund, *Juvenile Offenders and Victims: 1999 National Report* (Washington, DC: Office of Juvenile Justice and Delinquency Prevention, 1999), 32.

8. PRIDE Surveys, "2000–01 National Summary, Grades 6 through 12," reported in *Sourcebook of Criminal Justice Statistics 2001*. 245.

9. *Ibid.*, 31.

10. *Ibid.*, 33.

11. Jerry Halverson, associate superintendent of Los Angeles schools, in testimony before the Subcommittee to Investigate Juvenile Delinquency, quoted in *Better Homes and Gardens* 54, 9 (September 1976), 2.

12. "Crime and Violence n the Schools," *Bill of Rights in Action* 11. 1 (February 1977), 11.

13. "Janitor, 20, Charged in Classroom Killing," *Akron Beacon Journal*, 21, 2003, A5.

14. Brooke Donald, "School Crime Decreases, but Bullies Still a Threat," *Akron Beacon Journal*, December 10, 2002, A13.

15. William E. Amos, "Prevention through the School," in William E. Amos and Charles B. Welford, *Delinquency Prevention* (Englewood Cliffs, NJ: Prentice Hall, 1967), 129.

16. "Inner City Boys Beat the Odds," *A Safer Cleveland* (Cleveland, OH: Task Force on Violent Crime, January, 1993), 1, 3.

17. Wayne N. Welsh, "Effects of Student and School Factors on Five Measures of School Disorder," *Justice Quarterly* 18, 4 (December 2001), 911–947.

18. *Ibid.*, 934.

19. Keith McBurnett, Benjamin B. Llahe, and Linda J. Pfiffner, "Diagnosis of Attention Deficit Disorders in DSM–IV: Scientific Basis and Implications for Education," *Exceptional Children* 60, 2 (1993), 108–117.

20. Thomas E. Bratter, "Educating the Uneducable: The Little 'Ole' Red Schoolhouse with Bars in the Concrete Jungle," *Journal of Offender Counseling, Services, & Rehabilitation* 4, 2 (Winter 1979), 96.

21. Lynaia Romeo, Internship Log—Internship at Mahoning County (Ohio) Juvenile Center, May 1, 1992.

22. P. Kaufman, X. Chen, S. P. Choy, S. A. Ruddy, A. K. Miller, K. A. Chandler, C. D. Chapman, M. R. Rand, and P. Klaus, *"Indicators of School Crime and Safety, 1999.* (Washington, DC: U.S. Department of Education and U.S. Department of Justice, 1999), 153.

23. Mona J. E. Danner and Dianne Cyr Carmody, "Missing Gender in Cases of Infamous School Violence," 94.

24. Philip Kaufman, *Indicators of School Crime and Safety, 2001* (Washington, DC: U.S. Department of Education and Justice, 2001). Cited in *Sourcebook of Criminal Justice Statistics 2001*, 10.

25. Danner and Carmody, "Missing Gender in Cases of Infamous School Violence," 103–106.

26. Kaufman, *Indicators of School and Safety, 2001*, in *Sourcebook of Criminal Justice Statistics 2002*, 247, 252.

27. PRIDE Surveys, "2000–01 National Summary, Grades 6 through 12," reported in *Sourcebook of Criminal Justice Statistics*, 245.

28. L. Kann, S. Kinchen, B. Williams, J. Ross, R. Lowry, C. Hill, J. Grunbaum, P. Blumston, J. Collins, and L. Kolbe, "Youth Risk Behavior Surveillance—United States, 1997. Reported in Snyder and Sickmund, *Juvenile Offenders and Victims*, 68.

29. PRIDE Surveys, "2000–01 National Summary, 245.

30. U.S. Bureau of Justice Statistics, *The National Longitudinal Survey of Youth 1997.* reported in *Sourcebook of Criminal Justice Statistics,* 59.
31. Kann et al. "Youth Risk Behavior Surveillance—United States, 1997, in Snyder and Sickmund, *Juvenile Offenders and Victims,* 73.
32. Peter C. Kratcoski, "School Disruption and Violence Against Teachers," *Corrective and Social Psychiatry* 31, 3 (July 1985), 95.
33. Travis Hirschi, *Causes of Delinquency* (Berkley, CA: University of California Press, 1969).
34. Jack Frymier, *Growing Up is Risky Business, and Schools are Not to Blame* (Bloomington, IN: Phi Delta Kappa, 1992), 5.
35. *Ibid.,* vi.
36. Delos H. Kelly, *Creating School Failure: Youth, Crime, and Deviance* (Los Angeles: Trident Shop, 1982), 43.
37. *Ibid.,* 79.
38. "'Tracking' Harms Many Students," *USA Today* 123, 2591 (August 1994), 13.
39. *Ibid.*
40. *Ibid.*
41. Bruce G. Beezer, "Testing: Educational Goals and Change," *Intellect* 102, 2352 (November 1973), 114.
42. *Ibid.*
43. Joel Zimmerman et al., "Some Observations on the Link between Learning Disabilities and Juvenile Delinquency," *Journal of Criminal Justice* 9, 1 (1981), 1–17.
44. National Council of Juvenile and Family Court Judges, *Learning Disabilities and the Juvenile Justice System* (Reno, NV: National Council of Juvenile and Family Court Judges, 1987), 9.
45. National Center for Education Statistics, *Dropout Rates in the United States: 1996,* reported in Snyder and Sickmund, *Juvenile Offenders and Victims,* 12.
46. *Ibid.,* 13.
47. *Ibid.,* 12.
48. Frymer, *Growing Up is Risky Business.* 18.
49. National Center for Education Statistics, *Dropout Rates in the United States, 1992,* reported in Snyder and Sickmund, *Juvenile Offenders and Victims, 12.*
50. Lloyd D. Johnston, Patrick M. O'Malley, and Jerald G. Bachman, *National Survey Results on Drug Use from the Monitoring the Future Study 1975–2001,* in *Sourcebook of Criminal Justice Statistics, 2001,* 251.
51. L. Johnston, P. O'Malley, and J. Bachman, *National Survey Results on Drug Use for Monitoring the Future Study, 1975–1998.* Reported in Snyder and Sickmund, *Juvenile Offenders and Victims, 71.*
52. *Ibid.*
53. Kann et al., *Youth Risk Behavior Surveillance,* reported in Snyder and Sickmund, *Juvenile Offenders and Victims,* 72, 73.
54. Johnston, O'Malley, and Bachman, *Monitoring the Future,* reported in Snyder and Sickmund, *Juvenile Offenders and Victims,* 78.
55. Nechama Tec, *Grass is Green in Suburbia* (Roslyn Heights, NY: Libra Publishers, 1974), 140–141, 143.
56. Kenneth Polk and Steven R. Burkett, "Drinking as Rebellion: A Study of Adolescent Drinking," in Kenneth Polk and Walter E. Schafer, eds., *Schools and Delinquency* (Englewood Cliffs, NJ: Prentice Hall, 1972), 127.
57. Marvin D. Krohn, "The Web of Conformity: A Network Approach to the Explanation of Delinquent Behavior," *Social Problems* 33, 6 (1986), 581–593.
58. Fred M. Hechinger, "Saving Youth from Violence," *Carnegie Quarterly* 39, 1 (Winter 1994), 9.
59. Federal Bureau of Investigation, National Incident Based Reporting System Master Files, 1991–1996, as reported in Snyder and Sickmund, *Juvenile Offender and Victims, 1999,* 64–66.
60. Dan Bryant, *Community Responses Crucial for Dealing with Youth Gangs* (Washington, DC: U.S. Department of Justice, 1989), 5.
61. *Ibid.*

62. Danner and Carmody, "Missing Gender in Cases of Infamous School Violence," 95.
63. *Ibid.*, 97–98.
64. Peter C. Kratcoski, Duane Dukes, and Sandra Gustavson, *Evaluation of Cleveland Police Mini-Station Program*, Final Research Report for the Governor's Office of Criminal Justice Services, Columbus, OH, June 1994, 9–10.
65. U.S. Department of Justice, *The D.A.R.E. Program: A Review of Prevalence, User Satisfaction, and Effectiveness* (Washington, DC: National Institute of Justice, October 1994), 2.
66. "Study Findings Show DARE Program Effective with Elementary Students," *Tallmadge Express*, November 17, 2002, 7.
67. Mario D. Fantini, *Alternative Education: A Source Book for Parents, Teachers, Students, and Administrators* (Garden City, NY: Anchor Books, 1976), 4.
68. Gerald Smith, Thomas B. Gregory, and Richard C. Pugh, *Meeting Student Needs:* Evidence for the superiority of alternative Schools (New York: Phi Delta Kappa, 1981), 4–5.
69. Ernest DeZolt and Peter C. Kratcoski, "Alternative Education: Another Chance for Delinquents," paper presented at the annual meeting of the Academy of Criminal Justice Sciences, Pittsburgh, PA, March 1992, 16–18.
70. *Ibid.*, 19–20.
71. *Ibid.*, 21–28.
72. Ernest A. Wenk, *Schools and Delinquency Prevention* (Davis, CA: National Council on Crime and Delinquency, 1975), 244.
73. *Ibid.*, 244–255.

CHAPTER 10

MALTREATED/
ENDANGERED CHILDREN

(Photo credit: © K. L. Morrison)

WHAT ARE CHILD ABUSE AND NEGLECT?
MANDATORY VERSUS PERMISSIVE REPORTING OF CHILD ABUSE
EXTENT AND NATURE OF CHILD MALTREATMENT
    The Distinction between Child Punishment and Child Maltreatment
    Documentation of Child Maltreatment
SEXUAL EXPLOITATION AND ABUSE OF CHILDREN
    The Incidence of Sexual Abuse of Children
    Characteristics of Sexual Abuse of Children
WHO ARE THE ABUSED AND NEGLECTED CHILDREN?
WHO ARE THE ABUSERS?
THE RELATIONSHIP BETWEEN BEING ABUSED AND DELINQUENT AND CRIMINAL
    BEHAVIOR
DISCOVERY OF CHILD ABUSE AND NEGLECT AND SEXUAL ABUSE
LEGISLATION DIRECTED TOWARD PROTECTING MALTREATED CHILDREN
THE ROLE OF CHILD PROTECTIVE SERVICES
JUVENILE COURT PROCESS IN ABUSE AND NEGLECT CASES
    Steps in the Process
    Special Considerations in Abuse and Neglect Cases
WHAT CAN BE DONE?

When she was admitted to the hospital, T_____ was comatose and weighed only 35 pounds, witnesses said. She had suffered trauma to all parts of her body, . . . she had injuries consistent with someone who had been repeatedly gagged and bound or shackled by the wrists and ankles. . . . Her skin was worn away to bone at the base of the spine because she had been placed in a posture where all her weight was on the base of the spine.

[The abuse] included instances in which the girl was beaten, handcuffed, confined in a closet, and forced to stand outside naked because she had not "earned her clothes for the day."[1]

* * *

A 62-year-old _____ man was indicted Thursday . . . on 36 counts of rape for allegedly having sex with two of his step-granddaughters and their cousin.

An investigator for the _____ County prosecutor's office said police are looking for the man whom they allege had been having sex with the girls, ages, 6, 10, and 11, for the past three years.

The man, stepfather of the mother of two of the girls, gave them candy and money after he tied them to a bed with rope, performed oral sex on them, and forced them to perform oral sex on him, said _____, an investigator with the prosecutor's office.

_____ said the man also forced the girls to dance nude in his _____ cottage and regularly showed them pornographic magazines. . . .

The girls told investigators during the month-long investigation where the man kept pornographic magazines, the ropes he used to tie them up, and see-through night gowns he made them wear.

"We uncovered everything the kids told us would be there, exactly where they told us it would be," _____ said.[2]

* * *

205

A 35-year-old . . . woman was sentenced to six months in prison yesterday for leaving her three young daughters to fend for themselves while she spent a weekend with her boyfriend.

When _____ walked out of her apartment on a Friday morning in January, she left her 12-year-old daughter to look after 3-year-old and 4-year-old girls. When she had not returned by Sunday night, the 12-year-old called the police. . . .

Police found the apartment in disarray, smelling of urine, with beer cans strewn about, according to the charging document. _____, the father of the 3-year-old, said the apartment had trash on the kitchen floor, clothes piled in various rooms, no food in the refrigerator. He said the children slept on the floor.[3]

* * *

A foster father who disciplined a 2-year-old by leaving her in a sweltering attic, where she died, was given his punishment Tuesday: four years in prison. He punished Letia for misbehavior by putting her in the attic of his Orlando Avenue home and making her pick up small pieces of plaster. Lillard fell asleep and returned to the attic about five hours later to find Letia dead. He initially lied about what happened to the girl, saying she accidentally drowned in the bathtub. . . . an investigation revealed the child died of hyperthemia from prolonged heat exposure.[4]

* * *

Two Wadsworth mothers have been charged with obstructing an investigation into a party at which they allegedly supplied alcohol to minors and at which a 12-year-old said she was sexually assaulted. Police said the party . . . was held mainly in . . . [a] parked van in a field near Memorial Park and at . . . [an] apartment.[5]

In Chapter 7 we noted the profound influence the family unit has in shaping the behavior of young people and explored the various social and cultural changes in American life that have influenced family living and relationships. Physically, economically, and emotionally broken families were shown to have an important impact on the behavior of children. The strains and conflicts resulting from alcoholism, drug addiction, and mental illness also have a particularly detrimental effect on family relationships.

Another aspect of family-child relations that has been given increased attention is child abuse. Shocking cases such as those just described have aroused public concern and indignation when they are detailed in the news media, but many other instances of child abuse and neglect impact the lives of children daily without ever being officially reported or investigated. However, revelations that child abuse occurs more frequently and more savagely than the general public ever imagined has led to the enactment of legislation requiring physicians and social-agency personnel to report known or suspected cases. Neglect of the physical and emotional needs of youngsters also has a high incidence and occurs not only in family settings, but also in the foster homes and institutions where youths removed from homes judged "unfit" have been placed. The physical, emotional, and sexual abuse of children occurs in all social classes, and is not limited to any educational level, ethnic or racial group, or family type.

In this chapter, we will explore the legal definitions of abuse and neglect, the characteristics of abused children, the types of parents or caretakers most likely to be abusers, methods of handling child abuse and neglect cases, and the possible resolutions of these situations that hold the most hope for both the parents and the children involved.

WHAT ARE CHILD ABUSE AND NEGLECT?

Broad definitions of child abuse include not only physical injuries inflicted upon children by those who are in charge of them, but also psychological abuse. Physical abuse that results in reports or referrals to hospitals, social service agencies, or the police is the type of abuse most clearly documented and included in various regional and national statistical tabulations. Abuse has been defined as "any nonaccidental physical injury inflicted on a child by a parent or other caretaker deliberately or in anger."[6]

Chase describes abuse a bit more graphically, as:

> . . . the deliberate and willful injury of a child by a caretaker—hitting; beating with a belt, cord, or other implement; slamming against a wall; burning with cigarettes; scalding with hot water; locking in a dungeon; hog-tying; torturing; even killing.[7]

Neglect is difficult to define exactly, since it may involve disregard of physical, emotional, or moral needs of children. Physical neglect has been defined as "the failure to provide the essentials for normal life, such as food, clothing, shelter, care and supervision, and protection from assault."[8] Emotional neglect may include both the lack of expressed love and affection and the deliberate withholding of contact and approval. Moral neglect includes exposure to situations within the home (prostitution, alcoholism, obscenity) that present a pattern of moral conduct at variance with the norms of society. It may also include failure to train or discipline a child.

In the Child Abuse Prevention and Treatment Act (1974), Congress developed a combined definition of child abuse and neglect, terming it:

> . . . the physical or mental injury, sexual abuse, negligent treatment, or maltreatment of a child under the age of 18 by a person who is responsible for the child's welfare under circumstances which indicate that the child's health or welfare is harmed or threatened thereby.[9]

This definition has been interpreted as characterizing acts of "commission" (beatings, sexual use) as abuse and acts of "omission" (failure to provide food, clothing, or a proper home environment) as neglect.[10]

It becomes readily apparent that the distinction between "abuse" and "neglect" may be a matter of semantics. However, the distinction could be all-important in terms of the types of measures that can be undertaken for protection of the child. The amount and nature of the unacceptable parental behavior uncovered may depend on such factors as the identity and believability of the person making a complaint, the interview techniques employed by the person recording a complaint, the caseloads of workers assigned to investigate, the manipulative powers of the parents, or even the personality characteristics of the children. The existence of abuse as opposed to accidental injury is difficult to prove in cases in which the child's injury could in fact have been accidental, but the demeanor or behavior of the adults involved arouses suspicion that it may have been deliberately inflicted. Parents are sometimes unable to give a logical explanation of how an injury occurred. In such instances, hospital personnel are hard pressed to decide whether this is because the parents are distraught or feel guilty that the child was accidentally injured, or whether it indicates abusive behavior.

In the report of the Task Force on Juvenile Justice and Delinquency Prevention, the National Advisory Committee on Criminal Justice Standards and Goals proposed a new approach to the entire area of abuse and neglect. Labels such as "neglected," "abused," and "dependent" would be discarded in favor of a new concept: the "endangered child." Under the Committee's standards, parents would not be found "at fault" if the family situation required intervention. But official intervention would occur when:

1. A child has no parent, guardian, or other adult to whom the child has substantial ties, available and willing to care for him or her.
2. A child has suffered or is likely to suffer physical injury imminently, inflicted nonaccidentally by his or her parent, which causes or creates a substantial risk of disfigurement, impairment of bodily functioning, or severe bodily harm.
3. A child has suffered, or there is a substantial risk that the child will imminently suffer, disfigurement, impairment of bodily functioning, or severe bodily harm as a result of conditions uncorrected by the parents or of the failure of the parents to adequately supervise or protect the child.
4. A child is suffering serious emotional damage, evidenced by severe anxiety, depression, or withdrawal, or untoward aggressive behavior toward self or others, and the parents are unwilling to permit and cooperate with necessary treatment for the child.
5. A child has been sexually abused by a member of the household.
6. A child is in need of medical treatment to cure, alleviate, or prevent serious physical harm that may result in death, disfigurement, substantial impairment of bodily functions, or severe bodily harm and the parents are unwilling to permit the medical treatment.
7. A child is committing delinquent acts as a result of parental pressure, encouragement, or approval.[11]

The Juvenile Justice Standards prepared for the Standards Project of the Institute of Judicial Administration and the American Bar Association are virtually identical to those of the National Advisory Committee.[12]

MANDATORY VERSUS PERMISSIVE REPORTING OF CHILD ABUSE

All 50 states and the District of Columbia, Guam, and the Virgin Islands have enacted legislation requiring that suspected cases of abuse be reported.[13] Under this legislation, medical and social work personnel *must* report instances of suspected abuse to the appropriate authorities, whereas other community members (neighbors, relatives) *may* report them. Most states also have laws that require teachers to report suspected cases of abuse and neglect.[14] In the majority of states, child abuse reports are directed to the Child Welfare Services of the Department of Social Services at the county or state level,[15] but in some states, reports are first filed with the police department or the prosecutor and then investigated with the assistance of appropriate social service agencies. Many state codes direct that the report should first be made to appropriate authorities by telephone, followed by a written report submitted within a specific time period (24 to 48 hours). All the states and territories have provisions of immunity from legal retaliation for those making reports of suspected or confirmed child abuse.[16]

Mandatory reporting places a burden on professionals that is not always willingly assumed. Reporting suspected abuse means becoming involved in matters which are bothersome and time consuming and can raise the specter of false accusations, leading to embarrassment. Despite their personal concerns, health care professionals are instructed that they have a legal and moral obligation to report abuse.

> The most effective approaches to prevention in the area of interpersonal violence . . . could well spring from the disciplines of public health, medicine, nursing, and social service. . . . We know the face of violence. We accept and care for the victims who are beaten, assaulted, raped, and maimed. We in the health professions have tried to do this in a detached, even disinterested way. Some of us were mistakenly convinced that being detached and very "clinical" about these matters was also being very "professional." . . .
>
> Health professionals don't have the luxury of choice any more. As citizens of a humane and compassionate society—and as physicians, nurses, psychologists all bound to the highest ethics of our professions and as human beings—we are obligated to provide the best possible care for the *victims* of violence and to contribute whatever we can to the *prevention* of violence.[17]

EXTENT AND NATURE OF CHILD MALTREATMENT

The true amount of child abuse is impossible to determine, since available statistical information includes only reported cases and does not include those abused children who were never taken to a doctor or hospital for treatment, those who were treated by a physician who did not detect or suspect abuse, or those who were suspected of being abused but not reported as such. The National Committee for the Prevention of Child Abuse estimates that each reported case represents five unreported cases.[18]

A major reason why it is difficult to even estimate the amount of physical abuse of children is that the practice of disciplining children through physical punishment has been and continues to be considered a right of parents. The line between acceptable and unacceptable physical punishment may be difficult to determine.

The Distinction between Child Punishment and Child Maltreatment

Discussions with child welfare workers and police officers assigned to the juvenile bureau involved in investigating reports of suspected child abuse revealed that it is often very difficult to distinguish between abuse and legitimate physical punishment by parents. In many cases, the total home situation, rather than the present incident, might be the determining factor. If the family situation appears to be normal, with no evidence of other violence or neglect, police and child welfare workers may give the benefit of the doubt to the caregivers and not take any legal action.

Corporal punishment, as it applied to parent-child interaction, has been defined as:

> The use of physical force with the intention of causing a child to experience physical pain, but not injury, for the purpose of correction or control of the child's behavior.[19]
>
> . . . The most frequent forms of corporal punishment are spanking, slapping, grabbing or shoving a child roughly (with more force than is needed to move the child), and hitting with certain objects such as a hair brush, belt, or paddle.[20]

Corporal punishment of children begins at early ages. A survey of more than 200 mothers of children under four years of age revealed that 74 percent of the mothers believed that it was appropriate to spank young children, 42 percent said they had spanked their child in the past week, 19 percent said it was acceptable to spank a child less than one year old, 19 percent said spanking with something other than a hand is all right, and 8 percent said it was acceptable to spank so hard that it leaves a mark.[21]

The forms and extent of corporal punishment have been found to be applied consistently over the years. When Straus compared the rates of corporal punishment used by parents on their children 10 years after his initial study, he found that the overall proportion of parents using corporal punishment of any kind (65%) was virtually the same. However, there was a decrease in the percentage of parents using the more severe forms of punishment, such as throwing things at a children or hitting them with an object; there was also a decrease in the frequency with which corporal punishment was used. Straus also found great differences between families in the frequency (ranging from rarely to daily) and the severity (ranging from mild slaps to being hit with a belt of paddle) of the hitting that occurred.[22]

In his studies of family violence, Straus pointed out that spanking, slapping, grabbing, or shoving children roughly continued into the adolescent years. He noted that the common law and state statutes have a "parental exemption" that protects parents from being charged with assault for physically disciplining their children. According to Straus, corporal punishment of adolescents is associated with an increased probability of violent behavior, lower achievement, depression, and alienation on the part of the young person.[23]

Documentation of Child Maltreatment

According to the *National Report on Juvenile Offenders and Victims, 1999*, the concept of child maltreatment includes:

> physical, sexual, and emotional abuse and physical, emotional, and educational neglect by a caretaker.[24]

The National Center on Child Abuse and Neglect collects child maltreatment data from child protective service agencies each year, using the National Child Abuse and Neglect Data System. The maltreatment reports for the period 1980 through 1996 are summarized in Figure 10–1.

Number of child reports (in thousands)

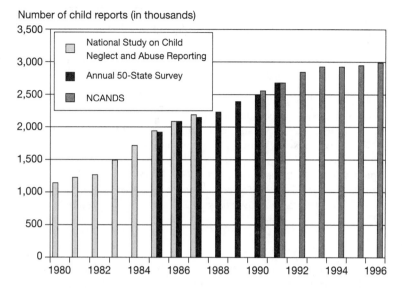

Figure 10–1. Reports to the National Center on Child Abuse and Neglect: 1980–1996 *(Source: Howard N. Snyder and Melissa Sickmund,* Juvenile Offenders and Victims: 1999 National Report *(Washington, D.C.: Office of Juvenile
Justice and Delinquency Prevention), 46.)*

As shown in Figure 10–1, there was a 161 percent increase in the number of reports of alleged mistreatment between 1980 and 1996 and the increase is believed to
be related to growing public awareness of this problem. The National Center on
Child Abuse and Neglect found that 80 percent of the estimated 2 million reports in
1996 were investigated by child protective service agencies. Of these, 35 percent of
allegations were substantiated or there were indications of maltreatment or risk of
maltreatment, while 58 percent were not substantiated.[25]

Of the substantiated or indicated cases of child maltreatment, more children
were classified as "neglected" and "abused" but some children were regarded as both
neglected and abused. In 1993, as shown in Figure 10–2, maltreated children were
victims of physical, emotional, or educational neglect or of physical, emotional, or
sexual abuse. The majority of the maltreated children (78%) were victimized by their
own parents.[26]

SEXUAL EXPLOITATION AND ABUSE OF CHILDREN

We noted in Chapter 5 that sexual abuse of children has always been a social problem. In contemporary society, sexual exploitation and abuse of children has taken on
new and disturbing forms. The Internet provides a lucrative market for pornographic
pictures and films that depict sexual activities involving children and it is also used
by sexual predators to prey on children through chat room contacts that may result
in exploitation of vulnerable and unsophisticated youths. Advertising that lures
young people into the pornography or prostitution market may offer them "model-

---

Most maltreated children were neglected in 1993

NIS-3 counts each incident of abuse or neglect that occurs. A single child may experience many types of abuse or neglect. In 1993, 70% of maltreated children were victims of neglect, and 43% were victims of abuse. More specifically:

- 47% were physically neglected.
- Almost equal proportions of maltreated children were physically abused (22%), emotionally neglected (21%), and emotionally abused (19%).
- 11% were sexually abused; 14% were educationally neglected.

Figure 10–2. Maltreated Children, 1993: Reports to the National Center on Child Abuse and Neglect: 1980–1996 *(Source: Howard N. Snyder and Melissa Sickmund,* Juvenile Offenders and Victims: 1999 National Report *(Washington, D.C.: Office of Juvenile Justice and Delinquency Prevention)* 40.)

ing" career opportunities. (See Chapter 8 for a detailed discussion of the problem of child prostitution and pornography.)

The Incidence of Sexual Abuse of Children

There is common agreement that the actual amount of sexual abuse of children is much greater than that officially reported. Some estimates place it as much as 10 times as high as the officially reported figures.

The chances of an incident of child sexual abuse being reported vary with the following circumstances:

1. Whether the case involves acquaintances, family members, or strangers;
2. Whether the offender is arrested and charged with a crime, or the situation is never made public and handled unofficially;
3. Whether the case came to the attention of officials through legal channels or through a social work or medical source; and
4. Whether the child came to the attention of social agency professionals as a specific referral for sexual abuse or for some other problem.

The forms of sexual abuse of children that may come under scrutiny by legal or social agencies are rape, gross sexual imposition, incest, sexual battery, or endangering children. If the incident involves a male victim or if the sexual offense was between family members, the matter is often not taken into court; if it is, the charge against the adult may be reduced to contributing to the delinquency of a minor or impairing the morals of a minor. Unless the case files are specifically read or released, the existence or extent of the sexual abuse remains hidden.

Professionals are the most common source of all types of abuse and neglect reports, as shown in Table 10–1.

A good deal of sexual abuse of children is discovered after the fact by professionals working in agencies or hospitals. A child may be referred for school problems,

Table 10–1. Sources of Abuse and Neglect Reports, 1996

Source of Referral	Percentage of Total
Professionals	52
Educators	16
Social service	12
Law enforcement	13
Medical	11
Family and community	25
Friends/neighbors	9
Relatives—not parents	10
Parents	6
Other sources	23
Anonymous	12
Victims	1
Other[a]	10

[a]Includes child care providers, perpetrators, and sources not otherwise identified.
Source: Authors' adaptation of U.S. Department of Health and Human Services' *Child maltreatment 1996: Reports from the States to the National Child Abuse and Neglect Data System.* Reported in Howard N. Snyder and Melissa Sickmund, *Juvenile Offenders and Victims: 1999 National Report* (Washington, DC: Office of Juvenile Justice and Delinquency Prevention, 1999), 46.

emotional problems, unacceptable social behavior, or a physical illness, and the sexual abuse is discovered in the course of examining or talking with the child.

Characteristics of Sexual Abuse of Children

Because of the rather sketchy information on the true extent and nature of sexual abuse of children, certain notions have emerged regarding its occurrence. These need careful examination in the light of the increased research on sexually abused children now becoming available.

The FBI has completed a special report on sexual abuse of children utilizing the National Incident-Based Reporting System (NIBRS). This reporting system provides detailed information on the characteristics of victims and offenders involved in criminal sexual assaults, including their ages and the relationship between victim and offender. The report is based on a representative sample of data from the police departments of 12 states. The report found that 32 percent of all of the juveniles who were victims of violent crimes had been sexually assaulted.

Table 10–2 reports the age and relationship characteristics of sexual assault offenders and their juvenile victims.

As shown in Table 10–2, the large majority of sexually assaulted juveniles had been assaulted by an acquaintance, often by a family member. Rarely was the offender a stranger. Twenty-two percent of the victims in the 12- to 17-year-old category were victimized by an acquaintance or family member who was in the same age category, 27 percent of the children in the 7- to 11-year-old category were victimized by youths in

Table 10–2. Age and Relationship Characteristics of Sexual Assault Offenders and Juvenile Sexual Assault Victims

Relationship to Victim	Age of Offender				
	Under 12	12–17	18–24	25–34	35 & older
In a typical 1,000 sexual assaults of children age 6 or younger					
Family member	40	126	71	136	125
Acquaintance	93	159	61	77	84
Stranger	3	8	5	7	6
In a typical 1,000 sexual assaults of young juveniles ages 7–11					
Family member	16	117	42	109	157
Acquaintance	46	148	68	100	148
Stranger	4	11	7	10	15
In a typical 1,000 sexual assaults of juveniles ages 12–17					
Family member	1	26	31	56	121
Acquaintance	5	196	270	122	101
Stranger	0	15	23	19	14

Note: Older juvenile acquaintances and family members age 25 and older were the most common offenders in sexual assaults against very young children.

About half of offenders who sexually assaulted juveniles ages 7–11 were older juvenile acquaintances and family members/acquaintances age 35 and older.

Nearly half of all offenders who sexually assaulted juveniles ages 12–17 were acquaintances between ages 12 and 24.

Source: Authors' analyses of the FBI's *National Incident-Based Reporting System master files* for the years 1991–1996 [machine-readable data files]. Reported in Howard N. Snyder and Melissa Sickmund, *Juvenile Offenders and Victims: 1999 National Report* (Washington, DC: Office of Juvenile Justice and Delinquency Prevention, 1999), 29.

the 12- to 17-year-old category, and 29 percent of the children age 6 and under were victimized by youths between the ages of 12 and 17. In summary, the study reveals that the relationship of victim to offender differs by the victim's age. For victims under age 12, the offender was a family member in 47 percent of the cases, an acquaintance in 49 percent of the cases, and a stranger in only 4 percent of the cases.[27]

Victim-Precipitated Abuse. The theory of victim precipitation assumes or insinuates that the abused child either cooperated with the offender or sought the sexual involvement that developed between them. The relationship developed over a period of time, beginning with sexual touching and fondling and not progressing to intercourse until months or years later. There is an absence of force and the sexual abuser is generally not viewed as threatening by the child. In fact, the abuser may be very affectionately involved with the child and show a strong interest in such aspects of the child's life as school or hobbies.

Rosenfeld, who termed such sexual abuse "endogamous," suggested that the child becomes adjusted to this sexual activity because it is integrated with other pleasurable experiences enjoyed with this adult. Rosenfeld characterized such an offender, often the child's father, as emotionally estranged from his wife and as a person who has experienced feelings of rejection or inadequacy. The child's mother is characterized as an insecure and needful woman, immature, incapable of managing, and futilely searching for approval. The sexually abused girl may take over the housekeeping and child-rearing roles of the mother. The mother overtly supports the daughter's assumption of her social roles, and may covertly support the daughter's taking over her sexual role.[28]

The characteristic of seductiveness is frequently attributed to the child-victim. Because of this alleged seductive behavior, there is a tendency to imply that the child is to blame or to attribute some degree of fault to the child for instigating the sexual interaction. Rosenfeld believed that a child develops these seductive tendencies in an effort to obtain the attention and affection which were not given in a normal manner. The child learns to act in a charming and sexually arousing way as a means of gaining attention that would otherwise have been denied. The "seductive" behavior is another symptom of the child's abnormal personality and arrested psychological development.[29]

It is quite likely that those professionals (psychologists, social workers, or institutional staff) who treat sexually abused children overestimate the degree of compliance and cooperativeness on the part of the child. This may occur because they get information on abuse after the fact and they may be dealing with an atypical portion of the sexually abused child population.

DeFrancis' research on 250 cases of child sexual abuse in New York City revealed that only 25 percent of the abusers were strangers; the remainder were either immediate family members, relatives, or friends of the child's family. He found that if the offender was a member of the immediate family unit (father, stepfather, brother), the use of force was less likely to occur than if the offender was a stranger. Yet even in 56 percent of the cases involving members of the immediate family, force or the threat of force was used.[30]

The Generational Hypothesis. Another assumption that needs to be questioned is the notion that sexual abuse occurs in families generation after generation and that those who have been abused will later abuse their own children. It has been substantiated through research that some children who have been physically abused grow up to be abusers, victimizing their own children as their parents victimized them. The concept has also been applied to sexual abuse. Elwell found that mothers who seemed to allow or not protest sexual abuse of their children by their husbands had themselves been sexually abused as children, or at least had observed abnormal sexual activity in their own families.[31] A study by the American Humane Association found that mothers of sexually abused children had themselves been child victims of such abuse in 11 percent of the cases.[32] Nevertheless, it is difficult to establish a direct cause-and-effect relationship between experiencing sexual abuse as a child and later deviance, emotional illness, or toleration of the sexual abuse of one's own children. Studies of delinquents, alcoholics, or mentally ill individuals reveal that, while sexual abuse might have been part of the life experience of some of these persons, it was not experienced by the majority of them. Many cases of child sexual abuse occur in what might be termed a "promiscuous family setting." The family unit is characterized by disorganization, chaos, antisocial parental behavior, violence, alcoholism, and various forms of deviance. The sexual abuse which may occur here is viewed as almost a minor part of this chaotic and unpredictable lifestyle.

The difficulty lies in determining how much adult deviant behavior can be attributed to experiencing sexual abuse as a child and how much is a result of other forms of deviance and disorganization. If a person who was physically and sexually abused as a child grows up to be a deviant or to have a distorted outlook, how much of this problem can be attributed to sexual abuse?

In regard to the generational hypothesis, then, it appears that the majority of sexual abusers of children were *not* abused themselves and that even though a high correlation between being abused as a child and later becoming an abuser has been documented, there is also evidence that the majority of abused children *do not* grow up to become abusers. A good portion of the sexual abuse of female children occurring today is the result of the increasing number of families in which a stepfather, live-in boyfriend of the mother, or stepbrother has entered the family setting through divorce or separation. The resulting sexual activity is not a result of an intricate family dysfunction but rather a situational occurrence between nonrelatives brought on by alcohol or drug abuse or a lack of moral conviction on the part of those involved. The socialization and value systems of these persons are such that they do not regard such behavior as morally wrong.

WHO ARE THE ABUSED AND NEGLECTED CHILDREN?

Babies and young children appear to run the greatest risk of being the objects of abusive behavior. The National Child Abuse and Neglect Data System reported that 19 percent of the victims were age two or younger.[33] Infants are vulnerable for several reasons. The helplessness of a very young child to escape from attack, coupled with its need for constant attention and its tendency to cry and to disrupt the social life or other activities of parents, makes it particularly at risk. In some cases of child abuse, the baby has been conceived by very young parents out of wedlock, forcing them into a too-early marriage. The child is seen as a physical symbol of their captivity and becomes a source of resentment. This attitude may persist throughout the child's entire life, helping to explain why one particular child is often a target of abuse while children born to the couple later are not mistreated. An illegitimate child who becomes a stepchild in a later marriage runs the risk of similar mistreatment. Premature, deformed, or sickly babies are also in danger of being abused, since they require excessive amounts of attention and care; twins are in the high-risk category for the same reasons. The National Child Abuse and Neglect Data also revealed variations according to race. Fifty five percent of the identified maltreatment victims were white, 28 percent were black, 12 percent were Hispanic, and 5 percent were of other races.[34]

There is no doubt that certain children have personality and behavioral characteristics that make them particularly difficult to handle. Parents who might be perfectly capable of caring for and disciplining a normal child can be pushed over the brink by constantly having to put up with a hyperactive, nasty-tempered child who needs little sleep and is constantly getting into mischief. Child abuse incidents involving such children tend to be isolated instances of too-severe reaction by the parents, rather than fitting into a pattern of abuse and neglect.

As we noted earlier, a number of researchers have documented the fact that there is a tendency for one specific child to be singled out as the object of abuse. Thomson found this to be true in 88 percent of 376 cases studied,[35] and Blair and Rita Justice noted the same condition in 80 percent of their cases.[36] When a single child is the target of abuse, it may be because he or she bears a striking physical resemblance to a former husband or lover, a despised parent or other relative, or even to the abuser, who sees all his or her worst characteristics personified in this child. Steele observed that abusing parents frequently express the idea that a crying infant sounds "just like my mother (or father) screaming at me to do something and criticizing me for failure."[37] Children who sense that they are disliked or resented may persist in angering and irritating their parents even though they are punished or abused because they perceive this activity as a method of gaining the parents' attention.

A homicide committed by most unusual means illustrates the potential for abuse present in such situations.

> When interrogated by the police [after the death of her three-and-a-half-year-old child] the mother stated that the child had developed the habit of taking the nursing bottle away from a 13-month-old sibling despite repeated attempts to discourage this practice. Following an additional instance of this activity, the mother unscrewed the top of a pepper shaker and *poured* the contents into the child's mouth. The child "swallowed" the material and immediately complained of burning in her throat and stomach. The mother said she gave her some sips of milk and some water, but the little girl started to gasp, turned blue, and collapsed. Screams for help aroused the neighbors who called the police. The child was rushed to a nearby hospital and was pronounced dead on arrival.[38]

Many youngsters become victims of abuse because they happen to be in the wrong place at the wrong time, as when a parent comes home in a drunken stupor or when a disagreement between the parents ends with one or the other taking his or her displeasure out on the child. Sometimes the frustrations of daily living reach a point where parents vent their anger on the nearest available object.

The age of abused children covers the entire juvenile range. Premature infants and those who are overactive, demanding, and exhausting may wear down a parent's self-control temporarily and trigger violent impulses.[39] Various phases of a child's development (e.g., the "terrible twos" or the adolescent years) have been identified as especially provocative of abuse, but there is no special developmental phase in which the bulk of child abuse is concentrated.[40] A number of researchers have found that males are slightly more likely than females to be abused, although abuse of girls increases in the teenage years, when physical force is used more frequently to keep them in line or when sexual abuse may occur within the family unit.[41]

The following characteristics have been summarized as frequently displayed by abused or neglected children:

1. They appear to be different from other children in physical or emotional makeup, or their parents inappropriately describe them as being "different" or "bad."
2. They seem unduly afraid of their parents.
3. They may often bear welts, bruises, untreated sores, or other skin injuries.
4. They show evidence of overall poor care.
5. They exhibit behavioral extremes: crying often, crying very little; being excessively fearful, or seeming fearless of adult authority; being unusually aggressive and destructive, or extremely passive and withdrawn.
6. Some are wary of physical contact, especially when it is initiated by an adult.
7. They may exhibit a sudden change in behavior: pants-wetting, thumb-sucking, frequent whining, becoming disruptive, or becoming uncommonly shy and passive.
8. They have learning problems that cannot be diagnosed.
9. They are habitually truant or late for school. Frequent or prolonged absences sometimes result when a parent keeps an injured child at home until the evidence of abuse disappears.
10. In some cases, they frequently arrive at school too early and remain after class rather than going home.
11. They are always tired and often sleep in class.
12. They are inappropriately dressed for the weather. Children who never have coats or shoes in cold weather are receiving subliminal care. Those who regularly wear long sleeves or high necklines on hot days may be dressed to hide bruises, burns, or other marks of abuse.[42]

WHO ARE THE ABUSERS?

Child abuse occurs in all social classes and is committed by members of every race, ethnic group, and age group. It is most likely to be reported and investigated—and in fact may occur more frequently—among the poor, uneducated, unskilled population and among minority-group members.

The identities of the perpetrators of physical abuse, sexual abuse, and neglect vary. Mothers are shown as more involved in child maltreatment than fathers, but they may be identified as such because the fathers were simply not present in the children's lives. Information from the National Child Abuse and Neglect Data System showed that over one half (52%) of the maltreatment cases substantiated or indicated by child service agencies involved a female only as the perpetrator, almost one fourth (24%) involved both male and female perpetrators, and the remaining 24 percent involved males only as perpetrators.[43] Fathers and stepfathers are more strongly involved in physical and sexual abuse than mothers or stepmothers. For sexual abuse cases, males were identified as the perpetrators in 62 percent of the substantiated or indicated cases, both male and female perpetrators were involved in 29 percent of the cases, and females only were involved in only 9 percent of the cases.[44]

Steele observed that a small group of abusive parents (less than 10%) suffers from serious psychiatric disorders, severe alcoholism, drug abuse, or significant sexual perversion, or is repeatedly involved in serious violent or criminal behavior, but that the majority of child abusers are applying an abnormal pattern of child rearing that they are likely to have experienced themselves.[45]

Some abusers are people who were physically or emotionally abused as children. They are consciously or unconsciously attempting to apply the same standards of child rearing to their own children. Such unreasonable expectations are manifested in comments that they will not "give in to" a crying baby and that they are "going to show him who's boss," even if it means physical punishment. "Spare the rod and spoil the child" would appear to be the biblical catch phrase for such thinking. Obviously, people who have not experienced loving care in their own early lives are ill equipped to give it to others and may make excessive demands upon a child who cannot possibly meet their expectations. Just as, say, an abusive father was constantly criticized and punished by his own parents, so he makes the same types of unreasonable demands and attacks on his off-spring, perhaps because this is the only pattern of child rearing with which he is familiar.

A small group of abusive parents may have been physically impaired by the abuse or neglect they suffered as children, perhaps by brain damage caused by blows to the head or other abnormalities caused by malnutrition at critical developmental periods. But for most abusing parents, the scars carried into adulthood are psychological rather than physical. These parents are characterized by a lack of trust in others and lack of confidence in self, which frequently leads to a way of life in which few neighborhood contacts or extended family relationships are maintained. The parents feel "alone" with their problems. Many female abusers are single parents, struggling with economic problems in addition to their psychological burdens.

Blair and Rita Justice researched the importance of life crises in cases of child abuse. They compared 35 abusing parents with a group of nonabusing parents matched for age, education, and income. They asked the members of both samples to note which of 43 various life events had happened to them during the 12 months prior to the abusive behavior by the offender sample. The events, ranging from death of a spouse, divorce, separation, and jail terms to changes in eating habits, were assigned numerical values according to the amount of life readjustment they required. The abusers were found to have experienced major, moderate, and mild crises in their lives more frequently than had members of the control group. Sexual difficulties between marriage partners, changes in financial status, changes in living conditions, and trouble with in-laws were the areas in which the abusers differed most from the nonabusers. The researchers also discovered that the changes found in the abusers' lives, which in turn precipitated more life crises for them, were not the sort over which they had no control, such as death or illness, but were related to their own personality characteristics, which brought on many of the problems they experienced.[46]

Sexual abusers of children present a slightly different profile. There is evidence that adults who molest children were themselves molestation victims or experienced or observed abnormal conditions with their families while growing up.

THE RELATIONSHIP BETWEEN BEING ABUSED AND DELINQUENT AND CRIMINAL BEHAVIOR

An important consideration in examining the types and extent of abuse of children is whether experiencing abuse leads a child to become involved in juvenile delinquency or adult criminality.

A research study sponsored by the National Institute of Justice examined this question by following nearly 1,600 young people from childhood through young adulthood. Two groups were involved: a study group of more than 900 substantiated cases of child abuse or neglect processed by the courts between 1967 and 1971 and a comparison group of nearly 700 children who had no official records of being abused or neglected. The two groups were matched according to sex, race, and family socio-economic status and followed through official records over a 15- to 20-year period. The researchers concluded that being abused as a child increased the odds of being involved in future delinquency or adult criminality by 40 percent. Likelihood of arrest as a juvenile was increased by 53 percent, likelihood of arrest as an adult was increased 38 percent, and likelihood of arrest for a violent crime increased by 38 percent.[47] Table 10–3 shows the extent of involvement in delinquency, adult criminality, and violent offenses by the abused and nonabused groups in the study.

As shown in Table 10–3, those who had been abused or neglected as children were found to be more likely to be arrested for juvenile, adult, or violent offenses than those in the comparison group. However, it is important to note that over 60 percent of those in both groups had no adult or juvenile criminal record. Other findings of the study included the fact that being abused or neglected in childhood increased the likelihood of arrest for females by 77 percent. For juvenile and adult offenses and for violent offenses, blacks who had been abused were more likely than whites to be offenders and were significantly more likely to be involved in all three types of offenses than black children who had not been abused.[48]

Sexual abuse also shows some relation to later involvement in sex offenses. Faller, in a study of the family backgrounds of sex offenders and the mothers of vic-

Table 10–3. Extent of Involvement in Delinquency, Adult Criminality, and Violent Criminal Behavior (%)

Type of Arrest	Abused and Neglected (n = 908)	Comparison Group (n = 667)
Juvenile	26.0	16.8
Adult	28.6	21.1
Violent crime	11.2	7.9

Note: All differences significant.
Source: Cathy Spatz Widom, *The Cycle of Violence* (Washington, DC: U.S. Department of Justice, 1992), 4.

tims of sex offenders, found that more than one third of the sex offenders had either experienced or been exposed to sexual abuse as children and nearly half of the mothers of the victims had also experienced or been exposed to sexual abuse as children.[49]

Abused children are at risk for becoming delinquent because they may have developed ways of coping with the abuse or distorted views of life that lead them toward illegal behavior. In his study of abused adolescents, Mouzakitis identified two distinct groups: youths who had been abused and neglected since infancy and early childhood and those whose abuse began when they reached puberty. He concluded that those who had been abused for an extended period of time were more psychologically damaged and more likely to be involved in violent behavior, promiscuity, running away, or criminal behavior than those who had endured abuse for shorter periods.[50]

Sexually abused children are at risk for involvement in delinquency because they may cope with the abuse in ways that lead toward unacceptable behavior. According to Moore, these include aggressive behavior as a way of displacing the anger they feel toward their victimizer; alienation from peers because they feel ashamed or fear that others will find out they have been sexually abused; distrust of adults and authority figures brought on by a sense of betrayal by adults; self-blame, created by feelings that they somehow brought about or encouraged the abuse; substance abuse, used to escape feelings of hurt, anger, and fear; or running away, which may remove the youth from the scene of the abuse but put him or her in jeopardy for committing offenses to survive on the street.[51]

DISCOVERY OF CHILD ABUSE AND NEGLECT AND SEXUAL ABUSE

Many cases of child abuse and neglect are handled informally within the family or the neighborhood. Parents are threatened with exposure or arrest by those who have observed the abusive or neglectful behavior or its results. For some this is a sufficient deterrent.

As noted earlier in this chapter, medical and social work personnel are mandated by law to report abuse and in most states teachers and police officers also have this obligation.

Researchers have examined the factors involved in police officers making decisions to report child abuse. Willis and Wells developed the following generalizations regarding these decisions based on their review of available studies:

1. The more serious the maltreatment, the more willing are police to report the act as abuse.
2. The greater the knowledge of the state's child abuse reporting law, the greater the willingness to report the act as abuse.
3. The more experienced the officer, the less the willingness to report the act as child abuse.
4. The more educated the police officer, the more the willingness to report the act as child abuse.

5. The greater the degree of dogmatism, the less the willingness to report the act as abuse, especially in cases of physical maltreatment.

6. Police are more willing to report child abuse in white than in black families.

7. Police are more willing to report child abuse in upper-class than in lower-class families.

8. The more criminal the situation is perceived to be, the greater the willingness to report the act as child abuse.

9. The willingness to report is influenced by the formal reporting structure within the police officer's organization:
    (a) The more formal the structure, the greater the willingness to report.
    (b) The greater the support within the organization for reporting child abuse, the greater the willingness to report.

10. Attitudes and experiences regarding child maltreatment influence the willingness to report a case as child abuse:
    (a) Experience reporting child abuse increases the willingness to report a case as child abuse.
    (b) Positive experience with the child welfare agency increases the willingness to report a case as child abuse.
    (c) The perception that reporting is counterproductive decreases the willingness to report a case as child abuse.[52]

A study of law enforcement officials who worked at the municipal and county levels found that police decisions to report abuse were based primarily on the officers' perceptions of the seriousness of the behavior; that is, whether the abuse or neglect was severe enough to be defined as criminal behavior. The race of the family was also a factor, with white families more likely than black families to be reported for abusive behavior.[53]

LEGISLATION DIRECTED TOWARD PROTECTING MALTREATED CHILDREN

Early in 1974, the U.S. Congress passed the Federal Child Abuse Prevention and Treatment Act. This led to the establishment of a National Center on Child Abuse and Neglect and provided funds to states to establish the agencies needed to investigate and prevent child maltreatment. To be eligible for these federal grants, the states had to demonstrate that they had enacted mandatory child abuse report laws.[54] Another provision of the Act was the requirement that the state must:

> . . . provide that in every case involving an abused or neglected child which results in a judicial proceeding a guardian ad litem shall be appointed to represent the child in such proceedings.[55]

The Victims of Child Abuse Act of 1990 included provisions for improving techniques for investigating and prosecuting child abuse cases; court-appointment of a special advocate for every child victim and use of *guardians ad litem* in more types of cases; training of court personnel and staff in issues related to child abuse and neglect; protection of victims' rights in testimony related to abuse, including use of closed-circuit television or videotaped depositions and grants for equipment to facilitate use of this type of testimony; training for those conducting competency examinations and direct examinations involving children; use of multidisciplinary child abuse teams during investigations; background checks for child care workers; and treatment for juvenile offenders who were found to be neglectful of abuse victims.[56]

Federal and state laws have also been enacted to protect children from becoming victims of sexual exploitation. These laws prohibit distribution or sale of pornographic material to a person under age 18 or depicting a person under age 18 engaging in or simulating sexual contact.[57]

THE ROLE OF CHILD PROTECTIVE SERVICES

Child protective services are those provided by agencies "authorized to act on behalf of a child when parents are unable or unwilling to do so."[58] The agencies are now required by law to investigate reports of child maltreatment that have occurred or are suspected.

The majority of the states designate specific child protective service agencies that are expected to assume the primary responsibility for investigating and servicing maltreated children. However, many other agencies, including law enforcement, schools, and health and social welfare agencies, are involved in child protective activity. Community response to child maltreatment generally involves:

Identification: Educators, law enforcement personnel, medical professionals, family members, neighbors, or others may first notice possible maltreatment of a child.

Reporting: Some professionals (medical personnel, educators, law enforcement personnel, day care workers, and social service providers) are required by law to report suspected abuse or neglect. Several states require reporting by any person having knowledge of child maltreatment. The initial report is usually made to child protective or law enforcement agencies.

Intake and Investigation: Child protective service staff members, sometimes with the assistance of law enforcement personnel, must complete an investigation to determine if the child is in immediate danger. If the allegation is not substantiated, the case is closed. If there is immediate danger, state statutes provide for removal of the child under temporary protective custody. In some states, this requires a court order; in other states there must be a court review of the action.

Assessment: The child service agency assessment addresses the cause of the maltreatment and the immediate needs of the victim.

Case Planning: A long range plan is developed to address the identified causes of the maltreatment.

Treatment: The child protective agency, in conjunction with other community service agencies, implements the case plan.

Evaluation: Established measurements are used and input from all involved agencies is obtained to assess whether the needed changes are being made and if the factors identified as leading to the abuse have been addressed.

Case closure: If it is determined that changes have occurred that make the probability of future maltreatment low, the case is closed. If the perpetrators of the abuse do not cooperate or if the risk of maltreatment remains high, a complaint against the perpetrators will be sent to the juvenile court. In some cases, the caretakers do not have the ability or resources to make the necessary changes. These cases will also be sent to the juvenile court.[59]

In spite of the mandates for action, many allegations of child maltreatment are never investigated. Because of the huge number of cases and understaffing, agency administrators focus on those cases for which the evidence is fairly substantial or the danger to the child appears immediate. The sources of the reports are good indicators of whether they will be followed up. The highest rates of investigation are for those reported by police and sheriff departments (52%), hospitals (46%), or mental health agencies (42%). Those with low rates of investigation include reports by day care centers (3%) and public health agencies (4%).[60]

JUVENILE COURT PROCESS IN ABUSE AND NEGLECT CASES

A small percentage of all the child abuse cases reported are eventually referred to family courts or juvenile courts (17% or less).[61] This occurs most frequently when a decision must be made on whether to remove the child from the home. According to Laudau, the function of the juvenile court in such cases is "to protect a child from further harm and rehabilitate family relationships, by way of court orders as to parental behavior, physical and/or psychiatric examinations, custody, and home supervision."[62]

Steps in the Process

The juvenile court process followed for cases involving endangered children usually involves six steps. These include court referral, a protective custody hearing, intake, petition and advisement, a pretrial conference, trial, and the disposition.[63]

Referrals to the juvenile court are generally initiated by children's service agencies or by the police. For example, the police may be called to a household where child abuse has allegedly occurred or is in process. The responding officers must assess the situation. If the parents or caretakers refuse to allow officers entry into the home and the officers have reasons to believe that a child or children are in danger, the police may enter the home to investigate without permission. If there is evidence that a child has been beaten, sexually molested or neglected or is in immediate danger of being beaten or molested, police can remove the child from the home using the power of temporary emergency custody. When such action is taken, the child is either transported to a hospital or to a temporary foster home and the appropriate children's service agency is notified.

The processing of child abuse or neglect cases in the juvenile court involves preparation of a petition (written complaint) against the parent or other abuser that details the specific acts of commission or omission with dates, times, and frequency of their occurrence. A child service agency is the most frequent source of such a petition, but it may also be filed by law enforcement officials. Often specific charges will not be filed until there has been time to investigate the charges. This investigation is generally completed by children's services, often with the assistance of the police. The prosecutor's office, after reviewing the information available on the case, may decide not to refer it to the juvenile court because there are not sufficient grounds to prove that physical or psychological abuse, neglect, or sexual abuse, as defined by law, actually occurred.

A protective custody hearing is generally held within 48 to 72 hours of the initial referral. At this hearing, it is determined whether emergency protective custody of the child is warranted, and, if warranted, whether it should be continued until the outcome of the case is decided.

During the intake, petition, and advisement stages the accused are informed of their right to private or court-appointed counsel and counsel is also assigned for the child. If the accused maintain that the charges are untrue, an adjournment is declared so that a defense can be prepared.

At the pretrial conference, the attorney for the complainant (generally a children's services agency) provides a written statement in which the alleged offenses are described. Consultations between attorneys for the accused and those for the agency may lead to a resolution of the issues. A common resolution takes the form of a consent decree agreement. Such an agreement is defined as "a judgment entered by consent of the parties whereby the defendant agrees to stop alleged illegal activity without admitting guilt or wrongdoing."[64] A consent decree agreement may be reached after there has been some bargaining on the specific charges in the complaint. For example, a charge of child neglect may be reduced to one of child dependency in exchange for the accused agreeing not to contest the action being proposed by the court to protect the interests of the child. In this way, no fault is attributed to the alleged offender, but the court has accomplished its primary goal of protecting the child from harm and assuring that the child's basic needs will be met.

If the case is not resolved at the pretrial conference, a trial, often referred to as a fact-finding hearing, takes place. In this hearing, the focus is not on proving the accused person or persons guilty of the charges, but on developing a solution to the problem. This juvenile court hearing is not a criminal procedure, where the offender must be proven guilty beyond a reasonable doubt, but a civil proceeding. The importance of the outcome in a civil proceeding determines the standard of proof to be applied. In child welfare cases that could result in placing the child for adoption because of alleged abuse or neglect on the part of the parents, a standard of clear and convincing evidence (approximately a 75% level of certainty) would be required.[65] Other child protective cases, in which the outcome could be placement of the child in temporary foster care, with the possibility of the family being reunited at a later

In some cases, protective custody of abused children is the best option. *(Photo credit: Bill Sherlock, courtesy of the American Correctional Association)*

date, use the "fair preponderance of the evidence" standard (51% or more level of certainty). This standard would mean that it is more credible and convincing to believe the accusations than not to believe them.[66]

At the trial (fact-finding hearing), the legal representative of the agency that brought the charges introduces the evidence, which may be in the form of medical reports or X-rays, testimony of witnesses, or other evidence. The accused have the right to confront all witnesses and cross-examine them. The child involved may be questioned in chambers or asked to testify before the court. The accused are not required to take the stand in their own defense, but if they do, they must submit to cross-examination. They may present witnesses and evidence in their own defense.

Special Considerations in Abuse and Neglect Cases

Testimony by Children. In cases involving sexual abuse, testimony by children is a particularly difficult problem. Unless the abuse occurred in a single, violent instance, there may be no physical evidence (bruises, venereal disease) to substantiate the child's story. The court is faced with the dilemma of testing a child's word against that of an adult. The competency of a child as a witness is open to question, and the effect on the child of being required to describe what has taken place in the presence of the accused can be particularly traumatic. In addition, the victim may recant the story or try to minimize what actually happened because he or she feels that the family has been hurt by the revelations and that everyone is angry with him or her for telling what took place. However, some experts believe that testifying can be therapeutic for some children and confirm a child's sense of justice.[67]

Certain innovations in court procedures have been used to minimize the possible traumatic effects of the testifying for the child. These include using a single trained interviewer to conduct a joint investigation for law enforcement, the prosecutor, and social service agencies, rather than requiring the child to recount what happened over and over to various persons,[68] videotaped or closed-circuit television testimony, use of anatomically detailed dolls or pictures to help the child explain what happened, or testimony by expert witnesses who have interviewed the victim and made judgments as to the veracity of the child's story.

The Guardian Ad Litem (Child Advocate).　One innovation in the processing of abuse and neglect cases by juvenile or family courts is the appointment by the court of a *guardian ad litem*. This individual, an attorney or a child abuse and child neglect professional, is present at all hearings for this case and has the specific obligation to protect the child's interests. This activity may involve assuring that the child's rights are not violated and giving active assistance in formulating the disposition that the case will receive.

Dispositions in Abuse or Neglect Cases.　If the court determines that abuse or neglect has taken place, the social agency that brought the information about the case to the court may be asked to make recommendations to the court or the court may determine the action to be taken. Dispositions might include supervision of the parents and child by a probation officer; medical or psychiatric examinations or treatment for members of the family; "orders of protection," which detail conditions that must be met by the parents; temporary removal of the child from the home to foster care; or permanent change of custody.

If removal of the child to foster care is indicated, a long history of displacement may begin. Parents with children who are in foster care are reluctant to release them for adoption, even though the chances of reestablishing a workable family unit may be remote. With every passing year, the child's chances of adoption diminish. The child may be placed in one foster home after another until reaching the upper age limit of the juvenile status. Difficult foster children all too frequently return to juvenile courts as truants, incorrigibles, or runaways, and eventually are placed in institutions simply because there is nowhere else to keep them. Here, the cycle may begin all over again, in the form of abuse or neglect by institutional personnel. Patterns of unreasonable expectations and demands all too familiar to these children again enter their lives.

WHAT CAN BE DONE?

Child abuse and neglect may be viewed in the larger context of the breakdown of the family unit within American society. Marriage, once regarded as a lifelong commitment, now may amount to nothing more than a series of legalized sexual encounters, each producing offspring that are unwanted and unloved. The increased incidence of violence in our society, promoted through the media—particularly television—as the way to solve problems, cannot fail to have an influence on young parents. The have-nots in our society are continually subjected to stress, as the task of day-to-day living becomes increasingly difficult for those on the bottom of the economic ladder. Explosive behavior in the form of child abuse can be triggered by a small incident that appears to be the "last straw" in an already stressful situation.

Other influences on the increase in reported abuse and neglect include the pressures on mothers who must work outside the home and then assume responsibility for the care of their children when they return and the general preoccupation with personal fulfillment rather than care for others that has become increasingly prevalent in our society. One method of approaching the problem is to view it realistically. Most women today cannot or do not wish to spend 20 years of their lives as homemakers. Extended educational opportunities for women with limited incomes, coupled with a much expanded day-care-center system, could help alleviate the frustrations of women who feel trapped in the "mothering" role and who do not have the resources to develop alternatives on their own.

For those under economic duress, expanded or revised welfare or family-maintenance programs offer the best hope for relief, if coupled with job training or other activity to break the cycle of generation-to-generation welfare dependence.

Since a portion of abuse and neglect is directly related to alcohol or drug abuse or to mental illness, increased public awareness of the availability of help and expanded facilities to serve these needs could offer some assistance.

Abusive parents are difficult to counsel for a number of reasons. They are already on the defensive because of the exposure of the abusive activity and the threat of court action against them and they may be unwilling to discuss other incidents that have occurred or other problems within the family because they fear that this information will later be used against them in court. In addition, the abuse to which they may have been subjected as youngsters has helped them learn how to "con" others into thinking that they are behaving as expected. Because as children they never experienced a trusting, confident relationship with adults, they may find it difficult to establish such a relationship with a counselor; or they may take the opposite tack and become totally dependent upon the worker and expect to be told exactly what to do and when to do it, rather than think through solutions to their own problems.

In addition to individual counseling, group therapy has been used with some success in dealing with child abusers. Organizations such as Parents Anonymous have sought to set up the type of program that has been used successfully by Alcoholics Anonymous. Behavior modification and psychodrama (role playing) have also been used.[69]

A number of states have had success with the use of volunteers to provide services to members of Parents Anonymous or other abuse-related organizations. Volunteer activities may include transporting parents to meetings; baby-sitting at the site of the meeting while the parents engage in group counseling or are instructed in homemaking or childcare skills; or even acting as parent aides, working directly in the home with a particular family.

Current efforts to uncover child abuse and neglect and get help for the abusers should be expanded. Here again, the cycle of passing on from generation to generation a style of child rearing that includes abusive or neglectful behavior must somehow be broken, through individual or group counseling, therapy, and training of mothers—particularly young mothers—in proper child care, family-life activities, and awareness of the medical needs of children and of their responsibility for meeting them.

Removal from the home and placement in foster care should be a last resort, since it may prove as psychologically damaging to the child in the long run as parental mistreatment. The National Advisory Committee on Criminal Justice Standards and Goals has recommended that after a child has been found by the courts to be endangered, every effort should be made to meet the needs of the child and the parents in the home setting. The Committee recommended court-ordered services to the family, day care, counseling, therapy, medical treatment, and provision of services by professionals as alternatives to removal from the home. When removal is dictated by the seriousness of the danger, the committee recommended that the status of each child in placement be reviewed at least every six months. It further suggested that if a child cannot be returned home within six months to one year, parental rights should be terminated, so that the child can be removed from temporary foster care and made available for adoption. Although a number of possible exceptions were noted, the committee based this strong stand on the need of children for continuity and stability in their lives, a need that cannot be met when children float from year to year in an atmosphere of uncertainty.[70]

SUMMARY

Child abuse and neglect are important concerns of the juvenile justice system and of the many community agencies that provide services to children. Abuse and neglect are defined in various jurisdictions as including physical mistreatment only or as extending to include emotional mistreatment or deprivation.

All states *require* medical and social work personnel to report suspected abuse to appropriate authorities, and any other person *may* do so. Immunity from legal retaliation is assured to those who make such reports.

The Task Force on Juvenile Justice and Delinquency Prevention proposed a new approach to handling abuse and neglect in which the term "endangered child" would be substituted for "abused" or "neglected." Intervention would be mandatory if certain family situations existed and parents would not be designated as "at fault," but would be required to accept help.

The true amount of child abuse is impossible to determine, but has been estimated to be much greater than the recorded number of cases. Reporting of abuse and neglect has increased in recent years as a result of growing public awareness of the problem and familiarity with agencies to which such reports should be made.

Sexual abuse of children is believed to be vastly underreported. Although reported instances of sexual abuse involve female victims more often than males, boys are also targets of this victimization. Explanations for the increases in reported cases include changes in lifestyles, alcohol and drug abuse, and a lack of socialization into a value system that regards the sexual use of children as improper.

Certain types of children have been identified as high risks for child abuse. These include babies; children of very young parents; illegitimate children or stepchildren; premature, deformed, or sickly infants; and hyperactive or behavior-disordered children. A tendency for one child in a family to be singled out for abuse has been documented by research studies, with the natural parents of children the abusers in the majority of cases.

Child abuse occurs in all social classes, ethnic groups, and age groups, although it is more likely to be reported and investigated, and may in fact occur more frequently, among the poor, uneducated, unskilled population and among minority-group members.

Researchers have discovered that many child abusers were themselves physically or emotionally mistreated as children. These people are consciously or unconsciously attempting to apply to their own children the same standards of child rearing applied to them when they were young. Parents who have experienced life crises (deaths in the family, divorce, sexual difficulties) and single parents have been found to be disproportionately represented among child abusers. Sexual abuse of children has also been found to occur in families where the abusers themselves experienced or observed abnormal sexual behavior within their own families.

A portion of child abuse and neglect is handled informally within neighborhoods and families through threats of exposure. When cases are reported to the police or social agencies, they are most frequently handled through counseling or casework techniques. If cases are referred to the family or juvenile courts, dispositions may include supervision of the family by a probation officer, medical or psychiatric examinations or treatment for family members, issuing of "orders of protection" to require that detailed conditions be met by the parents, or temporary or permanent removal of the child from the home.

Removal of neglected or abused children from the home and placement in foster care or institutions is a last-resort approach that in some cases may be as damaging as the original neglect or abuse. The National Advisory Committee on Criminal Justice Standards and Goals recommended that every effort should be made to meet the needs of endangered children in their home setting before removal is considered; that the status of children in placement should be reviewed at least every six months; and that if a child cannot be returned home within six months to one year, parental rights should be terminated so the child can be made available for adoption. This policy is designed to reduce the atmosphere of uncertainty and to provide the stability that neglected and abused children need.

DISCUSSION QUESTIONS

1. Is it possible for a parent who has never physically abused a child to be guilty of emotional abuse or neglect? Could a parent be criminally prosecuted on such a charge?
2. Why must caution be used in the investigation of any report of child abuse or neglect? What procedures might be followed by a physician on duty in an emergency room when he or she encounters a case that is suggestive of abusive or neglectful behavior?
3. Why is it important for a child who allegedly has been abused or neglected to have a guardian ad litem present when the case is heard in court?
4. Discuss several types of children who are considered "high risks" for child abuse. How do you explain the finding that in many instances only one child in a family is singled out as the target of abuse?
5. Are abused children likely to grow up to be abusing parents? Discuss.

NOTES

1. *Akron Beacon Journal*, September 9, 1983, D–5.
2. *Cleveland Plain Dealer*, September 18, 1988, B–5.
3. *Baltimore Sun*, August 31, 1994, 3B.
4. Andale Gross, "Girl's Family Sees Man Get 4 Years for Death," *Akron Beacon Journal*, February 19, 2003, A1, A5.
5. "Two Mothers Charged after Party," *Akron Beacon Journal*, February 4, 2003, B5.
6. Blair Justice and Rita Justice, *The Abusing Family* (New York: Human Sciences Press, 1976), 18.
7. Naomi Feigelson Chase, *A Child Is Being Beaten* (New York: McGraw-Hill, 1976), 1.
8. Abraham Levine, "Child Neglect: Reaching the Parent," *The Social Rehabilitation Record* 1, 7 (July–August 1974), 26.
9. Child Abuse Prevention and Treatment Act, Public Law 93–247, quoted in the U.S. Department of Health, Education, and Welfare, *Child Abuse and Neglect* 1 (Washington, DC: U.S. Government Printing Office, 1976), 3.
10. *Ibid.*
11. National Advisory Committee on Criminal Justice Standards and Goals, *Juvenile Justice and Delinquency Prevention* (Washington, DC: U.S. Government Printing Office, 1977), 335–336.
12. Juvenile Justice Standards Project of the Institute of Judicial Administration and the American Bar Association, *Juvenile Justice Standards* (Washington, DC: National Conference on New Juvenile Justice Standards, 1977), 2–3.
13. Vincent DeFrancis and Carroll L. Lucht, *Child Abuse Legislation in the 1970s*, (Denver, CO: American Humane Association, 1974), 177.
14. Ruth C. Blanche, "The Nightmare of the Sexually Abused Child," *USA Today* 114, 2486 (November 1985), 57.
15. DeFrancis and Lucht, *Child Abuse Legislation in the 1970s*, 177.
16. *Ibid.*, 12.
17. C. Everett Koop, "A Challenge to the Medical Profession," *Justice for Children*, 1, 3 (Fall 1985), 23.
18. Blanche, "The Nightmare of the Sexually Abused Child," 55.

19. Murray A. Straus, *Beating the Devil Out of Them*. (New York: Lexington Books, 1994), 4.
20. *Ibid.*, 5.
21. Rebecca Socoloar, "Many Mothers Spank Toddlers," reported in *Akron Beacon Journal*, January 19, 1995, A4.
22. Straus, *Beating the Devil Out of Them*, 32.
23. "Teens Still Being Struck by Parents," *USA Today* 122, 2579 (August 1993), 8–9.
24. Howard N. Snyder and Melissa Sickmund, *Juvenile Offenders and Victims: 1999 National Report* (Washington, DC: Office of Juvenile Justice and Delinquency Prevention, 1999), 40.
25. *Ibid.*, 45.
26. *Ibid.*, 41.
27. *Ibid.*, 29.
28. Alvin A. Rosenfeld, "Endogamic Incest and the Victim-Perpetrator Model," *American Journal of Diseases of Children* 133 (April 1979), 406–410.
29. *Ibid.*
30. Vincent DeFrancis, *Protecting the Child Victim of Sex Crimes* (Denver, CO: American Humane Association, Children's Division, 1969), 7.
31. M.E. Elwell, "Sexually Assaulted Children and Their Families," *Social Casework* 60, 4 (April 1979), 227–235.
32. Vincent DeFrancis, "American Humane Association Publishes Highlights of National Study of Child Neglect and Abuse Reporting (Washington, DC: U.S. Department of Health, Education, and Welfare, National Center on Child Abuse and Neglect, February 1977), Publication (OHD) 77–20086, 6–8.
33. Snyder and Sickmund, *Juvenile Offenders and Victims*, 45.
34. *Ibid.*
35. E. M. Thompson, *Child Abuse: A Community Challenge* (East Aurora, NY: Henry Steward, 1971), 116.
36. Justice and Justice, *The Abusing Family*, 95.
37. Brandt F. Steele, *Working with Abusive Parents from a Psychiatric Point of View* (Washington, DC: U.S. Department of Health, Education, and Welfare, 1976), Publication (OHD) 76–300070, 13.
38. Lester Adelson, "Homicide by Pepper," *Journal of Forensic Science* 9, 3 (July 1964), 393–394.
39. Charles P. Smith, *A Preliminary National Assessment of Child Abuse and Neglect and the Juvenile Justice System: The Shadows of Distress* (Washington, DC: U.S. Department of Justice, 1980), 14.
40. *Ibid.*
41. DeFrancis, *Protecting the Child Victim*, vii.
42. Excerpted from U.S. Department of Health, Education, and Welfare, *Child Abuse and Neglect*, 1, 4–5.
43. Snyder and Sickmund, *Juvenile Offenders and Victims*, 46.
44. *Ibid.*
45. Steele, *Working with Abusive Parents*, 2.
46. Justice and Justice, *The Abusing Family*, 25–34.
47. Cathy Spatz Widom, *The Cycle of Violence* (Washington, DC: U.S. Department of Justice, 1992), 1.
48. *Ibid.*, 2.
49. Kathleen Coulborn Faller, "Why Sexual Abuse? An Exploration of the Intergenerational Hypothesis," *Child Abuse & Neglect* 13 (1989), 543–548.
50. Chris M. Mouzakitis, "Characteristics of Abused Adolescents and Guidelines for Intervention," *Child Welfare* 63, 2 (March–April 1984), 149–157.
51. James Moore, "What Leads Sexually Abused Juveniles to Delinquency," *Corrections Today* 53, 2 (February 1991), 42.
52. Cecil L. Willis and Richard H. Wells, "The Police and Child Abuse: An Analysis of Police Decisions to Report Illegal Behavior," *Criminology* 26, 4 (1988), 698–699.
53. *Ibid.*, 710–711.

54. Inger J. Sagatun and Leonard P. Edwards, *Child Abuse and the Legal System* (Chicago: Nelson-Hall, 1995), 10.
55. 42 U.S.C.A. Section 5103(b)(2)(G). Quoted in Debra Whitcomb, *Guardian Ad Litem in Criminal Courts* (Washington, DC: National Institute of Justice, 1988).
56. Sagatun and Edwards, *Child Abuse and the Legal System*, 12.
57. *Ibid.*
58. Snyder and Sickmund, *Juvenile Offenders and Victims*, 43.
59. *Ibid.* 43–44.
60. *Ibid.*, 42.
61. Carol Colley, "Invoking the Court's Authority—A Diagnostic Approach," *5th National Symposium on Child Abuse* (Denver, CO: American Humane Association, 1970), 70.
62. Hortense Laudau, "Preparation and Presentation for the Juvenile Court," *5th National Symposium on Child Abuse* (Denver, CO: American Humane Assocation, 1970), 75.
63. Clifford K. Dorne, *Crimes Against Children* (New York: Harrow and Heston, 1989), 113–120.
64. Henry Campbell Black, *Black's Law Dictionary*, 6th ed. (St. Paul, MN: West Publishing Co., 1991), 284.
65. In *Santosky v. Kramer* [455 U.S. 745 (1982)], the U.S. Supreme Court held that "Before a State may sever completely and irrevocably the rights of parents in their natural child, due process requires that the State support its allegation by at least clear and convincing evidence."
66. According to Black's Law Dictionary, "fair preponderance of the evidence" would be "evidence which as a whole shows that the fact sought to be proved is more probable than not." Black, *Black's Law Dictionary*, 6th ed., 819
67. Office of Juvenile Justice and Delinquency Prevention, "The Child Victim As Witness," *NIJ Reports* (Washington, DC: U.S. Department of Justice, 1989), 11.
68. Debra Whitcomb, *Prosecution of Child Sexual Abuse: Innovations in Practice* (Washington, DC: U.S. Department of Justice, Nov. 1985), 7.
69. Ray E. Helfer, *The Diagnostic Process and Treatment Programs* (Washington, DC: U.S. Department of Health, Education, and Welfare, 1976), Publication (OHD) 76=30069, 15.
70. National Advisory Committee, *Juvenile Justice and Delinquency Prevention*, 484, 496, 500.

CHAPTER 11

KEY ISSUES
IN THE JUVENILE
JUSTICE PROCESS

(Photo credit: Ernie Mastroianni)

THE STATUS-OFFENDER DILEMMA
    Categories of Status Offenders
    History of the Treatment of Status Offenders by the Juvenile Court
    Runaway Behavior—Should the Juvenile Court Intervene?
    Other Status Offenses—The Role of the Juvenile Court
    Proposed Changes in the Handling of Status Offenders
HANDLING SERIOUS DELINQUENT OFFENDERS
    Scope of the Problem
    Legislation Directed to Control of Habitual and Violent Juvenile Offenders
    Court Action against Habitual and Violent Juvenile Offenders
    Methods of Working with Habitual Violent Offenders

The two most debated issues in the control and treatment of juveniles are whether the juvenile court should retain jurisdiction over status offenders and what steps should be taken to handle more effectively the hardcore, serious delinquent offenders. A juvenile status offender, as we have seen, is one who has engaged in an act subject to juvenile court jurisdiction that would not be considered criminal if it were performed by an adult. Habitual, hardcore delinquents, in contrast, are youths who commit serious felonies, have a history of frequent justice-system involvement, and are believed by some justice officials to require control and punishment beyond that which the juvenile court can provide. Some argue that both types of offenders should be removed from juvenile court jurisdiction: the status offenders because their involvement in juvenile court action may be more harmful to them than the acts they have committed and the hardcore delinquents because the seriousness and frequency of their offenses preclude their protection from criminal-court penalties on the basis of their age alone.

THE STATUS-OFFENDER DILEMMA

Categories of Status Offenders

The term "status offenders" has traditionally been used to refer to those juveniles who engage in behavior that would not be considered unacceptable for adults, but is considered inappropriate for those who fall within a specified age category, occupying the "status" of juvenile rather than adult. The types of behavior in question include violating curfews, being truant from school, running away from home, using tobacco or alcohol, or being considered incorrigible or beyond the control of parents. In their juvenile codes, most states make legal differentiations between delinquent offenders (those in a specified age category who have committed acts that would also be considered criminal violations for adults) and status offenders.

We noted in Chapter 1 that the majority of states differentiate in their juvenile codes between status and delinquent offenders, using such categories as Minors in Need of Supervision (MINS), Persons in Need of Supervision (PINS), Children in Need of Supervision (CHINS), or Juveniles in Need of Supervision (JINS). The

Ohio Revised Juvenile Code details a variety of acts for which a youth may be subject to juvenile court intervention as an "unruly child."

According to this code, an "unruly child" is one:

1. Who does not subject himself to the reasonable control of parents, teachers, guardian, or custodian, by reason of being wayward or habitually disobedient;

2. Who is an habitual truant from home or school;

3. Who so deports himself as to injure or endanger the health or morals of himself or others;

4. Who attempts to enter the marriage relation in any state without the consent of his parents, custodian, legal guardian, or other legal authority;

5. Who is found in a disreputable place; visits or patronizes a place prohibited by law; or associates with vagrant, vicious, criminal, notorious, or immoral persons;

6. Who engages in an occupation prohibited by law or is in a situation dangerous to life or limb or injurious to the health or morals of himself or others;

7. Who has violated a law applicable only to a child.[1]

In response to calls for changes in the ways status offenders are handled, some states have "decriminalized" certain status offenses so that they are no longer law violations. Juveniles involved in these behaviors are considered "dependent children" and child protective services rather than the juvenile courts have jurisdiction over them.[2] This approach is not used in all states, and the result is that runaways (e.g., a type of offender decriminalized in some states) may be handled through child welfare agencies in those states but taken to juvenile court intake in others.[3] In all states, however, when attempts at informal handling through service agencies fail and the unacceptable behavior persists, the cases can be referred to the juvenile courts for formal handling.[4]

In 1996, more than 162,000 status offense cases were formally processed by the juvenile courts. Twenty-eight percent of these involved juvenile liquor law violations, 24 percent truancy, 12 percent ungovernability, and 16 percent runaway behavior. The remaining 20 percent of the cases involved other status offenses, including curfew violations, smoking tobacco, or violation of a court order.[5] There was a more than 100 percent increase in formally processed status offense cases during the 10-year period from 1987 to 1996.[6]

History of the Treatment of Status Offenders by the Juvenile Court

As we have noted, the first juvenile court was created as a result of 19th-century reform movements to improve the education of children, eliminate child labor, and provide publicly supported care for neglected children. Later the "child savers" pressured various state legislatures to provide separate detention facilities and hearings for juveniles, who up to that time had been held in jails with adults and serviced by the criminal courts. The founders of the juvenile court were concerned with controlling and regulating the behavior of many types of children—not only those who had committed criminal offenses, but also young people who were homeless, parentless, idle, uneducated, wandering, subject to mischief and temptation, or easily misled by unscrupulous adults.

The juvenile court was established as an institution committed to acting in the best interests of the young people referred there. The type of behavior that brought them to the court's attention was not considered to be an important factor in determining the amount and forms of guidance and direction to be administered. Individualized justice—that is, action based on the unique problems of each child brought before the court—was to be dispensed. The first juvenile court was even authorized to deal with children who showed evidence of "predelinquent behavior." The disposition of each case was to have the purpose of effecting "changes in the behavior of the convicted person in the interests of his own happiness, health, and satisfaction, and in the interest of social defense."[7]

As a result of this orientation, juvenile codes set up by the various states made no distinction between undesirable juvenile acts that would be considered crimes if committed by adults and those that would not. Although individualized justice was the goal of juvenile court intervention, lack of funds, insensitive or poorly trained judges, lack of facilities for status offenders, and even the urging of parents that their children be treated severely by the juvenile court led in too many instances to the housing of status offenders with hardened delinquents, the institutionalization of status offenders, and their progression toward even more serious undesirable behavior as a result of ineffective treatment.

Runaway Behavior—Should the Juvenile Court Intervene?

Among status offenders, runaways as a group require special discussion, for with no other segment of its cases has the juvenile court been more ineffective. The *Uniform Crime Report* for 2001 gave an estimate of 133,259 arrests of youths under age 18 for runaway behavior.[8] Approximately 60 percent of those arrested were females.[9] It was also shown that approximately 50 percent of all of the arrests of juveniles under age 18 for status offenses were for the two offenses of running away and curfew violations/loitering law violations.[10]

Those arrested each year represent only a fraction of the runaway population. The National Incident Studies of Missing, Abducted, Runaway, and Throwaway Children estimated that, in a given year, more than 450,000 children were abducted by family members, abducted by nonfamily members, became runaways or throwaways, or were missing because they were lost or injured. The report estimated that as many as 20 percent of the children that other studies classified as runaways were in fact "throwaway" children—ones who were ordered by parents or caretakers to leave their homes, who were abandoned, or deserted, or who had run away and were not allowed to return home.[11] The following case illustrates a throwaway child's experiences.

When he was 15, Michael told his mother and stepfather that he was homosexual. His step-father couldn't handle it and kicked him out of the house—but Michael had nowhere to go. So he ended up on the streets of New York, where the dealers and the sex industry swallowed him up. When he first came to Covenant House [a shelter for homeless children], he was a desperate drug addict who supported himself and his habit by selling his body on the streets.[12]

While the trend has been toward dealing with runaways in an unofficial manner, through runaway shelters or social agencies, many runaways are still processed through the juvenile court. In 1996, 60 percent of the runaway cases formally disposed of by juvenile courts involved females.[13]

Some children who run away seek out large metropolitan areas with the hope of gaining anonymity and being able to "hustle a living." Youths who run to large cities frequently fall prey to the evils of inner-city life. Since they have little money and must turn to street contacts for life-sustaining funds, they often become involved in street crime, including drug dealing, prostitution, purse snatching or other types of larceny, and possession and sale of stolen property.

Runaways are easily influenced by those who operate outside the law because they are themselves fugitives from the juvenile justice system and cannot make contacts with legitimate social agencies for fear of being arrested, detained, and sent home. Their runaway status makes them particularly vulnerable to the street criminals with whom they deal, for they live under constant threat of being "turned in" unless they cooperate.

We noted earlier that runaways may in fact be "throwaways," whose parents caused them to become runaways and thus status offenders by mistreating them or pressuring them to leave home.[14] A case history of a juvenile prostitute describes such a situation.

Ann was 15 when she was interviewed. She had been born in a deprived area of New York City, the fourth child and first daughter of parents who had not wanted any more children. The father left home soon after Ann was born and her mother blamed the birth of an additional child for his leaving. For a while the mother worked as a waitress, but soon turned to prostitution. The three boys were sent to live with relatives, but no home could be found for the baby girl. Ann's mother complained often that the little girl was a nuisance and a burden. After 18 months on the street, the mother acquired a new boyfriend, who moved in with her; she gave up prostitution at this point. Now there were two adults bemoaning the lack of privacy and the inconvenience of having an adolescent girl living with them. As Ann says, "They didn't tell me to get out, but they didn't come looking for me when I did."[15]

Runaways have also been characterized as youths who manifest an inability to get along with adults in general, including parents, teachers, and professionals in various social helping fields. Rather than seeking help from adults, runaways tend to turn to their peer group for assistance and support. Counselors at havens for runaways confirm the fact that lack of communication between parents and children or conflicting lifestyles play an important part in running away. In a youth's mind, flight may be associated with a desire to identify with peers, which has been unduly suppressed or ridiculed at home.

Runaways as a status-offender group exemplify the dilemma that the handling of all types of status offenders presents to the juvenile court. Because of the nature of their behavior, runaways referred to the juvenile court are frequently held in detention rather than released to return for later hearings. The negative effects of detention itself may cause a youth to perceive himself or herself as deviant or criminal, making efforts to reach and help the young person more difficult. Commitment to institutions for repeated runaway offenses can result in stigmatization and association with more severely disturbed delinquents and can further reduce the chances of achieving a stable family situation. Yet, removing runaways from juvenile court jurisdiction would leave parents no legal means by which to seek the return to the home of children who need adult supervision. It reduces the control mechanisms available to cities to which large numbers of runaways are drawn.

In 1982, the U.S. Congress passed the Missing Children Act and in 1984 a National Center for Missing and Exploited Children was opened in Washington, DC, supported by the Office of Juvenile Justice and Delinquency Prevention. The center provides information on missing children to help parents, law enforcement agencies, and other organizations locate, identify, and return children who have been abducted or have run away from home. The center also works to increase public awareness of the problems of runaway and missing children. A toll-free telephone hotline to collect and disseminate information on sightings of missing children is part of the center's program. From 1984 through 1994, the center was credited with playing a role in the recovery of 24,000 missing children.[16]

Other Status Offenses—The Role of the Juvenile Court

In addition to running away, other forms of juvenile misbehavior that fall into the status offense category include truancy, ungovernability, violations of liquor laws, and curfew violations. Many of these offenses are related. For example, a youth who is experiencing serious difficulties at home because of the actions of overly strict or abusive parents may react to the situation in an aggressive way and be referred to the juvenile court as ungovernable. The child may decide to leave home as a way of escaping the situation there, and as a result may be truant from school or picked up by police as a curfew violator. Status offenses may lead to involvement in delinquent behavior. For example, running away may place a youth in a situation where stealing or prostituting is used for survival on the street.

The FBI's Uniform Crime Report, *Crime in the United States*, does not give statistics on arrests of juveniles for all types of status offenses, However, in 2001 there were more than 1,600 arrests of persons under age 18 for vagrancy and more than 65,000 arrests of persons in the same age group for curfew and loitering law violations. Almost 86,000 youths were arrested for violations of liquor laws and more than 13,000 were arrested for drunkenness.[17]

Many of the status offenders referred to juvenile courts are handled in an unofficial way or are diverted to other community agencies for assistance with their problems. Those whose cases are petitioned (formally handled) therefore represent only a portion of the youths who have some contact with the juvenile court. How-

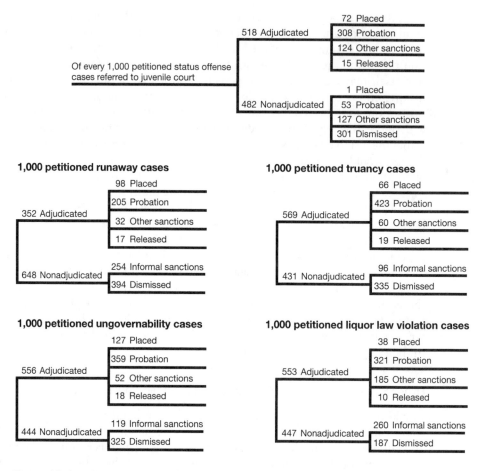

Figure 11–1.   Outcomes of Every 1,000 Petitioned Status Offenses Cases Processed in Juvenile Courts in 1996. *(Source: Howard N. Snyder and Melissa Sickmund,* Juvenile Offenders and Victims: 1999 National Report *(Washington, DC: Office of Juvenile Justice and Delinquency Prevention, 199), 169. Figure adapted from A. Stahl, M. Sickmund, T. Finnegan, H. Snyder, R. Poole, and N. Tierney,* Juvenile Court Statistics 1996 *(Washington, DC: Office of Juvenile Justice and Delinquency Prevention, 1999).)*

ever, *Juvenile Court Statistics* for 1996 provide information on recent trends. Overall, petitioned status-offense cases more than doubled between 1987 and 1996.[18] As shown in Figure 11–1, more than half of the petitioned status offense cases were adjudicated and the majority of those adjudicated receive probation as a sanction. The types of status offenses more likely to be formally adjudicated are truancy, liquor law violations, and ungovernability. Those youths brought to the court for running away, if adjudicated, are more likely to receive some type of out-of-home placement (28%) as a disposition than youths adjudicated for other types of status offenses.[19]

The arrest, detention, and handling by the juvenile courts of young people who have been involved in behavior that is only illegal because of their nonadult status has been hotly debated. It is felt by many that the contacts with law enforcement and the courts are more damaging to the youths than the behavior for which they are referred. However, it is important that there be methods to supervise and control behavior by juveniles that is inappropriate or dangerous for them.

Proposed Changes in the Handling of Status Offenders

Even though some judges, justice-system professionals, and interested community observers maintain that status offenders should continue to be handled by juvenile courts in the traditional manner, two alternatives have gained strong support: (1) complete removal of the status offender from juvenile court jurisdiction; and (2) retaining juvenile court jurisdiction over status offenders but excluding them from official proceedings and secure detention facilities. This approach involves revising the juvenile codes to define and limit the range of such offenses, lowering the upper age limit for status offenders, and setting a minimum age limit.

Arguments for Removing Status Offenders from Juvenile Court Jurisdiction.   Those who advocate complete removal of the status offender from the juvenile justice system argue that although status offenders do not violate criminal laws, they are often viewed by the public as minor criminals; that the codes defining status offenses use vague terminology; that stigmatization of the juvenile can result from court contact; that status offenders are often treated like and required to associate with hardened delinquents; that in many cases, social agencies and other community resources are in a better position to treat the status offender's problem than is the juvenile court; and that neglectful or abusive parents can precipitate behavior in a child for which the parents rather than the child should be punished.

Proponents contend that removing status offenders from the system would enable court personnel to concentrate their time and energy on delinquent youths who pose a greater threat to the community. The agencies to which status offenders would be referred would be forced to expand and improve their services to meet the increased demand.

One of the strongest arguments for removal involves the theory that bringing a child into contact with the juvenile court labels him or her deviant or delinquent in the eyes of the community, and that this labeling reinforces deviant behavior. Thus, a child first referred to the juvenile court for a minor status offense, kept in the same quarters as or associating with those referred for more serious status offenses or delinquencies, and, at least in his or her own perception, treated in the same manner begins to think of himself or herself as a delinquent. Proponents argue that the action of bringing such a youth to the juvenile court may have a detrimental effect that outweighs any assistance the court may give.

Support is given to this argument by Kelley's research on more than 2,000 juveniles referred to an urban juvenile court over a five-year period. Although the majority (57%) of those referred for status offenses were not referred to the court again after their first offense, those who did return had more serious offenses than at their initial referrals. The researcher concluded that status offenders may be pushed toward more serious offenses because of the effects of juvenile court involvement and that their more serious misbehavior after the initial court contact may be, in part, a reflection of the harmful effects of labeling resulting from their first court appearance.[20]

Another argument for removal is the vague nature of juvenile codes. Parents often use the threat of court action as a control mechanism and a way to force their children to behave properly. Parents frequently bring their daughters to the attention of juvenile authorities under the guise of incorrigibility because they suspect that they are sexually involved with a man or several men. Status offenses by girls frequently carry connotations of sexual involvement or victimization. Females are involved in 60 percent of all runaway cases and runaways constitute 40 percent of the status offenders held in public detention centers.[21] Rector found that "one of the major reasons for girls running away from home is to avoid sexual abuse from their fathers, their stepfathers, or their mother's boyfriends."[22] (See Chapter 8 for more detailed information on the backgrounds and difficulties of female status offenders.)

Clement contends that, in many cases, females were punished more severely because of the desire to protect them and young women were often sent to state institutions for sex-based types of offenses or "immoral conduct," while young males were not.[23] In Oklahoma, females were formerly under juvenile court jurisdiction until they reached age 18, but males left juvenile court jurisdiction after the age of 16. In *Lamb* v. *Brown* (1972), the 10th Circuit Court of the U.S. Court of Appeals declared that there was no constitutional justification for having different age limits for the juvenile status on the basis of sex and the Oklahoma juvenile code was changed.[24]

One of the most persuasive arguments for removing status offenders from court jurisdiction is the fact that they are often treated as harshly as or more harshly than their delinquent counterparts. Although not many judges will admit it, their dispositions are a full or partial reflection of a youth's attitude or sex, of a desire to punish, or of feelings of being at a loss as to what other action can be taken, rather than being based on only the severity of the offense under consideration.

Misguided efforts to assist status offenders may result in inappropriate court handling. A study of status and minor offenders in a large California county revealed that many first-time offenders were given out-of-home placements after their first offense, even though the offenses were minor. Those given the dispositions tended to come from dysfunctional homes where hardcore delinquents or alcohol- or drug-involved parents resided. Thus, out-of-home placement in group home or foster home was used as a way of taking the youths away from bad home environments.[25] The researchers discovered that:

> First time, nonserious offenders removed from the home were more than two times as likely to have parents with drug and alcohol abuse problems than juveniles placed on probation. It appears that the system is responding to the family's problem with the out-of-home placement decision [rather] than the individual juvenile's offense.[26]

The study reveals that, while the intentions of the court personnel were good, many first-time offenders who had committed offenses that were not considered serious were removed from their homes and brought under continued juvenile justice system supervision.

Arguments for Retaining Status Offenders under Juvenile Court Jurisdiction.   In the light of the many recognized problems and injustices associated with the processing of status offenders by the juvenile courts, it would appear that the advocates of removing them from juvenile court jurisdiction have some very strong arguments to support their position. Proponents of retention, however, are just as adamant in support of their point of view.

Those who favor retention of jurisdiction over status offenders maintain that status offenders are not as different from delinquent offenders as critics of the juvenile justice system would lead us to believe. Thomas compared the offense careers of three groups of first offenders: delinquent offenders charged with felonies, delinquent offenders charged with misdemeanors, and status offenders. He found that status offenders were more likely than the other two groups to recidivate, that 59 percent of those first charged with status offenses later committed misdemeanors or felonies, and that many of those who were first charged with felonies or misdemeanors later became status offenders.[27] A study that compared the offense patterns of status and delinquent offenders referred to a juvenile court discovered that the vast majority of the status offenders (65%) did not reappear before the court during the following two years. However, the status offenders who did recidivate committed delinquent offenses as well as status offenses. The researchers concluded that the harmful effects of court appearances on the status offenders were minimal.[28]

Another difficulty in defining status offenders as a group distinctly different from delinquent offenders is the fact that, with the increased use of legal counsel in the juvenile court, plea bargaining may result in the reduction of a delinquency charge to a status offense, although the juvenile did in fact commit an act that is a violation of the criminal code.

The argument that labeling youths deviant by referring them to the juvenile court has psychologically damaging effects is countered by the reply that these effects have been greatly exaggerated. Foster, Dinitz, and Reckless concluded that the characterization of youths as status or delinquent offenders did not cause any significant changes in the relationship between the offenders and their families, friends, or teachers.[29]

Gill maintained that the stigmatization reputed to accompany referral to the juvenile court would probably also occur if the child were referred to some other type of social agency. He reasoned that community members, school officials, and other youths would be quick to identify such agencies as the places where troubled or difficult children are referred and label the referrals accordingly. He also declared that the great majority of status offenders are children who are having problems with authority, and that only an agency such as the juvenile court, which has the power of law to enforce its decisions, can adequately deal with them. Community agencies do not have the necessary clout to require the youth or the family to seek help.[30]

Advocates of removal speak confidently about other agencies' expanding their services if status offenders are referred to them, but opponents say funding such expansion would be a great burden. In addition, if these agencies had no power to require a youth to seek help, parents who were at a loss for help in controlling their children would have nowhere to turn. Discussions with juvenile court administrators and personnel reveal that frequently the directors of group or foster homes must turn to the juvenile court for assistance in making youths placed in these homes conform to the rules. Another outcome of removal of status offenders could well be an increase in dependent-child suits, in which welfare agencies petition the court to have a child declared dependent and thus subject to juvenile court jurisdiction. Such a long, drawn-out legal process would delay getting help for a child.

The notion that status offenders are frequently victimized by institutionalization is also questioned by advocates of retention. Juvenile court judges contend that many juveniles who are sent to institutions following a court referral for a status offense have prior records of delinquent offenses. Even though the actual incident under consideration when the commitment decision is made may be a status offense, the judge ordering a disposition of institutionalization takes into consideration the previous juvenile court record of the youth, which may have involved serious delinquency.

Other Alternatives. One alternative method of handling status offenders, which takes the middle ground between complete removal from juvenile court jurisdiction and retention, is the practice of deinstitutionalization or removing status offenders from jails and correctional institutions. Federal legislation has been enacted toward meeting this goal. The Uniform Juvenile Court Act of 1968 recommended that placement of status offenders in state institutions for delinquents be prohibited unless proof is presented that other placements have failed and that such a commitment would facilitate the child's treatment.[31] The Juvenile Justice and Delinquency Prevention Act of 1974 stipulated that states applying for federal funds to assist with their juvenile justice plans must submit proof that within two years, facilities will be developed to separate status offenders from adults and delinquents in detention by placing them in separate shelter facilities. In 1977, this act was amended to extend the time period allowed for the states to comply and to include dependent and neglected children in the prohibition against detention with adults.[32] The Task Force Report of the National Advisory Commission on Criminal Justice Standards and Goals also recommended that placement of status offenders in institutions for delinquents not be permitted and urged diversion of status offenders from the justice system whenever possible.[33]

The effects of this legislation and the Task Force recommendations can be seen in the fact that, from 1975 to 1996, there was a decline in the proportion of status offenders held in detention from 40 percent in 1975 to less than 10 percent in 1996.[34] Nevertheless, there were still more than 39,000 status offenders held in detention in 1996. It is not certain how many of these were placed in detention under the guidelines established in the Juvenile Justice and Delinquency Prevention Act of 1974 that permit status offenders to be held for up to 24 hours.[35] A Report of the National Juvenile Justice Assessment Centers on the progress of deinstitutionalization of status offenders nationwide noted that in many instances alternatives developed for placement of status offenders were used for youths who might previously have been handled informally, while status offenders continued to be detained in secure facilities and the prohibitions against confinement of status offenders in secure facilities were circumvented by charging youths who might have been considered status offenders with minor delinquent offenses, thus allowing confinement.[36] It is apparent that the goal of removing all status offenders from secure facilities has not been realized.

Another possible resolution of the status-offender dilemma lies in revising current laws. There is no doubt that such terms as "unruly," "out of control," and "leading a lewd and dissolute life" can be applied to many acts that are dangerous to neither the child nor the community. The vagueness of the statutes currently in effect in many jurisdictions allows police officials and judges wide latitude in enforcing them. Enactment of clearly defined laws, elimination of many minor types of misbehavior from the status-offense category, and setting of standards for uniform application of the law would go far toward ending abuses.

Changes in the age ranges to which certain types of offenses apply could also reduce the number of status offenders referred to the juvenile courts. For example, setting the upper age limit for runaway or incorrigibility offenses at 15 would remove many youths from court involvement.

Recommendations of the Juvenile Justice and Delinquency Prevention Task Force.
As part of the work of the National Advisory Committee on Criminal Justice Standards and Goals, a Task Force on Juvenile Justice and Delinquency Prevention was established to develop national standards for juvenile justice system operation. Included in the Task Force's recommendations was a new plan for handling youths currently termed status offenders. This approach would involve eliminating the status offender, PINS, CHINS, and other labels completely. Instead, certain children and their families would be defined as Families with Service Needs. Rather than emphasizing the child as an offender, the new approach would bring the child and all family members under the jurisdiction and authority of the court.

The Task Force set forth five specific behaviors that would come under the jurisdiction of the court as appropriate for the Families with Service Needs designation:

1. *School truancy.* This is defined as a pattern of repeated or habitual unauthorized absence from school by any juvenile subject to compulsory education laws. The court's power to intervene in cases of truancy should be limited to situations where the child's continued absence from school clearly indicates the need for services.

2. *Repeated disregard for or misuse of lawful parental authority.* Family court jurisdiction under this category should be narrowly restricted to circumstances where a pattern of repeated disobedient behavior on the part of the juvenile or a pattern of repeated unreasonable demands on the part of the parents creates a situation of family conflict clearly evidencing a need for services.

3. *Repeated running away from home.* Running away is defined as a juvenile's unauthorized absence from home for more than 24 hours. Family court jurisdiction in this category should be the last resort for dealing with the juvenile who repeatedly runs away from home, refuses or has not benefited from voluntary services, and is incapable of self-support. Where the juvenile is capable of self-support, the family court should give serious consideration of the dispositional alternative of responsible self-sufficiency.

4. *Repeated use of intoxicating beverages.* This is defined as the repeated possession and/or consumption of intoxicating beverages by a juvenile. In this category, the family court should have the power to intervene and provide services where a juvenile's serious, repeated use of alcohol clearly indicates a need for these services.

5. *Delinquent acts committed by a juvenile younger than 10 years of age.* A delinquent act is defined as an act that would be a violation of federal or state criminal law or of local ordinance if committed by an adult. Family court delinquency jurisdiction covers juveniles of age 10 and above. This category is intended to cover the the situation where a juvenile younger than 10 years repeatedly commits acts that would support a delinquency petition for an older child or where the "delinquent acts" committed are of a serious nature.[37]

Hearings in court for Families with Service Needs would be designed to ascertain the truth of the facts presented in the petition, but would make no *designation of fault*. Rather than labeling a child who has not committed a crime a delinquent, the purpose of a Families with Service Needs hearing would be to develop the best possible disposition of the matter for the entire family. For example, in cases where running away from home was found to be the result of intolerable conditions caused by the behavior of the parents, the court's dispositional orders would focus on help for the parents rather than treatment for the child. A child whose school misbehavior problems were found to be related to learning disabilities or fear of failure would be handled by efforts to provide diagnostic or remedial assistance, rather than focusing on the misbehavior itself.[38]

The Task Force recommended that under no circumstances should children referred to the court for family service needs be committed to institutions for delinquents or confined in secure institutions. It also recommended that in certain cases the court be empowered to enter an order of "self-sufficiency" in which a child who has the maturity and ability to maintain himself or herself independently would be allowed to do so, free from parental control.[39]

The "middle-of-the-road" approach to the handling of status offenders advocated by the Task Force appears to be the most rational one. Rather than complete removal, which would throw the burden of treatment for such youths on agencies that have not demonstrated that they can handle such a volume of cases effectively, the retention of jurisdiction by the juvenile court, with very specifically defined offenses and standards for application of the laws, and elimination of many minor offenses would seem to be a logical starting point.

The juvenile codes of many states use language that is intentionally broad and general in its statements, giving juvenile courts the freedom to intervene in a wide range of instances when the welfare of the child seems to be threatened. Legal attacks on these codes have been based on the contention that the due-process rights of juveniles are violated by these codes because they are "void for vagueness." The principle of Anglo-American law states that "a statute may not be so indefinite in its language that men of common intelligence must necessarily guess at its meaning and differ as to its application."[40] The successful legal challenges to the codes have resulted in revisions which have detailed the exact behaviors that make a youth subject to juvenile court intervention.

The federal government and many state governments have already taken steps to eliminate such serious injustices as the widespread detention and institutionalization of status offenders. With the development of new resources, completion of research exploring the status offenders' problems and needs, and experimentation with innovative treatment methods, it is possible that at some future date, status offenders could be safely removed from the juvenile justice system and serviced by other types of agencies.

HANDLING SERIOUS DELINQUENT OFFENDERS

The arguments for removing status offenders from juvenile court jurisdiction are related to the realization that in too many instances, the dispositions they receive are overly severe and out of proportion to the offenses or behavior involved. Calls for changes in the handling of serious delinquent offenders are the result of activity at the opposite extreme. Citizens are incensed when habitual, serious offenders receive a "slap on the wrist," are repeatedly given probation, and in some instances flaunt their contempt for the inability of the juvenile courts to deal appropriately with them. Street-wise youths quickly discover that the juvenile justice system can be manipulated to their advantage.

Scope of the Problem

The FBI's *Uniform Crime Report* for 2001 indicated that approximately 17 percent of the total arrests in the United States in that year, more than 15 percent of the arrests for violent crimes (murder, forcible rape, robbery, and aggravated assault), and more than 30 percent of the arrests for property crimes (burglary, larceny-theft, motor vehicle theft, and arson) were of persons under 18 years of age. The arrests of youths under 18 for violent crimes were concentrated in the 15- to 17-year-old age group, with the exception of aggravated assaults and other assaults, where almost one third of those arrested were under age 15.[41] For property crimes, more than one third were committed by youths under age 15.[42] However, the five-year crime trend for the years 1997 through 2001 revealed a significant decline in arrests of youths under 18 for all categories of violent crime and for most property crimes.[43]

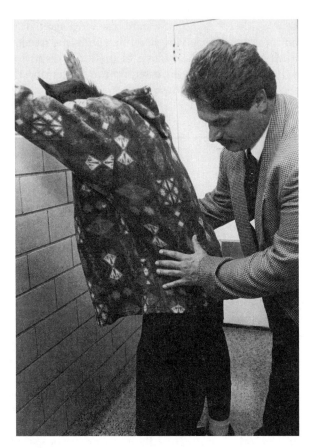

The growing use of weapons by youths is a cause for
great concern. *(Photo credit: Nick J. Cool, The Image Works)*

Legislation Directed to Control Habitual and Violent Juvenile Offenders

In response to the problem of habitual and violent youth crime, almost every state
has adopted new legislation that changes the function of the juvenile court away
from rehabilitation and toward punishment and public safety (the "justice model").
Included in this legislation are mandatory periods of incarceration for certain categories of violent and serious offenders, lowering the age of original jurisdiction of the
adult courts, juvenile code provisions that facilitate transfer of cases to adult criminal
courts, reducing the confidentiality of juvenile court proceedings and records, and
the introduction of the "blended sentence."

Blended sentencing statutes, which allow courts to impose juvenile and/or
adult correctional sanctions on certain young offenders, were in place in 20 states at
the end of 1997.[44]

The Violent and Repeat Juvenile Offender Act of 1997, applicable to all juveniles violating federal laws, gives federal prosecutors the discretionary power to try juveniles as adults for all felonies and allows juveniles arrested for felony crimes to be housed in adult jails for indefinite periods.[45] It was hoped that this Act would serve as a model for the states in terms of their approach to dealing with violent and serious juvenile offenders.

Court Action against Habitual and Violent Juvenile Offenders

One method of dealing with habitual and violent delinquents before their court appearances involves holding the youths in detention until the hearings take place. In 1984, the U.S. Supreme Court upheld the New York Family Court Act, which allows detention before hearings of juveniles who present a "serious risk" of committing another offense. In the decision *Schall v. Martin,* the Court ruled that juveniles, unlike adults, are always in some form of custody and that "the juvenile's liberty interest may, in appropriate circumstances, be subordinated to the State's 'parens patriae' interest in preserving and promoting the welfare of the child."[46] The Court also noted that every state and the District of Columbia permits some form of preventive detention of juveniles accused of crime.

In commenting on the ruling, U.S. Supreme Court Justice William Rehnquist noted:

> Society has a legitimate interest in protecting a juvenile from the consequences of his criminal activity—both from potential physical injury which may be suffered when a victim fights back . . . and from the downward spiral of criminal activity into which peer pressure may lead the child. . . . If parental control falters, the state must play its part as *parens patriae.*[47]

Once a violent or hardcore delinquent juvenile has been arrested, the question of whether the case will be retained in the juvenile court or waived to an adult criminal court becomes all important. If the case is adjudicated in the juvenile court and the charges are found to be true, the juvenile justice system can maintain jurisdiction over the offender only until the age of majority (21 in most states, but 18 in some). Thus a 14-year-old convicted of delinquency by reason of murder in a juvenile court would be under juvenile correctional supervision for only four years in some states, or for a maximum of seven years in the other states, before being released.

In the United States, juveniles may be processed by adult courts under the following conditions:

1. States may exclude certain offenses from juvenile jurisdiction—both the most serious crimes and the most trivial. Often an offense for which the death penalty or life imprisonment can be imposed is automatically a matter for the adult criminal court, although a few states provide for "reverse waiver"; that is, the adult court sends the case back to the juvenile court. At the other end of the scale, such matters as minor traffic offenses or fish and game violations usually do not come to juvenile court.

2. Juvenile courts may waive original jurisdiction and, after a hearing, transfer the case to adult criminal court. Almost half of the states do not specify a lower age limit for transfers, two states use age 10, three states use age 12, and 16 states use age 14.

3. In some states, the prosecutors can use discretion in determining whether to have a juvenile case filed in juvenile court or criminal court.

4. In states having a "blended sentence" provision, the case may be originally tried in either the juvenile or adult criminal court, and the sentence can include either juvenile, adult, or combined correctional sanctions.[48]

Judicial waiver is the predominant means through which juvenile cases are transferred to adult courts. The number of judicial waivers increased from approximately 6,500 in 1987 to approximately 10,000 in 1996, a 47 percent increase. The types of transferred offenses in 1996 included offenses against persons (43%), property offenses (37%), drug-related offenses (14%) and public order offenses (6%).[49]

The National Council of Juvenile and Family Court Judges developed recommendations for dealing with the problems of serious juvenile crime, noting that

> there are juveniles for whom the resources and processes available to the juvenile court will serve neither to rehabilitate the juvenile, nor to provide a suitable sanction for the offense, nor to adequately protect the public. Such juveniles should be tried and, if convicted, sentenced in the adult criminal court.[50]

It was recommended that waiver decisions be made by the juvenile court judge, using guidelines to protect the constitutional rights of the juvenile and that subsequent charges against previously transferred juveniles be subject to juvenile court jurisdiction and a new decision on transfer; that transfer hearing be open to the public; that juvenile court records be provided to adult criminal courts that convicted a waived juvenile; that legal records of these juveniles be opened to those who need access to them when public safety is involved; and that the effects of expunging [sealing] juvenile records should be reviewed.

The notion that youths whose cases are eligible for trial in adult courts will receive the same sentences that adults would receive for similar offenses is not borne out by research. Hamparian's study of violent juvenile offenders found that more than half of those tried as adults were given fines or probation.[51] Probation tends to be granted in these instances because the adult conviction is the first for the waived juvenile, even though a lengthy juvenile record may exist.

The state of Washington has developed a system of determinate sentencing that is based on an elaborate point system. The juvenile code, which excludes status offenses, provides that each conviction results in the assignment of a specified number of points to the juvenile, based on the youth's age, prior criminal record, and the severity of the offense. On the basis of the point system, delinquents are divided into minor, middle, and serious levels. Minor offenders seldom go to institutions, while serious offenders, with point accumulations over 110, almost always are institutionalized. They are sentenced to flat terms of up to three or four years. Time served cannot be adjusted more than 10 percent for good behavior. Set

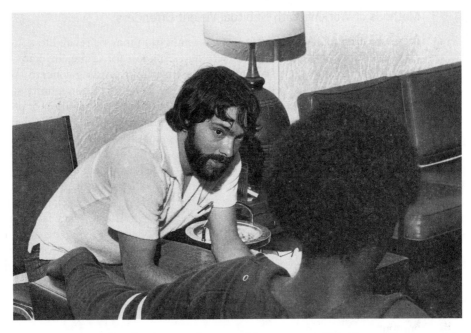

Even serious juvenile offenders can be treated in a community setting, with appropriate supervision and guidance. *(Photo credit: Jay Paris)*

penalties for middle or minor point levels may include fines, restitution, or community service.[52]

Although institutionalizing serious offenders temporarily prevents them from committing crimes, these offenders, because of their youth, are virtually certain to be released at some point and returned to the community. There is evidence that, once released, they continue to commit crimes and that their criminal activity tends to escalate. A study of young parolees released from state prisons found that the earlier a parolee's first adult arrest occurred, the more likely chances for rearrest were; 79 percent of offenders arrested and charged as adults before the age of 17 were rearrested, compared to 51 percent of those first arrested at age 20 or older.[53] A U.S. Bureau of Justice Statistics Special Report revealed that 21 percent of offenders released from prison when they were 18 to 24 years old were returned to prison within one year, 34 percent were returned within two years, and 50 percent were returned within seven years.[54] Fagan compared 15- and 16-year-old robbers and burglars who were automatically prosecuted in the criminal courts in New York because of the state statutes regarding age with a comparable group of offenders in New Jersey who were processed in the juvenile courts. He found that 76 percent of the New York youths processed in criminal courts were rearrested, compared to 67 percent of New Jersey youths, who were processed in juvenile courts. A larger proportion of the New York youths were reincarcerated after committing additional offenses. He concluded that transferred youths were likely to reoffend more quickly and more often than those retained in the juvenile justice system.[55]

Methods of Working with Habitual Violent Offenders

Increased criminal activity after institutionalization may be related to a "contamination" effect, with the institutions serving as schools for crime. In many instances, however, protection of the community must be the overriding concern. Youths may have to be institutionalized before they can be assigned to community supervision. The URSA Institute conducted an exhaustive national examination of programs for serious juvenile offenders and summarized the characteristics of those that appeared to have experienced some success. All of these involved long periods of supervision, beginning with perhaps 6 to 12 months of institutionalization followed by nonsecure residential treatment for three to six months and aftercare for one or more years. Offenders who were evaluated as not presenting a serious threat to community safety could begin their supervision in residential treatment or even be allowed to remain in their own homes during the entire period of supervision. A key factor in the successful programs was the consistent application of sanctions for negative behavior, including isolation, suspension of privileges, or return to an institution. It was recommended that a single caseworker be assigned to work with a youth during the entire period of supervision. Dedication and competence of staff members were viewed as very important elements in programs that had experienced some degree of success. The Institute also recommended adequate pay and rotation of assignments to avoid burnout.[56]

The National Council of Juvenile and Family Court Judges, in its recommendations for dealing with serious juvenile offenders, suggested that programs developed in community settings should provide strong controls and close supervision for the protection of the public and the staff and stressed the importance of gradual reentry into the community of youth released from institutions, through the use of halfway houses, group homes, and structured stages of supervision intensity.[57]

The Center for Studies of Anti-Social and Violent Behavior, established within the National Institute of Mental Health, has the specific goal of increasing the knowledge of the causes of antisocial and violent behavior and improving the ability of justice and human-service agencies to understand, cope with, prevent, and treat such behavior. No specific technique has been developed to treat violent behavior exclusively. Methods used in working with violent offenders are directed toward increasing their self-esteem, developing their educational and work skills, and improving their adjustment in family, peer-group, and community settings. We noted earlier that the theories of violence center on the causal influences of interpersonal relationships of the violent individuals with family members, peers, and significant others, with violence becoming a learned solution to problems. Because the difficulties in the lives of habitual and violent delinquent offenders are long-term and severe, success in working with them is never assured and the outlook is pessimistic. Nevertheless, efforts to reach and change them must continue.

The Office of Justice Programs Office of the U.S. Department of Justice, in conjunction with five other federal agencies, has developed the Serious and Violent Offender Reentry Initiative, under which 68 programs share more than $100 million in funding. The majority of the programs have juvenile components. They target high-risk offenders who are returning to the community after institutionalization and focus on helping them make a successful transition. Interagency cooperation and identification and use of existing resources are emphasized.[58]

SUMMARY

Two key issues in the control and treatment of juveniles today involve the handling of status offenders and serious, violent delinquents by the juvenile justice system. Some argue that both types of offenders should be removed from juvenile court jurisdiction. Others contend that the juvenile court is the proper setting for evaluating their behavior.

A juvenile status offender is one who has engaged in an act subject to juvenile court jurisdiction that would not be considered criminal if it were performed by an adult. Most states make legal differentiations in their juvenile codes between delinquent offenders and status offenders. Some states have "decriminalized" certain status offenses so that they are no longer law violations and youths involved in these behaviors are treated as "dependent children" and handled by child protective services. In all states, when unacceptable behavior in the status offense category persists, the cases can be referred to juvenile courts for formal handling.

The debate over the proper handling of status offenders within the juvenile justice system has led to strong support for two opposing viewpoints: complete removal of status offenders from juvenile court jurisdiction and retention of status offenders within the system, with exclusion of these youths from secure detention. This involves revising juvenile codes to specifically define and limit the range of offenses and setting specific minimum and maximum age limits for court intervention.

Those who favor removal of status offenders from juvenile court jurisdiction argue that although status offenders have not committed criminal acts, they are labeled delinquents as a result of juvenile court contact; that they are often treated like and forced to associate with hardened delinquents; that vague juvenile codes permit victimization of children through improper application of status-offender statutes; that status-offense statutes are applied to females in a discriminatory manner; and that in many cases, status offenders receive more severe dispositions than delinquents. They contend that such offenders could be handled adequately and more appropriately by other community agencies.

Those who argue for retention of juvenile court jurisdiction over status offenders maintain that status offenders are not necessarily less serious offenders than delinquents, and in some cases are more hardened and disturbed. They feel that the stigmatization attached to juvenile court involvement is not as damaging as lack of attention and treatment, if indeed it has any detrimental effects. They state that other agencies are inadequate to handle the number and types of offenders already serviced by the juvenile courts and that without the sanctioning powers of the juvenile court, service by these agencies would be largely ineffective.

A compromise position calls for the alteration of juvenile codes to eliminate certain types of activity as status offenses, the setting of maximum and minimum ages for application of status-offense statutes, the enactment of clearly defined laws, and the stipulation that status offenders not be detained in secure facilities or with delinquent offenders.

Habitual violent delinquents present a contrasting problem. Many people feel that the seriousness of their criminal activity should preclude them from juvenile court handling. Changes in statutes and procedures have been developed to provide more appropriate penalties for their misbehavior. These have included detention from the time of arrest until a hearing is held, mandatory incarceration for certain categories of violent and serious offenders, lowering the age of original jurisdiction of the adult courts, facilitating transfer of cases to adult courts, reducing the confidentiality of juvenile court proceedings and records, and using blended sentences that combine adult and juvenile sanctions.

When juveniles' cases are tried in adult courts, they are still unlikely to receive sentences that adults who committed similar crimes would receive. If they are required to serve terms in institutions, the probability that they will be rearrested and reinstitutionalized is high.

Because serious juvenile offenders pose a risk to the community, it is strongly recommended that their release from institutions be carefully monitored, accomplished in gradual stages, and include extended periods of supervision.

DISCUSSION QUESTIONS

1. What are some of the conditions that have inhibited the juvenile court from achieving its goal of individualized justice for each child?
2. Discuss the arguments given in support of complete removal of status offenders from juvenile court jurisdiction. How do those who favor retention of the juvenile court's jurisdiction reply to each of these arguments?
3. Discuss the legislation that has been enacted to help control habitual and violent juvenile offenders. In your opinion, should these offenders be completely removed from juvenile court jurisdiction and tried in adult courts without first being referred to the juvenile courts?
4. Several states have changed their juvenile codes to incorporate determinate types of dispositions for juveniles found to be delinquents. Discuss the underlying goals of the determinate disposition model.
5. What factors might explain the reduction in the number of youths arrested for committing violent crimes during the past five years? Is this reduction related to the changes that have occurred in the handling of youthful violent offenders? Explain.

NOTES

1. Ohio Revised Code §2151.022, in *Ohio Criminal Law and Motor Vehicle Handbook* (Longwood, FL: Gould Publications, 1994), 21–22.
2. Howard N. Snyder and Melissa Sickmund, *Juvenile Offenders and Victims: 1900 National Report* (Washington, DC: Office of Juvenile Justice and Delinquency Prevention, 1999), 166.
3. *Ibid.*

4. *Ibid.*

5. *Ibid.*

6. *Ibid.*

7. Francis A. Allen, *The Borderland of Criminal Justice* (Chicago: University of Chicago Press, 1964), 37.

8. Federal Bureau of Investigation, *Crime in the United States 2001* (Washington, DC: U.S. Government Printing Office, 2002), 233.

9. *Ibid.*, 243.

10. *Ibid.*, 240.

11. David Finkelhor, Gerald Hotaling, and Andrea Sedlak, *Missing, Abducted, Runaway, and Throwaway Children in America: First Report Numbers and Characteristics, National Incident Studies* (Washington, DC: U.S. Department of Justice, May 1990),

12. Sister Mary Rose McGeady, *God's Lost Children* (New York: Covenant House, 1991), 20.

13. Snyder and Sickmund, *Juvenile Offenders and Victims*, 167.

14. Ellen Gray, *Child Abuse: Prelude to Delinquency?* (Washington, DC: U.S. Department of Justice, 1986), 13.

15. Dorothy Heid Bracey, *Baby-Pros* (New York: John Jay Press, 1979), 48.

16. Ernie Allen, "Missing Children: A Fearful Epidemic, *USA Today* 123, 2590 (July 1994), 46.

17. FBI, *Crime in the United States 2001*, 242.

18. Snyder and Sickmund, *Juvenile Offenders and Victims*, 166.

19. *Ibid.*, 169.

20. Thomas M. Kelley, "Status Offenders Can Be Different: A Comparative Study of Delinquent Careers," *Crime and Delinquency* 29 (1983), 365–380.

21. Snyder and Sickmund, *Juvenile Offenders and Victims*, 207.

22. Milton Rector, *PINS Cases: An American Scandal* (Hackensack, NJ: National Council on Crime and Delinquency, 1974), 3.

23. Mary Clement, *The Juvenile Justice System: Law and Process* (Boston, MA: Butterworth-Heinemann, 1997), 78.

24. *Lamb v. Brown*, 456 F 2d 18 (1972).

25. Wesley Kraus and Marily D. McShane, "A Deinstitutionalization Retrospective: Relabeling the Status Offender," *Journal of Crime and Justice* 17, 1 (1994), 45–67.

26. *Ibid.*, 61.

27. Charles W. Thomas, "Are Status Offenders Really So Different?" *Crime and Delinquency* 22, 4 (October 1976), 438–355.

28. Stanton P. Fjeld, Lila Newsom, and Ruth M. Fjeld, "Delinquents and Status Offenders: The Similarities and Differences," *Juvenile and Family Court Journal* 32, 2 (May 1981), 3–10.

29. J. Foster, S. Dinitz, and W. Reckless, "Perceptions of Stigma Following Public Intervention for Delinquent Behavior," *Social Problems*, 20, 2 (Summer 1972), 203.

30. Thomas D. Gill, "The Status Offender," *Juvenile Justice* 27, 2 (August 1976), 10.

31. Lindsay A. Arthur, "Status Offenders Need Help, Too," *Juvenile Justice* 26, 1 (February 1975), 4.

32. Charles P. Smith et al., *Report on the National Juvenile Justice Assessment Centers* (Washington, DC: U.S. Department of Justice, 1980), 34.

33. National Advisory Committee on Criminal Justice Standards and Goals, *Juvenile Justice and Delinquency Prevention* (Washington, DC: U.S. Government Printing Office, 1977), 310.

34. Snyder and Sickmund, *Juvenile Offenders and Victims*, 207.

35. *Ibid.*, 207.

36. Anne L. Schneider, *Report of the National Juvenile Justice Assessment Centers: The Impact of Deinstitutionalization on Recidivism and Secure Confinement of Status Offenders* (Washington, DC: U.S. Department of Justice, 1985), vi.

37. National Advisory Committee, *Juvenile Justice and Delinquency Prevention*, 312.

38. *Ibid.*, 312.

39. *Ibid.*, 313.

40. Lee E. Tietelbaum and Aidan R. Gough, *Beyond Control* (Cambridge, MA: Ballinger, 1977), 201.
41. FBI, *Crime in the United States 2001*, 232
42. *Ibid.*, 244
43. *Ibid.*, 240.
44. Snyder and Sickmund, *Juvenile Offenders and Victims*, 108.
45. Vincent Schiraldi and Mark Soler, "The Will of the People? The Public's Opinion of the Violent and Repeat Juvenile Offender Act of 1997," *Crime and Delinquency* 44, 4 (October 1998), 590–601.
46. *Schall v. Martin*, 52 U.S.L.W. 4681, June 5, 1984.
47. *Ibid.*
48. Snyder and Sickmund, *Juvenile Offenders and Victims*, 106, 108.
49. *Ibid.*, 170–71.
50. National Council of Juvenile and Family Court Judges, "The Juvenile Court and Serious Offenders," *Juvenile and Family Court Journal*, Special Issue (Summer 1984), 13.
51. Donna Hamparian, Joseph M. Davis, Judith M. Jacobson, and Robert E. McGray, *The Young Criminal Years of the Violent Few* (Washington, DC: U.S. Department of Justice, 1985), 8.
52. Michael S. Serrill, "Washington's New Juvenile Code," *Corrections Magazine* 6, 1 (February 1980), 36–38.
53. Bureau of Justice Statistics, *Recidivism of Young Parolees*, BJS Special Report (Washington, DC: U.S. Department of Justice, May 1987), 71.
54. Bureau of Justice Statistics, *Examining Recidivism*. BJS Special Report (Washington, DC: U.S. Department of Justice, February, 1985), 11.
55. Jeffrey A. Fagan, *The Comparative Impacts of Juvenile and Criminal Court Sanctions on Adolescent Felony Offenders*. Final Report to the National Institute of Justice, Grant 87–IJ CX4044, Washington, DC: U.S. Department of Justice, 1991.
56. URSA Institute, "Characteristics of Successful Programs for the Serious Juvenile Offender," *Issues and Strategies/Special Report* (San Francisco: URSA Institute, 1981), 1–14.
57. National Council of Juvenile and Family Court Judges, "The Juvenile Court and Serious Offenders," 16–17.
58. U.S. Department of Justice, *OJJDP News at a Glance*, 1, 5 (Washington, DC: Office of Justice Programs, 2002, 4.

CHAPTER 12

THE POLICE ROLE
IN DELINQUENCY
PREVENTION
AND CONTROL

(Photo credit: Courtesy of the FBI)

THE NATURE OF POLICE WORK WITH JUVENILES
POLICE DISCRETION IN DEALING WITH JUVENILES
    Police Juvenile Diversion Programs
THE DECISION TO TAKE A JUVENILE INTO CUSTODY
    Interrogation Procedures
    Identification Procedures
    Fingerprinting and Photographing Juveniles
INVESTIGATING OFFENSES AGAINST CHILDREN
THE POLICE JUVENILE UNIT
YOUTH GANG UNITS
POLICE ROLE IN DELINQUENCY PREVENTION
    Community Policing
    Debate over the Appropriate Role of the Police in Delinquency Prevention

Police officers play an important role in all communities in the prevention and control of delinquency. Their presence at public gatherings of juveniles, such as sporting events, dances, or rock concerts, is designed to serve as a deterrent to destructive or violent behavior. They have broad discretion in the handling of youths observed or reported committing unlawful acts. They also serve as the major source of referrals to the juvenile courts and frequently discover and report behavior by adults that is contributing to the delinquency of minors.

Officers who have frequent contact with juveniles, whether they are regular patrol officers or members of a specialized juvenile unit, have opportunities to observe them in situations that are reported to parents or members of social service agencies only "after the fact." Whereas teachers, employers, and even parents interact with youths in rather structured situations in the schools, on the job, and at home, officers who observe young people with their peers in the community are aware of certain behaviors that are not displayed when these other adults are present. Parents frequently react to information about vandalism, violence, or other delinquent behavior with the response, "My son (or daughter) would never do such a thing!" But police are well aware that young people are capable of such behavior when under the influence of peer-group pressures.

The following case illustrates the way police officers may become involved in juvenile cases in the course of their patrol activities:

> Officers Mitchell and Lantano had just finished their dinner break and returned to the patrol car. As they waited to leave the restaurant's parking lot, a car sped by. Mitchell estimated that it was traveling at about 50 mph in a 35-mph zone. The officers gave chase and pulled over the auto. It was driven by a muscular white male who appeared to be 19 or 20. An attractive white woman was seated next to him. Both were neatly dressed. A clothing bag hanging in the rear of the car gave the officers the impression that they were a young couple traveling through town. Officer Mitchell told Lantano he would check them out. Lantano remained in the patrol car.
>
> Mitchell asked the driver to produce his license and the auto's registration. The driver, who seemed very nervous and stammered as he spoke, told the officer that it was his father's car. He said he had forgotten to get the registration from him and that he had left his license at home on the dresser. He told the officer that his name was Al Hollus, that he was 18, and that his father's name was Frank Hollus.

Mitchell had not told Al the reason he had stopped him, but the young man's demeanor aroused the officer's suspicions. He returned to the patrol car for a moment and asked Lantano to check out the registration on the auto from the license plate number. The information that came back did not correspond to the name Al had given as his father's. A radio call to the station and a telephone call from the dispatcher to the person the car was registered to produced the information that the car had been parked in front of the owner's home and had disappeared. Officer Lantano thereupon requested that the car be towed to the police station.

During the time Lantano was checking the car's registration, Mitchell remained with the couple, who became progressively more uneasy as they waited. Finally, Lantano approached the car and informed the driver that he was under arrest for auto theft and that both he and his passenger would have to come to the police station. He read Al his rights. Al mumbled some feeble protest and slipped into the back seat of the cruiser. His female companion, now very frightened, kept pleading with Al to tell her what was going on. Finally he began talking in a low voice. He informed the officers that he was really 16 years old and that he and his girlfriend were driving to a neighboring state to get married. Officer Lantano warned him that anything he said could be used against him, but he shrugged his shoulders and continued talking.

When they reached the police station, Mitchell called the number listed in the local directory for Frank Hollus. Mrs. Hollus answered. She said that her husband had left town about an hour earlier on a long-distance run for his trucking company. She confirmed that her son Al was indeed only 16 years old. She agreed to come to the station as soon as she could find someone to stay with her other children. At this point, the boy was turned over to Officer Frank O'Neil, a member of the force's juvenile division.[1]

It is obvious that police officers react to and deal with the various situations they encounter according to the seriousness of the offenses, the ages and attitudes of the offenders, and the possibilities for resolution open to them. Although most police departments have developed some type of specialized youth bureau or unit, the majority of initial contacts with young people involved in unacceptable behavior are still made by uniformed officers on patrol. Their handling of matters involving juveniles is a complex area of their overall responsibilities and an important facet of the police role.

THE NATURE OF POLICE WORK WITH JUVENILES

The major areas of police efforts in dealing with juveniles include discovery and investigation of delinquency, disposition of cases, protection of juveniles, and delinquency prevention.[2]

Many situations that generate police contacts with juveniles are resolved informally, and even when youths are taken into custody the police often make dispositions other than referral to juvenile courts. For example, 25 percent of the juveniles taken into custody in 1997 were handled within the department and released, usually to their parents, other adult relatives, or friends of the families. Another 1 percent were referred to other law enforcement or social service agencies. The remaining juveniles were referred to court intake. Ninety-one percent of these were referred to a juvenile court or to a probation department, and the other 9 percent were referred to criminal court for prosecution as adults.[3]

Another factor related to police decisions to arrest or release youths is the attitude toward juvenile misbehavior in the community, which may lead to the establishment of policies as to the types of juvenile misbehavior that should result in arrests. For example, communities that are vacation destinations for large numbers of adolescents may set policies that are very strict with regard to even minor instances of inappropriate behavior.[4]

Research on police encounters with juveniles in Chicago showed that such contacts have two basic sources. A citizen-initiated investigation occurs when a report is made to the police (usually by telephone) that unacceptable juvenile behavior is occurring. A police-initiated intervention takes place when an officer observes activity or a situation that is suspicious and investigates.[5] The researchers found that most police attention to juveniles occurs as a result of citizen complaints. They concluded that, in a sense, the citizens of a jurisdiction set the parameters of delinquent behavior by defining through their complaints the types of juvenile activity they regard as unacceptable. Of the 281 police-juvenile encounters studied, 72 percent were citizen-initiated. Only 5 percent involved felonies, and 60 percent had to do with juvenile rowdiness or mischievous behavior.[6]

A similar study of police-citizen encounters was conducted in a large midwestern city. Trained observers using portable electronic coding equipment rode with police for a full shift and recorded 2,000 police-citizen interactions, 200 of them involving juveniles. The vast majority of encounters could have ended in arrests, but only 16 percent actually did. All instances of felony offenses ended in attempted or actual arrests, while few of the minor delinquency or status offenses did. If a complainant was present when the police arrived, the suspect was more likely to be arrested than if a complainant was not present. Black juveniles were arrested at a higher rate than white juveniles when a complainant was present. Although a higher rate of arrests occurred for blacks, it was concluded that this was not due to differential handling because of their race, but rather was related to the combined influences of the severity of their offenses, the more frequent presence of a complainant in black juvenile-police encounters, and the black juveniles' demeanor. Juveniles who were antagonistic toward the officers were more likely to be arrested than those who were not, regardless of their race. This was true even if the offense was minor.[7]

Community policing has been introduced in many jurisdictions as a means of making officers more responsive to the needs of citizens in specific areas within larger jurisdictions. The question of whether police-juvenile encounters that involved community policing officers differed from encounters between juveniles and officers in traditional-style units was explored by Bazemore and Senjo through field observation of the first year that community policing was used in a highly urbanized city in South Florida. They concluded that officers in the neighborhoods where community policing was used were involved in activities designed to enhance prevention, create diversion possibilities, and increase youth advocacy and parental support. Although they did not cite arrest statistics, they noted that community policing may actually increase juvenile arrests because of the intense attention focused on the target areas. If this occurs, there are possible negative effects. It might be viewed as an order-maintenance tactic designed to remove troublesome youths from the neighborhood and lead juveniles to view the increased surveillance used in community policing as a form of harassment.[8]

POLICE DISCRETION IN DEALING WITH JUVENILES

The police have a number of alternatives open to them in dealing with reported or observed instances of juvenile misbehavior. The seriousness of the offense; the youngster's age, appearance, and attitude; the neighborhood in which the behavior occurs; and the child's home situation all are factors in the decision as to how the young person will be handled. In addition, the local laws, the type of police department in which the officer is employed (whether it exercises strong, detailed control over officers' activities or is discretion-oriented), the type of training the officer has received, and the officer's own personal prejudices and opinions affect the way an officer will operate at each discretionary opportunity.

An officer has a number of options in dealing with juvenile offenders. The officer may release the young person after questioning at the site of the misbehavior; admonish and then release the youth; divert the youth to a youth service agency; transport the youth to the police station for questioning and release; issue a citation for the youth to appear in juvenile court; or transport the youth to the juvenile detention center. If the police are unable to locate the parents of a juvenile, the chances of taking the child into custody increase. Formal handling is also more likely if the juvenile is known to the officers through earlier contacts or if he or she has a juvenile record.

Police discretion is sometimes limited by laws relating to the offense committed by the juvenile, as illustrated by a case that occurred in a state that has a law mandating arrest for anyone charged with domestic violence.

Sixteen-year-old Amber appeared to be a model teenager. She was doing well academically, was cooperative with teachers, and was a cheerleader who was well liked by her peers. She had no previous contacts with the juvenile court until she was arrested by police and placed in detention on a domestic violence charge. The incident related to this arrest was an argument with her mother over whether she could visit her girlfriend. When the girl insisted that she was going, the mother began hitting her with a bottle of dusting spray. She defended herself by pushing her mother away, walked out of the house, and went to her girlfriend's home.

When the girlfriend's mother overheard Amber describing the altercation with her mother, she decided to call the police. The police questioned both Amber and her mother and noted that her mother had a "slight scratch on her arm." In accordance with the law of the state, Amber was taken into custody on a domestic violence charge and was placed in the county's juvenile detention center. She remained there until an adjudication hearing was completed. She admitted having pushed her mother, but insisted that she did so to protect herself. Nevertheless, she was adjudicated delinquent and remanded back to the juvenile detention center for an indefinite period of time.

This case was abstracted from an internship paper completed by Heidi Ott, a justice studies student at Kent State University. The juvenile's name has been changed to protect her identity and the court and detention center have not been identified.

Eldefonso and Coffey noted that officers are likely to release a juvenile without further action rather than make an arrest if the offense is minor in nature, if the child has not demonstrated a pattern of habitual delinquency, if the family situation appears to be stable and a good relationship exists between the child and his or her parents, if the parents seem aware of the child's problems and able to cope with them, and if there is no apparent need for treatment or if the child is already receiving help from some agency in the community.[9]

The decision whether to use informal means to dispose of a case or to take formal action is more complex than it appears on the surface. Although such objective factors as the seriousness of the offense, previous record, and availability of alternative means of handling the problem enter into the decision, research has demonstrated that in many cases, the decision is grounded in less tangible factors. These include the attitude of the youth at the time of contact with the police; the officer's personal prejudices and biases; the race, sex, and social class of the youth; and the area in which the juvenile is apprehended.

Piliavin and Briar, who observed the activities of a metropolitan police department over a nine-month period, concluded that 90 percent of the youths with whom the police had contact were minor offenders and that the type of unacceptable behavior under investigation was not consequential in the police officers' decisions on the course of action to be taken. They found the youths' attitudes to be the most important factor in determining the dispositions chosen by the police. Those youths who were uncooperative, cocky, or argumentative in their encounters with the police were more likely to be arrested than those who appeared to be sorry for their actions and acted fearful and respectful. Fifty three percent of the cooperative youths were admonished and released, compared to only 5 percent of the uncooperative ones. Only 4 percent of the cooperative youths were arrested, compared to 67 percent of the uncooperative ones.[10] The researchers also observed that black youths and boys who matched the delinquent stereotype by looking "tough" (dressing in leather jackets, boots, and such apparel) were more frequently stopped and interrogated by officers than were others and were given more severe dispositions than other youths who had committed the same violations.[11]

Black and Reiss, through observations of police contacts with juveniles in Boston, Chicago, and Washington, DC, found that race and attitude had some influence on whether youths were arrested. The overall arrest rate for the police encounters with black youths they observed was 21 percent, compared to 8 percent for encounters with whites. They found that 22 percent of the youths who were antagonistic toward the police were arrested, compared to 16 percent of those who acted "civilly." They found, however, that the arrest rate for those who were *very* deferential toward the police was 22 percent, the same as the rate for those who were antagonistic. They interpreted this pattern as an indication that some juveniles adopt the ploy of great deference toward the police to try to avoid arrest but that the police see through this ruse.[12]

Several researchers have discovered that minority youths are overrepresented among those arrested and held in detention. Police decision making was found to contribute to this overrepresentation,[13] with minority youths held at the police station longer and placed in detention more often than nonminority youths.[14] This occurred for females as well as males. Kemph-Leonard et al. found that African-American juvenile females living in cities and urban areas were more likely than white juvenile females to be detained, while in rural settings white juvenile females were more likely to receive informal supervision than white males or African-American males and females with similar offense characteristics.[15] Bridges et al. found that the degree of urbanization, levels of violent crime, concentration of minorities in the county, and chronic juvenile offending all were important in the decision-making process related to minority youths,[16] but Dunn et al. found that, even when community characteristics were controlled, minority youths were more likely than white youths to be confined.[17]

Police Juvenile Diversion Programs

Many police departments operate diversion programs. The goal of these programs is to keep youths from being formally involved with juvenile courts and being labeled as "delinquents" and to deter them from further unacceptable behavior. This is accomplished by assigning them to programs that provide supervision and counseling to address the particular problem behavior in which the youths have been involved. Critics of these programs maintain that many youths who could have been counseled and released at the time of the incidents that brought them to the attention of the police are instead drawn into "treatment" that is not needed and may even be counterproductive.[18]

Kratcoski, Ammar, and Dahlgren studied the diversion programs of 24 police departments in five counties in Northeast Ohio. During a 15-month period, 2,258 juvenile offenders were referred to these programs. Ninety five percent of the referrals were made by police officers and the others came from school systems, parents, and the juvenile courts. Approximately 15 percent of these youths were advised, counseled, and released at the intake interviews. The remaining 85 percent were placed in police diversion programs.

The mean age of those referred was 15.4 years; 70 percent were males and 30 percent were females; 88 percent were Caucasian, 11 percent were African-Americans, and 1 percent were from other racial backgrounds. Forty nine percent were living with both parents, 29 percent lived with their mothers only, 7 percent lived with their fathers only, and the others lived in various combinations of relative situations. With regard to offenses, about 75 percent had committed misdemeanors (destruction of property, disorderly conduct, assault, or theft) and 20 percent were referred for status offenses (school truancy, running away, incorrigibility). One percent were referred for felony offenses and the remaining youths were defined as "at risk" or referred by parents or school officials.

The diversion program activities most frequently utilized were unofficial probation, community service, school-related disciplinary actions, referral to service agencies, and individual counseling. Ninety percent of the youths had satisfactory, above satisfactory, or very satisfactory performance ratings in the diversion programs. The remaining 10 percent were terminated because they had committed a new offense while in the program (4%), because they did not perform satisfactorily in the programs, or for other reasons.

During a follow-up period of six months to one year after completing the diversion programs, approximately 13 percent of the youths recidivated one or more times. Recidivism was defined as having a new referral to the juvenile court. The majority of these new offenses were misdemeanors. The apparent success of these programs, the average age and racial makeup of those referred, and the fact that they seemed to target youths who had manifested real problems rather than those only considered "at risk" indicated that these programs were addressing the stated goals of diversion.[19]

THE DECISION TO TAKE A JUVENILE INTO CUSTODY

Under the Uniform Juvenile Court Act, a child may be taken into custody:

1. Pursuant to an order of the court under this act;
2. Pursuant to an order of the court under the laws of arrest;
3. By a law enforcement officer (or duly authorized officer of the court) if there are reasonable grounds to believe that the child is suffering from illness or injury or is in immediate danger from his or her surroundings and that his or her removal is necessary; or
4. By a law enforcement officer (or duly authorized officer of the court) if there are reasonable grounds to believe that the child has run away from his or her parents, guardian, or other custodian.[20]

It is apparent that juveniles may be taken into police custody for reasons unrelated to unlawful behavior on their part. The various state codes allow an officer to enter a private home and remove a youth if there is evidence present to indicate that the child is in danger or in need of immediate medical assistance. Such an action is termed "emergency temporary custody."

When used in reference to juveniles, the term "custody" is preferable to "arrest," even if the action is taken as a result of alleged illegal behavior on the part of the youth. Use of the term "custody" would eliminate the confusion that results when some departments record as an arrest any police-juvenile encounter in which a youth is brought to the police station; others record an arrest only if an official charge is made; and still other departments consider an arrest to be any recorded contact between an officer and a juvenile, even if the juvenile is not brought to the police station. Such variations in recording are the reason for the inexact nature of nationwide statistics on the number of youths arrested.

Juvenile court statutes have detailed provisions for the handling of juveniles once they have been taken into custody. For example, the *Legislative Guide for Drafting Family and Juvenile Court Acts* provides that a person taking a child into custody, "with all reasonable speed and without first taking the child elsewhere," shall:

1. Release the child to parents, guardian, or other custodian upon their promise to bring the child before the court when requested by the court, unless detention or shelter care is warranted or required; or

2. Bring the child before the court to deliver him or her to a detention or shelter-care facility designated by the court or to a medical facility if the child is believed to suffer from a serious physical condition or illness that requires prompt treatment. The person shall promptly give written notice, together with a statement of the reason for taking the child into custody, to a parent, guardian, or other custodian and to the court.[21]

Interrogation Procedures

If a youth is taken into custody for allegedly having committed a delinquent act by violating a criminal law, there are constitutional limitations to the custodial interrogation to which the youth may be subjected. In *Miranda* v. *Arizona* (1966), the Supreme Court found that any person accused of a crime must be advised of the right to remain silent and the right to have legal representation.[22] As noted in Chapter 5, in the *Gault* decision (1967), the Supreme Court held that the constitutional privilege against self-incrimination is applicable in the case of juveniles just as it is with respect to adults.[23]

In the *Gault* decision, the Supreme Court specifically declined to address the issue of whether counsel is required in pre-adjudication stages of juvenile court proceedings. On the basis of the *Gault* decision, however, numerous lower courts have ruled that full *Miranda* warnings must be given to juveniles in custody during investigatory questionings. Several states have implemented legislation requiring that these *Miranda*-type warnings be given to juveniles.[24]

The circumstances surrounding the interrogation of a juvenile have also been considered in court cases. In *Haley* v. *Ohio* (1948), a 15-year-old defendant was held by police and continuously questioned for a long period of time without being allowed to see his parents or an attorney. The Supreme Court ruled that his subsequent confession was inadmissible because of the principle of "totality of circumstances"; that is, the absence of parents or lawyer, the age of the youth, the length of the questioning period, and the approach used by the officers.[25] In the later case of *Gallegos* v. *Colorado* (1962), the Court reached a similar decision.[26] As a result, great care must be taken by police in conducting interrogations or a youth's confession may be ruled inadmissible in court, even though he or she was informed of the right to remain silent, if it can be shown that the circumstances surrounding the interrogation were improper.

Identification Procedures

In *Wade* v. *U.S.*, the Supreme Court ruled that use of a line-up for the purpose of identifying a suspect is a critical stage of the criminal justice process, and therefore a suspect has a right to request that counsel be present to reduce the possibility that the line-up will be conducted in an unfair or discriminatory manner. *Wade* v. *U.S.* also set several standards as to how a line-up should be conducted, including the requirement that other members of the line-up be similar in physical characteristics to the suspect.[27] While *Wade* v. *U.S.* involved an adult, it is assumed that the same constitutional guarantees that resulted from the case are also applicable to juveniles.

Arranging a line-up when a juvenile is a suspect is difficult, since *Wade* requires that several other children who are similar in physical characteristics to the suspect must be found to serve as fill-ins. In most cases, children being held in detention are used as fill-ins, although it is doubtful that a youth can be legally compelled to act in such a capacity.

Because of the problems in arranging juvenile line-ups, the one-to-one identification process tends to be more common in juvenile cases. In this procedure, there is either a face-to-face meeting between the suspect and the witness, or the witness is allowed to observe the suspect without any contact between the two individuals. In *Stovall* v. *Denno*, the Supreme Court ruled that the principle of "fundamental fairness" was violated when a suspect was taken before the victim in a one-to-one situation while in handcuffs.[28] In *Simmons* v. *U.S.*, the Court ruled that this principle of "fundamental fairness" must also be maintained in photo identification.[29] For example, an investigator may show the witness several photographs of persons who are similar in physical characteristics rather than a single photograph of a suspect, or the investigator could ask the witness to identify the suspect in a group photograph. The one-to-one and photograph identification procedures are particularly important in identifying juvenile suspects because the line-up is used infrequently in these cases.

Fingerprinting and Photographing Juveniles

The juvenile codes of various states have specific provisions regarding the fingerprinting or photographing of juveniles, publication of their names in the press, the question of where and with whom they may be detained, and the types and locations of their police records.[30] Both the Uniform Juvenile Court Act and the Model Rules for Juvenile Courts of the National Council on Crime and Delinquency recommended that children not be photographed or fingerprinted unless such materials are necessary to prove the case, that the fingerprints of juveniles not be filed with those of adults or sent to central data banks, and that all fingerprint records of juveniles who are not found guilty be destroyed immediately. Many states require that for photographs to be taken, a court order must be obtained.[31]

The report of the Task Force on Juvenile Justice and Delinquency Prevention included specific guidelines for fingerprinting, photographing, and otherwise identifying juveniles. It recommended that fingerprinting take place only when fingerprints have been found on or are expected to be found on evidence; if they are taken, they should be immediately destroyed if the comparison is negative or if the youth is not referred to the juvenile court, even if the comparison is positive. Also, fingerprints and photographs that are retained should be destroyed if no petition is filed, if the case is dismissed after a petition is filed, if the youth is not adjudicated delinquent, or when a youth reaches age 21 without additional recorded delinquency after the age of 16.[32]

These stringent requirements are designed to minimize the possibility of labeling youths delinquent and submitting them to processes that will make them feel like criminals. The prohibitions against publication of the names of juvenile offenders are designed both to protect them and their families and to prevent the development of delinquent reputations that some offenders might feel required to live up to. Such idealistic motives are at times at odds with the harsh realities of the existence of hardened, violent juvenile offenders, particularly since some evidence has shown that treating such offenders severely reduces juvenile crime. One judge encouraged the press to publish the names and addresses of juvenile offenders, explaining, "Rather than simply emphasize the needs of the child, we also figure we have a paramount duty to protect society."[33] In one case, the U.S. Supreme Court struck down a decision of the Oklahoma Supreme Court barring three Oklahoma City newspapers from publishing the name of an 11-year-old boy charged in the shooting death of a railroad switchman.[34]

Even after an arrest has been made, in most states a juvenile has the opportunity to have the record expunged (destroyed or sealed from examination) after a specific period of time has passed with no other offenses. Other states automatically destroy juvenile records after a specific number of years, but in some states, a youth must petition the court to have a record destroyed or sealed. Police departments may keep juvenile arrest records separate from those of adults and refuse to release such information.

The degree of care and discretion with which juvenile arrests, arrest procedures, and arrest records are handled is dependent upon the philosophy of the police department in question. Those with a philosophy that juveniles should be given every opportunity to change their behavior will carry this over into their handling procedures, whereas departments less concerned with such matters will exercise less care.

INVESTIGATING OFFENSES AGAINST CHILDREN

There are numerous cases in which the police (either regular patrol officers or members of specialized units) become involved in situations in which a child is the victim of an offense rather than its perpetrator. For example, officers are frequently called upon to intervene in domestic situations that require a physically abused or sexually molested child to be removed from the home.

In most jurisdictions, the police have authority to act in the best interests of the child in emergency situations. An officer answering a domestic disturbance call in which children are involved must make a decision regarding the immediate danger to them or the need for medical attention. Transporting children to a hospital or shelter home may be necessary and agencies that will then assist the children, such as the juvenile court or Children's Services, must be notified of the emergency action taken.

Investigation of an offense against a juvenile may be undertaken by the officer initially involved in the complaint or by a special juvenile officer. This is a very delicate area, and skill is needed to collect needed facts without traumatizing the abused child further. If the person who has abused the child is criminally charged, it may be necessary for physicians, social workers, the prosecutor, or treatment specialists to question the child. To reduce the need for child victims to retell the story of their experiences many times, the U.S. Attorney General's Task Force and the National Legal Resources Center for Child Advocacy and Protection recommended limiting such interviews.[35] A report prepared for the National Institute of Justice suggests that the interview process can be consolidated by conducting a joint interview by two or more agencies, by assigning specialists within each agency so that there is only one interview per agency, by videotaping the child's first statement, by eliminating the need for the child to appear to the formal proceedings, and by coordinating juvenile and criminal court proceedings.[36]

Regardless of the procedures followed, it is obvious that police officers involved in the investigation of offenses against children must be skilled and highly sensitive to their needs.

THE POLICE JUVENILE UNIT

Today, virtually every police department has at least one officer whose primary function is to work with youth-related cases. In large departments, the juvenile bureau may be made up of dozens of officers and supporting personnel. They may operate out of the Special Investigations Unit or the Detective Bureau or be set up as an independent police bureau or unit. The prestige attached to juvenile-bureau assignments varies tremendously, depending on the department's goals and priorities. In some police departments, the officers in the juvenile bureau must have completed specialized education in dealing with juveniles and juvenile work is a sought-after assignment; in others, juvenile work has a low status and officers are demeaningly characterized as "social workers" or "kiddie cops."

A national survey of large police and sheriffs' departments revealed that special units were widely used, as shown in Table 12–1.

More than 90 percent of both types of agencies had written policy directives for handing juveniles.[37] If the procedures for dealing with youths are not specifically spelled out in department policies, such matters as providing assistance to juveniles,

Table 12–1.   Percentages of Police and Sheriff's Departments with Special Units Targeting Juvenile Concerns (1997)

	Type of Agency	
Special Units	**Local Police**	**Sheriff**
Drug education in schools	95%	79%
Juvenile crime	66	49
Gangs	55	50
Child abuse	48	53
Domestic violence	46	37
Missing children	33	28
Youth outreach	32	24

Source: Howard N. Snyder and Melissa Sickmund, *Juvenile Offenders and Victims: 1999 National Report* (Washington, DC: Office of Juvenile Justice and Delinquency Prevention, 1999), 139.

counseling, engaging in recreational and community activities, and the relationship between juvenile officers and patrol officers are handled according to the juvenile officers' own judgment.

The point at which officers from the juvenile bureau enter a case differs according to the administrative policies of the police department. Some departments require that all children involved in police-juvenile encounters be referred immediately to the juvenile bureau, while others allow regular patrol officers to handle initial contacts and use their discretion in dealing with juveniles, calling in the juvenile bureau officers only in serious or unusual matters. Another method allows line officers to handle contacts with juveniles in the community, with juvenile unit officers taking over when youths are brought to the police station. Sometimes the officers themselves are not sure of the department's policies because the juvenile unit operates as a seemingly independent entity.

The National Advisory Committee for Juvenile Justice and Delinquency Prevention suggested that law enforcement agencies with more than 50 sworn officers should establish a specialized unit to assist in handling matters involving juveniles and recommended that the person in charge of this unit should be of sufficient rank to assure that the unit has a status equal to that of other specialized units within the department. The Committee stated that the person in charge of the juvenile unit should be responsible for:

1. Assisting in the development and implementation of policies and regulations governing law enforcement practices and decisions relating to juveniles;
2. Serving as the liaison to other components of the juvenile justice system as well as agencies, groups, and organizations involved in delinquency prevention;
3. Taking charge of cases that go beyond initial and informal handling.[38]

The activities of juvenile officers vary according to the size of the city or community served and the size of the juvenile unit. The duties of such officers may include investigating crimes in which juveniles are suspects; processing adults charged with contributing to the delinquency of a minor, child neglect, or abuse; investigating school-related incidents reported to the police; investigating reports of missing or run-away children; supervising school and community social events involving juveniles; presenting delinquency control and prevention programs to community groups; and counseling parents and children.

In large cities, there may be areas of specialization even within the juvenile bureau or unit. For example, a team of officers specially trained in gang control may operate out of the bureau.

YOUTH GANG UNITS

Many large cities in the United States have established specialized units within their police departments to combat the problems posed by youth gangs. A survey of police departments in the 79 largest cities in the United States found that 72 percent of these departments had created specialized gang units.[39]

The extent of the gang problem is evident from the National Youth Gang Survey of law enforcement agencies. The 1996 survey reported that an estimated 31,000 gangs were operating in 4,800 U.S. cities. Seventy five percent of police agencies in large cities, 57 percent of those in suburbs, and 25 percent of agencies in rural areas reported that gangs were active in their areas.[40]

Gang activity is not equally intense throughout the cities. Some neighborhoods are problem-free, while others are constantly troubled by excessive noise, harassment, vandalism, theft, and violence resulting from gang activity. Reduction of these problems through minimization of the gangs' criminal conduct may be the focus of gang unit activity. In the past, the strategy police often used

> . . . was designed primarily to reduce intergang violence, to prevent the extortion of neighborhood citizens and merchants by the gangs, and to minimize the seriousness of the crimes committed by gang members. It was not designed to eliminate the gangs, although some efforts were made to turn them to legitimate and constructive activities. It depended for its success on such activities as establishing liaison with the gangs to communicate police expectations and aggressive police action against gang members, their clubhouses, and their activities when the gang stepped out of line.[41]

While these tactics may still be effective in dealing with youth gangs that are developed predominantly to provide security, protection, and status for their members, they are not likely to be effective in curtailing the activity of criminal gangs that are organized for profitmaking through drug and weapons sales. Police work with such gangs is likely to include:

1. The development of informants through criminal prosecutions, payments, and witness protection programs;
2. Heavy reliance on electronic surveillance and long-term undercover investigations; and
3. The use of special statutes that create criminal liabilities for conspiracy, extortion, or engaging in criminal enterprises.[42]

Curry and Decker noted that "gang [unit] responses must take into account variations in the structure and dynamics of gang crime problems that have been observed to exist across municipalities, communities, gender, and ethnicity."[43] Some regular patrol officers in a major Midwestern city with a police gang unit that had more than 60 officers in its administrative, enforcement, investigative, intelligence, and surveillance components revealed to researchers that they felt the regular street patrol officers were the heart of gang control efforts and that gang units were created more for show and to appease the public than to actually deal with gang problems.[44]

Suppression has been the dominant approach to gang problems. This has occurred because of increases in violent crime by young offenders, disillusionment with attempts at rehabilitation, and public demands that the police take some type of action that will produce visible results. Police gang unit efforts at total suppression of gangs have included the Los Angeles Police Department's Community Resources Against Street Hoodlums (CRASH) program, which targets both hard-core and peripheral gang members, and the Westminster, California, Tri-Agency Resource Gang Enforcement Team (TARGET), which focuses on gathering and sharing information that will lead to the arrest and prosecution of gang members.[45]

In Los Angeles County, California, the Sheriff's Department developed the Operation Safe Streets Program, a unit of 70 nonuniformed department personnel, to investigate gang activities and assist law enforcement agencies and the courts in their efforts to prosecute gang members for criminal acts. One of the unit's tools is GREAT (Gang Reporting, Evaluation, and Tracking), a computer system that helps investigators identify gang members and monitor their activities.[46]

Legislation has also been used to strengthen police powers. For example, the California Street Terrorism Informant Protection Act includes a provision that makes it a crime to participate in a "criminal" street gang for the purpose of promoting or assisting felonious criminal conduct.[47]

It is difficult to ascertain how effective gang units are in curtailing illegal activities and particularly the violence attributed to gangs. Typically, the units' effectiveness would be assessed in terms of arrests of known gang members, reduction of violent crimes attributed to gangs, and confiscation of weapons or drugs from persons identified as gang-associated. However, as Klein et al. pointed out, it is difficult to discover whether violence and other illegal behavior is really gang-related. For example, drive-by shootings, while often attributed to gangs by the police or the mass media, may be totally unrelated to gangs in some instances and it is virtually impossible to determine this if the perpetrators are not identified.[48] Some of the success stories about gang unit effectiveness have been viewed with skepticism, while others have been accepted as reliable.

We noted in Chapter 6 and Chapter 11 that some gangs, particularly those associated with organized crime, are migratory and have branches in many American cities. Exchange of information between the police gang units of major cities is now occurring, enabling police to identify and respond effectively to the threats posed by gang members who have migrated from other cities to establish new bases of operation. Thus, such groups as the Caribbean Gang Task Force—which includes representatives of local law enforcement agencies, as well as federal, state, and county representatives—function for the expressed purpose of gaining the evidence needed to arrest and prosecute offenders who are gang members. Agents from the Federal Bureau of Investigation; Bureau of Alcohol, Tobacco, and Firearms; the Internal Revenue Service; and prosecutors from the U.S. Attorney's Office, as well as city police officials, are involved. The Middle-Atlantic Great Lakes Organized Crime Law Enforcement Network (MAGLOCLEN) is another example of such cooperation.

Local police departments are very helpful to those involved in this interagency approach to dealing with gangs since their officers, through working in the cities' neighborhoods, have gained knowledge about the community and can find persons who may serve as informants.

The question of whether today's gangs are developing locally or are part of broader gang organizations is still being researched. The National Youth Gang Survey reported that, although some exceptionally well-organized gangs are believed to be involved in interstate drug trafficking and to be expanding their operations through member relocation, most law enforcement agencies still regard gang problems as "home grown" rather than imported from other cities.[49]

POLICE ROLE IN DELINQUENCY PREVENTION

Police-sponsored delinquency prevention activities can be traced back to the early years of the 20th century. The early programs tended to focus on recreational or sports activities. The best known example is the Police Athletic League (PAL), which originated in Philadelphia in 1942 as a boxing program. Gradually, officers were given specific assignments to coach or supervise various types of sports teams, and the PAL program was adopted in many American cities.[50] Officers also took part in other delinquency prevention measures through such activities as rigorous supervision of parks and recreation areas; establishing curfews; and forming cooperative relations with the schools, courts, and social agencies.[51]

There are also youth programs developed and directed by the police that focus on improving the quality of life for juveniles through opportunity provision. COPY Kids, implemented in 1992 by the Spokane, Washington, Police Department, enables children from the city's economically disadvantaged areas to earn money through work for the community. In the course of the eight-week program, the youngsters are involved in tasks to clean up and beautify the community, participate in recreational activities, hear talks by positive role models about various types of jobs, visit local businesses and public service organizations for tours and question-and-answer sessions, visit museums and other cultural sites, and have opportunities for informal interaction with the police officers who direct and supervise their activities. An evaluation of the program's success found that the participating youths had learned about employment opportunities and responsibilities. Forty-six percent of the parents of the participants indicated in interviews that they believed the program had produced positive changes in their children's attitudes. In addition, more than one third of the parents reported having a favorable image of the Spokane Police Department because of their children's involvement in the program.[52]

Police delinquency prevention programs can also target specific endangered youth populations. The reported presence of gangs in the schools, as documented by a national survey of students, rose from 15 percent in 1989 to 28 percent in 1995, with a reported violent victimization rate of 7.5 percent of students in the schools where gangs were present.[53] An in-school program designed to address this problem is GREAT, which originated in Phoenix in 1991. Local school administrators, in cooperation with local and federal law enforcement agencies, designed a school-based program for elementary grade children that would provide instruction and experiences to help them resist gang involvement.[54] Other GREAT programs following this model were quickly adopted throughout the United States. Typically, the local police department and the school system form a cooperative agreement in which police officers trained in the GREAT curriculum offer instruction and the schools provide personal development and cultural enrichment activities to show the students that there are alternatives to gang involvement. A worker who assisted with such a program described it in this way:

The GREAT Program lasted five hours each day for three weeks during the summer. The children (ages 9–12) were separated into four groups to hear speakers and take part in activities. They learned about crime and their rights, culture, conflict, drugs, responsibility, and setting goals. We also had fun days. All of the groups went on field trips twice each week, including movies and trips to the zoo and to amusement parks.[55]

Community Policing

Recently, there has been a trend toward the creation of programs designed to establish close cooperative relations between the police and residents of the community. Community policing involves close, person-to-person contacts between officers and community residents, accomplished by assignment of an officer to a specific section of the community for an extended period of time. It stresses high visibility of the officer and use of various patrol methods, including a return to foot patrol. The goals of community policing include crime prevention and control, involving citizens in problem solving, increasing the satisfaction of all citizens with police services, and improving the quality of life for all community residents.

The focus of this type of police work is service. The officers must know how to get in touch with social and governmental agencies in the community, so that appropriate referrals can be made, and must follow up on referrals to be sure that services have been requested and received.

In many police departments, community policing is still not viewed as "real police work." The media attention given to certain community policing activities,

Informal interaction with juveniles is an important facet of community policing. *(Photo credit: Jay Paris)*

focusing on midnight basketball and working with youngsters' other recreational programs, is seen by some as public relations rather than authentic police work. While such criticism is valid in certain instances, community policing, if properly implemented, can produce very positive crime prevention and control results, as illustrated by the following case:

> A veteran officer, with more than 10 years of mini-station experience, explained how he assisted the detectives from a homicide unit solve a murder.

> A restaurant in the neighborhood had been robbed and the owner was shot during the robbery. The detectives assigned to the case informed the mini-station officer that they were not coming up with any leads and asked if he would assist them. In the course of the officer's informal conversations with young people in the area, one boy eventually informed him that he knew the names of the hold-up assailants and that they had actually asked him to participate in the robbery. With this information available, the homicide detectives quickly cleared the case.[56]

A study that examined community policing in seven Ohio cities summarized the conditions needed for effective police work of this type.

> If community policing is to work, the officers must believe they have such a stake in the neighborhoods in which they work that if something negatively affects the residents it also negatively affects them. When the neighborhood hurts, the police hurt. This type of commitment to the job is not easily developed. If achieved, it is generally after years of continuous personal interaction with numerous individuals and groups in the community. Much of the interaction will be focused on working with the young people. They are the ones who are perceived as being the most subject to the negative influences in the community and also the ones most likely to be influenced by positive forces.[57]

Debate over the Appropriate Role of the Police in Delinquency Prevention

In the absence of any national operating guidelines or even state standards, the functions and goals of police work with juveniles have developed according to local needs. Some juvenile units have concentrated on the law enforcement facet of police work with juveniles and have largely restricted their roles to investigative work. Others have deemphasized the law enforcement facet and expanded the role to include various forms of social and recreational services. Indeed, some have made the organization and supervision of recreational activities a part of juvenile bureau duties. The degree to which this detracts from the other police work facets is a point of contention.

If officers devote a great deal of time to organizing recreational activities, speaking in the community to various public and civic groups on teenage crime and problems, counseling youth, and visiting schools, what time is left for such activities as crime prevention and law enforcement involving juveniles? Have police officers received any training in recreational organization that qualifies them to develop such programs, and if not, must such training be included in police academy programs? Does acquaintance with these officers as recreation directors blur their images as police officers in the community? Is there strong evidence that involvement in recreational activities by a limited number of youngsters is as effective a deterrent to delinquency as other activities in which these officers might engage?

The same types of questions can be asked about the kind of police involvement with juveniles that really amounts to social work and counseling. Are they adequately prepared for this work? Does it duplicate services already available from specialists within the community? When a police department focuses heavily on programs of counseling and "social work," does this cause suspicion that the officers have little confidence in the juvenile court of that jurisdiction and are attempting to take over some of its functions because they believe they can do a better job?

The most important consideration is that a police officer, whether assigned to regular patrol, a specialized juvenile bureau, or community policing, should be primarily engaged in police work. Involvement in other activities should be carried out in conjunction with persons who hold expertise in the specific area. For example, many police departments have established juvenile diversion bureaus that operate directly from the departments. Minor delinquent offenders or status offenders who come into contact with the police are handled by these bureaus rather than referred to the juvenile courts. While these bureaus are set up under the auspices of the police departments, those who provide counseling and assistance there are generally not sworn police officers, but social workers or counselors. When police are directly assigned to schools, it is predominantly to maintain security for students and teachers. Through community policing or drug prevention programs, some specialized officers have taken the role of educators in very limited subject areas, and, in an unofficial way, many officers assigned to schools do counsel or assist students or serve as role models, but their primary function is police work.

SUMMARY

Police work with juveniles involves the investigation of complaints initiated by citizens or of suspicious behavior observed by the officers themselves. Once a youth has been contacted by the police, officers must make immediate decisions as to whether to question and release the youth, release him or her after an admonition, take the young person to the police station for additional questioning, lodge a charge against the juvenile and release him or her in the custody of parents, or request secure detention. The majority of juvenile-police contacts do not lead to arrests or juvenile court referrals, but are disposed of in other ways.

When the officers do make a decision to take a juvenile into custody, they must have "probable cause" (sufficient evidence to substantiate the accusation) if the charged delinquency is a felony. A youth may be arrested for a misdemeanor or status offense when the behavior occurred in the officer's presence or when a complainant files a written petition. Specific safeguards of juveniles have been developed with regard to photographing, fingerprinting, publication of names, places of detention, and police records.

The decision as to the type of disposition made in each police–juvenile encounter is based on the seriousness of the offense; the offender's age, appearance, and attitude; the area in which the offense occurs; and facts the officer can discover about the child's home situation and previous juvenile record. In cases of minor delinquency, the youth's attitude has been found to be the most important factor determining the choice of disposition, with cooperative youths tending to be admonished and released far more often than uncooperative ones. Other researchers have found that sex, age, prior record, family status, and race, as well as the background and training of the officers themselves, are related to the types of police dispositions received.

Although officers on routine patrol are most likely to have initial contacts with juvenile offenders, most police departments also employ officers with special training to work with juveniles. These officers familiarize themselves with community centers of juvenile activity, are well-versed in juvenile court procedures, and develop communication and cooperation with the schools and with public and private social welfare agencies. They frequently operate out of a special police juvenile unit and they may become involved in investigation of all juvenile cases, all those in which youths are brought to the police station, or only those of a serious or unusual nature, depending upon the orientation of the particular police department. Juvenile officers' activities frequently include counseling parents and children and speaking engagements in the schools and community, in addition to investigative work.

Many large cities have established specialized youth gang units to gain intelligence on the activities of gangs and aid in the apprehension of gang members who have violated the law. Gang control units frequently share information with units from other cities and with special task forces developed to monitor and inhibit gang activities.

Through community policing, many officers play important roles in delinquency prevention by their presence in places or situations where juvenile misbehavior might occur or through providing special programs or positive experiences for young people.

DISCUSSION QUESTIONS

1. The question of whether police officers should be actively involved in counseling and recreation activities in the community has been widely debated. What are the strongest arguments for and against such police involvement?

2. Why have there been strong controls on the fingerprinting and photographing of juvenile offenders and prohibitions against publication of their names in some jurisdictions?

3. Discuss the circumstances surrounding a police-juvenile encounter that may lead an officer to release a juvenile rather than make an arrest and the circumstances that may lead an officer to make an arrest.

4. When it is appropriate for police officers to divert youths out of the juvenile justice system?

5. Discuss the concept of community policing. How does community policing relate to delinquency prevention and control?

NOTES

1. This story is based on a juvenile court referral, with the names and some of circumstances altered to protect identities. See Chapters 13 and 14 for more information about what happened to Al after his arrest.

2. C. J. Flammang, "Reflections on the Police Juvenile Enterprise," *Juvenile Justice* 24, 2 (May 1973), 22–27.

3. Howard N. Snyder and Melissa Sickmund, *Juvenile Offenders And Victims: 1999 National Report* (Washington, DC: Office of Juvenile Justice and Delinquency Prevention, 1999), 139.

4. *Ibid.*, 140.

5. Donald J. Black and Albert J. Reiss, Jr., "Police Control of Juveniles," in Richter H. Moore, Jr., Thomas C. Marks, Jr., and Robert V. Barrow, eds., *Readings in Criminal Justice* (Indianapolis, IN: Bobbs-Merrill, 1976), 417.

6. *Ibid.*, 418.

7. Richard J. Lundman, Richard E. Sykes, and John P. Clark, "Police Control of Juveniles: A Replication," in H. Ted Rubin, ed., *Juveniles in Justice: A Book of Readings* (Beverly Hills, CA: Sage, 1978), 158–168.

8. Gordon Bazemore and Scott Senjo, "Police Encounters with Juveniles Revisited: An Exploratory Study of Themes and Styles in Community Policing," *Policing: An International Journal of Police Strategy and Management*, 20 (1) 1997, 60–82.

9. Edward Eldefonso and Alan R. Coffey, *Process and Impact of the Juvenile Justice System* (Beverly Hills, CA: Glencoe, 1976), 52.

10. Irving Piliavin and Scott Briar, "Police Encounters with Juveniles," in William B. Sanders and Howard C. Daudistel, *The Criminal Justice Process* (New York: Praeger, 1976), 45.

11. *Ibid.*, 48.

12. Black and Reiss, "Police Control of Juveniles," 433.

13. Timothy Bynum, Madeline Wordes, and Charles Corley, *Disproportionate Representation in Juvenile Justice in Michigan*. Technical report prepared for the Michigan Committee on Juvenile Justice, 1993.

14. Eliot Hartstone and Dorinda Richetti, *An Assessment of Minority Overrepresentation in Connecticut's Juvenile Justice System*. Report prepared for the State of Connecticut, Office of Policy and Management, Policy Development and Planning Division (Hartford, CT: Spectrum Associates, 1995).

15. Kimberly Kempf-Leonard, Scott H. Decker, and Robert L. Bing, *An Analysis of Apparent Disparities in the Handling of Black Youth within Missouri's Juvenile Justice System*. (St. Louis, MO: University of Missouri–St. Louis, 1990).

16. George Bridges, Darlene Conley, Gina Beretta, and Rodney Engen, *Racial Disproportionality in the Juvenile Justice System*. Report to the commission on African-American Affairs and Management Services Division/Department of Social and Health Service (Olympia, WA: State of Washington, 1993).

17. Christopher Dunn, Stephen Cernkovich, Robert Perry, and Jerry Wicks, *Race and Juvenile Justice in Ohio: The Over-representation and Disproportionate Confinement of African American and Hispanic Youth* (Columbus, OH: Governor's Office of Criminal Justice, 1993).

18. Barry C. Fell, *Bad Kids*. New York: Oxford University Press, 1999.

19. Peter C. Kratcoski, Nawal Ammar, and Daniel Dahlgren, *Police Juvenile Diversion Programs* (Columbus, OH: Final Research Report, OCJS Grant No. 97DGG027272, Sept. 1, 2000).

20. National Conference of Commissioners on Uniform State Laws, *Uniform Juvenile Court Act* (Philadelphia: American Law Institute, 1968), Sec. 13.

21. *Legislative Guide for Drafting Family and Juvenile Court Acts*, Sec. 15 (1968), quoted in Paul Piersma et al., *Laws and Tactics in Juvenile Cases*, 3rd ed. (Philadelphia: American Law Institute, 1977), 66–67.

22. *Miranda v. Arizona*, 384 U.S. 436, 448 (1966).

23. *In re Gault*, 376 U.S. 1 (1967).

24. *National Advisory Committee for Juvenile Justice and Delinquency Prevention, Standards for the Administration of Juvenile Justice* (Washington, DC: U.S. Government Printing Office, 1980), 213.

25. *Haley v. Ohio*, 332 U.S. 596, 68 S. Ct. 302 (1948).

26. *Gallegos v. Colorado*, 370 U.S. 49, 82 S. Ct. 1209 (1962).

27. *Wade v. U.S.*, 388 U.S. 218 (1967).

28. *Stovall v. Denno*, 388 U.S. 293, 302 (1967).

29. *Simmons v. U.S.*, 390 U.S. 377 (1968).

30. Harold E. Resteiner, "Delinquent or Criminal. The Problems of Transfer of Jurisdiction," Position paper, Genessee County (Flint), Michigan, 1975.

31. Paul H. Hahn, *The Juvenile Offender and the Law* (Cincinnati, OH: W.H. Anderson, 1971), 178.

32. Task Force on Juvenile Justice and Delinquency Prevention, National Advisory Committee on Criminal Justice Standards and Goals, *Juvenile Justice and Delinquency Prevention* (Washington, DC: U.S. Government Printing Office, 1977), 221.

33. *Time*, July 11, 1977, 28.

34. *Juvenile Justice Digest*, March 18, 1977, 7.

35. Attorney General's Task Force on Family Violence, *Final Report* (Washington, DC: U.S. Government Printing Office, September 1984), 15; National Legal Resource Center for Child Advocacy and Protection, *Recommendations for Improving Legal Intervention in Intra-family Child Sexual Abuse Cases* (Washington, DC: American Bar Association, 1982), 10.

36. Debra Whitcomb, Elizabeth R. Shapiro, Lindsey D. Stellwagen, *When the Victim Is a Child* (Washington, DC: U.S. Department of Justice, 1985), 100.

37. Howard N. Snyder and Melissa Sickmund, *Juvenile Offenders and Victims: 1999 National Report* (Washington, DC: Office of Juvenile Justice and Delinquency Prevention, 1999), 139.

38. National Advisory Committee, *Standards for the Administration of Juvenile Justice*, Standard 2.25, 217.

39. G. David Curry and Scott H. Decker, *Confronting Gangs* (Los Angeles, CA: Roxbury Publishing Co., 1998), 151.

40. Howard N. Snyder and Melissa Sickmund, *Juvenile Offenders and Victims: 1999 National Report*, 77–78.

41. Mark K. Moore and Mark A.R. Koelman, *The Police and Drugs* (Washington, DC: U.S. Department of Justice, 1989), 7–8.

42. *Ibid.*, 8.

43. G. David Curry and Scott H. Decker, *Confronting Gangs* (Los Angeles, CA: Roxbury Publishing Co. 1998), 160.

44. Randall G. Shelden, Sharon K. Tracy, and William B. Brown, *Youth Gangs in American Society* (Belmont, CA: Wadsworth Publishing, 1997), 212.

45. Eric J. Fritsch, Tory J. Caet, and Robert W. Taylor, "Gang Suppression through Saturation Patrol, Aggressive Curfew, and Truancy Enforcement: A Quasi-Experimental Test of the Dallas Anti-Gang Initiative," *Crime and Delinquency*, 45 (1) 1999, 122–139.

46. *Street Gangs: The Law Enforcement Guide to Today's Urban Violence* (Boulder, CO: Paladin Press, 1995), 73.

47. *Ibid.*, 70.

48. Malcolm W. Klein, Margaret A. Gordon, and Cheryl L. Maxson, "The Impact of Police Investigations on Police-Related Rates of Gang and Nongang Homicides," *Criminology* 24, 3 (1986), 490.

49. Howard N. Snyder and Melissa Sickmund, *Juvenile Offenders and Victims: 1999 National Report*, 78.

50. Peter C. Kratcoski, interview with Mickey Grandinetti, May 1988.

51. Paul W. Tappan, *Juvenile Delinquency* (New York: McGraw-Hill, 1949), 8.

52. Quint C. Thurman, Andrew Giacomazzi, and Phil Bogen, "Research Note: Cops, Kids, and Community Policing—An Assessment of a Community Policing Demonstration Project," *Crime and Delinquency* 39, 4 (October 1993), 554–564.

53. Howard H. Snyder and Melissa Sickmund, *Juvenile Offenders 139 and Victims: 1999 National Report*, 139.

54. National Institute of Justice, *Solicitation for an Evaluation of GREAT: Gang Resistance Education and Training.* (Washington, DC: U.S. Department of Justice, 1994).

55. Carrie Lavery, Internship Paper, Jackson Township Police Department, 2002, 3–4.

56. Peter C. Kratcoski, *Evaluation of Cleveland Police Mini-Station Program*, Final Research Report for the Governor's Office of Criminal Justice Services, Columbus, OH, June 1994, 60–61.

57. Peter C. Kratcoski, *Evaluation of Community Policing in Ohio*, Final Report for the Governor's Office of Criminal Justice Services, Columbus, OH, 1995, 67–68.

CHAPTER 13

JUVENILE COURT
PROCESS AND ISSUES

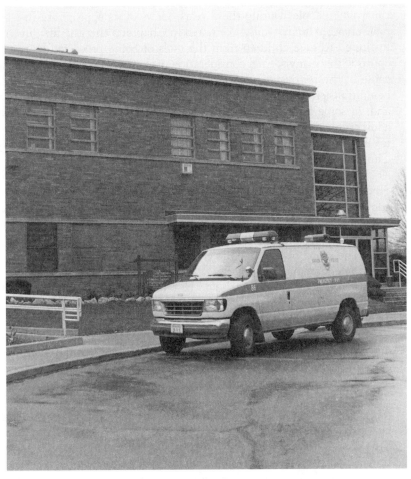

(Photo credit: Nick J. Cool, The Image Works)

SOURCES OF JUVENILE COURT REFERRALS
NATURE AND NUMBER OF CASES PROCESSED BY JUVENILE COURTS
THE JUVENILE COURT PROCESS
Total Diversion from Court involvement
Entering the Juvenile Court Process
The Petition
Temporary Detention
The Intake Process
Partial Diversion/Unofficial Probation
Juvenile Court Hearings
Adjudication Hearing
Dispositional Hearing
Sentencing of Juveniles Adjudicated in Criminal Court

Since 1899, the juvenile court has examined and regulated the behavior of American young people. During these years, views of its appropriate role and procedures have changed dramatically. We noted in Chapter 5 that the first juvenile courts were instituted to save children from the evils of being processed by the adult criminal courts without any special consideration of their age or lack of experience. Today, because of the seriousness and violence of their offenses, certain juveniles' cases are being transferred (waived) from juvenile court jurisdiction to adult criminal courts and, in some states, prosecutors have authority to file charges against juveniles in adult criminal court or juvenile court. Many states have also lowered the upper age of juvenile court jurisdiction, so that older adolescents are referred to adult courts. Thus, many delinquency cases are no longer heard by juvenile courts.

Another characteristic of the early juvenile court was its informal atmosphere. Since the 1960s, however, juvenile courts have taken on many of the trappings of adult courts, including use of prosecutors and defense attorneys. U.S. Supreme Court decisions are largely responsible for this trend, but the changes have also been influenced by demands that the rights of children be safeguarded.

The scope of the juvenile court's authority has also been questioned. Because status offenders have been charged with acts that would not be illegal for adults, many feel that these youths should be removed from juvenile court jurisdiction and handled by other agencies, or that such behavior does not require court involvement. This is a direct challenge to the purposes of the juvenile court, which was designed to intervene in and touch the lives of any youths believed to be disposed toward conduct defined as unacceptable or inappropriate for children. Finally, a huge increase in cases involving child abuse, neglect, and dependency has caused the juvenile court to devote a larger portion of its attention to such matters than it did in the past.

The State of Washington demonstrated its commitment to keeping status offenders out of the juvenile justice system by revising its juvenile code until, by the late 1970s, all status offenders had been removed from juvenile court jurisdiction. This process, termed *divestiture*, means that "the juvenile court cannot detain, petition, adjudicate, or place a youth on probation for the behaviors previously identified as status offenses."[1] Counseling and other services are made available for status offenders, through community health and human services agencies, but they are undertaken voluntarily. Although the divestiture actions successfully removed many young offenders from juvenile court involvement, an analysis of the effects of divestiture revealed that some youths who were basically status offenders were brought to the court and processed because some of their behavior could be construed as delinquent, whereas before divestiture, they would have been referred as status offenders. The result was that these youths tended to receive more severe sanctions from the court than they would have been given if supervision of status offenders had been retained by the juvenile courts.[2]

SOURCES OF JUVENILE COURT REFERRALS

A youth may become involved in the juvenile court process as a result of having allegedly committed a law violation which would be a criminal offense if committed by an adult or having allegedly committed a law violation which applies only to youths and would not be a criminal offense for an adult. These "status offenses," as we have seen, include running away, incorrigibility, truancy, and underage drinking. Children may also come under the juvenile court's protection because they are considered to be dependent, neglected, or abused.

Referrals to the juvenile court may come from parents, social agency personnel, school personnel, the police, or private individuals. If the alleged violation is a serious felony, it is very likely that the police will make the referral. Referrals for less serious delinquent offenses are also most likely to come from the police, while more than half of the referrals for status offenses come from other sources.[3]

In Chapter 12 we noted in our discussion of the police processing of youths who violate the law that the police have broad discretionary powers in deciding the course of action to be taken in incidents involving juveniles and that the majority of contacts of juveniles with police result in diversion out of the juvenile justice system. Even when a case is referred to the juvenile court by the police, parents, social agencies, school, or other persons, opportunities exist for the youth to be diverted away from official handling and avoid being labeled a "juvenile delinquent."

NATURE AND NUMBER OF CASES PROCESSED BY JUVENILE COURTS

The juvenile courts handled almost 1.8 million delinquency cases in 1996. Some youths are referred to the court several times during a given year and it is estimated that the 1.8 million cases represent approximately 1.2 million individual juvenile referrals.[4] As shown in Table 13–1, between 1987 and 1996 there was a 49 percent increase in delinquency cases handled by the juvenile courts. In 1996, 22 percent of the cases involved offenses against persons, 50 percent dealt with offenses against property, 10 percent were related to drug law violations, and 19 percent involved public order offenses. Eighty percent of the delinquency cases involved males and 60 percent of the referred youths were age 15 or older.[5]

Table 13–1. Delinquency Cases Handled by Juvenile Courts in 1996: Distribution of Cases by Type of Offense

Most Serious Offense	Number of Cases	Percentage of Total Cases	Percentage Change 1987–1996
Total delinquency	1,757,600	100	49
Person offenses	381,500	22	100
Criminal homicide	2,400	<1	74
Forcible rape	6,900	<1	60
Robbery	37,300	2	67
Aggravated assault	89,900	5	135
Simple assault	216,600	12	106
Other violent sex offenses	8,900	1	39
Other person offenses	19,400	1	51
Property offenses	874,400	50	23
Burglary	141,100	8	6
Larceny-theft	421,600	24	27
Motor vehicle theft	51,600	3	7
Arson	8,900	1	49
Vandalism	119,800	7	39
Trespassing	65,000	4	18
Stolen property offenses	32,900	2	6
Other property offenses	33,400	2	57
Drug law violations	176,300	10	144
Public order offenses	325,400	19	58
Obstruction of justice	125,800	7	70
Disorderly conduct	90,200	5	95
Weapons offenses	41,200	2	109
Liquor law violations	10,300	1	−44
Nonviolent sex offenses	10,600	1	−17
Other public order offenses	47,300	3	40
Violent Crime Index[a]	136,600	8	106
Property Crime Index[b]	623,300	35	20

Note: Juvenile court caseloads increased 49% between 1987 and 1996. The juvenile population increased only 11% in that time.

Although a substantial portion of the growth in court referrals is related to arrests, changes in juvenile court caseloads are also dependent on other forces. Between 1987 and 1996, the overall growth in juvenile court cases (49%) was greater than the growth in arrests of persons under age 18 (35%). During the same period, Violent Crime Index arrests rose 60%, arrests for Property Crime Index offenses rose 8%, and drug arrests rose 133%.

Detail may not add to totals because of rounding. Percentage change calculations are based on unrounded numbers.

[a]Includes criminal homicide, forcible rape, robbery, and aggravated assault.
[b]Includes burglary, larceny-theft, motor vehicle theft, and arson.
Source: Howard N. Snyder and Melissa Sickmund, *Juvenile Offenders and Victims: 1999 National Report* (Washington, DC: Office of Juvenile Justice and Delinquency Prevention, 1999), 144.

In addition to the approximately 1.8 million delinquency cases handled in 1996, the juvenile courts formally processed an estimated 162,000 status offenders. It is not possible to give accurate figures on the number of status offenders handled informally by the juvenile courts but, since the majority of the status offenders are handled informally, the number is much greater than that for formal status offender referrals.[6]

THE JUVENILE COURT PROCESS

Figure 13–1 outlines the juvenile court process and notes the possibilities for diversion.

Total Diversion from Court Involvement

Diversion may be either total or partial. *Total diversion* involves turning a youth in trouble away from a course of action that is leading toward justice system involvement. This can be done by police or school officials through a warning that any further trouble will lead to court involvement or through referral to some agency other than the juvenile court for assistance. Such referrals offer an alternative to juvenile court involvement. When a youth has been brought to the attention of the juvenile court, total diversion may still occur if the intake officer releases him or her with only a reprimand, if the prosecuting attorney decides not to prosecute the case, or if the complainant drops the charges. In total diversion, then, the juvenile justice system has no claim on the diverted youth and the youth has no obligation to submit to any type of treatment.

We noted in Chapter 12 that police officers can take a child into custody for improper behavior that is serious, for minor delinquency, for status offenses, or for the youth's own protection because the officer decides that such action is in the best interests of the child. With the exception of the serious offenses, most police have discretionary powers. In Cook County (Chicago), for example, police have the following options when they encounter status offenders.

> In the case of a child who is a runaway or beyond the control of parents, the Juvenile Court Act provides police officers and social agencies with various options to prevent the referral of such a child to the Juvenile Court. A police officer may take such a child into "limited custody" (but only for up to six hours) and, if the child agrees to return home, must transport and release the child to the parent and assist the family in contacting a social service agency if requested to do so. If the child refuses to return home or if the parents are unavailable, the officer must transport and release the child to a social agency offering crisis intervention services and shelter for the child.[7]

Entering the Juvenile Court Process

If the police decide not to divert a youth, referral is made to the juvenile court. Most juvenile codes require referral for youths charged with serious felony offenses and, in fact, also mandate that the police transport them to juvenile court. When police have diversionary discretion, the referral decision is based on such factors as the seriousness of the offense, the youth's physical condition (intoxicated, high on drugs), the child's or the parents' attitude, or the officers' belief that the child is in need of protective custody.

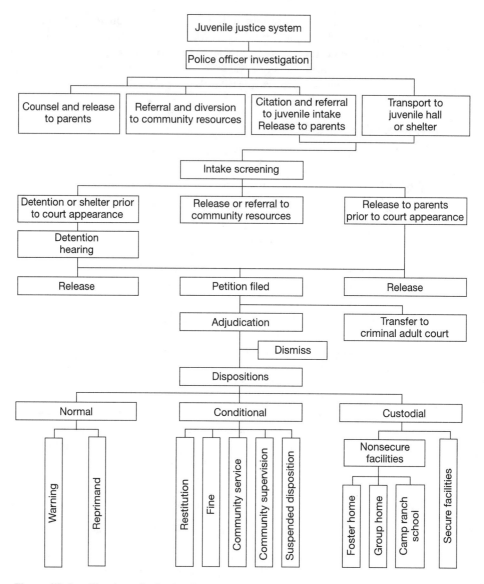

Figure 13–1.   The Juvenile Justice System *(Source: National Advisory Committee on Criminal Justice Standards and Goals,* Juvenile Justice and Delinquency Prevention *[Washington, DC: U.S. Government Printing Office, 1976], 9.)*

In less serious cases, the police often do not consider it necessary to transport youths who are going to be referred directly to the juvenile court. Instead, the officer releases the child to the custody of a parent or guardian and files a complaint with the juvenile court. The child and his or her parents or guardian are then issued a court summons (see Figure 13–2) to appear at a specific date and time to respond to the complaint.

Juv. 517-B-2　　　　　　　　　　　　　　　　　　　　BARRETT BROTHERS,　　, SPRINGFIELD, OHIO

SUMMONS

In the Court of Common Pleas, Juvenile Court Division _____ County, Ohio

IN THE MATTER OF

_____

_____　　　　　　　　Case No. _____

_____

_____

alleged[1] _____ Child __

To:** _____ Greetings:

WHEREAS, a complaint duly verified according to law, has been filed in this Court, which says that
_____ has knowledge of

(a) _____ certain child _____ , to-wit:
_____ age ___ years (D.O.B. _____)
who appear(s) to be (a) _____ child(ren)
in that

or

(2)

That the** _____
is directed to serve SUMMONS upon:

Juvenile: _____ age ___ years

Address: _____ ;

Parent(s): _____

Address: _____ ;

Guardian/Custodian/Guardian ad Litem: _____

Address: _____ ;

to personally appear (with said juvenile(s) before the said Court at _____ , Ohio, for the
_____ hearing on the _____ day of _____ , 19 ____ at _____ o'clock ___ M.
Said** _____ will make due return of this writ
on the _____ day of _____ , 19 ____ .
WITNESS my hand and the seal of said Court, this _____ day of _____ , 19 ____ .

_____
Judge

By _____

_____
Deputy-Clerk

(1) "Delinquent," "Neglected," "Dependent,"　　　"Unruly," "Abused"
(2) Wherefore, complainant prays for the permanent care and custody of child(ren).
** Officer to whom directed.　**NOTE: (Read other side of this form.)**

Figure 13–2.　Summons to Appear, Franklin County (Ohio) Juvenile Court, 1995.

It appearing to the Court that the juvenile(s) named herein (is) (are) in such conditions or surroundings that _____

welfare require __ that _____ custody be immediately assumed by the Court _____

_____ is ordered to take the said juvenile(s) into custody at once;

And, this cause is continued.

Ohio Revised Code Section 2151.353 (C). An adjudication of abuse, neglect, or dependency may result in an order of temporary custody. An order of temporary custody will cause the removal of the child from the legal custody of the parent until the court terminates the order of temporary custody or permanently divests them of their parental rights.

ANY PARTY (juvenile, parent, parent having custody of a juvenile, guardian or custodian, or person with whom a juvenile is) IS ENTITLED TO COUNSEL IN ALL PROCEEDINGS IN JUVENILE COURT; If a party is indigent, the Court will appoint counsel or designate a county public defender to provide legal representation upon request therefor;

WHEN A COMPLAINT CONTAINS A PRAYER OR REQUEST for the PERMANENT CUSTODY of a neglected or dependant child or children, the parents of said child or children are hereby notified that the granting of such permanent custody takes from the natural or adoptive parents all rights, duties and obligations of a parent, including the right to consent to an adoption of the child or children; To inherit from the child and the right of the child to inherit from the parent;

ANY PERSON SUMMONED TO APPEAR BEFORE THE COURT WHO FAILS TO DO SO, MAY BE PUNISHED AS IN OTHER CASES FOR CONTEMPT OF COURT, AND MAY LOSE VALUABLE RIGHTS AS A RESULT OF SAID FAILURE TO APPEAR.

WITNESS, my signature and seal of said court, this

_____ day of _____ , 19 _____

_____
Judge and Ex-Officio Clerk

By _____
Deputy-Clerk

RETURN

Received this writ on the _____ day of _____ , 19 _____ , at _____

o'clock ____ , and on the _____ day of _____ , 19 _____ , I served the same on

the within named by _____

_____

No. _____ Doc. _____ Page _____

Court of Common Pleas
Juvenile Division

_____ County, Ohio

In the Matter of:

_____ alleged _____ child

SUMMONS

Returnable _____ , 19 ___

Returned and Filed

∴ BARRETT BROTHERS, PUBLISHERS, SPRINGFIELD, OHIO

Figure 13–2.   Continued.

If persons other than the police (school officials, social service agencies, parents, neighbors, community members) are the source of the complaint, they will come to the juvenile court and sign a complaint and a summons will be issued for the child to appear.

The juvenile court process, once set in motion, has four distinct phases: (1) the filing of a petition, (2) referral to intake, (3) adjudication, and (4) disposition. The process may be halted at any of the three initial phases or proceed to the final step of disposition, depending upon decisions made by the person bringing the youth to the attention of the court, by intake officers, by the prosecuting attorney or the defense attorney, or by the juvenile court judge. At each stage of the juvenile court process, the juvenile's rights are safeguarded by various procedures that have been developed and refined in response to federal and state court decisions. The key decisions that have affected the juvenile justice process and juvenile court procedures are listed in Table 13–2 in chronological order. The procedures used in the juvenile court today gradually evolved as these decisions were implemented.

The Petition

A petition may be defined as "a formal written application to a court requesting judicial action on a certain matter."[8] In the juvenile court, a petition is not necessarily synonymous with a complaint. For example, parents or other persons may call the police or come to the juvenile court to "complain" about the actions of their children or others, but they may not seek formal action. The juvenile court petition is a legal document in which court action is sought as a result of the child's allegedly being delinquent; a status offender; or dependent, neglected, or abused. The petition is a formally stated complaint—a request for the court to become involved.

To give an example of police initiation of juvenile court proceedings, we will return to the case of Al Hollus, which was presented in Chapter 12. When we left Al's story, he had informed the officers that he was 16 years old. He had been taken to police headquarters and his mother had been summoned.

> Officer Frank O'Neil, a member of the police department's juvenile division, informed Al that a police complaint of delinquency by reason of auto theft had been filed against him by Officers Mitchell and Lantano and that his mother had been called. Questioning of Al's female companion in the auto, Rosemary Davis, convinced Mitchell and Lantano that she did not know the car was stolen. They also discovered that she was 23 years of age and had known Al for only a short time. She was not charged and she left the station.
>
> When Al's mother arrived, she was completely distraught and kept repeating that she could not believe Al would do such a thing to her and his father. She asked him over and over why he would take someone else's car and when she elicited the information that he had planned to run away and get married, she launched into a long, tearful tirade about that "no-good" girl who had gotten him into trouble. Officer O'Neil made no comment, except to inform both of them that Al's case had been referred to the juvenile court and that he would release Al in the custody of his mother until he was summoned to appear in juvenile court to answer the charges.

Table 13–2. Key Court Decisions Affecting the Legal Rights of Juveniles

Case	Year	Issue	Outcome
Ex parte Crouse	1838	Commitment of a juvenile to a House of Refuge without a jury trial	A State Appeals Court (Pennsylvania) ruled that no trial was necessary because the court was acting as a benevolent parent to protect the child from harm.
Haley v. Ohio	1948	Conditions under which a juvenile may be questioned	The Supreme Court ruled that a confession by a juvenile is inadmissible as evidence because of the circumstances surrounding the youth's questioning, including the absence of parents or counsel, the length of the questioning period, and the approach used by the officers.
Kent v. U.S.	1966	The due process rights of a juvenile whose case is considered for transferral to a criminal court for trial	The Supreme Court set the criteria to be used in the transfer decision.
In re Winburn	1966	An insanity defense in the juvenile court	A State Appeals Court (Wisconsin) ruled that an insanity defense did apply in the juvenile court.
Miranda v. Arizona	1966	Advising an arrested person of his or her rights	The Supreme Court ruled that a person must be advised at the time of arrest of the right to counsel and the right to remain silent, and be told that anything he or she says may be held against him or her.
In re Gault	1967	Due process rights of juveniles when commitment to an institution is the possible outcome of a juvenile court hearing	The Supreme Court noted the specific rights to which such juveniles are entitled, including a written notice of the charges in time to prepare a defense, the right to counsel, the privilege against self-incrimination, and the right to confront and cross-examine witnesses.
Stovall v. Denno	1967	Face-to-face identification of suspects	The Supreme Court ruled that the principle of "fundamental fairness" was violated because the suspect was taken before the victim in a one-to-one situation while in handcuffs.
Wade v. U.S.	1967	Line-up identification	The Supreme Court set standards for line-ups, including the requirement that other members of the line-up must be similar in physical characteristics to the suspect.

Table 13–2. Key Court Decisions Affecting the Legal Rights of Juveniles (*continued*)

Case	Year	Issue	Outcome
Simmons v. *U.S.*	1968	Photo identification of suspects	The Supreme Court ruled that the principle of "fundamental fairness" must be maintained by showing the witness photos of persons who are similar in physical characteristics rather than a single photograph, or by asking the witness to identify the suspect in a group photograph.
In re H.C.	1969	The insanity defense in the juvenile court	A State Appeals Court (New Jersey) ruled that this defense is not available to juveniles.
In re Winship	1970	Standard of proof required in the juvenile court	The Supreme Court ruled that when a juvenile is charged with an act that would make him or her liable to confinement, the charge must be proven beyond a reasonable doubt.
McKeiver v. *Pennsylvania*	1971	The right of a juvenile to a jury trial	The Supreme Court ruled that juveniles do not have a constitutional right to a jury trial.
In re Patricia A.	1972	Different upper age limits for institutionalization of male and female juveniles	A State Appeals Court (New York) held that a state law allowing such limits was unconstitutional because there were no factual differences between males and females that could justify such treatment.
Morales v. *Turman*	1974	The right to treatment	A U.S. Court of Appeals ruled that involuntarily confined juveniles have a statutory and constitutional right to treatment.
Breed v. *Jones*	1975	Double jeopardy	The Supreme Court held that a hearing for waiver of a juvenile's case to an adult criminal court must be held prior to adjudication in the juvenile court.
Smith v. *Daily Mail Publishing* Co.	1979	First Amendment issue regarding freedom of the press to publish information on juvenile court cases	The U.S. Supreme Court ruled that the interests of a free press supercede the need to protect the identity of juvenile offenders. Therefore the press may publish information, including the juvenile's name, if the information was obtained independently of the court.
Schall v. *Martin*	1984	Preventive detention of juveniles	The Supreme Court upheld a New York Family Court Act that allows detention before hearings of juveniles who present a serious risk of committing another offense.

continued

Table 13–2.   Key Court Decisions Affecting the Legal Rights of Juveniles (*continued*)

Case	Year	Issue	Outcome
New Jersey v. *T.L.O.*	1985	Search of students' persons and property by school officials	A New Jersey State Appeals Court ruled that school officials have a right to search students and their property if there is probable cause for believing that a law violation has occurred.
Thompson v. *Oklahoma*	1988	Execution of a person under age 16 at the time of his or her offense	The U.S. Supreme Court ruled that the 8th and 14th Amendments prohibit such an execution, noting that the imposition of the death penalty in such instances does not contribute to the goals of capital punishment—retribution and deterrence.
Stanford v. *Kentucky*	1989	Death penalty for juveniles ages 16 or 17	The U.S. Supreme Court joined this case with *Wilkins* v. *Missouri*, and ruled that it is not cruel and unusual punishment to impose capital punishment on a 16- or 17-year-old.
Verona School District 47 v. *ACTON*	1995	Does mandatory drug testing (urine analysis) for school athletes violate 4th Amendment prohibitions on unauthorized search and seizure	Mandatory drug testing does not violate 4th Amendment rights if the search is conducted according to accepted standards and serves a legitimate government interest (the special needs of the school district).

If the police elect to arrest a juvenile rather than use some type of discretionary handling, the youth must be advised at the time of arrest of the right to counsel (either private or court-appointed), informed of the right to remain silent, and told that anything he or she says may be held against him or her. This information, known as the "*Miranda* warnings," because it was guaranteed to arrested persons by the *Miranda* v. *Arizona* Supreme Court decision (1966),[9] is read to the youth again by the intake officer who first makes contact with the youth at the juvenile court. The officer who takes a child into custody is also required to notify the child's parents of this action and prepare a complaint that gives the name, age, and address of the child and the parents or guardians and specifies the law or ordinance that the youth is alleged to have violated. It may also include information on the attitude of the youth at the time of arrest and list accomplices, property recovered, or damage observed.

When a youth is arrested, the first decision to be made is whether he or she may be released into the custody of his or her parents or some other responsible person and return at a later date to answer the charges or whether the youth will be detained until a court hearing takes place.

Temporary Detention

The question of whether to detain or release a juvenile to the custody of a parent or guardian, pending court action on the case, is generally the responsibility of juvenile court personnel. However, when law enforcement officers bring a juvenile to the court and request that he or she be detained, the court personnel will generally honor such requests.

Detention can be defined as "the placement of a youth in a restrictive facility between referral to court intake and case disposition."[10] Although a detention center (a secure holding facility) is normally used for those youths who are awaiting formal action, at times youths may be placed in detention centers after there has been formal action on their cases, but before permanent placement can be made. By law, dependent, abused, or neglected children who are in need of temporary emergency care or protection are not held in detention centers. Instead, they are placed in shelter care centers or foster homes. Most juvenile codes also prohibit holding status offenders in detention centers with delinquent offenders, but some are detained in these centers.

Most of the juveniles who are referred to the juvenile courts are not detained. In the majority of cases, juveniles brought to the juvenile detention center will be

A counselor reprimands a youth at a county detention center. *(Photo credit: Akron Beacon Journal)*

released to the custody of their parents. A youth will be detained if the juvenile court personnel believe that he or she presents a serious threat to the community or if the youth is not likely to appear for a future court hearing on the charges. In 1996, juveniles charged with delinquency were detained in 18 percent of all the delinquency cases processed by the juvenile courts.[11]

The juvenile court judge has the final authority to decide whether detention is appropriate for a particular juvenile, but this power is usually delegated to a court intake official. A police officer's request for detention may be denied, but if it is approved, a formal hearing normally takes place within 24 hours (72 hours if the offense occurs on a weekend) to determine if detention should be continued.

The National Advisory Committee for Juvenile Justice and Delinquency Prevention recommended with regard to the detention of juveniles that juveniles subject to the jurisdiction of the family court over delinquency should not be detained in a secure facility unless:

1. They are fugitives from another jurisdiction.
2. They request protection in writing in circumstances that present an immediate threat of serious physical injury.
3. They are charged with murder in the first or second degree.
4. They are charged with a serious property crime or a crime of violence other than first- or second-degree murder that, if committed by an adult would be a felony, and
   (a) They are already detained or on conditioned release in connection with another delinquency proceeding;
   (b) They have a demonstrable recent record of willful failures to appear at family court proceedings;
   (c) They have a demonstrable recent record of violent conduct resulting in physical injury to others; or
   (d) They have a demonstrable recent record of adjudications for serious property offenses.
5. There is no less restrictive alternative that will reduce the risk of flight or of serious harm to property or to the physical safety of the juvenile or others.[12]

Although many juvenile courts have detention facilities, in numerous jurisdictions a section of the county jail is used for detention of juveniles.

Another option is the use of home detention (house arrest). In addition to supervision by parents, this process involves behavior restrictions and monitoring by a court official who makes visits or telephones periodically, or through use of an electronic device that records and reports the youth's movements. An example of such a program is the Cuyahoga County (Cleveland) Home Detention Project, which is administered through the staff of the detention center. Youths may be placed in this program while they are awaiting hearings or after they have been found delinquent or unruly. The home detention caseworkers are expected to assure the child's appearance at court hearings, supervise the child's behavior so that new offenses do not occur, and design constructive activities for the youth to pursue while detained at home.[13] An example of the type of agreement a youth and parents might complete if a child is assigned to home detention (house arrest) is given in Figure 13–3.

As shown in Table 13–2, in *Schall v. Martin* the U.S. Supreme Court upheld a New York State act that allowed detention of juveniles prior to their hearings if they presented a serious risk of committing another offense. Although juveniles do not have a right to bail (pretrial release with appearance at hearings secured by a specific amount of money that will be forfeited if the youth does not appear), some state juvenile codes have provisions for bail for juveniles. A judge may also require that parents or guardians sign a signature bond (a promise to pay a specific amount of money if the youth does not appear for hearings).

The Intake Process

Let us return now to the story of Al Hollus.

> On the following Monday, Al received a summons to appear in juvenile court. When he and his parents reported to the intake officer, Ms. Bronson, she informed him that he had a right to remain silent and that he could have an attorney present during their conversation. Al and his parents indicated that they understood these rights but did not plan to use counsel.
>
> During the subsequent interview, which involved a private meeting with Al, a talk with his parents, and finally a discussion with the entire family, it became apparent that Al was deeply emotionally involved with Rosemary, who was seven years his senior, and that he was willing to do anything to be with her. Even his arrest had not reduced his determination to continue seeing her. His parents stated that Al had always been a good boy until he met Rosemary, who worked at a drive-in restaurant, and that from the time he became interested in her, he stopped caring about school, stayed out until all hours, and was unwilling to tell his parents where he was going or what he was doing when he was away from home. Asked whether he was aware how serious an offense it was to steal a car, Al said he had only planned to borrow it until they were married and then leave it parked somewhere. He also commented that he would not have had to steal a car if his father had allowed him to use the family car, but his father had forbidden him to do so and had taken his keys as a punishment for staying out late.
>
> In the intake interview with Al's parents, Ms. Bronson discovered that Al's mother resented the fact that his father, who was a long-distance truck driver, was away from home so much, leaving her to care for their six children. She revealed that he was a strict disciplinarian who set penalties for misbehavior that she was required to enforce when he was not at home. Al commented that his mother was always on his back and that his father didn't care if Al was happy or not, as long as he kept out of his hair.
>
> On the basis of the seriousness of Al's offense, his apparent lack of remorse, and the unwillingness of his parents to guarantee that Al would submit to informal supervision, the intake officer made the decision to have the case handled officially. A hearing date was set.

The intake department is unique to juvenile courts; it has no parallel in adult criminal court proceedings. Cases come to the intake officers from four possible sources. Youths may be brought from the detention center, where they have been held for a short period of time awaiting an intake hearing; they may be brought

County of Hamilton

DAVID E. GROSSMANN, Judge   COURT OF COMMON PLEAS   SYLVIA SIEVE HENDON, Judge
JUVENILE COURT
800 BROADWAY
CINCINNATI, OHIO 45202-1332

HOUSE ARREST

I _____, having been on this date _____:

__ Referred to the Unofficial Court Officer for supervision.

__ Place(d) on ___ days House Arrest.

Agree immediately to the following conditions:

1.   You are not permitted to leave your home or yard unless accompanied by a parent or guardian.

2.   If you are attending school or have employment, you must go directly home and return immediately.

3.   You are not to have friends in your house without parental permission, except as follows:_____.

4.   You are not allowed to phone your friends nor to receive calls from them, except as follows:_____.

5.   You will report to an Unofficial Court Officer if notified.

6.   Other specific conditions:

_____

_____

_____
Juvenile

_____   _____
Unofficial Court Officer   Parent or Guardian

Figure 13–3.   House Arrest Form, Hamilton County (Ohio) Juvenile Court. *(Source: Thomas R. Lipps, Volunteer Referee Program Manual [Cincinnati, OH: Hamilton County Juvenile Court, 1994], 17.)*

directly to the intake department by police officers; they may be referred directly to the court by parents (most common in cases of incorrigibility); or youths may be responding to citations that have been issued to them earlier by police officers. (A citation, similar in appearance to a traffic ticket, lists the juvenile's name and address, the specific offense, and the date and time of scheduled appearance at intake. A parent or other responsible adult must accept and sign the citation.)

The function of intake is to screen all referrals and determine which cases should be handled judicially (officially) and which can be given nonjudicial (unofficial) treatment. The intake officer, who is a probation officer of the court assigned to performed this task, has wide discretionary powers in handling referrals. Some cases may be dismissed because of the pettiness of the charges or because conflicting or questionable information has been presented. Other youths are "admonished and released," receiving nothing more than a stern lecture about the unacceptability of their conduct, perhaps with a warning that next time they will be dealt with more severely. Once these referrals leave the intake officer's presence, they are freed from the control of the juvenile justice system, unless another offense brings them to its attention.

If it is decided to handle a case judicially (officially), the four phases of petition filing, intake interview, adjudicatory hearing, and disposition take place. In nonjudicial (unofficial) handling, parents and youths voluntarily agree to take certain action, often in the form of referral to programs of family or individual counseling conducted by community agencies. It is estimated that more than half of the juvenile cases referred to juvenile courts each year are handled nonjudicially.[14]

The court intake officer, in trying to determine whether the case should go to a formal process or be screened out and handled informally, must consider a number of factors. Certainly the seriousness of the offense will be of prime concern, but other matters that bear on the decision include whether the juvenile or family needs assistance or services but is not likely to seek them voluntarily, how much of an impact the case has on the community, whether the facts of the case are disputed, whether a "cooling-off period" appears to be necessary, and the degrees of cooperation likely to be received from the juvenile and the parents.

Generally, juveniles who are charged with status offenses (e.g., running away, truancy, or curfew violations) or minor delinquent offenses (e.g., shoplifting, trespassing, disorderly conduct, or minor assaults) are considered candidates for nonjudicial processing.

Partial Diversion/Unofficial Probation

After a young person does become the object of juvenile court involvement, the court may seek to prevent the child from being officially handled or labeled as a delinquent. Such activity, termed *partial diversion*, amounts to an agreement between the intake officer of the juvenile court, the youth, and the parents that if a certain course of action is followed, the youth may escape formal court processing. It is most often effected through referral to court-sponsored and court-supervised diversion programs, referral of the entire family to family-crisis or counseling centers, remanding of the youth to medical or psychological testing, or some other such activity. In partial diversion, the youth is *obliged* to seek the treatment indicated or be given an official court hearing.

Partial diversion occurs in cases where some type of informal supervision is considered necessary; but even here, the youth can avoid official processing and a juvenile court record. A partial diversion program in Kingston, Ontario, involves community representatives in the decision-making process when a youth is a candidate for unofficial processing. The young person enters this program after a petition has been filed against him or her, but before a juvenile court hearing takes place. A youth charged with a minor offense who has not previously been adjudicated delinquent is eligible for this program if he or she admits moral responsibility for the alleged offense and agrees to abide by a voluntary agreement formulated by a committee of three community representatives appointed by the court. Since the majority of the cases handled by the program are property offenses, the courses of action recommended by the committee generally involve restitution or community service. If an agreement is reached which is acceptable to the juvenile, his or her family, the police, the victim, and the committee, the committee recommends that the charges be withdrawn by the prosecutor, who normally complies. If the youth decides not to accept the committee's recommendation, the case is scheduled for a court hearing. This type of agreement is termed a "consent-decree agreement." An example of a consent decree agreement is given in Figure 13–4.

Another type of diversion at intake is referral to programs especially designed for certain types of offenders, such as drug or alcohol offenders or those with school-related problems. The price a youth pays for avoiding official processing may be participation in an alcohol- or drug-rehabilitation program, attendance at a particular type of school or work with an in-school counselor, or enrollment in a school program that combines a number of hours in the classroom with on-the-job experience. Successful completion of the diversion program usually means avoidance of a juvenile court record for the offense that brought the youth to the attention of the court.

In some cases, the entire family is referred to a family counseling center, and preparation of a petition against the youth is suspended until attempts are made to work out the problems. When physical or mental health problems are suspected as the cause of unlawful behavior, referral for diagnostic testing may be made before a decision on filing a petition is reached.

Diversion programs for status offenders and minor delinquents have not escaped criticism. The legality and propriety of treating a juvenile who has not had a formal judicial hearing have been questioned. In addition, concerns have been raised regarding the "net widening" that may result from placing children in diversion programs for treatment when their misbehavior is not serious enough to warrant such intervention. At times, administrators have been criticized for choosing cases for diversion programs where a successful outcome is almost certain, thus assuring that evaluations of the programs will show that they should be continued. The potential harmful effects of being involved in a treatment program that stemmed from a court referral may be overlooked in these evaluations.[15] Klein's research revealed that referrals to social service agencies can lead to the development of a negative self-image.[16]

County of Hamilton

DAVID E. GROSSMANN, Judge

COURT OF COMMON PLEAS
JUVENILE COURT
800 BROADWAY
CINCINNATI, OHIO 45202-1332

SYLVIA SIEVE HENDON, Judge

UNOFFICIAL JUVENILE COURT

Your child has been cited to appear in court this evening to answer to a referral made by the Police Department or by a private complainant. There has not been an official complaint signed against your child.

The unofficial docket has been instituted by the Hamilton County Juvenile Court to divert first offenders referred on misdemeanor crimes from the official court system. When the juvenile leaves court tonight, even if he/she admits to the charge, he/she will still have no juvenile record, however, a minor service contact card will be kept on file and destroyed after one year if there are no further contacts.

You do not have to have this hearing. If you wish your case to be heard on an official basis, you may ask that your case be referred to the Juvenile Court, 800 Broadway, Cincinnati, Ohio, for official action.

Your child has the right to a lawyer and will be granted a continuance for you to get a lawyer if requested. If a lawyer is not desired, the charge will be read, and the juvenile will be asked to enter a plea of admit or deny. If the plea is deny then it may be necessary to refer the matter for official trial.

If a plea of admit is entered, the facts will be discussed and any or all of the following dispositions may be made.

a) Admonishment

b) Work Details (serving 5 hrs.- 20 hrs. in unpaid manual labor for community under adult supervision)

c) House arrest

d) Probation - supervised by probation officer

e) parental driver's license suspension

f) Personal apology to victim

g) Referral to community resources for counseling or family therapy

h) Suggested arrangement of restitution

i) Written essay

j) Other

If you have any questions, please do not hesitate to ask at the beginning of the hearing. If you object to the disposition given, you may request that the matter may be referred for an official hearing in the Juvenile Court at 800 Broadway.

I hope your experience with this court is one which will benefit your child, the family as a whole, and ultimately the community.

Sincerely,

Figure 13–4. Consent Decree Agreement, Hamilton County (Ohio) Juvenile Court *(Source: Thomas R. Lipps, Volunteer Referee Program Manual [Cincinnati, OH: Hamilton County Juvenile Court, 1994], 15–16.)*

CONSENT FORM

<u>**RETURN THIS SHEET UPON ENTERING THE COURTROOM**</u>

I acknowledge receipt of the attached explanation of rights and procedure.

1.   I desire that my case be heard unofficially YES__NO__

        I desire that my case be referred for an official hearing. YES__NO__

2.   I wish to obtain a lawyer. YES__NO__

        I wish to proceed without an attorney. YES__NO__

_____

PARENT/GUARDIAN

_____

JUVENILE

_____

DATE

Figure 13–4. Continued

Net widening can be avoided when programs are designed to target specific types of juvenile offenders. For example, a Florida program, Project Diversion, was replaced by a punishment-based diversion program titled Juvenile Alternative Services Project. Instead of status or minor delinquent offenders, those referred to the program were youths who had committed more serious offenses, which would have resulted in official handling if they had not been deferred in this way. It was concluded that the program changes eliminated the courts' need to "select 'treatable' cases" for diversion programs and reduced the likelihood of net widening.[17]

Juvenile Court Hearings

The Initial Hearing. As we have seen, at his initial appearance before Juvenile Court Judge Martinson, Al Hollus readily admitted the truth of the accusations contained in the petition and the judge returned him to the custody of his parents pending the submission of a social investigation (predisposition) report at a dispositional hearing scheduled for a date three weeks later.

If a case is not dismissed at the intake level and diversion is not employed, the matter is handled judicially (formally). A formal case involves the filing of a petition, in which it is requested that the court hold an adjudicatory hearing. In 1996, 56 percent of the approximately 1.8 million cases were handled formally by the juvenile courts. This is an increase in the proportion of delinquency cases that were formally processed when compared with earlier years.[18]

If the case is handled judicially (formally), a hearing is scheduled—analogous to the pretrial or preliminary hearing held in adult criminal court—at which the charges contained in the petition are read. The youth is again advised of his or her constitutional rights, including the right to have an attorney present and, depending on the specific provisions of the state's juvenile code and the seriousness of the charges, the youth could be given an opportunity to make a plea at this time. In some states, the youth's possible responses to the charges can be "guilty" or "not guilty," while others use "true" or "not true" or "admit" or "deny." In states where juvenile traffic offenses are heard in the juvenile court rather than in a specialized traffic court, the plea of "no contest" is also available.

Although the majority of juveniles charged with offenses in juvenile courts eventually admit to the charges and enter pleas of "true" or "guilty," this normally does not occur at this phase of the process, but at later hearings. Analysis of the provisions of federal and state juvenile codes pertaining to the judge's obligations at the time a plea is entered reveal that some codes do not address the matter, but the majority of the codes spell out specific procedures that must be followed. These focus on the need for the judge to explain the charges to the defendant, to gain some assurance that the plea is voluntary, and, if the plea is the result of a plea bargain, to have this fact mentioned. It may also be required that a youth talk with parents or counsel before submitting a plea or that the youth be informed of the possible dispositions that may result from a guilty plea.

If a young person admits the truth of the allegations and the offenses are minor in nature, the adjudication and dispositional phases of the juvenile court process may be completed at this initial hearing. This can occur if state statutes permit a disposition to be made in minor-offense cases without completion of a social investigation (report by a court probation officer on the child's background, school performance, and past offenses). Combination of the adjudication and dispositional phases is likely if enough information is contained in the intake officer's report or in already existing juvenile court records for the judge to make a disposition decision.

If a plea of "guilty," "true," or "admit" is made, but the offense is rather serious in nature; if a social (predisposition) investigation is required by state statute; or if a social investigation is ordered by the judge, a youth may be returned to detention or released in the custody of his or her parents until a dispositional hearing takes place.

Juvenile Transfer to Criminal Courts. Every state has some provision in its statutes for having juveniles' cases heard in the criminal justice system. However, the states use various methods to accomplish this. The most frequently used mechanism is "judicial waiver." Here, the juvenile court judges have considerable discretion in waiving or transferring cases to the criminal courts. A second method is termed "statutory exclusion." For specified offenses committed by juveniles, the criminal court has the original jurisdiction in the case and juvenile offenders are automatically excluded from consideration by the juvenile court. Normally, those who commit serious offenses, older juveniles, and those with prior offenses fall into the "statutory exclusion" category. A third option is exercised in states with "concurrent jurisdiction" provisions. Here both the juvenile court and the criminal court have jurisdiction over juveniles. The statutes give the prosecutor the discretion to file a case in either the criminal court or the juvenile court. While most states rely primarily on judicial waivers, some use a combination of the three systems.[19] Figure 13–5 identifies the age and offense provisions for transfer of juveniles to the criminal courts. It is estimated that less than one percent of all delinquency cases initially referred to the juvenile court will be transferred to an adult criminal court.[20]

The Waiver Hearing.   In cases involving serious offenses, or those of youths who have shown a pattern of repeated delinquency and are over 16 years of age, the prosecuting attorney may request a waiver hearing if he wishes to transfer the proceed-

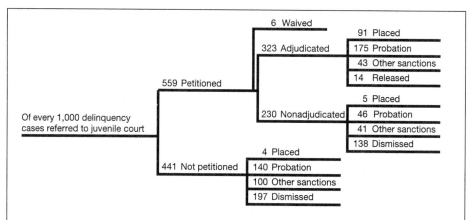

- In many formally handled delinquency cases that did not result in juvenile court adjudication, the youth agreed to informal services or sanctions, including out-of-home placement, informal probation, and other dispositions such as restitution.
- In a small number of cases (14 of 1,000), the juvenile was adjudicated but the court closed the case with a stayed or suspended sentence, warned and released the youth, or perhaps required the youth to write an essay. In such cases, the juvenile is not under any continuing court supervision.
- Although juvenile courts handled more than 4 in 10 delinquency cases without the filing of a formal petition, more than half of these cases received some form of court sanction, including probation or other dispositions such as restitution, community service, or referral to another agency.

Note: Cases are categorized by their most severe or restrictive sanction. Detail may not add to totals because of rounding.

Figure 13–5.   Processing and Dispositions of Every 1,000 Delinquency Cases Processed by Juvenile Courts in 1996. *(Source: Howard N. Snyder and Melissa Sickmund,* Juvenile Offenders and Victims: 1999 National Report *(Washington, DC: Office of Juvenile Justice and Delinquency Prevention, 1999),* 162. Adapted by the authors from A. Stahl, M. Sickmund, T. Finnegan, H. Snyder, R. Poole, & N. Tierney, *Juvenile Court Statistics, 1996)*

ings to the adult criminal court for trial. We have noted that in the *Kent* v. *U.S.* decision (1966), the Supreme Court set forth specific conditions for a valid waiver of jurisdiction by a juvenile court. The court ruled that a youth has a constitutional right to have counsel present at a waiver hearing and that the hearing must measure up to the essentials of due process and fair treatment.[21] In addition to the criteria contained in the *Kent* decision, most state statutes require that the presiding judge at the waiver hearing consider two other factors—the likely threat to public safety or dangerousness of the youth and whether the youth is likely to be amenable to treatment under the juvenile system. Critics of these provisions cite the difficulty inherent in predicting a youth's future behavior or responses to treatment and believe that inclusion of these factors provides too much discretion to the judge. Feld noted:

> . . .judicial waiver statutes that are couched in terms of amenability to treatment or dangerousness are simply broad, standardless grants of sentencing discretion characteristics of the individualized, offender-oriented dispositional statutes of the juvenile court.[22]

This opinion was borne out by a study of more than 200 juveniles remanded to adult court, which concluded that evidence did not support the contention that these offenders were more dangerous or intractable than other youths whose cases were retained in juvenile court.[23]

Even when a very serious offense has been committed, factors such as the age or mental competence of the offender may stand in the way of judicial transfer, as evidenced by the following case.

> A pregnant teenager who is accused of suffocating her young son is mentally retarded but not to the extent she should be spared prosecution, a Texas judge has ruled.
>
> . . . Now pregnant with her fourth child, she is accused of suffocating her 21-month-old son last summer.
>
> In ruling that she is mentally retarded, District Judge Andy Mireles also ordered the girl have further psychiatric and psychological testing.
>
> Tests have shown the girl functions academically at about the first-grade level with the social skills of a 10-year-old, according to testimony.
>
> . . . Prosecutors are unsure about just how to proceed with the case. . . . To try Debbie as an adult, prosecutors would have to prove that she is "sophisticated and mature" enough to be considered adult in the eyes of the law.[24]

In a waiver hearing, the question of the mental competence of the youth must be addressed. Before a waiver can be ordered, the youth must undergo psychological testing. If the competence of the youth cannot be established, it is likely that the waiver request will be abandoned. If the alleged delinquent appears to be mentally ill, the court may hold a hearing to determine insanity. If the court finds the defendant to be mentally ill, the original petition alleging delinquency may be dropped. The youth could then be admitted to a mental health institution for treatment.

Even though a case may qualify for waiver to an adult court because of the youth's age or the seriousness of the offense, it may not be transferred. The probability of waiver increases with the age of the offender for both violent and serious property offenses.[25] In addition, the juvenile court history of the offender is an important consideration. A study of waived cases found that youths with five or more juvenile court referrals and those whose first referral to the court was prior to age 14, as well as those with previous juvenile court adjudications for delinquent or status offenses, placements on probation, or placements in some type of juvenile facility outside their homes, are much more likely to have their cases waived.[26]

A study of South Carolina juvenile court waiver cases from 1985 through 1994 revealed that 595 cases involved requests for waivers and 80 percent of these requests were approved. A profile of juveniles for whom the waiver requests were made showed that 95 percent were male, 80 percent were blacks, and 80 percent were age 16 or older. Juveniles with extensive court histories and those who had previous cases formally handed by the juvenile court were significantly more likely to have their cases waived than those without such histories. Those who had committed serious offenses against persons or property were significantly more likely to have their cases waived than youths who had committed less serious offenses, but juveniles with two or more prior adjudications who committed less serious offenses were more likely to have their cases waived than those with similar offenses who had fewer prior adjudications.[27]

A study completed in a large city in a southwestern state identified the level of involvement of a youth in the alleged offense, the seriousness of the offense, and the youth's potential for aggressiveness as the most influential factors in the transfer of cases from juvenile courts to adult courts. Other factors bearing on the decisions were sex, previous offenses, IQ, and the specific court in which the case was heard, with some judges found to be more inclined to waive cases to adult courts. How actively the youth participated in the offense was the most important consideration.[28]

During the waiver hearing, the prosecuting attorney argues for the transfer and the defense attorney argues for retention of the case in the juvenile justice system. If a waiver is granted, the waiver order must be accompanied by a statement that shows the juvenile court has made an investigation of the matter and the reasons for the waiver must be listed.

The waiver hearing must take place early in the juvenile court process, before an adjudication has taken place. In *Breed* v. *Jones* (1975), a juvenile court waiver hearing was held *after* a youth had been adjudicated delinquent after it was determined that he was not amenable to treatment. The Supreme Court ruled that this action placed the youth in double jeopardy (subjected him to retrial for the same offense) and was unconstitutional. The court declared that a waiver hearing must be held *prior* to adjudication.[29]

Once a juvenile's case is transferred to the adult criminal court, the youth is entitled to some rights that were not available in the juvenile court, including the right to bail and to a jury trial. If found guilty, the juvenile may also be subjected to the penalties that apply to adult offenders, although some states provide certain exceptions, such as disallowing the death penalty for juveniles or not allowing them to be housed with incarcerated adult offenders until they reach a specified age.

The Prehearing Conference.   When a plea of "not guilty" or "not true" is made, and the case is to be heard by the juvenile court, an adjudicatory hearing is scheduled on the official court docket. If a youth makes a "not guilty" or "not true" plea, the option of a prehearing conference is available in many jurisdictions. Such a conference is generally held in the judge's chambers or in a conference room and is not an official court session. Court personnel who may participate include the judge, the prosecuting attorney, court workers assigned to the case, psychological personnel, and the juvenile's defense counsel if one has been retained or appointed. Generally, the youth charged with the offense is excluded from the conference.

At the prehearing conference, the judge will request a report from a court worker and the various attorneys involved in the case. The conference centers on legal issues, that is, the amount and types of evidence that the prosecutor has available and the type of disposition that can reasonably be expected if the youth changes the plea to "guilty" or "true." In many ways, the conference is similar to the plea-bargaining process in the adult criminal court. The majority of youths whose cases are given prehearing conferences will change their pleas to "guilty" or "true" at the adjudicatory hearing.

The complexity of the juvenile justice process today, even in its initial phases, highlights the fact that the roles of the judge, the prosecutor, and the defense counsel have developed and expanded with the evolution of juvenile court law.

Role of the Prosecutor. Until the 1960s, the charges against a juvenile were usually stated by the person filing the petition or by a court probation officer or were simply read aloud by the judge. This informal presentation conformed to the idea that what the child had done was not as important as what was to be done for the child. But the *Gault* decision (1967) made apparent the need for representation of the complainant's side of the case by the prosecuting attorney. We noted in Chapter 5 that Gault had received a disposition of commitment to a juvenile institution at an informal court hearing at which he was not represented by counsel and for which the woman making accusations against him did not appear. The Supreme Court, in commenting on the case, declared that in all instances where commitment to an institution is a possible disposition, the child and the parents must be advised of the right to counsel, either their own or court-appointed. It also ruled that a juvenile has a right to have witnesses cross-examined.[30]

The *Gault* decision's ruling with regard to the juvenile's rights in juvenile court proceedings made apparent the need for representation of the complainant by a prosecuting attorney. Juvenile court proceedings have thus moved away from informality toward an adversary (prosecutor versus defense attorney) style. In many states, statutes have been enacted that require the presence of a prosecutor at hearings for serious types of cases; in other states, court officials may request that a prosecutor be assigned.

A juvenile court prosecutor has broad powers. He or she can decline to prosecute a case, make plea bargains (only one state, Mississippi, prohibits plea bargaining in the juvenile court[31]), release a youth from detention, or recommend to the judge a particular type of disposition.

In the juvenile court process, the prosecutor may first enter the picture when a petition is written, checking to see that the officer or the private citizen filing it does so properly, or giving legal advice that another course of action might be more effective. The next step involves the decision whether to prosecute or drop any case in which a youth has responded "not guilty" or "not true" to a charge of delinquency. The prosecutor or a representative presents the state's case at the adjudicatory hearing and may recommend appropriate dispositions to the judge if a youth is adjudicated delinquent. Other matters of concern to a prosecutor include cases of dependency or neglect or of adults' contribution to the delinquency of minors. Prosecutors also serve as advocates for those who have allegedly been victimized by juveniles. They may assist them in making victim impact statements and help prepare them for court appearances.

Role of the Defense Attorney.   The defense attorney may be active in a juvenile's behalf at intake and try to help the youth avoid a formal court hearing. This may be done by convincing the person making the complaint to drop the charges or by assuring court officials that the youth will be referred to another agency or a private source for treatment. If a petition if filed, the defense attorney examines it and advises the client to enter a plea of "guilty" or "not guilty" or "true" or "not true," or may enter a plea on his or her behalf. The attorney may present facts in favor of release in the custody of the parents rather than detention until the adjudicatory hearing. Before the adjudicatory hearing, the defense attorney may persuade the prosecutor to drop the charges or may agree to have the client plead guilty to a reduced charge. This may occur at a prehearing conference, as described earlier in this chapter, or during an informal discussion between the prosecutor and the defense attorney.

As a result of the *Gault* decision (1967), a juvenile has a right to an attorney at every stage of the juvenile court process and an attorney must be provided for an indigent youth, if one is requested. In some courts, such counsel is made available at intake, but in most juvenile courts the attorney's services begin at the initial hearing.[32]

One effect of the *Gault* decision was an increased formalization and use of attorneys in the juvenile court. Nevertheless, a study of the cases of adjudicated delinquents completed more than 20 years after the Gault decision revealed that in some states less than half of these youths received the assistance of counsel.[33] A six-state study revealed that 85 to 95 percent of youths who lived in large, urbanized states (New York, California, Pennsylvania) received counsel's assistance, while 38 to 53 percent or those who lived in more rural, less populated states (Minnesota, North Dakota, Nebraska) had counsel to represent them. In all of the jurisdictions, the vast majority of the delinquency cases were handled by public defenders rather than by private counsel.[34]

It should be noted here that the Task Force Report on Juvenile Justice and Delinquency Prevention included a recommendation that plea bargaining in all forms be eliminated from the delinquency adjudication process because of the pressures it places on the juvenile to submit to a bargain that may result in a disposition not in his or her best interests, because hardened juvenile offenders can use bargaining to receive less severe dispositions than they actually deserve, and because juveniles who need to receive treatment that would be required if the case proceeded through the adjudication process may not receive it if plea bargaining results in a dismissal or a too-mild disposition.[35]

At the adjudicatory hearing, the defense counsel represents the client's side of the case. He or she may introduce witnesses. If a client is adjudicated delinquent, the defense attorney may present information at the dispositional hearing that will aid the court in deciding upon an appropriate disposition.

Besharov noted that the best way for a defense attorney to win a case for a client in juvenile court is to avoid or escape a formal hearing.[36] If this is not possible, the defense attorney must proceed cautiously, taking into account the current practices in a particular juvenile court and seeking to present an effective defense without antagonizing the judge. There is some evidence that youths represented by defense counsel may be treated more punitively than those who are not. For example, Stapleton and Teitelbaum, in a comparison of youths referred to the juvenile court of a large city who were matched for type of offense, number of earlier offenses, and family background, discovered that those represented by counsel were more likely than those not represented to be adjudicated delinquent and, if adjudicated delinquent, were more likely to be given dispositions of institutionalization.[37]

A study by Feld produced similar findings. Those youths who were charged with committing serious offenses, were held in detention prior to adjudication, and who had prior referrals to the court were found to be more likely to be represented by counsel than youths who did not fit this description. However, when these factors were controlled and the youths who were represented by counsel were compared to those who were not, it was found that "represented youths received more severe dispositions in every category" in the three large urban states included in the study and received more severe dispositions in the larger majority of categories in the three less populated, more rural states studied.[38] The reasons for the more severe dispositions could not be definitely ascertained, but Feld offered plausible explanations. These included the possibility that defense attorneys may have antagonized the judges just by being present or that judges may tend to assume the "parent substitute" role and be more lenient with unrepresented youths than with those who have counsel present. Another hypothetical scenario raised was that the judges had studied the cases before the hearings and, in anticipation of guilty findings and subsequent institutionalization, had arranged for counsel for the youths so that questions about the proceedings would not be raised in the future.[39]

Role of the Juvenile Court Judge.   When juvenile courts were created, the judge was assigned the role of single-handedly deciding the course of action that would turn a child away from unacceptable behavior. As McCarthy observed:

> The idea emerged of a judge acting as a benevolent father figure who, through informal chats with the child and other interested parties, would determine, unhampered by legalistic constraints, what was in the best interest of the child.[40]

Today, the juvenile court judge is still the sole decision maker as to whether a child is adjudicated delinquent. Although the courses of action a judge may follow have been modified somewhat by legal constraints set up as a result of various court decisions, the powers of juvenile court judges are still extensive. The dispositional decision, particularly when it involves institutionalization or removal from the parents' residence, cannot be made lightly. As Klein noted:

> The process by which a judge decides whether or not to deprive a child of his freedom is an intricate one. It is a complex of his expectations for himself, his expectations for others, and others' expectations of him. His decision making is also related to the community rehabilitation alternatives available to his disposition and to his rating of state institutional resources. It is also a product of the seriousness of the juvenile's offense, the chronicity of his record, the youth's attitude toward his conduct and toward the court, and the extent to which his parents appear able to provide effective controls over his behavior.[41]

Although a background in social or justice work would seem to be ideal preparation for such decision making, few juvenile court judges are selected because they have demonstrated a concern for, or even an interest in, the social welfare of children. Instead, they are often chosen to run for these elective offices on the basis of political and social contacts.

After election, a juvenile court judge must continue to weigh the political consequences of his or her decisions. A judge who develops a reputation for leniency may become unpopular with local police, who may feel that their efforts at investigation and apprehension have borne little fruit. A judge who pushes for expansion of court services may alienate the county commissioners, who may fear that tax increases would jeopardize their positions. A judge who is strict and unbending may arouse the anger of child-advocacy groups. The result of miscalculating the electorate's reactions may well be defeat at the polls.

Revision of juvenile codes, increased use of prosecuting attorneys and defense counsel in the juvenile courts, and heightened community awareness of the problem of juvenile crime have caused many judges to adopt a policy of strict interpretation of the law in juvenile cases, even when such application seems to conflict with the needs of the community.

The alarming amount of violent juvenile crime, especially among youths in the early teens, as well as the growing number of families with needs that must be ascertained and provided for by the juvenile courts, underline the importance of the presence of well-qualified and experienced judges in these courts. The Task Force Report on Juvenile Justice and Delinquency Prevention contained a recommendation that all family (juvenile) court judges be lawyers and be interested in the problems of children and families and aware of the responsibilities of working in this special area. It suggested that family court judgeships be permanent assignments and that all family court judges be required to receive special education and training.[42]

When the enormous responsibility, range, and implications of the juvenile court judge's decisions are considered, it becomes apparent that hopes for change through juvenile court action must extend far beyond the mere handing down of decisions in court proceedings. Rather than mediocre, mechanical decision makers, the juvenile court needs judges who are dynamic, progressive, and even prophetic in their approaches.

When asked to assess the reasons for his success in dealing with the youths who appeared before him, Leodis Harris, a former Ohio juvenile judge, cited "communication." He defined communication in the following way:

> I try not to talk to them, but with them. If you are not successful in communicating, then you can't succeed. When I say communication, I mean on a level where they actually are accepting you as well as what you're saying . . . and it's not a lot of mumbo jumbo and they're not going through an act. If either side, myself or the young person, is going through an act, then we're both bound to fail.[43]

When asked what he considered to be the disappointments of work as a juvenile court judge, Judge Harris stated:

> One of my greatest disappointments is to find that the system is so bogged down in the way things used to be or the way things are supposed to be that they're not involved with the way things are. And when you try to move the system you get involved with the natural built-in inertia or resistance. I don't mean only the court system. . . . Many of the social service agencies get so involved with the day-to-day mechanics that they forget or seem to lose the ultimate or original objective. . . . We get so involved with the paperwork, the rules, or the protocol that we tend to lose sight of the person we are trying to serve. . . . We treat the manifestation of the problem and never get to the problem itself. And as long as we can get on television and in the newspapers . . . and say we're working on the problem, then everybody's happy. If you were to turn around and say, "This is the basic cause of this problem," nobody wants to be bothered with that.[44]

Judges are painfully aware that the types of offenses bringing youths to juvenile court are changing. A judge in a rural county commented:

> Rape is the most serious crime I saw last year. It seems that more and more of our kids are being charged with a lot of sex crimes, but I'm not sure why that is.[45]

Another stated:

> Our society has become more violent and our juvenile justice system has not changed to deal with it effectively.[46]

One judge noted the difficulties is dealing with certain offenders:

> I came into the juvenile system real optimistic that I could change the world and that all kids could be rehabilitated, but at some point I realized that there are some kids that border on sociopathic and have no conscience.[47]

One justice, reflecting on the point that some children seem to have no sense of right or wrong, observed.

Juvenile court judges must develop innovative responses to the problems presented to them. *(Photo credit: Ernie Mastroianni)*

You would think that if they don't have any guilt or shame for what they do, they would at least think about what will happen to them if they get caught.[48]

To make children more aware of the seriousness of juvenile court appearances, Judge Saundra Robinson initiated changes in the physical setting. Formerly, the juvenile court hearing room resembled a conference room. It was renovated to provide a more official and imposing environment. The judge now sits behind a raised bench, witnesses are required to stand, and circular tables are provided for prosecutors and defense attorneys. With the exception of areas for the jury and for spectators, it now closely resembles a criminal court setting. "Juvenile court is a court," the judge observed, "not a meeting place."[49] Noting the sophistication of some young offenders, she observed:

We don't want kids coming to court saying they know they have three or four chances before they can be sent away. We have to stop slapping their hands.[50]

Judge Robinson's commitment to holding children responsible does not mean that she embraces a philosophy of punitive handling. She noted:

> Because of the very nature of the people that we deal with being children, even the most hardened criminals that we see, the kids that have done the worst crimes, are still children; when they're held in the detention center, you realize that these are just children who have never been parented. If we go with the punitive way, then we're just throwing away our whole generation. Punitiveness without rehabilitation or working with the children will not work. However, there is no way you can just be very lenient at the same time. Children don't respect that. Children want limits and you have to show them and make them accept responsibility for their own actions once they reach a certain age.[51]

In regard to what can be done to prevent child abuse, neglect, and dependency and aid children who lack family, church, or community support systems, she believed:

> Most of the children do not have parents to serve as role models. Many of the children under our supervision are parents themselves. It is not unusual for us [through the Children's Services Board] to have custody of 13 to 15-year-old children who have children. Obviously, a 15-year-old child has never been shown how to be a parent. There is no way she is going to know how to be a parent herself. Breaking the cycle of teenage children having babies, to me, is the biggest thing we can do to cut down on child abuse, neglect, and dependency.[52]

Adjudication Hearing

If a youth makes a "not guilty" or "untrue" plea (sometimes stated as "affirm" or "deny") at the initial hearing, and the case is not later resolved in a prehearing conference, or if a youth makes no plea at the initial hearing, an adjudication hearing is held, presided over by a juvenile court judge. The state's case is presented by a prosecutor or a representative of the prosecutor's office. The youth may be, and frequently is, represented by a defense attorney.

In adjudication hearings, juveniles have been guaranteed the rights of due process and privilege against self-incrimination. As a result of the *In re Winship* decision (1970), the Supreme Court also established "proof beyond a reasonable doubt" as the standard required in any juvenile court case in which a finding of "true" could result in institutionalization. We noted in Chapter 5 that, prior to the *Winship* decision, the standard of proof required in the juvenile court was the same as that in civil law: a preponderance (majority) of the evidence, rather than proof beyond a reasonable doubt.[53]

One right available in adult criminal courts that is not extended to youths having hearings in the juvenile court is that of a jury trial. We saw in Chapter 5 that, in *McKeiver v. Pennsylvania*, the Supreme court declared that juveniles do not have a *constitutional right* to a jury trial.[54] Several state juvenile codes, however, do provide for the use of a jury in a juvenile proceeding if this is requested by defense counsel or if the state has a blended sentence provision. With a blended sentence, the adjudicated delinquent completes part of his or her sentence under the juvenile system and part under the adult system.

We noted in our discussion of the role of the juvenile court judge that adjudication is a complex process. Some of the cases involve youths who have allegedly committed heinous crimes. For these, the court proceedings are formal and adversarial in nature. The role of the judge may be quite similar to that of a judge in a criminal trial—making sure that procedural rules are followed and that the evidence and witnesses are properly presented. Since the judge will be making the adjudication decision, he or she must also explore aggravating or mitigating circumstances surrounding the incidents. In cases involving children who have been abused or neglected, the demeanor of the judge toward the children must be quite different. Here the judge seeks to reassure the child and make the court appearance as nonthreatening as possible.

If a determination is made that the charge is not true, the case is dismissed by the judge. If a determination of "guilty" or "true" is reached and the charge is a minor one, disposition may be made at this point. Otherwise a date for the dispositional hearing is set.

The majority of states provide juveniles with the statutory right to appeal adjudications. The Task Force Report on Juvenile Justice and Delinquency Prevention recommended that all states extend this right.[55]

Dispositional Hearing

Many states require that the disposition or sentencing in a juvenile case be made at a hearing that is separated from the adjudication hearing. This separation has been termed the *bifurcated hearing* process. The reason for separating the adjudication and dispositional hearings is to afford the court an opportunity to obtain the information that will be needed to make an appropriate disposition. If considerable knowledge of the youth's background is already available to the court, as in instances where the young person has had a number of previous juvenile court appearances, an adjournment between the adjudication hearing and the dispositional hearing may not be necessary. In those cases in which the hearings are bifurcated, the major task to be completed during the interval between the two hearings (usually one to two weeks) is the preparation of a predisposition social investigation.

The social investigation is a key part of the juvenile court process. A probation officer assembles all the facts regarding the incident currently under consideration by the court, as well as the record of previous offenses; information about the offender gathered at the intake interview or by detention personnel if the youth was detained prior to the adjudication hearing; information about school progress and attitude; reports from any other social agencies in the community that have had contact with the youth or the family; and personal data on the child's abilities, interests, problems, and family situation. The probation officer may also suggest a dispositional alternative or treatment plan in the social investigation report. The social investigation report submitted for Al Hollus is given here.

PREDISPOSITION
SOCIAL INVESTIGATION

Name of Child   <u>Albert Hollus</u>   Charge   <u>Delinquency by reason of auto theft</u>
   <u>   </u> Detention   <u>X</u>   Custody of Parents
Intake Disposition   <u>Judicial</u>   Date   <u>4-26-03</u>
Counselor   <u>Marian Bronson</u>

Intake Report

On March 30, 2003, the _____ Juvenile Court received a Complaint Form
from the _____ Police Department which alleged that on March 28, Albert Hollus
was stopped by Officers Mitchell and Lantano for a speeding violation and found to be
driving an auto for which he could not produce registration. Police investigation uncovered the information that the auto belonged to Walter Carswell of the same city and that
it was missing from a parking area in front of his residence. Albert Hollus was taken to
the _____ Police Station and charged with delinquency by reason of auto theft.
His female companion was released after questioning revealed she did not know she was
traveling in a stolen auto. The boy's mother was summoned to the station and he was released in her custody, pending a juvenile court hearing. A notification for the parents to
appear with Albert at intake on April 6, 2003, was mailed to their home address, 1207
Lindon Street.

Albert Hollus, age 16, and his parents, Mr. and Mrs. Frank Hollus of 1207 Lindon Street,
appeared for the intake interview. They talked freely with Marian Bronson, the Intake
Officer, about the incident, and also about Al's behavior. A check of juvenile court
records revealed that Al had no prior referrals and his parents reported that he had always been a well-behaved boy and a good student until he began dating Rosemary Davis,
who was 23 years old. They met in late February of this year at the drive-in restaurant
where Rosemary works and since that time Al had been spending every evening with
Rosemary, in spite of his parents' objections. The parents reported that they had attempted to control Al's behavior by forbidding him to use the family car and taking away
his set of keys, but he had still managed to go to the girl's home or to the drive-in to visit
her. They had assumed that the whole matter was a crush or a phase Al was going
through, and had been greatly shocked to hear that Al was in the process of running
away to marry the girl in another state when he was apprehended with the stolen auto.
Al insisted that he had only planned to "borrow the car for a short time and then leave it
parked somewhere after they were married." He repeated over and over that he loved
Rosemary and would do anything to be with her.

The Intake Officer determined that the case would be handled judicially and a hearing
was set for April 18.

Strengths and Resources

Al has no previous court referrals and his parents report that he never presented any type
of discipline or behavior problems until the present incident.

Mr. Hollus is a long-distance trucker who is away from home approximately 20 days out of every month. He appears to be a hard-working individual who has set firm standards of discipline for Al and the other five children in the family, all of whom are younger than Al. It is his belief that if Al can be "made to forget about" the older girl with whom he has become involved, all his problems will be over. He is very much concerned about the fact that Al stole an auto and called the owner of the car to apologize for his son's actions.

Mrs. Hollus is a rather nervous-acting woman in her late 30s who seems completely dominated by her husband. She appears to be resentful of the fact that he is away so much and she is responsible for care of the six children, although she stated that she realizes her husband works hard and has to spend a lot of time on the road to provide them with a nice home and the things the children need. She reported that she had never had to scold Al excessively about anything and could always "reason with him" about behavior of which she did not approve, until Rosemary came along. She blames the girl for the entire incident and believes that she is "making a fool out of Al."

Al is a quiet boy who appears to be very unhappy. When questioned, he reported that his mother is always after him to help out with the housework even though he has four younger sisters who could take care of most of it. He stated that his mother depends on him to drive her to church and to visit her friends when his father is away from home, since she does not have a driver's license, and he has to wait around all evening for her. He stated that he believed his mother made such a fuss about Rosemary because she was jealous of the attention he was giving her and because he wasn't around to "help and wait on" her when he was out with Rosemary. Al had little to say about his father, except that he was "never home" and that he made him "toe the line." He admitted that his parents loved him and cared about him.

Action Taken

A delinquency petition was filed by the Assistant State Attorney, alleging that Albert Hollus was delinquent by reason of auto theft, and a hearing was scheduled for April 18. At this hearing Al admitted that he stole the auto and Judge Martinson ordered a presentence investigation for disposition of the case. A disposition hearing was scheduled for April 30, 2003.

Juvenile's Statement and Attitude

Al continues to assert that he loves Rosemary Davis and plans to spend his life with her, no matter what his parents or anyone else do to stop him. He reported that he has telephoned her every day since the auto-theft incident, but that she has refused to go out with him because she is angry about getting into trouble because of him. She told him she couldn't understand why he would steal a car to go away and get married when he knew he would get caught. Al still shows no remorse for the auto theft and maintains that he didn't plan to hurt the car, just use it for about two hours, and he can't see why everyone is making such a fuss. He kept repeating that he plans to marry Rosemary as soon as all this is straightened out. When confronted with the fact that he has no job and still has more than a year of high school to complete, he replied that Rosemary promised to work and take care of him until he finishes school.

Background of This Juvenile

Physical Data. According to Mrs. Hollus, Al has never suffered any type of physical or mental trauma. He had most of the childhood diseases and broke his right arm in a fall from a bicycle when he was 10, but otherwise has a history of normal physical and mental development. Al is tall and physically mature and gives the appearance of being two or three years older than his actual age.

Psychological and Psychiatric Data. Al did not receive any psychiatric or psychological examinations administrated by the court.

Special Interests. Al has been active in a number of sports in high school. He is currently in the 11th grade and was a member of the varsity basketball team during the past season. He did not go out for track this spring, as he had done in previous years, because he wanted to spend his time with Rosemary. Al was a reporter on the school newspaper during 10th grade, but did not continue this activity. He stated that he likes all types of sports and is good at them.

Family Structure

Home Environment. The family resides in a comfortable home in a middle-class neighborhood of _____. The house is neatly kept and the six children seem to have enough room for play activities both inside and outside the home. All the child have assigned "chores" which they are required to complete each day, and they are punished if they fail to do them. Punishments usually involve being "grounded" (forbidden to go to friends' homes or to have visitors). The mother seems to be very anxious about the children's well-being and to want them to succeed in school.

Family Relationships. Al is the oldest in a family of six. He has four younger sisters and a baby brother who is 18 months old. Al's father is absent from home a good deal of the time and it appears that Al is called upon to alternately serve as a substitute for his father in driving his mother to her activities and as a helper with the housework. Al contends that his mother makes him do many things at home (ironing, cooking) which his sisters could do "if they weren't so lazy."

Al's father admitted that he has little time to spend with the children and that when he is at home he spends a good deal of his time sleeping or watching television. He has not been actively involved in any sports activities with Al and the boy stated that he "hardly ever does anything with his father." Al indicated that he would like to spend more time with him.

Mr. and Mrs. Hollus appear to be happily married, although Mrs. Hollus complained that she has to spend a lot of time alone with the children while he is away and it wears her out. She is very anxious and worried about Al and kept stating that a complete change has come over him and she doesn't know what to do with him.

School History

Al ranked 50th in a class of 270 when he completed _____ Junior High School. His 10th grade final grades at _____ High School were all As and Bs, and he had comparable grades during the first half of his 11th grade year. During the nine-week period just completed, he received four Cs and two Bs. He has no record of truancy, although he had six tardy notices during the nine-week period just completed. The high school guidance counselor noted that Al was a "natural athlete" who could compete well in virtually any sport and that he was quiet but well liked by his classmates. His Standard Achievement Tests, last completed in the 10th grade, revealed above-average scores in both verbal and quantitative ability. The guidance counselor reported that Al had never been referred to the discipline principal during his high school career and could find no record of his having been given a school detention.

Impressions and Recommendations

The court is dealing with a 16-year-old youngster who is physically mature and strongly emotionally involved with an older girl. He has never evidenced any behavior problems at home or at school until this involvement. The girl maintains that they like each other, have a lot in common, and believe they are ready to get married, but Al's immature behavior in stealing a car to go away to get married shocked her. She stated that she is still in love with Al, but that he may need to "grow up a little" before he is ready for marriage.

Al readily admitted his delinquent act, but still has displayed no remorse for it. He maintains that he loves Rosemary and will do "anything" to be with her. His parents are willing to help him in any way they can, although they are bitter toward Rosemary for causing their son to get into trouble and want the court to forbid Al to associate with her. They believe Al would benefit from counseling and have indicated that they would be willing to participate in family counseling, although Mr. Hollus' schedule would make this difficult.

It is the recommendation of this officer that Al be granted probation and supervised under a behavior contract which allows him to associate with Rosemary on a limited basis, but also provides for him to participate in a variety of activities with youths of his own age. It is also recommended that efforts be made to find part-time employment for Al so that he will spend less time at home with his mother and sisters and can experience the responsibility of holding a job.

At the dispositional hearing, the judge has the social investigation report before him and may also hear information from the defense counsel, the prosecutor, or probation officers about possible treatment alternatives available to the youth. This hearing is considerably less adversarial than the adjudication hearing. The defense counsel may ask character witnesses (teachers, social workers, relatives) to speak on the youth's behalf and counsel may also examine the predisposition social investigation report to be sure that the information contained in it is accurate. If a plea bargain that included a suggested disposition was made, the defense counsel is present to assure that the terms of the plea bargain are carried out. If a prosecutor is present, he or she functions predominately to protect the interests of the community or of a specific victim. While, in general, prosecutors may argue for more severe dispositions than the defense counsel wishes they may be supportive of dispositions that involve treatment rather than punishment if the circumstances surrounding certain cases seem to warrant this.

In some states, juvenile codes *mandate* specific dispositions for certain offenses. For example, if a juvenile is adjudicated delinquent on a serious felony charge, commitment to a secure institution may be required by the code. In other cases, juvenile codes may *prohibit* certain dispositions. For example, many states prohibit secure institutionalization of status offenders. Generally, state codes allow juvenile court judges to make discretionary dispositions for the majority of delinquent offenses. As noted in Figure 13–1, dispositions can range from those that are nominal, such as warnings or reprimands, to those that are custodial and will result in the youth being placed in a secure correctional facility.

Studies of the factors affecting the severity of dispositions given in juvenile courts have produced varied findings. One study reported that prior referrals, age, being held in detention, and the seriousness of the youth's offense were all related to severity,[56] while another identified race, sex, and socioeconomic class as significant predictors.[57] A third study found that minority juveniles, males and juveniles whose families were on public assistance were given harsher dispositions and identified other related items, including prior record, detention status, seriousness of the offense, age, and representation by counsel.[58]

Figure 13–5 reports the types of dispositions give for every 1,000 delinquency cases referred to the juvenile courts in one year. The dispositions a judge may make include (1) release of the youth to the supervision of his or her parents with a warning; (2) imposition of a fine or a requirement that restitution of some sort be made to an injured party; (3) referral to a community social agency for counseling or treatment; (4) assignment to official probation supervision by the court; (5) placement in a residential treatment center; (6) removal from the home and placement in a foster home; (7) making the child a ward of the court, who will receive needed medical or psychological treatment; or (8) commitment to a public or private institution, or to the state youth authority for placement. In 1996, 175 of every 323 adjudicated cases (54%) resulted in formal probation, 91 (28%) resulted in residential placement, 43 (13%) received other sanctions, and 14 (5%) were released.[59]

The dispositional hearing closes when the judge signs a decree of disposition, which is a written statement of the disposition chosen and the basis for it.

Al and his parents, all looking nervous and worried, appeared before Judge Martinson for the dispositional hearing. Probation Officer Bronson, who had interviewed Al at intake and conducted the social investigation, was present.

Judge Martinson asked Ms. Bronson for the social investigation report and glanced through it. He informed the Holluses that he had talked Al's situation over with Ms. Bronson and that she had recommended that Al be placed on probation. Judge Martinson asked Al and his parents if they had any comments to make, but they remained silent. The judge then stated that a disposition of probation was granted and that Al would be required to report to officers of the court periodically. A decree of disposition to this effect was entered in the court record. Al and his parents were informed that they had a right to appeal this disposition and were told of the process by which an appeal could be made. The Holluses indicated that they had no desire to appeal and expressed great relief that Al had been "given another chance." The judge reminded Al that he must abide by the rules of probation set up by his officer.

According to Besharov, state juvenile codes do not generally specify the conditions constituting grounds for appeal of a disposition considered unfair or too harsh by the youth or the youth's defense lawyer. Many times, the appellate courts have tried to establish broad general standards for appeal of a disposition when the appeal appears to be in the "best interests of the child and the state or the particular needs of the individual juvenile."[60] Besharov noted that appellate decisions reversing juvenile court dispositions almost always involve dispositions that led to the institutionalization of the juvenile.[61] The report of the Task Force on Juvenile Justice and Delinquency Prevention recommended that a juvenile, his or her parents, the correctional agency responsible for the juvenile, or the family court be permitted to petition the court for reduction or modification of the disposition at any time during the period, and that a hearing on such a petition should be held within 30 days of the time it is filed.[62]

The majority of youths referred to juvenile courts (54% of males and 73% of females) do not return.[63] However, researchers have found that youths who are referred to juvenile courts a second time before age 16 are very likely to continue their delinquent behavior. Those most likely to have a second referral were originally charged with burglary, truancy, motor vehicle theft, or robbery, while those least likely to return to the court had such offenses as underage drinking, running away, or shoplifting.[64]

If a juvenile is referred to the court for a new offense or violation of conditions established by the court, the process begins anew. At its conclusion, if the petition is found to be true, the judge must consider the rather limited range of dispositions available and choose one that may, in this instance, prevent another return. Youths identified as chronic offenders are likely to receive successively more severe dispositions.

If an offender is not referred to the juvenile court again after a specific period of time, most state codes provide for *expungement* (destruction or sealing of the juvenile's record). In some states, the juvenile court judge is required to inform the juvenile that this right exists and to describe the process involved. In Ohio, as shown in Figure 13–6, destruction of all records is provided for those juveniles whose cases were either dismissed or adjudicated not guilty. For those cases in which the charges were found to be true, the records are sealed rather than destroyed. Sealed records can only be viewed if a court order is obtained.

Sentencing of Juveniles Adjudicated in Criminal Court

Although juveniles tried and convicted in criminal courts can receive sentences similar to those adults convicted of identical offenses would receive, age is often used as a mitigating circumstance to justify a less severe sentence for a juvenile. A study of violent juvenile offenders who were tried in criminal courts found that more than half of the convicted felons received sentences of fines and/or probation.[65] Nevertheless, juveniles are sentenced to adult correctional institutions and in a few cases have been given death sentences. Thirty-eight states and the District of Columbia authorize the death penalty for juveniles. Between 1976 and July, 2002, 21 adults were executed for crimes they committed as juveniles. As of July 1, 2002, there were 80 persons on death row under death sentences for crimes they committed as juveniles. All of these were ages 16 or 17 when they committed the crimes and their current ages ranged from 18 to 42 years.[66]

COURT OF COMMON PLEAS FRANKLIN COUNTY, OHIO
DIVISION OF DOMESTIC RELATIONS
JUVENILE BRANCH

IN THE MATTER OF:

_____   CASE NO. _____

_____

_____

☐   # REQUEST FOR EXPUNGEMENT MOTION

_____ HEREBY APPLIES TO HAVE HIS RECORD EX-
JUVENILE'S NAME
PUNGED IN THE ABOVE CASE NUMBER PURSUANT TO O.R.C. 2151.358(F).

MEMORANDUM

THE CHARGE(S) OF _____

_____

IN THE ABOVE CASE NUMBER HAVE BEEN DISMISSED OR WAS ADJUDICATED NOT GUILTY OF

THE NAMED CHARGES ON _____ .

☐   # REQUEST FOR SEALING MOTION

_____ HEREBY APPLIES TO HAVE HIS RECORD SEALED
JUVENILE'S NAME
IN CASE NUMBER PURSUANT TO O.R.C. 2151.358(D).

MEMORANDUM

THE COURT'S ORDERS IN THE CHARGE(S) OF _____

_____

WERE TERMINATED ON _____ _____ , OR I WAS UNCONDITIONALLY

DISCHARGED FROM _____ ON _____ .

_____   _____
JUVENILE'S NAME   DATE

NOTICE OF HEARING

YOU ARE HEREBY NOTIFIED THAT THIS MATTER WILL COME ON FOR HEARING ON

_____ 19 ___ AT _____ ___ M. BEFORE REFEREE _____

COURTROOM NO. _____ AT _____ .
J-270

Figure 13–6.   Request for Juvenile Court Record Expungement. (*Source: Franklin County (Ohio) Court of Common Pleas, Juvenile Branch, Columbus, Ohio.*)

In *Thompson* v. *Oklahoma* (1988), the U.S. Supreme Court prohibited the execution of a child who committed a capital offense while under the age of 16,[67] but in considering *Stanford* v. *Kentucky* and *Wilkins* v. *Missouri* (1989), the Supreme Court ruled that the execution of a youth who was 16 or 17 years of age at the time of the offense would not violate the Eighth Amendment, which prohibits cruel and unusual punishment.[68]

SUMMARY

Views of the appropriate role and procedures for the juvenile court have changed over the years. Youths charged with serious offenses are being transferred to adult courts more frequently and some states allow prosecutors to choose to bring charges in either adult or juvenile court. The upper age of juvenile court jurisdiction has also been lowered in certain states and the propriety of including status offenders in the court's jurisdiction is debated. Hearings have become more formal and there has been an increase in the number of abuse, neglect, and dependency cases handled.

Youths may be referred to the juvenile court for offenses that are also law violations for adults or for behavior that is unlawful only for juveniles (status offenses). The majority of juvenile court referrals are made by law enforcement agencies, but referrals may also come from parents, social agencies, schools, or private individuals.

Total diversion from court involvement can occur if the youth is counseled by police and released or through referral to another agency. If this occurs, no juvenile court action is taken.

The juvenile court process begins when the agency or person making the referral files a petition (complaint) that specifies the law or ordinance that the youth has violated. The offender may be arrested and brought to the court by police or may receive a summons to appear.

At the intake level, the intake officer of the juvenile court may decide to authorize detention, dismiss the case, or partially divert the youths from juvenile court action. Detention involves holding a youth in a center provided by the court or arrangement for home detention (house arrest) until action is taken on the case. *Partial diversion* involves some type of informal supervision or treatment. A youth is required to follow the diversion recommendations of the court or face official handling.

If a case is not dismissed at the intake level and diversion is not employed, the matter is handled judicially (officially). An *initial hearing* is scheduled, at which the charges contained in the petition are read and the youth responds by answering "guilty" or "not guilty," "true" or "untrue," or "admit" or "deny." If a youth admits the truth of the allegations and the offenses are minor, the case may be disposed of at this hearing. If a plea of "guilty" or "true" is made to a serious offense, a social investigation is required to aid the judge in deciding upon an appropriate disposition. If a plea of "not guilty" or "untrue" is entered, an *adjudication hearing* is scheduled.

In cases involving serious offenses, the prosecuting attorney may request a *waiver hearing* to apply for transfer of the case to an adult criminal court for trial. Such hearings must be conducted according to the constitutional safeguards established in *Kent* v. *U.S.* and *Breed* v. *Jones*.

In some instances, a *prehearing conference* between the judge, court personnel, the prosecuting attorney, and the defense attorney may occur, in which the facts of the case are considered and the disposition that can be expected if a plea of "guilty" or "true" is made is outlined. The conference is analogous to the plea-bargaining process on the adult level.

At the *adjudication hearing*, the judge decides upon the truth of the charges and acts accordingly, basing the decision on the standard of "proof beyond a reasonable doubt." If the charges are found to be untrue, they are dismissed. If a determination of "true" is reached and the offense is a minor one, a disposition may be given at this point. Otherwise a date for a dispositional hearing is set, with a social investigation conducted in the interim. The separation of adjudication and disposition into two separate hearings is termed the *bifurcated hearing* process.

At the *dispositional hearing*, the judge reviews the social investigation report, informs the youth of the disposition decided upon, and signs a decree of disposition, which states the disposition chosen and its basis. Juvenile court dispositions may be appealed and this occurs most frequently when the disposition involves institutionalization.

Although the majority of youths referred to juvenile courts are not referred again, certain types of offenses are related to repeated referrals. If an offender is not referred again after a specific period of time, *expungement* (destruction or sealing) of the juvenile's record can be requested.

Youths whose cases are waived to adult criminal courts are liable to the same penalties adults can receive if they are found guilty, but the age of the waived youth may be a mitigating factor. However, juveniles can be sentenced to adult correctional institutions and those age 16 or 17 at the time a capital offense was committed can be executed.

DISCUSSION QUESTIONS

1. Define total diversion and partial diversion. What are the primary goals of diversion?

2. Discuss the role of a juvenile court intake officer in decisions to divert juveniles from official handling. On what basis does an intake officer make these decisions?

3.. How has the role of the defense attorney in the juvenile court expanded since the *Gault, Kent,* and *Winship* decisions?

4. When is it appropriate to place a juvenile charged with a delinquent act in a detention center? The U.S. Supreme Court ruled that preventive detention is acceptable for juveniles. Do you agree? Why?

5. Discuss the waiver process. When is it appropriate to have a juvenile case transferred to the criminal court?

NOTES

1. Anne Larason Schneider, "Divesting Status Offenses from Juvenile Court Jurisdiction," *Crime & Delinquency* 30, 3 (July 1984), 349.
2. *Ibid.*, 347–370.

3. Jeffrey A. Butts, *Offenders in Juvenile Court, 1992* (Washington, DC: U.S. Department of Justice, 1994), 9.
4. Howard N. Snyder and Melissa Sickmund, *Juvenile Offenders and Victims: 1999 National Report* (Washington, DC: Office of Juvenile Justice and Delinquency Prevention, 1999), 144.
5. *Ibid.*, 146, 148.
6. *Ibid.*, 166.
7. Circuit Court of Cook County, Juvenile Division, *Juvenile Court of Cook County Information Booklet,* (Chicago, IL: Circuit Court of Cook County, 2989), 16.
8. Henry Campbell Black, *Black's Law Dictionary,* 6th ed. (St. Paul, MN: West Publishing Co., 1991), 793.
9. *Miranda* v. *Arizona,* 358 U.S. 436, 448 (1966).
10. Butts, *Offenders in Juvenile Court, 1992,* 11.
11. Snyder and Sickmund, *Juvenile Offenders and Victims,* 152.
12. National Advisory Committee for Juvenile Justice and Delinquency Prevention, *Standards for the Administration of Juvenile Justice* (Washington, DC: U.S. Government Printing Office, 1980), 297.
13. Richard A. Ball, C. Ronald Huff, and J. Robert Lilly, "A Model House Arrest Program for Juveniles: What Makes It Work?" In Richard A. Ball, C. Ronald Huff, and J. Robert Lilly, *House Arrest and Correctional Policy* (Newbury Park, CA: Sage Publications, 1988), 53–76.
14. Butts, *Offenders and Juvenile Court, 1992,* 6.
15. John R. Fuller and William M. Norton, "Juvenile Diversion: The Impact of Program Philosophy on Net Widening," *Journal of Crime and Justice* 16, 1 (1993), 30.
16. Malcolm W. Klein, "Labeling Theory and Delinquency Policy: An Experimental Test," *Criminal Justice and Behavior* 13 (1986), 47–79.
17. Fuller and Norton, "Juvenile Diversion: The Impact of Program Philosophy on Net Widening," 40.
18. Snyder and Sickmund, *Juvenile Offenders and Victims,* 157.
19. Howard Snyder, Melissa Sickmund, and Eileen Poe-Yamagata, *Juvenile Transfers to Criminal Court in the 1990s. Lessons Learned from Four Studies* (Pittsburgh, PA: National Center for Juvenile Justice, 2000), xi.
20. Snyder and Sickmund, *Juvenile Offenders and Victims,* 162.
21. *Kent* v. *U.S.,* 383 U.S. 541 (1966).
22. Barry C. Feld, "The Juvenile Court Meets the Principle of the Offense: Legislative Changes in Juvenile Waiver Statutes," *Journal of Criminal Law & Criminology,* 78, 3 (1987), 491.
23. M.A. Bortner, "Traditional Rhetoric, Organizational Realities: Remand of Juveniles to Adult Court," *Crime and Delinquency* 32, 1 (January 1986), 53–73.
24. "Case Against Retarded Mother in Texas is at Legal Crossroads," *Akron Beacon Journal,* February 16, 1995, A4.
25. Ellen Nimick, Linda Szymanski, and Howard Snyder, *Juvenile Court Waiver: A Study of Juvenile Court Cases Transferred to Criminal Court* (Pittsburgh, PA: National Center for Juvenile Justice, 1986), 4.
26. John A. Webb and Edwin P. Willems, "Certifying Juveniles for Adult Court: An Attribution Analysis," *Journal of Applied Social Psychology* 17, 10 (1987), 896.
27. Snyder, et al., *Juvenile Transfer to Criminal Court in the 1990s,* 11–15.
28. Marilyn Houghtalin and G. Larry Mays, "Criminal Dispositions of New Mexico Juveniles Transferred to Adult Court," *Crime & Delinquency* 37, 3 (July 1001), 393–407.
29. *Breed* v. *Jones,* 421 U.S. 519 (1975).
30. *In re Gault,* 376 U.S. 1 (1967).
31. Joseph P. Sanborn, Jr., "Pleading Guilty in Juvenile Court: Minimal Ado About Something Very Important to Young Defendants," *Justice Quarterly* 9, 1 (March 1992), 133.
32. David P. Aday, Jr., "Court Structure, Defense Attorney Use, and Juvenile Court Decisions," *Sociological Quarterly* 27, 1 (1986), 107–119.
33. Barry C. Feld, "*In re Gault* Revisited: A Cross-State Comparison of the Right to Counsel in Juvenile Court," *Crime & Delinquency* 34, 4 (October 1988), 394.

34. *Ibid.*, 400.
35. Task Force on Juvenile Justice and Delinquency Prevention, National Advisory Committee on Criminal Justice Standards and Goals, *Juvenile Justice and Delinquency Prevention* (Washington, DC: U.S. Government Printing Office, 1977), 410.
36. Douglas Besharov, *Juvenile Justice Advocacy* (New York: Practicing Law Institute, 1974), 38.
37. W. Vaughan Stapleton and Lee E. Teitelbaum, *In Defense of Youth* (New York: Russell Sage Foundation, 1972), 60–72.
38. Feld, "*In re Gault* Revisited . . .," 405.
39. *Ibid.*
40. Francis Barry McCarthy, "Should Juvenile Delinquency Be Abolished?" *Crime & Delinquency* 23, 2 (April 1977), 197.
41. Malcolm W. Klein, "The Eye of the Juvenile Court Judge: A One Step Up View of the Juvenile Justice System," In Malcolm W. Klein, ed., *The Juvenile Justice System* (Beverly Hills, CA: Sage, 1976), 19.
42. Task Force, *Juvenile Justice and Delinquency Prevention*, 284.
43. Interview with Judge Leodis Harris, conducted by Peter C. Kratcoski, April 11, 1978.
44. *Ibid.*
45. Collette M. Jenkins, "Juvenile Courts Confront Troubling Societal Trends," *Akron Beacon Journal*, February 14, 1995, C3.
46. *Ibid.*
47. *Ibid.*
48. Marilyn Miller Roane, "Controversy Shrouds Youth Court," *Akron Beacon Journal*, April 12, 1992, A10.
49. Charlene Nevada, "Juvenile Court More Imposing," *Akron Beacon Journal*, August 1, 1994, A4.
50. Roane, "Controversy Shrouds Youth Court," A1.
51. Interview with Judge Saundra Robinson, conducted by Peter C. Kratcoski, February 10, 1993.
52. *Ibid.*
53. *In re Winship*, 397 U.S. 358 (1970).
54. *McKeiven v. Pennsylvania*, 403 U.S. 528 (1970).
55. Task Force Report, *Juvenile Justice and Delinquency Prevention*, 428.
56. Bortner, *Inside a Juvenile Court*, 82.
57. Terence P. Thornberry, "Sentencing Disparities in the Juvenile Justice System," *Journal of Criminal Law and Criminology* 70 (1979), 164.
58. Christopher S. Dunn, Stephen A. Cernkovich, Robert L. Perry, and Jerry W. Wicks, *Race and Juvenile Justice in Ohio* (Bowling Green, OH: Bowling Green State University, 1993), 83.
59. Snyder and Sickmund, *Juvenile Offenders and Victims*, 162.
60. Besharov, *Juvenile Justice Advocacy*, 408.
61. *Ibid.*
62. Task Force, *Juvenile Justice and Delinquency Prevention*, 475.
63. Snyder and Sickmund, *Juvenile Offenders and Victims*, 80.
64. U.S. Department of Justice, "Study Sheds New Light on Court Careers of Juvenile Offenders," *OJJDP Update on Research* (Washington, DC: U.S. Government Printing Office, August, 1988), 1.
65. Donna Hamparian, Joseph M. Davis, Judith M. Jacobson, and Robert E. McGraw, *The Youth Criminal Years of the Violent Few* (Washington, DC: U.S. Department of Justice, 1985), 8.
66. Victor L. Streib, *The Juvenile Death Penalty Today: Death Sentences and Executions for Juvenile Crimes January 1973–June 30, 2002.* www.deathpenaltyinfo.org/juvchair.html, January 15, 2003.
67. *Thompson v. Oklahoma*, 487 U.S. 815 (1988).
68. *Stanford v. Kentucky (Wilkins v. Missouri)* 109 S. Ct. 2969 (1989).

CHAPTER 14

PROBATION
AND COMMUNITY-BASED
PROGRAMS

(Photo Credit: Nick J. Cool, The Image Works)

HISTORICAL DEVELOPMENT OF PROBATION
DEFINITION OF PROBATION
EXTENT OF PROBATION USE
ROLE OF THE PROBATION OFFICER
THE PROBATION PROCESS
    The Probation Officer as Investigator
    The Probation Officer as Supervisor
    Intensive Probation
PROBATION REVOCATION
ALTERNATIVE COMMUNITY-BASED SUPERVISION
    Early Experiments with Community-Based Services for Delinquents
    Current Community Supervision Programs
    Specialized Treatment Programs
    Services for Multiproblem Youths
    Community Residential Treatment
THE EFFECTIVENESS OF PROBATION AND OTHER COMMUNITY-BASED ALTERNATIVES

Al and his mother sat in hard-backed chairs in the reception area, awaiting their turn to speak with Mr. Carson, the probation officer assigned to Al's case. Al was somewhat apprehensive about this first meeting. He had been told to report to Mr. Carson's office at 2:30, but it was already 3:30, and several youths and their parents who had been there when he arrived were still waiting. Al's mother kept checking her watch. She had left her five younger children with a neighbor while she came to the appointment with Al. The notice to appear requested that Mr. Hollus also come, but he was out of town on a long-distance run for his trucking company.

Mrs. Hollus felt apprehension tinged with guilt and wished that she had kept closer tabs on Al's activities. She was also angry with Al for "letting her down" and resentful toward her husband for not sharing more of the responsibility for raising the children.

At one point in the long wait, Al whispered to his mother that he wanted to pick up and leave, but he was afraid to carry out his threat because he knew it would lead to more trouble. Finally their turn arrived, and Al and his mother went into Mr. Carson's office.

Carson, appearing tired and somewhat bored, proceeded to review the case by reading from various reports that were spread out on his desk. "Let's see, you're 16 years old. . . eleventh grade. . . average student. . . mother and father both living at home. . ." At this point he stopped and asked Mrs. Hollus where her husband was. She replied, "Driving his truck." Carson launched into a rather mechanical recitation of the importance of having both parents attend these meetings, and then abruptly returned to Al's records. "Let's see. . . you stole a car, and you and a girl by the name of Rosemary tried to run away and get married. The owner of the car is pretty mad, and says he wants to see that punks like you are taken off the streets. Do you want to talk about it?".

Al began to explain how he had met Rosemary at a local drive-in restaurant where she worked, and that although she was older (23), they liked each other a lot. Since he had met Rosemary, he was bored with school, and he didn't want to live at home any more because his parents kept hassling him and his mother made him do a lot of housework and "hauling her around." One night, he and Rosemary had decided they would run away and get married. Al's father had forbidden him to use the family car and had taken away his keys, so in desperation he had decided to steal an auto for the trip. He figured they could drive to another state, get married, and then abandon the car.

During Al's explanation of his problems, the probation officer kept glancing at his watch, and Al's mother fidgeted in her chair, mindful of the long time the other children had been with the neighbor. Al, taking note that his audience was losing interest, broke off the story by saying, "I already told all this to the police, and the judge, and other people around the court here." Mrs. Hollus broke in to observe that Al really was a pretty good boy, except that he didn't help out with the housework and the other children as much as he should and stayed out too late at night, especially since he started hanging around with this "Rosemary girl." Mrs. Hollus wanted Al to finish school and stay away from Rosemary, who was too old and wild for him. She added that Mr. Hollus would "kick the hell out of Al" if he found out that he had seen that girl again.

Al interrupted at this point to say that Rosemary was the only girl he really felt good with, and he didn't understand why he had to stay away from her. The probation officer's only comment when he finished this outburst was that it was 4:30, and since there were others still waiting to see him, it was time to close the discussion and set up the rules and visitation schedule.

Al's case illustrates a number of the difficulties in juvenile probation work. Most of the youths who are brought into the courts are not too different from teenagers who have never had official contact with the law. Their unlawful acts are entangled with social, psychological, and cultural factors. Some young people faced with behavioral decisions receive little help or understanding from their parents and, being immature, select courses of action that lead to law violations and their apprehension. They may not recognize the seriousness of their behavior, and even if they do, their need for status, recognition, or money, or their desire to retaliate, seems more important at the time than the possible consequence of being caught.

Al's case also illustrates the fact that the typical probation officer is expected to deal with complex situations in limited time and with strong pressures not to fail. The probation officer has many restraints regarding the courses of action he or she can follow and must constantly keep in mind the many publics he or she serves. For example, a youthful offender is viewed by community members in different ways, depending on the person doing the defining:

As an illustration take just one little vandal: call him 12 years old and you will see him as a baby who did not know what he was doing (according to his parents); as a kid who broke some 20 windows and was arrested (according to the police); as a little beast who should be locked up (according to the victim); as just another kid on the block (according to the neighbors); as one of 10,000 juveniles who are processed every year (according to the particular probation office); as one of 30 or more cases to decide on a given day (according to the Juvenile Court judge); as a fairly healthy physical specimen (according to the family doctor); as a reflection of the morality of the community (according to the social worker); as a child expressing frustration, aggression, and hostility (according to the psychiatrist); as a status seeker (according to the sociologist); as good copy for the newspaper; and as a project for a service club.[1]

Just as young people who come to the attention of juvenile authorities are perceived in various ways by those who have an interest or stake in their behavior, they differ greatly in their attitudes, values, and amenability to counseling. Because of the wide range of backgrounds and personal attributes of probationers and the differences in the training and resources of probation officers, it is difficult to make generalizations about probation work.

HISTORICAL DEVELOPMENT OF PROBATION

The roots of the practice of probation can be found in the Middle Ages, when certain types of offenders could be released to the custody of a member of the clergy, a peace-keeping officer, a relative, or a friend rather than given the harsh corporal or capital punishment prescribed by law. Such releases apparently were quite common with children who violated the law. They were given over to the custody of their parents or other supervisors with the stipulation that they be appropriately punished.

John Augustus (1774–1859) is credited with first using the term "probation" and initiating the practice as we know it today. He offered to supervise the activities of a man referred to the Police Court of Boston in 1841 to keep him from being sent to the House of Correction. When this case had a successful outcome, Augustus continued throughout his lifetime to supervise offenders and report their progress to the judges. By the time of his death, he had supervised almost 2,000 adults and several thousand children.[2]

Following Augustus' lead, Massachusetts was the first state to institute a probation program for youths. In an act passed in 1869, a representative of the State Board of Charities was allowed to appear before the court in criminal cases involving juveniles. This agent could be given the responsibility of locating and placing youths in foster homes, if necessary, and was also empowered to supervise and assist the child after placement.[3] By 1900, six states had enacted probation legislation for adults and juveniles. The Illinois Juvenile Court Act of 1899, which established the first juvenile court, provided for the appointment of juvenile probation officers and also specified their duties:

> The court shall have authority to appoint or designate one or more discreet persons of good character to serve as probation officers during the pleasure of the court; said probation officers to receive no compensation from the public treasury. . . . It shall be the duty of the said probation officer to make such investigation as may be required by the court; to be present in court in order to represent the interests of the child when the case is heard, to furnish to the court such information and assistance as the judge may require; and to take such charge of any child before and after trial as may be directed by the court.[4]

Gradually, as other states enacted legislation that created separate courts for juveniles, juvenile probation because an integral part of the juvenile justice process and persons specifically trained in social work, psychology, or child welfare were hired as probation officers.

DEFINITION OF PROBATION

The term "probation" can refer to a disposition given to an adjudicated delinquent by a juvenile court judge or it may be used to describe the probation process.

Under probation as a court disposition, the offender is allowed to remain in the community, subject to supervision by a court official. He or she must abide by certain rules and conditions established by the juvenile court. There are two ways in which a juvenile may be placed on probation. One is termed "suspension of the imposition of the disposition." Here the juvenile is given a disposition of commitment to an institution; this commitment is then suspended, and the youth is placed on probation. If the juvenile violates the terms of the probation, the suspension can be lifted and the juvenile is then institutionalized. The second type of juvenile probation is an "order of probation" issued by a juvenile court judge. Conditions are set by the court and an agreement to meet them is signed by the juvenile and his or her parents. Violations are referred to the juvenile court. The judge can establish a specific period of probation (e.g., one year), or the probation may be for an indeterminate period, which would make the youth subject to court supervision until the upper age limit of the juvenile court's jurisdiction, unless the probation is terminated earlier by the court. Both methods of probation can be used within the same juvenile court jurisdiction, with the suspension of the imposition of the disposition used in more serious cases.

A study of the length of juvenile probation conducted by the National Assessment of Juvenile Corrections found that the mean length of time the youths in the sample were placed on probation was 11.5 months. Approximately 25 percent of the probation officers surveyed noted that this length of time referred to active probation. Youths would not necessarily be discharged at the end of this time period, but rather would be placed on inactive status, in which case there are no required contacts with the court or probation officer, but the youth is still technically on probation. Keeping a youth on inactive status expedites the handling of youths who commit new offenses, since they are still under formal supervision of the juvenile court and some of the initial due process requirements can be bypassed.[5]

EXTENT OF PROBATION USE

For cases that are officially processed by the juvenile court, probation is the most frequent disposition. In 1996, in 57 percent of the cases informally processed that were not dismissed the youth agreed to a term of voluntary probation supervision and 41 percent agreed to other sanctions, such as voluntary restitution, community service, or referral to another agency.[6] Of those formally processed and adjudicated delinquent, 54 percent were given probation and 28 percent were given residential placement.[7] As shown in Table 14–1, the proportion of adjudicated delinquents receiving either residential placement or formal probation varied by age, sex, and race. It should be noted that the criminal histories of the youths and the severity of the offenses they committed may account for some of the variations recorded.

Scarpitti and Stephenson, who analyzed the social backgrounds, delinquency histories, and scores on a standard personality inventory of 1,210 boys who received dispositions from a juvenile court over a three-year period, discovered that 78 percent (943) received probation disposition, and that the number of court appearances, age at first court appearance, and number of times on probation had a greater influence than did the types of past offenses on whether the judge granted probation or

Table 14–1. Case Characteristics of Adjudicated Delinquents–1996

Case Characteristics	Percent of Adjudicated Delinquency Cases in 1996	
	Residential Placement	Formal Probation
All cases	28	54
Age		
13 or younger	23	60
14	29	56
15	30	55
16	30	52
17	27	50
Sex		
Male	29	59
Female	22	54
Race		
White	26	55
Black	32	52
Other	32	48

Source: Howard N. Snyder and Melissa Sickmund, *Juvenile Offenders and Victims: 1999 National Report.* (Washington, DC: Office of Juvenile Justice, 1999), 159.

required institutionalization. They also found that those granted probation were somewhat less antisocial, less delinquent, and better adjusted emotionally than those given more severe dispositions.[8]

In courts serving large metropolitan areas, hundreds of officers may be involved in juvenile probation activities, whereas a small rural jurisdiction may have a single, part-time officer. Caseloads may be set at 40 or 50 or expanded to several hundred. And because no nationally recognized qualifications or standards for probation officers have been established, their preparation and training may range from a college education and long experience as a specialist to no specific education or training at all for this type of work. Furthermore, the auxiliary court resources on which probation officers can draw are determined by the tone and philosophy set by the juvenile court judge, county or municipal budgets, the limitations of the court's physical plant, the degree of community knowledge of and involvement in the court's work, and the administrative and organizational abilities of court personnel.

ROLE OF THE PROBATION OFFICER

A probation officer wears many hats in the course of his or her duties. As a member of a specific probation department and a subordinate of a particular chief probation officer, he or she is committed to the defined goals of the department and satisfactory performance of specified duties within the department. In dealings with probationers, the officer must perform varied duties, including counseling, making referrals to service agencies, investigation of the probationers' activities, job or school placement assistance, mediation of family disputes, invocation of the court's authority, or reporting a youth's illegal behavior, which may result in probation being terminated. Role conflict can result when an officer who enters probation work because of a strong interest in helping others becomes so bogged down in report writing and other administrative duties that he or she is forced to handle the caseload in "assembly line" fashion.

Because of large caseloads and other pressures, probation officers in large jurisdictions may have to alter their role definitions. Miller made the point that probation officers, on the basis of the preparation for their positions, are not qualified to perform the wide range of services that many courts try to provide, including psychological therapy, recognition of health problems, interpretation of vocational testing, and other specialized tasks. He sees the probation officer redefined as a "broker," with the primary function of matching the probationers with treatment resources available in the community.[9]

The duties of a juvenile probation officer can be broadly categorized as investigation and supervision. As an investigator, the probation officer is responsible for completing the predisposition social history report and for providing an assessment of the risks this youth poses to the community and the specific needs of the probationer. In a supervisory capacity, the probation officer provides counseling and guidance to the youth and monitors his or her activities. Probation officers' caseloads may include youths who are on official probation after adjudication, others who are on informal probation as part of a diversion arrangement, and youths involved in restitution or community service.

THE PROBATION PROCESS

When a disposition of probation is granted to a juvenile offender, the youth is instructed to report within a short period of time to the probation officer assigned to the case. Even before this postdisposition interview takes place, however, a youth who has been granted probation may have had some exposure to, or even numerous interactions with, the juvenile court's probation personnel.

As noted in Chapter 13, the intake officer of a juvenile court is a probation officer who has been assigned to this specialty. Data on the juvenile gathered by this officer at the time of intake are available to the judge at the time the disposition decision is made. If the youth was previously involved in any sort of diversion program before official referral to the juvenile court, he or she may also have encountered probation officers who worked as diversion specialists. Such officers frequently serve as supervisors of volunteer-run diversion programs, or may themselves be the agents of diversion by working with youths judged as salvageable without formal court intervention. Probation personnel, under such titles as "street workers," "detached workers," "community workers," or "youth workers," make contact with and supervise youths who have been granted some type of diversion rather than official processing. Youths who are part of a court diversion program but are not officially adjudicated delinquent are placed in programs known as "unofficial" or "informal" probation. Under this form of supervision by the court, the youth's and the family's participation is voluntary; they agree to abide by the probation officer's recommendations without a formal court hearing.

Many courts have standardized informal probation to the extent that a child who has been accused of a delinquent act but has not had an adjudicatory hearing, the child's parents or guardian, and the supervising probation officer agree to the terms of informal probation by entering into a consent decree agreement. This written agreement lists the rules and activities that must be adhered to by the youth during a specific period of time and describes the consequences to the youth if the provisions are violated. It also states that at any time the youth may be released from the agreement and have the original charge of delinquency scheduled for a formal hearing before the juvenile court judge.

The Probation Officer as Investigator

Probationers may have had earlier contact with officers assigned to their cases when the predisposition investigation was conducted. In some courts, probation officers are trained and assigned to specialize in predisposition investigations; in others, officers are assigned to investigation or supervision activities according to current needs. As noted in Chapter 13, the predisposition investigation involves a detailed report on the youth's family situation, school record, social relationships, and previous offense record. The probation officer who prepares it may recommend a disposition in the report or may appear at the dispositional hearing to offer information and suggestions.

There are advantages and disadvantages in having the same probation officer conduct the predisposition investigation and supervise the probationer. It is advantageous in that the officer has been familiar with the case for a period of time and has more complete background information on the youth at the time the probation period begins; it is also advantageous because the juvenile realizes that this officer is aware of any past problems. Disadvantages include a possible transfer of the youth's negative feelings regarding the juvenile court experience to the probation officer who was a part of that experience, the juvenile's viewing the probation officer as a "law enforcement" rather than a "helping" person, and the lack of opportunity for the youth to make a "new start" with new counselors. Specialization in investigation or counseling may be a more efficient use of probation personnel, since officers may have special talents or training for one of these functions.

Some large juvenile courts use standardized case management systems to classify probationers on the basis of the potential risk they pose to the community and the extent of need for services they present. These are assessed through use of a "risk" instrument, (which weights the importance of such factors as prior felony convictions, substance abuse problems, and prior probation revocation) and a "needs" instrument (which weights the importance of peer associations, family situation, and school problems). An example of such instruments is given in Figure 14–1.

Based on the information gathered from these instruments, the youth is placed on a specific level of supervision, ranging from intensive to minimal. Once the youth's level is determined, case assignments may be made to officers who are specifically trained or skilled in working with youngsters who require a certain level of supervision.

The judge, with the assistance of the probation officer's predisposition report, can use great discretion in shaping an adjudicated youth's probation program. The judge may combine probation with other obligations, such as restitution to the offended party, involvement in a drug or alcohol rehabilitation program, or enrollment in a special school or work program. The judge may also make a disposition of probation contingent upon the juvenile's being placed in a halfway house or community residential facility, where he or she will be supervised by staff and visited by court personnel.

In addition to combining probation with other requirements, juvenile court judges have a good deal of discretion in setting up the rules for each juvenile's probation period.

Probation rules begin with a number of general behavior guidelines that apply to all juveniles on probation. Following is an example of general probation rules.

1. The Juvenile must obey all state, federal, and municipal laws.
2. The Juvenile must obey all rules, regulations, and orders of the parents.
3. The Juvenile must attend school, attend all classes, and obey all school rules and regulations until 18 years of age. A working permit issued by school authorities would be an exception to the above.
4. Use of intoxicating beverages and drugs is prohibited.
5. The Juvenile will develop and maintain a proper attitude and respect the rights and properties of others.
6. The Juvenile is to report to the Probation Officer as scheduled or immediately upon notice to the Juvenile or parents.
7. Permission must be given by the Probation Officer in order to leave Trumbull County.
8. Curfew for the Juvenile will be designated by the Probation Officer.
9. Violation of any of the foregoing rules must be reported to the Probation Officer immediately by the parents.[10]

Following the general rules of probation, specific regulations may be added. For example, association with a person who has been demonstrated to be a bad influence on the probationer may be forbidden, a youth who has been involved in car theft or joyriding may be prohibited from driving a car, or an exact curfew hour may be set. The constitutionality of some types of probation regulations, such as attending church services or prohibitions on dressing in a certain way, is open to question.

The length of a youth's assignment to probation supervision conforms to statutory regulations of the jurisdiction served by the particular juvenile court; it may vary

SUPERVISION RISK/CLASSIFICATION INSTRUMENT

SECTION 1 – IDENTIFYING DATA

_____
DATE COMPLETED

NAME _____   SS#/CIS _____
CASE MANAGER _____   DISTRICT _____

SECTION II – RISK ASSESSMENT   POINTS

A. INSTANT OFFENSE (_____)   _____
MOST SERIOUS

1.	Capital or Life felony	32 Points
2.	1st Degree Felony/2nd Degree Felony (Violent)	17 Points
3.	2nd Degree Felony	14 Points
4.	3rd Degree Felony	7 Points
5.	1st Degree Misdemeanor (Violent)	5 Points
6.	1st Degree Misdemeanor	3 Points
7.	2nd Degree Misdemeanor	1 Point

B. PRIOR HISTORY (Highest Applicable Score)   _____

1. Has met the Definition of a Serious Habitual Offender with this offense   6 Points
2. Two or more Prior Non-related Felonies Resulting in Adjudication or W/H Adjudication within the Previous 36 Months   3 Points
3. One Felony or two or more Non-related Misdemeanors Resulting in an Adjudication or W/H Adjudication in the Previous 36 Months   2 Points
4. One prior misdemeanor resulting in an adjudication or W/H adjudication within previous 36 months   1 Point

C. OTHER SCORING FACTORS (Combined score)
(Maximum 1 Point each unless noted)   _____

1. Current Legal Status 2 CC/F - 4 Committed   Point _____
2. Previous Technical Violation of Supervision   Point _____
3. Youth was 12 Years Old or under at the Time of 1st Diversion Placement or Adjudication (including W/H)   Point _____
4. Substance Abuse Involved   Point _____
5. History of Escape/Absconding   Point _____
6. Current or Previous JASP or Community Arbitration   Point _____

SECTION II – A + B + C =   SUB-TOTAL _____

Figure 14–1.   *State of Florida Delinquency Supervision and Risk Assessment Instrument, May 1, 1991.*

D. MITIGATING AND AGGRAVATING FACTORS   SUB-TOTAL _____

1. Mitigating (No More than 5 Pts. Total) Justification:

SUB-TOTAL D1 (-) _____

2. Aggravating (No More Than 5 Points Total) Justification:

SUB-TOTAL D2 (+) _____

A + B + C SUB-TOTAL - D1 + D2 =   TOTAL RISK SCORE _____

SECTION III – NEEDS ASSESSMENT

A. FAMILY RELATIONSHIP (Score highest in section)   _____

1. Parents Unwilling or Unable to Control Youth	3
2. Parent(s) Cooperative, Some Control (includes latch-key)	1
3. Parent(s) Cooperative, Relationships good	0
4. Youth in unstable independent living situation	2

B. PARENTAL DYSFUNCTIONS (Score total points in section)   _____

1. History of Abuse/Neglect	1
2. Parent w/Criminal History (if relevant)	1
3. Parent Mental Illness/Untreated	1
3. Parent Substance Abuse/Untreated	1
4. Out of home dependency placement	2
5. Current Abuse/Neglect/Under Investigation	3

C. PEER RELATIONSHIP (score total points in section)   _____

1. Socially Immature	1
2. Socially Withdrawn	1
3. Easily Led by Others	1
4. Exploits or is Aggressive to Others	2
5. Socially appropriate w/peers	0

D. SIGNIFICANT ADULT RELATIONSHIP (Scores highest within section)   _____

1. Youth relates well	0
2. Authority figure relationships are inconsistent	1
3. Youth is unable or unwilling to relate to outside adult authority figures	2

Figure 14–1. Continued

E. EDUCATIONAL (Score total points in section) _____

1. Poor Attendence   2
2. Disruptive School Behavior   2
3. Literacy Problems   2
4. Learning Disability/Special Ed. classes   1
5. Learning Disability/Identified - no services   3
6. Withdrawn/Expelled (under age 16)   2
7. Enrolled and Failing   2

F. YOUTH'S EMPLOYMENT (Score total points in section) _____

1. Currently Employed   0
2. Currently Developing Marketable Skills/No School   1
3. Needs to Develop Marketable Skills/No School   2
4. Currently Unemployed/Nor School   2

G. DEVELOPMENTAL DISABILITIES (Highest appropriate score within section) _____

1. Known Developmental Disabilities no services   3
2. Known Developmental Disabilities   2
2. None   3

H. PHYSICAL HEALTH AND HYGIENE (Score total points in section) _____

1. Medical or Dental Referral Needed   1
2. Needs Health or Hygiene Education   1
3. Handicap or Illness limits Functioning   2

I. MENTAL HEALTH (Score total points in section) _____

1. Assessment Needed   2
2. Prior Mental Health Placement History   2
3. Currently in Treatment/Residential   2
4. Currently in Treatment/Non-residential   3
5. Comprehensive Assessment indicates treatment
   needed residential or non-residential   3

J. SUBSTANCE ABUSE (Alcohol or Drug) (Score highest within section) _____

1. No Use   0
2. Occasional Use   1
3. Frequent Use   2
4. Assessment Needed   2

Figure 14–1. Continued

5. Comprehensive Assessment indicates treatment needed
   residential or non-residential   3
6. Currently in Treatment/Residential   2
7. Currently in Treatment/Non-residential   3

TOTAL NEEDS SCORE   _____

SECTION IV – RANGES AND CLASSIFICATIONS

Needs Scoring Ranges	Community Control Ranges	Commitment Ranges
0 - 13 Low Needs	Category A - 18 - 20	Level 8 - 32 +
14 - 20 Medium Service Needs	Category B - 14 - 17	Level 6 - 28 - 31
21 - 26 High Service Needs	Category C - 10- 13	Level 4 - 25 - 27
26 + Intensive Service Needs		Level 2 - 20 - 24

See Placement Grid, Attachment 2

Total Risk Score _____

Total Needs Score _____

Classification Decision _____

SECTION V – CASE MANAGER/COMMITMENT MANAGER OVERRIDE JUSTIFICATION

This section should be used when additional mitigating and/or aggravating factors are present which would indicate the need to override the level of classification indicated in Section IV. For the case manager override, supervisory approval is required. Override classification decision _____ Justification:

Figure 14–1. Continued

from six months all the way to termination at the upper age limit of the juvenile court's jurisdiction. Since the maximum potential for changing a youth's behavior is focused in the early stages of probation and a long-drawn-out period of probation may lead to resentment or discouragement, a maximum of two years might be an effective general guideline for the term of probation.

The Probation Officer as Supervisor

The initial interview with the probation officer is an important event in the probation process. It gives the officer an opportunity to review the juvenile court procedures with the child and the parents, explain the court's judgment, and spell out very clearly what the court's expectations are from this point on. Also at this time, the officer can define his or her role in the youth's probation adjustment, noting that these

TO THE CLIENT

You have been placed on intensive Probation, consisting of four Phases which you must complete before discharge from probation can occur. This is a program designed to help you in changing your behavior and avoiding further violation of the law. This program calls for the establishment of an **agreement** to identify terms of probation, methods and tools to be used and consequences for your behavior. While your Probation Counselor will press for changes in your behavior, parent(s)/guardian(s) and significant others will have to help out by actively participating in the program.

It is understood that you, your parent(s)/guardian(s) and significant others will carefully consider the terms of the agreement, discussing each provision with the Probation Counselor. When the agreement is signed, you, your parent(s)/guardian(s) and significant others will have agreed to fully participate in the services described herein unless and until a request for revision is made and granted.

PHASE I RULES

1. Conduct yourself according to the laws of this state, the United States, and any ordinances of the City or Village in which you live.

2. Obey your parents, teachers, guardians or custodians.

3. Conduct yourself in such a way as not to injure the morals or health of yourself or others.

4. You are not to go anywhere unless you are with a parent(s)/guardian(s). The only exceptions to this rule are going to and from school and the Probation Counselor's office.

5. You are not to have anyone at your house unless permission is given by parent(s)/guardian(s) and the Probation Counselor. This permission is only given when you comply with Phase rules and conditions.

6. You are to attend school regularly and on time. You will attend all your classes on time. Good behavior in the school and classroom is expected.

If you leave school early, you must go directly home. Illness is to be reported to school and Probation Counselor by 8:30 a.m. and verified by parent(s)/guardian(s).

7. You must learn Phase I rules and discuss them with the Team Leader.

8. You can earn your way out of house arrest by accumulating 30 good days to advance to Phase II.

Special Court Orders:

PROBATION CONDITIONS

While on house arrest you are being given the privilege to participate with your parent(s)/guardian(s) and Probation Counselor to define responsibilities and rules you must follow:

You will have the following responsibilites:

1.
2.
3.
4.
5.
6.

Your parent(s)/guardian(s) will have the following responsibilities:

1.
2.
3.
4.
5.
6.

Others responsibilities:

1.
2.
3.
4.
5.
6.

Figure 14-2. Phase I Behavior Contract. Cuyahoga Court of Common Pleas. *(Source: Cuyahoga County Juvenile Court "Intensive Probation Supervision: A Team Approach." [Cleveland, OH: Cuyahoga County Juvenile Court, 1996], mimeographed program description.)*

335

PROBATION AGREEMENT
PHASE I

NAME:

RECORD NUMBER:

CASE NUMBER:

ADDRESS:

TELEPHONE NUMBER:

SCHOOL:

GRADE: HOMEROOM NUMBER:

PARENT(S)/GUARDIAN(S):

HEARING DATE:

JUDGE/REFEREE:

CHARGES:

SPECIAL ORDERS:

PROBATION TEAM: PHONE NO:

NAMES:

THIS AGREEMENT IS:

A — ORIGINAL _____ DATE

B — REVISED _____ DATE

JC62061 3949

I, _____ , have discussed the conditions and terms of this agreement regarding my participation in Intensive Probation and agree to the following:

1. I will comply with all the rules and conditions set forth in the probation agreement.

2. I will provide accurate information about my progress.

3. I will keep all scheduled appointments with my Probation Counselor and others.

We, _____ , the parent(s)/guardian(s), agree to supervise our/my child under the rules and conditions of the Phase I agreement and further agree to:

1. Provide accurate information about the progress of our/my child.

2. We further agree to keep all scheduled appointments with the Probation Counselor and **others.**

_____
Date   Child

_____
Parent(s)/Guardian(s)

_____
Probation Counselor

CONSEQUENCE

Failure or compliance with the Phase rules and the conditions of probation will result in logical and progressive steps delivered by the Probation Counselor as follows:

Positive	Negative
1. Can earn up to 30 days to complete Phase I.	1. Not earning a day.
	2. Loss of Privileges.
	3. Loss of good days.
	4. Transport youth to office or Detention Center.

Privileges can be earned as follows:

Figure 14–2. Continued.

336

The initial interview often sets the tone for the probation officer-client relationship. *(Photo credit: Jay Paris)*

responsibilities include both supervision and counseling. The officer may discuss the parent's responsibilities with them, and if family counseling has been recommended by the judge or is requested by the family, plans for implementing it should be formulated. If the judge's disposition included instructions that restitution of some type be made, the probation officer will draw up a payment schedule at this time or work out a system whereby the youth will provide services to the injured party.

Another vital part of the initial interview is advising a youth of his or her responsibilities for reporting to the probation officer and for observing the general and specific rules set by the court. The officer may offer some encouragement that this period of supervision can be a helping experience, if the child cooperates. One function of the initial interview is to give the officer an opportunity to develop rapport with the youth.

The frequency of subsequent meetings between the probationer and the supervision officer depends upon the seriousness of the youth's problems and the size of the officer's caseload. At such meetings, goal setting is an effective device for allowing a juvenile to measure his or her progress and move toward release from probation. Goal setting is most effective if the goals set are attainable and are to be realized within a short period of time. Defining these goals should be the task of the probationer. They may be put in the form of a behavior contract, which sets certain specific rewards to be received when goals are achieved; for example, daily undisruptive attendance at school for a week may result in being released from home detention for one day during the weekend. Parents play an important role in such contracting, for they must be firm enough to withhold the desired reward if the youth does not fulfill the obligations. The achievement of realistic, short-term goals provides the probationer with feelings of success and is more helpful than working toward such abstract goals as "becoming a better person" or "changing my ways."

A youth's limitations must also be recognized in setting goals and promising rewards. A young person whose academic ability would be reflected by a C level at maximum cannot be promised rewards for getting all B grades within the next school marking period, since this is obviously an unattainable goal.

As part of the interaction between the probation officer and the probationer, the young person should be made aware of the consequences of conforming and also of the consequences of not conforming.

After considerable research and analysis of what works and what fails in the rehabilitation of delinquents, the specific method or technique applied has been found to be not as crucial in determining the outcome of the process as are the attributes of the people who occupy probation officer positions. Officers from a wide variety of educational, social, and philosophical backgrounds have demonstrated that they can successfully reach young people and assist them with their problems and needs. What works for one officer may not be viable for another. Some may be successful with group sessions in a structured setting, whereas the personalities, temperaments, and basic orientations of others would not be conducive to success using this method. Some officers may take a "buddy" position; others are more authoritarian; and some are successful in the role of rather formal, detached listeners. What seem to be the crucial ingredients are honesty and being oneself.

Stratton noted that some probation officers become "con artists" in their dealings with clients. Their phoniness might take the form of maintaining a superior attitude and preaching to clients; trying to impress clients with their culture, image, clothes, or knowledge of street language and happenings; using meetings as mere social exchanges rather than occasions for providing help; doing things for their clients that they should be made to do for themselves, thereby developing an unhealthy dependency; or assuring a youth that certain rules do not have to be adhered to "to the letter" and then showing inconsistency by punishing the child for minor rule violations. In contrast to this, Stratton characterized a true therapeutic encounter between probation officer and youth as one in which "there is the opportunity for having honest expression of thought and feelings, regardless of the discomforts to either person involved in the relationship, whether it be the officer or the person he supervises."[11]

Of the variety of tools available to a probation officer in seeking to change the behavior of probationers or inhibit future misbehavior, the most powerful is the threat of institutionalization. A youth who is placed on probation is frequently returned to the same setting and associates with the same peer group that contributed to his or her problems with the juvenile court. But now the price to be paid for repeating the previous behavior is loss of freedom. The probation officer must impress upon the youth the necessity for changing his or her behavior or suffering this fate.

The position of the probation officer as the person who "checks up on" a probationer, either personally or through contacts with the schools, other agency representatives, or parents, may inhibit to some degree the establishment of a trusting relationship with the probationer. A youth may decide to conceal from the officer information that will make him or her "look bad," even though talking over existing problems might be the best way to move toward better adjustment. Parents also may conceal information from the probation officer and the juvenile court, for fear that the child's probation will be revoked. The officer too may play upon the authoritarian aspects of his or her position in attempts to gain respect and control if "helping" efforts have proved ineffective. Thus, the probation officer, who ideally acts as a representative of the court with a mandate to provide assistance and support as well as supervision, may find the supervision facet of the role taking precedence over other aspects or even interfering with his or her success in providing assistance and support.

In jurisdictions where the judge, police, school officials, or citizens exert considerable vocal pressure for control of juvenile offenders, a probation officer may find it necessary to devote a disproportionate amount of time to probationers who are "troublemakers," constantly keeping them under surveillance or checking on them while granting little attention to other youths who are not committing violations or creating any disturbances but who are badly in need of attention. In such dilemmas, the referral of such youths to other agencies may help to equalize the provision of services.

The influence of probation officers and their services to the community may extend far beyond the officer-probationer relationship. Effective probation work may help alleviate school problems and make the families of probationers more aware of the assistance available to them through community service agencies. A probation supervisor in a juvenile court serving a metropolitan area made this observation with regard to probation work:

> I feel one of the most overlooked aspects of probation, and where I feel it is most effective, is in the area of prevention. You may be helping other youths, younger siblings that are . . . in a predelinquent status, or just helping the family resolve some other crises they have which they would otherwise not be able to handle to have assistance with if their child was not involved with the court. There is no way of measuring that success.[12]

Over the years he has been involved in juvenile justice work, probation supervisor Tom Cerne has experienced a wide range of approaches to dealing with juvenile offenders. At the beginning of his career, the "medical model" was in vogue. The emphasis was on individualized treatment for the juvenile offenders and on providing services to their families. At that time, delinquency was viewed as a social problem and the youth's family situation, including the physical and social environment, was considered to be related to the youth's misbehavior. Later, he saw the court and the juvenile justice system move toward the "retribution model," with more emphasis on punishment and less concern about treatment. He stated that currently:

> The court has taken in a "restorative justice" approach. There is much greater emphasis on the rights of the victims. The court works hand in hand with the victim assistance programs and the judge has appointed a court liaison person who notifies the victims on all matters

pertaining to their cases. By law, a victim has the right to complete a Victim Impact State-ment if the offense committed by the juvenile is of a serious felony nature. If the offender is sent to a Department of Youth Services institution, the Victim Impact Statement is sent along and the victim must be notified when the youth is released from the institution.[13]

Cerne also mentioned that the Domestic Violence Offense statute that has been en-acted in his state has had a dramatic effect on the way some juveniles are processed. Police are required to make an arrest if the act falls within the statute's definition of domestic violence. He contends that some parents use domestic violence as a club against their children. He stated:

> Most of the cases of youths charged with domestic violence that I see involve slapping, shov-ing, or threatening parents. Usually no medical attention is involved. In the past, we could work with the youth and the parents to try to get them to solve their problems without hav-ing to resort to formal court intervention. Now we must make these cases formal.[14]

Intensive Probation

Juvenile court administrators have come to realize that the amount of supervision and assistance needed by youths placed on probation differs from one client to an-other. Some probationers are able to make successful adjustments without much contact with the supervising officer. Experienced officers are able to assess the needs of various youths and adjust the intensity of their contacts with them accordingly, freeing additional time for contacts with multiproblem youths who most need their help.

Intensive probation is used in many courts as a substitute for institutionalization. It is grounded in the belief that, if juvenile offenders are closely supervised and given very strict rules and regulations to follow, the community can be protected. Probation officers who are assigned to intensive probation programs will generally have small caseloads, ranging from 10 to 25 probationers per officer. In addition to the frequent supervision, intensive probation may involve home detention (house arrest) or requir-ing the youths to wear electronic devices that monitor their movements.

Many of the larger juvenile court systems, which process thousands of cases each year, have adopted standardized case classification procedures using "risk" and "needs" instruments similar to the measurements discussed earlier in this chapter. In one court, probationers are placed into supervision categories (intensive, high, medium, and low), based on probability of recidivism, as measured by standardized case classification instruments. Those identified as potential chronic offenders, who show a very high risk for recidivism, are placed in the intensive supervision category.[15]

Those assigned to intensive supervision are serviced by a team of officers made up of a team leader, two surveillance officers, and a probation counselor. Each team provides services to approximately 30 clients. In the beginning, the surveillance offi-cer has daily contact with the probationer and the probation counselor provides weekly counseling services to the client and the family. The frequency of contacts is reduced as progress is demonstrated. The team leader supervises, coordinates, and evaluates these case services.[16]

PROBATION REVOCATION

If a youth violates the conditions of probation or is involved in new illegal activity, probation can be revoked. Generally, the supervising probation officer will receive information that the juvenile has been arrested or will become aware of violations of conditions or probation while conducting routine supervision. The probation officer will then prepare a report of the violations, which includes a recommendation as to whether the juvenile should be brought into court to discuss the violations and whether revocation of probation should be sought. Minor violations usually do not result in revocation, but may bring about the assignment of additional conditions of probation. If the violations made known to the court are very serious, or if new offenses have occurred, a youth's probation may be revoked by the juvenile court judge. Institutionalization will probably be the result.

The decision to revoke probation is based on a substantial violation of the general or special rules of probation. For example, the commission of another delinquent act or violation of a court order to attend school could result in revocation. In *Mempa* v. *Rhay* (1967), the U.S. Supreme Court ruled that an adult probationer charged with a violation of his probation had a right to have an attorney present at the revocation hearing.[17] In *Morrisey* v. *Brewer* (1972), the Court granted the accused due process rights at a probation hearing.[18] However, the actual right to have a hearing, if revocation of probation is being considered, was not established by the Court until 1973, in *Gagnon* v. *Scarpelli*. In that case, the Court decided that the accused had a right to both a preliminary and a final hearing on a violation of probation charge.[19] Although none of these cases specifically involved juveniles, the courts have generally conceded that the rulings extend to juveniles and most juvenile courts have incorporated these rights into the juvenile justice process.

ALTERNATIVE COMMUNITY-BASED SUPERVISION

As research began to reveal that there are limitations in the probation approach, some courts and communities began combining probation with other rehabilitation programs. A youth might be assigned to probation coupled with a work program, a highly structured group counseling program, foster home placement, or placement in a community residential treatment center.

Early Experiments with Community-Based Services for Delinquents

The first community-based programs for juveniles emphasized treatment using behavior modification, guided group interaction, or reality therapy. (These treatment modalities will be described in detail in Chapter 17.) The programs were operated under the auspices of the juvenile court or of the state's youth authority and the youths were under probation supervision. Community-based supervision followed the principle of "minimization of penetration"; that is, the least restrictive alternative disposition was chosen for offenders to give them only the penetration into the juvenile justice system necessary to change their behavior and protect the community. Often the juvenile courts were given subsidies to develop treatment programs for youths in community settings as an alternative to placing them in institutions.

The Provo Experiment.   One of the earliest programs that employed intensive community-based treatment began in Provo, Utah, in 1959. LaMar Empey developed a system of group counseling in which the youths themselves set the standards for all members of the group. The program, limited to 20 habitual delinquents, used the technique of guided group interaction. Under staff guidance, the youths set group standards. They were permitted to participate in problem-solving interaction and involved in decisions regarding discipline, responsibilities of group members, and even the readiness of those in the group for release from the program.[20]

Research on all subjects released from the Provo Experiment for up to four years after release (the point where most of them reached the legal age of adulthood) showed that in the long run, the Provo Experimental Program did not prove to be greatly superior to regular probation in terms of postrelease recidivism. It was shown, however, to be clearly superior to institutionalization. When compared with matched groups of youths who were institutionalized during the same period, the boys in the Provo Experiment had "significantly fewer arrests, their offenses were less serious, and far fewer of them were confined for adult crimes."[21]

Kentfields.   Another program conducted in a community setting relied on the application of the theories and principles of the treatment technique known as "behavior modification." The Kentfields Rehabilitation Program had the goals of increasing desirable behavior and drastically reducing deviant behavior through the use of behavior modification, of providing a less costly alternative to institutionalization, and of reintegrating the boys into the community as productive members. The Kentfields Program attacked the problem of delinquency through four tactics: work projects, group sessions, monitoring of home behavior, and reintegration into the community. The work projects involved four hours of work, four days each week. The work was graded each hour by a supervisor and the boys were given points according to the quality of their work performance. Monitoring of home behavior included contracts between the parents and the boy that were evaluated through the use of charts kept each day and collected weekly. The reintegration aspect of the Kentfields Program involved each boy's choosing a goal when he reached the highest level of the program and working toward its achievement. Goals included return to school, job placement, or vocational training.[22]

The California Youth Authority's Community Treatment Project.   The California Youth Authority's Community Treatment Project tried yet another treatment approach. The project, begun in 1961, selected youths from the juvenile courts in California. The project participants were allowed to remain in the community either in their own homes, or in foster or group homes; received intensive services from their probation officers, particularly in the early stages of their probation; and were assisted by the officers in obtaining needed community services. A youth's involvement in the program extended for a period of about two years.

A follow-up of the juveniles involved in the first 12 years of the program revealed that it had resulted in less recidivism overall than institutionalization had, but that it was not equally effective with all types of offenders. Some youths were handled most successfully by beginning their treatment in a medium-sized residential facility and then transferring them to community treatment. "Power-oriented" youths (gang members, cultural identifiers) were found to be treated more effectively by institutionalization than by community treatment.[23]

The community treatment programs used today, like these earlier programs, tend to base their approaches on one or several treatment modalities. However, current programs tend to focus on a specific type of offender (e.g., drug or sex offenders) rather than placing youths with varying problems together in the same treatment program.

Current Community Supervision Programs

Another characteristic of current community supervision programs is an emphasis on accountability. Youths are required to show that they are abiding by the rules set for them, and, in some instances, must make reparation for their offenses by community service or other types of restitution.

Home Detention. In a number of courts, probation supervision is supplemented by home detention. Home detention programs are utilized in lieu of institutionalization for juvenile offenders who need more supervision than can normally be given under the conventional probation plan.

A youth placed in home detention is contacted on a daily basis. In exchange for being allowed to live at home, he or she is subjected to an extensive list of rules, which are rigidly enforced. A contract between the youth and the counselor is written up in some home detention programs. The rules include attending school, obeying a curfew, and keeping parents and the probation officer informed of his or her activities.

The Home Detention Project of the Cuyahoga County Juvenile Court receives youths before or after adjudication. Both male and female status and delinquent offenders are referred. The program uses behavior modification and requires the youths and their parents to sign behavior contracts that detail the conditions of probation and the behavior expected. A caseworker makes frequent contacts with the child and provides counseling, when needed. Behavior at home and in school is carefully monitored and checks are made with the court to see if any new offenses have occurred.

Evaluation of a random sample of youths who were referred to the program over a five-year period revealed that 82 percent of the home detention students were rated as successes, since they did not require placement in the detention center, were available for their court appearances, did not commit new offenses, and did not violate their behavior contracts. The success rates were lower for females than males and lower for status than for delinquent offenders. The least successful cases proved to be unruly girls and this was attributed to the fact that they tended to have rather severe emotional problems or problems related to their home situations. The easiest youths to supervise, surprisingly, proved to be older male youths who had committed offenses that could have resulted in institutionalization, and some of these had been previously institutionalized.[24] The evaluators concluded that the number of caseworker-youth contacts was significant in determining the success of the program.

Restitution and Community Service.   In instances where the offenses committed by juveniles involve property damage, property loss, or personal injuries to victims, restitution programs are increasingly being used as a method of holding the juvenile offenders responsible for their actions.

In restitution programs, youths involved in offenses that have resulted in property damage or personal injury are required to work at job sites chosen by the court. They receive no payment. Instead, the amount they earn, usually the minimum wage, is held until the figure set by the court as payment to the victim is reached. The victim then receives the restitution payment from the court. This completes the youth's activity.

A national survey of juvenile restitution programs found that all states and the District of Columbia had at least one restitution or community service program. The majority of programs identified by this survey involved both financial restitution and community service (75%).[25] In about one fourth of the programs, direct victim-offender mediation was involved.[26] The structures and management of the programs varied considerably. The larger majority of the programs were under the control of juvenile courts. However, some were administered by private or public nonprofit organizations.[27]

Community service is another disposition available in lieu of probation or in conjunction with probation. Community service programs are closely related to restitution, since they hold a youth accountable for delinquent behavior by requiring work as compensation. In community service, however, the victim does not receive a direct cash payment. Instead, the offender is required to complete some type of public service. For example, a youth involved in school vandalism may be required to help repair the damages. In most cases, however, the offender is required to work as a volunteer at a hospital or other type of health care facility or to engage in cleanup or maintenance work at public parks or buildings. No direct payment of the youth's wages is made to either the victim or the court. The judge can require the youth or his or her parents to pay damages to the victim up to the amount allowed by law.

Community-service programs are less expensive to operate than restitution, since they do not involve the amount of paperwork or the intensive levels of offender supervision needed for restitution programs. They provide some of the same benefits, including development of a feeling of personal responsibility and good work habits. The community receives the benefit of the work completed and is also made aware that youthful offenders are being held responsible for their actions.

Although administrators and staffers of restitution and community service programs are highly enthusiastic about their effectiveness, little research is available to

Community service programs benefit both the youth and the community. *(Photo credit: Eckerd Youth Alternatives)*

compare the recidivism rates of youths involved in the programs with those for offenders handled in other ways. One study evaluated experiments in four juvenile courts in which youths were randomly assigned to restitution programs, some of which also involved community service, or given traditional sanctions. In two of the courts, those ordered to pay restitution or perform community service had lower recidivism than those not assigned to such programs. In a third court, the number of cases assigned was too small to draw conclusions, while in the fourth there was no difference in the recidivism of those given restitution/community service and those given other dispositions.[28]

Specialized Treatment Programs

Many community-based programs focus on juveniles who have committed specific types of offenses, with criteria for involvement based on the exhibition of unacceptable behavior or symptoms. The programs are structured to provide specially developed treatment and counseling.

Family Counseling. The evidence is quite clear that the majority of youths who are processed through the juvenile courts come from dysfunctional families. Those who work with probationers recognize the need to elicit the cooperation of parents, but

The Summit County Child Responsibility Project

The Summit County (Ohio) Child Responsibility Project is an example of a highly successful court-administered program. Offenders between the ages of 12 and 17 who have committed offenses for which restitution can be made are required to work at job sites until the amount owed is paid. This takes approximately 115 hours of work over a six-week period. There is a limit of $600 per offense on the amount a youth must pay back through the project and no juvenile may be referred to the program more than three times. Victims must present valid proof of loss and the parents of the participating youth must agree to the program's conditions.

According to Nicholas DelGrosso, the director of the project, between 500 and 550 youths are placed in the program each year. The offenses committed by these youths include offenses against property, theft, and personal injury. A large number of these would be felony offenses if committed by adults. Nearly one fourth of the youths referred to the project are females and their offenses are similar to those committed by males. For some of these youths, referral to the Child Responsibility Project is the only sanction they receive and they are not under the supervision of probation officers. Others involved in the project have been placed on probation and are under supervision in addition to this sanction.

At the job sites, the youths are monitored by the program staff. Three work crews of five youths and one supervisor are assigned to various job sites, predominantly public institutions (schools) or public recreations facilities (city parks). DelGrosso stated:

In the past we had employees of the job site agencies supervise the youths. We had to drop that because those we place today are much younger and tend to have disciplinary and emotional problems. They need very close supervision. Sometimes when they were doing janitorial work in a school the custodian who was supervising them was preoccupied and the youths would go into classrooms and steal things. We now have our own staff doing the monitoring. Currently, we pick up the youths at their homes, take them to the work sites, and transport them back home after the work is completed.

One major problem is that we do not get much support or backing from many of the parents. If we report to the parents that a youth is troublesome at the work site and/or reluctant to work they regard this as our problem, not theirs.

The Ohio Department of Youth Services requires a yearly statistical report on the program. Del Grosso reported that, six months after completing the program, almost 90 percent of the youths had no new referrals to the juvenile court.

A recent addition to the original program is community service. DelGrosso noted:

For some youths, there is no victim to compensate, but the judge felt that community service would be an appropriate way to emphasize the restorative justice approach being followed by the court. Such youths are obligated to complete 20 hours of community service. They are placed in the same work crews as those in the restitution facet of the project

Such a program has a variety of benefits. In addition to having to pay compensation to the victims, the youths are introduced to a work experience and the concept of accountability. DelGrosso noted that this type of program improves the image of the justice system in the community because the victims are made to feel that the court really cares about them. The self-image of the youths is also improved because they experience a sense of satisfaction when the have paid off the debt. Parents are relieved that they themselves do not have to pay the damages. Also, many of the juveniles referred to the program come from homes where unemployment is the norm. The youth's exposure to the work ethic and introduction to work habits may lead to changes in expectations and goals.

This material is based on an interview with Nicholas DelGrosso, Director of the Summit County Juvenile Court Child Responsibility Project. The interview was conducted by Peter C. Kratcoski on November 18, 2002.

they also recognize the difficulties involved. Dr. Jacqueline Y. Warren, counseling psychologist and family therapist in a family counseling program, observed:

> Our families do not meet the traditional definition of the two-parent family that usually comes to mind when we speak of families. Juveniles who are involved in the juvenile justice system usually come from single-parent homes where a female, usually the mother, is head of the household. Many of these single mothers have not graduated from high school and finances are strained. Many of these mothers either have low-paying jobs or are on public assistance. Most of these parents are overwhelmed with many children and/or other problems. Some are reluctant to get involved and have no motivation to help their children. Others feel they are being punished for having children involved in the juvenile justice system. However, a small proportion of parents will become involved with their juveniles in a therapeutic setting once a therapist has taken the time to explain how it would be beneficial. I always tell the parents that their being involved shows the juveniles that their parents care about them.[29]

Another consideration is that in some instances the parents themselves are partially responsible for the youth's misbehavior. For example, a girl may run away from home to escape sexual abuse by a father or stepfather. In these instances, the court may make a disposition that requires both the youth and the parents to take part in family counseling.

The family counseling program operated by the Cuyahoga County (Ohio) Juvenile Court is designed for youths whose families appear to have the potential to benefit from involvement. Both delinquent and status offenders may be referred. The counseling consists of weekly sessions over a 12-week period, with the goal of reducing or eliminating unacceptable behavior by improving communications between juveniles and their parents, developing parenting skills, and enhancing the quality of the supervision the youths receive.[30] Most of the parents who become involved are females. Separate and joint sessions are held for the parents and youths and here family-related factors that are problematic are discussed. Dr. Jacqueline Y. Warren, who has worked with this program since it began, noted that there is evidence it has been successful in "helping the parents establish boundaries in the home setting and being consistent in rules and discipline toward their juveniles."[31]

Substance Abuse Counseling.   Many youths referred to juvenile courts display substance abuse problems. Analysis of data from The National Longitudinal Survey of Youth 1997 revealed that, among youths between the ages of 12 and 16, 40 percent had smoked cigarettes; 30 percent had drunk alcoholic beverages; 21 percent had used marijuana; 5 percent had sold marijuana; and 3 percent had sold hard drugs such as cocaine, LSD, or heroin at least once.[32] In many instances where juveniles come to the court's attention for other offenses (violent behavior, crimes against property), drug or alcohol use is also a factor.

In summarizing the characteristics of adolescent substance users, Chaiken and Johnson noted that about half of such youths only abuse alcohol, but approximately a third use both alcohol and marijuana and slightly over 10 percent use multiple drugs.[33]

Although many adolescent substance users and abusers never come to the attention of the juvenile courts, Chaiken and Johnson commented:

> Two types of adolescents described do require more juvenile justice resources: the small number of the most seriously drug-involved who are already coming to the frequent attention of police and juvenile authorities and the few young high-rate violent dealers who evade arrest for most of their crimes. Unless they are identified and diverted into programs that provide the context and skills for more constructive lifestyles, research indicates that both groups are more likely than any other type of delinquent to continue committing crimes as adults, including numerous violent offenses and vast numbers of drug deals.[34]

The juvenile court's response to juvenile substance abuse depends on the degree of the youth's involvement with drugs and the severity of the delinquency in which he or she has engaged. For many, the misbehavior is so serious that incarceration in a juvenile justice facility is required and substance abuse treatment is offered in that setting. For those whose primary difficulty is the substance abuse itself, residential treatment in a facility that focuses on that specific problem may be necessary. A survey of the ages of persons in drug or alcohol units revealed that six percent of them (nearly 44,000 clients) were under 18 years of age.[35] Some hospitals have detoxification units for adolescents and hospital-related programs may involve intensive individual and group therapy. Many drug and alcohol treatment programs use ex-addicts as counselors and participation in Alcoholics Anonymous or Drug Abusers Anonymous may be part of the program.[36]

For youths with less severe substance abuse problems, treatment can be offered in the community, either through programs that youths attend while living at home or in conjunction with placement in a nonsecure community residential facility. The specific nature of the treatment is related to the level of dependency on drugs or alcohol. In most cases community-based substance abuse treatment is coupled with probation supervision and family counseling, educational counseling, or community service may also be required by the court. Specific treatment techniques for substance abusers are discussed in Chapter 17.

Programs for Sex Offenders.   Determining the appropriate treatment for adolescent sex offenders is very difficult. The factors underlying this behavior are difficult to pinpoint and, in fact, there is disagreement as to whether some adolescent sex-related misbehavior should be considered deviant. As Stops and Mays observed:

The special problems of adolescent sexually abusive male youths have been consistently un-
deracknowledged, neglected, or often responded to inappropriately. More often than not,
such behaviors are dismissed as sexual curiosity or experimentation, interpreted as purely situational in nature, or excused because they are perceived as part of the normal aggressiveness of a sexually maturing adolescent.[37]

Those who have worked with adolescent sex offenders feel that treatment is
most effective if it is mandated by the juvenile court because offenders are more
likely to attend the sessions if they are required to do so. Steen and Monnette observed that community treatment rather than residential treatment is appropriate for
lower-risk sex offenders because of the high cost of residential treatment, the stigma-
tizing and disruptive effect on the child's life of being placed in such treatment, and
because the youth must be able to apply new and more appropriate behavior patterns
that are developed in therapy at home and in school.[38]

Group therapy is frequently successfully used with sex offenders. In addition to
its cost efficiency, group therapy brings some of the shame and secrecy connected
with these offenses out into the open for group discussion and the group setting addresses the social isolation and difficulties in communicating with peers that are
characteristic of such youths.[39]

In addition to group counseling, other treatment strategies for sex offenders include behavior modification, reality therapy, and individual psychological counseling. Normally, the more intensive forms of treatment for adolescent sex offenders are
reserved for institutional use. These treatment strategies are described in Chapter 17.

Services for Multiproblem Youths

Those who are involved in the management and administration of youth service
agencies, including physical and mental health facilities, recreation programs, drug
and/or alcohol treatment centers, family counseling services, welfare work, or juvenile justice agencies, are well aware of the fact that a sizable number of the youths
they serve are multiproblem adolescents. In a survey of youths who were being served
by one or more public or private agencies in a midwestern state, it was found that 28
percent of the youths had five or more problems in the areas of school, family, health,
substance abuse, mental health, or legal needs and an additional 27 percent had four
problems in these areas.[40]

If an agency follows the course of trying to work on all problems identified in a
particular youth, the result may be to spread available personnel and resources so
thin that little is actually accomplished. In addition, staff members may feel uncom-
fortable or inadequate when called upon to provide assistance in areas outside their
professional expertise. If administrators caution personnel to provide services only in
the area in which the agency specializes, the staff may be prohibited from providing
services or accepting clients for problems beyond these parameters. In such cases,
other difficulties experienced by multiproblem youths may be identified, but ignored.

The Neighborhood Network Center.   In Lansing, Michigan, community policing efforts in one of the city's most troubled neighborhoods led to the development of a

multi-agency team, composed of representatives of the schools; public health, mental health, and social services; and the juvenile court.[41]

The problem-solving team meets weekly to discuss such concerns as apparent drug-dealing activity in the neighborhood, vandalism, truancy, family violence incidents, or child neglect. Problem youths and their families are identified and efforts are made to intervene in their lives in a positive way. The type of assistance given and their progress are reviewed at subsequent team meetings.

A network for interagency referrals was developed and neighborhood and school-based social events are used to bring area residents together. Special youth activities provided include High Adventure Groups—clubs for up to 10 boys or girls in the fifth grade who are from single-parent families. The groups meet each week and have an outing each month. Big Brothers and Sisters recruits adult volunteers to work with the young people in their groups.

The Network also supervises youths assigned to community service as part of their case dispositions from the juvenile court. Youths may work individually at janitorial or secretarial work at the Center or in work crews involved in neighborhood clean up or beautification. College interns serve as supervisors of these youths.

Although no formal evaluation of the Network's effectiveness has been made, reported offenses in the area have declined each year since the Network was formed. The many volunteers involved in this program—including local residents, college students, and representatives of area businesses and churches—are regarded as key factors in the program's success.[42]

Community Residential Treatment

The home situations of some delinquent or status offenders may be evaluated by the court as inadequate, inappropriate, or even dangerous. This may occur when parents lack the ability or inclination to care for or supervise their children or when situations in the home, such as alcohol or drug abuse, family conflicts, or sexual abuse, threaten the welfare of juveniles. Nonsecure residential facilities operated or approved by the court meet the needs of such children. Foster homes and group homes are examples of such facilities. Some are designed to serve dependent, abused, or neglected children, while others may be used for status or delinquent offenders.

Foster care refers to the placement of a juvenile in a residential setting outside his or her own home where adults assume the role of parents. Foster parents may take children on a temporary, emergency basis for short periods of time or may assume long-term responsibility for them. Some foster parents will accept only one child at a time, while others have working arrangements with the court to house several children. The Task Force on Juvenile Justice and Delinquency Prevention recommended that foster homes be limited to one to four beds and that the facilities be located in close proximity to the community from which the delinquent population using the home is drawn.[43]

Since the youths placed in foster homes are not likely to pose any danger to the community, the atmosphere and programs in such facilities should represent as closely as possible a parent-child relationship, with emphasis on having the youths develop trust, respect, and affection toward those assuming the role of surrogate parents. Juvenile probation agencies use foster care for juveniles who have severe family problems but who still voluntarily respond to an adult's supervision.

Foster parenting is a very demanding job. Children placed in foster homes generally have had negative experiences in their own homes and often have experienced rootless movement from relative to relative, or agency to agency, or even periods of institutional placement. Since the need for foster homes and foster parents exceeds the availability, many children who could benefit from such placement are denied the opportunity. According to a study by the Office of Juvenile Justice and Delinquency Prevention, foster-home placements are most likely to be successful if the foster mother

1. Grew up in a family with a number of brothers and sisters and was an elder or the eldest child in her family;
2. Has had experience caring for a child not her own for several weeks, both day and night;
3. Shows skill and understanding in handling a number of specific behavior incidents typical of schoolage children and in understanding and handling the hypothetical behavior problems shown by a "defiant" and "withdrawn" child;
4. Discusses each of her own children as distinct individuals.

The study found that a successful foster father

1. Grew up in a family with a number of siblings;
2. Expresses warmth in talking about his own father and describes his father as affectionate toward him;
3. Indicates favorable attitudes toward having a social worker visit the home and make definite suggestions regarding the handling of the foster child;
4. Shows understanding and skill in responding to specific behavior incidents and in understanding and handling a "defiant" child and a child who is "careless with his clothes and the furniture in his foster home";
5. Focuses on the foster child's problems, such as adjusting to a strange situation, in talking about what might be difficult in being a foster parent;
6. Reports that he and his wife together make major decisions in the family, rather than either of them having greater authority.

Additional factors that contribute to successful foster placement include circumstances in which

1. The foster child becomes the youngest child in the family group;
2. There are no preschool children in the home;
3. The foster child's natural family retains parental rights, rather than there being a transfer of custody to guardianship;

4. The social worker available to make and supervise the placement has had at least several years experience in the field and is able to have several contacts with the prospective foster parents to prepare them for the placement.[44]

Group home placement is another option available to the court for youths when removal from the home situation is indicated. Group homes are somewhat larger facilities than foster homes and feature round-the-clock availability of residential and treatment staff members who work in shifts and may not reside at the facility on a full-time basis. Such homes are used for adolescents who have difficulty adjusting to foster care because of behavior difficulties, who have experienced unsuccessful foster care placement in the past, who require more intensive supervision and treatment than foster parents can provide, and who seem to make a better adjustment to life with a group of peers than to a traditional family setting. Group homes in the community that receive delinquent offenders provide more extensive supervision of the youths and are termed "staff secure" facilities. Although the doors may not be locked from the inside and the facility does not normally have an outside fence, there is 24-hour staff supervision of the residents, with the youths in someone's vision at all times. The Task Force on Juvenile Justice and Delinquency Prevention recommended that group homes be limited in size to 4 to 12 beds and that they be located close to the community from which the residents come.[45]

In group home settings, the development of constructive interpersonal relationships with adults and peers is stressed and decisions about daily life, conduct, discipline, and home activities are made in discussions between residents and staff members. Diagnostic and treatment services are provided by the staff members or through referrals to cooperating agencies. Participation of the group home residents in school and community events is stressed. The activities of the group home are carried out within the boundaries of the supporting agency's guidelines and the requirements for the residents' behavior set by the juvenile court.

THE EFFECTIVENESS OF PROBATION AND OTHER COMMUNITY-BASED ALTERNATIVES

It is obvious that probation is not the panacea or ideal disposition for all types of offenders. The concept of minimization of penetration entails involving a youth in the juvenile justice system to the least degree necessary to effect positive behavioral changes. Although institutionalization should be used only as a last resort according to this principle, it appears to be the only viable disposition for some youths. Between probation and institutionalization, various levels of structured supervision and treatment may be utilized. According to Bernstein, the key to working successfully with more difficult delinquents is to "develop systematically a plan that is carefully tailored for the individual juvenile"—a plan balancing the degree of danger the youth presents to the community with the development of strategies to provide the services the youth needs in an appropriate physical setting.[46]

It is very difficult to determine the effects of supervision on probationers because other factors in the youth's life may also have exerted influences on his or her behavior. Family members, peers, teachers, and other persons in the young person's life may have helped produce behavior changes. In addition, the likelihood that the youth will be able to avoid additional offenses is, to some extent, predictable at the time assignment to probation occurs. Therefore, the success of some probationers in specific programs may be related to their selection for inclusion to enhance the possibility of successful outcomes, so that grant money to continue the programs is assured.

Studies that have attempted to measure the effectiveness of probation have yielded contradictory findings. An examination and comparison of five studies of male and female juvenile offenders placed on probation showed that those who received more intensive probation supervision had lower rates of recidivism.[47] Three studies that measured recidivism in terms of rearrest for a new offense reported recidivism rates of from 34 to 41 percent for those in special programs, as compared to rates of 38 to 44 percent for those in control groups.[48] But one study produced the surprising finding that in a sample of 2,290 juvenile offenders, those who received *no special probation treatment* had *lower rates* of recidivism than those who had contact with probation officers.[49]

If probation is coupled with other types of supervision, such as house arrest, family counseling, substance abuse counseling, or group home residency, the likelihood of positive behavior changes increases. An evaluation of an intensive supervision program revealed that 57 percent of the juveniles supervised did not recidivate during a one-year period.[50]

After reviewing 17 research studies of juvenile probation effectiveness, Romig concluded that the studies did not demonstrate probation is an effective means of eliminating or reducing delinquent behavior. He did express the opinion, however, that reduction of delinquent behavior should not be the sole criterion used in evaluating the success or failure of probation activity, since services such as counseling or job training given to the youth and/or the family may show long-term benefits and reduce the chances that the youth or other family members will become involved in more serious delinquency or criminal activity.[51] Probation supervisor Tom Cerne noted the difficulties of measuring degrees of success:

> It's hard to make a drastic turnaround in any of these kids, although some do amaze you—they can turn around so much—but we get a lot of kids with character disorders and long-range personality defects and a one-year intervention is not going to make that much of a change in a child.[52]

SUMMARY

Probation, the most frequently used juvenile court disposition, involves supervision of an adjudicated delinquent who has been allowed to remain in the community by an officer of the juvenile court. Probation may be given as a suspension of the imposition of a disposition of institutionalization or as a direct order of probation. Youths placed on probation are required to abide by general and specific rules, to report to their probation officers according to a set schedule, and to commit no additional offenses. The length of the probation period varies according to the terms set by the court. The penalty for violating probation regulations may be the imposition of additional rules or institutionalization.

During meetings with the probation officer, a probationer is encouraged to set short-term goals and evaluate his or her progress toward achieving them. The probation officer may attempt to provide the youth with counseling and other necessary assistance. Or, the officer may act as a "broker," referring the youth to other community agencies. The officer, who has a mandate to supervise, assist, and support those youths assigned to his or her care, may be required to exercise authority to control the youth and report any misbehavior, as well as to operate in a helping role. The officer-probationer interaction is a relationship that must be developed through mutual trust and honesty.

Although some youths can be successfully supervised with few officer contacts, others require intensive surveillance and counseling. Many large juvenile court systems now classify probationers according to their risk for recidivism and adjust the level of their supervision accordingly.

Probation can be revoked if a youth violates the conditions of probation or commits a new offense. A revocation hearing must be held before a juvenile's probation can be terminated.

Probation is often combined with other structured, community-based programs for youths. In one of the earliest experiments with intensive community-based treatment and probation, the Provo Experiment used guided group interaction. The Kentfields Rehabilitation Program used behavior modification techniques for the same purpose, while the California Youth Authority's Community Treatment Project used differential programs of treatment.

Many current community supervision programs emphasize accountability. In home detention programs, youths are carefully monitored and required to strictly follow all probation rules. In restitution programs, youths involved in offenses that have resulted in property damage or personal injuries to victims are required to work at job sites chosen by the court. The victims receive the offenders' wages until a restitution amount set by the court is reached. Community-service programs require offenders to complete some type of work activity set by the court without pay. In addition, offenders may be required to make cash payments to victims.

Other programs focus on juveniles who have committed specific types of offenses or who are in need of specialized counseling or therapy. These include family counseling, substance abuse counseling, and programs for sex offenders. Adolescents who are considered multiproblem offenders are given intensive supervision and services.

The special needs of some youths require that they be placed in community residential treatment. These needs are met by foster and group homes. In these group settings, efforts are made to develop constructive interpersonal relationships, to provide the diagnostic and treatment services needed, and to integrate the youths into the social life of the community. The activities of community residential treatment facilities are subject to requirements set for the residents' behavior by the juvenile court.

A certain number of youths cannot be placed on probation because they pose too great a threat to the community or because they have violated probation rules so seriously or frequently that probation is no longer feasible. For these juveniles, the disposition of institutionalization is made. Incarcerated with these hardcore delinquents are other children for whom no successful placement in the community can be found, or whose problems are such that they are not considered good risks for nonsecure placement. The disposition of institutionalization and the characteristics of the youths currently held in juvenile institutions are discussed in detail in Chapter 15.

DISCUSSION QUESTIONS

1. In some jurisdictions, the same probation officer who conducts the predisposition social investigation may also supervise the probationer after disposition, while in others separate officers are assigned to each of these activities. Discuss the advantages and disadvantages of both types of arrangements.

2. Discuss some of the pressures faced by probation officers that may inhibit their effectiveness. How may certain probationers be adversely affected as a result of officers' responses to these pressures?

3. Since many juvenile probationers come from dysfunctional homes, should their parents be *required* to take part in family counseling or parent training? What can be done to assist probationers who are in need of parenting but receive little or no support or interest from their parents?

4. Should probation officers emphasize the surveillance and control of youths in their caseloads, or should they emphasize providing guidance and assistance?

5. Discuss intensive probation. Should intensive probation be used in place of institutionalization? Discuss.

NOTES

1. Louis B. Sies, *From the Probation Officer's Desk* (New York: Esposition Press, 1965), 17.
2. John Ortiz Smykla, *Probation and Parole: Crime Control in the Community* (New York: Macmillan, 1984), 67.
3. George Killinger, Hazel Kerper, and Paul F. Cromwell, Jr., *Probation and Parole in the Criminal Justice System* (St. Paul, MN: West Publishing Company, 1973), 45.
4. Illinois Laws 1899, 131–37. Quoted in Monrad G. Paulsen, *The Problems of Juvenile Courts and the Rights of Children* (Philadelphia: American Law Institute, 1975), 15–16.
5. Rosemary Sarri and Yeheskel Hasenfield, eds., *Brought to Justice? Juveniles, the Courts, and the Law* (Ann Arbor, MI: National Assessment of Corrections, 1976), 160.
6. Howard W. Snyder and Melissa Sickmund, *Juvenile Offenders and Victims: 1999 National Report* (Washington, DC: Office of Juvenile Justice and Delinquency Prevention, 1999), 156.
7. Ibid., 159.
8. U.S. Department of Justice, *Report to the Nation on Crime and Justice*, 2nd ed. (Washington, DC: U.S. Bureau of Justice Statistics, 1988), 95.
9. E. Eugene Miller, "The Probation Officer as Broker," in E. Eugene Miller and M. Robert Montilla, *Corrections in the Community* (Reston, VA: Reston, 1977), 82.
10. Probation Rules for the Court of Common Pleas, Juvenile Division, Trumbull County (Warren), Ohio.
11. John Stratton, "Correctional Workers: Counseling Con Men," *Federal Probation* 37 (September, 1973), 14–15.

12. Interview with Thomas Cerne by Peter C. Kratcoski, January 3, 1978; reinterviewed January, 1989.
13. Interview with Thomas Cerne by Peter C. Kratcoski, November 20, 2002.
14. *Ibid.*
15. Cuyahoga County Juvenile Court, "Intensive Probation Supervision: A Team Approach" (Cleveland, OH: Cuyahoga County Juvenile Court, 1986), mimeographed program description, 1–4.
16. *Ibid.*
17. *Mempa v. Rhay*, 389 U.S. 128 (1967)
18. *Morrisey v. Brewer*, 408 U.S. 471, 92 S.Ct. 2593, 33 L.Ed. 2d 484 (1972).
19. *Gagnon v. Scarpelli*, 411 U.S. 778 (1978).
20. LaMar T. Empey, "The Provo and Silverlake Experiment," in Miller and Montilla, *Corrections in the Community*, 109.
21. *Ibid.*
22. William S. Davidson II, *Kentfields Rehabilitation Program: An Alternative to Institutionalization* (Grand Rapids, MI: Kent County Juvenile Court, 1970), 4.
23. Ted Palmer, "The Youth Authority's Community Treatment Project," *Federal Probation* 38, 1 (January 1974), 3–12.
24. Richard A. Ball, C. Ronald Huff, and J. Robert Lilly, "A Model House Arrest Program for Juveniles: What Makes It Work?" in Richard A. Ball, C. Ronald Huff, and J. Robert Lilly, *House Arrest and Correctional Policy: Doing Time at Home* (Newbury Park, CA: Sage Publications, 1988), 64.
25. U.S. Department of Justice, *National Directory of Juvenile Restitution Programs, 1987* (Washington, DC: U.S. Department of Justice, 1987), 3.
26. *Ibid.*, 1.
27. *Ibid.*, 4.
28. Douglas C. McDonald, *Restitution and Community Service* (Washington, DC: U.S. Department of Justice, 1988), 3.
29. Interview with Dr. Jacqueline Y. Warren conducted by Peter C. Kratcoski, February 23, 1995.
30. Jacqueline Y. Warren, *Family Counseling with Juveniles and Their Parents in a Juvenile Court Setting*, unpublished doctoral dissertation, May, 1992, Kent State University.
31. Interview with Dr. Jacqueline Y. Warren, February 23, 1995.
32. Howard N. Snyder and Melissa Sickmund. *Juvenile Offenders and Victims: 1999 National Report* (Washington, DC: Office of Juvenile Justice and Delinquency Prevention, 1999), 59.
33. Marcia R. Chaiken and Bruce D. Johnson, *Characteristics of Different Types of Drug-Involved Offenders* (Washington, DC: U.S. Department of Justice, 1988), 9.
34. *Ibid.*, 3.
35. U.S. Department of Health and Human Services, National Institute on Drug Abuse and National Institute on Alcohol Abuse and Alcoholism, *Highlights from the 1991 National Drug and Alcoholism Treatment Unit Survey* (Washington, DC: U.S. Department of Health and Human Services, 1992), 8.
36. Eli Ginzberg, Howard Berliner, and Miriam Ostrow, *Young People at Risk, Is Prevention Possible?* (Boulder, CO: Westview Press, 1988), 99.
37. Maria Stops and G. Larry Mays, "Treating Adolescent Sex Offenders in a Multi-Cultural Community Setting," *Journal of Offender Rehabilitation* 17 (1991), 87–88.
38. Charlene Steen and Barbara Monnette, *Treating Adolescent Sex Offenders in the Community* (Springfield, IL: Charles C. Thomas, 1989), 3.
39. Garry P. Perry and Janet Orchard, *Assessment and Treatment of Adolescent Sex Offenders* (Sarasota, FL: Professional Resource Press, 1992), 67.
40. Peter C. Kratcoski, "Planning for Change: Increasing Cooperation in Youth Service Agencies," paper presented at the annual meeting of the Society for Applied Sociology, October 1985, 4.

41. Roberta C. Cronin, *Innovative Community Partnership: Working Together for Change* (Washington, DC: U.S. Department of Justice, Office of Juvenile Justice and Delinquency Prevention, 1994), 11.
42. *Ibid.*, 17.
43. National Advisory Committee on Criminal Justice Standards and Goals, *Juvenile Justice and Delinquency Prevention* (Washington, DC: U.S. Government Printing Office, 1977), 706.
44. Arthur D. Little, *Foster Parenting* (Washington, DC: Office of Juvenile Justice and Delinquency Prevention, 1978), 114–115.
45. National Advisory Committee, *Juvenile Justice and Delinquency Prevention*, 706.
46. Samuel Bernstein, "Can Probation Work?" *Juvenile Justice* 26, 3 (August 1975), 20–22.
47. Douglas Lipton, Robert Martinson, and Judith Wilks, *The Effectiveness of Correctional Treatment* (New York: Praeger, 1976), 27.
48. *Ibid.*, 62–63, 72.
49. *Ibid.*, 70.
50. Bernadette Jones, "Intensive Probation, Philadelphia County, November 1986–February 1989," unpublished paper given at the annual meeting of the American Society of Criminology, Baltimore, Maryland, November, 1990.
51. Dennis A. Romig, *Justice for our Children* (Lexington, MA: Lexington Books, 1978), 138.
52. Interview with Thomas Cerne by Peter C. Kratcoski, November 20, 2002.

CHAPTER 15

SECURE FACILITIES
FOR JUVENILES

(Photo credit: Mary Kate Denny/PhotoEdit)

HISTORY OF JUVENILE INSTITUTIONS IN AMERICA
THE ORGANIZATION OF JUVENILE DETENTION AND CORRECTIONAL FACILITIES
    Short-Term Incarceration Facilities
    Long-Term Incarceration Facilities
THE JUVENILE'S RESPONSE TO INSTITUTIONAL LIFE
    Violence in Institutions
    Adaptation to Institutional Life
    Institutional Effectiveness
    Normalization

In Chapter 13, we noted that at the disposition phase of the juvenile court process out-of-home placement is one of the options available to the juvenile court judge. Adjudicated offenders can be placed in nonsecure foster or group homes, staff secure residential treatment centers, or juvenile correctional facilities that have various levels of security. The juvenile codes of some states now require placement in secure institutions for adjudicated delinquents who have committed certain serious or violent offenses, while other states continue to allow the judge discretion in the disposition choices.

If a youth receives a disposition of institutionalization, the length of time spent there is dependent on the determinate or indeterminate disposition standards of the state. If indeterminate sentencing applies, the period of confinement is relatively open-ended, with the maximum stay generally being the age statutorily defined as the upper age of juvenile court jurisdiction in that state. Release of the youth occurs after a period decided by the youth's behavior in the institution and the institution staff's or committing judge's assessment of the youth's progress toward rehabilitation. In contrast, a determinate disposition is a specification of institutionalization for a narrowly defined length of time, set when the juvenile court disposition is made, with release occurring after completion of this time.

Although the majority of states still use indeterminate dispositions, a national survey revealed that a few states have implemented totally determinate dispositions for commitment or release of juvenile offenders and other states have adopted determinate sentencing for specific types of juvenile offenders.[1] These provisions, called "serious delinquency statutes,"

> mandate that a subset of delinquents (usually statutorily labeled serious, violent, repeat or habitual) be adjudicated and committed in a specific manner different from other committed delinquents. . . . They receive commitments which may vary significantly from the type given other adjudicated delinquents.[2]

The statutes may require a minimum length of confinement or placement in a specific type of facility.[3]

On the basis of the trend toward statutorily required placement of serious and violent offenders in institutions, it would seem that those held in correctional facilities would be juveniles who had committed very serious offenses, or repeat offenders for whom no other disposition would be appropriate. However, analyses of the offenses of those held reveal that this is not the case, as shown in Figure 15–1.

As shown in Figure 15–1, approximately 14 percent of juveniles committed in 28 states surveyed were institutionalized for serious and violent offenses, while approximately 79 percent were committed for property, drug, public order, or traffic offenses (moderate severity, as shown in Figure 15–1). In addition, 52 percent of those with moderate severity offenses were in state institutions for the first time.[4] Another research study of youths confined in 14 states found that the percentage of those held who had committed serious and violent offenses ranged from 11 to 44 percent. On the basis of specific public safety risk factors, this study also concluded that about a third of these juveniles could have been placed in less secure settings.[5] The offense profile in a census of juveniles in residential placement revealed that 25 percent of those in residential facilities were committed for violent offenses, 8 percent for other offenses against persons, 30 percent for property offenses, 21 percent for public order offenses, 9 percent for drug offenses, and 7 percent for status offenses.[6]

The success rate for rehabilitation of juveniles placed in institutions is not encouraging. Few programs of treatment, education, training, or punishment have been shown to be very effective in rehabilitating youths housed in institutions.

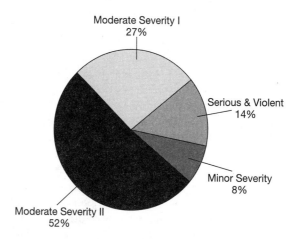

Total Number of Cases: 50,260

Serious & Violent: Murder, Manslaughter, Homicide, Forcible Rape, Other Violent Sex Offenses, Sodomy, Kidnapping, Endangerment, Robbery (with priors), and Assault (with priors).
Minor Severity: Shoplifting, Technical (Probation or parole), Minor Public Order, Status Offenses, Driving w/o license, Minor Traffic, Dependency, and Special Court Proceedings.
Moderate Severity: I = Offenses not categorized in Serious & Violent or Minor Severity, such as Property, Drug, Public Order, and Traffic Offenses with prior state commitments. II = No prior state commitments.

Figure 15–1.   Estimated Proportions of Admissions to State Juvenile Corrections Systems by Severity of Offense, CY1992 *(Source: Juveniles Taken Into Custody Research Program; State Juvenile Corrections System Reporting Program; estimates based on 29 states for 1992. National Council on Crime and Delinquency in cooperation with the Office of Juvenile Justice and Delinquency Prevention. Presented in Michael A. Jones and Barry Krisberg, Images and Reality: Juvenile Crime, Youth Violence and Public Policy [San Francisco, CA: National Council on Crime and Delinquency, 1994], p. 28.)*

Commitment to a juvenile institution has been found to be strongly correlated with continued criminal behavior as an adult. In *The Young Criminal Years of the Violent Few*, Hamparian et al. continued to follow the arrest and incarceration histories of a cohort of juveniles who had been arrested for at least one violent offense and followed through their juvenile years. As adults, 76 percent of those who had been committed to juvenile training schools were arrested and 69 percent of those arrested went to prison at least once.[7]

The rapid increase in the number of juveniles in secure institutions and the combination of serious, moderate, and minor severity offenders in the same facilities have resulted in a growing emphasis on control and impersonality, as evidenced by use of uniforms, regulation haircuts, regimentation of movement, and enforced silence. Threats of physical violence from other residents, assignment to demeaning tasks by institution staff, extortion, and physical and sexual assaults by stronger inmates occur. The endless, carefully programmed routine of institutional life offers little opportunity for developing personal skills or using creativity or imagination unless they are applied to schemes for obtaining or secreting contraband, planning criminal activities to be carried out after release, or fantasizing about the world outside and what life will be like after release.

As juvenile institutions become more and more like those for adult offenders, a look at the history and development of these institutions will place the problems they face today in perspective.

HISTORY OF JUVENILE INSTITUTIONS IN AMERICA

In the American colonies, children found guilty of repeated incorrigibility could actually be sentenced to death. Those who were regarded as having tendencies toward such behavior could be placed in adult houses of correction for indeterminate periods of time. The 1650 Connecticut Blue Laws made specific provisions to this effect:

> Whatsoever Childe or servant within these Libberties, shall be convicted of any stubborne or rebellious carriage against their parents or governors, which is a forruner of the aformentioned evils, the Governor or any two Magistrats have libberty and power from this Courte to committ such person or persons to the House of Corrections and there to remaine under hard labour and severe punishment so long as the Courte or the major parte of the Magistrates shall judge meete.[8]

It should be noted that even though execution or imprisonment of children for committing various offenses, even minor ones, was allowed in the statutes, the most common court responses to youthful misbehavior were whippings or the release of the child to the custody of parents.[9]

Throughout the Colonial period and in the first years of the new republic, some children accused of crimes were sentenced in adult courts and remanded to adult prisons. The first institution specifically for juveniles was created in 1824 in New York City, financed by public funds and the Society for the Reformation of Juvenile Delinquents. This institution, dubbed a "House of Refuge" by its founders, James W. Gerard and Isaac Collins, separated juveniles from adults but did not offer them less severe treatment. Such devices as the ball and chain, handcuffs, leg irons, and whipping have been documented as being used there.[10] Children followed a regimented routine from sunrise to dark, without hope of release until they reached adulthood. The House of Refuge movement spread rapidly in the eastern United States and persisted until the close of the 19th century. In areas where such facilities were not constructed, children continued to be held in jails and prisons.

In 1857, the innovation of a "cottage system" was implemented at a state reform school for boys in Lancaster, Ohio. Instead of housing the youths in one structure with cell blocks, the cottage system placed them in small groups in separate small buildings, under the supervision of cottage parents. This arrangement provided for more homelike surroundings and individualization of treatment. The cottage design is still widely used for many juvenile institutions.[11]

The Child-Saving Movement, discussed earlier as leading to the creation of the juvenile court system at the turn of the century, also had some influence on the design and treatment methods of institutions for juveniles. The fact that many juvenile institutions today are located in rural areas may have its origins in the "child savers" firm belief that urban life was conducive to delinquent behavior and that children would benefit from an acquaintance with rural life. A female advocate of the Movement expressed this notion in the following way:

> Children acquire a perverted taste for city life and crowded streets; but if introduced when young to country life, care of animals and plants, and rural pleasures, they are likely . . . to be healthier in mind and body for such associations.[12]

From 1854 through 1929, New York's Children Aid Society operated "orphan trains" that transported homeless and deprived youngsters to the Midwest. These trains stopped at preselected towns and the local people, usually farm families, had opportunities to look over the passengers and, if they chose, select one or more to live with them. Children placed on the trains were either orphans or those whose parents had relinquished custody of them to the Society. One passenger on an "orphan train" described the experience in later years:

> The trip was a great adventure. . . . We couldn't get done gawking out the windows. Boys were in one compartment and girls in another. We had no idea where we were going. At Savannah [Missouri] they took us to the courthouse and lined us up, you know, like they was going to mow us down with a machine gun. People walked up to us and said a few words and moved on. My brothers were all picked the first day, but I wasn't taken till the second. People came up and felt our arms and legs, and mine were kind of spindly. I was hoping that whoever picked me would have plenty to eat, that was my main goal.[13]

Some of the foster families treated the children well and eventually adopted them. Others kept them in an "indentured servant" status, overworking them and giving them little affection. Children who were separated from brothers and sisters sometimes lost contact with them or did not see them for many years.[14] Other ideas for juvenile institutionalization included school ships, which were anchored in the harbors of port cities and took the inmates on short voyages under the regulations of naval life, and military schools, which viewed strict martial discipline as beneficial. A wide variety of private institutions for youth was also established. In the main, these were reserved for wayward children, orphans, or unwed mothers. They were generally under the auspices of religious groups and often were not available for the urban poor or for minority group members. Foster home placement was also introduced, but it did not gain wide popularity.[15]

The development of the juvenile court, based upon the idea that the state, acting as a benevolent substitute parent, would provide individualized attention to each child under its jurisdiction, ushered in the era of treatment and rehabilitation. In the early 20th century, this took the form of inculcating what were viewed as desirable work habits, coupled with a liberal amount of religious training.

The techniques of placing youths on farms using military or seamanship discipline, training them in specific trades, or using cottage arrangements were all fads of certain decades, but they persist in some manner in today's juvenile institutions. The programs in these institutions appear to have run in cycles, with a certain form of program coming into existence, gaining wide acceptance, proliferating to other institutions, and then dying out in favor of some new strategy.

THE ORGANIZATION OF JUVENILE DETENTION AND CORRECTIONAL FACILITIES

There are 1,121 public state and local detention and correctional facilities and 2,310 private correctional facilities in the United States, which house nearly 126,000 juveniles. Of the persons under age 21 in these facilities who have been charged with or court-adjudicated for an offense and are in residential placement because of that offense, 93 percent are held for a delinquent offense and the remainder are status offenders; voluntary commitments; retarded or emotionally disturbed; or dependent, neglected, or abused children. Eighty six percent are males and 14 percent are females.[16] Seventy four percent of these youths are held in public facilities, while 26 percent are held in private facilities.[17] Public and private juvenile correctional facilities differ in their environments. Public facilities are generally characterized by restraints on the residents' movements and limited access to the community. In contrast, private facilities often have more open, relaxed environments. Some juveniles are also held in adult jails or prisons.[18]

Short-Term Incarceration Facilities

Short-term facilities include detention centers, shelter homes, and reception and diagnostic centers. Juveniles may also be held for short periods of time in adult jails.

Detention Centers. Detention centers are secure facilities that hold youths for whom release prior to juvenile court hearings is judged too risky because of the nature of the offense (violent behavior or running away), the inadvisability or impossibility of return home (physically or emotionally threatening situations, or refusal of parents to accept responsibility), or the need for physical or mental examination or treatment. Youths held in detention centers or jails are guaranteed a hearing within an established time period. Detention centers also hold juveniles who have been adjudicated delinquent and are awaiting residential or institutional placement.

A "secure facility" is one that is designed and operated so that all entrances and exists are under the control of the staff. Detention facilities are temporary custody facilities, which limits their use to short-term placements. The Advisory Commission on Accreditation for Corrections has stated that "placement in a juvenile detention facility should not exceed 30 days."[19]

Figure 15–2 compares the length of stays in detention for juveniles awaiting adjudication or disposition and those awaiting placement elsewhere, with length of placement in secure facilities for committed juveniles. Although those detained awaiting adjudication or disposition had the shortest stays, 28 percent were held for at least 30 days, 14 percent remained in detention after 60 days, and 10 percent were still detained after 90 days. Of those awaiting placement elsewhere, 48 percent were in detention for at least 30 days, 25 percent for 60 days, and 15 percent after 90 days.[20]

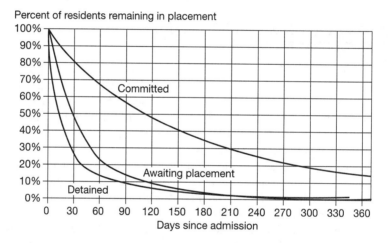

- Among juveniles detained while awaiting adjudication or disposition, 70% had been in placement in the facility for at least 7 days, 50% for at least 15 days, and 28% for at least 30 days. By 60 days, only 14% of these detained juveniles remained in placement; by 90 days, less than 10% remained.

- Among juveniles awaiting placement elsewhere, 69% had been in the facility at least 15 days, 48% for at least 30 days. By 60 days, 25% remained; and after 90 days, 15% remained.

- Among committed juveniles (those adjudicated, disposed, and placed in the facility), 90% had been in the facility at least 15 days, 81% at least 30 days, 68% at least 60 days, and 57% at least 90 days. After a full year, 15% of committed juveniles remained in placement.

Figure 15–2. Number of Days Held in Detention or Residential Placement for Juveniles Awaiting Adjudication or Disposition, Juveniles Awaiting Placement, and Committed Juveniles. *(Source: Office of Juvenile Justice and Delinquency Prevention, Census of Juveniles in Residential Placement 1997. Reported in Howard N. Snyder and Melissa Sickmund, Juvenile Offenders and Victims: 1999 National Report (Washington, DC: Office of Juvenile Justice and Delinquency Prevention, 1999), 201.)*

In the cases of habitual and violent juvenile offenders, placement in detention without possibilities for release prior to hearings has been upheld by the U.S. Supreme Court. We noted in Chapter 11 that the Court's support of such action, in *Schall v. Martin*, was based on the need to promote the welfare of the child by barring him or her from the opportunity to be involved in additional criminal activity.[21]

As mentioned in Chapter 13, the decision to place a child in detention is made by the juvenile court's intake officer or a member of the detention facility staff. Although most courts have guidelines as to the characteristics of youths who should be detained, research indicates that the detention decision is often somewhat arbitrary. A study that focused on detention decisions in Florida found that those most likely to be detained were older, black, female, or rural youths; those charged with felonies or multiple offenses; and those who had prior juvenile court referrals.[22] In a study that focused on race and juvenile justice in Ohio, it was discovered that, with all other factors controlled, the odds of minority youths being detained were about 25 percent greater than the odds of white youths being detained.[23]

The reauthorized Juvenile Justice and Delinquency Prevention Act of 1988 required states to reduce the overrepresentation of minorities in secure facilities and, beginning in 1995, states applying for federal funding for juvenile justice programs must show in their proposals that attempts are being made to deal with disproportionate confinement of minorities.[24]

Florida's Department of Health and Rehabilitative Services uses a Detention Risk Assessment Instrument (see Figure 15–3) to evaluate the need for detention.

As shown in Figure 15–3, such factors as likelihood of escape or absconding, the severity of the alleged offense, prior record, and a history of violent conduct are all given weight in the decision.

Since detention centers are short-term holding facilities, where a youth's stay may range from a few hours to 180 days, programs implemented in detention centers must be adaptable to a constantly changing resident population. Many of the youths are being held for relatively minor offenses, such as probation violations or property or public order offenses; others have committed serious, violent offenses; and members of a third group may be experiencing detention as a disposition. Several states permit placement of adjudicated delinquents in detention facilities for periods up to 180 days as a disposition.[25] Rationales for such placements include the possibility that this will give a youth exposure to the deprivations of institutionalization without a long-term commitment and this experience may turn the youth away from activity that would lead in that direction. It also lets youths know that the juvenile court can deal with them in a more severe way than release on probation.[26]

The National Council on Crime and Delinquency recommended that the following services be provided by detention centers:

1. Administrative services, which should include staff for secretarial, bookkeeping, and telephone-answering services as well as staff for community relations, staff development, and supervision of staff.

2. Group work services that are well balanced with recreational and creative activities, which include daily living activities as well as supervision of group discussion and group activities.

DETENTION RISK ASSESSMENT INSTRUMENT

SS#/CIS _____
Record Check _____
Not Available _____

Detention Center

I.   IDENTIFYING DATA

Last Name   First   Middle   AKA
_____

Number/Street   Telephone
_____

City, State, Zip   Race/Sex/   D.O.B.
_____
                                                    _____Yes
                          AM   _____No
_____ PM
MO/DAY/YR Screened/Time   Assigned Counselor/ Program Area/ Contacted

                                                    _____Yes
                                                    _____No
_____
School or Work   Assigned Counselor/ Program Area/ Contacted

Parent/Guardian   Alleged Offense(s) (Continuous)
_____

Number/Street
_____

City, State, Zip
_____

Telephone: Home & Work   Law Enforcement Agency
                                 Name and ID or Badge No.

Parent/Guardian Interviewed
_____ Yes _____ No
             _____ 1. Face to Face   Youth advised of right to legal counsel __ Yes __ No
       AM   _____ 2. Telephone
_____ PM   _____ 3. Unable to Contact   FPSS Record Check _____ Yes _____ Not Available
Time   _____ 4. Message Left
                    With whom: Current Allegation of Abuse/Neglect Pending ____ Yes ____ No
_____ History of Confirmed or Indicated Abuse/Neglect ___ Yes ___ No
       Name   Relationship   Type: Physical Abuse __ Sexual Abuse __ Neglect __ Emotional __
                                          (If available provide input on assigned
                                          counselor and status in Narrative)

II.   Admission Criteria
      A.   Youth has been delivered and the following criteria as outlined in s. 39.044 (2) indicate the youth's eligi-
           bility for detention care:
      Yes _____ No _____ 1. The youth is alleged to be an escapee or an absconder from a commitment program, a
                            community control program, furlough, or aftercare supervision, or the child is wanted in
                            another jurisdiction for an offense which if committed by an adult, would be a felony;
      Yes _____ No _____ 2. The youth has been charged with a delinquent act or violation of law and requests in
                            writing through legal counsel to be detained for protection from an imminent physical
                            threat to his personal safety; (Attach documentation)
      Yes _____ No _____ 3. The youth is charged with a capital felony, life felony, felony of the first degree, felony
                            of the second degree, or a felony that is also a crime of violence; or

HRS-CYF Form 2049, Jan 91 (Obsoletes previous editions which may not be used)
(Stock Number: 5749-001-2049-4)

Figure 15–3. State of Florida Detention Risk Assessment *(Source: State of Florida, Detention Risk Assessment In-strument, January 1991.)*

Factor #4 requires an affirmative answer to at least one of the qualifiers before a yes answer can be recorded (s. 39.044(2)(d), F.S.).

Yes _____ No _____ 4. The youth is charged with a serious property crime as described in s. 810.02 (2) or (3) (Burglary) or s. 812.014 (2) (c) 4. (Grand Theft Auto), any offense involving the use of a firearm, or any second-degree or third-degree felony involving a violation of chapter 893 (Felony Drugs) and:

Yes _____ No _____ (a) youth has a record of failure to appear at court hearings after being properly notified in accordance with the Rules of Juvenile Procedure;

Yes _____ No _____ (b) youth has a record of law violations prior to court hearings;

Yes _____ No _____ (c) youth has already been detained or has been released and is awaiting final disposition of his case; or

Yes _____ No _____ (d) youth has a record of violent conduct resulting in physical injury to others.

> If any of the above (1–4) are answered yes proceed to Section III. If each of the above (1–4) are answered no the youth must be released.

A youth delivered with a judicial order requiring detention care must be detained. The risk assessment instrument still must be completed for informational purposes, but the youth must be detained regardless of the points score.

The responsibilities of law enforcement and case managers from releasing a youth from custody will be discharged in accordance with s. 39.038.

Section III   Risk Assessment

    A. Most serious current offense

      1. All capital, life, and first degree felony PBL   15 _____

      2. All other first degree felonies, vehicular homicide, violent second degree felonies, youth is wanted by another jurisdiction for a felony offense   12 _____

      3. Second degree felony drug charges, escape or absconding, any third degree felony involving the use of a firearm, burglary of an occupied residential structure   10 _____

      4. Violent third degree felonies   9 _____

      5. All other second degree felonies (except dealing stolen property)   8 _____

      6. Dealing in stolen property, other third degree felonies that qualify for detention in s. 39.044(2)(d) (See factor #4 above)   7 _____

      7. Reckless display or unlawful discharge of a firearm   4 _____
      _____

    B. Other current offenses and pending charges (separate, non-related events)

      1. Each felony   2 _____

      2. Each misdemeanor   1 _____

      3. Prior felony arrest within last 7 days   6 _____
      _

    C. Prior History

      1. 3 felony adjudications or adjudications withheld last 12 months, or   4 _____

      2. 2 felony adjudications or adjudications withheld last 12 months, or   2 _____

      3. 1 felony adjudication or adjudication withheld or misdemeanor adjudications or adjudications withheld   1 _____
      _____

    D. Legal Status

      1. Committed or detention   8 _____

      2. Active community control cases with last adjudication or adjudication withheld within 90 days   6 _____

      3. Active community control case with last adjudication or adjudication withheld more than 90 days ago   2 _____
      _____

HRS-CYF Form 2049, Aug 91 (Replaces Jan 91 edition which may be used)
(Stock Number: 5749-002-2049-9)

Figure 15–3.   Continued

HRS

E. Aggravating or Mitigating Circumstances

    1. Aggravating factors (add to score)   1–3   ____

    2. Mitigating factors (subtract from score)   1–3   ____

      The case manager must fully document the reasons for scoring
      aggravating or mitigating points

                                                                      Total (Sum A-E)   _____

F. Detain/release decision

    0–6 points = release

    7–11 points = nonsecure or home detention

    12 or more points = secure detention

Section IV.   State Attorney Review/Decision (Complete based upon item # 1 being appropriate)

    1.   If the case manager believes that a youth who is eligible for detention based upon the results of the risk assessment instrument should be released, the state attorney must be contacted to approve release (s. 39.044(1)(c). The state attorney also may approve home or nonsecure detention for a youth who scores eligible for secure detention. The case manager must document the reasons for the recommendation in the narrative section.

    2.   (a) State Attorney contacted   Yes _____ No _____

                Name _____

                (b) State Attorney decision Detain _____ Release _____

Section V.   Screening Decision

        Detention: _____ Yes _____ No

        Placement: _____ Secure   Notification of Detention Hearing:

                              _____ Home   Hearing Date: _____ Time: _____

                              _____ Non-secure

                              _____ Release

        Release to: Name _____

                    Address _____

                    Telephone _____ Time _____

Section VI.   Narrative (Continue on back if needed)

_____

_____

_____

_____

_____

Case Manager	Date	Reviewed by	Date
		Detention Review Specialist	Date

HRS-CYF Form 2049, Jan 91
(Stock Number: 5749-003-2049-3)

Figure 15–3. Continued

    3. Housekeeping services, which should include maintenance of buildings and grounds as well as preparing meals, processing laundry, and general housekeeping chores.

    4. Arrangements for health services, which would include medical examination as well as emergency medical and dental treatment.

5. Access to psychiatric and psychological services to assist the staff in handling certain minors. Besides this consultative role for those from the mental health field, there may well be occasions when psychiatric evaluation or psychological testing for diagnostic purposes is needed.

6. Casework services, which would include the observation of the minor's behavior, potential, and needs and having these observations recorded and made available to the probation department and/or the juvenile court.

7. Religious activity for minors, to be made available as part of the staff function.

8. Educational services, to comply with the law and to give each minor a structured objective that is in keeping with the minor's designated responsibility as regards his or her age.[27]

Programming in juvenile detention centers has two functions—maintaining control and providing some basic treatment. Well-developed programs in detention demonstrate to the youths involved that efforts to assist them and change their behavior have begun and they also keep the detainees occupied and reduce the possibilities for boredom and misbehavior.

The Responsible Behavior Program used by the Multi-County Juvenile Attention System in Ohio is grounded in behavior modification. As shown in Figure 15-4, A resident can progress from the lowest status (New Arrival) to the highest status (Youth Aide), depending on behavior and conformity to the rules and regulations of the Center. A higher status gives more privileges, freedom, and trust. Residents are evaluated daily on personal hygiene, room appearance, behavior at meals, job performance, participation in activities, performance in the educational classes, and respect for staff and other residents.[28]

Juveniles in Adult Jails.   In local jurisdictions that have no detention centers exclusively for juveniles, youths are held in detention by being placed in a separate section of the local jail. The 1974 Juvenile Justice Act required that to be eligible for federal funds for juvenile justice programs, jurisdictions must provide plans for separate, nonsecure detention facilities for status offenders and not house them with delinquent offenders.[29] The Act was amended in 1980 to prohibit confining any juveniles in adult jails.[30] In 1985, six conditions were set under which youths could be held up to 24 hours in adult jails. These include being charged with a delinquent (criminal) offense; being held awaiting a court appearance; residing in a state that requires court appearance within 24 hours, exclusive of holidays and weekends; being placed in a jail that is outside a major metropolitan area; no other acceptable alternative exists; and juvenile is separated by sight and sound from adult detainees. Youths who have been waived for trial in adult criminal court may be held in adult jails and a child may be held in jail up to six hours for identification, processing, or transfer.[31] In 1996, these requirements were modified to provide that brief and inadvertent or accidental contact with adult offenders in nonresidential areas was not a violation, that the 6-hour hold rule was expanded to include 6 hours before and after court appearances, and that adjudicated delinquents held in juvenile facilities could be transferred to adult facilities in states where such transfers were authorized or required by

MULTI-COUNTY JUVENILE ATTENTION SYSTEM
RESPONSIBLE BEHAVIOR PROGRAM

STATUS REQUIREMENTS

1. YOUTH AIDE	-is the highest level. Must maintain Youth Aide Candidate Status for seven consecutive days. He/she should possess qualities of trust, responsibility and leadership.
2. YOUTH AIDE CANDIDATE	-A Youth Aide Candidate must maintain a grade average of 2.85 for five consecutive days preceding his placement to Youth Aide Candidate.
3. "A" STATUS	-performing at an excellent level.
	1) Trusted by staff.
	2) Gets along with other youth at Center.
	3) Respects self, staff and others at Center.
	4) Has respect for property, personal and others' at Center.
	5) Maintains room and self neatly at all times.
	6) Participation and cooperates well in the Center's program.
4. "B" STATUS	-performing at a good level.
	1) Follows all Center procedures and rules.
	2) Cooperates with staff, others and Center program.
	3) Have not attempted to improve their status.
	4) Lack of trust.
5. "C" STATUS	-performing at a fair level.
	1) Follows all rules and regulations of the Center.
	2) Lacks improvement.
	3) Causes no problems to staff or others.
6. "D" STATUS	-performing at a poor level.
	1) Non-compliance to rules.
	2) Destruction of property.
	3) Causes problems to the staff or others.
	4) Uncooperative with staff.
	5) Planned or attempted escape.
7. NA STATUS	-New Admission Evaluation Period
	Cooling off period for New Admissions. All new arrivals are confined to their rooms for three (3) hours. NA's up and ready for school no matter what time admitted. After this period, they will be rated and their status will be determined.

Figure 15–4. Responsible Behavior Program of the Multi-County (Ohio) Juvenile Attention System. *(Source: David Vanderwall, Multi-County Juvenile Attention System Responsible Behavior Program. Canton, OH: Multi-County Juvenile Attention System, 2001, 8.)*

law once they reached the state's age of full criminal responsibility.[32] In 1997, 2 percent of the total jail population was made up of youths under age 18 and the number of jail inmates under age 18 increased 35 percent from 1994 to 1997.[33]

Incarceration in an adult jail can have devastating psychological effects on young people. The requirement that youths be held out of sight and sound of adult inmates has, in some instances, resulted in placement in solitary confinement.

> Compliance with this rule often meant that juveniles were placed in solitary confinement with all of the punitive consequences such as curtailing the time a child could actually spend outside of his cell. Sight and sound separation in many instances has proved to be detrimental rather than beneficial.[34]

Although the practice of holding children in adult jails has been roundly condemned, it is apparent that efforts to remove juveniles from adult jails have not been successful. Ira Schwartz, former administration of the Office of Juvenile Justice and Delinquency Prevention, noted the urgency of new action in this regard.

> It is particularly important that strategies be implemented to inform and educate state and local elected officials, law enforcement personnel, and judges about the hazards and liabilities of jailing children. Jails lack adequate physical plant facilities; adequate numbers of appropriately trained staff members; as well as adequate health, recreational, and other programs to meet the minimum standards of juvenile confinement.[35]

Shelter Homes. Shelter homes provide short-term care of youths in a nonsecure environment. These shelters are used primarily for juveniles referred to the courts as dependent or neglected children, although, as noted earlier, the Juvenile Justice Act of 1974 recommended that status offenders in need of temporary shelter be placed in such facilities rather than in detention centers with delinquents.

Public shelter homes are usually small facilities (housing 1 to 12 youths) and are most often administered at the local level. Private shelters are financed by contributions of public and private agencies, individual contributions, or support from the United Way or similar plans.[36] Although youths placed in detention are almost always sent there by the police or the juvenile court, children placed in shelter facilities may be directly referred there by parents, children's service agencies, or other social agencies.

Reception or Diagnostic Centers. Some states have reception or diagnostic centers to which the youths given a disposition of institutionalization are referred for study and evaluation before placement in some type of long-term incarceration facility. In those states without reception or diagnostic centers, or in cases of referral to private institutions, the judge designates the specific facility in which the youth will be placed at the dispositional hearing.

A reception or diagnostic center generally operates under the administration of a state agency responsible for youth corrections. Youths are tested and evaluated for a period of one to six weeks after assignment to the center. The evaluation includes medical, psychological, and attitude testing to help the staff decide upon the most auspicious placement for each youth.

Long-Term Incarceration Facilities

Long-term incarceration facilities include training schools, ranches, forestry camps, farms, halfway houses, and group homes. Training schools (often termed "Youth Development Centers") are the more secure types of juvenile correctional facilities. Those known as ranches, forestry camps, or farms provide residential treatment for youths who are not regarded as needing secure confinement and separation from the community.

Physical Structure. The type of structure used to house institutionalized delinquents may range from cell-like living quarters in an old facility resembling a fortress, with uniformed custody personnel who perform security functions, to the prep school or summer resort atmosphere of small cottages, which attempt to imitate a homelike setting, complete with houseparents. The majority have a relatively open architecture, without a perimeter wall or fence, and include a number of dormitory-like buildings called cottages, a school building, an administration building, and a vocational training area. Generally, 15 to 40 or more youths are assigned to each cottage. A cottage set aside for those students who present discipline problems may contain rooms resembling cells.

This description cannot be applied to all types of training schools, since many of the newer facilities, designed to house older, more hardcore types of delinquents, resemble prison structures, with individual rooms, an outer fence that may have sensing devices, and other means of closely controlling movement within the institution. There is a growing emphasis on control and an impersonal atmosphere, as evidenced by use of uniforms, regulation haircuts, regimentation of movement, and enforced silence.

Organizational Goals.   It is difficult to generalize about the specific goals on which an institution has focused. Long-term institutions for youth have a general mandate to control those placed under their jurisdiction, protect the community, provide treatment, and rehabilitate inmates. The extent to which these goals are actually pursued depends in many ways upon the state youth authority under which the institution is operated, or upon the sponsoring organization in the case of private institutions. Some institutions are almost totally custody-oriented, some are strongly committed to treatment, and others attempt to balance custody and treatment in their programming. Street, Vinter, and Perrow characterized three types of organizational models found in juvenile institutions as *obedience/conformity, re-education/development,* and *treatment.* The *obedience/conformity* institutions were seen as focusing on

The security for some juvenile institutions is comparable to that for adult facilities. *(Photo credit: Craig Yingling, The Image Works)*

close control, emphasis on rules, and enforcement of negative sanctions for inappropriate behavior. In contrast, they characterized the *re-education/development* institutions as emphasizing changing the youths through training, skill development, and rewards for appropriate behavior. *Treatment* institutions were committed to defining the sources of youths' misbehavior and addressing them through specific treatment techniques to help the youths to become better adjusted and prepare them for return to the community. They also noted the existence of "mixed goal" institutions, which focused on both custody and treatment.[37]

It is also possible for all of the organizational models described by Street, Vinter, and Perrow to exist within the same facility. In his study of 10 cottages within a juvenile institution, Feld reported that some had programs similar to those of industrial training schools, while others concentrated on individual or group treatment.[38] He also described a cottage that closely resembled the *obedience/conformity* type described by Street, Vinter, and Perrow. The youths in this cottage had been runaways or discipline problems. He described the cottage in this way:

> Staff used physical coercion and isolation cells—the "Tombs" to enforce obedience, conformity, and respect. . . . Staff members used their limited repertoire of controls to counter major forms of deviance such as riots and fights, as well as inmate provocation, disrespect, or recalcitrance. . . . Other control techniques were virtually absent, since there were no amenities or privileges that might be lost.[39]

The Paint Creek Youth Center in southern Ohio typifies the *re-education/development* model. The Center, developed by New Life Youth Services, Inc. for youths convicted of serious felonies, used a small, residential setting to apply interventions that had demonstrated some success with such youths, including defining risk factors, having staff members model appropriate behavior, peer-centered therapy, drug and alcohol counseling, family counseling, and work experience while in custody. A research study matched these youths with a sample committed to high-security training schools that did not offer as many services to the youths. Although the Paint Creek group received more varied and intensive services and more intensive aftercare supervision than the youths in the matched sample, recidivism comparisons after one year showed no significant difference in reoffending or in length of time between release and first new arrest. A self-reported delinquency questionnaire completed by both groups showed that 75 percent of the Paint Creek youths had committed at least one new offense, compared to 62 percent of those in the control group.[40] Although the more intensive work with the Paint Creek attendees evidently did not reduce postinstitutionalization offending, the Paint Creek program and similar programs can address institutional overcrowding by providing viable alternatives.

A program that meets the description of a *treatment* model is Specialized Treatment Services in Mercer, Pennsylvania. This private, state-licensed residential facility for males is designed for emotionally disturbed adjudicated delinquents. A specialized, individual treatment plan is developed for each resident. Goals are defined and the specific strategies for treatment, anticipated length of stay, involvement of parents, and aftercare plans are included. Therapists, teachers, probation officers, and parents contribute toward designing the plan. The committing court and parents receive monthly progress reports and the youths under treatment are also advised of how they are progressing.[41]

Although most residents of juvenile institutions participate in school, work, or vocational programs and at times receive individual or group counseling, when matters of security arise, the overall concern tends to gravitate toward keeping down escapes and internal disturbances. The prevailing goal becomes maintaining order and security and treatment programs must conform to this reality. Institution administrators, as well as the directors of state agencies, are particularly sensitive to negative community reaction or political criticism. Smoothly running facilities tend to be equated with good facilities in the eyes of the public.

The institutional environment may both influence and respond to the characteristics of the youths held there. Poole and Regoli, in their study of four institutions for males, found that inmates held in custodial-emphasis institutions were more violent than those held in treatment-oriented institutions. However, they found that, regardless of the organizational model, preinstitutional violence was the most important predictor of inmate aggression in the institution. They also discovered that the more a facility was concerned with security and less involved in treatment, the stronger the inmate subculture, developed as a response to the deprivations of imprisonment, flourished.[42]

Classification.   When a youth is admitted to long-term institutionalization, the facility to which he or she is committed and the specific assignment or type of treatment given are determined in a number of different ways. If there is a statewide reception and diagnostic system, the judge will remand the youth to the state youth authority at the time of disposition. The juvenile is then sent to a diagnostic center where a battery of physical, psychological, personality, and vocational tests is administered. After a period of observation, a decision is made as to which institution would best serve the youth's needs. In the larger states, institutions may be differentiated on the basis of security needs, the sex and age levels of the inmates, and the seriousness of the offenses committed by the youths housed there.

Within a specific training school, the same types of categorizations are frequently made. The aggressive, older youths are assigned to one cottage or section and the younger, less mature ones are kept in another. Some states have incorporated classification treatment models that provide information to help make the initial placement. The models also furnish guidelines to the type of treatment that would most probably be beneficial to the youth. These models are grounded in the concept of differential treatment, which means tailoring the treatment program to the individual problems and psychological needs of the residents.

Initial classification is made by:

1. Studying the child and analyzing his or her problems through the use of every available technique and procedure;
2. Formulating in a staff conference a program of custodial care, treatment, and training that is best suited to the child's particular needs, abilities, and potentials;

3. Assuring that this program is put into operation;
4. Providing guidance for the child through interviews and counseling;
5. Observing the progress of the child, and modifying or changing his or her program from time to time when necessary;
6. Making recommendations with respect to the child's release at the appropriate time.[43]

Treatment Programs.   We noted in Chapter 3 that the "medical model" of juvenile court intervention popular in the 1950s and 1960s regarded the problems that brought youths into the juvenile justice system as treatable once they were properly diagnosed. When treatment efforts appeared to produce little change in the behavior of the youths involved in a wide variety of programs, administrators became increasingly skeptical about the effectiveness of treatment. This was particularly true of institutional treatment programs. By the mid-1970s, a national survey of correctional administrators found that only about half of them viewed rehabilitation as the primary goal of juvenile institutions, while another quarter considered rehabilitation and public protection to be their major goal. The remainder regarded public protection, punishment, and other goals as most important. Skepticism over the effectiveness of institutional treatment continued to grow in the 1980s and 1990s, with resulting changes in the emphasis placed on treatment programs within institutions. As the inmate population continues to grow and becomes increasingly composed of more hardened and violent offenders, institutional treatment has focused on controlling and changing the behavior of the youths while they are incarcerated and less emphasis has been placed on resolving their personal difficulties or maladjustments.

The *right to treatment* for involuntarily confined juveniles was confirmed by the *Morales v. Turman* (1974) court decision. In this case a U.S. District Court ordered two Texas institutions closed because of the lack of treatment there and the harsh and cruel punishments given the inmates, including beatings, use of crowd-control chemicals, and long-term solitary confinement. It ordered the establishment of community-based treatment facilities for the youths involved and set detailed procedures and standards for providing treatment.[44] In *Nelson v. Heyne* (1974), the U.S. Court of Appeals declared that institutionalized juveniles have a constitutional as well as a statutory right to treatment under the 14th Amendment.[45]

The treatment techniques used in some institutions, including behavior modification and aversive conditioning, have been criticized as constituting control mechanisms rather than true treatment. Debates over the nature and types of treatment which should be offered in institutions continue.

Most long-term institutions provide some educational opportunities of an academic or vocational nature, work experiences, recreation, and some form of individual or group counseling. Which of these is given the highest priority depends upon the age, sex, and other characteristics of the residents. If the average age is approximately 13 to 15, the institutions tend to emphasize educational programs, supplemented by counseling, arts and crafts, and recreation.

Institutionalized youths do not differ from the general population in their intellectual ability, but they are usually functioning several grade levels below their age group in academic achievement. This condition is frequently due to long absences from school or deprived home environments. In some institutions, students must attend school for the entire day, but half-day sessions with short classroom periods are more common. Small classes allow individualized instruction. The curriculum centers on the development of basic skills along with the internalization of good work habits and respect for authority. Juveniles who graduate from institutional school programs receive diplomas from the local school district, which do not contain the information that attendance took place within the institution. Some institutions (including many private ones) allow youths to attend the public schools in the community.

Vocational programs in institutions frequently stress skills that help maintain and serve the institutions' needs, such as cooking, gardening, or laundry service. Others incorporate training in computer skills, barbering, cosmetology, metalworking, woodshop, or auto mechanics. Such a program may be handicapped by a lack of modern equipment or well-trained instructors, but in some cases it has enough depth to prepare a youth for a work position after release.

In institutions for older offenders, those who will not be expected to return to school after release, the major focus of the treatment plan is centered on providing work experiences. In ranch, farm, or forestry-camp settings, work constitutes much of the daily activity of the resident. Some institutions allow youths to work in state facilities such as hospitals, parks, or forest reserves during the day and return to the institution at night. Because of the concern for security, however, the majority of the work activities tend to be concentrated on the grounds of the institutions.

Counseling is crucial to any treatment program for institutionalized youths. Much of the counseling is directed toward helping them adapt to the institutional setting and preparing them for return to the community after release. Group counseling is widely used because group techniques play upon the strong peer group influence present in adolescence, as well as upon the acknowledged importance of the inmate subculture in influencing institutional behavior. In addition, group counseling is less expensive in terms of counselor hours than is individual counseling.

Some institutional group counseling focuses on specific offender needs. After it was discovered that nearly 60 percent of those held in Kansas' only state institution for delinquent girls had been sexually abused, a counseling program was developed. In addition to helping the girls discuss the abuse they experienced in group sessions, the counseling focused on inappropriate feelings or behavior that may result from being sexually abused, including developing a negative self-image, distrust of adults, substance abuse, or running away. Participation is voluntary and, since dealing with sexual abuse is a long-term process, the group sessions continue through the girls' stay at the institution and the girls are encouraged to join support groups after release.[46]

Guided group interaction is a group technique that has received favorable comment as a treatment method. In guided group interaction, there is an awareness of the dynamics of the peer group culture and the importance of the peer group in influencing youths' values, attitudes, and behavior. Thus, in guided group interaction, the professional staff (group leaders) is rather unintrusive; it only gets the group started and from time to time keeps it directed. Each group member is considered responsible for all other members and each has an opportunity within the group setting to examine and evaluate his or her life experiences, personal deficiencies and handicaps, and strengths. Members of the group are expected to provide constructive support in helping each other achieve maturity and overcome their problems. If one member of the group fails, it is a reflection on the entire group.

Another method of group treatment that has aroused considerable public interest is the creation of "boot camps" designed to imitate the physically and emotionally challenging programs the armed services use for their new recruits. The appeal of boot camps is easy to understand. Offenders are given "no-nonsense" tough disciple in a no-frills atmosphere, yet are held for relatively short periods of time (usually 90 to 120 days), making the programs less costly than long-term institutionalization. Those committed to boot camps are usually nonviolent, older adolescents incarcerated for the first time.[47]

Although the majority of the states now operate boot camps,[48] there is little research information to show that they are successful in preventing recidivism once the enrollees return home. In Oklahoma, it was found that nearly half of the graduates had returned to institutions after two years, while in Georgia, comparisons of those who had completed boot camps with those released from the state's correctional institutions showed little difference in the recidivism of the two groups.[49]

These findings are disappointing, since the boot camp experience would seem to address many of the problems youthful offenders have, including low self-esteem and lack of self-discipline. Programming is designed to demonstrate to the youths that they can succeed in nondelinquent activity. It may be that the experience is too short to have a lasting effect. As Hengesh observed:

> Consider military boot camps. They are not intended to make a young person into a fully functional soldier. Rather, they provide a foundation of discipline, responsibility and self-esteem the military can build on during the advanced training that follows.[50]

Using this analogy, observers have concluded that boot camps will be much more effective if they are seen as the first step in a lengthier process of change. That is, after the initial boot camp experience, the released youth should be given intensive supervision in the community in an aftercare status so that the habits of personal discipline and responsibility for one's actions can be monitored and reinforced in the environment to which the youth has returned.[51]

This view would seem to be confirmed by a study that found boot camp participants' attitudes, perceptions of the future opportunities available to them, and views of their own abilities positively changed during the boot camp experience.[52] Once such change is in process, continued supervision and interaction with probation personnel in an aftercare setting could greatly enhance the possibility of reduced delinquency.

Factors that Inhibit the Effectiveness of Institutional Programming. The power of juvenile institutional programs to provide treatment is often limited by pressures to maintain tight control and custody to present a good image to state officials and prevent adverse reactions from the citizenry. The quality or amount of education, vocational training, or even civilized interaction between confined juveniles is frequently reduced in the name of security.

The toleration of such behavior by staff members comes about because the outward appearance of a smoothly running, secure institution becomes the primary goal and other goals become subordinated to it. In addition, lengthy exposure to the deplorable conditions in many institutions for delinquent youths creates a kind of psychic numbness in the staff and they become blasé. James vividly described this process.

> After many months of daily exposure to agencies and institutions in our so-called juvenile system of justice, I began to find the reform schools and jails less depressing. I began to grow accustomed to it all. This helped me better understand the men and women who work in these places. Slowly I began to realize that they were not (at least not *all*) sadistic, brutal, or stupid. In fact, many decent people had simply grown accustomed to the system and saw it as normal. The children's prison was the place where they worked and they saw their job as keeping the institution running without extreme confusion or breakdown—not unlike that of the man who tends a factory production line. When the system was operating smoothly for the staff—that is, when the children moved about the grounds in an orderly manner; when they assaulted only each other; when the runaway rate was low; and (most important) when the neighboring townspeople were not complaining—then they felt they were doing a "good job," even when children left the institution as bad as or worse than when they entered it.[53]

It should also be noted that when the goal of conformity is achieved, the goal of rehabilitation frequently is not. Youths can be trained to act in a restrained, submissive manner within institutions, but such schooling is not preparing them for life in the "real world" after release, when they will not be followed around by "keepers" telling them exactly how to behave.

THE JUVENILE'S RESPONSE TO INSTITUTIONAL LIFE

There is a great deal of evidence that correctional institutions have a negative impact on the residents. Even under optimal conditions, there are dangers that the youth might be physically or sexually assaulted by the staff or other residents, be victimized through extortion, be humiliated or confused, develop a negative self-image, and experience other forms of deprivation and anguish. Even in institutions that have highly trained professional staffs and are oriented toward treatment, residents might be hostile to the staff and each other and react to the experience badly.

Residents are not always treated equally or fairly. Deals are frequently made between youth workers and strong juveniles in institutions to preserve the "peace." This may involve giving these youths special privileges that have not been merited through their behavior, smuggling in contraband for them, or looking the other way when the toughs keep other residents in line. Underpaid youth workers struggling for advancement or older workers afraid of losing their positions are particularly vulnerable to such manipulation, as are nonprofessional custodial personnel.

Violence in Institutions

Studies of violence and aggression by the inmates of secure institutions have attributed this behavior to either the *deprivation perspective* or the *cultural-importation perspective*. According to the deprivation perspective, aggressive behavior is a response

---

These problems are illustrated by a youth's description of his first taste of institutional life.

During the four months I was initially incarcerated in juvenile hall, I experienced another side of life that is known only by the people confined to such an environment. I experienced my first physical beating, my first sexual molestation, my first placement in solitary confinement, and I watched, for the first time, an act of rape. I also committed my first act of violence, and my victim nearly died. . . .

Driving past the entrance to the Los Angeles County Juvenile Hall was a terrifying experience. As I got out of the car, I glanced several times at the high wall, while two men led me to a large metal door that was unlocked from the inside. The door opened, and I was nudged through the doorway into a small room.

A counselor appeared and escorted me to another building. Its door was unlocked from the inside, too. I stepped through the doorway. The noise was deafening. There was a fight going on just a few feet from the counselor. He ignored it. Kids were hollering and running all over the place. . . .

The counselor who had escorted me inside took me by my arm and led me to his office. There he told me the rules, most of which were being violated when I entered the dorm. . . . He then took me to my assigned bed and said, "Make it up before you do anything else."

Seconds later, I made my first mistake. I took the blankets and sheets folded at the foot of my bed and laid them on the bed next to mine. A black kid, twice my size and several years older, picked up the bedding and threw it on the floor. "You better watch what you put on my bed," he said, staring at me. I looked at him, saying nothing. I had never seen a black person before. He scared the hell out of me.

He shoved me, asking, "What do you think you're doing?"

I started to tell him as he took a step forward and hit me hard, right on my mouth.

I had never been hit with a closed fist until then. The punch knocked me to the floor. I laid there with the pain. The bully began kicking me. I did my best to cover my head. The counselor allowed this to go on for a few minutes before he pulled the kid away from me. Crying, I stood up and saw the other kids looking at me. My nose was swollen and bleeding.

"You'll be okay," the counselor said. "You better learn not to mess with anybody. Stop being such a baby."

I was confused. I *was* a baby. I'd never been spanked before, let alone punched or kicked. When I was unable to control my crying, the counselor slapped me hard. I fell down onto my bed, rolled over it, and landed on the floor.

He said, "You better fight next time, boy. I'm not here to babysit you."[54]

to the harsh conditions, degradation, and deprivation the inmate experiences. The cultural-importation perspective, in contrast, argues that violent and aggressive behavior is merely a manifestation of previously held values and behavior patterns that the inmate brings to the institution and uses to gain as many advantages and material rewards as possible.

A study of aggressive behavior by youths in four juvenile correctional institutions that varied in organizational structure and programming from custodial to treatment-oriented found that a history of aggressive behavior was the most important variable in explaining inmate aggression within an institution, regardless of the type of institution in which the youth was held. A history of aggressive behavior, however, appeared to have a stronger influence on the aggressive behavior of individuals in treatment-oriented institutions than it did on those in institutions with a custodial emphasis. The researchers noted that

> The depersonalization and deprivation in this coercive environment may make the pains of imprisonment so acute, encompassing, and restrictive that the potential influences of preprison variables are largely blocked.[55]

The problem of violence in juvenile institutions is well documented. One report found that, in a one-year period, there were 27 homicides of youths in custody and nearly 1,400 assaults committed by juveniles on other juveniles required medical attention.[56] To address the problem of institutional violence, security and treatment personnel are being trained in crisis intervention and management techniques and policies and procedures for handling disruptive incidents are being clearly defined. The physical environments in which youths with a history of violence are held must be designed to ensure the safety of the youths, other residents, and staff members. A staff team approach and staff education in how to deal with such emergency situations as resident assaults on staff, riot control, or hostage taking should be provided.[57]

The rural location of many training schools contributes to the isolation of residents, the majority of whom are urban youths, from their families. The predominance of blacks or other nonwhites in institutional populations[58] is in sharp contrast to the high number of whites in the executive, treatment, teaching, and supervisory staffs.[59] This reduces inmates' opportunities to observe and identify with role models of their own race so they may instead identify with older or stronger inmates. Also, there is always a potential for inmate victimization.

Adaptation to Institutional Life

Juveniles placed in institutions find that they must adapt to two forces working upon them with conflicting goals and modes of operation—the staff and fellow residents. To achieve the goal of release, the juvenile resident must seem to be cooperating with the staff and progressing in the treatment program set up for him or her. At the same time, there are pressures from fellow residents that must somehow be dealt with. The resident subculture may make demands upon the juvenile that are at odds with those made by staff members.

The boredom and barrenness of the institutional experience can have negative effects on juveniles. *(Photo credit: Jay Paris)*

Sieverdes and Bartollas, in a study of juveniles institutionalized in two coeducational training schools, developed a typology of juvenile modes of adaptation to life in these institutions. They identified youths as conformists, innovators, ritualists, retreatists, and rebels. While the *conformists* tend to identify with the staff, act in a cooperative way, and avoid the inmate subculture, the *innovators* are manipulative and deceptive in their dealings with both staff members and their peers and the *ritualists* are youths who have been spending a good deal of time in institutions and feel rather comfortable in the institutional setting. *Retreatists,* in contrast, have difficulty in adapting to the life style and may seek to escape through running away, suicide, or other self-destructive activity. *Rebels* seek to control the resident subculture through force or intimidation, resist institutional programming, and tend to act in a hostile way toward the staff.[60]

Another study, which considered the resident social structure in a juvenile institution for girls, revealed that the adaptation patterns focused on establishing family-like types of relationships within the institution. Giallombardo defined the social world of imprisoned girls as being set up in "family groups." Almost all the inmates had culturally defined roles—the "true butch" (homosexual in the outside world also), the "trust-to-be-butch" (assumes the male role in the institution, but prefers heterosexual relationships on the outside), the "jive butch" and "jive fem" (who move around from one partner to another without forming any serious attachments), the "fem" (who maintains the female role), and the "trust-to-be-fem" (who assumes the female role in the institution, but might go either way on the outside).

Giallombardo described the initiation process into the family structure of the institution:

> A new arrival is approached by a few girls in each cottage to determine what she is like. She will be asked her name, age, home town, and whether she originates from upstate or downstate. Inmates at Eastern who are from the metropolis downstate are especially interested to learn whether any of their friends are in youth house juvenile center. The newcomer will also be asked what her offense is, whether she has used any drugs, and if so, the kinds of drugs. If she is not an Eastern recidivist, she will be asked, "Do you know what racket is?'" "Are you in the gay life?" The latter question is to ascertain whether her experience is limited to institutions or whether it extends to the community.[61]

Giallombardo concluded that the informal social structure provides functional relationships for the girls, since it gives them substitutes for the community and family ties that have been broken. It supplies protection, mutual aid, and affection. She noted that the homosexual family structure is tolerated in institutions because it helps the administration maintain order and discipline. "If an inmate continually breaks the rules, she may be disowned by the parents; this action would mean exclusion from the entire family group. For most inmates the emotional and social support gained within the family is of such magnitude that they will conform."[62]

Institutional Effectiveness

It is difficult to separate the effects of institutionalization from all the other factors in a youth's life that must be considered in attempting to ascertain if those effects are predominantly positive or negative. Most youths released from institutions return to their former environments, family situations, and peer-group influences, all of which may have contributed to the development of their delinquency.

Recidivism statistics for youths released from institutions are difficult to obtain. Once released, a youth may have no future contact with institutional personnel unless he or she is recommitted for a new offense. And since many youths leave institutions when they are close to the upper age limit of the juvenile status, future offenses are referred to the adult system and may not be brought to the attention of the juvenile justice system personnel, since there is little communication and exchange of information between the two systems on such matters. These conditions, in addition to the geographic mobility of families, and particularly of young adults, make compilation of recidivism data a difficult task. We noted earlier in this chapter that Hamparian et al. found that 76 percent of the violent juveniles in their study who had been committed to juvenile training schools were arrested as adults and 69 percent of those arrested went to prison at least once.[63] A study of juveniles who were sentences to two maximum security obedience/conformity model institutions in Illinois tested what was termed the "suppression" effect of institutionalization. The researchers tabulated the number of delinquent acts committed by each juvenile during the 12 months before institutionalization and also the number recorded during the 12 months after release. They found that the mean number of arrests for each delinquent during the 12 months before commitment was 6.3, compared to a mean number of 2.0 during the 12 months after release. On the basis of this finding a "suppression" effect could be hypothesized, with the researchers taking the position that the institutionalization experience had a deterrent effect on future delinquent behavior.[64] However, there are other possible explanations for the reduced delinquency after release, including a maturing of the offender during commitment, or the possibility that, for the older youths, delinquent behavior was not as easily detected and recorded.

There is a general perception that the failure rate for all types of institutionalized juveniles, measured in terms of new offenses, is quite substantial. This raises the question of how success and failure should be measured. If a child has learned to cope better with his or her environment, social situation, and family problems, and has developed ego strength and internalized a prosocial value system, should the institutionalization process by considered successful even if the child engages in some future delinquencies? Or should a young person who stays within the law after release but emerges from the institution hostile, dependent, emotionally scarred, or fearful of authority be rated a success merely because of lack of recidivism?

Traumatic institutionalization experiences can change a youth profoundly. An adult offender, serving a 10 year sentence for assault with a deadly weapon, described his ordeal in solitary confinement at the age of nine and its effects on him.

> After wrestling the bat from my hands, two counselors took me to solitary confinement. Solitary consisted of an almost soundproof room with a bed, a sink, and a toilet. Encased in a steel door was a metal flap that could be opened only from the outside so a counselor could look inside. The only other time it was unlocked was during meals. I thought I would go crazy. . . . I had contact with another person only when I was fed, showered, and counted. At those times, the counselors refused to talk. At no time did I hear or see anyone else inside the building.
>
> I remained in solitary for three months.
>
> One day, the cell's door was opened and the clothes I'd worn into the dorm were thrown at me. Then, the first human voice I'd heard for months told me my father had come to take me home. I stood there, frightened. I was unwilling and unable to leave the cell where I had sat staring at the walls, seeing no one. . . . The counselor shouted at me to move. Then he entered the cell, took me by the arm, and guided me from the building. I remember how bright the sun was. I had to cover my eyes with my hands all the way to the juvenile hall's waiting room.
>
> Then, walking into the room, I saw my father. I stood looking at him and watched as a puzzled expression covered his face. Years later, I recalled that look when Dad told me he'd had a strange feeling come over him when he first saw me and looked into my eyes. He said it was as if his eyes told him I was his son, but my eyes told him his son was no longer there.[65]

The contaminating effect of the association of less serious offenders with hardened delinquents is another harsh fact of institutional life. Even youths who do not learn specific modes of unacceptable behavior or criminal techniques from others are bound to be influenced by the crudity and barrenness of institutional life. There is little room here for refinement, cultural development, or creativity.

Normalization

Normalization means providing those youths who are drawn into the justice system with experiences that approximate as nearly as possible those of normal community life.[66] For example, the situation farthest from "normal" is removal of a child from home and community and placement in an artificial, structured environment that is far removed in activities and interactions from ordinary life. The situation closest to "normal" would be supervision within the home community, either in the youth's own home or in some type of community residential treatment. In the case of youths who need secure custody, the institutional experience should be made as nearly normal as possible, through placing them in small group units, allowing them to retain their individuality in dress and possessions, encouraging them to develop their talents, and providing opportunities for contact with the outside world.

In the 1970s, the state of Massachusetts took a radical step toward normalization by closing almost all of its training schools and placing the formerly institutionalized youths in other types of programs. In an attempt to humanize treatment, therapeutic communities were developed within the existing institutions. Youths were allowed to wear their hair as they chose and wear street clothes rather than institutional garb. Marching in silent formation was discontinued. Several facilities for the most disturbed or rebellious youngsters were eventually closed. Attempts were made to develop programs for girls and boys in the same institution and even in the same cottage. The length of stay for youths was reduced from an average of eight months to an average of three months.[67]

Attempts were made to change the authority system in the institutions by emphasizing group processes within the cottages. The juveniles were given a good deal of decision-making responsibility for their individual units in the hope of counteracting the negative effects of the inmate subculture.

Evaluations of the Massachusetts experiment revealed both positive effects and continuing problems in this normalization and deinstitutionalization experiment. It was found that approximately 90 percent of the youths who would formerly have been placed in secure institutions could be handled in community residential or nonresidential placements. Programming for the delinquents who had to be kept in secure facilities, however, was found to be inadequate and the youths who were placed in community programs made better adjustments than those who were held in secure facilities. Youths in programs that offered a number of treatment options were found to have made more successful adjustments than those in programs that had few treatment options.[68]

Over a period of time, the recidivism rates for the youths who were removed from the institutions were found to be similar to those for the youths who had been institutionalized in the past. Romig suggested that the reason for this was the lack of quality community-based programs.[69] The experiment also showed that some youths must be institutionalized because they pose a threat to the community.

In spite of its problems, the Massachusetts experiment must be regarded as a milestone in juvenile correctional reform. It advanced the goal of more humane treatment of youthful offenders and showed that community placement is a viable disposition that can safely and effectively be used in lieu of institutionalization for many juvenile offenders.

SUMMARY

The youths institutionalized in the United States vary widely in their personal and behavioral characteristics. Populations of long-term, secure institutions are largely made up of hardcore offenders who have been placed there after repeated attempts to change their behavior or supervise their activities have been fruitless. These adjudicated delinquents receive determinate (set length) or indeterminate (open-ended, possibly extending to the upper age of juvenile court jurisdiction) sentences, depending on the standards of their state. Other institutions, particularly private institutions, house youths who pose no threat to the community but have been placed in these facilities after options for their care or placement in other situations have been exhausted.

Juvenile correctional facilities include long-term facilities (training schools, ranches, forestry camps, farms, halfway houses, and group homes) and short-term facilities (detention centers, shelter homes, and reception and diagnostic centers). Juveniles are also held in adult jails. Short-term facilities function as holding points for youths before their juvenile court hearings or after adjudication but prior to longer term placement, although in some states detention can be given as a disposition. Youths in adult jails may be held there because their cases have been transferred to adult criminal courts, or because there is no available detention facility for juveniles. Long-term facilities may be rather open or highly secure. The most secure type of juvenile facility, the training school, exists in all states. Training schools may vary in appearance from old fortress-style buildings to modern cottage settlements. Their programs and goal orientations also vary according to the attitudes and guidelines of the controlling state authority, the institution, and the staff. Youths are normally classified and treated according to their dangerousness, observed social or psychological problems, age, and sex. Educational and vocational programs are used, together with various types of individual or group therapy and counseling.

Institutions have not demonstrated their effectiveness in deterring youths from further criminal behavior. Punishment or control, rather than rehabilitation, is too often the most important consideration. Physical brutality and mentally debilitating cruelties have frequently been documented as occurring in juvenile institutions.

Young people respond to their institutional experiences in various ways, ranging from open rebellion, manipulation, or mindless conformity, to a genuine change of attitude and behavior. Harmful effects of institutionalization include isolation from family and community, exploitation by other inmates, acquaintance with more hardened delinquents and schooling in crime, and development of a general feeling of hopelessness and abandonment.

Experiments with removal of all but dangerous offenders from institutions and their placement in community-based treatment have been attempted, with the most radical approach being Massachusetts' closing of its juvenile institutions. The Massachusetts experiment revealed that community placement can be safely and effectively used instead of institutionalization for many juvenile offenders.

DISCUSSION QUESTIONS

1. Why have some states passed serious delinquency statutes? Do you think this trend is a reaction to the criticism that juvenile courts are "soft" on serious delinquency offenders?

2. Why is the decision to hold a juvenile in detention rather than release him or her such an important one? Do you agree that the factors presented on risk assessment instruments used by juvenile detention centers are the appropriate ones to consider in making this decision?

3. Juveniles held in institutions for long periods of time tend to develop an informal social system, with the leaders having power and privileges over the other residents. What are the conditions in institutions that tend to bring about the formation of such informal groupings?

4. Why does the placement of juvenile offenders in "boot camps" have such appeal to the general public? Why do you think the boot camp experience does not seem to have long-term effects in changing behavior?

5. Are long-term juvenile correctional institutions effective in deterring delinquent behavior? Discuss.

NOTES

1. Martin L. Forst, Bruce A. Fisher, and Robert B. Coates, "Indeterminate and Determinate Sentencing of Juvenile Delinquents: A National Survey of Approaches to Commitment and Release Decision-Making," *Juvenile and Family Court Journal* 35, 3 (Summer 1985), 1–12.
2. *Ibid.*, 9.
3. *Ibid.*
4. R. DeComo, S. Tunis, B. Krisberg, and N. Herrara, *Juveniles Taken into Custody Research Program: FY 1992 Annual Report* (Washington, DC: Office of Juvenile Justice and Delinquency Prevention, U.S. Department of Justice, 1993), reported in Michael A. Jones and Barry Krisberg, *Images and Reality: Juvenile Crime, Youth Violence, and Public Policy* (San Francisco: National Counil on Crime and Delinquency, 1994), 27.
5. B. Krisberg, D. Onek, M. Jones, and I. Schwartz, *Juveniles in State Custody: Prospects for Community-Based Care of Troubled Adolescents*, (San Francisco: National Council on Crime and Delinquency, 1993), reported in Jones and Krisberg, *Images and Reality*, 28.
6. Howard N. Snyder and Melissa Sickmund, "Analysis of Data from OJJDP's Census of Juveniles in Residential Placement 1997," *Juvenile Offenders and Victims: 1999 National Report* (Washington, DC: Office of Juvenile Justice and Delinquency Prevention, 1999), 190.
7. Donna Martin Hamparian, Joseph M. David, Judith M. Jacobson, and Robert E. McGraw, *The Young Criminal Years of the Violent Few* (Washington, DC: U.S. Department of Justice, Office of Juvenile Justice and Delinquency Prevention, 1985), 18.
8. Larry Cole, *Our Children's Keepers* (Greenwich, CT: Fawcett, 1974), 13.
9. Anthony Platt, "The Rise of the Child-Saving Movement: A Study of Social Policy and Correctional Reform," in Frederic L. Faust and Paul J. Brantingham, eds., *Juvenile Justice Philosophy* (St. Paul, MN: West Publishing Company, 1974), 129.
10. Cole, *Our Children's Keepers*, 14–15.
11. Robert G. Caldwell and James A. Black, *Juvenile Delinquency* (New York: Wiley, 1971), 269.
12. Clara T. Leonard, "Family Homes for Paupers and Dependent Children," Annual Conference of Charities, *Proceedings* (Chicago, 1879), p. 174; quoted in Platt, "The Rise of the Child-Saving Movement," 123.
13. Donald Dale Jackson, "It Took Trains to Put Street Kids on the Right Track Out of the Slums," *Smithsonian* 15, 4 (July 1984), 95.
14. *Ibid.*, 94–102.

15. Cole, *Our Children's Keepers*, 13.
16. Snyder and Sickmund, "Analysis of Data from OJJDP's Census of Juveniles in Residential Placement 1997, "*Juvenile Offenders and Victims*, 186, 198.
17. *Ibid.*, 191.
18. *Ibid.*, 209.
19. Commission on Accreditation for Corrections, *Manual of Standards for Juvenile Detention Facilities and Services* (Rockville, MD: Commission on Accreditation for Corrections, 1979), xx.
20. Office of Juvenile Justice and Delinquency Prevention, *Census of Juveniles in Residential Placement 1997*, reported in Snyder and Sickmund, *Juvenile Offenders and Victims*, 201.
21. *Schall v. Martin*, 52 U.S.L.W. 4681, June 5, 1984.
22. Charles E. Frazier and John C. Cochran, "Detention of Juveniles: Its Effects on Subsequent Juvenile Court Processing Decisions," *Youth and Society* 17, 3 (March 1986), 286–305.
23. Christopher Dunn, Robert L. Perry, Stephen A. Cernkovich, and Jerry W. Wicks, *Race and Juvenile Justice in Ohio* (Bowling Green, OH: Bowling Green State University, 1993), 78.
24. Vicky Turner Church, "Meeting Disproportionate Minority Confinement Mandates," *Corrections Today* 56, 7 (December 1994), 70.
25. David W. Roush, "Juvenile Detention Programming," *Federal Probation* 57, 3 (September 1993), 30.
26. *Ibid.*
27. National Council on Crime and Delinquency, *Standards and Goals for the Detention of Children and Youth* (Washington, DC: U.S. Government Printing Office, 1975), 41–42.
28. David Vanderwall, *Multi-County Juvenile Attention System Responsible Behavior Program*. Canton, OH: Multi-County Juvenile Attention System, 2001, 5–6.
29. Correctional Council of the National Council on Crime and Delinquency, *Status Offenders and the Juvenile Court* (New York: National Council on Crime and Delinquency, 1975), 6.
30. Michael J. Dale, "Children in Adult Jails: A Look at Liability Issues," *American Jails 4, 5 (January–February, 1991)*, 30.
31. *Ibid.*
32. Snyder and Sickmund, *Juvenile Offenders and Victims*, 208.
33. *Ibid.*
34. Ken Kerle, "Juveniless and Jails," *American Jails* 4, 5 (January–February 1991), 3.
35. Ira M. Schwartz, in *Justice for Juveniles* (Lexington, MA: Lexington Books, 1989), 82–83.
36. U.S. Department of Justice, *Children in Custody* (Washington, DC: U.S. Bureau of Justice Statistics, 1986), 62.
37. David Street, Robert D. Vinter, and Charles Perrow, *Organization for Treatment* (New York: Free Press, 1966), 21.
38. Barry C. Feld, "A Comparative Analysis of Organizational Structure and Inmate Subcultures in Institutions for Juvenile Offenders," *Crime and Delinquency* 27, 3 (July 1981), 346–347.
39. *Ibid.*
40. Peter W. Greenwood and Susan Turner, "Evaluation of the Paint Creek Youth Center: A Residential Program for Serious Delinquents," *Criminology* 31, 2 (1993), 263–279.
41. *Specialized Treatment Services*, folder describing the program at Specialized Treatment Services, Mercer, Pennsylvania, 1991.
42. Eric D. Poole and Robert M. Regoli, "Violence in Juvenile Institutions," *Criminology* 21, 2 (May 1983), 213–232.
43. Caldwell and Black, *Juvenile Delinquency*, 278.
44. *Morales v. Turman*, 383 F.Supp.53 (Ed. Texas 1974).
45. *Nelson v. Heyne*, 491 F.2d 352 (7 Cir.1974).
46. James Moore, "Overcoming the Past," *Corrections Today* 53, 1 (February 1991), 40–47.
47. Donald Hengesh, "Think of Boot Camps as a Foundation for Change, Not an Instant Cure," *Corrections Today* 53, 6 (October 1991), 106–108.
48. Velmer S. Burton, Jr., James W. Marquart, Steven J. Cuvelier, Leanne Fiftal Alarid, and Robert J. Hunter, "A Study of Attitudinal Change Among Boot Camp Participants," *Federal Probation* 57, 3 (September 1993), 46.

49. Anthony W. Salerno, "Boot Camps: A Critique and a Proposed Alternative," *Journal of Offender Rehabilitation* 20 (1994), 151.

50. Hengesh "Think of Boot Camps as a Foundation for Change, Not an Instant Cure," 1–6.

51. *Ibid.*, 108.

52. Burton et al., "A Study of Attitudinal Change Among Boot Camp Participants," 46–52.

53. Howard James, *Children in Trouble: A National Scandal* (New York: Christian Science Publishing Company, 1970), 2.

54. Dwight Boyd Roberts, "Imprisoning Violent Youths Exposes Them to Physical and Sexual Abuse," in David L. Bender, Bruno Leone, Bonnie Szumski, Carol Wekesser, Michael D. Biskup, and Charles P. Cozic, *Youth Violence* (San Diego: Greenhaven Press, Inc., 1992), 234–235.

55. Eric D. Poole and Robert M. Regoli, "Violence in Juvenile Institutions," 214.

56. George M. Camp and Camille Graham Camp, *The Corrections Yearbook, 1993* (South Salem, NY: Criminal Justice Institute, 1993), 25.

57. Henry R. Cellini, "Management and Treatment of Institutionalized Violent Juveniles," *Corrctions Today* 57, 4 (July 1994), 98–102.

58. In 1997, minorities made up 67% of the juveniles committed to public residential facilities. This figure was nearly twice their proportion in the juvenile population. Minorities also made up 55% of those in private residential placement. Snyder and and Sickmund, *Juvenile Offenders and Victims*, 194.

59. American Correctional Association, *1994 Directory of Juvenile and Adult Correctional Departments, Institutions, Agencies, and Paroling Authorities* (Laurel, MD: American Correctional Association, 1994), xliii.

60. Christopher M. Sieverdes and Clement Bartollas, "Modes of Adaptation and Game Behavior at Two Juvenile Institutions," 27–35, in Paul C. Friday and V. Lorne Stewart, eds., *Youth Crime and Juvenile Justice: International Perspectives.* Copyright 1977 by the American Society of Criminology.

61. Rose Giallombardo, "The Social World of Imprisoned Girls," in *Juvenile Delinquency* (New York: Wiley, 1976), 566.

62. *Ibid.*, 577.

63. Hamparian et al., *The Young Criminal Years of the Violent Few*, 18.

64. Charles A. Murray and Louis A. Cox, Jr., *Beyond Probation: Juvenile Corrections and the Chronic Delinquent* (Beverly Hills, CA: Sage Publications, 1979), 31–43.

65. Roberts, "Imprisoning Violent Youths Exposes Them to Physical and Sexual Abuse," 238–239.

66. Daniel Katkin, Drew Hyman, and John Kramer, *Juvenile Delinquency and the Juvenile Justice System* (North Scituate, MA: Duxbury Press, 1976), 458.

67. U.S. Department of Justice, *Juvenile Correctional Reform in Massachusetts* (Washington, DC: U.S. Government Printing Office, 1977), 5–7.

68. Office of Juvenile Justice and Delinquency Prevention, *Juvenile Justice Before and After the Onset of Delinquency* (Washington, DC: U.S. Department of Justice, 1981), 45.

69. Romig, *Justice for Our Children*, 179–181.

CHAPTER 16

AFTERCARE
AND NONSECURE
RESIDENTIAL PLACEMENT

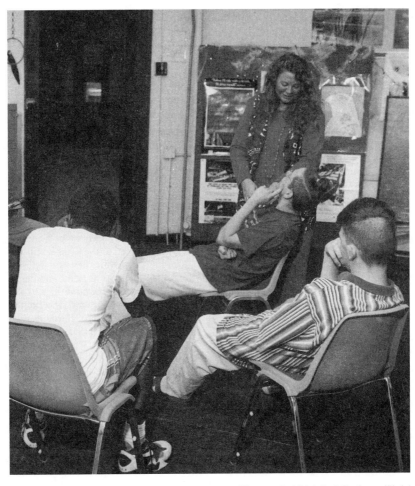

(Photo credit: Nick J. Cool, The Image Works)

THE JUVENILE AFTERCARE DECISION
THE AFTERCARE PROCESS
Preparation for Release
The Aftercare Treatment Plan
General and Special Rules of Aftercare
Discharge from Aftercare
AFTERCARE REVOCATION
The Revocation Process
Youths' Rights at a Revocation Hearing
AFTERCARE EFFECTIVENESS
INTENSIVE AFTERCARE FOR HIGH-RISK JUVENILES
Developing Intensive Case Management Plans
Implementing Intensive Case Management
Effectiveness of Intensive Aftercare
AFTERCARE AND RESIDENTIAL TREATMENT
History of the Halfway House Movement
Highfields
Community Hostels

A _____ High School student was charged in juvenile court Friday with the stabbing of an elderly couple in their home. [He] faces delinquency charges of two counts of attempted aggravated murder, one count of aggravated burglary, and one count of aggravated robbery. The [elderly couple] were attacked when they answered the front door of their _____ home. . . . Police said Johnson, a 10th grader, came to the home after fleeing the school following a fight. . . . While handcuffed, (he) bolted from the principal's office and out of the school. . . .

_____ spent four years in the custody of the Ohio Department of Youth Services after being convicted of rape in 1998. [He] was paroled in September (approximately two months before this incident) according to Kevin Miller of the youth services agency.[1]

A 16-year-old recently released from a youth prison was charged Saturday in connection with the kidnapping and robbery of two young women in the Chapel Hill Mall parking lot. . . . Police said _____ approached _____ and _____ while they were walking to their vehicle. [He] then allegedly pressed a handgun to the cheek of _____ and demanded money . . . _____ forced the women into their car and made them drive him to a cash machine . . . _____ got away with an undetermined amount of cash from the victims. After being apprehended, _____ told police he was just released from Indian River Juvenile Correctional Facility in Massillon, where he'd been serving time for an aggravated robbery charge.[2]

In Chapters 11 and 13, we noted that recent trends in juvenile justice policy include longer dispositions (sentences) for juvenile offenders, more juveniles being institutionalized, transfer of more and more juvenile cases to adult criminal courts, and use of blended sentences. Even though many serious juvenile offenders are held in institutions for long periods of time, nearly all of them will be released and returned to the community at some point. Most of these will still be under juvenile justice system supervision after release. In the large majority of cases they will be returning to the communities, schools, and family situations they were involved in before incarceration. In spite of the best efforts of institutional personnel to positively influence these youths, the institutional experience may have had detrimental effects on them and they may quickly return to the same patterns of unacceptable behavior that led to their incarceration. As a result, they may pose an immediate threat to the community. The two aforementioned cases illustrate the importance of the release decision and the careful supervision of youths after release.

THE JUVENILE AFTERCARE DECISION

There is no standard for determining when a youth should be released from an institution. In most states, commitments are indeterminate in length and can continue until the juvenile is judged to be rehabilitated or reaches the age of majority, which is 21 in some states and 18 in others. Most juveniles are not held to the age of majority but are released prior to that time under the supervision of aftercare officers in the community. Although determinate dispositions, mandating a specific length of institutionalization, are now the most widely used type, some states have responded to the overcrowding problems caused by increased commitment by releasing youths to aftercare after shorter periods of incarceration.[3] The Office of Juvenile Justice and Delinquency Prevention's Census of Juveniles in Residential Placement 1997 found that the average length of stay varied by type of facility (public or private), gender, race, and the type of offense that led to incarceration. Those in public facilities were held an average of six months, compared to five months for those in private facilities. Males had an average commitment time of more than six months, compared to an average of approximately five months for females. Minority youths were held an average of two weeks longer than nonminority whites and those who had committed violent offenses had been in the facilities an average of nearly nine months, compared to six months for those who had committed other types of offenses.[4]

The process of releasing a juvenile from an institution varies according to the organization of the juvenile justice system in the state from which the youth was originally committed. In those states with a state youth authority or youth commission, the release decision is generally made by an institutional release committee composed of those staff members who have had opportunities to assess the juvenile's progress in the institution, subject to the approval of a representative of the state youth authority or commission. In those states where commitment is made directly by a judge to a specific institution, the recommendation of the institutional release committee or board is subject to the approval of the committing judge. Even in states where the youth authority or commission makes the release decision, the committing judge may be informed of the youth's release as a matter of courtesy.

The institutional release committee is usually composed of such staff members as the cottage supervisor, social worker, teachers, youth counselors, and a representative of the administrative staff. In cases where the offense for which the youth was committed was extremely serious (murder, rape), an examination by and a recommendation from a staff psychiatrist may be required by the committee making the decision.

The factors the committee generally considers in making its decision include the youth's adjustment within the institution, changes of attitude as perceived by testing and observation by the staff members, and the youth's willingness and ability to plan for the future and set attainable goals. Other considerations, notably committee members' reactions to the youth's appearance or to the offense that resulted in the commitment, may also influence their decisions.

THE AFTERCARE PROCESS

In keeping with the trend toward differentiating juvenile offenders from adults through the use of separate terminology, the release of juveniles from institutions under the supervision of officers in the community is commonly called *aftercare*, whereas release of adults under the same type of supervision is termed *parole*. However, in keeping with the movement toward more formalization of juvenile justice proceedings, several states now use the term *parole* rather than *aftercare* to describe supervision of juveniles returned to the community after institutionalization.

Youths released from institutions operated under the supervision of a state authority are supervised by aftercare officers employed by that body. Since there are no federal juvenile courts, children under 18 who violate federal laws are dealt with in the U.S. district courts or have their cases transferred to state juvenile or criminal courts and their aftercare is also supervised by state authorities.[5] In states where no central authority handles juvenile institutions, local jurisdictions employ aftercare officers. In some jurisdictions, the same people may serve as both probation and aftercare officers.

State juvenile codes provide for several different types of aftercare (parole). These are shown in Figure 16–1, according to their determinate or indeterminate nature and the percentages of states using each type. The determinate types (1 through 4) differ slightly. In Type 1 the length of parole (aftercare) is part of the specific length of commitment set by the court, while in Type 2 the length is set by the supervising agency, based on offense and criminal history. Types 3 and 4 have a set minimum period, but the maximum period may be extended. The amount of extension is limited for Type 3, but may be extended for an indeterminate period in Type 4. The indeterminate types also vary. Types 5, 6, and 7 have some limits regarding minimum or maximum lengths, while in Type 8 they are completely discretionary.[6] As shown in Figure 16–1, the vast majority of states use some type of indeterminate aftercare supervision.

The positive aspects of release to aftercare as opposed to continued institutionalization are readily discernible. The shorter the period of institutionalization, the smaller the chance that the youth will become deeply involved in the inmate subculture within the institution. Return to the community at the earliest opportune time allows the positive values, norms, and attitudes of the community to influence a youth's behavior. Return to regular school classes, as opposed to education in the artificial environment of the institution, can also aid the youth in the adjustment process. Aftercare officers' efforts to promote part- or full-time employment for the released juvenile may open doors for him or her and make the difference between continued delinquency and a turnaround in the young person's life. Finally, long periods of institutionalization, except in cases where they are dictated for the protec-

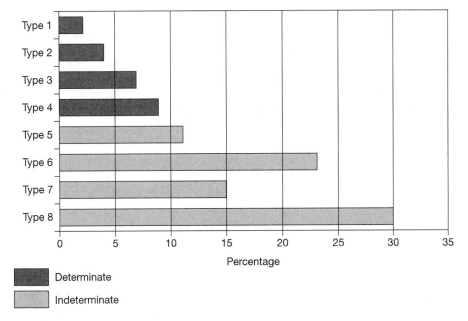

Figure 16–1. Percentages of Parole Types across the United States *(Source:* Jose B. Ashford and Craig Winston LeCroy, *"Juvenile Parole Policy in the United States:" Determinate Versus Indeterminate Models," Justice Quarterly 10, 2 [June 1993], 191.)*

tion of the community, decrease the possibilities for successful adjustment after release.

Although the aftercare process is similar in some respects to the probation process discussed in Chapter 14, there are a number of differences. Youths referred to aftercare may have had a number of unsuccessful probation experiences before institutionalization. Strategies of aftercare may call for different methods from those used when the youth was on probation. In addition, juveniles referred to aftercare tend to have committed more offenses, and more serious offenses, than juveniles placed on probation. Since the young person has been removed from the community and socialized in the institutional culture and life-style, readjustment to life outside the institution must be undertaken as part of the aftercare process. For some youths, this involves helping them stay away from or resist influences toward misbehavior that are present in the peer culture to which they return. For others, institutionalization may have produced an unhealthy dependence upon others that must be reversed through aftercare activities.

Preparation for Release

Preparation for aftercare may begin weeks or even months before release. Those most deeply involved in the juvenile's treatment program should help the youth assess his or her strengths and weaknesses and make realistic plans for the future. If the juvenile is returning home, weekend visits or even a longer furlough period may precede release. In some institutions, those who are approaching release are assigned to a pre-release or honor cottage where they are given more responsibility and flexibility in their activities and may be allowed to leave the grounds for various social activities.

Many factors must be taken into account in preparing a young person for release from an institution. Of primary importance is the home situation to which he or she will return. During institutionalization, contacts with families should be maintained and children must be informed of and made to face any changes in the home that have occurred in their absence (such as death or desertion of a parent, unemployment, or change of place of residence). If returning home seems inadvisable because the environment there is judged unsuitable, or because the parents are reluctant to accept responsibility for the youth, placement in foster care or a residential treatment center (halfway house) may be the best solution. In either case, prerelease activity may include a visit or weekend stay at home or at the prospective placement site.

When home visits are made a part of the prerelease program, coordination of efforts and exchange of information with local law enforcement authorities are a necessity. In large metropolitan areas, youths who are released for home visits may commit new offenses that are never reported to the institution's personnel.

The National Council of Juvenile and Family Court Judges, in its recommendations for handling serious offenders, emphasized that their aftercare supervision must be intensive, stating:

> Attention should be directed toward gradual re-entry of youths into the community through a staging process utilizing halfway houses, group homes, day treatment, and other appropriate aftercare programs.[7]

In elaborating on this recommendation, a special report by the National Council of Juvenile and Family Court Judges noted that:

> Far too often serious juvenile offenders are returned to the community "cold turkey," straight from secure placement without adequate resources and efforts for gradual reintergration into community living. . . . Failure to assist youths in this reintegration process often causes those gains made in residential placement to "wash out" upon the youth's return to the community.[8]

Readjustment to the community can be more easily achieved if institutionalized juveniles have not been completely isolated during their commitment. Athletic contests, cultural events, field trips, and various types of recreational outings can keep juveniles in touch with community life. Preparation for employment after release should be stressed, in terms of teaching prereleased juveniles the techniques of applying for jobs or preparing them through development of specific skills and through development of good work habits and a positive attitude toward work. Educational programs in the institutional setting that focus on remedial work or vocational training may also be helpful in preparing juveniles for release. Returning released youths to public schools poses a dilemma for those involved in the transition. Normally, school officials are informed that the returning youth is being released from an institution, but are not given access to the youth's delinquency records and they may not be informed about the past offenses committed by the youth because of confidentiality laws that are designed to protect the returning youth from being stigmatized or labeled as a deviant by teachers and fellow students. In a case described at the beginning of this chapter, a recently released juvenile who had been returned to public school after being released from a state juvenile correctional facility escaped from the school where he had been detained for fighting, stabbed two elderly people when they answered their door, and stole the couple's car. Investigation of the incident led to revelation of the information that from 45 to 75 juveniles from the state's youth prisons were directly returned to the public schools in the same city each year. As a result of this incident, two state legislators drafted a bill that would require all youths released from state juvenile facilities who have committed violent offenses to be sent to a special alternative school rather than returned to the regular school system.[9]

The Aftercare Treatment Plan

An aftercare treatment plan should be formulated for the juvenile before release. This may involve a return to public school or enrollment in a special type of educational program, registration in a school program that provides time for work release, or direct job placement for those older youths who will not return to school.

Aftercare is an important facet of the juvenile justice process. Most juveniles discharged from correctional facilities are placed in aftercare. The duties of an aftercare officer are similar to those of a probation officer; they include counseling, making referrals to community resources, and assisting the juvenile in developing a healthy adjustment within the community. Because those placed in aftercare are more likely than probationers to be hardcore, serious ex-offenders, the aftercare officer has extensive duties involving control, supervision, and surveillance. The officer must keep very close watch on the youth's behavior and associations, investigating matters that may indicate the need for a change in aftercare regulations or the desirability of a return to confinement. If the aftercare adjustment appears to be very successful, the officer may recommend early termination of aftercare supervision.

General and Special Rules of Aftercare

The juvenile who is in aftercare status is expected to follow a set of general rules, including adhering to curfew regulations; attending school if still enrolled; abstaining from the use of drugs and alcohol; abiding by all local, state, and federal laws; and reporting regularly to the aftercare officer. Just as in probation supervision, the aftercare officer may request some specific conditions. These could involve forbidding association with certain persons or the frequenting of certain places or requiring attendance at Alcoholics Anonymous or drug-treatment programs, school attendance, or employment.

The aftercare officer's effectiveness at supervising and assisting the youths assigned to him or her is determined by such factors as the number of cases, the resources available in the community, the cooperation and support received from the youth's family and significant others, and the juvenile's motivation to make a satisfactory adjustment in the community.

Discharge from Aftercare

When a juvenile is placed in aftercare status, the length of the period of supervision is indeterminate; that is, it extends to the age of majority in that state (18 or 21). Active aftercare supervision, however, is usually terminated earlier. A year of active supervision is generally considered adequate if there is evidence of a positive adjustment.

When the juvenile aftercare officer is satisfied that the juvenile has met aftercare rules and made an adequate adjustment in the community, he or she submits a written request to the agency from which the youth was released (the state youth authority or youth commission) stating the reasons why discharge from supervision is indicated. Complete discharge from supervision may be granted, or a youth may be transferred to inactive status, with very infrequent contacts or surveillance continuing until the youth authority is satisfied that the youth no longer presents a threat to the community.

AFTERCARE REVOCATION

Youths on aftercare are in a precarious position because the possibility of return to the institution is always present. Although a standard revocation-of-aftercare process for juveniles has not been clearly established, several U.S. Supreme Court decisions relating to adult parole revocation have also been interpreted as applicable to juveniles. In Chapter 14, we noted that the cases of *Mempa* v. *Rhay, Gagnon* v. *Scarpelli*, and *Morrisey* v. *Brewer* all guaranteed a youth on probation a hearing and due process rights if revocation of that status was threatened.[10] The same safeguards are extended to a youth in aftercare status. Before these decisions, revocation of a juvenile's aftercare status was based on testimony of the aftercare officer alone, presenting the possibility that personality clashes or prejudice on the part of such an officer could lead to unjust recommitment.

The Revocation Process

A number of jurisdictions have now developed formalized procedures for the aftercare-revocation process. An alleged violation of aftercare regulations may be discovered by the aftercare officer or reported by parents, foster parents, halfway house personnel, or law enforcement officers. The aftercare officer will investigate the charge and may follow one of several courses of action, depending on the nature of the violation and other relevant circumstances. If the alleged violation is of a technical nature (violating the general or special rules of aftercare), the officer, after establishing that there is some evidence to support the allegations, may simply warn the youth that a violation has occurred and attempt to discover the reason for it. If it becomes apparent that certain factors in the youth's environment are contributing to violations, the officer may request that the circumstances of the juvenile's placement be changed. For example, a youth who has returned to association with peers who are a bad influence may be removed from that environment by placement in a foster home or residential treatment center.

If a youth in aftercare is suspected of being involved in a delinquent offense, the aftercare officer may request that he or she be held in detention while the police investigate the incident, or kept in detention if the police have already made an arrest. An adjudicatory hearing on the offense may result in recommitment to an institution if the charges are found to be true.

Youth's Rights at a Revocation Hearing

At an aftercare-revocation hearing, a juvenile has the right to respond to and contest the allegations. While the U.S. Supreme Court has not specifically ruled on the rights of a delinquent during an aftercare-revocation hearing, the majority of the states use the U.S. Supreme Court ruling in *Morrissey* v. *Brewer* as a guideline. In that instance, the Court ruled that a defendant faced with parole revocation is entitled to the due process rights of a hearing, written notice of the charges, knowledge of evidence to be presented, and a written statement of the reasons that revocation is proposed. The parolee must also be given an opportunity to present witnesses in his or her behalf and to cross-examine other witnesses.[11]

A revocation hearing is the culmination of a process that begins with a report of the aftercare violation by the aftercare officer to his or her supervisor. The supervisor may review the case and make the decision or a revocation committee may be formed to examine the problem. The aftercare officer may be required to submit a written recommendation of revocation.

The aftercare officer assigned is not allowed to serve on the revocation committee, but he or she may testify. The youth may also appear and speak in his or her own defense. The juvenile aftercare revocation is still relatively informal in nature; it has not yet been changed to the legalistic formulas now used in adult revocation hearings.

When juvenile aftercare is revoked, the youth may be recommitted to the institution from which he or she was released or may be sent to a different institution. An order of revocation is shown in Figure 16–2.

AFTERCARE EFFECTIVENESS

The effectiveness of aftercare programs is difficult to assess, since many youths are close to the upper age limit of the juvenile status at the time they are released from institutions and may spend only a very short period in aftercare before becoming adults, when they are no longer carried in the juvenile offense statistics.

Romig's review of eight studies of juvenile parole, which examined the effectiveness of the aftercare of more than 2,300 juveniles, found no clear-cut patterns or styles of supervision that seemed to decrease recidivism. A study that compared youths placed under aftercare supervision with a control group that received no

STATE OF FLORIDA

DEPARTMENT OF HEALTH AND REHABILITATIVE SERVICES

Division of Youth Services
Bureau of Field Services

ORDER OF REVOCATION

It appearing that said _____ , having been furloughed

to the Bureau of Field Services by the Bureau of Training Schools/Bureau of Group Treatment on

_____ , and that said child failed to abide by his/her furlough agreement

by virtue of the following facts:

THEREFORE, THIS IS TO CERTIFY that as of the _____ day of _____ , _____ ,

the furlough status of the above is hereby revoked and said child is to be returned to the

_____ as soon as time permits.

cc: Youth - Original
     CO
     D()
     Parent
     Institution

By: _____

Title: _____

DYS Form 129
(Supersedes DYS-A-121)

Figure 16–2. Order of aftercare revocation. *(Source: State of Florida, Department of Health and Rehabilitative Services)*

supervision revealed that those with no supervision had as good a record of remaining offense-free as those supervised, and that even those assigned to aftercare officers tended to seek help with their problems from family members rather than from the officers. A study that compared the offense patterns of offenders before institutionalization and after placement in aftercare found that youths who had committed certain types of offenses, particularly those involving violent gang delinquencies, had little success in aftercare in the community and that many of these youths had to be returned to residential treatment. Aftercare appeared to be most successful when it was combined with some other type of assistance or involvement, such as living in a halfway house or being enrolled in job-training or educational programs.[12]

INTENSIVE AFTERCARE FOR HIGH-RISK JUVENILES

The backgrounds and delinquency histories of certain juvenile offenders cause them to be at high risk for reoffending, once they are released from institutions. These youths began their delinquent careers at early ages and the seriousness of their offenses progressively increased.

> This high-risk group tends to exhibit a persistent pattern of intense and severe delinquent activity and is plagued by a multitude of other problems. Often, they have emotional and interpersonal problems that are sometimes accompanied by physical health problems; most come out of family settings characterized by high levels of violence, chaos, and dysfunction; many are engaged in excessive alcohol and drug consumption and abuse; and a substantial proportion have become chronically truant or have dropped out of school altogether.[13]

The Office of Juvenile Justice and Delinquency Prevention funded several intensive community-based aftercare programs that it felt could be used as models for work with high-risk juveniles. As the programs developed, it became apparent that various organizational structures could be used and that the specific content of the programs would be affected by such factors as the level of resources available, the number of youths under supervision, the specific state statutes and laws governing juvenile aftercare in a particular state, whether the aftercare services would be provided by public or private agencies, and whether the population being served was predominantly urban or rural.[14]

Developing Intensive Case Management Plans

To maximize aftercare effectiveness, the development of case management plans for high-risk offenders should begin while the youths are still institutionalized. The first step is an assessment of the risks the released offender will present to the community and the services or support the youth will need to succeed in aftercare. A standardized risk assessment approach is now being utilized in several states, using an instrument similar to the probation risk/classification instrument presented in Chapter 14. Needs assessment focuses on the juvenile's problems and deficiencies and many of the identified needs are related to items in the risk assessment, such as substance abuse or a tendency toward violence. Thus, the risk and needs are usually interrelated.

Once the risks and needs are assessed, a behavior or contingency contract may be developed. This specifies required behavior and/or treatment and spells out the positive or negative sanctions that will result from compliance or noncompliance. For high-risk offenders, surveillance and supervision may receive more emphasis in the case plan than intervention strategies that address the offenders' needs. Representatives of any community or treatment agencies that will be involved should be consulted as the case plan is developed. Specific provisions should be made for assuring that the aftercare plan is followed once the offender returns to the community.[15]

Implementing Intensive Case Management

A variety of methods or tools can be used to assure that the appropriate surveillance and supervision, as detailed in the case management plan, are carried out. These include frequent home or telephone contacts, house arrest, electronic monitoring, and drug or alcohol testing. During the intensive supervision, minor infractions or small technical violations of the behavior or contingency contract may be uncovered. Normally, these do not result in aftercare revocation, but if violations continue, harsher sanctions may be applied. To meet the offender's defined needs, the aftercare officer generally functions as a service broker, making the appropriate referrals to social service or treatment agencies and seeking support from schools, family members, or employers.

The key to success in intensive aftercare appears to be combining high levels of supervision with utilization of community resources. A program that addresses community reintegration needs of released youths is the Student Transition Education Employment Program (STEEP), a cooperative effort of the Ohio Department of Youth Services, Lutheran Metropolitan Ministries, and Cleveland Public Schools. Youths are given opportunities for vocational education through work in housing rehabilitation. Before release, youths apply for the program and, if they are selected, are enrolled in a specialized vocational class within the institution. When they are released, they are placed in public schools and receive academic credit for their work at construction sites. This work may eventually lead to job placement.[16]

Effectiveness of Intensive Aftercare

Intensive aftercare has demonstrated its effectiveness when researchers have compared it with other programs. Youths in the Violent Juvenile Offender Program, designed to provide intensive supervision for chronically violent juveniles placed in aftercare from four institutions, were compared in aftercare outcomes to juveniles randomly assigned to other programs. Those in the Violent Juvenile Offender Program showed significant reductions in the number and severity of arrests and a significantly greater time until rearrest.[17] The researcher concluded that this carefully implemented and well-managed program helped protect the community and avert quick returns to delinquent behavior by the youths after release.[18]

Another evaluation of the effectiveness of intensive aftercare involved male delinquents committed to the Bensalem Youth Development Center by the Philadelphia Family Court and placed in an intensive aftercare program after release. All of the youths had been adjudicated delinquent for very serious felony offenses. The intensive aftercare involved assigning the supervising officer a maximum caseload of 12, as contrasted to the caseload of 70 to 100 common for regular aftercare. The officer worked very closely with the juveniles and their families, making frequent home contacts. When the intensively supervised youths were compared with a group of juveniles who were supervised in the traditional aftercare manner, it was found that the officers in the intensive program made approximately 10 times more contacts with the youths than did the regular officers. Reoffending occurred for both groups, but the intensive supervision group had a 50 percent recidivism rate, compared to 74 percent for those in regular aftercare.[19] Only 25 percent of the intensive program participants were arrested for committing a new felony offense, compared to 41 percent in the regular probation group, and the mean number of rearrests was lower for the intensively supervised group.[20] The researchers interpreted their findings by stating:

> We cannot conclude that intensive aftercare, as operationalized in the Philadelphia program, turns youths away from their propensity to crime. Rather, it appears that the program succeeds in providing IAP [Intensive Aftercare Program] officers with the resources, guidelines, administrative backing, and motivation to intervene rapidly, when appropriate, to prevent youths who are failing to make successful adjustments to community life from incurring multiple rearrests.[21]

AFTERCARE AND RESIDENTIAL TREATMENT

In Chapter 15, we noted the use of residential treatment centers as a final alternative for those who were "halfway in" in terms of risk of commitment to institutions. These centers may also be used to provide shelter and care for youths who must be removed from their homes for a "cooling-off period" but who will eventually be returned to supervision in their own homes. The function of halfway houses that we will consider in this chapter is their use for juveniles who are "halfway out"—in aftercare supervision but still under obligation to abide by the conditions set at the time of release.

When evidence mounted that aftercare alone was not an effective technique for preventing recidivism in many instances, a movement developed to combine aftercare with residential placement in nonsecure facilities. Placement of juveniles in residential treatment centers (halfway houses) for a period of time after release from a juvenile institution presents distinct advantages. It provides a less structured environment than the institution but gives some direction and control to juveniles who may not be ready to completely regulate their own activities. It serves as an alternative to a disruptive home or neighborhood environment and returns the youth to the community without necessarily returning him or her to association with peers who were unhealthy influences. It provides friendship and counseling from residential staff "on the spot" when a releasee needs immediate help to resist delinquent influences.

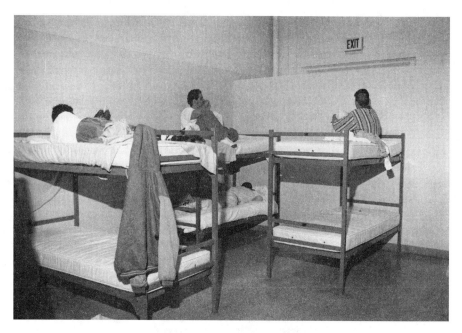

For some youths, aftercare involves residential treatment. *(Photo credit: Nick J. Cool, The Image Works)*

Residential treatment takes place in foster homes, group homes, and half-way houses. Foster and group homes are most concerned with providing a "homelike" environment to return the releasee to residence in the community; group homes and halfway houses, termed "residential treatment centers," incorporate a program of treatment into the day-to-day activities and employ professional staff who actively assist those placed on aftercare in arranging educational programs, job placements, and counseling.

History of the Halfway House Movement

The development of halfway houses in the United States came in two distinct eras. The halfway houses established before the 1950s were predominantly concerned with meeting the ex-offenders' basic human needs and providing a place of residence during re-entry into the community. These halfway houses, begun in the early 19th century in New York, Pennsylvania, and Massachusetts, were founded by private religious and volunteer groups, or even by individuals who sought to come to the aid of released prisoners. They operated independently of the correctional system and at times were open to critical attack from correction officials. The most frequently voiced objection was that in these houses, the exoffenders associated closely with other former prisoners—an activity forbidden by parole regulations.

Milestones in the development of the concept in this early period included the opening of a halfway house for women in Boston in 1864; and in 1896, the founding of the Isaac T. Hopper Home in New York by the Quakers and the opening of the first Hope Hall in New York City by the Volunteers of America. Hope Halls were subsequently established in six other large American cities.[22]

In the 1950s, there was a renaissance of interest in the halfway house, sparked by a growing awareness among correctional administrators that institutional treatment was not successful in preventing recidivism. The halfway houses established in this second era were more frequently funded by public agencies or through grants from private foundations or government agencies. They added the concept of *treatment* within the residential center itself to the already established goals of providing shelter, food, and companionship for those trying to reintegrate into society. The halfway house movement continued to expand and gain support in the 1960s and 1970s, but declined in the 1980s, as federal funding losses and local economic pressures forced many facilities to close. In the 1990s, the pressure of overcrowding in institutions resulted in increased halfway house use, and this trend continued into the 2000s.

Highfields

Strong impetus to the halfway house movement for juveniles was provided by the success of an experimental program begun in New Jersey in 1950. The idea of Highfields was conceived by F. Lovell Bixby and Lloyd W. McCorkle. They sought to establish a center where delinquent boys would be intensively treated with a type of group therapy termed *guided group interaction*. The plan called for residential treatment in small groups, with the boys supervised by houseparents and a treatment director. The boys were given a work experience and hobby and craft activities were available. The heart of the program was the use of evening sessions, five times a week, of guided group interaction.[23]

One of the basic premises of this experiment was that the strong peer influence of adolescents, which might lead them into additional delinquency if they returned directly home, could be used in the residential-treatment-center setting to influence the youths toward rehabilitation.

Community Hostels

Many of the youths released from juvenile institutions have reached the upper age limit of the juvenile status. Placement with their families may not be feasible or desirable for various reasons. The youths may not be returning to school, and an independent living status would be the most appropriate arrangement if they are not violent, hardcore offenders who require intensive supervision. In these cases, a community hostel may be the answer. This residential facility would function in a manner similar to a halfway house, except that there would be no treatment program or supervision within the house, although residents may be required to follow certain rules (no alcohol, sharing of housekeeping duties). In this type of setting, the released youths have opportunities to make educational, social services, or employment contacts, but this is their own responsibility.

Youths in residential treatment can benefit greatly from the friendly, caring atmosphere provided there. *(Photo credit: Nick J. Cool, The Image Works)*

The community hostel concept has been used quite extensively with juvenile delinquents in Israel and a three-year follow-up of youths who resided in them after discharge from institutions revealed that the larger majority did not have additional recorded criminal offenses.[24]

SUMMARY

In this chapter, we examined juvenile aftercare. In states with a state youth authority or commission, the release decision is made by an institutional release committee or board, subject to the approval of the authority or commission. In states where judges commit youths directly to specific institutions, the committing judge must approve the committee's decision. In making release decisions, release committees normally take into consideration the young person's adjustment within the institution, perceived changes of attitude, and ability to plan for the future. The decision to release may also be influenced by the nature of the offense prior to commitment and the juvenile's attitude.

To differentiate youthful offenders from adults, the process of supervision in the community after release is called "aftercare" when juveniles are involved, rather than "parole." In states with a central youth authority, the aftercare officers are employed by that body. In states without a central youth authority, aftercare officers are employed by the local jurisdiction. The same people may serve as both probation and aftercare officers.

Juveniles in aftercare present special supervision problems because they tend to be serious past offenders and must be assisted in readjusting to the community after institutionalization. This is best accomplished through careful planning prior to release.

Intensive aftercare supervision is used for juveniles defined as high-risk for reoffending. Case plans developed before they are released detail the behavior and treatment expected and state the positive or negative sanctions that will result from compliance or noncompliance. To protect the community, surveillance is coupled with addressing the offenders' needs.

Return of a youth to the environment in which he or she became involved in delinquency presents special problems. Many youths can receive support from family and friends to resist unwholesome influences, but others have little chance of aftercare success if they return home. For these youths, foster home placement or residential treatment centers offer the best hope.

Residential treatment combined with aftercare has been used in halfway houses in the United States since the early 1800s. Those that have been most successful have developed careful screening processes to discover which juveniles can best succeed in residential treatment and have fostered strong ties of communication and cooperation with the local law enforcement agencies, the juvenile court, and community agencies.

Violation of the general or special rules of aftercare or commission of a new offense may result in aftercare revocation. In some jurisdictions, recommitment is made on the basis of the recommendation of the aftercare officer or is ordered at an adjudication hearing at which a judge finds a new charge against the juvenile to be true. If a revocation hearing is held, a committee hears testimony concerning the aftercare violation or new offense and makes the decision to recommit or continue aftercare. A young person whose aftercare status has been revoked may be recommitted to the institution from which he or she was released, or sent to a different institution.

DISCUSSION QUESTIONS

1. What are the factors that a release committee would consider in making the decision as to whether an institutionalized youth is ready to be recommended for aftercare?
2. Describe the process followed in preparing a youth for release to an aftercare status. How can youths be prepared for readjustment in the community even while they are institutionalized?
3. What are the duties of an aftercare officer before and during the aftercare process? How do the duties of an aftercare officer differ from those of a probation officer?
4. How does intensive aftercare supervision of high-risk youths address the problem of protecting the community from released youths who present a serious risk of reoffending?

5. Describe the aftercare revocation process. How might an aftercare officer deal with a technical violation or minor offense if it does not appear serious enough to warrant aftercare revocation?

NOTES

1. *Akron Beacon Journal*, "Teen Charged in Attack," November 2, 2002, B4.
2. *Akron Beacon Journal*, "Teen Suspected in Chapel Hill Robbery," January 20, 2003, B6.
3. Jose B. Ashford and Craig Winstin LeCroy, "Juvenile Parole Policy in the United States: Determinate versus Indeterminate Models," *Justice Quarterly*, 10 (1993), 187–191.
4. Office of Juvenile Justice and Delinquency Prevention, *Census of Juveniles in Residential Placement 1997*, reported in Howard N. Snyder and Melissa Sickmund, *Juvenile Offenders and Victims: 1999 National Report* (Washington, DC: Office of Juvenile Justice and Delinquency Prevention, 1999), 201–204.
5. Section 5001, *Federal Criminal Codes and Rules, 1991* (St. Paul, MN: West Publishing Co., 1991), 921.
6. Ashford and LeCroy, "Juvenile Parole Policy in the United States . . .," 179–195.
7. National Council of Juvenile and Family Court Judges, "The Juvenile Court and Serious Offenders: 38 Recommendations," *Juvenile and Family Court Journal*, Special Issue (Summer, 1984), 17.
8. *Ibid.*
9. Stephanie Warsmith, "Akron Stabbings May Prompt Reform," *Akron Beacon Journal*, November 4, 2002, Al, 9.
10. *Mempa v. Rhay*, 389 U.S. 128 (1967); *Gagnon v. Scarpelli*, 411 U.S. 778 (1973); *Morrisey v. Brewer*, 408 U.S. 471, 92 S.Ct. 2593, 33 L.Ed. 2d 484 (1972).
11. *Morrisey v. Brewer*, 408 U.S. 471, 92 S.Ct. 2593, 33 L.Ed. 2d 484 (1972).
12. Dennis A. Romig, *Justice for Our Children* (Lexington, MA: Lexington Books, 1978), 190–193.
13. David M. Altschuler and Troy L. Armstrong, *Intensive Aftercare for High-Risk Juveniles: Policies and Procedures* (Washington, DC: Office of Juvenile Justice and Delinquency Prevention, 1994), 2.
14. *Ibid.*, 5.
15. *Ibid.*, 15.
16. Lynn Sametz, Steven Yuan, and Joseph Ahern, *An Evaluation of the Student Transition Education Employment Program*, submitted to the Ohio Governor's Office of Criminal Justice Sercies, July, 1993.
17. Jeffrey A. Fagan, "Treatment and Reintegration of Violent Juvenile Offenders: Experimental Results," *Justice Quarterly* 7, 2 (June 1990), 258.
18. *Ibid.*, 251.
19. Henry Sontheimer and Lynne Goodstein, "An Evaluation of Juvenile Intensive Aftercare Probation: Aftercare Versus System Response Effects," *Justice Quarterly* 10, 2 (June 1993), 216.
20. *Ibid.*
21. *Ibid.*, 221.
22. Hassim M. Solomon, *Community Corrections* (Boston, MA: Holbrook Press, 1976), 241–242.
23. H. Ashley Weeks, *Youthful Offenders at Highfields* (Ann Arbor, MI: University of Michigan Press, 1963), 3, 4.
24. Yochanan Wozner and Bilha Arad-Davidson, "Community Hostels: An Alternative to Rehabilitating Young Offenders," *Journal of Offender Rehabilitation* 20 (3-4), 1994, 37–60.

CHAPTER 17

TREATING
THE JUVENILE OFFENDER

(Photo Credit: Nick J. Cool, The Image Works)

DEFINITION OF TREATMENT
THE APPLICATION OF MANAGEMENT PRINCIPLES TO THE TREATMENT OF JUVENILES
     Management of Treatment Programs
     The Decision to Use Individual or Group Treatment
THE ROLE OF TREATMENT PERSONNEL
SPECIFIC TREATMENT TECHNIQUES
     Psychotherapy
     Reality Therapy
     Crisis Intervention
     Assertiveness Training
     Behavior Modification
     Milieu Therapy
     Group Work
     Guided Group Interaction and Positive Peer Culture
     Family Counseling
     Anger Management
     Treatment Techniques for Specific Types of Offenders
TREATMENT EFFECTIVENESS

In the earlier chapters of this book, we noted that the state assumes responsibility for providing care and services for children in need of them at various levels of involvement in the juvenile justice system. Treatment is an important part of the handling of juvenile offenders referred to programs of diversion sponsored by either the juvenile court or community agencies and it is also vital in probation and community-based services, institutionalization, aftercare, and community residential programs.

Theorists in delinquency causation have attempted to explain juvenile misbehavior in accordance with their own fields of interest and specialization. For example, psychoanalysts have advanced explanations that are heavily weighted in favor of emotional problems, whereas phrenologists, who were most familiar with the physical makeup of the body, developed explanations based on physical factors. Treatment theories and strategies have also evolved according to the interest and specializations of those using them. As Trojanowicz noted:

> Sociologists usually take a "social engineering" approach to delinquency prevention and treatment, while psychologists treat the individual. In other words, sociologists attempt to determine the conditions of the social structure that breed delinquency, while psychologists emphasize the individual and his interpersonal dynamics. . . . The social worker, then, translates the theories and assumptions of both psychological and sociological theory into action.[1]

The concept of treatment for juvenile offenders, as opposed to "punishment," has passed through a number of developmental variations in recent years. As juvenile behavior was analyzed by psychologists and psychiatrists in the years after 1920, it came increasingly to be viewed as a manifestation of underlying emotional illness, to be diagnosed and "cured." This "medical model" of delinquency treatment reached the height of its popularity in the 1960s when elaborate efforts were undertaken to analyze each child's "illness," and various treatments were undertaken to effect "cures." The ever-increasing tide of delinquent behavior and the high rates of re-cidivism among juvenile offenders caused juvenile justice system treatment person-nel to take a long second look at the medical model. In the 1970s it began to be abandoned or downplayed in favor of treatment methods that hold that a youth is re-sponsible for his or her own behavior and should be actively involved in attempts to change it, and that look to environmental factors as strong influences in the produc-tion of delinquency.

Since the first edition of this book appeared in 1979, opinions on the appropri-ate response to juvenile delinquency have changed considerably. Increases in serious violent offenses have motivated revisions in state juvenile codes that emphasize cus-tody and control rather than treatment and, as evaluations of various types of treat-ment programs have revealed little or marginal improvement in the offenders' be-havior, the focus of treatment has shifted. Although the concept of providing treatment has not been abandoned, it has been refocused. Currently, the majority of treatment programs combine the element of holding a youth responsible for his or her actions with discovering and dealing with factors that may have precipitated the deviant behavior. Treatment techniques such as positive peer culture, guided group interaction, reality therapy, and behavior modification continue to be used because they combine personal responsibility with treatment. There is also a growing empha-sis on treatment that focuses on special problems such as substance abuse, sex of-fenses, or violent behavior.[2]

Treatment programs may also involve some degree of punishment or sanction-ing. Glaser maintained that treatment and punishment are compatible if their appli-cation is grounded in a sound theoretical base. He noted that in Massachusetts, where the institutional commitment rate for juvenile offenders is very low, with the majority of youths being placed in community supervision and treatment-type pro-grams, recidivism rates are much lower than in California, which institutionalizes a much higher percentage of its youth offenders. However, for youths who become chronic offenders, handling in community-based treatment programs is less success-ful and both the community and these youths are best served by their placement in institutional settings. He concluded that the development of appropriate combina-tions of punishment, community service, restitution, house arrest, and confinement with treatment will protect the community, satisfy the public's desire to have offend-ers punished, and lead to positive change.[3]

In the 1990s, the National Center for Juvenile Justice and the National Coun-cil of Juvenile and Family Court Judges sought to identify effective programs. Juve-nile court judges, probation administrators, and court workers nominated more than 1,000 programs in 49 states and 425 of these were selected to be included in a direc-tory titled, *What Works: Promising Interventions in Juvenile Justice.* The successful pro-grams proved to have certain things in common. They combined offender account-ability, graduated sanctions, and service provision. Various approaches and types of interventions were used, including skill development; individual, group, and family counseling; and mentoring. Aftercare was also important. The majority of the pro-grams served fewer than 50 clients and were community base. Staff training was also emphasized.[4]

This chapter will focus on the treatment techniques and programs currently used in juvenile justice that have been found effective in addressing the particular characteristics and special needs of today's juvenile offenders.

DEFINITION OF TREATMENT

A large segment of juvenile justice system personnel is designated as "treatment staff." Whether these people work with children who have been referred to a diversion program as a result of a minor offense or with hardcore delinquents in a secure institution, they are expected to "treat" the young people under their supervision. Treatment personnel attached to a juvenile court might include probation officers, family counselors, community (street) workers, residential facility houseparents and counselors, social workers, and psychologists. Treatment staff members in a juvenile correctional institution might include social workers, group counselors, activity supervisors, and youth leaders. Those assigned to treatment positions typically hold degrees in fields related to the study or analysis of human behavior such as psychology, social work, sociology, criminal justice, or human services. Paraprofessionals are also frequently involved in treatment programs. Individualized treatment plans are designed to provide the youth with the amount of support, direction, and supervision necessary to turn him or her away from socially unacceptable modes of behavior.

When applied to juveniles who have come under the purview of the juvenile justice system, how should "treatment" be defined? Gibbons said that treatment in a justice-system setting involves the use of "explicit tactics or procedures deliberately undertaken to change those conditions thought to be responsible for the violator's misbehavior."[5] He noted further that since the treatment is undertaken because of unacceptable behavior that is believed to stem from certain factors or conditions in the subject's life, it should be designed to change some or all of these conditions.[6] Whittaker delineated some specific areas to be included in social treatment by defining it as:

> an approach to interpersonal helping which utilizes direct and indirect strategies of intervention to aid individuals, families, and small groups in improving social functioning and coping with social problems.[7]

After the treatment process begins, it proceeds through various stages, which have been characterized by Newman as investigation, diagnosis, and treatment supervision.[8] In the investigation phase, the causes of the manifested unacceptable behavior are sought. An important part of this phase is the use of the case study—a detailed report on a child's personality and physical characteristics, developmental history, home situation, family, school performance, recreational interests and activities, and current or past problems. This information, which is frequently made available to the judge at the time of the dispositional decision in the form of a social investigation report (see Chapter 13), is supplemented and correlated by treatment personnel in looking for reasons behind a youth's unacceptable behavior.

The diagnosis stage involves the organization and analysis of what has been learned in the investigation. A treatment plan is developed that has practical, attainable goals. For example, treatment investigation revealing that a child has persistently run away from home because of intolerable domestic conditions that are not likely to change might lead to a diagnosis that the treatment goal for this child should be development of self-reliance to the point where an independent-living placement, away from his or her parents, could be worked out.

The third phase, treatment supervision, was described by Newman as "the elaboration of knowledge about the individual through the process of communication, so that the individual will gain a more realistic appraisal of his behavior, thereby enhancing his own ability to function more acceptably in the community."[9] Ideally, the treatment plan finally recommended for each child is grounded in discovery of what appear to be the causes of current behavior.

A difficulty arises in implementing a three-phase model of treatment in juvenile justice because those responsible for investigation, diagnosis, and treatment recommendations are frequently not the same people as those responsible for actually implementing the treatment plan. For instance, a separate diagnostic staff may be composed of clinical psychologists and may therefore lean toward psychotherapeutic explanations of delinquent behavior and formulation of sophisticated, technical diagnoses that are not clearly understood by the treatment personnel in courts or institutions who have the responsibility of working directly with the youngsters.

Effective implementation of treatment may involve both direct interaction with the client and interaction on his or her behalf with community agencies that can offer assistance. In Chapter 14, we noted that a probation officer may be as successful in this "brokerage" role as in direct interaction with the young person. An effective treatment worker must also be aware of the social milieu within which the young person under his or her supervision operates, either in the community or within an institution, and adapt treatment strategies to the realities of the youth's situation. A probationer who is sleeping on a bare mattress in a room with four siblings may not be an appropriate candidate for individual counseling and analysis of emotional needs until his or her basic physical needs are met. Although a treatment worker need not alter his or her own value system and ways of looking at things, the worker must recognize that other systems and outlooks exist and must develop an understanding of how adaptation to life in a social setting different from his or her own can be related to effective treatment. Finally, a worker must function within the bounds of a professional code of ethics and adhere to the regulations set by the department or agency by which he or she is employed.

THE APPLICATION OF MANAGEMENT PRINCIPLES
TO THE TREATMENT OF JUVENILES

The children who appear before the juvenile court represent the whole spectrum of the juvenile population with regard to age, gender, and racial and ethnic backgrounds. Some have committed extremely serious acts; others have been involved in minor offenses. Some are negative, antisocial, and bitter in their attitudes; others are scared, despondent, and remorseful. Some have strong family support to fall back on, but many do not.

On the assumption that most organizations can apply common management principles to improve their effectiveness, juvenile justice agency administrators should have a coordinated plan under which the specific goals for each operation are established. It is not the unique character of the programs developed that accounts for the success any particular court experiences in its attempts at delinquency control and the rehabilitation of offenders, but rather the skillful utilization and integration of the many resources within the courts and the community.

Often, the number of programs developed by an agency has little relevance to solving the problems confronting it because the programs are implemented in a haphazard way as funds become available, without sufficient thought being given to the underlying purposes and goals the administrators hope to achieve through these programs. Some administrators in the juvenile justice field are ill prepared in management skill, and this condition is reflected in their failure to make use of the resources available to them. Successful administrators have systematically developed and coordinated each program in the light of the needs of the youths involved, the community's interests, and the resources available. Through a skillful use of community resources outside the court structure, the administrator can avoid duplication of services.

Management of Treatment Programs

Before any treatment strategy can be developed and implemented, the underlying goals and philosophy of the treatment agency must be set and communicated to all the various levels of personnel who will be involved in the program.

Too often, juvenile treatment personnel are required to participate in lengthy, seemingly endless series of "client-centered" sessions that have long ago lost their meaning. The sessions become reviews of probation requirements, rap sessions, forums where the clients can vent feelings (positive or negative) about the treatment personnel, or merely "booster shots" in the sense that at each meeting the worker gives the client some positive feedback and encouragement to make it through another week. Since the purpose of the counseling is lost, so are the results. Accomplishments are vague: better ego strength, improved interpersonal relations, acceptance of self, or learned self-discipline.

In contrast, modern justice system management, like business management, insists on accountability. Filtering it through the system, administrators hold management accountable, management holds line staff workers accountable, and justice system members hold the youths accountable.

Accountability is measured in terms of results rather than in time and effort. If after six months in a diversion program, probation, or institutionalization a youth is still burglarizing homes, the result is unacceptable and the victims of the child's delinquency should hold the juvenile justice system accountable.

Management by objectives is one approach to accountability in a result-oriented system. Objectives are identified as clear, concise tasks, with time lines where possible, and they emphasize working toward a goal. A goal is defined as an ideal behavior to be achieved. Goals are not readily attained or easily measured for success.

Sound management principles can be applied at the organizational level by the administrators and managers of an agency or by an individual practitioner in case management.

Use of management by objectives in case management involves clear definitions of attainable goals and the objectives that can be used to achieve them. For example, the goal of a particular youth's treatment might be to be released from probation and the agreed upon objectives to reach the goals would be a series of tasks to be completed by the young person, such as:

1. I will apply for three jobs each Saturday until I find one.
2. I will apologize to the victim by next week and offer to work out restitution.
3. I will attend at least 95 percent of my classes and keep a record for the probation officer.
4. I will not steal from *anyone* (objective: 100%).

The probation officer will measure the results of the objectives, perhaps monthly, and will delete and add as appropriate.

The supervisory staff and administration also set objectives for themselves, such as:

1. Conducting monthly evaluations of staff treatment objectives.
2. Accompanying each staff worker into the field every two months to observe the interaction, as part of the process of supervision.

The administration establishes a plan to measure the success of the supervisory staff's objectives and, in turn, its own objectives, which become the objectives for the entire justice agency.

In summary, management by objectives involves a high degree of accountability. The results are tangible measurements, not estimates. The rewards are built into the system. If an objective is met, a feeling of accomplishment results. Additional rewards may ensue. For the client, they might include early release from probation and a decreased possibility of recidivism; for the case worker, merit-pay increases; and for the administration, a tight management system and the most productive use of public funds.

At each system level, from administration to the client, all parties have a share in management by objectives. They work together on the objectives, measure the results together, take credit, and give credit for accomplishments. Every person in the system is responsible for his or her results.

The Decision to Use Individual or Group Treatment

The decision on whether to assign a juvenile to individual or group treatment is the product of many factors, including the type and seriousness of the youngster's most recent offense, the success of previous attempts at individual or group treatment if the juvenile is a repeat offender, the range of group treatment programs available at this particular court and the possibilities for placement in one, and, most important, whether individual or group treatment seems to offer the best hope of securing help for the child.

A juvenile's initial entrance into the juvenile justice system takes place in a one-to-one situation, with an intake officer or judge talking with or questioning the child. Group treatment may enter the picture if it is decided that either immediate family crisis intervention or counseling of the entire family over a period of weeks offers the best solution.

Another type of group treatment occurs when a probation officer meets with his or her probationers in small groups rather than individually. The group sessions are helpful to officers with large caseloads and are also beneficial to youngsters with problems related to subcultural (gang) delinquency. Those with problems related to the inability to relate well to peers, or to resist the influence of delinquent peers, may also be helped by group treatment. Some justice system personnel combine individual sessions (possibly weekly) for clients with a monthly group session that may involve recreation or cultural enrichment.

The obvious advantage of group treatment is that it is less expensive and allows an officer to increase the number of contacts with youths within the same time frame. It may prove impractical because of scheduling difficulties or because certain juveniles have problems that can best be handled in individual treatment sessions. Group discussions may allow youngsters to open up and make comments that they would not make without the group's presence and support. Peer pressure can be utilized to help a child conform to the group's expectations. Young people who have never had peer discussions or involvement may experience a sense of relief in a group situation and discover that their problems and fears are common to many other youths.

THE ROLE OF TREATMENT PERSONNEL

The question of the most appropriate background training and education for those involved in juvenile justice treatment is still being debated. We noted earlier that the education of juvenile justice workers tends to include higher education in psychology, sociology, social work, and criminal justice.

Juvenile justice treatment personnel may assume a variety of roles in the course of their interaction with young people. They may serve as listeners, observers, information disseminators, service brokers, givers of emotional support, supervisors, behavior regulators, and imposers of sanctions. The roles they assume and the type of direction they give are dependent upon the needs of the juveniles, as ascertained by the treatment personnel. The counseling given may range on a continuum from nondirective to highly directive. Nondirective counseling is characterized by listening, giving information, and offering advice, without placing pressure on the person being counseled to choose a certain course of action. Vocational counseling is frequently of this type. Directive counseling, in contrast, involves activity ranging from strongly worded advice to commands and demands. In directive counseling, the counselor takes charge of the pace and the direction of the interview and even the content of the interaction. Highly directive counseling might occur when a youth who has violated rules or conditions of probation is told that unless he or she behaves in a certain way or conforms to certain ultimatums, the probation will be revoked.[10]

Work with juveniles who have become involved in the juvenile justice system tends to include a more directive type of counseling relationship, since the youth or the family has not sought help voluntarily but has become involved in treatment because of court orders. Juvenile justice counseling usually contains an element of supervision or control. This supervision, which may be defined as a limited control through the exercise of the authority and sanctions of the court,[11] involves assisting the child and perhaps the entire family to develop internal control of their behavior in order to conform to societal norms. Helping them to develop such inner controls may include the use by the counselor of external controls in the form of behavior contracts, conditions of probation, enforcement of strict adherence to a schedule of visits, or other requirements.

The counseling-supervision process may entail simple, short, infrequent meetings or more detailed and frequent sessions, depending upon the types and seriousness of the behavior that has brought the child under the supervision of the court. Ideally, even with juveniles who are not regarded as needing elaborate counseling-

Counseling juveniles involves developing listening skills. *(Photo credit: Courtesy of Capitol Communications and the American Correctional Association)*

supervision plans, the process should proceed through the two stages of (1) developing empathy and trust between the juvenile and the counselor and (2) formulating and implementing a behavior plan that has definite, observable steps and sets a certain improved behavior condition as the goal. In the case of detailed and extended counseling sessions, Step 1 involves the entry of the youth into the counseling relationship, definition of his or her problems, exploration of possible solutions, setting of definite goals, and development of specific behavioral activities that can be measured as working toward these goals. Step 2 begins when the counselor and the youth agree on and accept the goals set and begin to implement certain strategies to achieve them. The youth's progress is continually monitored and evaluated during this step until termination of the counselor-juvenile relationship. Even after the formal sessions are concluded, follow-up, in terms of recidivism checks or progress reports, is helpful to the counselor in gauging the effectiveness of the helping process.[12]

SPECIFIC TREATMENT TECHNIQUES

Psychotherapy

We noted in Chapter 3 that the theories of crime and delinquency causation developed by Freud and his followers in the area of psychoanalysis placed the roots of deviant behavior within the personality. The general term "psychotherapy" is used to designate a variety of treatment techniques that are derived from the assumptions underlying psychoanalytic theory and general psychiatric theory. They range from the classic forms of psychoanalysis developed by Freud and his successors to reality therapy, which tends to be an eclectic, common-sense approach to therapy. As with other types, the goal of psychotherapy is the alleviation of the emotional or personal problems that are believed to be the cause of misbehavior.

Johnson differentiated two broad types of psychotherapy—insight therapies, which help a person uncover the reasons for his or her behavior, and action therapies, which undertake certain types of activities to improve the person's condition once the causes of the problem have been identified.[13]

Insight psychotherapy is a specialized area that requires training beyond the education of the typical juvenile justice system counselors. Psychologists or psychiatrists attached to juvenile institutions or to courts may attempt psychotherapy in certain cases or may refer children to specialists for such treatment. As we noted in Chapter 3, the effectiveness and applicability of psychotherapeutic techniques for most juveniles referred to the justice system have been questioned and most juveniles are not considered to have difficulties requiring such extensive treatment. A number of the therapies that are popular and widely used today do, however, attempt to incorporate some form of personality or behavior analysis.

Reality Therapy

William Glasser, a physician trained in psychiatry who became somewhat disillusioned with psychotherapy as a general treatment approach for the majority of those who came to him for counseling, developed a new treatment alternative, *reality ther-*

apy. Reality therapy states that a person's disruptive behavior stems from feelings of being unloved and of having no one to love, of not being worthwhile to oneself or others. Such a person is irresponsible. Thus, the goal of reality therapy is to make the person become responsible. Responsibility is defined as fulfilling one's own needs without depriving other people of their needs.[14]

Many of the principles of reality therapy are applications of common sense; its value as a treatment technique lies in this fact. It is easy to learn, does not require preparatory training in sophisticated theories, and can be employed in only a fraction of the time needed with more conventional therapies. Workers in the juvenile justice field can apply and develop the reality therapy approach rather easily because it does not involve collecting a great deal of historical social data, but rather begins where the child is now and proceeds from there. Both professional and lay workers are able to utilize reality therapy because its goals are clear. It requires the counselor to get involved, to care about the people being counseled, to let them know that he or she cares, and to help them fulfill their needs by helping them reject unacceptable behavior.

Making a person responsible is the aim of reality therapy and one becomes responsible by overcoming an identity with failure. A quick accomplishment is a good start toward a success identity. Developing a sense of worthiness increases a belief in self and helps the child see that he or she has a stake in the system. Glasser carefully noted that the goal of reality therapy is to act responsibly, not to be happy, although happiness and a feeling of well-being may be by-products of behaving responsibly.

Art therapy is used as a treatment technique. *(Photo credit: Nick J. Cool, The Image Works)*

Critics of reality therapy maintain that the assumptions underlying it are too simplistic to be applicable to all human behavior and that it does not take into account factors such as emotional disturbance, hyperactivity, or cultural influences that present a youth with a value system in conflict with that of the larger society. Also, the therapy is heavily dependent on the individual therapist's or counselor's interpretation of what constitutes "responsible" behavior. Certain children, particularly those who have turned to delinquent behavior because they could not meet the continually stated expectations of teachers or parents, are unlikely to respond favorably to a therapy that uses basically the same approach. Another danger is that "caring about the client" and therefore doing what is best for the client may be misinterpreted by some counselors. Rather harsh sanctions could be imposed under the principle of "doing it for the child's own good." With certain exceptions, however, reality therapy does offer an approach that can prove useful in working with many types of offenders.

Crisis Intervention

Crisis intervention, as the name implies, involves *immediate* attention to the misbehavior of the child, within hours of its occurrence. It may involve the young person only or may include the entire family in efforts to determine immediately the cause of the youth's problems and activate efforts to alleviate them.

Crisis intervention therapy is based on the belief that at the time of a crisis, a child or the family may be more open to suggestions for assistance than they would be at a later time. Crisis intervention centers are operated by certain juvenile courts, which summon members of the family to a consultation session as soon as possible after a young person is apprehended and work with the family in setting up goals and methods of dealing with the problem.

We noted in Chapter 10 that child abuse has been associated with the existence of certain stresses or crises in the lives of the abusing parents. A portion of delinquency can no doubt be attributed to comparable family crises. It is this segment of the cases that can best be served by crisis intervention techniques. Even though parents and youths may be more open to and willing to accept help at the time of a crisis, it must be remembered that crisis intervention must frequently be followed up with other types of therapy to prevent the recurrence of delinquent behavior after the crisis atmosphere is over.

Assertiveness Training

Some young people become involved in delinquent activities because they are passive and easily led by peers. When they are placed in situations that involve pressures to engage in illegal acts, they "go along with the crowd," even though they know that what they are doing is wrong. They do this because they are afraid they will lose the friendship of peers if they do not.

Children may become nonassertive and easily led as a result of conditioning at home or in school. When a child has been physically punished or verbally reprimanded by adults for expressing opinions or ever asking questions they judge to be inappropriate, he or she may fall into a pattern of refraining from contributing ideas and simply going along with what others suggest. Passivity may be reinforced when a child who is submissive and nonassertive is praised by parents or teachers for being "good." A child who develops a pattern of overconformity because he or she believes this is a way to please parents or teachers is also likely to overconform to gain the approval of peers. Another basis for lack of assertiveness on a child's part is inexperience with certain social situations and lack of opportunity to observe the proper ways to behave. In such situations, the leadership of peers who appear to "know the score" can be very strong. In addition, passivity, particularly for girls, is regarded as a virtue in some cultural or ethnic settings and a child may assume this posture as an ascribed status.

Why is assertiveness important? Merna D. and John P. Galassi note that appropriate self-expression is an important component of mental health and that "individuals who have difficulty expressing themselves . . . report feelings of low self-esteem, depression, and undue anxiety in interpersonal situations. . . . They feel unappreciated, taken for granted, or used by others. They often report various somatic or psychosomatic complaints.[15]

Assertive behavior is defined as:

> The direct communication of one's needs, wants, and opinions without punishing, threatening, or putting down the other person. It also involves standing up for one's legitimate rights without violating the rights of others and without being unduly fearful in the process.[16]

Assertiveness involves three categories of behavior: (1) expressing positive feelings (giving and receiving compliments, carrying on conversations), (2) self-affirmation (standing up for one's rights, refusing to do certain things), and (3) expressing negative feelings (annoyance or anger that is justified by another's behavior).[17]

Assertiveness training for juveniles may involve an assessment of the types of situations in which they are most likely to go along with the suggestions of peers even though they may not really wish to, or situations in which they are unable to express their feelings or desires to parents or teachers. Assertiveness training sessions generally begin with a discussion of the rights and responsibilities of the juvenile in these types of situations. Youths are taught to analyze the short- and long-term consequences of various ways of acting and then decide how to behave.

Behavior Modification

One of the most widely publicized and discussed techniques of treatment is behavior modification. This process involves a "cost-and-rewards" approach to behavior, with the subject receiving certain types of reinforcement (reward or lack of reward) as a consequence of behavior.

Behavior modification has been described as:

> a special form of behavior influence that involves primarily the application of principles derived from research in experimental psychology to alleviate human suffering and enhance

human functioning. Behavior modification emphasizes systematic monitoring and evaluation of the effectiveness of these applications. The techniques of behavior modification are generally intended to facilitate improved self-control by expanding individual skills, abilities, and independence.[18]

The basic principles of behavior modification are derived from Pavlov's conditioned-reflex experiments in which he rang a bell and provided a dog with a treat repeatedly until the dog would salivate at the sound of the bell even when no treat was forthcoming. Extensive animal experiments along these lines (notably by B. F. Skinner) have been performed since about 1920. Later the techniques were applied to modifying the behavior of emotionally disturbed or retarded children, but behavior modification as a technique for changing the behavior of delinquent, criminal, or mentally disturbed people has been widely used only since the 1960s.

Behavior modification may involve the use of positive reinforcement or aversion stimuli. In positive reinforcement, a subject is given some type of reward each time a desired behavior takes place. In an institutional setting, this might involve a point system, with increased privileges given for a certain number of points; for school truants, a certain amount of money may be given for each day of prompt attendance at school each week. The reward (reinforcement) given is selected to appeal to the age and needs of the person whose behavior is being modified. In the use of aversion stimuli, some unpleasant occurrence is associated with improper behavior. For delinquents, this might be a fine or loss of points for misbehavior. In an institutional setting, it could take the form of a short period of isolation or restriction of privileges such as television viewing or sports participation.

Behavior modification, in terms of the use of positive rewards or aversion stimuli, has always been used by parents as a way of controlling and directing the behavior of children. Outside institutional settings, it is most frequently utilized in juvenile justice work through the use of *behavior contracts*. Behavior contracts are written agreements between two parties that certain stated regulations will be followed and that, in return, various rewards will be given. They also provide that if the regulations are not followed, rewards will be withheld or sanctions imposed.

The success of behavior modification depends greatly upon the subject's receiving the positive reinforcements when the desired behavior occurs or the negative sanctions if undesirable behavior takes place. In the case of behavioral contracts, this may mean impressing on parents the importance of strictly enforcing the rules agreed upon in the contract and faithfully reporting even minor violations to the probation officer. A sample of a behavioral contract that might be set up between a probation officer and a youth, with the consent and cooperation of the child's parents, is given in Figure 17–1.

Although the limited comparative research on the success of behavior modification indicates that it is useful as a delinquency treatment technique, a number of criticisms must be noted. Some have claimed that it has a dehumanizing quality and reduces the regulation of human behavior to the same level as training an animal. Particularly in regard to aversive stimuli, questions have been raised about the morality of such devices as electric shocks or drugs. These have not been widely used with

BEHAVIORAL CONTRACT

Date _____

John agrees:

1. To return home immediately after school
2. To work on homework from 7–8 p.m. Sunday through Thursday.
3. To complete chores assigned by parents each day.
4. To telephone the probation officer three times each week during designated hours.

Parents agree:

1. If John completes the contract conditions, they will give him a bonus in his allowance.
2. If John completes all his homework, he has Friday and Saturday nights out until 11 p.m. If not, he must stay at home.

P.O. agrees:

1. To be available to receive the calls.
2. To review the contract monthly and increase privileges if the contract is adhered to.
3. If John's conditions 1–4 are met for 2 weeks, he will take John bowling.

(Signed) _____

John

_____

Parents

_____

P.O.

Figure 17–1. Behavioral Contract

juveniles, but are sometimes used in behavior modification programs in mental hospitals or in dealing with drug addicts or alcoholics. Civil libertarians have argued that some types of behavior modification border on "mind" or "thought control." Another expressed fear is that behavior modification can be used in institutions as a punitive rather than a therapeutic measure, with rewards withheld or aversive stimuli applied to strengthen control over the residents rather than to aid in modification of their behavior in a therapeutic sense. Certainly, any use of behavior modification in a setting of total control and involuntary participation should be carefully monitored. Finally, longitudinal studies should be conducted of those who have completed behavior modification programs to determine whether the subjects returned to their former behavior patterns after the positive and negative reinforcements offered in the program were withdrawn for a period of time.

Milieu Therapy

Milieu therapy may be defined as the involvement of all aspects of a youth's environment in treatment and efforts to change his or her behavior. This group-oriented therapy can obviously be performed most easily in a controlled environment such as an institution, but it can also be attempted in community-based treatment centers such as group homes, even though outside influences in such settings may prevent the creation of a total-milieu treatment plan.

In milieu therapy, everything in a young person's surroundings is manipulated or designed to assist in changing his or her behavior and leading the youth toward a more satisfactory way of behaving. Once this is accomplished, the changes in behavior, attitudes, or outlook must be internalized so that when the child leaves this closed setting, he or she will be able to function without reverting to old behavior patterns. Its obvious drawback is the difficulty inherent in transferring the youth's reactions to this artificial setting to the realities of life outside the institution or community treatment facility. Milieu therapy is frequently a prelude to other types of treatment that help a youth readjust to life in the community. It is often attempted with youths whose previous environments are considered to have contributed greatly to their delinquent behavior.

Group Work

We noted earlier that the decision whether to use individual or group treatment is an important one to be made by the counselor. In some cases, as in group work with gangs, the group already exists and the counselor must adapt his or her methods to its structure. This is also true of group work with family units. A counselor or probation officer who decides to use group formation can work out various combinations of youths that he or she believes will result in effective operation of the group process. Some background information or even diagnostic testing may be undertaken before the group is formed, so that a well-balanced unit can be put together.

Group work is a form of therapy in which the desired ends are sought through interaction of the group members and the counselor, rather than through one-to-one counseling between a youth and a counselor. The group is both the context in which the treatment takes place and the means by which treatment is given.[19] In other words, certain dynamic processes occur in a group setting that can be valuable in promoting identification of problems, goal setting, and movement toward solutions. The counselor uses the process of social interaction that occurs in the group setting as a means of bringing about the changes needed in the juvenile's life. In some groups, a counselor may play a very passive role, with the group members doing most of the problem identification and analysis; in others, the members may need to be prodded through the use of role playing to get the group process working effectively. The worker's skill in guiding the group toward the desired goals is all-important if the method is to succeed.

Vinter saw group work as involving a five-stage treatment sequence: intake (acceptance of the client), diagnosis and treatment planning by the worker, group composition and formation, group development and treatment, and evaluation and termination.[20] The length of time that group treatment continues depends upon the nature of the group, the needs of the group members, the length of time needed for achievement of the goals and activities set for the group, the amount of time the counselor can devote to the sessions, and even the desires of the group members to continue to interact. Group counseling is used quite frequently in the treatment of sex offenders and in anger management training.

Guided Group Interaction and Positive Peer Culture

Guided group interaction as a specialized method of group therapy was developed during World War II by Lloyd McCorkle and Dr. Alexander Wolf, who were searching for an effective way to treat offenders in the military services. After the war, the approach was adapted in various forms by civilian correctional institutions, including Highfields, a community treatment center for juveniles in New Jersey.

The key element of guided group interaction is that the group members themselves are the agents in changing behavior; they are agents of change for themselves and for each other. The members become a cohesive group, providing support for each other in working toward treatment goals—specifically, the goal of being able to live successfully in society—and they feel responsible as a group if an individual member fails.

A therapy technique that has many similarities to guided group interaction is known as positive peer culture. It was developed by Harry H. Vorrath and Larry K. Brendtro and first applied at a Minnesota training school for delinquent boys. Small groups (9 to 10 members) are formed, with a staff group leader present to guide the members' interaction. Members of a group are committed to helping and being concerned about each other. They learn to accept responsibility for their own actions and those of other group members.

The designers of positive peer culture developed a "universal language of problems" for use in the group discussions. It allows those involved to label and define their difficulties in terms that are easy to understand. The language comprises three general problems—low self-image, lack of consideration of others, and lack of consideration of self—and nine specific problem labels. These constitute the "positive peer culture problem-solving list" that sets forth exact definitions of the problems and gives measurements for deciding when a problem is solved.[21]

The group evaluates the behavior of each member and decides whether each has been successful in solving his or her defined problems. The group opinion is crucial at the time a youth appears to be ready to be terminated from a positive peer culture group. The group itself is responsible for recommending release from therapy. Its recommendation has great importance when this therapy process has taken place in an institution. When a member requests release, the group meets; evaluates his or her values, self-concept, and efforts and success in helping others; and votes on a decision. If the decision is in favor of release, it is referred to a staff team for final action.

Family Counseling

Realizing that a substantial portion of delinquent behavior is a result of malfunctioning of the family unit, family counseling agencies broke with the tradition of singling out the misbehaving child for treatment and instead began offering treatment for the family as a unit.

Family therapy is not merely one more method of treatment to be added to individual and group therapy. Its focus is not on changing a person's perceptions or behavior, but rather on changing the structure of a family and the sequences of malfunctioning behavior within it. The living situation of the troubled child is the target for positive change.

In Chapter 14, it was noted that the large majority of youths who are under juvenile court supervision come from dysfunctional families. Thus, family counseling is often recommended or mandated as part of a youth's disposition. In many cases, the juvenile offender may have been victimized by a family member or close relative, through physical or sexual abuse or neglect, and in these instances one or more family members may be required to take part in counseling. If the juvenile was involved in substance abuse, runaway behavior, or sex offenses, the family is often involved in the treatment strategies, setting limits and applying needed sanctions.

Conjoint family therapy is an action-oriented form of treatment that emphasizes change in the dynamics of the family. Underlying the approach is the important concept that the family is a system, more dynamic and complex than the mere sum of its component parts, each of which is still an entity in itself.

Virginia Satir has identified five response patterns in communication that can be used in analyzing family structures and interaction patterns: the placater, the blamer, the computer, the distracter, and the leveling person.[22] From these she developed the "family categories schema"—an attempt to categorize family systems, thereby allowing a consistent, systematic investigation of the family unit. Through the application of perceptual, conceptual, and executive skills, the therapist recognizes, describes, and helps the family evaluate interactions, transactions, the experience of being pulled into the family system, idiosyncratic reactions to family members, and the effect of the family group on each member. The therapist assesses the strengths and weaknesses of the family unit in problem solving, affective expression and involvement, communication, role behavior, autonomy, modes of behavioral control, and areas of psychopathology. The interaction patterns developed by Satir are communicated to the family members and they are asked to try to identify these patterns in themselves and other family members and to use this knowledge to aid in positive, open communication.[23]

Scherz stressed that if a worker is to assess family dynamics effectively and use family interaction in a therapeutic way, the five aspects of family vulnerability and strength, roles, goals, communication patterns, and need-response patterns must be taken into consideration.[24]

Anger Management

Anger management has "earned face validity as a reasonable treatment alternative for domestic abusers, child abusers, animal abusers, substance abusers, aggressive juveniles, vandals, perpetrators of hate crimes or road rage, and other violent offenders."[25] Anger management programs for delinquent youths vary in content and structure, but they all have the common goal of teaching those who are participating in the programs how to control their responses to anger provoking situations. Skills closely associated with the development of anger management are conflict resolution and violence prevention. The main focus of all these programs is to teach the participants to think of the consequences before they act.

Anger management training is grounded in cognitive behavior theories. It emphasizes that one's response to anger-provoking situations is shaped by socialization and a learned pattern of response. Hollenhorst reports that those in need of anger management often have a family history of violence, disorganized family structure, inadequate role models, and alcohol and drug problems.[26]

Anger management treatment usually takes place in a group setting and begins with a lecture on understanding the nature of anger, that is, what types of stimuli cause a person to become angry, the biological and physiological changes anger produces, and the how anger is associated with aggression. Anger management training is a re-socialization process, geared toward changing inappropriate behavior response patterns to appropriate ones. During the sessions, participants are urged to "open up," reduce their defensiveness, and come to understand how anger-induced responses intensify the possibility of aggression and violence.

Aggression replacement therapy is an example of an anger management program designed for young, assaultive male offenders. Hollenhorst described the program, which involved 12 ninety-minute weekly sessions:

> Participants . . . are required to sign an agreement stating that they will attend, take the pre- and posttests, maintain a daily log tracking moments of anger, complete all other homework assignments, respectfully participate in group discussions and role-playing, and keep all information discussed in the group confidential. Lessons include learning constructive interpersonal skills such as expressing a complaint, responding to anger, and dealing with group pressures. Participants learn to recognize physical signs of becoming angry and to employ anger reduction techniques.[27]

Treatment Techniques for Specific Types of Offenders

While the techniques discussed up to this point could be used with a wide range of juvenile offenders, certain specialized treatment modalities are needed for offenders whose problems are focused in a specific behavior area. These include substance abusers; sex offenders; and serious, violent offenders. There may also be an interrelationship of these behavior patterns. For example, a sex offender may also be violent and aggressive.[28] In the treatment of the special offender types, some programs are grounded in a very specific treatment modality that focuses on what may be considered the root cause of the misbehavior, but the majority of them tend to be eclectic; that is, they use several approaches. These may include behavior modification, psychological counseling, employment skills development, self-esteem building, assertiveness training, art therapy, and therapy that focuses on cognitive distortions (errors in thinking). Group, individual, and family counseling may be used.

Techniques for working with serious, violent offenders were discussed in Chapters 11 and 13. Here, we will focus on treatment for sex offenders and substance abusers.

Art Therapy as a Treatment Modality. A large proportion of the youths who are processed through the juvenile courts have experienced physical abuse, sexual abuse, and other forms of maltreatment from parents and other adult authority figures. Many of these youthful offenders are highly suspicious of all adults and unwilling to communicate with them in conventional types of therapy. Those involved in working with such youths have discovered that children who may be reluctant to express their feelings, emotions, wishes, or fears verbally will project them through their art work.

A student intern who was working with the director of a juvenile detention center described how a 13-year-old girl who had been involved in sexual activities with members of a gang revealed information about her relationships with members of her family through drawing.

> Ron [the director] wanted her to draw to see if she would express herself through drawing, particularly if she would draw about her relation to gang life or about her family. I had her draw a picture about anything she wanted to draw about, not the typical five subjects that the juveniles are required to draw on. She chose to draw about her family, which was not a surprise to me. She drew her father, mother, brother, sister, and herself. Her mother, she drew with larger hands and larger feet and she drew her brother and sister very normal, with more emphasis on their features, for instance, moles and birthmarks. She drew herself very small, barely recognizing that it was her. Rod, the director, explained what those characteristics meant on each person she drew. I do not want to go into grave detail about each person that Sue drew about. However, I would like to talk about the characteristics of her mother. The large hands on her mother symbolized physical abuse and the large feet symbolized sexual abuse. The large mouth on her father symbolized that he was verbally abusive to her.[29]

Treatment Programs for Sex Offenders. We noted in Chapter 14 that some of the behavior of juvenile sex offenders may initially be regarded as normal or acceptable for a sexually developing adolescent. A large number of youths who are referred to juvenile courts as sex offenders have also been involved in other types of delinquency. Because the sexual deviance may be only one aspect of the youth's offense patterns, an eclectic approach to treatment is generally followed. Treatment modalities may include behavior modification, victim empathy, anger management, and confrontation. They often focus on breaking down denial and rationalization and concentrate on bringing the offender to accept responsibility for his or her actions.[30]

Denial is an important aspect of sex offending, with the perpetrator refusing to admit that the incident occurred or to accept blame for it. Consequently, confronting and breaking down the denial factor is a key part of the treatment process. To accomplish this, a group setting may be used to lead the offender to critically examine what has occurred. This may include probing, challenging, and role playing. Because this involves thoughtfully examining what has taken place, it is unlikely to be successful with persons who are emotionally disturbed or who possess limited intelligence.[31]

When VanNess analyzed group treatment of violent juvenile sex offenders, she found that the most frequently discussed topics included honestly admitting what had occurred and taking personal responsibility for it, understanding the legal basis for the charges against the offender, realizing the effect of the offense on the victim

Art Therapy as a Treatment Modality: The Multi-county Juvenile Justice System's Drugs and Alcohol in Your Schools and Neighborhood Program

Rod Schneider, Administrator of the Stark County Juvenile Attention Center, one of the short-term detention centers in the Multi-County Juvenile Attention System, which covers six counties in Ohio, has introduced a number of innovative programs for special types of offenders, including gang members and substance abuse offenders. He has supervised and worked with troubled youths for more than 25 years. Reflecting on his experiences, he observed:

> The kids we see today are much younger, more violent, and more sexually active than those we would hold at the Center in the past. Many of them have contacted not just one "social disease," like gonorrhea, but they have several types of venereal diseases. Also, a sizeable number have severe personality problems and are under medication to reduce depression or anxiety or to control their aggressive behavior.

He began using art therapy 13 years ago, as a way of working with the youths on weekends, when there were no regularly structured classes. He found that:

> Most kids, even those that are withdrawn or very distrustful of all adults, particularly those who have authority over them, and kids who are aggressive and bullies, have something to say about themselves through drawing pictures.

Currently, the artwork of the youths is being analyzed by a clinical psychologist and it has been useful in developing treatment strategies. It can also be used to diagnose risk of suicide or mental breakdown, uncover trauma suffered from an abusive family, and assess potential for gang involvement.

Another project involving artwork, the Drugs and Alcohol in Your Schools and Neighborhood Program, is based on the premise that art can be a useful tool in helping youths to understand how substance abuse can affect their lives. The program was introduced to help young people share their feelings about their day-to-day experiences with drugs and alcohol through art. The youths are given a free range of expression. No instructions are given to them, just paper, pencils, and colored markers. Over 200 pieces of artwork were collected during a single year. The results of the artwork collected suggest that young children and teenagers from all neighborhoods and schools in the area have easy access to alcohol and a variety of drugs. The level of sophistication about and in-depth knowledge of drugs displayed in their artwork is a possible indication of their involvement with these substances.

Source: Interview with Rod Schneider, Administrator of the Stark County Juvenile Attention Center, January 17, 2003, and Rod Schneider, *A Call to Action* (Canton, OH: Stark County Citizens' Council for Non-Violence, 2000), 1–2.

and on family members, learning how to handle anger and how to solve problems without violence, examining the relationship of substance abuse to the offense (if this was a factor), and deciding how to build positive relationships with others.[32]

For those who have committed serious sex offenses or have been identified as habitual sex offenders, treatment may be much more structured and intense. Hagan, King, and Patros examined a program for such offenders that was conducted in a secure facility. The youths were required to take part in the program. All of them had been convicted of a serious sexual assault, and most had committed other offenses. They received intensive group treatment that was provided in several phases. Beginning with leading the offenders to accept responsibility for their sexual offenses, the program progressed to focusing on the motivation for the behavior; then to the influence of family, peers, or substance abuse on the occurrence; and finally to improving the offender's self-image and preparing him for release.[33] In addition to the group sessions, some youths received individual psychotherapy. In spite of the treatment they received, 46 percent of the 50 youths studied committed a new criminal offense within two years of release. The majority of new offenses were against property rather than against people. The researchers concluded:

> The fact that almost half of the male offenders in this sample engaged in criminal behavior two years postdischarge to the community strongly argues for intensive therapy for these offenders while incarcerated and, perhaps more important, longer term intensive supervision when returned to the community[34]

Treatment Programs for Substance Abusers.   Use of alcohol and drugs by adolescents is very prevalent in our society. Self-report studies revealed that 54 percent of all high school seniors had tried illicit drugs. Marijuana was by far the most used drug, with 23 percent of the seniors reporting that they had used it in the last month and 6 percent reporting that they had used it on 20 or more occasions in the previous 30 days. Thirty-one percent of the seniors had drunk alcohol in the last month, and even 25 percent of eighth graders had used alcohol in the month prior to the survey.[35] A study of youths in three cities (Denver, Pittsburgh, and Rochester, New York), conducted over a five-year period, found that half of the youths in the study were using alcohol regularly by age 16, but marijuana use began somewhat later, and only about 10 percent of the youths in the sample ever became involved in harder drugs.[36]

Juvenile arrests for drug abuse violations increased more that 121 percent between 1992 and 2001.[37] Police officers and juvenile court personnel believe that, regardless of the specific charge, the majority of arrests of juvenile offenders are related to substance abuse in some way. Research has shown that involvement with drugs was associated with delinquent behavior.

> Among all age, gender, and ethnic groups, the more seriously involved in drugs a youth was, the more seriously that juvenile was involved in delinquency, and vice versa.[38]

It is fairly routine for those youths being held in detention or being formally processed through the juvenile court system to receive a substance abuse evaluation. Such assessments examine the following areas of a youth's background:

... history of alcohol or drug use, history of over-the-counter drug use, medical history, mental health history, family history, school history, sexual history, peer relationships, gang involvement, inter-personal skills, leisure-time activities, neighborhood environment, and home environment.[39]

Substance abuse is rarely the only problem in an adolescent's life. Instead, substance abusers are likely to be multiproblem youths who may require attention to their family situations, educational needs, and personal adjustment problems. Therefore, treatment for such abusers is designed to combine various approaches. It may be provided in secure or open settings, operated by private or public groups or agencies, and be residential or nonresidential. Depending on the severity of the youth's problem, it may involve detoxification or monitoring by urinalysis or be predominantly educational in nature.

Creation of drug courts for juveniles and family drug courts is becoming more prevalent since juvenile justice and social services administrators and workers have realized that substance abuse and dependency are interrelated with deviant behavior of juveniles. Drug courts for juveniles were begun for the purpose of offering an alternative to formal juvenile court processing. Referral to drug court may be an option for youths who have some substance abuse problems but have not committed serious violent offenses that would make them a danger to the community. They must voluntarily agree to complete the treatment program. Although the drug treatment may be administered by professional therapists, the juvenile court judge still maintains control of the case. If a youth successfully completes the program, the initial charges are often dropped and the young person will not have an official delinquency record.[40]

The family drug court is structured in a similar way. However, the major focus of this court is on parents who face criminal prosecution for substance abuse-related offenses that have been shown to have detrimental effects on their children. After acceptance, those families that enter the family drug court program receive intensive interventions, with the goal of changing a dysfunctional family into a stable, productive family. A family drug court director gave this profile of the clients:

> Participants in the Family Drug Court are of both genders, come from many different ethnic and socioeconomic backgrounds, use every kind of drug (although the main "drug of choice" is methamphetamine), and face other complicating factors. . . . Often women in the program have personal histories of child and adult sexual or physical abuse. Their continued tendency to make poor choices in male companions has a direct impact on their sobriety and success in the programs. . . . Many children suffer from birth defects associated with prenatal alcohol exposure. Often the mother also has defects associated with her mother's alcohol abuse.[41]

The family drug court process frequently involves continued contact with and mentoring of the parents for long periods of time.

Substance abuse treatment programs identified as successful vary widely in their approaches. Such programs generally offer services for juveniles who have some involvement with court drug- or alcohol-related charges and have a history of substance abuse. Nonresidential programs assess each youth and make referrals to community agencies, provide intensive casework testing, and use graduated sanctions for failure to meet required behavior.[42] Some programs use group living in a nonsecure residential setting. Treatment follows the 12 steps used by Alcoholics Anonymous, and living, communication, and social skills are emphasized.[43] Following residential treatment, follow-up services may be provided. For example, as part of the Adelphi Village Drug and Alcohol Aftercare in Latrobe, Pennsylvania, counselors work with the recently discharged adolescents to help them develop coping strategies for handling peer pressure, reintegrating into family life and school, and dealing with anger or crisis situations.[44]

Because substance abuse is involved in a great deal of delinquent behavior, the Office of Juvenile Justice and Delinquency Prevention sponsored the development of a training program for juvenile justice professionals that would assist them in identifying youths who have substance abuse problems. A 12-step process was suggested.

1. Take a drug history, using structured questions about prior drug involvement.
2. Administer a breath alcohol test.
3. Perform a preliminary prescreen, using questions, observation, and asking the juvenile to perform simple tests.
4. Examine the eyes. Certain drugs will change the appearance or functioning ability of the eyes.
5. Administer the divided-attention psychophysical tests. These involve activities that check balance and coordination.
6. Perform the dark room examination. This checks the size of the eyes' pupils and their reaction to light.
7. Examine vital signs. Certain drugs raise blood pressure and heart rate or cause rapid breathing.
8. Examine for muscle rigidity, since some drugs cause muscles to become hypertense and rigid.
9. Look for injection sites. Scars or tracks may be found on the arms, legs, or neck.
10. Interview the juvenile and make observations.
11. Form an opinion, based on the evidence and observations.
12. Request a toxicological examination, since chemical tests can provide evidence to substantiate the conclusions reached.[45]

Once substance abuse is identified as a problem, court personnel must decide whether the youth needs to receive special intensive treatment for the abuse, or if a more general type of treatment and supervision is indicated.

TREATMENT EFFECTIVENESS

While most administrators of treatment programs for juvenile delinquents can describe success cases associated with their programs and provide statistics to back up their claims that their particular approach is effective, they must also concede that there are failures. Claims of great program success are met with skepticism in many instances and criticisms of the ways that programs are evaluated abound.[46] Was effectiveness measured over a period of time after the treatment was completed? What were the criteria on which success claims were based? How can the influence of a particular treatment be isolated from other things that are occurring in an adolescent's life? For example, a youth who is placed on probation may be required to make restitution for some property damage and participate in a substance abuse treatment program. If, after a designated period of time, it is found that the young person completed the restitution and has shown no evidence of engaging in substance abuse, but has committed another delinquent offense, should this youth's treatment be judged a failure or a success?

Critics of treatment programs maintain that many programs fail because they are not grounded in theory, but instead are implemented without defined goals or clear determinations of the target populations they should serve. For example, a study of the effectiveness of a treatment program for sex offenders was developed by comparing the youths in the program to another group sent to secure institutions or community-based intervention programs, most of which did not have sexual treatment programming. When the recidivism of the two groups was compared, they differed little in the percentage who committed another sexual offense, but a higher percentage of those who received the treatment for sexual offenders recidivated. The evaluators concluded that the type of treatment used with the sexual offenders (a psycho-socio-educational approach) did not focus on the causes of the youths' deviance and was therefore ineffective.[47]

It is important that treatment address the offender's needs, be administered in an appropriate setting, and be provided by those who have the required training and expertise. We noted in Chapter 14 that some courts have adopted classification systems that measure the potential risks posed by juvenile offenders and the needs they exhibit that may point to the desirability of treatment. Classification systems were used quite extensively in institutional treatment in the 1960s and 1970s. The most popular, the Quay System[48] and the I-Level (Interpersonal Maturity Level) Classification System,[49] had elaborately developed categories of offenders and the institutions attempted to group and treat the youths according to specific behavior typologies. These complex systems were gradually abandoned because they were too difficult to apply using the available staff, and because the populations of secure institutions became increasingly made up of chronic, violent offenders, thus reducing the need for elaborate classification categories.

Nevertheless, it is important to select the proper program type and setting for offenders. Van Voorhis contended that the manipulative, exploitative, asocial type of offender, often labeled untreatable, can be reached effectively in a program that is designed to alter antisocial value systems and behavior, if this treatment is applied in a positive peer culture setting. She maintained that this type of offender will respond to confrontational therapy.[50] In contrast, this type of approach is unlikely to be effective if it is used with juveniles who are neurotic or have personality disorders.[51] Once experience has revealed that certain types of therapies are effective with specific groups of offenders, treatment planners can use this information to focus their energies.

Earlier in this chapter, we noted that the National Center for Juvenile Justice and the National Council of Juvenile and Family Court Judges identified more than 400 treatment programs that appeared to be successful. Ninety percent of these had some form of evaluation in their format. The criteria for determining effectiveness varied, but two factors were always considered: the level of new delinquent offenses after release from the program was examined and the social and psychological adjustment of the treated youth was assessed.[52] These effectiveness determinants could be used by any juvenile justice agency or institution as the basis for program decisions.

SUMMARY

In this chapter, we have examined the characteristics of treatment and the process by which it is implemented. We noted the importance of effective planning and management in producing the best treatment possible and discovered that many types of individual and group treatment have been used by juvenile justice agencies.

Because of the pressures of large caseloads and tight budgets, many agencies have been forced to search for new methods of handling juveniles referred to them for treatment. Group work has increased in popularity, as have the "action" therapies, which involve the use of volunteers and paraprofessionals. Interface (cooperation and communication) with other community agencies has enabled the juvenile courts to divert some youthful offenders to other sources of treatment rather than handling them within the justice system. The movements toward community-based treatment and deinstitutionalization have also highlighted the importance of cooperation with various local agencies for maximization of treatment potential.

The key position of the counselor in the treatment process cannot be overemphasized. The helping person must be well versed in the particular techniques, able to relate to the juveniles (and parents) assigned to his or her care, and capable of measuring the effectiveness of various approaches and abandoning those that prove ineffective.

A wide variety of treatment techniques has been used with juvenile offenders. *Psychotherapy* may involve insight therapy to uncover the reasons for behavior or action therapies to improve psychological functioning. *Reality therapy* involves analysis of behavior with the goal of becoming responsible. While such therapies may be applied over a period of weeks or months, *crisis intervention* is immediate attention to misbehavior, with both the offender and his or her family usually involved. The crisis event is seen as an occasion when parents and youths can come to acknowledge the need for help and agree to accept counseling. *Assertiveness training* is recommended for young people who may have been led into delinquency by peers because they lack the courage to refuse to become involved. *Behavior modification* is a "cost and rewards" approach to behavior, with the person being treated receiving positive or negative reinforcement, according to the behavior that occurs. *Milieu therapy* attempts to involve all aspects of a youth's environment in efforts to change his or her behavior.

In addition to individual therapies, group work is also used in treating delinquents. In *guided group interaction*, the members of the group itself work to change each other's behavior. In a similar program, *positive peer culture*, members of the treatment group are committed to helping and being concerned about each other. They learn to accept responsibility for their own actions and those of other group members. *Family counseling* seeks to change family interaction patterns that have resulted in juvenile misbehavior. In *conjoint family therapy*, the family is examined and treated as a system and the positions of various members of the family are analyzed. Anger management therapy seeks to teach youths how to control their responses to anger provoking situations and think of the consequences before they act.

An important trend in juvenile offender treatment is the development of techniques designed for offenders whose problems are focused in a specific behavior area. These include sex offenders, substance abusers, and serious violent offenders. The treatment may include group, individual, and family counseling, which may be applied in institutional or community settings. The therapy combines elements of various treatment approaches to address the offenders' problems. Art therapy is useful when working with youths who are withdrawn, noncommunicative, or depressed.

The best hope for treatment success appears to lie in a careful selection of treatment techniques, dedication and skill on the part of the treatment workers, and evaluation of methods to determine if they are achieving results or should be supplemented or replaced. Also, actively involving the juvenile in his or her own treatment must be stressed.

DISCUSSION QUESTIONS

1. Discuss the underlying assumptions of the "medical model." Why has it been down-played in favor of other treatment approaches in recent years?
2. The management by objectives approach to juvenile treatment focuses on results. Do you feel that the results of treatment can be effectively measured? How do case management approaches that use management by objectives define or measure treatment effectiveness?
3. Discuss the factors that are considered in making decisions to use group or individual treatment for juveniles. Which types of offenders seem to respond most positively to group treatment?
4. Behavior modification is frequently used in delinquency treatment programs. Discuss the positive facets of behavior modification. What are some negative aspects?
5. What is the first step in treatment therapy for sex offenders? Why do you think a confrontational approach in a group setting is frequently used with sex offenders?

NOTES

1. Robert C. Trojanowicz, *Juvenile Delinquency*, 2nd ed. (Englewood Cliffs, NJ: Prentice Hall, 1978), 264–265.
2. George Camp and Camille Camp, *The Corrections Yearbook, 1993* (South Salem, NY: Criminal Justice Institute, 1993), 45.
3. Daniel Glaser, "What Works, and Why it is Important: A Response to Logan and Gaes," *Justice Quarterly* 11, 4 (December 1994), 712–723.

4. Imogene Montgomery and Marilyn Landon, "What Works: Promising Interventions in Juvenile Justice," (Washington, DC: U.S. Department of Justice, December 1994), Fact Sheet #20, 1.

5. Don C. Gibbons, "On the Nature and Forms of Treatment," in Robert G. Leger and John R. Stratton, *The Sociology of Corrections* (New York: Wiley, 1977), 305.

6. Ibid., 306.

7. James K. Whittaker, *Social Treatment* (Chicago: Aldine, 1974), 49.

8. Charles L. Newman, "Concepts of Treatment in Probation and Parole Supervision," in Edward E. Peoples, *Readings in Correctional Casework and Counseling* (Pacific Palisades, CA: Goodyear, 1975), 62.

9. Ibid., 63.

10. Charles J. Stewart and William B. Cash, *Interviewing: Principles and Practices*, 5th ed. (Dubuque, IA: W.C. Brown, 1988), 199–220.

11. Thomas A. Johnson, *Introduction to the Juvenile Justice System* (St. Paul, MN: West Publishing Company, 1975), 110.

12. Wittaker, *Social Treatment*, 110–181.

13. Johnson, *Introduction to the Juvenile Justice System*, 269–280.

14. Richard L. Rachin, "Reality Therapy: Helping People Help Themselves," *Crime and Delinquency* 20, 1 (January 1974), 51–53.

15. Merna D. Galassi and John P. Galassi, *Assert Yourself* (New York: Human Sciences Press, 1977), 4.

16. Ibid., 3

17. Ibid., 4.

18. Bertram S. Brown, Louis A. Wienchowski, and Stephanie B. Stolz, "Behavior Modification: Perspective on a Current Issue," in Peter C. Kratcoski, *Correctional Counseling and Treatment*, 4th ed. (Prospect Heights, IL: Waveland Press, 2000), 438.

19. Robert D. Vinter, "An Approach to Group Work Practice," in Paul Glasser, Rosemary Sarri, and Robert D. Vinter, *Individual Change through Small Groups* (New York: Free Press, 1974), 5

20. Robert D. Vinter, "The Essential Components of Social Group Work Practice," in Glasser, Sarri, and Vinter, *Individual Change through Small Groups*, 10–11.

21. Harry H. Vorrath and Larry K. Brendtro, *Positive Peer Culture* (Chicago: Aldine, 1974), 37–38.

22. Virginia Satir, *Peoplemaking* (Palo Alto, CA: Science and Behavior Books, 1972), 599–79.

23. Ibid.

24. Frances H. Scherz, "Exploring the Use of Family Interviews in Diagnosis," in *Casework Treatment of the Family Unit* (New York: Family Service Association, 1966), 12–18.

25. Pamela Stiebs Hollenhorst, "What Do We Know About Anger Management Programs in Corrections?" in Peter C. Kratcoski, *Correctional Counseling and Treatment*, 4th ed., 350.

26. Ibid., 356.

27. Ibid., 360.

28. Peter C. Kratcoski, "Special Areas of Correctional Treatment," *Correctional Counseling and Treatment*, 4th ed., 535.

29. Kristal Y. Brown, Internship Paper, Kent State University, Stark, October, 2002, 8.

30. Fay Honey Knopp, *Remedial Intervention in Adolescent Sex Offenses: Nine Program Descriptions* (Syracuse, NY: Safer Society Press, 1982).

31. M. Borzecki and J.S. Wormith, "A Survey of Treatment Programs for Sex Offenders in North America," *Canadian Psychology*, 28 (1987), 30–44.

32. Shela R. VanNess, "Rape as Instrumental Violence: A Perspective for Theory, Research, and Corrections," paper presented at the annual meeting of the Academy of Criminal Justice Sciences, San Antonio, Texas, 1983, 14.

33. M.P. Hagan, R.P. King, and R.L. Patros, "Recidivism among Adolescent Perpetrators of Sexual Assault Against Children," in Nathaniel J. Pallone, ed., *Young Victims, Young Offenders* (New York: The Haworth Press, 1994), 127–138.

34. Ibid.

35. L. Johnston, P. O'Malley, and J. Bachman, *National Survey Results on Drug Use from the Monitoring the Future Study. 1975–1998. Volume I: Secondary School Students*. Rockville, MD: Na-

tional Institute on Drug Abuse. Reported in Howard N. Snyder and Melissa Sickmund, *Juvenile Offenders and Victims: 1999 National Report* (Washington, DC: Office of Juvenile Justice and Delinquency Prevention, 1999), 70.

36. Stuart Greenbaum, "Drugs, Delinquency, and Other Data," *Juvenile Justice* 2, 1 (Spring/Summer 1994), 3.

37. Federal Bureau of Investigation, *Crime in the United States 2001* (Washington, DC: U.S. Government Printing Office, 2002), 233

38. Greenbaum, Drugs, Delinquency, and Other Data, 3.

39. Rodney A. Ellis and Karen M. Sowers, *Juvenile Justice Practice* (Belmont, CA: Brooks/Cole, 2001), 75

40. National Association of Drug Court Professionals, *Defining Drug Courts: The Key Components* (Washington, DC: Office of Justice Programs, 1997), 7.

41. Charles M. McGree, "Family Drug Court: Another Permanency Perspective," in Peter C. Kratcoski, *Correctional Counseling and Treatment*, 4th ed., 555.

42. Imogene M. Montgomery, Patricia McFall Torbet, Diana A. Malloy, Lori P. Adamcik, M. James Toner, and Joey Andrews, *What Works: Promising Interventions in Juvenile Justice* (Washington, DC: Office of Juvenile Justice and Delinquency Prevention, 1994), 221.

43. *Ibid.*, 228.

44. *Ibid.*, 219.

45. Robert W. Sweet, Jr., "Drug Recognition Techniques: A Training Program for Juvenile Justice Professionals," *NIIJ Reports* 221 (Summer 1990), 16–18.

46. See Richard Londman, *Prevention and Control of Juvenile Delinquency* (New York: Oxford University Press, 1993) for a review of various types of programs and their effectiveness.

47. S.P. Lab, G. Shields, and C. Schondel, "Research Note: An Evaluation of Juvenile Sexual Offender Treatment," *Crime and Delinquency* 39, 4 (October 1993), 551.

48. See Roy Gerard, "Institutional Innovations in Juvenile Corrections," *Federal Probation* 34, 4 (December 1970), 37–44.

49. See Riverview School for Girls, "The I-Level Classification System," mimeographed staff orientation materials, 1977, 37–44.

50. Patricia VanVoorhis, "Efficient Applications of Differential Treatment to Correctional Treatment Settings," Paper presented at the annual meeting of the Academy of Criminal Justice Sciences, Boston, March 1995, 13.

51. *Ibid*, 16.

52. Imogene Montgomery and Marilyn Landon, "What Works: Promising Interventions in Juvenile Justice," Fact Sheet #20, 1.

DELINQUENCY PREVENTION AND CONTROL

(Photo credit: Tony Anderson/Getty Images, Inc. – Taxi)

DELINQUENCY PREVENTION PROGRAMS
The Evolution of Delinquency Prevention Programming
Contemporary Delinquency Prevention Programming
THE ROLE OF VOLUNTEERS IN DELINQUENCY PREVENTION
DELINQUENCY PREVENTION THROUGH DETERRENT METHODS
DELINQUENCY CONTROL
Juvenile Code Revision and Juvenile Court Administration
Possible Changes in the Jurisdiction of the Juvenile Court
The Balanced Approach/Restorative Justice Approach
Privatization in Juvenile Corrections
PLANNING FOR DELINQUENCY PREVENTION AND CONTROL

DELINQUENCY PREVENTION PROGRAMS

The Evolution of Delinquency Prevention Programming

Once a separate juvenile justice system was created, attempts were made to discover the causes of delinquency and develop programs to prevent it. Over the years, prevention strategies have been altered to conform to the currently popular theories. After much research, effort, and evaluation, the general conclusion is that delinquency is generated by multiple factors in a child's life and that prevention and treatment are most effective if they are multifaceted, focusing on individual needs; peer relations; and school, family, and community adjustment.

Early in the 20th century, such national organizations as the Family Welfare Association, the Big Brothers and Sisters Federation, and the Child Welfare League of America were formed to provide community services to youths and families and they focused some of their activities on prevention and treatment of juvenile delinquency.

The Chicago Area Project. Begun in 1932 and continued into the 1960s, the Chicago Area Project was grounded in the assumption that the neighborhoods with high delinquency rates lacked the stability and cohesion to combat and prevent delinquency. After the areas of the city with high amounts of delinquency were identified, neighborhood committees were formed, relying on the indigenous leadership, and strategies were developed to improve neighborhood conditions, provide recreational opportunities, and reduce the influence of youth gangs and criminal role models that was apparent in the neighborhoods. Neighborhood centers were established and recreational and educational facilities were opened. While the Chicago Area Project staff assisted the local residents, they did not assume control. Eventually, 20 different neighborhood projects were established. The area concept introduced in Chicago is still being used as a delinquency prevention model in many other cities.[1]

The Cambridge-Somerville Youth Study. Begun in 1937, the program focused on individual prevention and treatment. It sought to give intensive and long-term assistance to youths in two Massachusetts towns who were identified as delinquency-prone or endangered. The male youths in the sample, beginning at about age 11, were given intensive individual help and guidance, including medical attention, tutoring and other education related services, recreational opportunities, and individual counseling. Their families were also counseled and assisted. Originally planned to continue for 10 years, the project ended in 1945, because of the problems presented by the disruptions of World War II.[2]

The Boston Midcity Project.   Begun in 1954, this project was grounded in Miller's theory of the lower-class culture as a generating milieu for delinquency. (See Chapter 4 for a discussion of this theory.) Its delinquency prevention approach was quite similar to that of the Chicago Area project, but greater emphasis was placed on the roles of detached gang workers, who were social workers professionally trained to work with gangs. The project focused on intensive contacts with the gang members and also provided assistance to families identified as "chronic problem families." The neighborhood residents were encouraged to form groups to attempt to change neighborhood conditions and decrease the delinquency-producing elements.[3]

The Mobilization for Youth Program.   This 1960s program was based on the theory that delinquent behavior arises because there is a gap between the social and economic aspirations of young people and their opportunities to achieve these goals through legitimate means. (See Chapter 4 for a detailed discussion of Cloward and Ohlin's "delinquency and opportunity" theories.) The Mobilization for Youth project, implemented in a 67-block area of New York City that included many Puerto Ricans and blacks in its population, sought to improve the opportunities of the young people of the area in work, education, services available to individuals and families, and community organizations. The activities in regard to employment included a subsidized work, vocational-guidance, and job-training program for all unemployed, out-of-school youths, male and female, between 16 and 21 years of age residing in the target area. The educational facet involved working for increased parent-school contacts, developing curriculum and methods consistent with lower-class culture, and providing younger students with homework help from high school youths, who were paid for their services. To reach adults in the area, Neighborhood Service Centers were set up to provide assistance with paperwork in applying for Social Security or welfare benefits. Babysitting, family counseling, and classes in home-making skills were also provided at these centers.

For young people aged 8 to 12, the Mobilization for Youth project developed the Adventure Corps, which provided exciting recreational and educational activities. A Detached Worker Program sent workers into the streets to mingle with older youths and try to offer them alternatives to antisocial behavior. The Coffee House Program, designed as an alternative to gang membership, provided an attractive meeting place where young people could engage in many types of recreational and social activities. Attempts at community organization by the Mobilization for Youth program included drives for increased voter registration and development of tenant organizations to help residents of the target area fight for improved housing conditions.[4]

Even though millions of dollars were spent on the Mobilization for Youth program, and it seemed to embody all the elements for the prevention and control of delinquency that had been identified by researchers, it was judged only a partial success. The same was true of other youth opportunity programs that seem to go directly to the defined sources of delinquency.

The War on Poverty.   Throughout our history, state governments, and, to some degree the federal government, have been concerned about the plight of the poor, especially poor children. In 1909, President Theodore Roosevelt convened the first White House Conference on Children. Topics considered at this conference included initiating a nationwide effort to deter the use of child labor in factories, coal mines, and other dangerous occupations, providing some public assistance to widows with young children and reducing the reliance on orphanages.[5] In the following years, government programs were implemented to improve the lives of poor children and prevent or reduce delinquent behavior. By far the most ambitious of these efforts were the programs of the War on Poverty, which were implemented from 1963 until the early 1970s. The programs sought to attack the problem of delinquency by improving youths' school, employment, environmental, and personal development opportunities. Extensive local involvement, in the form of the coordination of already existing resources available from private and public sources and efforts to develop the programs within the existing sociocultural environment of the target area, were hallmarks of those programs that achieved some measure of success. The best known of these programs is Headstart (a program for preschool youngsters, designed to promote readiness to learn, cultural enrichment, and medical and dental care) which is still popular and widely used today. Another well-publicized and heavily funded program, the Neighborhood Youth Corps (which provided students and dropouts with employment opportunities designed to improve the quality of life in the neighborhoods), did not achieve the hoped-for results in terms of dramatic reductions in delinquent behavior.

After the report of the President's Commission on Law Enforcement and the Administration of Justice (1967) highlighted the need for delinquency-prevention efforts, many research studies were undertaken to define the causes of delinquency and suggest solutions. New programs were designed, funded, and implemented. Huge sums of money were made available through the Office of Economic Opportunity and the Law Enforcement Assistance Administration (LEAA). Many of the funded projects were hurriedly set up and put into operation without adequate preliminary research or theoretical bases. Some of the most expensive and extensive programs contained no provisions for evaluation. Some were regarded as the definitive answer to the problems of delinquency defined by theorists.

As the Vietnam War escalated and budgets were cut, program after program of the War on Poverty fell victim. Today it is difficult to decide whether these efforts showed no striking results in delinquency prevention because the principles upon which they were developed were faulty, because they were implemented haphazardly and poorly administered in many instances, or because, in the relatively short period of time they were in operation, they could not hope to change behavior patterns of groups that had lived with poverty and deprivation for generations.

As noted in Chapter 7, despite the numerous federal and state aid programs for children and families living in poverty, the number of children currently in poverty is higher than it has been for several decades. Poverty is closely related to the unemployment rate and general economic conditions of the country. As the economy worsens, the amount of poverty increases.

Perhaps the lesson to be learned from these expensive experiments is that social change is such a complex phenomenon that just when a cause-effect relationship seems to have been defined and programs to effect changes have been implemented, another side of the problem presents itself and redefinitions are necessary. Programs must begin somewhere; but when it becomes apparent that they are not fulfilling their purposes, they must, through the process of constant evaluation, be redirected and revised even while they are in operation.

Youth Service Bureaus.   The President's Commission on Law Enforcement and the Administration of Justice (1967) presented the concept of youth service bureaus as a means of diverting children who are already involved in minor unacceptable behavior or who are in danger of becoming involved in some type of delinquent activity. The youth service bureau was envisioned by the Commission as a new community device to coordinate existing services and provide new programs that would compensate for deficiencies in available services.[6]

The true potential and effectiveness of youth service bureaus as diversionary agencies, shelters for runaways, and places where intensive counseling of runaways and other troubled youths and their families could take place outside the framework of arrest or juvenile court intervention was never realized. Most of the bureaus fell victim to funding cuts. Then, with the elimination of the Law Enforcement Assistance Administration, the chief source of grants for these bureaus, the majority were forced to close. Those that have survived in some form were incorporated into other juvenile-court-related programs already in existence.

Other Federally Sponsored Programs.   In the 1980s and 1990s, federal programs concentrated on economic development opportunities as a key to delinquency prevention. Two such programs for youth employment are reminiscent of the Depression era's Civilian Conservation Corps. The National Youth Conservation Program provides jobs for youths aged 16 to 24 in outdoor conservation work and the Youth Community Conservation and Improvement Program offers jobs for 16- to 19-year-olds in improving their own communities and neighborhoods and restoring natural resources on public lands. The Job Corps, one of the few War on Poverty programs still in, operation, has trained thousands of disadvantaged youngsters for jobs.[7]

Contemporary Delinquency Prevention Programming

Mentoring Programs.   One program that has had a long, illustrious history is the Big Brothers/Big Sisters Program. The concept of using "big brother" volunteers to reach out to children who were in need of positive socialization, firm guidance, and adult role models was originated in 1904 by Ernest K. Coulter. Big Brothers/Big Sisters of America, with more than 500 participating agencies, is the largest mentoring organization in the country. Volunteers are recruited, carefully screened, trained, and then matched with a boy or girl on a one-to-one basis. The children involved usually come from single-parent households. The adult volunteer creates his or her own set of activities, gearing them toward the interests and needs of the little brother or little sister. While the one-to-one relationship is emphasized, occasionally there may be group activities, such as bowling, picnics, or attending social or sporting events.[8]

There has been some research on the effectiveness of this organization as a delinquency prevention medium. One study compared youths who were involved in Big Brothers/Big Sisters with a similar group of youths (single-parent, low income families) who were eligible for the program but had not yet been assigned a mentor. It was found that the youths in the Big Brothers/Big Sisters program were less likely than the youths in the control group to engage in drug or alcohol use, to hit someone, or to be truant from school. They were also more likely to have improved their relationships with their peer groups and with their parent or caretaker.[9]

The Juvenile Mentoring Program (JUMP) is a federal program administered by the Office of Juvenile Justice and Delinquency Prevention that provides an opportunity for a one-to-one relationship to develop between an adult and a juvenile on a regular basis. The mentors in JUMP include law enforcement personnel, college students, senior citizens, business persons, and those from other occupations.

> JUMP is designed to reduce juvenile delinquency and gang participation, improve academic performance, and reduce school dropout rates. To achieve these purposes, JUMP brings together caring, responsible adults and at-risk young people in need of positive role models.[10]

The young people mentored range from age 5 to 20 and come from all races and social backgrounds. School dropouts and those with delinquency records are not excluded. A major emphasis is placed on providing academic assistance and vocational counseling and training.[11]

The D.A.R.E. program is perhaps the most widely used delinquency prevention program. This drug education program, based on cooperative efforts of local police departments and local school systems, operates in almost three fourths of schools in the United States and has also been adopted in a large number of other countries.[12] The D.A.R.E. program focuses on drug use and violence prevention. Law enforcement agencies, the schools, and the local community collaborate to offer a drug prevention curriculum in the schools. Uniformed police officers teach this curriculum to elementary school students.

A number of evaluations of D.A.R.E. have been completed. In general, they have not shown that the D.A.R.E. programs have long-term effects in reducing the levels of drug use for those youths who participated in the program. A six-year analysis of D.A.R.E. programs operating in elementary schools in urban, suburban, and rural areas in Illinois revealed that D.A.R.E. had immediate and short-term effects (up to two years) on some variables, such as youths' resistance skills and attitudes about drugs, but these positive effects were not apparent when the youths reached the high school years. The researchers concluded that the positive effects of the program recorded for fifth and sixth graders were not likely to persist into the high school years, in the absence of a strong reinforcement program. They suggested that, while the D.A.R.E. organization has strong backing and support among police, educators, and community leaders, the police departments must now design a more effective drug prevention program.[13] Concern over the effectiveness of D.A.R.E. has led to some program modifications, including a greater presence of the D.A.R.E. officers in high schools and more person-to-person contacts between officers and students to promote a more personalized, mentoring relationship between the officers and the students.

The Future of Delinquency Prevention.   In planning and implementing delinquency prevention programs, it is important to keep in mind that the whole matter of preventing delinquency is a delicate one. Youths who are chosen to participate in prevention programs because they are "at risk" must not be characterized as "potential delinquents." Such labeling can be as damaging as the "delinquent" label applied to those referred to the juvenile court. Delinquency prevention agencies, then, can perhaps be most successful when they are not defined as such, either within the neighborhoods they serve or in the larger community. They must be designed to offer opportunities to all the juveniles there, not just to those who can be identified as "potential delinquents."

Those who design prevention programs must also have realistic expectations. Programs that will operate in inner city areas, serving the urban poor, are not likely

Police investigating a gang activity site. *(Photo credit: Nick J. Cool, The Image Works)*

to produce dramatic results in a short period of time. Through the process of what Pope terms *hyperghettoization*,[14] the amount of violent crime, family disruption, educational decline, substance abuse, and residential and commercial deterioration in some areas has reached such a high level that support networks no longer exist. Any effort to develop programs for such a setting must take into account the formidable obstacles that stand in the way of success.

THE ROLE OF VOLUNTEERS IN DELINQUENCY PREVENTION

A look at the early development of delinquency-control agencies at the local level reveals that volunteers have always been actively involved, both in direct contact with youths and in groups that have worked for funding to support such programs. Through civic organizations and churches, many volunteers have become involved in efforts to establish halfway houses, refuges for runaways, and job-training programs.

As the handling of youths who are defined as "problems" is conducted more frequently in the community, people are becoming more knowledgeable about and interested in the fate of juveniles in trouble and a number seek to become actively involved in assisting them. This involvement may take the form of direct assistance through counseling, tutoring, friendship, companionship, or emotional support, or formation of organizations or committees within existing organizations to educate the general public on the causes and prevention of delinquency. Lobbies or pressure groups promote new legislation or work for passage of tax levies to increase funds for local community-based prevention and control programs.

Because of the cost factor alone, many social agencies must depend upon volunteers to staff programs. In addition, experimentation with volunteers has shown that they bring to their work a degree of motivation and commitment that cannot be purchased. College students have been found to be particularly effective in diversion programs for young people, because their closeness in age to the clients permits them to empathize with the problems of the youths they counsel.

DELINQUENCY PREVENTION THROUGH DETERRENT METHODS

For some youths, fear can be a delinquency prevention tool. They may be deterred (turned away) from unacceptable behavior because they fear the personal consequences. Playing on this possibility, programs have been developed to show youths what has happened to others who have committed criminal acts, in the hope that observing and talking with them will instill the type of fear that will turn the youths away from delinquency. These programs are based on the threat or fear of punishment, not actual punishment.

A unique effort of this type was the Juvenile Awareness Project, which was brought to national attention by the television documentary *Scared Straight*. In this program, youths were brought to Rahway Prison, where prisoners confined there with long sentences, known as the "Lifers' Group," told them of the brutality and pain of imprisonment. More than 15,000 young people came to Rahway and took part in the program.

In the television documentary, extravagant claims were made about the success of the program in turning the young people involved away from a life of crime. After a close examination of the program, however, James Finckenauer reported in his book *Scared Straight and the Panacea Phenomenon* that many of the youths brought to the prison had not been involved in delinquency before taking part in the program and that neither the attitudes nor the behavior of other participants who did have records of serious delinquency were changed by the experience.[15] Subsequently, such organizations as the National Council on Crime and Delinquency and the American Correctional Association criticized this and similar programs, noting that they had the potential for psychological harm for some youths and that they did not give proper attention to the social and economic conditions which are related to a good deal of juvenile delinquency.[16]

While the overblown claims of the Rahway Prison program and similar experiments grounded in fear seem largely unsubstantiated, the approach is still widely employed by judges and juvenile courts. However, prison visitation programs are usually carefully monitored, so that only youths who have actually performed delinquent acts are included. There is more serious and quiet conversation between the youths and inmates and less yelling and attempts to intimidate youths. It appears that this controlled and objective discussion approach is more conducive to producing long-term results.

Another type of deterrence program is shock incarceration designed to prevent further delinquency, most commonly taking the form of "boot camps." (See Chapter 15 for a description of boot camps.) In these programs, the juvenile offenders experience tough discipline, rigorous physical challenges, and very few rewards or privileges. Most boot camps are used for late adolescent, nonviolent offenders. Although the programs are designed to raise the youths' self-esteem and confidence and familiarize them with a disciplined, orderly lifestyle, they have been found to have little effect on behavior after release, unless the youths are given continued supervision in the community.[17] The boot camp concept may be flawed because it does not address the problems in a youth's life or provide supervision after return to the old environment. One assessment of boot camps for juvenile delinquents concluded that:

> Although they may be effective in instilling compliance in the short term, if boot camps fail to provide programs to address services and needs, such as education and employment, and if they do not provide intensive follow-up supervision, their value in reducing recidivism clearly seems to be limited.[18]

DELINQUENCY CONTROL

We noted in Chapter 3 that the juvenile justice system has increasingly moved away from the medical model premise that each offender has a specific problem that can be diagnosed and treated. Instead, the notion that youthful offenders should receive dispositions that are just punishments for what they have done is gaining strong support. "Treatment" programs and repeated assignments to probation have come to be viewed as inappropriate dispositions for habitual serious juvenile offenders. A "just desserts" model for juvenile justice, with punishments geared to the seriousness of offenses, has gained support. Proponents of this model maintain that since juveniles are now guaranteed the same legal rights as adults, the attention of the juvenile court should be focused on their offenses rather than on social factors in their lives. The gradual movement toward this philosophy has resulted in changes in juvenile codes and the manner in which juvenile justice is administered.

Juvenile Code Revision and Juvenile Court Administration

In earlier chapters, we noted the variations from state to state with regard to the upper age limit of the juvenile status, the definition of what constitutes a delinquent offense, the types of facilities in which juveniles may be detained, and the dispositions given to juvenile offenders. As a result of the landmark Supreme Court decisions of the 1960s and early 1970s, many states have already revised their juvenile codes to clarify and specify the definitions of delinquency. Laws governing treatment of juveniles who are apprehended outside their state of residence have also been formulated. It is probable that in the future, a standardized code of juvenile justice will be adopted nationwide.

Possible Changes in the Jurisdiction of the Juvenile Court

In the 1960s and early 1970s, the *Kent, Gault,* and *Winship* Supreme Court decisions brought about serious questioning of the juvenile court's philosophy of acting in what is believed to be the best interests of the child, without exercising care to safeguard the constitutional rights of the juvenile or assure due process. As a result, juvenile court proceedings in the 1970s and 1980s took on many of the trappings of adult criminal courts, including increased use of defense lawyers and prosecutors, plea bargaining, guarantees of due process, requirement of proof beyond a reasonable doubt in cases that could result in institutionalization, and a general formalization of proceedings.

As a result of the emphasis on guilt or innocence, the courts have moved to a two-phase (bifurcated) hearing, which separates the adjudication from the disposition. The adjudicatory hearing is concerned exclusively with guilt or innocence, whereas the disposition hearing still retains some aspects of the application of individualized justice that was the hallmark of the juvenile court.

The formalization of juvenile court procedures, the promotion of standardized dispositions, the demands from the public to "get tough" with delinquents—particularly violent offenders—and the increasing numbers of hardened juvenile offenders who come before them have led the juvenile courts to become closer to criminal courts in style and proceedings, particularly in large cities.

Feld contends that:

> In the three decades since *Gault*, judicial decisions, legislative amendments, and administrative changes have transformed the juvenile court from a nominally rehabilitative welfare agency into a scaled-down, second-class criminal court for young people. These revisions have converted the historical ideal of the juvenile court as a social welfare institution into a penal system that provides young offenders with neither therapy nor justice.[19]

Feld maintains that, under the guise of treatment, youths convicted of crimes in juvenile courts may be sent to institutions for long periods of time. If they had been processed in adult criminal courts, they might have received less severe sanctions. The findings of one study showed that youths' use of attorneys in juvenile court proceedings might result in more severe sanctions. The researchers found that "out-of-home placement was more likely to occur if a youth had an attorney, even when other relevant legal and individual factors were the same."[20]

Possible solutions to eliminate the contradictions in the juvenile court system have been proposed. These include (1) a return to the original welfare-oriented juvenile court system, (2) establishing a juvenile version of the criminal court in which the social control and punishment goals of the court are acknowledged as legitimate functions, and (3) establishing an integrated criminal court in which juvenile court jurisdiction over criminal conduct by juveniles would be abolished. All criminal offenses committed by juveniles would be tried in the criminal court. Juveniles would have all the legal rights granted to adult offenders. Also, several procedural and substantive modifications would be introduced for the benefit of younger offenders.[21] Feld endorses the integrated criminal court model and proposes:

> . . . an age-based "youth discount" of sentences—a sliding scale of developmental and criminal responsibility—to implement the lesser culpability of younger offenders in the legal system.[22]

The Juvenile Justice Standards Project, prepared by the Institute of Judicial Administration and the American Bar Association, addressed the question of the future scope and jurisdiction of the juvenile justice system. A set of recommendations was prepared that, if adopted, would dramatically alter the nature of juvenile justice and virtually eliminate the operation of the juvenile court under the *parens patriae* (benevolent parent) principle. The Project produced the following recommendations:

1. Sanctions for juvenile offenders should be proportional to the seriousness of the offense committed.
2. Sentences or dispositions should be determinate.
3. The least restrictive alternative should be the choice of decision makers for intervention in the lives of juveniles and their families. If a decision maker, such as a judge or an intake officer, imposes a restrictive disposition, he or she must state in writing the reasons for finding less drastic remedies inappropriate or inadequate to further the purposes of the criminal justice system.
4. Noncriminal misbehavior (status offenses, PINS) should be removed from juvenile court jurisdiction.
5. Visibility and accountability of decision making should replace unrestrained official discretion and, where appropriate, closed proceedings.
6. There should be a right to counsel for all affected interests at all crucial stages of the proceedings.

7. Juveniles should have the right to decide on actions affecting their lives and freedom, unless found incapable of making reasoned decisions.

8. The role of parents in juvenile proceedings should be redefined, with particular attention to possible conflicts between the interests of parent and child.

9. Limitation should be imposed on detention, treatment, or other intervention prior to adjudication and disposition.

10. Strict criteria should be established for waiver of juvenile court jurisdiction to regulate transfer of juveniles to adult criminal court.[23]

The standards, of course, are recommendations and do not have the force of law. They were not accepted without challenge by judges, law enforcement officials, probation and aftercare officers, and attorneys.

The Balanced Approach/Restorative Justice Approach

The balanced/restorative justice approach to juvenile justice is being advocated by many scholars and practitioners as an alternative that lies between the rehabilitative, child-focused model and the "just deserts," retributive model that focuses on the offense.

As developed by Bazemore and Umbreit, the balanced approach emphasizes the need for the justice system to develop policies that provide community protection, offender accountability for his/her behavior, and rehabilitative intervention programs that make the youths more capable when they leave the system than when they entered it.[24] In the balanced approach model, responsibility for one's deviant behavior is always emphasized and those courts that apply this model will always concentrate on restitution or community service in dispositions. The rehabilitative intervention facet employs various diversion possibilities, such as mediation, which allows the less serious offenders to have their cases decided informally by a nonpartisan mediator. Such programs as drug courts for juveniles, family violence courts, and juvenile gun courts are designed to address all three elements of the approach.

The juvenile gun court programs, modeled after the drug courts, are the most recent innovations in restorative justice. They involve early intervention with those who are charged with nonfelony, gun-related offenses. This intervention takes the form of resolving these cases very quickly (within a day or two after the charges are made) so that the offender becomes immediately aware of the seriousness of the charges and the harm that this unlawful behavior can cause. These cases can be handled formally or informally. If they are treated informally, the charges will be dropped if the youth completes a mandatory rehabilitation program. If a case is handled formally, completion of the gun court program is a condition of the youth's probation. The gun court programs focus on making the youths aware of the potential harm to the community, the severe punishments that are given to those convicted of gun-related offenses, and nonviolent alternatives that youths can use in settling conflicts. The gun court team includes the juvenile court judge, law enforcement officials, probation officers, prosecutors, and defense counsel all working together with volunteer community members who may provide educational input.[25]

Privatization in Juvenile Corrections

There has been a steady growth of services for the control and treatment of juvenile delinquents by private agencies since the early 1960s. The private sector has been involved in providing such services as medical and mental health programs, food preparation, counseling, and psychological testing for a considerable period of time; however, a more recent trend is for private corporations to build and administer correctional facilities.

Some private corporations offer "full-service juvenile corrections and treatment," as illustrated in the following advertisement for the Rebound Corporation.

> Deciding where to place adjudicated and preadjudicated youth is never easy, especially when faced with limited resources, soaring juvenile crime, and shrinking budgets. . . . We provide a wide range of youth services to government agencies, counties, and school districts. From facility design, construction, and operation to providing effective treatment, educational, and vocational programs, Rebound is your full-service juvenile corrections and treatment system provider.[26]

Although private firms involved in corrections have maintained that they can do a better and more cost-efficient job than public agencies, there is, as yet, little research evidence to support this assertion. However, it does seem that they can provide services of comparable quality. For example, a research comparison of youths who completed an intense private program for serious offenders, the Paint Creek Youth Center, with youth placed in state secure facilities found that there was no significant difference in recidivism for the two groups.[27] (See Chapter 15 for a description of the Paint Creek program.)

The use of private agencies for youth counseling, family counseling, substance addiction treatment, group home administration, and even long-term institutionalization seems assured, and can be expected to expand. This is true because of overcrowding pressures, brought on by increased placements of youths in institutions and longer commitments. A study of a nationally representative, randomly selected sample of 95 public and private juvenile facilities, which included detention centers, training schools, ranches, camps, farms, and reception centers, found that a high proportion of the facilities had fire safety violations and that, in a large majority of the facilities, inadequate living space, health care, security, crowding, and control of suicidal behavior were pervasive problems.[28]

PLANNING FOR DELINQUENCY PREVENTION AND CONTROL

Several longitudinal studies have been completed to explore how delinquency prevention and intervention into the lives of at-risk youths can be accomplished. The Project on Human Development in Chicago Neighborhoods focused on individual differences in the subjects, including psychological, biomedical, and health characteristics; family, school, peer, and community influences; the length, extent, and

Providing today's youths with exciting physical challenges is a top priority at the Eckerd Family Youth Alternatives, a private treatment program for youths located in Florida. *(Photo credit: Eckerd Youth Alternatives)*

types of offenses of any criminal careers that are identified; and factors that appear to predict dangerousness.[29]

While the Chicago Neighborhoods Project sought to identify indicators of delinquency endangerment that can be used as the basis for prevention through intervention, another longitudinal study supported by the Office of Juvenile Justice and Delinquency Prevention has already reached some conclusions with regard to the design of such programs. The Program of Research on the Causes and Correlates of Juvenile Delinquency began in 1986, directed by research teams in three cities. In Denver, annual interviews were conducted with samples of boys and girls who were 7, 9, 11, 13, and 15 when the study began. Their parents were also interviewed. The sample was selected from areas of Denver with housing and population characteristics associated with delinquency. In Pittsburgh, 1,500 boys in grades one, four, and seven from Pittsburgh schools were followed over a five-year period. Teachers and parents were also involved. In Rochester, New York, a sample of 1,000 boys and girls in the seventh and eighth grades in Rochester public schools, including more from high-crime areas than from low-crime areas, were interviewed at six-month intervals, over a four-and-one-half year period. Parents were also interviewed and data from schools, the police, courts, and social services were collected.[30]

On the basis of the initial findings, four conclusions were reached.

- Prevention programs need to start early in life because of the observed early age of onset of serious forms of delinquency and drug use. . . . Intervention programs beginning as early as the elementary school years will be most effective in the long run.
- Delinquent careers follow a set of behavioral pathways that progress from less serious to more serious forms of behavior. Prevention programs should be designed to intercept or short-circuit youth in these pathways before their behavior becomes more ingrained. . . .
- Intervention programs for delinquents, especially serious delinquents, need to be comprehensive. . . . They need to deal with the multiple, co-occurring problem behaviors experienced by serious delinquents. . . . They are likely to be involved in drug use, precocious sexual activity, school failure, juvenile gangs, owning guns, and other related problem behaviors. While not all serious delinquents will experience all of these problems, they are likely to experience more than one of them and intervention programs should provide services to deal with them.
- Delinquency intervention programs should be comprehensive in terms of multiple and interlocking causes associated with delinquency. Factors such as family, school, peers, and neighborhoods are all related to delinquency. . . . They appear to be interrelated; for example, it appears that youth who are poorly supervised by their parents *and* who associate with delinquent peers have higher rates of delinquency and drug use than youth who have only one of these risk factors.
- Intervention programs should be designed for the long term because risk factors usually have a long-term effect on juveniles' behavior. . . . Intervention programs lasting 6 to 10 months with youth returning to the same high-risk environment from which they came are not likely to produce any lasting results. . . . We must develop comprehensive programs that provide social and psychological support to these adolescents for years, not months.[31]

These conclusions reinforce the findings of other studies and it appears that delinquency prevention has the best hope of success if programs are grounded in research findings and designed to meet the identified needs of specific types of offenders.

SUMMARY

Since the creation of the juvenile justice system, efforts have been made to discover the causes of delinquency and to develop delinquency prevention programs. Over the years, many elaborate projects, including the Chicago Area Project, the Cambridge-Somerville Youth Study, the Boston Midcity Project, the Mobilization for Youth Program. Youth Service Bureaus, and federal programs that were part of the War on Poverty were implemented. Although many youths were involved in these programs, there is little evidence that they contributed significantly to delinquency prevention and current prevention programs tend to focus on improving conditions for the entire community rather than identifying and working with an "at-risk" population.

Volunteers are important to the continued operation of delinquency prevention and control programs. They have been involved in a wide variety of programs where they provide direct assistance to youths through counseling, tutoring, friendship, companionship, or emotional support, or indirect help by working on committees or lobbying for legislation that will increase funds for community-based delinquency prevention and control programs.

Deterrence has been tried as a delinquency prevention tool in programs that bring youth to meet with prisoners in institutions or in "boot camps" that enforce rigid discipline. The effects of these experiences in deterring delinquent behavior have been found to be negligible.

Juvenile code revisions for delinquency control, grounded in a "just deserts" philosophy, have been enacted in many states. As a result, juveniles accused of violent crimes are more likely to be immediately referred to adult criminal court or to specialized youth courts developed for hardcore offenders.

The future status of the juvenile court is uncertain. It may continue to exist in its present form, be modified to handle only cases of juvenile misbehavior that would also be criminal for adults, or take the reverse tactic of referring all criminal behavior to other courts and specializing in assisting youths involved in minor delinquencies or status offenses. The balanced/restorative justice approach to juvenile justice is proposed as an alternative that lies between the rehabilitative, child-focused model and the retributive, "just deserts" approach. The balanced/restorative justice approach seeks to balance community protection, offender accountability, and rehabilitative intervention. Specialized drug courts for juveniles, family violence courts, and juvenile gun courts have been created as part of the programming in this approach.

Privatization of correctional services will continue in the areas of medical and mental health services, food service, counseling, testing, and substance addiction treatment. If private agencies can conclusively demonstrate that the services they offer are more effective and cost-efficient than state- or community-operated services, the involvement of the private sector in juvenile corrections will increase.

Current efforts at delinquency prevention include the implementation of large longitudinal studies designed to chart the development of delinquency from birth and identify factors that produce it. Initial findings from this research seem to indicate that delinquency is a highly complex, many-faceted problem, and that programs designed to prevent or control it must be long-term and consider every facet of the youth's life and environment.

DISCUSSION QUESTIONS

1. Why is it logical to involve the community in delinquency prevention and control programs?
2. Why do programs to deter youths from future delinquency by seeking to instill fear prove ineffective? Should prison visitation programs be abandoned because of possible harmful consequences?

3. Discuss the proposal that all juvenile cases involving criminal activities should be heard in adult criminal courts. What would be the advantages and disadvantages of such a change?

4. Various states are relying more and more on the private sector to provide delinquency prevention, control, and treatment services. Discuss the pros and cons of the privatization movement.

5. Research on the effectiveness of delinquency prevention and control programs reveals that they usually are found to be marginally successful, at best. What factors account for the failure of these programs to prevent and control juvenile delinquency?

NOTES

1. Richard J. Lundman, *Prevention and Control of Juvenile Delinquency* (New York: Oxford University Press, 1993), 67.

2. *Ibid.*, 39–43.

3. *Ibid.*, 78.

4. Marylyn Bibb, "Gang-Related Services of Mobilization for Youth," in *Juvenile Gangs in Context* (Englewood Cliffs, NJ: Prentice Hall, 1967), 175–182.

5. Susan Gluck Mezey, *Children in Court* (Albany, NY: State University of New York Press, 1996), 32.

6. President's Commission on Law Enforcement and Administration of Justice, *Task Force Report: The Challenge of Crime in a Free Society* (Washington, DC: U.S. Government Printing Office, 1967), 83.

7. Statement of Ray Young, National Job Corps Administration, in an interview reported in *The Sullivan Review*, 100, 50 (December 22, 1977), 20.

8. Jean Baldwin Grossman and Eileen M. Barry, "Mentoring—A Proven Delinquency Prevention Strategy," *OJJDP Juvenile Justice Bulletin*, April 1997, 1.

9. P.A. Roaf, J.P. Tierney, and D.E. Hunte, *Big Brothers/Big Sisters: A Study of Volunteer Recruitment and Screening* (Philadelphia: Public-Private Ventures, 1994).

10. Grossman and Barry, "Mentoring—A Proven Delinquency Prevention Strategy," 2.

11. *Ibid.*

12. Law Enforcement News, "When It Comes to the Young, Anti-Drug Efforts Are Going to Pot," *Law Enforcement News*, 22 (1996), 442–447.

13. Dennis P. Rosenbaum and Gordon S. Hanson, "Assessing the Effects of School-Based Drug Education: A Six-Year Multi-Level Analysis of Project DARE," *Journal of Research in Crime and Delinquency*, 35, 4 (1998), 381–412.

14. Carl E. Pope, "Juvenile Justice in the Next Millennium," in John Klofas and Stan Stojkovic, eds., *Crime and Justice in the Year 2010* (Belmont, CA: Wadsworth Publishing Company, 1995), 273.

15. James O. Finckenauer, *Scared Straight and the Panacea Phenomenon* (Englewood Cliffs, NJ: Prentice Hall, 1982).

16. Gray Cavender, "Scared Straight: Ideology and the Media," *Journal of Criminal Justice* 9 (1981), 433.

17. Donald Hengesh, "Think of Boot Camps as a Foundation for Change, Not an Instant Cure," *Corrections Today* 53, 6 (October 1991), 106–108.

18. Edward J. Loughran and Susan Guarino-Ghezzi, "A State Perspective," in Barry Glick and Arnold P. Goldstein, eds., *Managing Delinquency Programs That Work* (Laurel, MD: American Correctional Association, 1995), 47.

19. Barry C. Feld, *Bad Kids* (New York: Oxford University Press, 1999), 287.

20. George W. Burruss, Jr. and Kimberly Kempf-Leonard, "The Questionable Advantage of Defense Counsel in Juvenile Court," *Justice Quarterly* 19, 1 (March 2002), 37.

21. Barry C. Feld, *Bad Kids*, 289.
22. *Ibid.*, 289–290.
23. Juvenile Justice Standards Project, *Juvenile Justice Standards* (Washington, DC: National Conference on the Proposed IJA/ABA Juvenile Justice Standards, October 30–November 3, 1977), 2.
24. G. Bazemore and M. Umbreit, *Balanced and Restorative Justice for Juveniles* (Washington, DC: Office of Juvenile Justice and Delinquency Prevention, 1995).
25. David Sheppard and Patricia Kelly, *Juvenile Gun Courts: Promoting Accountability and Providing Treatment* (Washington, DC: Office of Juvenile Justice and Delinquency Prevention, 2002), 1–12.
26. "Providing Solutions for Juvenile Offenders," *Corrections Today* 56, 7 (December 1994), 102.
27. Peter W. Greenwood and Susan Turner, "Evaluation of the Paint Creek Youth Center: A Residential Program for Serious Delinquents," *Criminology* 31, 2 (1993), 263–279.
28. Dale G. Parent, Valerie Leiter, Stephen Kennedy, Lisa Livens, Daniel Wentworth, and Sarah Wilcox, *Conditions of Confinement: Juvenile Detention and Corrections Facilities* (Washington, DC: Office of Juvenile Justice and Delinquency Prevention, 1994), 2, 4–7.
29. Felton J. Earls and Albert J. Reiss, Jr., *Breaking the Cycle: Predicting and Preventing Crime* (Washington, DC: National Institute of Justice, 1994), 5.
30. David Huizinga, Rolf Loeber, and Terence P. Thornberry, *Urban Delinquency and Substance Abuse* (Washington, DC: Office of Juvenile Justice and Delinquency Prevention, 1994), 2–4.
31. *Ibid.*, 22–23.

Index

NAME INDEX

Ackely, E., 134
Adamcik, Lori P., 435
Aday, David P. Jr., 320
Addams, Jane, 82
Adelson, Lester, 232
Agnew, Robert, 59, 72
Ahern, Joseph, 406
Alarid, Leanne Fiftal, 387
Alexander, Thad, 123, 135
Allen, Ernie, 255
Allen, Francis A., 255
Altschuler, David M., 406
Ammar, Nawal, 263, 277
Amos, William E., 180, 201
Andrews, Joey, 435
Arad-Davidson, Bilha, 406
Archambault, F. X., 173
Archbold, Carol. A., 127, 135
Arjunan, Mehala, 131, 134, 135
Armstrong, Troy L, 406
Aro, A., 36
Arthur, Lindsay A., 255
Asbury, Herbert, 132
Ashford, Jose B., 406
Atkinson, Maxine P., 163, 173
Augustus, John, 325
Austin, James, 133

Bachara, Gary H., 36
Bachman, Jerald G., 10, 19, 173, 202, 434
Baer, John S., 36
Bailey, W.C., 26, 36
Bakan, David, 91
Ball, Richard A., 320, 356
Bandura, Albert, 64–65, 73
Baron, Stephen W., 134
Barr, Helen M., 36
Barrow, Robert V., 277
Barry, Eileen M., 452
Bartollas, Clement, 381, 388
Bazemore, Gordon, 92, 260, 277, 447, 453
Beccaria, Cesare, 25, 34
Beck, Allen J., 73
Beezer, Bruce G., 202
Belknap, Joanne, 164, 165, 173
Bender, David L. 388
Bensinger, Gad J., 131, 132
Benson, Peter L., 36
Bentham, Jeremy, 26, 34
Beretta, Gina, 277
Berliner, Howard, 356
Bernard, William, 121, 134
Bernstein, Samuel, 352, 357
Besharov, Douglas J., 92, 305, 321, 316, 321
Bibb, Marylyn, 452
Bing, Robert L., 277
Biskup, Michael D., 52, 388
Bixby, F. Lovell, 403,
Black, Donald J., 262, 277
Black, Henry Campbell, 233, 320
Black, James A., 386, 387
Blanche, Ruth C., 231
Block, Carolyn Rebecca, 107, 126, 127, 131, 133, 135
Block, Richard, 107, 126, 127, 131, 133, 135
Blomgren, Paul G., 52
Bloom, B. L., 58, 72

Blumston, P., 19, 201
Bogen, Phil, 278
Bohman, Martin, 33, 36
Bonger, Willem, 35
Bookstein, Fred L., 36
Bortner, M.A., 320, 321
Borzecki, M., 434
Bour, Daria S., 173
Bowen, Louise DeKoven, 82
Bracey, Dorothy Heid, 166, 173, 255
Brantingham, Paul J., 386
Bratter, Thomas E., 183, 201
Brendtro, Larry K., 423, 434
Brenner, Charles, 39, 51
Briar, Scott, 262, 277
Bridges, George, 263, 277
Bronner, A.L., 152
Brown, Bertram S., 434
Brown, Kristal Y., 434
Brown, S., 173
Brown, William B., 134, 278
Brunson, Rod K., 134, 167, 174
Bryant, Dan, 202
Burgess, E.W., 72
Burkett, Steven R., 191, 202
Burr, Wesley R., 153, 154
Burruss, George W., Jr., 452
Burton, Velmer S., Jr., 387, 388
Butts, Jeffrey A., 320
Bynum, Timothy, 277

Caet, Tory J., 278
Caldwell, Robert B., 386, 387
Calhoun, Thomas C., 153
Camp, Camille Graham, 388, 433
Camp, George M., 388, 433
Campbell, Anne, 121, 123, 134, 135
Canter, Rachelle J., 142, 153, 154
Carmody, Dianne Cyr, 184, 200, 201, 203
Cash, William B., 434
Cavan, Ruth Shonle, 19, 24, 35, 173
Cavender, Gray, 452
Cellini, Henry R., 388
Cerne, Thomas, 339, 340, 353, 356, 357
Cernkovich, Stephen A., 277, 321, 387
Chaffee, S., 65, 73
Chaiken, Marcia R., 348, 356
Chandler, K.A., 201
Chapman, C.D., 201
Chapple, Constance L., 153
Chase, Naomi Feigelson, 231
Chen, S.P., 201
Chesney-Lind, Meda, 165, 166, 173, 174
Chilton, Ronald, 59, 72
Chitwood, Dale D., 174
Choy, S.P., 201
Christiansen, K.O., 36
Church, Vicky Turner, 387
Clark, John P., 277
Cleckley, Hervey, M., 48
Clement, Mary, 242, 255
Cloward, Richard A., 60, 72, 106, 107, 108, 133, 157, 438
Coates, Robert B., 386
Cochran, John C., 387
Coffey, Alan R., 262, 277
Cohen, Albert K., 23, 35, 60, 72, 105, 133, 157
Cohen, Lawrence, 72

Cole, Larry, 91, 386, 387
Colley, Carol, 233
Collins, H. Craig, 119, 132, 134
Collins, Isaac, 360
Collins, J., 19, 201
Conley, Darlene, 277
Cook, Jacqueline, 138, 152
Corley, Charles, 277
Coulter, Ernest K., 441
Cox, Louis A., Jr., 388
Cozic, Charles P., 388
Cozic, Michael D., 52
Cressey, Donald R., 35, 36, 73
Crews, Gordon A., 19
Cromwell, Paul F., Jr., 355
Cronin, Roberta C., 357
Cull, John G., 142, 153
Cullen, Francis T., 153
Curry, G. David, 125, 135, 270, 278
Cuvelier, Steven J., 387

Dahlgren, Daniel, 263, 277
Dalgard, Odd Steffen, 33, 36
Danner, Mona J.E., 184, 200, 201, 203
Darwin, Charles, 27
Daudistel, Howard C., 277
David, Joseph M., 386
Davids, Leo, 146, 147, 153
Davidson, Robert, 148, 154, 173
Davidson, William S. II, 356
Davis, Nannette J., 165, 173
Davis, Joseph M., 256, 321
Dawley, David, 99, 132
Day, Susan E., 92
Decker, Scott H., 132, 270, 277, 278
DeComo, R., 386
DeFrancis, Vincent, 215, 231, 232
DelGrosso, Nicholas, 346, 347
DeMause, Lloyd, 91
Deschenes, Elizabeth Piper, 135
Dezolt, Ernest, 203
Dinitz, Simon, 73, 243, 255
Doemer, William G., 91
Donald, Brooke, 201
Donnermeyer, J.F., 20
Dorne, Clifford K., 233
Dugdale, Richard, 29, 36
Dukes, Duane, 203
Duncan, G., 72
Duncan, J., 72
Dunn, Christopher, 263, 277, 321, 387
Durkheim, Emile, 59, 72

Earls, Felton J., 453
Edwards, Leonard P., 233
Egley, Arlen, Jr., 131, 132, 134, 135
Eldefonso, Edward, 262, 277
Elliott, Delbert S., 19
Ellis, Rodney A., 435
Elwell, M.E., 215, 232
Empey, Lamar T., 36, 91, 342, 356
Engen, Rodney, 277
Erikson, Eric H., 40, 51
Esbensen, Finn-Aage, 118, 134, 135
Eve, Raymond, 147, 154, 163, 173

Fagan, Jeffrey A., 153, 256, 406
Faller, Kathleen Coulborn, 232
Fantiti, Mario D., 203
Faust, Frederic L., 386

Feld, Barry C., 277, 301, 305, 320, 321, 373, 387, 445, 446, 452, 453
Felson, Marcus, 72
Ferdinand, Theodore N., 19, 24, 35
Ferracuti, Franco, 65, 73
Ferraro, G., 36
Figlio, Robert M., 10, 72
Finckenauer, James O., 452
Finkelhor, David, 153, 255
Finnegan, T., 240, 300
Fishbein, E., 36
Fisher, Bruce A., 386
Fjeld, Ruth M., 255
Fjeld, Stanton P. 255
Flammang, C.J., 276, 278
Flaste, Richard, 172
Fliegel, B., 134
Fogel, David, 26, 35
Forde, David R., 134
Forney, Mary Ann, 174
Forst, Martin L., 386
Foster, J., 243, 255
Fox, James Anan, 134
Fox, Sanford J., 35
Frazier, Charles E., 387
Freeman, Beatrice, 143, 153
French, Alfred P., 152
Freud, Anna, 40
Freud, Sigmund, 39–40, 416
Friday, Paul C., 19
Fritsch, Eric J., 278
Fryberg, Susan, 156
Frymier, Jack, 202
Fuller, John R., 320

Gaarder, Emily, 164, 173
Galassi, John P., 419, 434
Galassi, Merna D., 419, 434
Gale, William, 134
Gallup, George Jr., 201
Galvin, Charles, 66, 73
Garner, Connie Chenoweth, 153
Garrett, Gerald R., 132
Gault, Gerald, 86
Gault, Robert H., 36
Gelles, Richard J., 153
Gerard, James W., 361
Gerard, Roy, 51, 435
Giacomazzi, Andrew, 278
Giallombardo, Rose, 72, 381, 382, 388
Gibbons, Don C., 410, 434
Gill, Thomas D., 243, 255
Gillis, A. R., 163, 173
Ginzberg, Eli, 356
Glaser, Daniel, 133, 409, 433
Glasser, Paul, 66, 73, 434
Glasser, William, 416, 417
Gleason, Debra K., 132
Glick, Barry, 452
Glueck, Eleanor, 22, 28, 29, 35, 36, 44, 51, 66, 73, 152, 157
Glueck, Sheldon, 22, 28, 29, 35, 36, 44, 51, 66, 73, 152, 157
Goddard, Henry, 29, 36
Golden, Roy E., 150, 154
Goldstein, Arnold P., 452
Gonzales-Cossio, T., 36
Goodstein, Lynne, 406
Gordon, Margaret A., 132, 278
Goring, Charles, 22, 35
Gottfredson, Michael, 72
Gough, Aidan R., 256
Gray, Ellen, 255
Gray, L. N., 26, 36
Greenbaum, Stuart, 435
Greenfeld, Lawrence A., 73
Greenwood, Peter W., 387, 453
Gregory, Thomas B., 203

Griffin, P., 19
Grisso, Thomas, 41, 51
Griswald, D.B., 73
Gross, Andale, 231
Grossman, Jean Baldwin, 452
Grunbaum, J., 19, 201
Guarino-Ghezzi, Susan, 452
Gustavson, Sandra, 203

Hackler, James C., 68, 73, 89, 92
Hagan, M. P., 428, 434
Hagedorn, John, 112, 115, 131, 133, 134
Hagen, John, 163, 173
Hahn, Paul H., 278
Halverson, Jerry, 201
Hamm, Mark S., 124, 135
Hamparian, Donna, 250, 256, 321, 382, 386, 388
Hansen, K. V., 153
Hanson, Gordon S., 452
Hardman, Dale G., 118, 124, 134, 135
Hardy, Richard E., 142, 153
Hardyck, Jane Allyn, 150, 154
Harris, Leodis, 307, 321
Hartman, Heinz, 40
Hartstone, Eliot, 277
Hasenfield, Yeheskel, 355
Healy, W., 152
Hechinger, Fred M., 131, 135, 202
Helfer, Ray E., 233
Hengesh, Donald, 377, 387, 388, 452
Henningsen, Rodney, 173
Herbert, Bob, 133
Hernandez-Avila, H., 36
Herrara, N., 386
Hewitt, Lester C., 44, 51
Hill, C., 19, 201
Hill, Gary D., 163, 173
Hill, Reuben, 154
Hippchen, Leonard J., 36
Hirschi, Travis, 67, 72, 73, 143, 144, 147, 153, 154, 202
Ho, H., 36
Hoiles, Robert, 73
Hollenhorst, Pamela Stiebs, 425, 434
Hooton, Earnest, 29, 36
Hope, Trina L., 144, 153
Horowitz, Ruth, 133
Hotaling, Gerald, 255
Houghtalin, Marilyn, 320
Howell, James C., 132, 133, 135
Huff, C. Ronald, 112, 118, 128, 132, 133, 134, 135, 194, 320, 356
Huizinga, David, 118, 134, 453
Hunte, D. E., 452
Hunter, Robert M., 387
Hutchings, Bernard, 33, 36
Hyman, Drew, 388

Inciardi, James A., 133, 134, 174
Inhelder, B., 51
Ireland, Timothy O., 167, 173
Isaacs, Mareasa R., 60–61, 72

Jackson, Donald Dale, 386
Jackson, Robert K, 112, 117, 123, 133, 134, 135
Jacobson, Judith M., 256, 321, 386
James, Howard, 378, 387, 388
James, Jennifer A., 91, 165, 173
Janus, M., 167, 173
Jeffery, C. R., 63, 73
Jenkins, Collette M., 321
Jenkins, Richard L., 44, 51
Jensen, Gary F., 91, 92
Jensen, Gary J., 147, 154, 163, 173
Jesness, Carl F., 46, 52
Johnson, Bruce D., 348, 356

Johnson, Thomas A., 91, 416, 434
Johnston, Lloyd D., 19, 173, 202, 434
Johnston, Norman, 153
Jones, Michael A., 360, 386
Junger, M., 67, 73
Justice, Blair, 217, 219, 231, 232
Justice, Rita, 217, 219, 231, 232

Kaczor, Bill, 51
Kalinich, David, 134
Kallikak, Martin, Sr., 29
Kann, L., 19, 201, 202
Katkin, Daniel, 388
Kaufman, P., 201
Kay, Barbara, 73
Keiser, R. Lincoln, 99, 132
Kelley, Thomas M., 241, 255
Kelly, Delos H., 187, 202
Kelly, Patricia, 453
Kemph-Leonard, Kimberly, 263, 277, 452
Kennedy, Leslie W., 134
Kennedy, Stephen, 453
Kenney, Emmet, 52
Kerle, Ken, 387
Kerper, Hazel, 355
Kichen, S., 19, 201
Killinger, George, 355
King, R. P., 428, 434
Klaus, P., 201
Klein, Malcolm W., 132, 271, 278, 306, 320, 321
Klemke, Lloyd W., 73
Kline, Susan A., 73
Klofas, John, 134, 452
Knopp, Fay Honey, 434
Knudten, Richard D., 35
Koelman, Mark A. R., 278
Kohlberg, Lawrence, 41, 51
Kolbe, L., 19, 201
Konopka, Gisela, 157, 161, 172, 173
Koop, C. Everett, 231
Kosofsky, Barry E., 31, 36
Kovar, Lillian, 164, 173
Kramer, John, 388
Kratcoski, John E., 10, 19
Kratcoski, Lucille, 8, 92, 153, 158
Kratcoski, Peter C., 10, 19, 61, 72, 73, 92, 133, 135, 153, 173, 202, 203, 263, 277, 278, 356, 357, 434, 435
Kraus, Wesley, 255
Kringler, Einar, 33, 36
Krisberg, Barry, 133, 360, 386
Krohn, Marvin D., 193, 202

Lab, S.P., 435
Lamb, Kevin, 153
Landon, Marilyn, 434, 435
Laudau, Hortense, 233
Lavery, Carrie, 278
Leader, A., 63, 73
LeCroy, Craig Winston, 406
Leiter, Valerie, 453
Leonard, Clara T., 386
Leone, Bruno, 388
Lerman, Paul, 91
Levine, Abraham, 231
Lewis, Michael, 106, 111, 133
Lilly, J. Robert, 320, 356
Lipps, Thomas R., 294
Lipton, Douglas, 357
Little, Arthur D., 357
Livens, Lisa, 453
Llahe, Benjamin B., 201
Loeber, Rolf, 149, 154, 453
Lombroso, Cesare, 22, 27, 28, 29, 30, 35
Londman, Richard, 435
Lopiparo, Jerome J., 64, 73

Loughran, Edward J., 452
Love, W. Chris, 36
Lowry, R., 19, 201
Lucht, Carroll L., 231
Lundman, Richard J., 277, 452
Lurie, Theodora, 152, 154

Mack, Julian, 84, 92
Macon, Perry, 112, 115, 131, 133, 134
Malloy, Diana A., 435
Mann, Coramae Richey, 145, 153
Marks, Thomas C., Jr., 277
Marquart, James W., 387
Marshall, I. H., 67, 73
Martin, J.D., 26. 36
Martinson, Robert, 357
Maslow, Abraham H., 117, 134
Mathers, Richard A., 153
Matza, David, 58, 72
Mawson, Robert, 60, 72
Maxson, Cheryl L., 132, 278
Mays, G. Larry, 320, 348, 356
McBride, Duane C., 174
McBride, Wesley D.,112, 117, 123, 133, 134, 135
McBurnett, Keith, 201
McCaghy, Charles H., 36
McCarthy, Francis Barry, 305, 321
McCord, Joan, 48, 52, 153
McCord, William, 48, 52, 153
McCorkle, Lloyd W., 403, 423
McDonald, Douglas C., 356
McGeady, Mary Rose, 255
McGraw, Robert E., 256, 321, 386
McGree, Charles M., 435
McKay, Henry D., 57, 72, 104, 106, 133, 152
McKeiver, Joseph, 87
McKenzie, R.D., 72
McLeod, J., 65, 73
McShane, Marilyn D., 255
Megargee, Edwin I., 150, 154
Mendick, S.A., 36
Merton, Robert K., 59, 72
Meyer, Michael, 127, 135
Mezey, Susan Gluck, 152, 452
Milich, Richard, 35
Miller, A.K., 201
Miller, Edwin, 128
Miller, E. Eugene, 355
Miller, Jody, 122, 134, 135, 167, 174
Miller, Norma, 36
Miller Robert, 52
Miller, Walter B., 99, 100–01, 105–06, 121, 122, 132, 133, 134, 135, 438
Moffit, L., 41–42
Mones, Paul, 47–48
Monnette, Barbara, 349, 356
Montgomery, Imogene, 434, 435
Montgomery, Reid H., Jr., 19
Montilla, M. Robert, 355
Moore, James, 232, 387
Moore, Joan, 96, 112, 116, 131, 133, 134, 167, 174
Moore, Mark K., 278
Moore, Richter H., Jr., 277
Morris, Norval, 154
Mouzakitis, Chris M., 232
Mulligan, William, 32, 36
Munner, Robert J., 73
Murray, Charles A., 36, 388
Murray, Ellen, 73

Neilson, Kathleen, 142, 153
Nettler, Gwynn, 23, 35
Nevada, Charlene, 321
Newman, Charles L., 410, 411, 434
Newsom, Lila, 255
Nimick, Ellen, 320

Norton, William M., 320
Nye, F. Ivan, 154
Nye, William, 144, 153, 173

O'Brien, Shirley, 173, 174
O'Conner, J., 174
Ohlin, Lloyd, E., 60, 72, 106, 107, 108, 133, 157, 438
O'Malley, Patrick M., 19, 173, 202, 434
Onek, D., 386
Orchard, Janet, 356
Ostrow, Miriam, 356
Ott, Heidi, 261

Palazuelos, A., 36
Palmer, Ted, 356
Parent, Dale G., 453
Park, R. E., 72
Patros, R. L., 428, 434
Pelham, William, 35
Peoples, Edward E., 51, 73
Perrow, Charles, 373, 387
Perry, Garry P., 356
Perry, Robert L., 277, 321, 387
Peterson, K.E., 36
Pfiffner, Linda J., 201
Philpott, William H., 36
Piaget, Jean, 40–41, 51
Pierce, Glenn, 134
Piliavin, Irving M., 150, 154, 262, 277
Platt, Anthony, 91, 92, 201, 386
Poe-Yamagata, Eileen, 320
Polk, Kenneth, 191, 202
Poole, Eric D., 387, 388
Poole, R., 240, 300
Pope, Carl E., 452
Pottieger, Anne E., 133, 174
Powers, Edwin, 91
Pugh, Richard C., 203
Pugh, Tony, 71

Quay, Herbert, 45

Rachin, Richard L., 434
Rand, M. R., 201
Rankin, Joseph H., 149, 154
Rebellon, Cesar J., 173
Reckless, Walter, 66, 68, 73, 243, 255
Rector, Milton, 242, 255
Regoli, Robert M., 387, 388
Reid, Sue Titus, 35
Reiss, Albert J. Jr., 262, 277, 453
Reiss, Ira, 154
Renquist, William, 249
Resteiner, Harold E., 277
Rettig, Richard R., 132
Richetti, Dorinda, 277
Roaf, P.A., 452
Roane, Marilyn Miller, 321
Roberts, Dwight Boyd, 388
Roberts, M. K., 73
Robertson, Pricilla, 91
Robinson, Saundra, 308, 309, 321
Robinson, Sophia M., 92
Roche, Michael P., 72
Roehlkepartain, Eugene C., 36
Rojek, Dean G, 91, 92
Rollins, Boyd, 149, 154
Romeo, Lynaia, 201
Romig, Dennis A., 353, 357, 388, 406
Roosevelt, Theodore, 141, 439
Rosen, Lawrence, 142, 153
Rosenbaum, Dennis P., 452
Rosenfeld, Alvin A., 214, 215, 232
Ross, J., 19, 201
Roth, Loren H., 35
Rothman, David J., 91
Roush, David W., 387

Rubin, H. Ted, 277
Ruddy, S. A., 201

Sagatun, Inger J., 233
Salerno, Anthony W., 388
Samenow, Stanton E., 46–47, 48, 52
Sametz, Lynn, 406
Samm, L.H., 36
Sampson, Paul D., 36
Sampson, Robert J., 59, 72
Sanborn, Joseph P., Jr., 320
Sanders, William B., 277
Sarri, Rosemary, 355, 434
Satir, Virginia, 424, 434
Saunders, Susan, 154
Savastano, George, 153
Savitz, Leonard D., 153
Scarpitti, Frank R., 326
Schafer, Stephen, 35
Schafer, Walter E., 202
Scherz, Frances H., 424, 434
Schiraldi, Vincent, 256
Schneider, Anne L., 255, 319
Schneider, Rod, 427
Schoenfeld, C. G., 51
Schondel, C., 435
Schur, Edwin M., 70, 73
Schwartz, Ira M., 371, 386, 387
Scott, Elizabeth S., 41, 51
Sedlak, Andrea, 255
Sendi, Ismail B., 52
Seng, Mangus J., 173
Senjo, Scott, 260, 277
Serrill, Michael S., 256
Shah, Saleem A., 35
Shakur, Sanyika, 52
Shapiro, Elizabeth R., 278
Sharma, Anu R., 36
Shaw, Clifford, 57, 72, 104, 106, 131, 133, 152
Shelden, Randall G., 115, 134, 166, 173, 174, 278
Sheldon, William H., 28, 36
Sheley, Joseph F., 132
Sheppard, David, 453
Shields, G., 435
Shoemaker, Donald J., 23, 35, 51, 72
Short, James F., Jr., 118, 132, 134
Sickmund, Melissa, 16, 19, 20, 71, 92, 135, 152, 173, 201, 211, 212, 213, 214, 232, 233, 240, 254, 255, 256, 268, 277, 278, 282, 300, 320, 321, 327, 355, 356, 386, 387, 388, 406
Sies, Louis B., 355
Sieverdes, Christopher M., 381, 388
Simons, Ronald L., 173
Simpson, John, 163, 173
Skinner, B.F., 420
Skoloff, Brian, 132
Smith, Carolyn A., 173
Smith, Charles P., 232, 255
Smith, Gerald, 203
Smykla, John Ortiz, 355
Snyder, Howard N., 16, 19, 20, 71, 92, 135, 152, 173, 201, 211, 212, 213, 214, 232, 233, 240, 254, 255, 256, 268, 277, 278, 282, 300, 320, 321, 327, 355, 356, 386, 387, 388, 406
Socoloar, Rebecca, 232
Soler, Mark, 256
Solomon, Hassim M., 406
Sontheimer, Henry, 406
Sorrells, James M. Jr., 52, 72
Sowers, Karen M., 435
Spergel, Irving A., 125, 135
Stahl, A., 240, 300
Stapleton, W. Vaughan, 321
Steele, Brandt F., 219, 232

Steen, Charlene, 349, 356
Steib, Victor L., 321
Stellwagen, Lindsey D., 278
Stephenson, Richard M., 326
Stevens, Ronald, 194
Stewart, Charles J., 434
Stewart, D.K., 153
Stojkovic, Stan, 134, 452
Stolz, Stephanie B., 434
Stops, Maria, 348, 356
Stratton, John, 355
Straus, Murray A., 144, 145, 153, 210, 232
Street, David, 373, 387
Streissguth, Ann P., 36
Strodtbeck, Fred L., 118, 134
Strouse, Jean, 173
Strouthamer-Loeber, Magda, 149, 154
Stuart, V. Lorne, 19
Sullivan, Mercer L., 114, 134
Sutherland, Edwin H., 35, 36, 62–63, 64, 73
Sweet, Robert W., Jr., 435
Sykes, Gresham M., 58, 72
Sykes, Richard E., 277
Szumski, Bonnie, 388
Szymanski, Linda, 19, 320

Taft, Donald R., 72
Tanay, E., 72
Tannenbaum, Frank, 105, 133
Tappan, Paul W., 278
Tarde, Gabriel, 61
Taylor, Carl S., 107, 133
Taylor, Robert W., 278
Tec, Nechama, 191, 202
Teele, James E., 73
Thomas, Charles W., 255
Thomas, Darwin, 149, 154
Thomas, W. I., 72, 157, 172
Thompson, E. M., 217, 232
Thornberry, Terence P., 173, 321, 453
Thornton, William E. Jr., 91
Thorsell, Bernard A., 73
Thrasher, Frederick M., 98, 103–04, 114, 118, 121, 132, 133, 134
Thurman, Quint C., 278
Tierney, J. P., 452
Tierney, N., 240, 300
Tietelbaum, Lee E., 256, 321
Tobias, I.J., 153
Toby, Jackson, 152
Toft, Doug, 36
Toner, M. James, 435
Tonry, Michael, 154
Torbet, Patricia McFall, 19, 435
Torres, Manuel J., 132
Tracy, Paul E., 19, 72
Tracy, Sharon K., 134, 278
Trojanowicz, Robert C., 408, 433
Tunis, S., 386
Turner, Susan, 387, 453

Umbreit, M., 447, 453

Vadum, Arlene C., 150, 154
VanBemmelen, J. M., 35
Vanderwall, David, 370, 387
VanNess, Shela R., 46, 52, 426, 434
VanVoorhis, Patricia, 142, 153, 431, 435
VanWinkle, B., 132
Vinter, Robert D., 373, 387, 422, 434
Vorrath, Harry H., 423, 434
Voss, Harwin L., 157, 172
Walker, Yvonne Elder, 73
Warren, Jacqueline Y., 347, 356
Warsmith, Stephanie, 406
Webb, John A., 320
Weeks, H. Ashley, 406
Weisheit, Ralph A., 20, 131

Wekesser, Carol, 388
Wells, L. Edward, 20, 131, 149, 154
Wells, Richard H., 232
Welsh, L., 173
Welsh, Wayne N., 182, 201
Wenk, Ernst A., 197, 203
Wentworth, Daniel, 453
Whitbeck, Les B., 173
Whitcomb, Debra, 233, 278
White, Joseph L., 42, 43, 51
Whittaker, James K., 410, 434
Whyte, William F., 98, 105, 132, 133
Wiatrowski, M., 73
Wicks, Jerry W., 277, 321, 387
Widom, Cathy Spartz, 72, 174, 220, 232
Wienchowski, Louis A., 434
Wilcox, Sarah, 453
Wilks, Judith, 357
Williams, B., 19, 201
Williams, Edwin P., 320
Williams, Timothy, 71, 152
Willis, Cecil L., 232
Wilson, James Q., 26, 36
Wilson, William J., 115, 134
Wolf, Alexander, 423
Wolfgang, Marvin E., 19, 35, 58, 65, 72, 73
Wooden, Wayne S., 131, 135
Wordes, Madeline, 277
Wormith, J. S., 434
Wozner, Yochanan, 406
Wright, James D., 132

Yablonsky, Lewis, 111, 118, 133, 134
Yochelson, Samuel, 46–47, 48, 52
Young, Jeanne P.K., 173
Young, Ray, 452
Yuan, Steven, 406

Zeleny, L.D., 29
Zimmerman, Joel, 202
Znaniecki, Florian

SUBJECT INDEX

Abuse, child. See Child abuse and neglect
Academic failure and delinquency, 31–32, 186–89
Adjudicated delinquents, 3, 305, 309–10, 325
Admonish and release, 295
Adolescence:
    definition, 75
    drug and alcohol use, 8, 10, 13–14, 112–15, 158–59, 191–92, 195
    internalized values in, 41
    "normal" behavior, 5
    unique problems of females, 161
    unlawful activities, 23, 6
Adolescent coping mechanisms, 42–43
Adolescent Girl in Conflict, The, 157, 161
Adopted child research, 33–34
Aftercare:
    decision, 391
    definition, 392
    discharge from, 396
    effectiveness, 397–99, 400–01
    eligibility, 391–92
    intensive, 399–401
    officers, 392
    preparation for, 393–95
    process, 392–96
    readjustment, 391
    recidivism, 397–99
    and residential treatment, 401–04
    revocation, 396–98
    revocation hearing, 397
    rules, 395–96
    supervision by federal parole officers, 391
    treatment plans, 395–96, 399–401

types, 392–93
    violations, 396–97
Aggressive behavior on television, 64–65
Aid for/to Dependent Children, 55, 141–42
Akron Beacon Journal, 19, 20, 51, 71, 72, 133, 152, 201, 231, 406
Alcoholism of parents, 33, 145
Alcohol use by juveniles, 8, 10, 13–14, 112–15, 158–59, 191–92, 195
Alternative schools, 196–97
American Bar Association, 208
American Humane Association, 215
Anomie, 59
Anthony v. Marshall County Board of Education, 188
Appeal of juvenile court dispositions, 316, 319
Apprenticeship, 77
Arrest, juvenile, See Custody, taken into
Arrest records, juvenile, 266–67
Arrests, juvenile:
    by age, 7–8
    conditions for, 264–65
    drug and alcohol related, 8, 10, 13–14
    male-female ratio, 9, 15
    methods of reporting, 7–9
    overrepresentation of minority youths, 15–16
    property crime, 7, 8, 10, 11
    suburban-rural comparison, 15–17
    trends, 11–17
    violent crime, 8, 11–13
Aspirations and delinquency, 118, 185
Assertiveness training, 418–19
Atavism, 27

Baltimore:
    delinquency areas, 58
    juvenile courts, 49
Behavior contracting, 335–36, 337, 420–21
Behavior disorders, 45–46
Behavior modification, 342, 419–21
"Beyond control" offenses, 6
Biochemical explanations of delinquency, 22, 31
Biological school of delinquency theory, 27–29
Blended sentence, 248–49
Blocked aspirations theory of delinquency, 118, 164
"Boot" camps, 377, 444
Boston:
    gang formation, 97–98
    houses of refuge, 80
    juvenile hearings, 83
    Midcity Project, 438
Breed v. Jones, 289, 302, 320
Bureaucratization of schools, 181–82

California Youth Authority's Community Treatment Project, 342–43
Cambridge-Somerville Youth Study, 437–38
Capital punishment, 25
Case management, intensive, 399–491
Catharsis theory, 64
Causes of delinquency. See Delinquency, causes
Chancery courts, 82
Chicago:
    delinquency in Polish neighborhood, 56
    gang activity, 96–99, 104–05, 107–08, 118, 121
    location of first juvenile court, 83
    police contacts with juveniles, 260
    Project on Human Development in Chicago Neighborhoods, 448–49
    social disorganization in, 57

Chicago Area Project, 57, 104–05
Chicago School of sociologists, 57, 104–05
Child abuse and neglect:
  abused children:
    characteristics, 216–18
    custody of, 224–27
    in foster care, 227
    in institutions, 227
  abusive parents
    characteristics, 145–46, 218–20
    childhoods, 219
    difficulties in counseling, 228
    life crises, 219
    Parents Anonymous, 229
    psychiatric disorders, 219
    therapy for, 229
  child protective services, 223–24
  definitions, 207
  diagnosis, 223–24
  discovery, 221–22
  documentation, 210–11
  extent and nature, 144–46, 209–11
  handling, 207–08
  legislation to protect maltreated
    children, 222–23
  juvenile court procedures, 224–28
  recorded, 209–11
  relationship to delinquent and criminal
    behavior, 220–21
  reporting, 208–09
  sexual abuse
    characteristics of victims, 213–16
    endogamous, 214
    extent, 165–68, 212–13
    forms, 189
    generational hypothesis, 215–16
    by parents, 142, 164, 165–68, 216–18,
      242
    by pornography, 169, 211
    by prostitution, 164–69, 211
    reporting, 212
    testimony by children, 226–27
    victim precipitated, 214–15
Child Abuse Prevention and Treatment
  Act, 207
Child advocacy, 227
Child pornography, 169, 211
Child prostitution, 164–69, 211, 238
Children:
  abused and neglected, 216–18
  in Colonial America, 78–79
  death penalty for, 79
  in the Middle Ages, 76–77
  in the nineteenth century, 79–80
  in the Renaissance, 77–78
  on "orphan trains," 362
  punishment of, 77–81
"Children in need of supervision," 6, 235
Child Saving Movement, 82–83, 236–37,
  362
Child Welfare Services, 209
Citizen-initiated police investigations, 258,
  260
Classical School of delinquency theory,
  25–26
Codes, juvenile, 3, 6–7, 280–81
Colorado School Laws, 83
Columbine High School shootings, 11,
  176
Community-based treatment:
  Child Responsibility Project, 346
  early experiments, 341–43
    community service, 344–45
  effectiveness of, 352–53
  family counseling, 345–47
  in Massachusetts, 384
  for multi-problem youths, 349–50
  programs, 341–52

  residential, 350–52
  restitution, 344
Compound, The, 116
Compulsory school attendance, 80–81, 177
Concentric zone concept, 57
Concurrent jurisdiction, 4
Conduct disorders, 39
Confessions by juveniles,
Conflict gangs, 106, 110–12
Connecticut Blue Laws, 78
Consent decree agreement, 296
Counsel, juvenile's right to, 86–87, 243,
  288, 304–05, 314
Counseling:
  for abusive parents, 228
  directive and nondirective, 414–15
  family, 345–47, 415, 423–24
  group, 342, 376–377, 422–23
  in institutions, 376–77
  for multiproblem youths, 349–50
  for sex offenders, 348–49, 426, 428
  substance abuse, 348, 428–30
Counselor-client interaction, 414–16
Crime, violent juvenile, 8, 11–13, 94–95,
  100–03, 110–12, 158–59, 247–53,
  281–82, 300–02, 305–06
Criminal:
  behavior influences, 61–64
  complaints, 84
  court trials for juveniles, 4, 85–88,
    249–51, 300–02, 316
  gangs, 107–09
  offenses by juveniles, 8–13
  personality, 46–47
  predisposition, 27
  types, 22
Criminal court trials for juveniles, 4,
  85–88, 226–28
Culture of violence, 65–66
Custody, child taken into, 264–67

D.A.R.E. (Drug Abuse Resistance
  Education), 195–96, 441–42
Death penalty for juveniles, 79, 290, 316,
  318
Deinstitutionalization:
  in Massachusetts, 384
  of status offenders, 244–45
Delinquency:
  and alcohol use, 8, 10, 13–14, 112–15,
    158–59, 191–92
  areas, 56–58, 66–67, 104–05
  body types, 28–29, 66
  and broken homes, 141, 142–43, 163–64
  causes, 15–16, 25–34, 39–50, 54–70,
    103–18, 160–68
  definition, 2–3, 5–6
  and discipline, 147–49
  and drift, 58
  and dropping out of school, 189–90
  and drug use, 13–14, 112–15, 158–59,
    191–92
  and environment, 56–58, 66–67, 115–16
  and family functioning, 137–52, 163–64
  female, 9, 15, 120–23, 155–72
  gang, 94–130
  influence by peers, 58–59, 62–63
  link to learning disabilities, 188–89
  longitudinal study, 9–10, 143
  male-female ratio, 9, 15, 158
  and mass media, 64–65
  measurement of, 7–10
  middle class, 15–17
  and mother's employment, 137, 147–48
  officially recorded, 7–9
  and opportunity, 60
  oriented social system, 58–59
  and parental expectations, 138, 149

  and parental rejection, 146–47
  and parental supervision, 147–49
  and poverty, 54–56, 149
  prevention, 192–196, 437–43
  problem areas, 56–58
  rural, 15–17
  and schools, 176–200
  self-reported, 7, 9–10, 24, 159–60
  subcultural, 150
  suburban, 15–17
  theories of, 25–34, 39–50, 54–70, 103–18
  trends, 11–17, 158
  and values, 150
  violent, 8, 11–13, 65–66, 94–95, 100–03,
    110–12, 158–59, 247–53, 281–82,
    300–302, 307
Delinquency and Opportunity, 60, 106–07,
  157
Delinquency Control:
  the "balanced approach," 447
  changes in juvenile court jurisdiction,
    235–36, 241, 244–45, 248–51, 254,
    445–47
  court action against habitual and violent
    offenders, 249–51
  juvenile code revision, 241–42, 247,
    248–51, 254, 445
  legislation to control habitual and
    violent juvenile offenders, 248–49
  planning, 448–50
  privatization in juvenile corrections, 448
  restorative justice, 447
  working with habitual violent offenders,
    252
Delinquency Prevention Programs
  Big Brothers and Sisters, 440–41
  "Boot" camps, 377, 444
  Boston Midcity Project, 438
  Cambridge-Somerville Youth Study,
    437–38
  Chicago Area Project, 57, 104–05, 437
  Chicago Neighborhoods Project, 448–49
  D.A.R.E. (Drug Awareness Resistance
    Education), 195–96, 441–42
  Evolution 437–40
  Job Corps, 440
  Juvenile Mentoring Program (JUMP),
    441
  Mobilization for Youth Program, 438–39
  National Youth Conservation Program,
    440
  Planning, 442–43, 448–50
  Program of Research on the Causes and
    Correlates of Juvenile Delinquency,
    449
  Scared Straight Program, 443–44
  War on Poverty, 439–40
  use of volunteers, 443
  Youth Service Bureaus, 440
Delinquent:
  offenses, 6–7
  subculture, 106–07
Delinquent Boys, 60, 105, 157
Delinquents:
  adjudicated, 3, 305, 309–10, 325
  habitual, 249–53
  hard-core, 247–49
  serious, 247, 252
  unofficial handling of, 241–43, 259–60
  violent, 8, 11–13, 65–66, 94–95, 100–03,
    110–12, 158–59, 247–53
Dependent children, 6, 244
Designation of fault, 246
Detention:
  in adult jails, 369–71
  before juvenile court hearings, 161–63,
    170, 249, 254, 289, 291–93
  centers, 291, 363–71

Detention: *(cont.)*
  of habitual and violent delinquents, 249,
    254, 292, 365–69, 365–71
  home, 343
  risk assessment instrument, 366–68
  of status offenders, 142, 170, 241–42, 247
  temporary, 291–92, 363
Determinate sentencing for juveniles, 89,
  248–251, 315
Determinism, biological, 27–29
Detroit:
  delinquency areas, 58
  gang activity in, 108, 112
Deviant norms, 105
Diagnostic centers, 371
Differential association, 62–63
Differential reinforcement, 63–64
Differential treatment, 142, 161–63, 170–71,
  235–36, 239, 245, 280–81, 289
Discretion, police, 261–64
Disposition:
  appeal of, 316, 319
  decree of, 315
  determinate, 359
  indeterminate, 359
Dispositional hearing, 310–16
Dispositions, juvenile court, 84, 310–16
Diversion:
  from juvenile courts, 84, 237–38,
    241–43, 283
  partial, 295–98
  by police, 259–64
  of runaways, 237–39, 242
  of status offenders, 170, 237–39, 241–43
  total, 273
Double jeopardy, 289, 302
Drinking, teenage. *See* Alcohol use by juveniles
Drug use by juveniles, 8, 13–14, 112–15,
  158–59, 184–85, 191–92, 195
Dyslexia, 32

Ecology, human, 56
Educational system, American, 80–81
Endangered/Maltreated Children, 205–31
England:
  chancery courts in, 82
  handling of child offenders, 82
  eighteenth-century justice, 25–26
Environment and delinquency, 56–59, 67
Ex parte Crouse, 82, 91, 288
Expunged juvenile records, 316–17

Families with Service Needs, 245–46
Family:
  broken, 137, 140–41, 142–43
  child abuse and neglect, 144–46, 205–31
  conflict, 140–41, 144–46
  counseling, 345–47
  and delinquency, 136–52, 163–64
  disorganization, 15, 54–56, 163–64
  disruption and delinquency, 4, 56, 163
  "healthy," 138–39
  homeostatic mechanisms, 138
  internal conflicts, 140–41
  maintenance programs, 228
  processes, 138–39
  sexual abuse patterns, 165–69, 213–16
  size and delinquency, 137
  structures, 137–38, 140–41
  as a system, 138
  typical American, 137
Father figure, 146–47
Federal Bureau of Investigation, 7–8, 11, 16,
  18, 19, 20, 158, 239, 247, 255, 256
Female delinquency:
  arrests: 9, 15, 158–59
  causes, 160–70

extent, 15, 158–60
handling by juvenile justice system, 157,
  161–63, 170–71
influenced by family disruption, 163–64
nature, 160
sex related offenses, 164–70
violent, 121, 158–59
Female gangs, 120–23
Female-male arrests ratios, 9, 15, 158
Females, institutionalized, 162–63, 170–71,
  244
Females, sexual abuse of, 142–43, 164–70,
  238, 242
Female status offenders, 157, 158–60,
  161–63, 170–71, 237–38, 242
Fingerprinting of juveniles, 266–67
Four to One Causal Law, 66
Foster care, 350–52, 394
Free will, 26
Freudians, 39–40
"fundamental fairness," principle of, 266

Gagnon v. Scarpelli, 341, 356, 396, 406
Gallegos v. Colorado, 265, 277
Gang:
  activity control, 125–130
  activities in school, 11, 103, 184–85
  behavior, 94–130
  defense of territory, 110–12
  definition of, 96
  development, 97–103
  fights, 95, 110–12
  formation theories, 103–118
  hard-core members, 118–19
  intelligence units, 127–28
  leadership, 118–19
  membership, 97–99
  solidarity, 118–19
  structure, 118–120
  suppression. 127–28
  typologies, 101
  variations in behavior, 120–125
  violence, 94–95, 100–03, 110–12, 252
Gang, The, 98
Gangs:
  Boston, 97–98
  Chicago, 96–99, 104–06, 107–08, 118,
    121
  conflict, 107, 110–112
  criminal, 107–09
  Detroit, 108, 112
  diffuse or solidified, 104
  female, 120–123
  Hispanic, 97, 123
  history of development, 97–99
  in the 1970s, 100–101
  in the 1980s, 1990s, and 2000s, 101–02
  legislation for control, 129
  Los Angeles, 119
  Miami, 114
  middle class, 124
  Milwaukee, 109, 113–14, 115, 121
  New York City, 97–98, 110, 114–15,
    116–17
  Ohio, 108, 128
  retreatist, 112–115
  scope of the problem, 96–97
  sex-oriented, 119–20, 121
  solidified, 104
  suburban and small town, 123–24
  theories of formation, 97–101
  underclass generation, 115–17
  violent, 94–95, 100–03, 110–12, 252
Gangs of New York, The, 97
Gault decision. *See In re Gault*
Group homes, 171, 352
Group therapy, 376–77, 403
Guardian *ad litem*, 227

Guided group interaction, 342, 376–77,
  403, 423

Haley v. Ohio, 265, 277, 288
Halfway houses:
  history, 402–03
  organization, 401–02
  treatment in, 401–03
Hard-core delinquents, 247–53, 399–401
Hard-core gang members, 118–19
Health problems of delinquents, 168–69
Hearings, juvenile court. *See* juvenile court
  hearings
Heredity based theories of delinquency,
  29–30, 33
Home detention, 343
Homeostasis, 138
Hostels, community, 403–04
Houses of Refuge, 80, 362
Hyperactivity and delinquency, 31–32
Hyperkinesis, 32, 183, 188–89

Identification of juvenile suspects, 265–66,
  289
Illinois Juvenile Court Act of 1899, 83, 325
Indeterminate commitment, 80, 392
Indeterminate disposition, 326, 359
In re Gault, 86–87, 88, 92, 265, 277, 288,
  303–04, 320, 445
In re H.C, 50, 52, 289
In re Patricia A., 289
In re Winburn, 49–50, 52. 288
In re Winship, 87, 88, 92, 289, 309, 321, 445
Insanity defense in juvenile cases, 49–50,
  88, 289
Inside the Criminal Mind, 47
Institute for Social Research, University of
  Michigan's
  self-report delinquency studies, 9–10
Institutionalization:
  adaptation to, 380–382
  alternatives for status offenders, 171,
    244–45
  classification of juvenile inmates, 371
  as a disposition, 252, 359
  of females, 157, 162–63, 170, 381–82
  of hard-core offenders, 27, 128, 251–52,
    359–60
  length, 359, 391
  recidivism after, 360–61, 382–83, 385
  of status offenders, 6, 237, 246, 360
Institutions, correctional, 25–26, 359–84
Institutions, juvenile:
  adaptation to, 380–82
  classification in, 371
  cottage system, 371–72
  counseling in, 373–77
  detention centers, 363–69
  effectiveness, 360–61, 378, 382–84
  goals, 372–77
  harmful effects, 361, 378–82
  history, 361–63
  homosexuality in, 381–82
  indeterminate commitment to, 80, 359
  inmate's response to, 378–82
  life in, 378–79
  long-term, 252, 371–78
  number of facilities, 363
  number of residents, 363
  organization, 363–78
  physical structure, 371–72
  profile of youths committed, 360
  punishment in, 359, 378
  private, 363
  rehabilitation in, 360–61
  release from, 391
  school programs in, 373–74
  short-term, 363–371

social structure in, 380–82
staff, 378
training schools, 363, 371
treatment in, 157, 372–78
victimization in, 378–80
violence in, 379–80
vocational programs in, 157, 374
Intake officers:
    duties, 293–95, 328
    role in diversion, 328–29
Intelligence, relation to delinquency, 22, 29–30
Internalization of values, 40–41
Interrogation of juveniles, 265
Interstitial areas, 57

Jails, children held in, 369–71
Jesness Inventory, 4, 46
Jonesboro, Arkansas shootings, 11
Jukes family, 29
Justice model, 26
Just desserts, 88
Just punishment, 26
Juvenile:
    adjudication hearing, 309–10
    age limits, 3–4
    alcohol and drug use, 8, 10, 13–14, 112–15, 158–59, 191–92, 195
    arrests, 6–16, 159–60, 264–67
    attitudes toward police, 262
    codes, 3–4, 6–7, 88, 236, 241–42, 245, 248–51, 264–65, 280–81
    confessions, 265
    corrections, 359–86
    dispositional hearing, 310, 314–16
    fingerprints, 266–67
    identification of suspects, 265–66, 289
    initial hearing, 298–99
    interrogation of, 265
    legal rights, 85–88, 264–67
    lineups, 265–66, 247, 249, 289
    murderers, 49
    photographs of, 266–67
    police units, 268–72
    records, 267
    referral to adult courts, 4, 85–86, 248–51, 288, 299–302
    records, 49
    rights, 264–67
    unlawful behavior for, 2–3, 5
Juvenile court:
    adjudication, 287, 305, 309–10, 326
    age for referral, 3–4, 88
    appeal of decisions, 310, 316
    behavior subject to court action, 2–3, 5
    citation, 295
    consent decree agreement, 225, 296–98
    creation of, 83
    decree of disposition, 315
    defense attorney's role, 304–05, 314
    defense of insanity, 49–50, 288
    detention before hearings, 161–62, 170, 249–50, 254, 363–71
    differential treatment of males and females, 142, 161–63, 170–71
    dispositional hearing, 310–16
    dispositions, 84, 227–28
    diversion from, 84, 170, 237–41,
    divestiture for status offenders, 254–55
    expungement of record, 316–17
    focus on treatment, 84–85
    guardian ad litem, 227
    handling of abuse and neglect cases, 224–28
    handling of status offenders, 88
    hearings, 84, 298–310

insanity defense in, 49–50, 52, 88, 288
intake process, 293–95
judge, 305–09
jurisdiction, 3–4, 6–7, 235–36, 241, 244–45, 248–51, 280–81
jury trial in, 87, 88, 289, 309–10
number of referrals, 9, 159, 281–83
official action, 3–4, 9, 283–87
origins of, 81–83
petition, 287, 290, 298
philosophy, 81, 84, 89, 137, 236–37
plea bargaining in, 243, 303, 314
pleas, 302–03
prehearing conference, 302–03
process, 2, 283–318
prosecutor's role, 4, 303–04, 314
ratio of male-female referrals, 9, 159
referrals by parents, 161–62, 238–39, 281
removal of status offenders from, 241–43, 280–81
retention of status offenders in, 243–44
sources of referrals, 281
standard of proof in, 87, 225–26, 289, 309
stigmatization from contact, 241–43
summons, 285
testimony by children in sexual abuse cases, 226–27
today, 88–90
use of legal counsel in, 86–87, 243, 288, 304–05, 314
waiver of jurisdiction, 4, 16, 85–86, 248–51, 288, 299–302
Juvenile Court Statistics, 9, 159, 240, 281–82
Juvenile justice:
    standards, 4, 208
    statutes, revision of, 88–89, 241–43, 248–51, 280–81
Juvenile Justice and Delinquency Prevention Act of 1974, 244
Juvenile Justice Standards Project, 208, 446–47
Juveniles In Need of Supervision (JINS), 6, 235

Kallikak family, 29
Kentfields Rehabilitation Program, 342
Kent v. U.S., 4, 19, 85–86, 88, 92, 288, 301, 318, 320, 445

Labeling:
    effects of, 241–44, 266–67
    theory, 70
Law of Imitation, The, 61
Learning disabilities, 31–32, 183, 188–89
Legal counsel in juvenile court, 86–87, 243, 304–05, 314
Legal rights of children, 88–89
Legislative Guide for Drafting Family and Juvenile Court Acts, 264
Life crises, 138
Longfellow Alternative Learning Center, 196–97
Longitudinal study of delinquency, 9–10, 143, 448–50
Lower class culture, 105–06

Management by objectives, 411–13
Massachusetts:
    compulsory education laws, 80
    normalization in juvenile corrections, 384
    probation in, 325
    Stubborn Child Law, 78
Mass media and delinquency, 64–65
McKeiver v. Pennsylvania, 87–88, 92, 289, 309–10, 320

Medical model of delinquency treatment, 48, 408–10
Mempa v. Rhay, 341, 356, 396, 406
mens rea, 81, 88
Mental illness and delinquency, 48–50
Mentoring, 126
Mercer, Pennsylvania Specialized Treatment Services, 373–74
Mesomorphic body type, 28–29, 44–45
Middle class:
    delinquency, 15–17, 143
    gangs, 124
    life styles, 105–06
    standards, 82
Minimization of penetration, 88, 296
Minnesota Multiphasic Personality Inventory (MMPI), 45
Minority youth:
    crime, 15, 16
    overrepresentation in the juvenile justice system, 15, 16
Minors In Need of Supervision (MINS), 6, 235
Miranda v. Arizona, 265, 277, 288, 290, 320
Miranda warnings, 265, 288, 290
Missing Child Act of 1982, 239
Mobility and delinquency, 17, 57
Mobilization for Youth Program, 438–39
Model Rules for Juvenile Courts, 266
Moral development theories of delinquency, 40–43
Morales v. Turman, 289, 387
Morrisey v. Brewer, 341, 356, 396, 397, 406
Moses v. Washington Parish School Board, 188

Nation of Lords, A, 99
National Advisory Committee for Juvenile Justice and Delinquency Prevention, 268, 284, 292
National Advisory Committee on Criminal Justice Standards and Goals, 208, 230, 230, 245, 268–69
National Advisory Committee on Handicapped Children, 31
National Assessment of Juvenile Corrections, 326
National Center for Juvenile Justice, 409
National Center for Missing and Exploited Children, 239
National Center on Child Abuse and Neglect, 210–11
National Committee for Prevention of Child Abuse, 209
National Council on Crime and Delinquency, 266, 365
National Council of Juvenile and Family Court Judges, 250, 252, 394, 409
National Crime Survey, 10
National Incident Studies of Missing, Abducted, Runaway, and Throwaway Children, 237
National Institute of Justice, 268
National Institutes of Mental Health, 252
National Legal Resources Center for Child Advocacy and Protection, 268
National Longitudinal Survey of Youth, 159
National Office of Juvenile Justice and Delinquency Prevention, 239
National Youth Survey Project, 10, 19
Needs satisfaction, 62–63
Neighborhood Network Center, 349–50
Nelson v. Heyne, 346, 387
Neoclassical delinquency theory, 26–27
Neo-Freudians, 40

Neurosis, 40
New Jersey v. T.L.O., 290
New York City:
    Children's Aid Society, 362
    first juvenile institution, 361
    gang activity, 97–98, 110, 114–15, 116–17
New York Society for the Prevention of
    Cruelty to Children, 83
New York State:
    compulsory education laws, 80
    Court of Appeals, 162
    Family Court Act, 249
    halfway houses, 402–03
    houses of refuge, 80, 361
    Persons in Need of Supervision Law,
      162
    status offenders in, 162–63
Normalization:
    definition, 384
    in Massachusetts, 384

Office of Juvenile Justice and Delinquency
    Prevention, 282, 351, 371, 449
Ohio Revised Juvenile Code, 236
Order of self–sufficiency, 246
Orders of protection, 227, 230
Orphan trains, 362

Paint Creek Youth Center, 373, 448
Parens patriae, 81, 84, 89, 237
Parental rejection, 146–47
Parental supervision and delinquency,
    147–49
Parent-child relationship, 137–39
Parents Anonymous, 229
Patterned reaction, 70
Peer group pressures, 117, 182, 184–85,
    258, 380–382, 423
Personality:
    criminal, 46–47
    development theory, 43–48
    disorders, 45–46
    measurement, 45–46
    trait theories of delinquency, 43–48
Persons in Need of Supervision (PINS), 6,
    162
Petition, juvenile court, 84, 289, 290, 298
Philadelphia:
    houses of refuge, 80
    police contact with juveniles, 9, 57–58
    violence in schools, 182
Phoenix Program, 197
Photographing of juveniles, 266–67
Phrenologists, 27–29
Physical characteristics of delinquents,
    28–29
Physique and Delinquency, 157
Plea bargaining in juvenile courts, 243,
    303, 314
Pleasure-pain principle, 25–26
Police:
    Athletic League, 272
    community policing, 273–74
    contacts with juveniles, 7–8, 57–58,
      258–76
    delinquency prevention and control,
      268–76
    discretion in dealing with juveniles,
      261–63
    initiated intervention, 262
    investigation of offenses against children,
      267–68
    juvenile diversion programs, 263–64
    juvenile units, 268–69
    patrol officers, 260
    role in delinquency prevention, 274–75
    training for work with juveniles, 268–69

work with juveniles, 259–61
    youth gang units, 269–73
Polish Peasant, The, 56
Population density and delinquency, 57
Pornography, child, 169, 211–12
Poverty:
    and delinquency, 54–56, 137, 148–49,
      160
    federal definition, 55
Pre-adolescent years, 40–41
Pre-delinquent behavior, 82–83, 237, 442
Predisposition (social) investigation,
    310–14
Pregnancy:
    and dropping out of school, 190, 196
    unmarried adolescent, 140, 141–42,
      148–49, 160, 176–77
Prerelease programs, 393–95
Preventive detention of juveniles, 249,
    289, 292–93, 365
Prisons, 26–27
Probation:
    activities, 328–40
    brokerage of services, 328, 354
    caseloads, 328
    and community based treatment, 343–52
    and community service, 344–45
    definition, 325–26
    difficulties, 324
    as a disposition, 325–26
    effectiveness, 352–53
    extent of use, 326–27
    historical development, 325
    informal, 329
    initial interview, 323–24, 334, 337
    intensive, 340
    length, 326, 330–31
    officers, 327–30, 338–40
    order of probation, 326
    process, 328–341
    unofficial, 295–98, 329
    with restitution, 344–45
    revocation, 341
    risk assessment, 331–34
    rules, 330
    specialized programs, 345–52
    suspension of the imposition of
      disposition, 326
    termination, 330
    unofficial, 329
    violations, 341
Probation officer:
    as investigator, 329–34
    role of, 327–40
    as supervisor, 334–40
Proof, standard in juvenile court, 87–88,
    225–26, 289, 309
Property crime by juveniles, 7–8, 10, 11,
    15, 158–59, 281–82
Prosecutor in the juvenile court, 4, 303–04,
    314
Prostitution, child, 164–69, 211
Protection of Children Against Sexual
    Exploitation Act, 169
Protection, orders of, 227, 230
Provo Experiment, 342
Psychiatric treatment, 48–49
Psychoanalytic theory, 39–40
Psychological:
    disturbances, 48–49
    theories of delinquency, 39–50
Psychopathic personality, 48
Psychotics, 48–49
Punishment:
    capital, 25
    certainty of, 26
    just, 26

by parents, 144–46
    physical, 144–46
    right to, 26

Quay System, 45

Reaction-formation behavior, 60, 105
Reality therapy, 416–18
Reception centers, 371
Recidivism:
    after institutionalization, 360–61, 382–83
    of probationers, 341, 352–53
    of status offenders, 243
    of youths in community treatment,
      353
Rehabilitation 197, 198, 360–61
Reliability of testing, 45
Removal of status offenders from juvenile
    court, 241–43
Residential treatment:
    alternative to institutionalization,
      350–52
    for delinquent girls, 171
    as a disposition, 315
    in halfway houses, 402–403,
    at Highfields, 403
    history, 401–04
    in Massachusetts, 384
    recidivism after, 382–83, 405
    types, 372–78, 401–04
Revision of juvenile codes, 88, 241–42,
    247, 248–51, 264–65, 280–81
Right to punishment, 26
Right to treatment, 289
Rites of passage, 116–17
Runaway behavior:
    amount, 8, 158–59, 237
    causes, 160, 164–66, 170, 238–39
    differential treatment of males and
      females, 170, 239
    by females, 158–59, 160, 164–66, 170,
      238–39
    handled by diversion, 170–71, 238–39
    and sexual abuse, 164, 165–68, 238–39
Runaway shelters, 239
Rural delinquency, 15–17

Scared Straight, 443–44
Schall v. Martin, 249, 256, 289, 365, 387
School:
    bureaucratization, 180–82
    climate, 182–83
    commitment, 185
    curriculum, 186–88
    discipline, 180
    disorder, 182–83
    dropouts, 189–90
    environment and delinquency, 181–82
    fear of social failure at, 185
    fears related to guns, drugs, and gangs,
      184–85
    gang activity in, 11, 103, 184–85
    involvement, 191
    searches of students, 290
    socialization in, 179–81
    vandalism, 190
    victimization at, 183–185
    violence, 103, 176–78
Schools:
    alternative, 196–97
    and delinquency, 176–200
    dropout prevention projects in, 192–94
    failure in socialization, 179–81
    role in delinquency prevention and
      control, 197–98
    security in, 194–95
    students' academic failure in, 186–189

tracking in, 186–88
Scientific perspective on delinquency,
    22–23
Self-concept, 68–69
Self-image, 37–38, 45–46, 70, 139
Self-reported delinquency, 7, 9–10, 13, 24,
    150, 159
Sentencing of juveniles adjudicated in
    criminal court, 316
Serious delinquent offenders:
    characteristics of, 12
    court action against, 249–51
    methods of working with, 252–53
    scope of the problem, 8,10, 247–48
Sex-related offenses by females, 158,
    161–62, 164–69, 242
Sexual abuse of children:
    characteristics of victims, 213–14
    extent, 164–69, 212
    forms, 164–68, 211–12
    generational hypothesis, 215–16
    in the Middle Ages, 76–77
    by parents, 165–67, 218–20
    reporting, 212
    victim-precipitated, 214–15
Sexual mores, 6, 15, 157, 160, 161–63
Shelter homes, 371
Simmons v. U.S., 266, 277, 289
Slums and delinquency, 54–58
Smith v. Daily Mail Publishing Co., 289
Social:
    disorganization, 56
    ecology, 56
    influences in delinquency, 15, 16–17, 160
    networking, 193–94
    norms, 2–3, 5
    organization, 56–57
    processes, 56, 179–81
    reaction to youthful misbehavior, 5–6
Social investigation reports, 310–15, 329
Socialization process, 105–06, 137–39
Society for the Reformation of Juvenile
    Delinquents, 80, 361
Sociological studies of delinquency, 54–66
Sociopaths, 48
Somatotypes, 28–29, 44–45
Special investigation units,
Stages in life, 39–40
Standards Project of the Institute of
    Judicial Administration, 208
Stanford v. Kentucky, 290, 321
Status offenders:
    alternative methods of handling,
        241–43, 280–81
    categorization of, 235–36
    definition of, 6, 235–36
    diversion of, 241–43
    divestiture from juvenile court, 254–55
    female, 158–59, 161–67, 243
    handling by juvenile courts, 88–89,
        170–71, 236–37, 239–41
    institutionalization of, 7, 162, 237, 246,
        360
    methods of handling, 6–7, 88–89, 236–37
    removal from juvenile court, 88, 171,
        241–43
    residential treatment for, 171
    retention by juvenile court, 243–44
    sexually abused, 243
Sterilization of the feebleminded, 30
Stigmata, 27
Stigmatization from juvenile court contact,
    241–43
Stovall v. Denno, 266, 277, 288

Street Corner Society, 98
Substance abuse by juveniles, 8, 10, 13–14
Suburban delinquency, 15–17, 95
Summit County (OH) Juvenile Court
    Child Responsibility Project,
    346–47

Task Force on Juvenile Justice and
    Delinquency Prevention, 245–46,
    306
Television:
    and delinquency, 64–65
    violence, 64–65
Testing, statistical, 22–23, 45–46
Theorists, delinquency, 22–34, 39–50, 54–70
Theory, delinquency:
    biochemical, 22, 31
    biological school, 27–29
    catharsis, 64
    classical school, 25–26
    cognitive development, 41–42
    containment, 66–67
    costs and rewards, 150
    delinquency and opportunity, 106–07
    differential association, 62
    differential reinforcement, 63
    gang formation, 103–118
    genetic, 32–34
    heredity based, 29–30, 32–34
    labeling, 70
    learning, 61–64
    lower class culture, 105–06
    mental illness, 48–50
    methods of development, 23–25
    moral development, 40–41
    multiple-factor approach, 66
    needs, 117–18
    neoclassical, 26–27
    opportunity, 60
    personality development, 43–48
    personality trait, 41–48
    psychoanalytic, 39–43
    psychological school, 25, 39–50
    reaction formation, 60
    routine activities, 58
    social control/bonding, 67–68
    social-learning, 61
    social-psychological, 66–70
    sociological, 25, 54–66
    stress theory, 60–61
Thompson v. Oklahoma, 290, 318, 321
Tracking, school, 186–88
Treatment:
    choice of, 413–14
    community residential, 350–52, 401–04
    concept of, 48, 408–11
    definitions, 410–11
    differential, 142, 161–63, 170–71,
        235–36, 239, 245, 280–81, 289
    effectiveness, 430–32
    focus by juvenile court, 84–85, 411–13
    goals, 411–13
    implementation, 410–11
    individualized, 237, 410–11, 413–14
    in institutions, 372–78
    medical model, 48, 408–10
    process, 410–11
    staff, 410, 414–15
    strategies, 408–32
    supervision, 412–13
Treatment personnel:
    juvenile court, 409, 411–12
    in institutions, 372–76
    qualifications, 414–16

    role of, 414–16
Treatment techniques:
    art therapy, 426–27
    anger management, 424–25
    assertiveness training, 418–19
    behavior contracting, 335–36, 421
    behavior modification, 342, 343, 419–22
    community residential, 350–52
    conjoint family therapy, 424
    crisis intervention, 418
    family counseling, 345–47, 376–77,
        423–24
    group work, 342, 349, 422–23
    guided group interaction, 342, 376–77,
        423
    milieu therapy, 422
    for multi-problem youths, 349–50
    positive peer culture, 423
    psychotherapy, 416
    reality therapy, 416–18
    for sex offenders, 348–49, 426, 428
    substance abuse counseling, 348, 428–30
Trends in delinquent behavior, 11–17, 158,
    448–49
Twin research, 32–33

Underclass, 54–56, 115–117, 149, 160
Unemployment and delinquency, 54–56
Uniform Crime Reports, 7–8, 11, 16, 18,
    19, 20, 158, 237, 239, 247, 255,
    256
Uniform Juvenile Court Act of 1968, 244,
    264
Unruly child, 6
Urbanization and delinquency, 56–58, 79,
    139–40
Utilitarianism, 26
URSA Institute, 252
U.S. Bureau of Census, 10, 71
U.S. Bureau of Justice Statistics, 10, 251,
U.S. Department of Housing and Urban
    Development, 55
U.S. Office of Economic Opportunity, 99
U.S. Supreme Court, 4, 49, 85–88, 249–50,
    265, 266, 267, 288–90, 293, 301,
    302, 303, 309, 318

Values, 40–43, 56–57, 62–64, 150
Verona School District 47 v. ACTON, 290
Victimization surveys, 7, 10–11
Victimless offenses, 157
Violence:
    against parents, 144
    gang, 94–95, 100–03
    in institutions, 379–80
    in schools, 103
    television, 64–65
Violent crime by juveniles, 8, 10, 11–13,
    65–66, 94–95. 100–03, 110–12,
    158–59, 247–254, 281–82,
    299–302, 306–07
Violent Gang, The, 111
Volunteers
    role in delinquency prevention, 443
    and runaways, 239

Wade v. U.S, 265–66, 277, 288
Waiver to adult criminal courts, 4, 16,
    85–86, 88, 249–51, 288, 299–302
War on Poverty, 439–40
Women's changing roles and delinquency,
    137–40

XYY chromosome theory, 22